SECOND CANADIAN EDITION

PSYCHOLOGY OF CRIMINAL BEHAVIOUR

A Canadian Perspective

SHELLEY BROWN, PH.D.
Carleton University

RALPH SERIN, PH.D., C. PSYCH.
Carleton University

ADELLE FORTH, PH.D.
Carleton University

KEVIN NUNES, PH.D.
Carleton University

CRAIG BENNELL, PH.D.
Carleton University

JOANNA POZZULO, PH.D., C. PSYCH.
Carleton University

PEARSON

Toronto

Editorial Director: Claudine O'Donnell
Acquisitions Editor: Darcey Pepper
Marketing Manager: Lisa Gillis
Program Manager: Madhu Ranadive
Project Manager: Pippa Kennard
Manager of Content Development:
　Suzanne Schaan
Developmental Editor: Cheryl Finch

Production Services: Cenveo® Publisher Services
Permissions Project Manager: Katheryn O'Handley
Photo and Text Permissions Research: Lumina
Interior Designer: Cenveo Publisher Services
Cover Designer: Carie Keller, Cenveo Publisher
　Services
Cover Image: © Shutterstock/sakhorn

Vice-President, Cross Media and Publishing Services: Gary Bennett

2　16

Library and Archives Canada Cataloguing in Publication
Brown, Shelley L., 1969-, author

　　Psychology of criminal behaviour: a Canadian perspective / Shelley Brown, Ph.D. (Carleton University), Ralph Serin, Ph.D., C. Psych. (Carleton University), Adelle Forth, Ph.D. (Carleton University), Kevin Nunes, Ph.D. (Carleton University), Craig Bennell, Ph.D. (Carleton University), Joanna Pozzulo, Ph.D. (Carleton University). — Second edition.
Revision of: Psychology of criminal behaviour : a Canadian perspective/Ralph Serin ... [et al.]. — 1st ed. — Toronto: Pearson Canada, [2010], ©2011.

Includes bibliographical references and index.
ISBN 978-0-13-298005-0 (paperback)
　　1. Criminal psychology—Textbooks. 2. Criminal psychology—Canada—Textbooks.
I. Serin, Ralph C. (Ralph Charles), 1953-, author II.Forth, Adelle Elizabeth, 1961-, author
III.Nunes, Kevin L., author IV. Bennell, Craig, author V. Pozzulo, Joanna, author VI. Title.

HV6080.B76 2016　　　　　　364.3　　　　　　C2015-907770-2

ISBN 978-0-13-298005-0

Contents

Preface

Over the past several years, likely spawned by interest in our second-year Forensic Psychology course and popular television shows on criminal behaviour, enrollment in our Criminal Behaviour courses has been consistently high. As we prepare each year for teaching, the same question arises among the faculty: which text should we use? It seemed we had all used different texts for different reasons, but with similar results. Student response was modest at best. Complaints were that the texts were too dense, too American, too expensive, or too British. We even tried a course pack of some of our favourite selected readings, believing this compromise would be successful. Perhaps we were simply delaying the inevitable, because students' comments were equally critical of the course pack. They rightly noted it wasn't a textbook and lacked all the requisite bells and whistles such as a glossary and sample quizzes, and it certainly wasn't inexpensive. This collective experience led to the realization that a new textbook was needed, and that this textbook should highlight the many contributions made by Canadian researchers.

We owe a significant debt of gratitude to numerous Canadian researchers, many of whom we have highlighted in this text. Based on their collective contributions, Canadian corrections research and practice continues to be at the forefront in North America and abroad. Canadian theory and research is prominently represented in risk and needs assessment, correctional rehabilitation programs, and evaluation strategies throughout the world. We feel it is important that students understand this legacy and that they appreciate the contribution Canadian researchers have made. This textbook also highlights subgroups of offenders, such as Aboriginal and female offenders, for whom specific research is emerging. Also, the importance of a more integrated model of criminal behaviour that considers biology, as well as the person and situation interaction, is emphasized. In this new Second Edition we have included two new chapters devoted exclusively to psychopathic offenders and substance abusing offenders. We have also enhanced the consistency between chapters and have attempted to make the material more accessible to a wider audience. This was no small task with six authors—each with our own style, inclinations, and varying degrees of stubbornness! It is our hope that this textbook intrigues and engages a new generation of corrections researchers and practitioners. Certainly, relentless media coverage, political and ideological debates, fiscal challenges in corrections, and continued public concern regarding safety make this an exciting time in corrections research.

As a group we mused and reflected on the needs of our students and what a new textbook might look like. For instance, of the 1500 or so students that take our Criminal Behaviour course at Carleton each year, very few continue their studies at the graduate level. Also, our students are an interdisciplinary mix of psychology, criminology, sociology, and law students, many of whom aspire to careers in the areas of policing, corrections, probation and parole, and nongovernment organizations such as the John Howard Society and Elizabeth Fry Society. Many of us recruit guest lecturers—often the most popular class is one by senior corrections officials describing work in corrections and how to get a summer job (usually there is a mob scene at the end of class as students clamour for a business card). These experiences meant that our textbook needed to meet a range of needs and interests for our students. It had to highlight Canadian research, both influential and contemporary; it had to link research to practice; and it had to be accessible. We hope that we have achieved these goals with this textbook.

DISTINGUISHING FEATURES

Although the textbook has been written by six different authors, a common outline has been utilized. Key pedagogical aids have been incorporated to promote student learning and to assist instructors in presenting important material. Key features include the following:

- **Chapter objectives.** Each chapter starts with a list of learning objectives to guide students' learning of the material and closes with a summary linked to the learning objectives.

- **Vignettes.** Case studies or vignettes are presented at the beginning of each chapter to provide a context for the key concepts reflected in the chapter. These vignettes are based on real-world cases and scenarios to help students make the link from research to practice.

- **Key terms and Glossary.** Key terms are highlighted in bold type throughout each chapter and definitions are provided in the Glossary at the end of the textbook for easy reference.

- **Evidence-based practice.** A major focus of the text is the use of empirical research to support key theories and practice. Data reported in original studies are often presented in graph or table form and is cited throughout the textbook.

- **Profiles of Canadian researchers.** Canadian researchers are among the best in the world and their contributions have been innumerable. Each chapter provides a profile of a key Canadian researcher whose work is relevant to the chapter. These profiles also highlight information such as educational background, research interests, and some aspects of their personal lives.

- **Boxes.** Boxed features within the chapters provide interesting asides to the main text. These boxes help develop student appreciation for current techniques and issues.

- **Discussion questions.** Several discussion questions are provided at the end of each chapter. Instructors can assign these for group discussion in class, or students can consider them in order to examine their understanding of the chapter material.

- **Linking research to practice.** A dedicated chapter demonstrates how empirical research and theory are linked to contemporary correctional practice. This should be of interest to students who plan on pursuing careers in the fields of corrections and criminal justice.

SUPPLEMENTS

The following supplements specific to this text can be downloaded by instructors from a password-protected location of Pearson Canada's online catalogue (http://vig.pearsoned.ca). Contact your local sales representative for further information.

- **Instructor's Manual.** The Instructor's Manual is a comprehensive resource that provides chapter outlines, class activities, and summaries of key concepts. We hope our colleagues will use the textbook and Instructor's Manual as a foundation that they can build on in the classroom.

- **Test Item File.** This test bank, offered in Microsoft Word format, contains multiple-choice, true/false, short-answer, and essay questions. Each question is classified according to difficulty level and is keyed to the appropriate page number in the text.

- **PowerPoint Presentations.** PowerPoint slides highlight the key concepts in each chapter of the text.

MySearchLab

MySearchLab offers extensive help to students with their writing and research projects and provides round-the-clock access to credible and reliable source material.

Research Content on MySearchLab includes immediate access to thousands of full-text articles from leading Canadian and international academic journals, and daily news feeds from The Associated Press. Articles contain the full downloadable text—including abstract and citation information—and can be cut, pasted, emailed, or saved for later use.

Writing MySearchLab also includes a step-by-step tutorial on writing a research paper. Included are sections on planning a research assignment, finding a topic, creating effective notes, and finding source material. Our exclusive online handbook provides grammar and usage support. Pearson SourceCheck™ offers an easy way to detect accidental plagiarism issues, and our exclusive tutorials teach how to avoid them in the future. MySearchLab also contains AutoCite, which helps to cite sources correctly using MLA, APA, CMS, and CBE documentation styles for both endnotes and bibliographies.

To order this book with MySearchLab access at no extra charge, use ISBN 978-0-13-801340-0.

Take a tour at **www.mysearchlab.com**.

Acknowledgments

This book would never have come to fruition without assistance from many people. In particular, we would never have been able to complete such a text without the mentoring of outstanding forensic and correctional researchers.

We would like to acknowledge that the forensic program at Carleton University, of which we are part, would not exist without Don Andrews. He was an exceptional and generous colleague whose work will continue to guide the field for decades. His infectious giggle is never far from our hearts. Robert Hoge has also been a long-time supportive colleague and an important advocate for attending to the issue of juvenile crime in Canada. We would also like to thank Ralph Serin for graciously passing the reigns over to his dear friend and colleague, Shelley Brown who guided the second edition of this book.

We are thankful to the exceptional researchers we profiled in this textbook for giving us permission to give students a glimpse into their lives, and for offering us great insight by reviewing content we provided: Don Andrews, Kelley Blanchette, Shelley Trevethan, Zoe Hilton, Paul Gendreau, Sheilagh Hodgins, Martin Lalumière, Michael Seto, Tracey Skilling, Mark Olver, Stephen Wong, Debra Pepler, and John Weekes. All have made significant contributions to understanding criminal behaviour.

We would like to formally recognize the significant contributions of Marnie Rice and Grant Harris, who both passed away recently and unexpectedly. Their work has forever changed the landscape of forensic psychology in immeasurable ways.

We would like to make special mention of our Carleton student research assistants who tirelessly and carefully provided invaluable support during the research and writing processes. In particular we would like to thank:

Brittany Blaskovits

Carolyn Blank

Sacha Maimone

Cathrine Pettersen

Anna Pham

We would like to thank the reviewers who provided us with helpful feedback that allowed us to make this textbook stronger. Reviewers of the manuscript and/or the original project proposal include:

Curtis Fogel, Lakehead University

Hilary Kim Morden, Simon Fraser University

Brent Snook, Memorial University

Mitchell Walker, Okanagan College

We would like to thank the family at Pearson Canada: Ky Pruesse (editor-in-chief) for enthusiastically supporting the original concept for this text; Madhu Ranadive (program manager) for patiently guiding us through the contractual process; Cheryl Finch (developmental editor) for keeping us focused on timeframes and being patient regarding our transgressions (of which there seemed to be several); and Laura Neves (copy editor) for helping us transform our ideas into a more readable form.

Finally, we would like to thank our many undergraduate and graduate students. The undergraduates prompted us to undertake this challenge and we feel our program will be stronger because of their wish for a real Canadian criminal behaviour textbook. Our graduate students continue to encourage us with their thoughtful discussions regarding the contents of this textbook and challenge us to look forward to the next frontiers of a psychological perspective on criminal behaviour.

Completion of a textbook is a considerable challenge not only to the authors, but to the people in their lives. Ralph Serin would like to thank his wife, Carolan, for her continued patience and support as he spent countless hours hidden away in front of a computer. Joanna Pozzulo would like to thank her partner David for patiently waiting out the long hours of writing. Adelle Forth would like to give a huge thanks to her partner, John Logan, for editing her chapters, giving insightful feedback, not getting too frustrated with repeated requests for help, and for generally being supportive, including taking over the care of numerous four-footed critters while the textbook was being written. Shelley Brown would like to thank her husband, Murray, for his unwavering support during the writing of this book that included taking their two children (Will and Lydia) away on the occasional weekend when she desperately needed to write; Will and Lydia thank you for being so grown-up. I never thought I would see the day when we could actually work productively side-by-side in the office. Craig Bennell would like to thank his wife, Cindy, for her love, patience, and support; Noah and Elijah, for being such great kids while Dad had to write and for making sure he took lots of breaks to have some family fun. Kevin Nunes would like to thank his wife, Anne, for all her support, and his daughter, Ruby, for visiting him at the computer in the morning ("go see dad in the off-off") and bringing so much happiness and wonder into his life.

Chapter 1
Crime in Canada

TYPICAL OFFENDER PROFILE

Bill Jones, aged 28, is serving a 36-month sentence for armed robbery. This is not his first incarceration, having served time in both secure custody as a youth as well as provincial jails for property crimes (theft, break and enter, drug possession, and a couple of assaults). He dropped out of high school prior to completing Grade 10 and has infrequently held odd jobs. Presentence reports describe a fairly chaotic child-hood and family situation, a long history of drug and alcohol abuse, and multiple brief relationships.

Assessments indicate that Bill presents as impulsive with poor problem-solving skills, which, along with his hanging out with antisocial peers, seem related to his fairly consistent involvement with the courts as an adult. He claims to want treatment, but is somewhat unclear regarding what this would entail. Prior involvement in counselling has not been successful in reducing his criminality. Recently, he met a woman and he hopes this relationship, along with improved employment skills, will help him straighten out. Until now, his main form of leisure activity was to go to bars with his friends.

SENSATIONAL CASE PROFILE

In June 1991, Paul Bernardo kidnapped, raped, and murdered 14-year-old Leslie Mahaffy. He and his girlfriend, Karla Homolka, held Mahaffy for 24 hours, during which time they repeatedly raped her. Homolka and Bernardo taped the assaults. One scene even shows Homolka putting on makeup to look pretty before raping Mahaffy. The two killed the teen and planned to dismember her body and dispose of it piece by piece after encasing the parts in cement. Two people canoeing in a local lake found her body. The very same day, Homolka and Bernardo were married.

A short time later, in April 1992, Bernardo and Homolka kidnapped another teenager, Kristen French. French was also raped and tortured over several days. The pair killed Kristen French just before attending Easter Sunday dinner with Homolka's parents.

The Canadian press started calling the couple the "Ken and Barbie" murderers. Homolka later plea bargained with the prosecution, testifying against Paul Bernardo (including information about their part in the killing of Karla's sister) in return for a lighter

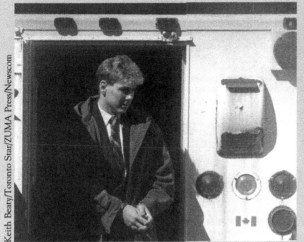

Paul Bernardo and Karla Homolka, the Ken and Barbie of Canadian serial killers

sentence. Bernardo, who claimed to be a fan of serial killer stories, later changed his name to Paul Teale. Bernardo was convicted of three counts of murder on September 1, 1995, and sentenced to life in prison at the Kingston Penitentiary in Kingston, Ontario. Reports indicate that although his parents were not close to one another, he seemed to have been a "perfect" child and was beginning a career as an accountant.

Learning Objectives

1 Describe a typical offender, with a discussion of implications for understanding criminal behaviour in general.

2 Provide an interdisciplinary context to understanding criminal behaviour.

3 Describe public perceptions of criminal justice agencies.

4 Describe crime trends throughout Canada, including variations in rates according to different sources.

5 Describe the empirically-derived determinants of crime and discuss their implications for assessment and treatment of offenders.

6 Describe the financial and social impact of crime on Canadians.

CONTEXT

<small>As noted by this excerpt from the speech from the throne, the canadian</small> government continues to see crime as an important issue requiring attention.

> Our Government believes that the justice system exists to protect law-abiding citizens and our communities. For too long, the voices of victims have been silenced while the system coddled criminals. Our Government has worked to re-establish Canada as a country where those who break the law are punished for their actions; where penalties match the severity of crimes committed; where the rights of victims come before the rights of criminals. (Speech from the Throne October 16, 2013)

When the first edition of this book was published, criminal justice issues were of concern to Canadians but lagged behind concerns regarding health care, the environment, poor government leadership, unemployment, and the military (Queen's University 2006). A more recent poll indicated that crime and violence ranked seventh, behind health care, employment, taxes, and political corruption concerns (IPSOS Reid, cited in Kondro 2015). Government and police statistics have documented a continuing decline in crime rates over the past two decades, which may help explain this trend in public opinion, especially in those under 45 years of age (older Canadians tend to be disproportionately concerned with crime) (Environics Institute 2010). The same survey also indicated that Canadians now feel that crime prevention is more effective than law enforcement for combatting crime.

Despite this relatively benign public view of crime and crime prevention, new laws have been passed that reflect the majority Conservative government's tough-on-crime agenda and were intended to restore "balance" in the criminal justice system. These new laws abolished early parole of non-violent first time federal offenders (Bill C-59), increased offender accountability and inmate costs (i.e., room and board, telephone usage) (Bill C-39), overhauled the inmate grievance system to eliminate frivolous applications (Bill C-293), and increased the rights of victims of crime in terms of access to information, participation in decisions, and restitution (Bill C-32). As well, the language of the *Corrections and Conditional Release Act* (CCRA) has been amended such that protection of society is the paramount consideration in decisions regarding offender release and supervision. Given this stark contrast in government versus public approaches to crime, it is worth questioning how well informed Canadians (especially those over age 45) are about criminal justice issues.

THE INFLUENCE OF THE MEDIA

<small>Nothing galvanizes public opinion more that the media's portrayal of</small> criminal justice issues. Perhaps it is for this reason that in 2008 the *Toronto Star* undertook to publish a special series highlighting the complexity of crime and criminal justice issues in Canada. Crime and criminal justice issues receive considerable media scrutiny, sensational crimes receive front-page billing, and the general public is inundated with facts,

Inmates Eat Better than Seniors?

"Even inmates eat better than seniors in nursing homes." Wallace 2008: 4

James Wallace's 2008 story "Even inmates eat better than seniors in nursing homes" in the *Kingston Whig Standard* noted that the Ontario government raised its food allowance for feeding seniors in long-term care facilities by 12 cents per day. This increased the meal per diem to $5.46, which includes two choices of meals at breakfast, lunch, and dinner each day, as well as snacks and drinks. In contrast, Ontario prisons received meals worth more than $10 per day.

figures, and (more importantly) opinions regarding what to do about crime and how to increase public safety.

See Figure 1.1 for the results of a recent survey regarding how Canadians rate different sources of information regarding the criminal justice system (Latimer and Desjardins 2007). In this telephone survey, researchers interviewed more than 4500 Canadians regarding their perceptions of crime. The results show government information as having moderate influence and academic contributions as having none, although some academics provide commentaries in newspapers and magazines. Clearly these data confirm the importance of the media as an information source for Canadians.

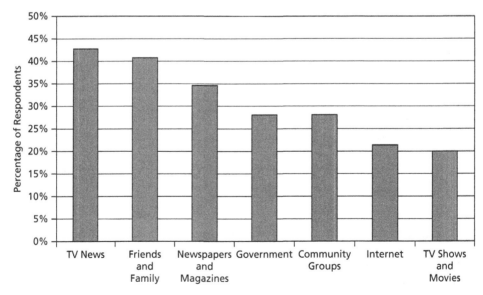

Figure 1.1 Information Sources Rated as Highly Important

Source: Latimer and Desjardins (2007).

DEFINITIONS
What Is Crime?

Variation in rates of crime and incarceration across countries suggests there are differences in the definitions and/or tolerance of crime. McGuire (2004) describes a variety of factors that have been used to define crime and to help explain when certain behaviours may be viewed as criminal or not. These factors include an individual's motivation, opportunity, politics, social convention, and context. Further, Muncie (2001) has delineated 11 separate definitions of crime, highlighting the challenges in arriving at a perfect definition of crime. Types of definitions typically include legal, moral, social, and psychological explanations: *legal* refers to acts prohibited by the state and punishable under the law; *moral* refers to the violation of norms of religion and morality that are punishable by supreme beings; *social* refers to the violation of certain norms and customs that are punishable by the community; and *psychological* refers to acts that are rewarding to the perpetrator but harmful to others.

While it is clear that crime is a socially constructed phenomenon, early research (Newman 1976; 1977) has shown that there is consistency across countries regarding what is viewed as criminal. Using brief vignettes to describe situations (e.g., a person forcefully taking money from another, resulting in injury to the victim; a father having sexual relations with his grown-up daughter), Newman surveyed people in six countries and found there was a high degree of agreement in respondents' perceptions of what is considered a crime. In particular, robbery, theft, and incest were all viewed to be criminal.

For the purposes of this text, our working definition of criminal behaviour comes from Bartol and Bartol (2008). Of note is that this definition incorporates intent, thereby addressing Canadian concerns regarding criminal responsibility.

> Criminal behaviour refers to intentional behaviour that violates a criminal code; intentional in that it did not occur accidentally or without justification of excuse (Bartol and Bartol 2008).

The issue of what is considered a crime may seem unwarranted, since the courts adjudicate cases and determine sanctions and probation officers, jails, and prisons manage these sentences. A definition of crime is *critical* because the specific definition will influence prevalence—a more conservative or restrictive definition will decrease the rate of crime. Further, any definition of crime must concede that there are inter-cultural variations regarding normative and acceptable behaviour, and that these acceptable norms can change over time within a culture (e.g., abortion laws in Canada). Further, immigrants to Canada may behave in a manner consistent with the cultural norms of their native country, but such behaviour may be illegal in their newly adopted country (e.g., age of consent for sexual intercourse). Since treatment is often provided by correctional agencies to address the underlying reasons for criminality and to reduce the likelihood of repeating such behaviour, sensitivity to both legal and cultural issues must be reflected in psychological responses to criminal behaviour.

WHY DO WE CARE?

IN ADDITION TO PUBLIC OPINION SURVEYS INDICATING THAT CRIME IN GENERAL is a major concern to Canadians, there are several additional considerations worth discussing: prevalence, victimization, and costs.

Prevalence refers to the proportion of a population found to be involved in crime. This can be reflected historically (ever in their lifetime) or currently (in the past year, how many convictions occurred). According to the Uniform Crime Reporting Survey (Boyce, Cotter, and Perreault 2014), the police-reported crime rate in 2012 was 6409 crimes per 100 000 people, or 2 235 325 crimes. However, one offender may have committed multiple crimes, so we should also consider the number of individuals charged, which was 1 678 425 individuals, or 4.84 percent of the Canadian population. It is also important to keep in mind that a criminal charge (which occurs every three minutes in Canada) does not always lead to a conviction.

Victimization refers to those affected by crime. As the number of victims of crime increases, so too does public concern. Data from the General Social Survey (Statistics Canada 2009) indicate that 225 per 1000 Canadians have reported being victims of (in descending order) theft of personal property, assault, sexual assault, and robbery. Most victims of crime are under 30 years of age. In 2009 there were approximately 373 000 victims of violent crime (*Uniform Crime Reporting Survey*, Statistics Canada, cited in Public Safety Canada 2014). In the 2009/2010 *Victim Services Survey*, 911 service providers indicated they had assisted close to 410 000 victims of crime between April 1, 2009 and March 31, 2010. According to the survey respondents, three times more women received assistance from a victim service than did men. We cover victimization in greater detail later in this chapter.

The total cost of crime can be difficult to calculate. The Fraser Institute (Easton, Furness, and Brantingham 2014) estimated that in 1998, Canada spent over $42.4 billion on crime, of which $15.5 billion was associated with what we think of as the "direct cost" of crime (police, courts, and corrections). Federal and provincial corrections alone cost $4.62 billion per year. Earlier it was noted that Canadians support crime prevention initiatives. Recently, a cost–benefit study was completed that underscores this view. Koegl and Day (2015) calculated the criminal justice costs of a cohort of 386 juvenile offenders who were tracked for 15 years beginning in 1986. Based only on official convictions, the aggregate cost (which includes victim, correctional, and other criminal justice system costs) of offending for this group was $671 million (or $1.74 million per person over 15 years). In a related study, Day and Koegl (2015) examined the costs relating to different trajectory groups of offenders, based on age of onset and persistence. While the average aggregate cost per person was $5.86 million, costs ranged from less than $4 million for those with low persistence to more than $16 million for those with high persistence and late onset. Clearly, long-term costs are highly related to the trajectory group that an offender falls into.

Approximately 2.6 million crimes are reported annually in Canada, with property crimes representing the greatest proportion. The General Social Survey (Statistics

Canada 2009) suggests that 22.5 percent of Canadians report being a victim of crime in a given year. Other credible estimates range from 28.8 percent (Latimer and Desjardins 2007) to 48 percent (Statistics Canada 2005a) when the timeframe is extended beyond one year. If we accept the lowest estimate of 22.5 percent, we might further assert that for each victim of a crime, there is a perpetrator, and both the victim and perpetrator and likely have someone in their life who is negatively affected by the incident. For the victim, this could be a partner, child, or friend who is also affected by the property loss, trauma, or fear of future victimization; for the perpetrator, this could be a partner or child who is financially or socially disadvantaged by the perpetrator being fined, on probation, or in jail. In this context, we can readily appreciate that the scope of negative influence of crime is significant, perhaps affecting more than 80 percent of Canadians. Thus, crime is a major social concern that might be best considered to be a public policy concern, rather than simply a criminal justice concern.

FEDERAL AND PROVINCIAL CORRECTIONS

CORRECTIONAL SERVICES ARE OPERATED BY BOTH THE FEDERAL AND PROVINCIAL governments. Offenders who receive sentences of less than two years or who receive community sentences such as fines, community service work, or probation fall under provincial jurisdiction. Offenders who receive prison sentences of two years or more are the responsibility of the federal government and are incarcerated in federal prisons. Young offender services (including pre-trial supervision, community and custody sentences, and extrajudicial sanctions programs) are the responsibility of the provincial government.

Unlike in the United States, where state and federal prisons have markedly different populations due to sentencing guidelines, in Canada the major difference relates to sentence length. Provincial jails are also remand centres, where offenders are held while awaiting trial. Some offenders who are subsequently found guilty and sentenced may eventually be transferred to federal prisons. This means that a variety of offense categories are represented in both settings, but federal offenders are more likely to have engaged in more violent crime and/or have more serious criminal histories. If federal offenders on supervised release (i.e., parole, statutory release after two thirds of their sentence is completed) have their parole revoked or commit new crimes and receive sentences of less than two years, they will still return to federal custody. As well, some sex offenders may be given a sentence of less than two years but also be designated a Long Term Offender, requiring community supervision for up to 10 years. This supervision is completed by federal parole officers following the offender's release from a provincial jail. In some cases (e.g., in New Brunswick) there is an exchange of service agreement such that federal corrections manage provincial offenders. In other areas of Canada, there is an exchange of service agreement whereby federal corrections utilizes provincial resources (i.e., halfway house bed space). See Table 1.1 for an overview of Canadian provincial correctional facilities. In Canada there are 115 provincial correctional facilities and 58 federal facilities.

Table 1.1 Provincial Jails

Province	Provincial Correctional Facilities
Alberta	4 adult correctional centres, 4 remand centres, 1 adult community correctional centre operated by an aboriginal organization, 2 camps
British Columbia	9 adult correctional centres, 3 pre-trial facilities, 2 youth correctional centres
Manitoba	7 adult and 2 youth correctional centres
New Brunswick	4 adult correctional centres, 1 youth correctional centre, 1 community residential centre
Newfoundland and Labrador	4 adult correctional centres, 1 penitentiary, 2 detention centres, 2 youth facilities
Northwest Territories	3 adult correctional centres, 1 youth correctional centre, 1 wilderness camp
Nova Scotia	4 adult correctional centres, 2 youth correctional or detention centres
Nunavut	1 correctional centre
Ontario	9 adult correctional centres, 10 adult detention centres, 9 adult jails, 6 youth correctional facilities
Prince Edward Island	2 adult correctional centres, 1 youth correctional centre
Quebec	18 correctional centres and jails
Saskatchewan	4 adult correctional centres, 5 community correctional centres and community training residences, 2 camps, 6 youth facilities
Yukon	1 correctional centre

Sources: Alberta Justice and Solicitor General (2015); British Columbia Ministry of Justice (2013); Manitoba Justice (2015); New Brunswick Public Safety (2015); Newfoundland Labrador Department of Justice and Public Safety (2015); Northwest Territories Department of Justice (2015); Nova Scotia Department of Justice Correctional Services (2013); Nunavut Department of Justice (2013); Ontario Ministry of Community Safety and Correctional Services (2015); Prince Edward Island Department of Justice and Public Safety (2015); Saskatchewan Ministry of Justice (2012); Sécurité Publique Québec (2015); Yukon Department of Justice (2014).

Typically, federal prisons are larger facilities with greater numbers of offenders and staff (see Table 1.2 for basic facts), although some provinces such as Ontario have adopted a super-jail model. Both the federal and provincial systems include correctional staff, as well as parole officers. Social workers are more common in the provincial facilities and psychologists work in both settings. Licensing is a provincial responsibility, so social workers and psychologists must meet the certification requirements of the province in which

Table 1.2 Basic Facts: Correctional Service Canada

- Responsible for approximately 15 215 incarcerated offenders and 7754 offenders in the community
- 43 institutions (8 maximum, 12 multilevel, 18 medium, 20 minimum security), 15 community correctional centres, 92 parole offices, and 4 healing lodges across 5 regions
- 18 244 staff (15.4 percent in headquarters, 76.4 percent in institutions, 8.2 percent in the community)
- 40 percent of staff are correctional officers, 15 percent of staff are parole officers or program staff
- Annual budget of $2.7 billion

Source: Public Safety Canada (2014).

they work. This means there is some variation across the country. Correctional Service Canada (CSC) is the largest single employer of psychologists in the country.

CAREER PROFILES

THE FOLLOWING HYPOTHETICAL PROFILES ARE INTENDED TO PROVIDE A SYNOPSIS of different career options in the field of criminal justice, either as a researcher, practitioner, or clinician. It is important to note that many staff (not just psychologists) conduct counselling with offenders. For instance, all parole officers in CSC provide forms of counselling to offenders. Indeed, there are almost 1500 parole officers in CSC but only about 250 psychologists (including full-time and contract staff). Social workers and chaplains also provide counselling services to offenders in both federal and provincial corrections. With almost 20 000 offenders in prisons and the community, there is a clear need for many different staff to provide counselling services.

The face of corrections staff is changing: it is younger, more diverse, and more gender equal. It should be noted that there has been a significant influx of new staff in the past several years. Observations and testimonials from real CSC staff can be viewed at www.csc-scc.gc.ca/careers/index-eng.shtml.

Correctional Officer *(blended to reflect duties in both provincial and federal corrections)*

Mary is a 29-year-old correctional officer working in a medium security prison for men. She has an undergraduate degree in criminology and has been working in corrections for three years. Before her employment, she volunteered with the John Howard Society counselling ex-offenders. She enjoys her job and her fellow officers, and feels that she can make a difference because she interacts with offenders on a daily basis. Mary hopes to eventually become a parole officer. She realizes that security is a major part of her job, but she also likes the opportunity to talk to offenders. She sees herself as someone who does more than open locked doors and frisk offenders.

It took Mary a while to get used to working shifts but now she appreciates having time to get things done while others are working. One of the aspects that she likes best about her job is the variety of the work. When she is assigned to different posts, she interacts with different people, and gets a full appreciation for how the prison functions. One day she could be working at a control post, ensuring that offenders have passes authorizing their movement and keeping an area secure, while another day she could be working in a unit that observes and interacts with offenders one on one. Mary has always known that corrections is about people, so it requires good communication skills, but sometimes she has to write reports on offenders and she is now realizing the importance of good writing skills as well.

Parole Officer *(federal, institutional)*

Fred is 48 years old and has been a parole officer for more than 20 years. He has seen many changes during his career. When he started, computers were just being introduced. Now, everything regarding his interactions with offenders is entered into a computer and tracked. This is more efficient, and also permits tracking to ensure he meets his deadlines, but he wonders if technology has actually reduced the amount counselling contact he has with offenders. Fortunately, there are now correctional programs for offenders that can be delivered by other staff. Nonetheless, Fred is expected to meet regularly with all of the offenders on his caseload so that he is up to date regarding their adjustment in prison. The procedures he is required to follow to conduct his work are very detailed since they need to meet legal requirements and because of the increased complexity of using different risk assessment instruments. He has also noticed changes in the offender population: they have more serious criminal histories, are older on average, and have more serious mental health concerns. These all make it more challenging for him to prepare offenders for release and to determine their suitability for transfer to facilities with reduced security.

Still, he loves his work. He has had the opportunity to work on some special assignments and he feels he makes a difference for those offenders who want to change. Yes, sometimes he gets yelled or sworn at, but despite such challenges, he feels he has an interesting and rewarding career.

Probation Officer *(similar to a federal parole officer in the community)*

Susan is a 32-year-old probation officer who previously worked as a substitute teacher for 5 years. Before her teaching work, she volunteered through her church to visit offenders at a minimum security prison. After years of trying to get a full-time job as a teacher, the chance came up to apply for position as a probation officer and she jumped at it. She loves her job, but the shift in careers took some adjustment. She has always been a positive, people-oriented person. She now realizes that rehabilitation must be balanced with supervision. Not only is this required in terms of how her duties are defined, but it also works best for offenders. Offenders need support and structure and this is how she approaches her supervision of offenders in the community. Her days are varied.

Some days she meets clients in the office; some days she sees clients at Tim Hortons, drinking way too much coffee; other days she interviews employers and family members of accused in order to complete presentence reports for the courts; and sometimes she provides her comments at court regarding the suitability for a sentenced offender to be placed on probation. She loves the variety and connection to the community that experiences in her work.

Sometimes there are disappointments, such as when an offender she has worked very hard to help ends up returning to crime. At times it also difficult to be in court, particularly when she must recommend imprisonment for an offender in front of the offender's family. She sees her job as helping offenders to see that they have choices but that they are accountable for their actions.

Psychologist

Jane is a 35-year-old correctional psychologist who works at a medium security prison for male offenders. She completed her clinical psychology degree at the University of Saskatchewan, including several placements at the Regional Psychiatric Centre in Saskatoon. There she gained invaluable experience completing risk assessments, conducting group treatment with offenders, and conducting research, all under supervision.

Since her early years as an undergraduate, Jane knew she wanted to work in corrections. As an undergraduate she participated in a tour of a prison in Kingston, which led her to volunteer with the Elizabeth Fry Society. She found this highly rewarding and it solidified her interest in helping others, especially those who have been in conflict with the courts. She realizes that most offenders return to the community and that community support is vital to their success. While some see the role of psychology in corrections as simply conducting risk assessments, she sees the risk assessment as the start of a process of change for the offender. Jane is a positive person and believes that people can and do want to change, but that change is difficult. The risk assessments she completes help offenders better understand the areas of their lives that they must address if they are to remain crime-free. She knows that further research is required to better understand offender change and crime desistance, and she sees her role as a correctional psychologist as ideally situated to pursue such research.

Professor

William is 37 and has recently been hired as an Assistant Professor in the Department of Psychology at a Canadian university. His has expertise regarding sex offenders and has joined a small department that is interested in expanding the forensic psychology program, given its popularity with students. William's work has been mainly in the area of theory; that is, understanding models of why certain individuals (usually males) commit sexual crimes. Through his research he has become an expert on various assessments (static and dynamic risk, phallometrics) and has conducted research in both prisons and forensic hospitals (but he is not a clinical psychologist).

He has taught courses in Forensic Psychology for the past several years, and he realizes this is a major reason he was selected by the university. His previous teaching evaluations have helped him appreciate the importance of making course material engaging for students, rather than just informing them of contemporary issues and current research topics. William realizes that not all undergraduates will want to pursue graduate school but he believes it is important to share his passion for the subject, especially for those who may eventually choose a career in the field.

The past year has been hectic to say the least. William has worked hard to prepare for the new courses he must teach, has been working on manuscripts from his recent doctoral thesis, and has been preparing grant applications. Without funding, it will be nearly impossible to continue his research on sex offenders due to the cost of equipment and travel to prisons. He cannot remember when he last worked this hard! Nonetheless, he is excited about his new position and career.

A Career in Corrections

For those who find corrections and criminal justice topics interesting and exciting, there are numerous career pathways to consider. Some careers require a degree in one of the social sciences and knowledge of the criminal justice system (i.e., relevant laws, mission statements, policy initiatives). Good verbal and written communication skills are also critical, since many roles involve interacting with others. In addition, recruitment notices for employment in corrections typically include skills such as the ability to motivate offenders to change antisocial behaviour, an interest in helping others, good analytic and problem solving abilities, and knowledge of evidence-based practice (e.g., the information covered in this course!).

Table 1.3 provides a summary that may be helpful in appreciating the variety of career options available to graduating students. These include an academic professor and researcher, a clinical forensic psychologist (in private practice or within a corrections agency), a government researcher, a counsellor with a nongovernment organization (such as the John Howard Society), a correctional officer, a probation or parole officer, and a project officer in government. The minimum degree requirement for each career is provided, as is an estimate of salary level.

Table 1.3 Different Career Paths in Correctional Psychology

Type of Job	Degree Requirement	Other Notes	Typical Starting Salary*
Professor	• Ph.D. (typically completed in 7–8 years post-B.A.)	• Average age of new hires is 37, meaning several years may be spent seeking employment	• Assistant Professor in Psychology: $70 000–80 000

Type of Job	Degree Requirement	Other Notes	Typical Starting Salary*
Clinical Psychologist	• Preferably Ph.D. • Some provinces only require an M.A.	• Licensing requires 1 year of supervised practice	• PS-3: $72 000–84 000 • Salaries vary slightly between provincial and federal systems
Associate Psychologist	• M.A. (typically completed in 2 years post-B.A.) • Must be eligible to be registered in province of practice within 2 years of start of employment	• Requires 2 years of supervised practice	• PS-2: $61 000–74 000
Government Researcher	• M.A. for entry level • Ph.D. for senior level		• ES-4: $65 000–75 000 • ES-5: $77 000–89 000
Counsellor in Not-for-Profit	• B.A. • Volunteer experience an asset	• Positions can often be obtained quickly after B.A. is complete	• $35 000–46 000 • Positions vary, some have additional benefits (shift work, etc.)
Correctional Officer	• High school diploma	• Pay increases with security level	• CX-2: $59 000–75 000
Parole or Probation Officer	• B.A.	• Criminal justice experience an asset	• WP-4: $62 000–82 000
Administration Officer	• Secondary school degree	• Bilingualism an asset	• AS-2: $54 000–59,000
Project Officer in Government	• B.A.	• Bilingualism an asset	• AS-3: $58 000–63 000 (entry level) • AS-4: $64 000–69 000

*Abbreviations in this column are used by the Government of Canada to designate employment departments and levels. PS = Psychology. ES = Economics and Social Science Services. CX = Correctional Services. WP = Welfare Programmes. AS = Administrative Services. The number following an abbreviation indicates employment level (1 indicates an entry-level position).

Note: Some salaries may be 1–2 years out of date due to contract issues with employers.

Source: Salary information from Government of Canada (2015c).

THEORIES OF CRIMINAL CONDUCT
What Is Correctional Psychology?

This text focuses on a *psychological* understanding of criminal behaviour. Specifically, psychology is interested in intra-individual differences (variations in criminal conduct within an individual across time and different situations) and inter-individual differences (variation in criminal conduct between individuals) in behaviour. This perspective does not ignore broader social influences on criminality, but asserts that greater understanding of criminal behaviour comes from psychological explanations that consider individual differences. The exploration of social influences is of greatest interest to sociologists. As McGuire (2004) noted, a key difference between psychology and sociology is the level or focus of comparisons: psychology focuses on individuals whereas sociology focuses more on groups. McGuire used the analogy of a microscope, arguing that psychology uses a much higher level of magnification in order to see things (about crime) that are not apparent from a different view. Examining the broader social context is an insufficient approach for understanding individual differences in criminal behaviour (e.g., not all individuals who are poor commit criminal acts, nor do all well-off individuals avoid crime).

The terms used to define the study of criminal behaviour vary somewhat across different texts. Broadly speaking, **forensic psychology** refers to any application of psychology to the legal system (Pozzulo, Bennell, and Forth 2008). While some reserve this term for the practice of clinical psychology in the legal system (Huss 2009), this more reflects issues of risk assessment and expert testimony—key activities of psychologists in the courts intended to guide legal decision-making—than the investigation of an understanding of criminal behaviour. In the United Kingdom (McGuire 2002), the specific psychological study of criminal behaviour is referred to as criminological psychology; in the United States and Canada, the area is often described as **correctional psychology** (Magaletta and Boothby 2003). Magaletta and Boothby recognized that correctional psychologists conduct crisis management and individual and group psychotherapy with general population inmates as well as with offenders with mental disorders and substance abuse problems. The focus of this text is to understand the assessment and management of individuals who engage in criminal behaviour by following dispositions made by the courts (rather than examining issues relating to the operation of justice). Accordingly, our preferred "model" is that of correctional psychology, as described by Magaletta and Boothby (2003).

Sociological explanations regarding such factors as age, gender, and social class provide insight into groups of individuals. For instance, relatively speaking, younger males are more likely to be involved in **criminal behaviour**, and crime decreases with increased age (Blumstein and Cohen 1987). Prisoners tend to be less educated and have poorer employment histories (Motiuk, Cousineau, and Gileno 2005). However, not all young males commit crimes, some quite elderly males are involved in criminal behaviour, and some highly educated individuals (e.g., university professors!) commit crimes and receive sanctions from the courts.

Juxtaposing correctional psychology with sociological and criminological explanations underscores the different perspectives and levels of analysis of these approaches

(McGuire 2002). As the level of analysis varies, so too does the theoretical explanation. For instance, at the macro level, the objective is to understand crime as a large-scale social phenomenon, reflecting strain theory (Merton 1957). As the perspective narrows, the importance of socialization and the influence of community, family, and peer groups becomes of greater interest, reflecting differential association theory (Sutherland and Cressey 1970). An even narrower focus examines patterns of individual behaviour, first over time and situation, and then in terms of the influence of psychological factors such as thoughts, feelings, or attitudes (Andrews and Bonta 2006; McGuire 2002). These last two levels of analysis are of greatest interest when examining inter- and intra-individual differences in criminal behaviour.

Notably, as illustrated by the offender profiles at the beginning of this chapter, offenders comprise a particularly heterogeneous group (Piquero, Blumstein, Brame, Haapanen, Mulvey, and Nagin 2001). Aggregate age–crime data tend to conceal the distinct trajectories of widely different offenders (Barnett, Blumstein, & Farrington 1987; Hussong, Curran, Moffitt, Caspi, and Carrig 2004). Importantly, as many as 70 percent of offenders follow some approximation of the age–crime curve, with only a small percentage of offenders maintaining criminal activity well into adulthood (Piquero et al. 2001). This suggests that group-based explanations must be informed by explanations of individual differences in order to situate a psychological understanding of crime.

A psychological explanation, then, considers the factors that might influence criminal behaviour (both crime acquisition and cessation). For example, within a group of males, how might we determine which younger males are more likely to engage in criminal activity and which older males are more likely to stop committing crimes? Psychology attempts to refine our understanding of criminal behaviour by considering individual differences in order to account for heterogeneity and provide differentiated assessment and intervention. Such a psychological understanding is derived from considerations of variability of criminal behaviour among individuals as well as variability within an individual over time and across situations.

The Personal, Interpersonal and Community-Reinforcement model (PIC–R; Andrews and Bonta 2006)—sometimes referred to as a general personality and social psychology of criminal conduct—is a prominent psychological depiction of the interplay among factors influencing criminality. This model posits that criminal behaviour reflects the "immediate situation"—that factors (e.g., temptations, facilitators, inhibitors, and stressors) combine to influence a decision to engage in criminal behaviour. The decision is further influenced by attitudes supportive of crime, a history of criminal behaviour, a balance of the costs and rewards of crime, and the presence of social supports for crime. Further, Andrews and Bonta's PIC–R perspective on criminal conduct highlights the contributions of community (family of origin, social economic factors), interpersonal (family/child relations, childhood attachment, neglect, abuse, ties to criminal others), personal (early conduct problems; biological factors such as temperament, verbal intelligence, gender, age, and cognitions), and consequences (whether criminal behaviour is rewarded). It is an integrative and situational model of criminal behaviour that recognizes the influence of both historical and immediate factors on an individual who is arriving at the decision to engage in a criminal act and to view such behaviour as appropriate (Andrews and Bonta 2006). In this manner, PIC–R reflects a learning theory of crime that attends to both social and cognitive factors as well as behaviour, underscoring it as a contemporary **cognitive social learning theory** of crime.

It is interesting and important to note that this model is quite similar to contemporary criminological viewpoints (Farrington 2003) that consider short- and long-term risk factors as well as cognitive processes and consequences of behaviour. In Farrington's (2003) theory, long-term risk factors (biological, individual, family, peer, school, community, and society) interact with short-term risk factors (energizing and inhibiting factors, opportunity, antisocial tendency, and cognitive processes) to influence antisocial behaviour.

CRIME TRENDS

CONSIDERING MEDIA REPORTS AND POLITICAL CALLS TO GET TOUGH ON CRIME, IT would be reasonable for Canadians to believe that crime rates, especially for serious gun crimes, are increasing. However, the data overall are encouraging, except for some specific subgroups for which there is marked concern (e.g., young girls, Aboriginals of all ages). Figure 1.2 presents police-reported crime rates from 1998–2012, which show a general decline (28 percent) since 1998. Since 2000, the rate of violent crimes has decreased 20.4 percent. It is important to note that these figures reflect crimes reported to the police; since not all crimes are reported, the data underestimate actual crime.

A similar trend of declining crime occurs for both youth (12 to 17 years) and adults (Public Safety Canada 2014). Further, for both youth and adults, violent crime is less prevalent than property crime. It would appear that age has some influence on type of crimes committed. Administration of justice charges (e.g., failure to appear, breach of probation), impaired driving, and weapons charges are more common for adults. Break and enter, robbery, and sexual assault are more common for youth. Table 1.4 presents a summary of crime statistics for youth and adults.

The pattern of rates of crime among youth and adults in 2012 was consistent with previous years. Overall, youth account for more criminal charges (2840 per 100 000) than adults (1990 per 100 000). Among youth, males and females accounted for comparable percentages of different court dispositions (e.g., fines, community service, probation, custody).

In terms of violent offending, 9.6 percent of all adult offences are violent when all violent offences, including major assaults, are combined. This figure rises to 26 percent when violence includes possession of weapons charges, uttering threats, and common assault.

Crime Severity Index

A new tool, the Police Reported Crime Severity Index (PRCSI) has recently been developed for measuring police-reported crime in Canada (Statistics Canada 2009). This index tracks changes in the severity of police-reported crime from year to year by taking into account the change in volume of a particular crime (i.e., police-reported crime) and the relative seriousness of that crime in comparison to other crimes. In contrast, the

Rate per 100 000 Population

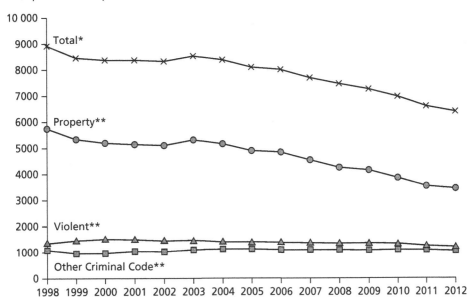

Figure 1.2 Police-Reported Crime Rates

*The type of decision group "guilty" includes guilty of the offence, of an included offence, of an attempt of the offence, or of an attempt of an included offence. This category also includes cases where an absolute or conditional discharge has been imposed.
**This figure only includes cases in provincial court and partial data from Superior Court. Superior Court data are not reported to the *Adult Criminal Court Survey* for Quebec, Ontario, Manitoba, and Saskatchewan. Information from Quebec's municipal courts is not collected. The concept of a case has changed to more closely reflect court processing. Statistics from the *Adult Criminal Court Survey* used in this report should not be compared to editions of the *Corrections and Conditional Release Statistical Overview* prior to 2007. A case is one or more charges against an accused person or corporation, processed by the courts at the same time, and where all of the charges in the case received a final disposition. Police data are reported on a calendar year basis whereas court and prison data are reported on a fiscal year basis (April 1 through March 31).

Source: Figure data from *Uniform Crime Reporting Survey*, Canadian Centre for Justice Statistics, Statistics Canada, cited in Public Safety Canada (2014), Figure A1, p. 1.

traditional "crime rate" provides information on the number of police-reported incidents that have occurred for a given population. It measures the volume of crime coming to the attention of the police. The rate is simply a count of all criminal incidents reported to and by police divided by the population of interest. Each criminal incident, regardless of the type or seriousness of the offence, counts the same in the rate. For example, one homicide counts the same as one act of mischief.

The PRCSI helps answer such questions as "Is the crime coming to the attention of police more or less serious than before?" and "Is police-reported crime in a given city or province more or less serious than in Canada overall?" The principle behind the Crime Severity Index was to have more-serious crimes carry greater weight than less-serious

Table 1.4 Types of Crimes Committed by Youth and Adults, 2012–13

Type of Crime	Youth (%)	Adults (%)
Administration of justice	10.9	21.7
Impaired driving	0	10.9
Break and enter	7.8	2.8
Theft	13.6	10.3
Fraud	0	3.2
Common assault	8.3	9.6
Drugs (possession and trafficking)	8.3	7.5
Robbery	5.0	1.0
Weapons	3.4	2.5
Sexual assault	2.6	1.0
Homicide and related	0.1	0.07

Source: Public Safety Canada (2014).

crimes. As a result, changes in more-serious crimes have a greater impact on the Index than on the traditional crime rate. This allows the Index to better reflect changes in the incidence of more serious crimes and minimizes the impact of differences in the way the public and police in various jurisdictions report high-volume, less-serious crime, thereby improving comparisons among provinces and municipalities.

The weights assigned to different crimes are derived from actual sentences handed down by courts in all provinces and territories. More-serious crimes are assigned higher weights, while less-serious offences are assigned lower weights. The specific weight for any given type of offence consists of two parts. The first component is the incarceration rate for the offence type. This is the proportion of people convicted of the offence who are sentenced to time in prison. The second component is the average (mean) length of the prison sentence (in days) for the specific type of offence. The weights are updated every five years to ensure that they reflect changes in sentencing patterns and new legislation. It is not necessary to update them each year as trends in court data do not tend to change substantially from year to year. Figure 1.3 presents police-reported crime severity indexes from 1998 through 2014. It is useful to contrast this chart with the police-reported crime rates illustrated in Figure 1.2.

The Crime Severity Index appears to be a useful tool for analyzing crime trends in Canada since it addresses not only the amount of crime coming to the attention of police, but also the severity of this crime. In addition, it shows whether crime in general is relatively more or less serious than in previous years, and it is useful in determining if reported crime is more or less serious in one jurisdiction than in another.

Index (2006 = 100)

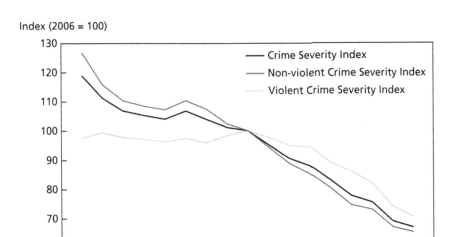

Figure 1.3 Police-Reported Crime Severity Indexes, 1998–2014

Source: Statistics Canada (2015d).

Crime Victimization

Incident-based data (Public Safety Canada 2014) noted marked variation in the age of crime victims. While only 36.9 percent of the Canadian population is under the age of 30, more than half (52.6 percent) of all victims of violent crime reported in 2011 were under the age of 30. Canadians aged 65 and older (who account for 14.15 percent of the general population) represented 2.5 percent of victims. Females aged 15–44 were more likely than males of the same age to be victims of a violent crime. Male victims of violent crime tended to be younger. The age groups with the highest rates of victimization for violent crime were ages 15–19 (15.2 percent), ages 20–24 (15.0 percent), and ages 25–29 (12.4 percent). According to the General Social Survey (Statistics Canada 1999, 2004, 2009), rates of being a victim of property crime increased from 75 per 1000 population to 108 per 1000 population. Rates for other crimes remained relatively constant during the same time frame (sexual assault, 24 per 1000; robbery, 13 per 1000; assault, 80 per 1000).

As noted earlier, police-reported crime does not necessarily reflect the extent of criminal conduct because some crime goes unreported. Victimization surveys present an additional understanding of crime and will typically yield higher rates of crime. According to a 2004 survey, 17 percent of Canadians aged 16 and over had been victims of at least one crime measured by the International Criminal Victimization Survey during the year preceding the survey (Statistics Canada 2005a). This rate was similar to the overall international victimization rate (16 percent). Across all participating countries, slightly more than half the population (53 percent) reported a victimization incident to the police, whereas 48 percent of Canadians reported being a victim of one of five offence types: theft

Table 1.5 Involvement in the Criminal Justice System

Involvement	N (%)
Victim of crime	1069 (28.8%)
Witness to a crime	435 (9.7%)
Working in the justice system	214 (4.8%)
A juror	150 (3.3%)
Charged with a crime	141 (33.1%)

Source: Latimer and Desjardins (2007).

from a car, theft of a bicycle, burglary, attempted burglary, and theft of personal property. Interestingly, a recent Canadian survey (Latimer and Desjardins 2007) provides additional insight into crime victimization and its potential impact on Canadians' perceptions of the criminal justice system, specifically their confidence in its various components (police, courts, corrections, and parole). This study utilized a household telephone survey of 4502 Canadians across all 10 provinces (with only a 9 percent response rate, which is consistent with industry norms). The respondents were asked if within the last ten years they had been an accused, a witness, a juror, a victim, or had worked within the justice system in some capacity. The survey results are presented in Table 1.5.

While extrapolation of this small sample to the larger Canadian population should be performed with caution because of the small sample size, it is important to note the almost 30 percent of respondents reported being a victim of crime. Within this group, 76.2 percent reported a property offence (e.g., break and enter, theft), while 23.8 percent reported a violent offence (e.g., assault). Nonetheless, police-reported violent crime in 2007 in Canada was 930 per 100 000 population (Public Safety Canada 2008), or approximately 294 000 victimizations annually—roughly equivalent to the sixteenth-largest city in Canada. Estimates for victimization-related costs in Canada were suggested to be an additional $47 billion in 2003 (Government of Canada 2009). These costs must be added to the actual costs of the operation of the criminal justice system to fully appreciate the impact of crime on Canadians. Accordingly, in 2003, crime in Canada cost an estimated $60 billion, $13 billion of which was related to criminal justice system expenditures such as police, courts, and correctional services. This cost is slightly less than half the direct and indirect costs for health care in Canada, which were estimated at $123 billion in 2003 (Canadian Institute for Health Information 2006).

Public Perceptions of the Criminal Justice System

Latimer and Desjardins' (2007) study reveals interesting insight into Canadians' perceptions of the criminal justice system. For instance, contrary to the evidence, 57.8 percent of those surveyed believed the overall crime rate had gone up (74.4 percent for property crime, 62.7 percent for violent crime). Surprisingly, only 6.5 percent indicated that they

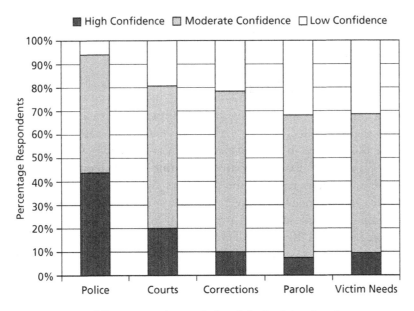

■ High Confidence ▨ Moderate Confidence ☐ Low Confidence

Figure 1.4 Public Perceptions of the Criminal Justice System

Source: Latimer and Desjardins (2007).

believed their neighbourhoods were less safe, despite their view that crime was increasing. A quarter of respondents indicated a low level of confidence in the criminal justice system and one-third rated their confidence in the youth criminal justice system as low. Indeed, public confidence in the criminal justice system was lower than for the education, health care, and welfare systems. Figure 1.4 provides a more specific breakdown for different components of the criminal justice system. Parole appears to have generated the least confidence in the Canadians who responded to this survey.

A further examination of confidence in specific components of the criminal justice system suggests the public has the least confidence in police preventing crime, the courts imposing appropriate sentences, corrections rehabilitating offenders, and parole supervising offenders in the community. Nonetheless, greater confidence was reported in terms of police solving crimes, the courts determining guilt, and corrections preventing escapes. This report also identified characteristics that lead Canadians to be more optimistic and confident regarding the criminal justice system. Those individuals who value government information, who support less punitive sentencing practices, are treatment-oriented, have a university degree, who use the Internet as a source of information, and who support the government's Tackling Crime agenda (i.e., tougher penalties and crime prevention) are more confident in the criminal justice system. For more specific information regarding Canadians' perceptions of sentencing and other aspects of the criminal justice system, review Latimer and Desjardins' (2007) full report. See also Roberts, Crutcher, and Verbrugge (2007), whose recent research demonstrates that 74 percent of Canadians believe that sentencing is too lenient, although there was support for restorative sentence objectives promoting a sense of responsibility in the offender (84 percent) and securing reparation for the crime victim (66 percent).

Variation in Crime by Source

As discussed earlier, crime rates vary according to the definition of crime and the source of the information. Police-reported crime is lower than victimization rates. Moreover, if one uses incarceration rates as an index of the seriousness of crime in Canada, then crime appears less problematic. One method of presenting the attrition in crime is to review the numbers of crimes reported, the number of convictions, the number of provincial sentences, and the number of federal sentences (the lengthiest sentences, presumably reserved for the more serious offences). Figure 1.5 presents what has been referred to as a crime funnel. Of the 2.24 million crimes reported to the police in 2012, only 4999 resulted in warrants of committal for a federal sentence (2.2 percent). Some cases were still pending before the courts, but using similar data from 2005–06, only

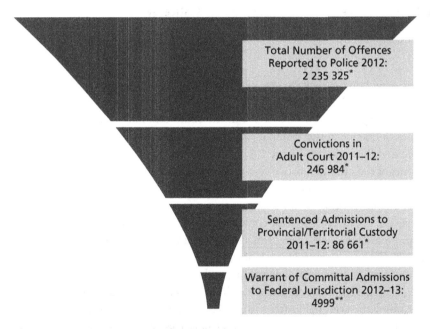

Figure 1.5 Crime Funnel of Criminal Outcomes

*Uniform Crime Reporting Survey, Adult Criminal Court Survey, and Adult Correctional Services Survey, Canadian Centre for Justice Statistics, Statistics Canada.
**Correctional Service Canada.

Source: Public Safety Canada (2014), Figure A7, p. 13.

1.7 of police-reported offences resulted in federal sentences, and 2.8 percent resulted in provincial custodial sentences.

Length of Sentences

Over half (54.6 percent) of all custodial sentences imposed by adult courts are less than one month. Prison sentences for men tend to be longer than for women. Over two-thirds (69.9 percent) of women and just over half of men (52.9 percent) who are incarcerated upon conviction receive a sentence of one month or less, and 92.1 percent of women and 85.1 percent of men receive a sentence of six months or less. Of all convictions that result in custody, only 4.2 percent result in federal jurisdiction (i.e., a sentence of two or more years) (Public Safety Canada 2014).

These figures are very important in terms of the provision of assessment and treatment services to offenders. The shorter the sentence received by the offender, the less time is available for comprehensive assessments and participation in prison-based programming prior to the offender's return to the community. The proportion of offenders that receives sentences of greater than 12 months (a reasonable time to arrange and complete programming) is relatively small (men: one to two years (3.6 percent), two years or greater (4.5 percent); women: one to two years (1.9 percent), two years or greater (2.0 percent)). Although community-based programming is effective in reducing future reoffending, some offenders clearly require prison-based programming if the correctional agencies are to address public safety concerns. This is not a call for increased sentence lengths, but rather recognition that certain correctional operational realities are linked to sentencing.

Variations Across Provinces

One important consideration in understanding the impact of crime is to consider variations across Canada. Figure 1.6 presents the crime rate by province compared against the national average. There is a general trend towards increased crime rates the further west and north one moves. Most notable is that the crime rate of the Northwest Territories is eight times the national average. Underscoring these data is the over-representation of Aboriginals in the Canadian criminal justice system (see Chapter 12).

International Context

It is important to consider how Canada compares to other countries regarding crime and, in particular, rates of incarceration. Canada's incarceration rate is 118 per 100 000 population, which represents a slight increase despite a decreasing crime rate. Compared to the United States, Canada's incarceration rate is modest, but the U.S. rate has been decreasing while Canada's has been increasing. Figure 1.7 presents a summary of international incarceration rates.

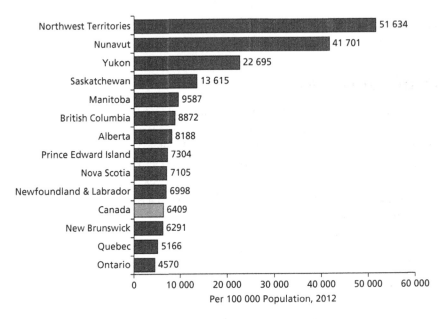

Figure 1.6 Crime Rates by Province

Source: *Uniform Crime Reporting Survey*, Canadian Centre for Justice Statistics, Statistics Canada, cited in Public Safety Canada (2014), Figure A2, p. 3.

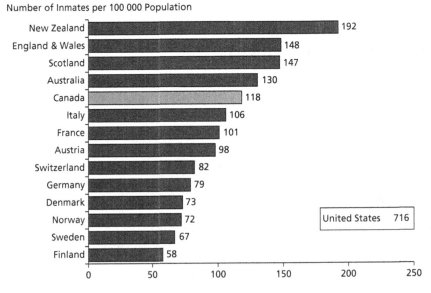

Figure 1.7 International Incarceration Rates

Source: "World Prison Population List," cited in Public Safety Canada (2014), Figure A3, p. 5.

Statistical Information for Understanding Research

In order to understand common tables and terms used in the study of criminal psychology, it may be useful to review some key terms and approaches to presenting and summarizing research findings. This section briefly describes effect sizes, meta-analysis, and how to measure predictive accuracy.

Effect Sizes and Meta-Analysis

Most research questions (e.g., Does treatment work? What predicts recidivism?) have been tested in multiple studies, which makes synthesizing the current research a challenging task. For example, by 1990, there were nearly 500 studies evaluating offender treatment (Andrews and Bonta 2006), with some studies concluding that treatment reduced recidivism, others concluding that it increased recidivism, and others finding no effect. How does one interpret such a large and contradictory body of research?

One way to synthesize this information is **meta-analysis**, which uses statistics to aggregate the results of individual studies and develop one averaged effect size for all the studies combined. It should be noted that meta-analytic statistics typically do not report an unweighted average (i.e., a straight average from all studies); instead, they usually give some studies more weight than others. The rationale behind weighted average effect sizes is that certain studies (such as those with larger sample sizes) may deserve greater weight.

A note about **effect sizes** is necessary here. Statistics such as the t-test or the F-test (ANOVA) tell you whether groups are significantly different from each other, but they do not tell you anything about the magnitude of that difference. Effect sizes *do* provide information about the magnitude of the difference and they can also be tested for significance. The best effect size to use depends on the type of research question you are asking. Studies involving two dichotomous variables (e.g.,

assessing the impact of treatment versus no treatment on recidivism) typically use effect sizes such as a phi correlation or an odds ratio. For studies looking at a continuous variable and a dichotomous variable (e.g., risk assessment scores and recidivism), effect sizes are typically reported as the area under the receiver operating characteristic curve (AUC for ROC), a Cohen's d, correlation, or the B_1 coefficient from logistic regression. These statistics have their advantages and disadvantages and it is important to be aware of them when selecting which effect size to use (for more information, see Hanson 2008; Rice and Harris 2005). For example, correlations are fairly robust when recidivism base rates are roughly 50 percent, but they become unreliable for extremely low or high base rates. When using correlations for low-base-rate research (e.g., sex offender recidivism), statistical adjustments for correlations are recommended.

Meta-analysis is useful because the aggregated effect size provides a quantitative summary of a large body of research. It also has some other interesting features. Different studies tend to use different statistics to report their results, which makes them difficult to directly compare (e.g., some report ROCs, while others might report Cohen's d). In meta-analysis, however, formulae can be used to convert information from one measure of effect size into another. This allows you to directly compare individual studies that used different statistics, and it allows you to combine studies no matter what statistics they reported.

There are also some limitations to meta-analysis. For example, aggregating data only from published studies is problematic if there is a publication bias (i.e., studies with significant effect sizes are more likely to be published). Seeking out unpublished studies can help provide a more accurate answer to your research question. Another important limitation of meta-analysis is that the conclusions of the meta-analysis are only as strong as the quality of the individual studies that are aggregated. You would not put much faith in a study with poor methodological quality (e.g., a study with questionable validity or with systematic biases in its results). Likewise, a meta-analysis that aggregates results from 50 poor-quality studies should be interpreted with caution. One way to address this issue is to code study quality (several guidelines exist for this task) and test whether the effect sizes vary based on the quality of the study. For example, in a meta-analysis of sex offender treatment, Hanson, Bourgon, Helmus, and Hodgson (2009a) found a trend for *smaller* effect sizes in better quality studies. Although meta-analysis has certain limitations, it remains an effective way to synthesize research in a given area and is generally considered the gold standard for answering a research question.

Measuring Predictive Accuracy

Receiver operating characteristic (ROC) analysis is a technique for measuring the accuracy of risk assessments by examining false positives and true positives across decision thresholds. For each possible cut-off value (score), one can plot the false positive rate (x-axis) as a function of true positive rate (y-axis). We can then measure the area under that curve (AUC) to get an overall measure of predictive accuracy. Compared to other methods like correlations, ROC analyses are less influenced by decision thresholds and base rate and has become a standard in comparing across risk measures. See Figure 1.8 for an example of an ROC curve.

AUC ranges from 0.50 (indicating chance accuracy) to 1.00 (indicating perfect accuracy). In other words, an AUC of 0.80 indicates that 80 percent of the time, a randomly selected recidivist will have a higher risk score than a randomly selected non-recidivist. An AUC greater than .80 is considered very good. An AUC can also be directly converted to a Cohen's d effect size by referring to a table (Rice and Harris 2005).

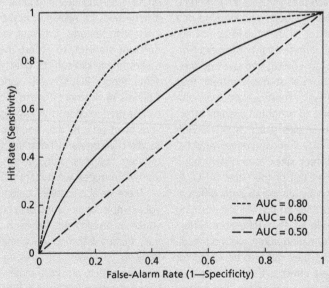

Figure 1.8 Exemplar Receiver Operator Characteristic Curve

METHODOLOGY
Determinants of Crime

As noted in the PIC–R model, determinants of crime have often been described as distal (historical) and proximal (immediate, situational). From psychology's perspective, it is of interest to identify those factors that are most strongly associated with criminality in order to develop assessments that reflect these domains and interventions that address (i.e., change, modify, diminish) these domains and reduce future reoffending. While literature reviews are helpful in understanding key issues within a field, a more useful strategy to empirically identify determinants of crime is through meta-analysis. Meta-analytic reviews are less biased, in that they provide quantitative estimates of the importance of study results, rather than narrative interpretations by the authors. This method of reviewing studies and aggregating the findings in terms of effect sizes (i.e., the strength of the association between independent variables such as substance abuse and a dependent variable such as criminal behaviour) is now considered the standard for reviewing the literature. Moreover, statistical techniques exist such that differences between groups (percentages, t-scores) can be converted to a Pearson correlation coefficient (r), permitting a common metric for easily understanding the relative importance of different independent variables.

Correlates, Risk Factors, and Causal Factors

The research to date is primarily correlational, meaning there is a demonstrated relationship between some factor and criminal conduct. However, we don't know what came first—the factor or criminal conduct. For example, suppose a researcher interviews women in prison and learns that most of the female inmates are very depressed. Does this mean that depression is a risk factor for criminal conduct? Not necessarily. It could simply mean that the women became depressed after imprisonment. Thus, depression is considered a correlate of criminal conduct in this example, not a risk factor. In order for depression to be considered a risk factor, the measurement of depression would have to precede the measurement of crime, and the statistical relationship would have to be positive (i.e., as depression increases, so does crime). Table 1.6 summarizes known risk factors of crime, while Table 1.7 presents the empirical support for these risk factors from meta-analyses. To date, explicit causal factors have not been demonstrated. Nonetheless, it is clear that as the number of risk factors accumulate, the likelihood of a person engaging (or re-engaging) in criminal conduct increases proportionately.

FACTORS ASSOCIATED WITH CRIMINAL CONDUCT

THE WORK BY ANDREWS AND HIS COLLEAGUES RANKS VARIABLES PURPORTED TO be related to criminality and identifies a **Central Eight** risk/need factors that are most important in understanding criminal behaviour. Embedded within this group of variables are the **Big Four**, proposed as the major causal variables in the analysis of the criminal

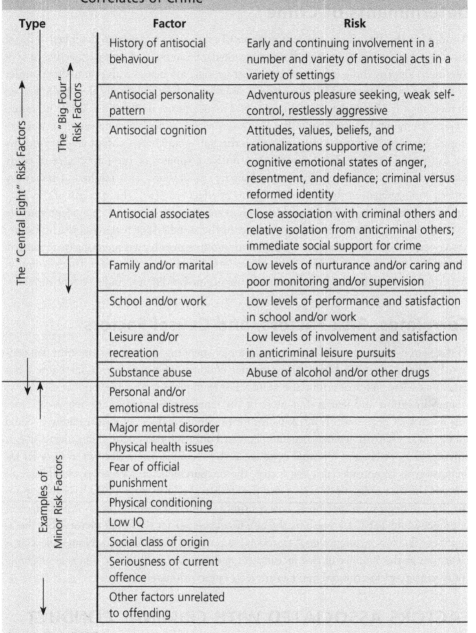

Table 1.6 An Overview of Meta-Analytic Findings Regarding Correlates of Crime

Type			Factor	Risk
The "Central Eight" Risk Factors	The "Big Four" Risk Factors		History of antisocial behaviour	Early and continuing involvement in a number and variety of antisocial acts in a variety of settings
			Antisocial personality pattern	Adventurous pleasure seeking, weak self-control, restlessly aggressive
			Antisocial cognition	Attitudes, values, beliefs, and rationalizations supportive of crime; cognitive emotional states of anger, resentment, and defiance; criminal versus reformed identity
			Antisocial associates	Close association with criminal others and relative isolation from anticriminal others; immediate social support for crime
			Family and/or marital	Low levels of nurturance and/or caring and poor monitoring and/or supervision
			School and/or work	Low levels of performance and satisfaction in school and/or work
			Leisure and/or recreation	Low levels of involvement and satisfaction in anticriminal leisure pursuits
			Substance abuse	Abuse of alcohol and/or other drugs
Examples of Minor Risk Factors			Personal and/or emotional distress	
			Major mental disorder	
			Physical health issues	
			Fear of official punishment	
			Physical conditioning	
			Low IQ	
			Social class of origin	
			Seriousness of current offence	
			Other factors unrelated to offending	

Source: Bonta (2007).

Table 1.7 Summary of Correlations among Risk Factors and Criminal Conduct

Risk Factor	Pearson Correlation	No. of Correlation Coefficients
1. Lower-class origins	0.06	97
2. Personal distress/psychopathology	0.08	226
3. Personal education/vocational achievement	0.12	129
4. Parental/family factors	0.18	334
5. Temperament/personality	0.21	621
6. Antisocial attitudes/associates	0.22	168

Source: Andrews and Bonta (2006).

behaviour of individuals. Equally important, a series of meta-analyses have also confirmed that certain variables previously considered important correlates of crime in sociological theory have proved to be relatively unimportant. These factors are referred to as minor risk factors. Table 1.6 presents James Bonta's synthesis of this meta-analytic research.

Perhaps the most compelling demonstration of the relative importance of major (first order) and minor (second order) risk factors comes from an ongoing research project and collaboration between the University of New Brunswick and Carleton University (Andrews and Bonta 2006). Approximately 1000 studies were identified from 1970 on, which yielded 372 studies for content analysis and meta-analysis. These 372 studies yielded more than 1770 Pearson correlation coefficients, each of which reflected correlations between purported risk factors and some measure of criminal behaviour. In general, the Central Eight, as reflected in PIC–R, yielded more robust correlations than other factors. Similar findings have also been reported by McGuire (2002). Table 1.7 presents a summary of the findings.

As is clear, the more robust co-variation with criminal behaviour is from variables embedded within a cognitive social learning theory of crime. This means that if the goal is to understand and reduce criminal behaviour, then assessments and treatment must attend to those factors that are most highly correlated with criminal conduct. Specifically, antisocial attitudes and associates are much more important that such factors as social class or mental health symptoms.

Another series of analyses reported by Andrews and Bonta (2006) using eight different datasets from eight independent meta-analyses further reflects the relative importance of the Central Eight and the emergence of the Big Four as the strongest correlates of criminal conduct. These findings are highlighted in Table 1.8.

Two key points are worth highlighting from Table 1.8. First, the eight independent meta-analyses yielded very consistent findings regarding the relative importance of risk

Table 1.8 Mean Estimates of Correlations among Risk Factors and Criminal Conduct

Risk Factor	Mean Pearson Correlation	Confidence Interval (95%)
1. Big Four risk factors	0.26	0.19–0.33
2. Moderate risk factors	0.17	0.12–0.21
3. Minor risk factors	0.04	−0.04–0.12

Source: Andrews and Bonta (2006).

factors. Second, the confidence interval for the minor risk factors includes 0.00, which indicates that on average there is no relationship between these predictor variables and criminal behaviour. That is, these minor risk factors cannot explain criminal conduct. In combination, Tables 1.7 and 1.8 provide strong empirical support for a cognitive social learning model of criminal behaviour. These major risk factors are often termed **criminogenic** in that they are empirically related to criminal conduct and, when reduced, lead to reductions in future reoffending. For this reason, **criminogenic needs** typically inform treatment referrals.

Linking the Research to the Case Studies

It may be helpful to review case studies from the beginning of this chapter to determine how research regarding determinants of crime actually applies in the real world (see Table 1.9). For instance, in the case of the Bill Jones, the offender is a younger male with prior criminal involvement. Family background is problematic, as are educational achievement and employment history. In addition to these distal risk factors, he presents with self-regulation deficits and substance abuse problems and maintains antisocial peer relationships. These more proximal risk factors have not been satisfactorily ameliorated through treatment. A recent relationship may have the potential to change the contingencies for prosocial behaviour, thus acting as a protective factor.

In the case of Paul Bernardo, less information is provided regarding his background, although it is readily available elsewhere. His co-accused could be viewed as an antisocial associate given the nature of her participation, although her plea bargain asserted she had been a victim of abuse by Bernardo. His family background was dysfunctional in terms of parental modelling and attachment, although he presented as the perfect child. He had good job as an accountant and there was no evidence of substance abuse, although recreational drug use could have occurred. Independent accounts have speculated that Bernardo meets the criteria for a diagnosis of psychopath, but court evidence confirming this is unavailable. As well, it is important to note that at the time of his arrest, Bernardo scored low on a variety of standardized sex offender risk scales, further supporting the

Table 1.9 Case Studies (Bill & Paul): Presence of Risk Factors

Risk Factors	Bill Jones	Paul Bernardo
	Applies	
History of antisocial behaviour	Yes	No
Antisocial personality	Yes	Likely
Antisocial attitudes	Likely	Likely
Antisocial associates	Yes	No (co-accused?)
Family/marital problems	Yes	No
Education/employment problems	Yes	No
Substance abuse	Yes	No
Leisure/recreation problems	Yes	No

view that he was atypical of the majority of sex offenders who come in formal contact with the courts.

One noteworthy aspect of this review is that a clearer understanding of typical criminal behaviour comes from a review of primary or first-order risk factors. As will be clear in reviewing prevalence rates for different types of crimes, the majority of crimes reflect ordinary individuals committing less serious offenses. Despite the fascination by the public (and psychology students!) with serial and unusual crimes, most individuals involved in criminal behaviour are ordinary individuals with ordinary problems (i.e., poor self-regulation, substance use, lack of employment, or poor choice in friends) whose decision to engage in criminal conduct reflects disinhibition, a failure to consider short- and long-term consequences, support from criminal peers, and attitudes for such behaviour. As support for prosocial behaviour increases, offenders' decisions and behaviours, especially when buttressed by intervention, become less criminal.

FUTURE DIRECTIONS

In Canada, there is an increasing disconnect between crime rates and policy. Despite lower crime rates, incarceration rates are increasing. Chapter 4 more fully explores the utility of a punitive approach to reduce criminal behaviour. The corrections field has fully incorporated criminogenic needs into risk assessment and case planning, but risk assessments lack a standardized instrument or approach. The distinction between static and dynamic risk, as well as potential protective factors has only recently begun to be considered. Again, this is more fully discussed in Chapter 4. While the personal and fiscal costs of crime are high, the field of correctional psychology has not utilized a cost–benefit approach to evaluation of strategies to reduce crime and manage risk, especially as it applies to individual offenders.

SUMMARY

1. The goal of this chapter was to highlight some key reasons why crime is of concern to Canadians and to provide an empirical backdrop for understanding criminal conduct using Canadian data and Canadian researchers' contributions.

2. Public confidence regarding corrections and parole is not high. This suggests there is a need for better communication of empirical findings to the Canadian public.

3. Key studies illustrated the role of media, Canadians' perceptions of components of the criminal justice system, and rates and types of crimes for youth and adults. Crime and incarceration in Canada has been situated in an international context, showing that relative to the United States (716 per 100 000 incarceration rate), Canada is in fairly good shape (118 per 100 000), although less so relative to Western Europe (e.g., 79 per 10 000 in Germany). With respect to crime rates in Canada, there are differences in terms of age and gender, and less serious crimes (i.e., administration of justice) are most prevalent.

4. While media portrayals of crime often reflect sensational cases, correctional psychology in general focuses on more typical offenders, their needs, and strategies to manage risk within prisons and following offender release.

5. Restricting the text to correctional psychology is intended to inform the explanation and understanding of criminal behaviour in a manner that will be of interest and assistance to students interested in careers in corrections, including parole and probation staff and psychologists. Overall, the purpose of the text is to highlight key literature that describes and supports evidence-based practice for reducing reoffending.

Discussion Questions

1. Why does the public have such low confidence in corrections? How could this be improved? How might the media help Canadians to better understand the true picture about crime?

2. How does Canada fare relative to other countries in terms of rates of incarceration? Is this a satisfactory situation?

3. Why should crime be considered a major public policy concern in Canada? What is the impact of crime on Canadians?

4. How are victims' concerns addressed in the criminal justice system? Is this sufficient?

Chapter 2
Theories of Crime: Biological and Evolutionary Explanations

Bob was recently released from prison after serving a five-year sentence. He has a long history of getting into fights, committing break and enters for excitement, and drinking to excess. His psychological report indicates that he was abused as a child, is impulsive, and has an anger management problem. Bob participated in a research study while in prison that revealed his MAOA gene was of the "low activity" variety. Immediately after his release, he went to a bar and met a woman. As the evening progressed, Bob became increasingly intoxicated and noticed another male patron was hitting on his new friend. He told the man (in a somewhat threatening manner) that the woman was with him and that he should look elsewhere. As Bob walked away, the man yelled, "You can have the tramp." Bob stopped for a second and resisted the burning urge to punch the man in the face. However, the man persisted and said, "What's the matter, too cowardly to defend your woman?" A crowd had gathered. Bob responded immediately and threw the first punch. Within 24 hours, he was back in prison for breaching the conditions of his release and for incurring a new criminal assault charge.

Learning Objectives

1   Describe the range of biological explanations of crime, including genetics, neurochemistry, hormones, psychophysiology, and more.

2   Explain the basic principles of evolutionary psychology and demonstrate how these principles are used to understand crime in general as well as specific forms of crime and specific types of criminal offenders.

3   Demonstrate that biological and evolutionary theories of crime are as much about the environment as they are about biology and evolution.

4   Demonstrate that biological and evolutionary explanations are not incompatible with traditional theories of crime (e.g., social learning theory, presented in Chapter 3), but rather are complementary.

INTRODUCTION

How we explain Bob's behaviour depends on our perspective. We could focus on factors in the immediate situation, such as his alcohol-induced disinhibition or his childhood, where he learned that violence is an effective conflict resolution strategy. These sorts of accounts are addressed in Chapter 3. Alternately, we could focus on Bob's innate nature (his genes), or take an entirely different perspective by asking if his behaviour is part of an adaptation that has been selected during human evolutionary history. For example, did defending honour and reputation somehow increase the reproductive success of our ancestors, perhaps by deterring or eliminating competition or by enhancing attractiveness as a worthy mate?

This chapter focuses on biological and evolutionary explanations for antisocial behaviour, crime, and violence. Biological explanations are varied, ranging from genetics (as exemplified by twin and adoption studies) to brain neurochemistry and the importance of diet. Basic evolutionary psychology principles are described, followed by an illustration of how these principles are used to understand certain types of offenders, such as psychopaths, and specific types of crimes, such as homicide. Paradoxically, it will become evident that this chapter is as much about the environment as it is about biology and evolution. Discussions will explore how the environment—our hunter-and-gatherer **ancestral environment**—profoundly shaped the evolution of the human species, and how our environment continues to influence our biology.

CONTEXT

Italian physician, Cesare Lombroso (1835–1909) is commonly known as the father of criminology. Lombroso argued that criminals possess distinctive physical features (such as sloping foreheads and twisted lips) that were not often observed in his "normal" subjects. He referred to these features as atavisms, and suggested that criminals were evolutionary throwbacks who had more in common with Neanderthals than modern-day humans (Lombroso 2006).

Charles Darwin published *On the Origin of Species* in 1859, almost 17 years before Lombroso published the first volume of *Criminal Man*. Darwin argued that humans had evolved from ancestral species via the mechanisms of **natural selection**. Unfortunately, others began to misuse his work, most notably Darwin's own cousin, Francis Galton. Galton founded **eugenics**—the theory that was ultimately responsible not only for the forced sterilization (or worse) of thousands of individuals deemed "unfit" to

Yayayoyo/Shutterstock

Lombroso believed criminals were physically inferior to non-criminals, likening criminals to evolutionary throwbacks.

reproduce in the United States during the early twentieth century, but also for the atrocities that occurred under Hilter's regime—forced abortion, sterilization, and concentration camps (Niehoff 1999).

It is not surprising that a number of social scientists, particularly criminologists working from a sociological perspective, have been dismissive and in some instances scornful of biological and/or evolutionary approaches. However, as Anderson (2007) and Durrant and Ward (2015) cleverly demonstrate, the tides are changing. The study of biology and evolution has advanced considerably since Darwin and Lombroso. Moreover, it is becoming increasingly clear that biology is not destiny.

DEFINITIONS

Defining *CRIME* is a complex task. While some researchers have examined the link between biology and crime by comparing "normal" individuals to individuals who have been officially diagnosed with **antisocial personality disorder (ASPD), conduct disorder (CD),** or **psychopathy**; others have used measures of **aggression** or composite indices of **antisocial behaviour** obtained using self-report surveys or, in the case of children, from parents or teachers. Researchers often define crime using current legal definitions and examine whether biological factors correlate or predict official criminal offending in the form of arrests or convictions. Targets of study are also varied, with some researchers focusing on males and others studying females. Researchers sometimes study children, adolescents, adults, or specific groups of offenders such as violent or sexual offenders. Thus, the research methods and participant pools are vast and complex.

WHY DO WE CARE?

Theory may seem boring but it is very important. Theory keeps research findings organized. Theories also allow scientists to make sense of the world in a way that will eventually translate into real benefits for society. Theories come in many different shapes and sizes, however there are certain defining features that can make a theory particularly strong.

What Makes a Strong Theory?

Numerous textbooks and experts have defined the meaning of theory, particularly strong theory. Thus, our definition represents an amalgamation of perspectives (see Andrews and Bonta 2010; Blanchette and Brown 2006; Pozzulo, Bennell, and Forth 2015; Rappaport 1987). In sum, a theory is simply an explanation of a particular phenomenon, in this case antisocial behaviour. A strong theory: 1) is parsimonious; 2) clearly identifies the **causal mechanisms** and corresponding **mediators** and **moderators** underlying the phenomenon of interest; 3) is testable and hence falsifiable via hypotheses and predictions; 4) is based on empirical data and is modified in response to new data; 5) possesses interdisciplinary compatibility; and 6) respects gender, ethnicity, and culture. Throughout this chapter, it may be helpful to ask, "Does this perspective provide a good theory of crime?" For example, are certain explanations stronger in the sense that the corresponding evidence is stronger?

METHODOLOGY
How Is Biology-Focused Research Conducted?

A number of researchers working from very different perspectives have studied biological explanations of crime using diverse and complex research methods. Behavioural genetics researchers might employ twin methodology to ask whether identical twins are more likely to commit crime than non-identical twins. Molecular biologists might compare the genetic makeup of a group of "criminals" to one of "non-criminals" to look for distinct genetic differences between the two. Neurochemical approaches might examine how genes actually express themselves in terms of the brain's **neurotransmitter** systems. Still other researchers may rely on brain-imaging techniques such as computer tomography (CT) to assess whether the functions of the brain are somehow impaired in antisocial individuals.

BIOLOGICAL THEORIES OF CRIME
Genetics and Crime—Twins, Adoption, and Molecular Genetics

Twin Studies To examine the role that genetics plays in criminal conduct, it is necessary to employ methodologies that allow researchers to separate genetic and environmental influences. Consider the following example. A researcher asks 500 pairs of biologically related fathers and sons to complete a self-report criminal behaviour survey. The researcher then correlates the answers between fathers and sons and finds that the average correlation is .30. The question remains: Is the observed correlation due to fathers passing on "criminal genes," or is it due to fathers passing on criminal attitudes and criminal life skills through years of living together? Unfortunately, this research design does not permit a clear answer. However, the field of **behavioural genetics**, which relies heavily on the study of twins and adoptions, can help separate genetic from environmental influences, at least to some degree.

Every human being shares about 99 percent of his or her DNA sequence with the rest of the human species. The 99 percent that we have in common is fixed (not free to vary), accounting for our basic similarities (e.g., we all have two arms, two legs, one heart, one brain, two eyes, and so forth) (Plomin, DeFries, McClearn, and McGuffin 2001). Behavioural genetics focuses on the remaining 1 percent of the variance that is free to vary.

Monozygotic (MZ) or identical twins are genetically identical. They share 100 percent of their genes. Specifically, the 1 percent of DNA that is free to vary from human to human is 100 percent identical for MZ twins. In contrast, dizygotic (DZ) or fraternal twins are no more alike than non-twin siblings, sharing about 50 percent of that 1 percent that is free to vary. Keeping this in mind, let's discuss the research.

In the earliest forms of twin studies, a researcher would identify a sample of MZ and DZ twins, both raised by their respective biological families, and obtain some estimate of criminal behaviour (perhaps using self-reports or official police records). Next, the researcher would record whether each twin was criminal or non-criminal, indicating the number of times both members of each twin pair were classified as criminal. This frequency would then be converted into a concordance rate that represented the percentage of both twins classified as criminal. Concordance rates would be calculated separately for MZ and DZ twins and then compared. A concordance rate of 30 percent for the DZ twins would mean that if one of the DZ twins was criminal, then there was a 30 percent chance that the other DZ twin was also criminal. Similarly, a concordance rate of 70 percent for the MZ twins would mean that if one of the MZ twins was criminal, there was 70 percent chance that the other MZ twin was also criminal. Evidence for a genetic contribution to crime is inferred if concordance rates are higher among the MZ than DZ twins.

Concordance rates are typically converted into a heritability coefficient—a descriptive statistic that represents the proportion of **phenotypic** variance in a given behaviour (e.g., criminal) in a sample and/or population that can be attributed to genetic variation among individuals (Polmin et al. 2001). Recently, however, more complex statistical approaches such as biometric modelling have been used to estimate heritability coefficients (DeFries and Fulker 1985; Rhee and Waldman 2002). Statistical modelling methods permit the estimation of two types of environmental factors: 1) shared environmental factors (i.e., aspects of the environment shared by all family members, such as living in poverty); and 2) non-shared environmental factors (i.e., aspects of the environment not shared by all family members, such as exposure to different peer groups or differential treatment by parents) (Quinsey, Skilling, Lalumière, and Craig 2004). Thus, contrary to popular belief, genetic studies are just as much about genes as they are about environment.

A common criticism levied against this type of twin study is that it may overestimate (or in some cases underestimate) the genetic contribution for several reasons. First, parents are arguably more likely to provide similar environments for MZ twins (the same toys, clothes, and learning opportunities) than their DZ counterparts (Anderson 2007; Raine 1993), thus artificially inflating the genetic contribution. Second, heritability estimates for MZ twins may be confounded by prenatal factors that by definition aren't necessarily genetic. For example, MZ twins usually share one placenta and DZ twins usually have two separate placentas, thereby introducing a potential biological difference that is not necessarily genetic. Earlier twin studies were also criticized for using small sample sizes and for being subject to political influence (e.g., two studies were conducted in Nazi Germany in 1936) (Anderson 2007). Fortunately, adoption studies have been able to address some of these criticisms.

Adoption Studies Adoption research has taken one of two forms: 1) parent–offspring adoption studies; and 2) sibling–offspring adoption studies. In the parent–offspring paradigm, concordance rates (or correlations) between adoptive parents and adoptees' antisocial behaviour are compared to concordance rates (or correlations) between biological parents and adoptees. If the concordance rates/correlations are higher for the biological parents and the adopted offspring than the adoptive parents and the adopted offspring, genetic contributions to antisocial behaviour are inferred (Rhee and Waldman 2002). In the sibling–offspring paradigm, concordance rates between adoptive siblings are compared with concordance rates between biological siblings.

Mednick et al. (1984) performed a particularly strong adoption study of 14 427 non-familial adoptions in Demark between 1924 and 1947. The main results were as follows: if both the biological and adoptive parents had no criminal record, then only 13.5 percent of adopted sons had criminal records; if the adopted parent had a criminal record and the biological parent did not, this percentage increased marginally to 14.7 percent. In contrast, 20 percent of adopted sons had a criminal record if the biological but not the adopted parent also had a criminal record. However, the highest level of criminality (24.5 percent) was observed if *both* sets of parents—biological and adoptive—had criminal records.

Since 1929, over 100 twin and adoption studies have been conducted worldwide (Moffitt 2005). Rhee and Waldman (2002) recently completed the most comprehensive meta-analytic review of these studies by aggregating the results of 10 independent adoption samples and 42 independent twin samples. In sum, across all studies (involving a staggering 55 525 pairs of participants!), the variance in antisocial behaviour could be divided as follows: heritability (41 percent), shared environment (16 percent), and non-shared environment (43 percent). Notably, the removal of potential outliers (e.g., eight studies involving psychopathy) did not alter the findings.

Thus, genetics and the environment both contribute to variance in antisocial behaviour. It is important to highlight that research increasingly shows that the gene–crime link is most likely not a direct conduit but rather a function of the mediational effects of inherited characteristics that *predispose* an individual to antisocial behaviour (e.g., lower intelligence, impulsivity, attention deficit hyperactivity disorder) (Lyons 1996; Taylor, Iacono, and McGue 2000). This theme recurs throughout this chapter and the rest of this book—pathways to antisocial behaviour are not usually direct, nor are they uni-dimensional. Rather, antisocial behaviour often results from a series of complex interactions between numerous factors that may seem benign in and of themselves, but in combination produce devastating consequences.

One particularly exciting new avenue in the field of behaviour genetics is the role that genetics might play in either reducing or magnifying the effects of environmental risk factors (Beaver, Nedelec, Schwartz, and Connolly 2014; Moffitt 2005). Instead of simply studying the additive effects of "genes" plus "environment," a new generation of behavioural geneticists are increasingly asking if there are **interactive** effects between genes and the environment: Is there a "gene" *by* "environment" effect?

The evidence unequivocally demonstrates that childhood maltreatment (e.g., physical abuse, emotional abuse, sexual abuse, neglect) contributes to the development of antisocial and criminal behaviour. What is less clear is why 50 percent of maltreated children do not engage in delinquency, aggressive behaviour, or criminality (Widom 1997). Jaffee et al. (2005) shed some light on this issue in a prospective follow-up study of 1116 five-year-old British twin pairs. Children were classified along a genetic risk continuum (e.g., from low to high risk). In sum, the authors reported that the experience of maltreatment increased the probability of receiving a conduct disorder diagnosis by 1.6 percent among children deemed "lowest genetic risk". However, the probability of receiving a conduct disorder diagnosis increased to 23.5 percent among children deemed "highest genetic risk."

Molecular Genetics Research Twin and adoption studies illustrate that there is a clear link between genetics and antisocial behaviour. However, the actual functional gene(s) involved has not been identified. The main function of a gene is to produce proteins comprised of **amino acids**—the basic building blocks of life. Proteins are ultimately responsible for the phenotypic expression of our **genotype**. Faulty genes generally do one of two things—produce too much or too little of a particular protein. Human genes are stored in 46 chromosomes (23 pairs). One of these pairs is the sex chromosome—males have an X and Y chromosome while females have two X chromosomes. X-linked genes are carried on the X chromosome (Campbell, Reece, and Mitchell 1999).

Caspi and colleagues (2002) published the first groundbreaking study demonstrating an interaction between a specific gene and a well-known risk factor—childhood maltreatment. Caspi et al. (2002) were specifically interested in knowing how a low-activity version of the monoamine oxidase A (MAOA) gene may or may not intensify the effects of childhood maltreatment. The MAOA gene is located on the X chromosome; hence it is sex-linked. The MAOA gene is responsible for encoding the MAOA enzyme, which in turn is responsible for metabolizing or breaking down key brain neurotransmitters such as norepinephrine (NE), serotonin (5-Ht), and dopamine (DA), all of which have been implicated in aggression and various forms of antisocial behaviour. The two existing versions of the MAOA gene—low activity and high activity—are the result of a **polymorphism**.

Caspi et al. (2002) used a strong research design to test the MAOA gene by environment interaction. The study was **epidemiological** in nature. They followed an entire cohort of children from birth until age 26 in the small New Zealand town of Dunedin. The birth cohort of 1037 children (52 percent male) was assessed regularly at ages 3, 5, 7, 9, 11, 13, 15, 18, and 21 and was virtually intact by age 26 (96 percent). The assessment process was extensive, involving an entire day's assessments conducted at the main research facility. Researchers found evidence for a strong gene by environment interaction across all four measures of antisocial behaviour—conduct disorder, violent convictions, violent disposition, and antisocial personality disorder symptoms. As Figure 2.1 illustrates, over 80 percent of youth classified as having low MAOA activity *and* as being severely maltreated were classified as conduct disordered; however, only 40 percent with high MAOA activity plus severe maltreatment were similarly classified. While maltreatment by itself had deleterious effects, its effects were exacerbated by the presence of a low-activity MAOA gene. Furthermore, merely having the low-activity MAOA gene type did not elevate risk of antisocial behaviour. Notably, Caspi et al.'s research (2002) has been replicated using different samples and different research designs (Foley et al., 2004); Frazzetto et al., 2007; McDermott, Tingley, Cowden, Frazzetto, and Johnson 2009).

Neurochemistry and Crime—Hormones and Neurotransmitters

Genes are largely responsible for the expression of hormones and neurotransmitters. While the body's endocrine system regulates hormone production and distribution, the nervous system regulates the production and function of neurotransmitters. As we shall

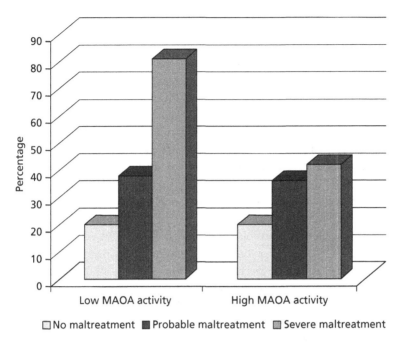

Figure 2.1 Percentage of Males Diagnosed with Conduct Disorder as a Function of MAOA Gene Functioning and Maltreatment History

Source: Adapted from (Caspi et al. 2002).

see, a number of studies have explored whether or not certain types of hormones (e.g., testosterone) and neurotransmitters (e.g., serotonin) are linked to criminal behaviour.

Hormones and Crime The endocrine system governs more than 50 hormones in the human body. These hormones are released into our bodily fluids, typically through the bloodstream) (Campbell et al. 1999). Hormones not only regulate metabolism, growth, and development, they also impact behaviour. Hormonal imbalances may be minor, resulting in mood swings (e.g., irritability experienced during a woman's menstrual cycle), or severe, resulting in serious illness or death (e.g., diabetic shock brought on by low blood-sugar levels) (Anderson 2007).

Testosterone is a hormone responsible for developing and maintaining male primary (e.g., growth of penis, testes, and sperm) and secondary sexual characteristics (e.g., deepening of the voice, growth of facial and body hair, increased muscle mass and strength). Two meta-analyses have found a positive correlational relationship between testosterone and aggression (Archer 1991; Book, Statzyk, and Quinsey 2001). However, the average effect is relatively small. It is also important to note that other researchers have cogently argued that the relationship between testosterone levels and aggression is complex (and far from causal), most likely playing an indirect role in the expression of aggression and antisocial behaviour (Archer 2006; Peper and Dahl 2013).

Should "Bad Genes" Excuse Violent Crime?

Stephen Anthony Mobley grew up in a white, middle-class American family and was never abused nor mistreated. Inexplicably, he became increasingly violent. At the age of 25 he shot and killed the manager of a Domino's Pizza store and was subsequently executed by lethal injection on March 1, 2005. During his trial, his aunt testified that the last four generations of Mobley's family evidenced extreme violence, aggression, and criminality (Conner 1995). Interestingly, Mobley's defense team petitioned the court to fund genetic testing to ascertain if Mobley suffered from a genetic disorder described as "a deficiency of enzymatic activity for monoamine oxidase." The court rejected the petition "finding that the

theory behind the request for funds will not have reached a scientific stage of verifiable certainty in the near future and that Mobley could not show that such a stage will ever be reached" (*Mobley v. The State*, 265 Ga. 292, S94P1271 (1995)).

Jumping forward almost 15 years to 2009, Bradley Waldroup, a Tennessee murder defendant, had his sentence successfully reduced from homicide to manslaughter based on the MAOA defense. Bradley Waldroup severely wounded his estranged wife and brutally murdered his wife's friend (Brooks-Crozier 2011). The MAOA defense has not yet been tested in a Canadian court of law, but it will be interesting to see how Waldroup's sentencing might affect similar cases in the future.

Neurotransmitters and Crime Neurotransmitters are chemical messengers that operate in the brain. While hormones are the messengers of the endocrine system, neurotransmitters are the messengers of the nervous system. Both systems often work in concert.

Neurons or nerve cells transmit commands from one part of the body to another. Neurotransmitters play a critical role in this communication process. As Figure 2.2

Synapse

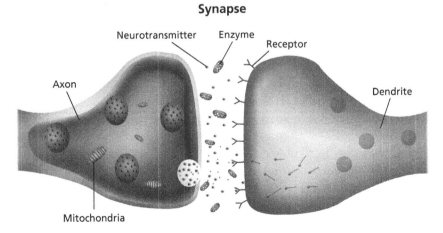

Figure 2.2 The Presynaptic (Axon) and Postsynaptic (Dendrite) Cell

Should Premenstrual Syndrome (PMS) Be Considered a Valid Legal Defence?

Craddock was a British barmaid charged with murdering her co-worker. In 1980, a United Kingdom court found her guilty of manslaughter based on a plea of diminished responsibility because "PMS turned her into a raging animal each month and forced her to act out of character" (Benedek 1985, as cited in Easteal 1991). Incidentally, Craddock also had an extensive record for various offences including theft, arson, and assault. Craddock is not the only case where PMS was used successfully in a court of law. Additional cases, albeit rare, have occurred in the United Kingdom, Canada, and the United States (Anderson 2007; Easteal 1991). While PMS has typically been successful in demonstrating diminished responsibility (e.g., in Canada), it has also resulted in full acquittals. In the early 1990s, an American woman was fully acquitted of drunk-driving charges on the grounds that PMS magnified the effects of alcohol (Easteal 1991).

Premenstrual syndrome (PMS) refers to a collection of physical (e.g., cramping, bloating, back pain), psychological (e.g., concentration difficulties, anxiety), and emotional (e.g., irritability, depression) symptoms related to a woman's menstrual cycle. The American Psychiatric Association included Premenstrual Dysphoric Disorder (PMDD) as one class of depressive disorder in the fifth edition of the Diagnostic and Statistical Manual of Mental Disorders (DSM-V) (American Psychiatric Association 2003). The DSM-V estimates that PMDD affects less than six percent of menstruating women and describes the symptoms as "mood affective lability, irritability, dysphoria, and anxiety symptoms that occur repeatedly during the pre-menstrual phase of the cycle..."(pp. 172–173).

Research suggests that the link between PMS and crime, particularly violent crime, is equivocal. Critics have noted that the stress following arrest may induce menstruation rather than menstruation preceding crime (Raine 1993). As well, menstruation impacts the body in several others ways, including reductions in blood glucose levels, which have also been linked to antisocial behaviour. While menstruation is associated with hormonal changes that cause a small group of women to be more prone to anger during menstruation, it is quite another matter to infer that PMS-induced anger is causally related to crime (Anderson 2007).

illustrates, there are two types of neurons—presynaptic and postsynaptic. The presynaptic cell is the sender and uses its axon's synaptic terminals to transmit the message to the receiver—the postsynaptic cell. The postsynaptic cell receives the message using its dendrites. Narrow gaps, called synapses, exist between the presynaptic and postsynaptic cells. Some of these synapses are electrical and some are chemical. We are interested in the chemical synapses. An electrical impulse or signal travels along the presynaptic cell but cannot cross the synaptic cleft to the postsynaptic cell without being temporarily converted into a chemical signal. The converter, or chemical messenger, is the neurotransmitter (Anderson 2007; Campbell et al. 1999). Neurotransmitters are stored in synaptic vesicles. Imagine this process happening a million times in a nanosecond, just so you can scratch your nose! Although the brain is home to several neurotransmitters, we are most concerned with those that facilitate information processing, mood regulation, and communication. Although three neurotransmitters in particular have been studied in relation to crime (serotonin, dopamine, and norepinephrine) we focus on serotonin given that it has been researched most extensively.

The neurotransmitter serotonin, plays an important role in behavioural inhibition and mood regulation. It is produced from an essential amino acid called tryptophan. Tryptophan is not produced naturally within the body but must be obtained from diet. Most notable sources include protein-based foods such as turkey and chocolate. Since 1959, research has shown that there is a link between a malfunctioning serotonin system and impulsivity, irritability, and aggression (directed at self or others). This research has operationalized malfunctioning serotonin systems in several ways, including low levels of serotonin, low levels of its precursors such as tryptophan, low levels of its metabolites (once a neurotransmitter has completed its job, it breaks down into metabolites), and faulty serotonin receptor sites on the postsynaptic neuron. As well, serotonin, its precursors, and its metabolites have been measured in the blood, urine, and cerebrospinal fluid (CSF). CSF studies are considered the most reliable method of measuring serotonin levels (Anderson 2007).

Moore, Scarpa and Raine's (2002) meta-analytic review of 16 studies illustrated that, on average, serotonin levels (as measured via CSF serotonin metabolites) were substantially lower among antisocial individuals than non-antisocial individuals (mean weighted effect size (Cohen's $d = -0.45$). The effect did not change as a function of gender, target of violence, history of suicide, or alcoholism. While the size of these effects is impressive, considered in the moderate to large range (Cohen 1988), it is important to note that in addition to being correlational in nature, the vast majority of studies included in the meta-analysis were based on relatively small non-random samples (e.g., less than 30).

Taken together, this research clearly suggests that there is, at the very least, a correlational link between a malfunctioning serotonin system and aggression. However, the extent to which serotonin is predictive or causally related to violence and/or aggression requires further study. Studies that artificially manipulate the level of tryptophan and then examine its impact on aggression in a laboratory setting suggest a causal link (e.g., Bjork, Dougherty, Moeller, and Swann 2000). However, this research is preliminary and requires replication. Similarly, other research illustrating that low levels of serotonin increase impulsivity (a known correlate of aggression) (Linnoila et al. 1983) suggests that serotonin may exert its influence indirectly on aggression through the mediator of impulsivity or perhaps negative mood. In sum, the research, while exciting, remains preliminary.

Psychophysiology and Crime A psychophysiological theory uses physiology (e.g., low resting heart rate) to explain psychological constructs (e.g., emotions, motivation, learning). Various psychophysiological theories have tried to link measures of autonomic response such as heart rate and electrodermal activity (sometimes known as galvanic skin response or skin conductance) to various measures of antisocial conduct (Berkowitz 1994; Fowles 1988; Gray and McNaughton 2000). Electrodermal activity (EDA) measures the amount of electrical current between two points on the skin. Typically, electrodes are placed on two fingers, and changes (even minor ones) in electrical activity brought on by sweating are recorded by a polygraph (Raine 1993). Increases in heart rate and EDA are related to general emotional responses such as fear, anger, or anxiety (Lange 1994).

Over the past 50 years, a number of methods have been used to test psychophysiological theories of antisocial behaviour in a diverse range of samples ranging from children with conduct disorder (e.g., running away from home, fighting, lying, stealing) to incarcerated offenders classified as psychopaths. These studies have typically measured heart rate (HR) or EDA in one of three paradigms: (1) *rest*: HR/EDA is measured in the absence of a stimuli; (2) *task*: HR/EDA is measured in the presence of a stimuli, usually stressful (e.g., performing some form of arithmetic in public); and (3) *reactivity*: HR/EDA is measured before and after a stimuli.

Two meta-analytic reviews (Lorber 2004; Ortiz and Raine 2004) concluded that there is a small to moderate correlation between various indices of antisociality and low levels of autonomic arousal (i.e., low heart rate, low electrodermal activity). Thus, individuals who engage in antisocial behaviours also have a tendency to exhibit low heart rates and low electrodermal activity (essentially, they don't sweat much).

Two prominent, albeit competing theories have emerged to explain these findings: fearlessness theory and stimulation-seeking theory (Armstrong and Boutwell 2012). Fearlessness theory argues that some individuals do not experience much fear (i.e., elevated heart rate, sweaty palms) when stressed. Thus, it is argued that these individuals possess the requisite level of fearlessness to engage in crime. Research conducted by Choy, Raine, Portnoy, Rudo-Hutt, Gao, and Soyfer (2015) suggests that children who have experienced chronic childhood stressors (the same life stressors known to elevate one's risk for engaging in antisocial behaviour) have learned to habituate to life stress. Consequently, they are predisposed to fearlessness and a proclivity to antisocial conduct. In contrast, Portnoy, Raine, Chen, Pardini, Loeber, and Jennings (2014) found evidence in support of the simulation-seeking perspective. They reported that the relationship between a low resting heart rate and aggression could be explained by the need for stimulation rather than fearlessness. The simulation-seeking theory hypothesizes that being in a chronic state of low arousal (e.g., having a low resting heart rate) is unpleasant. Consequently, individuals seek to alleviate this unpleasant state by engaging in risky activities such as crime (Armstrong and Boutwell 2012).

The Brain and Crime—Neuroimaging and Neuropsychology

In 1848, Phineas Gage was packing gunpowder into a rock with a tamping iron when it ignited prematurely. The iron shot into his left cheek through to the top of his skull, destroying his frontal lobe in the process. Remarkably, he survived. Although his memory and intellect remained unchanged, Gage's friends and family reported that he was "no longer Gage." Before the accident, he was reportedly kind, polite, and responsible. After the accident, he became irritable, profane, and violent. This was the first documented "natural experiment" linking the brain to personality and behaviour. Since Gage's unfortunate accident, scientists have accumulated much knowledge about the brain and antisocial behaviour along two main avenues—brain imaging studies and neuropsychology (Anderson 2007).

Brain Imaging Brain imaging (or "neuroimaging") research examines the structural (e.g., reduced grey matter size, tumours, lesions) and functional characteristics of the brain (e.g., blood flow, glucose metabolism). Brain structure is typically studied with magnetic resonance imaging (MRI) and computed tomography (CT), while brain function is studied through positron-emission tomography (PET) and single photon emission computed tomography (SPECT) (Anderson 2007; Raine 1993).

Brain imaging studies are complex and diverse. Typically, they involve assessing a small number of "known" antisocial individuals (e.g., sex offenders, violent offenders, psychopaths) against a comparison group (e.g., non-sex offenders, non-violent offenders, non-psychopaths, or non-offenders). While earlier studies (see Raine 1993 for a review) simply compared the brain structures and/or functions of the two groups, more recent studies have compared brain function while the test subjects were engaged in some cognitive activity (such as while viewing emotionally negative pictures) (see Birbaumer et al. 2005). These studies have been reviewed by several researchers (see Anderson 2007; Henry and Moffitt 1997; Raine 1993, 2013). Notably, Yange and Raine (2009) recently meta-analyzed 43 of these studies. They concluded that functional and structural impairments to the prefrontal cortex are more common among antisocial populations than comparison groups. In particular, they implicate three specialized areas within the prefrontal cortex that are more likely to be impaired among antisocial populations. Notably, these three areas regulate emotional processing, decision making, impulse control, and cognitive flexibility. Thus, it is no surprise that deficits in these domains could lead to an "antisocial tendency" as hypothesized by Raine and Yang (2006).

It is also important to underscore that while this body of research is intriguing, it is not flawless. It is built on small samples of incarcerated offenders (predominately sex and violent offenders), typically without non-criminal comparison groups. This precludes our ability to determine whether brain abnormalities cause antisocial behaviour or, alternatively, whether engaging in antisocial behaviour ultimately changes the brain's structure and/or function (Henry and Moffitt 1997).

Neuropsychology Unlike neuroimaging studies that examine the brain using direct physical means, neuropsychology studies brain function indirectly. For example, if you are suspected of having a brain injury following an accident, a neuropsychologist may administer a battery of paper/pencil and/or motor tests designed to diagnose what part of the brain is malfunctioning. Experts in the field of neuropsychology have studied whether deficits in executive functioning are related to antisocial behaviour. In brief, executive functioning refers to cognitive functioning involving future goal-oriented behaviour, purposive attention, organizational skills, and inhibitory control (Morgan and Lilienfeld 2000). While these functions have been associated with the frontal lobe, it is impossible to rule out that other components of the brain such as the connector pathways also play a role in executive functioning. Although two narrative reviews reached inconclusive results regarding the link between executive functioning and antisocial behaviour (Kandel and Freed 1982; Lilienfeld 1992), a recent meta-analytic study has shed new light. Morgan and Lilienfeld (2000) meta-analytically reviewed 39 studies comparing antisocial groups with non-antisocial or "less antisocial" groups on six measures of executive functioning considered to have the highest validity in the field. Overall, they aggregated the results of 4589 participants. A robust effect (weighted Cohen's $d = 0.62$) was observed, indicating that poor executive functioning is related to antisocial behaviour. However, the authors noted that there was considerable variability from study to study, suggesting that further research is needed to enhance our confidence in this finding. The studies were also largely correlational in nature.

Other Biological Considerations—Pregnancy, Birth Complications, Toxins, and Diet

The evidence reviewed thus far clearly suggests a correlation between biology and various forms of antisocial behaviour. It should also be clear by now that the biology/environment or nature/nurture dichotomy is false. Biology and the environment are inextricably linked. We have shown how biology can predispose an individual to future antisocial behaviour. We have also started to illustrate how environmental insults change our biology in a manner that heightens our propensity toward antisocial behaviour (e.g., chronic childhood stress results in a lower resting heart rate). Moreover, researchers are beginning to suggest that inadequate prenatal (during pregnancy) conditions, perinatal (during birth) complications, improper diet, and environmental toxins (e.g., lead) result in changes to our biology that may make us more likely to engage in antisocial behaviour.

There is some evidence linking hypoglycemia (low blood sugar—known to result in panic, irritability, nervousness) with aggression (Raine 1993) and antisocial behaviour (Anderson 2007). Schoenthaler (1983) conducted a particularly intriguing analysis demonstrating this effect. Using a double-blind study, Schoenthaler examined the effects of a healthy diet (designed to regulate blood sugar levels) on a sample of incarcerated juvenile offenders for two years. For half the sample, soft drinks and junk-food snacks were replaced with fruit juices and nutritious snacks. High-sugar desserts and cereals were eliminated. The other half of the sample received the usual meal plan. This study was double-blind because neither the researcher nor the participants were told which group they belonged to. Impressively, the program reduced antisocial behaviour by 48 percent.

Researchers have also investigated the impact of certain neurotoxins, particularly lead, on brain development. Needleman, Riess, Tobin, Biesecker, and Greenhouse (1996) conducted a study of 212 boys in the Pittsburgh school system aged 7 to 11. During the course of the study, the researchers assessed lead concentration levels and antisocial behaviour in the children. While no effect was observed at age 7, there seemed to be a cumulative effect of lead so that by age 11, children with elevated lead levels exhibited significantly more antisocial behaviour than their peers with normal lead levels, as rated by themselves, their parents, and their teachers, even after controlling for other factors such as socioeconomic status and parental quality. This study demonstrated that even small amounts of lead can have deleterious effects.

An equally important body of research has examined how abnormal fetal development (due to factors such as maternal smoking, drinking, **fetal alcohol spectrum disorder**, poor nutrition, and birth complications) may predispose an individual to antisocial behaviour. For example, it is well known that hypoxia or lack of oxygen to the brain at birth can have a profound impact on development, increasing the probability of learning disabilities, impaired cognitive functioning, and intelligence. Arguably, such factors would enhance one's propensity toward antisocial behaviour. It is also important to note that research has shown two things. First, the environment (e.g., positive parenting) can reverse the potentially deleterious effects associated with pregnancy and birth-related insults and thus serve to protect individuals from their "biology" (Mednick and Kandel 1988). Second, the environment (e.g., poor parenting) can aggravate biological risk, such as children born with subtle neurological impairments (Anderson 2007).

In sum, the research is impressive, but it is important to underscore the complex interactions occurring not only within the biological subsystems but also between them. For example, improved diet has a multitude of effects not only on blood glucose and hormonal levels but also on serotonin levels, all of which have been linked to antisocial behaviour. Furthermore, there are complex interactions occurring at the environmental level. For example, the positive impact of diet on hyperactive children is magnified when accompanied by a supportive home environment (Rumsey and Rapoport 1983). It is critical to ascertain how all these factors fit together—specifically, what are the true causal risk factors, mediators, and moderators of these effects? Not only will this approach result in a stronger theory of crime but it will also allow causal factors to emerge that in turn lead to efficient allocation of limited treatment resources.

EVOLUTIONARY THEORIES OF CRIME

SO FAR WE HAVE EXPLORED BIOLOGICAL EXPLANATIONS OF ANTISOCIAL BEHAVIOUR and crime that have focused on genetics, the brain, hormones, autonomic arousal, and other factors that find their triggers in the environment, such as diet and pregnancy complications. This level of explanation can be considered proximate. Proximate explanations identify which factors in a person's immediate environment cause certain behaviours. Proximate explanations also ask how the behaviour develops over an organism's lifespan, questioning causation and development at the individual level. In contrast, ultimate or more distal explanations ask questions about function and adaptation for an entire species. This level of analysis asks questions such as, "Why did humans develop the capacity for speech, emotion, or aggression?" (Durrant and Ward 2015; Mishra and Lalumière 2008; Quinsey et al. 2004).

1840   1854

1881

Everett Historical/Shutterstock

Charles Darwin (1809–1882)

Some modern biology textbooks (e.g., Campbell et al. 1999) state that "biology came of age" the day Charles Darwin published *On the Origin of Species* in 1859. Darwin made two critical points in his book: 1) species did not always exist in their current form but evolved or transformed from ancestral species; and 2) the evolutionary mechanism for this transformation was natural selection (Campbell et al. 1999). Even more impressive, Darwin foresaw the emergence of evolutionary psychology: "In the distant future I see open fields for more important researches. Psychology will be based on a new foundation, that of the necessary acquirement of each mental power and capacity by graduation." (Darwin 1859, as cited in Buss 2005).

Evolution 101: Natural Selection, Adaptation, and Beyond

Evolutionary psychology is a relatively new yet thriving discipline that seeks to understand human psychology from a Darwinian perspective. In essence, evolutionary psychologists are trying to "map a universal human nature" (Tooby and Cosmides 2005: 5). To date, this perspective has been applied to a vast array of psychological constructs ranging from altruism, phobias, emotions, and group dynamics to the focus of this chapter—antisocial behaviour. Before we explore what evolution or, more accurately, forensic evolutionary psychology (Duntley and Buss 2008) has to say about antisocial behaviour, it is necessary to review a few basic principles of evolution.

Evolutionary psychology posits that the human mind comes equipped with numerous psychological mechanisms that have been designed and maintained through selection over hundreds of thousands of years of evolution. These psychological mechanisms are sometimes conceptualized as a series of mini computer programs that have been designed by one master programmer. The master programmer wasn't a person but rather the environment that our hunter–gatherer ancestors inhabited many years ago. Our ancestral environment was comprised of various **selection pressures** or adaptive problems—finding a mate, hunting, gathering, protecting children, avoiding predators, and finding shelter. "Hunters" and "gatherers" who successfully responded to adaptive problems or selection pressures not only survived, but lived long enough to produce children and pass these successful adaptations on to the next generation. Unsuccessful responses resulted in death or reduced capacity to reproduce. Herein lies the basic assumption of natural selection: a successful **adaptation**—be it biological or psychological—is housed in an individual's genetic makeup, so the only way adaptations can be passed on is through genetic rather than cultural transmission. A prerequisite to becoming a potential adaptation is that the "candidate" adaptation must first appear in the organism's genetic makeup by chance, for example as a genetic mutation. If the mutation enhances the organism's reproductive fitness—how good an organism is at reproducing plentifully and keeping offspring alive long enough for them to reproduce—it will be retained and passed on to the next generation, and so on. Gradually, as a result of its enhanced reproductive fitness, the adaptation works its way into the species' genome. It is important to note that this process takes, on average, a few thousand generations (although it can happen much faster), and adaptations that increase reproductive fitness by as little as 1 percent (on average) are naturally selected over other less beneficial characteristics (Campbell et al. 1999; Duntley and Buss 2008; Tooby and Cosmides 2005).

It is important to note that there is increasing acceptance for nongenetic mechanisms of inheritance. For example, Durrant and Ward (2015) nicely summarize the role of epigenetic (when the expression of genes are modified during development and these phenotypic variations are inherited by the next generation), ecological, and cultural methods of transmission. However, the field of evolutionary forensic psychology remains firmly rooted in genetic mechanisms of evolutionary change.

Given that evolution takes so long, our existing psychological mechanisms are the result of selection pressures that existed during the hunter and gatherer era rather than the industrial or even the agricultural revolutions. Our existing psychological mechanisms *were* adaptive in a typical hunter–gatherer environment characterized by life in small nomadic bands of less than 100 people, most of whom were genetically related. However, it does not necessarily follow that these evolved mechanisms will be adaptive in contemporary society (Buss 2005; Daly and Wilson 1988)! We are the way we are because our existing attributes (ability to walk upright, to feel fear, to fight) were adaptations in the distant past that enhanced our reproductive fitness and consequently were naturally

Top Three Criticisms and Misconceptions— Evolutionary Psychology Takes the Stand

Critique: Determinism

Critics argue that evolution (and biology, for that matter) is not useful because of its determinist nature—we can't change what happened in an ancestral environment, so how can we use a theory about the past to solve current problems? If evolution's blueprint is housed in our genes, we cannot change its impact because our genes are immutable. Determinists also argue that evolution ignores environmental factors.

Defence:

It has hopefully become apparent that our evolved psychological mechanisms developed in response to the environment, albeit a distant one. Thus, arguably, evolution is all about the environment! As we shall soon see, present-day environmental cues tell an organism about what the future likely holds and, in turn, directs the organism to adopt a course of action most likely to enhance reproductive fitness. Importantly, evolution has designed us to be highly flexible and adaptive to whatever our current environment throws at us. Life history theory is an evolutionary theory that explicitly describes how what we have inherited in the distant past is what makes us extremely flexible and adaptive in the present.

The section of this chapter that addressed biology clearly demonstrated that biology is not destiny and that while biology may predispose an individual in certain ways, these predispositions will most likely not manifest in the absence of the appropriate environmental trigger. Additionally, numerous biological ailments are readily solved with environmental treatments that are sometimes as simple as changing one's diet.

Phenylketonuria (PKU) is a biologically based disease that prevents individuals from metabolizing phenylalanine, an essential amino acid. Buildup of this amino acid results in severe brain impairment in young children. Once the biology of the disease was understood, the remedy was simple: keep phenylalanine out of an affected child's diet until age seven, at which point the buildup is no longer harmful. The solution to this biological problem was environmental.

Critique: Naturalistic Fallacy

Evolutionary theory is flawed because it legitimizes aggression and violence along with a myriad of social injustices. For example, in reference to evolutionary explanations of female crime, Belknap (2001) states ". . . this perspective is . . . insulting to girls and women, viewing them as pathetic, needy competitors for male attention . . ." (p. 57).

Defence:

The most straightforward response to this position is that just because a scientist studies a given behaviour—good or bad—it doesn't mean he/she endorses it. For example, researchers who study cancer and the evolution of viruses do not condone the spread of such diseases (quite the contrary). The fact that something was adaptive in an ancestral environment does not make it morally right, yesterday or today.

Misconception: Natural Selection Is a Conscious Process

Evolutionary psychology assumes that individuals consciously decide to act in a certain way, which ultimately results in our present-day adaptations.

Defence:

Sometimes the principles of natural selection are misunderstood and it is erroneously concluded that our ancestors consciously made decisions to act adaptively because they knew that doing so would ensure the survival of the species. The only true drivers of evolutionary adaptations are automatic—be it the gene, culture, or ecological forces. (Dawkins 1989; Durrant and Ward 2015).

selected and became part of the human genome. See the Hot Topics feature for a discussion of common criticisms and misconceptions about evolutionary psychology.

METHODOLOGY

How Is Evolutionary Research Conducted?

Researchers use an array of methods to test evolutionary theories and hypotheses, including historical, anthropological, and cross-cultural methods. Researchers also use methods that are routine among psychologists (e.g., paper/pencil questionnaires, interviews, computer simulation studies), with the key difference being in how evolutionary theorists frame questions and interpret results. While a social learning psychologist might interpret aggressive behaviour between two males as pathological, stemming from each individual's interpretation of the rewards outweighing the costs for such behaviour, an evolutionary psychologist would look for an ultimate explanation and explore whether the behaviour served some adaptive function in an ancestral environment such that the reward/cost ratio favours the species. If it is not an adaptation, evolutionary psychologists would test whether it is a byproduct of another adaptation or the result of a malfunctioning adaptation.

Evolution and Crime: What Do We Know?

The application of evolutionary principles to criminal behaviour is a growing yet novice field. Evolutionists posit that recurring conflict (over resources, mates, or offspring, for example) drove the selection pressures that shaped evolutionary adaptations, manifesting in a wide range of antisocial behaviours including violent (rape, homicide) and non-violent offenses (sexual harassment, theft) (Durrant and Ward 2015; Shackelford and Duntley 2008). In this section, we describe how researchers have applied certain micro-level theories that exist within the grand framework of evolutionary psychology. First, life history theory is used to explain antisocial behaviour. Second, frequency dependence selection is used to explain psychopathy. Third, homicide is explained through the notion of male–male competition. Last, parental investment and mating effort theories are used to explain gender differences in crime.

Life History Theory and Antisocial Behaviour

Like us, our ancestors had several competing demands on their time. Not only did they have to hunt and gather, and find and attract a mate, they also had to protect and nourish offspring. It is easy to see how these activities could enhance survival and reproductive fitness. The challenge, however, was in how individuals could establish the most effective trade-off between these activities. Allotting time to one activity, such as nourishing and protecting offspring (also known as parental investment), would offer an important reproductive benefit—increasing the probability that the offspring would live long enough to mate and transfer his/her (and ultimately your) genetic material to the next generation. A cost would simultaneously be incurred, however. Protecting offspring would take time away from siring other children, or, for females, would reduce survival or fertility (Mishra and Lalumière 2008). Thus, there was always a trade-off between the costs and benefits associated with the various activities that defined our ancestors' lives. Life history theory argues that natural selection favours allocation strategies that, on average, optimize reproductive fitness (Kaplan and Gangestad 2005).

However, what is most intriguing about life history theory is the unequivocal assumption that the psychological mechanisms that regulate how we spend our time have evolved to be highly flexible and responsive to environmental cues. This phenomena has been coined "adaptive phenotypic plasticity" (Durrant and Ward 2015). Thus, if the environmental cues suggest that life is likely to end at any time (e.g., constant food scarcity and/or predatory threats) or that the future is bleak and unpredictable, our evolved psychology will direct a life strategy characterized by riskier activities that are more likely to attract and retain a mate, for example by demonstrating mate worthiness by physically attacking competing male suitors in front of a prospective mate. Although this life strategy would get your genes a little more quickly into the next gene pool before it is too late (e.g., before you starve to death) it also comes with a price. In our evolutionary past it meant that we spent less time protecting and nourishing our existing offspring. In present day society, these riskier activities are more likely to result in criminal justice involvement.

Simpson, Griskevicius, Kuo, Sung, and Collins (2012) tested life history theory empirically. The researchers followed 165 individuals from birth into their early 20s. The study found that early childhoods characterized by chaos and unpredictability (parents who were sporadically employed, multiple changes in residences, changes in cohabitation status) also had more sexual partners and engaged in more aggression, delinquency, and crime later in life.

A group of Canadian researchers (Lalumière, Mishra, Harris, Quinsey, and Rice) have used life history theory to explain criminal behaviour. But they have also used more general principles of evolution to explain sexually coercive behaviour (see the Canadian Researcher Profile feature for a profile of Dr. Lalumière).

Psychopathy

The construct of psychopathy has intrigued the public and the academic community for some time. In brief, psychopathy is typified by a constellation of affective, interpersonal,

Box 2.1

Canadian Researcher Profile Dr. Martin Lalumière

Dr. Martin Lalumière is an internationally recognized expert on sexual aggression, paraphilias, and risk-taking. Some of his research projects are heavily influenced by an evolutionary standpoint. He currently serves as Professor in the School of Psychology at the University of Ottawa and Senior Scientist at The Royal's Institute of Mental Health Research.

Before moving to Ottawa in 2013, Dr. Lalumière was a Professor in the Department of Psychology at the University of Lethbridge; a Research Psychologist at the Centre for Addiction and Mental Health, Associate Professor of Psychiatry and Criminology at the University of Toronto; and a Research Psychologist at the Mental Health Centre Penetanguishene (now called Waypoint Centre for Mental Health Care). He was also briefly a Post-Doctoral Fellow at Correctional Service Canada. He obtained his Ph.D. in

Courtesy of Martin Lalumière

Dr. Martin Lalumière

1995 under the supervision of Professor Vernon Quinsey. Dr. Lalumière's dissertation, *The Sexual Interests of Sexually Coercive Men*, earned him the Governor General's Academic Gold Medal for graduate work at Queen's University.

Dr. Lalumière has published extensively, including 5 books and over 100 book chapters and journal articles. His work has appeared in several influential journals, ranging from *Psychological Bulletin, Psychological Assessment,* and *Journal of Abnormal Psychology* to *Archives of Sexual Behaviour, Evolution and Human Behaviour,* and *Social Science and Medicine*. He is best known for his work on the phallometric assessment of rapists and the evolution of psychopathy, and for establishing a link between handedness and sexual orientation. His approach to research involves a mix of proximal (mechanistic or developmental) and ultimate (functional) questions to fully understand the hows and whys of behavioural phenomena. For example, what are the developmental, motivational, and contextual factors that influence sexual aggression or risk taking? What are the evolved functions, if any, of these behaviours?

Here is an example involving a contentious topic: Sometimes, victims of rape date their perpetrators after the event. What explains this? Some researchers have found that future dating is more likely when penile-vaginal penetration occurs during the rape event, compared to when penetration does not occur. These researchers suggested that there is something unique about penetration that triggers bonding with the perpetrator (a proximate explanation), which could increase the chance of survival of the offspring if pregnancy occurs (a functional explanation). Dr. Lalumière and his students tested an alternative

Box 2.1   (Continued)

proximal explanation by examining whether a prior relationship between victims and perpetrators could explain the association between the occurrence of penetration during the rape event and future dating. From an online survey of nearly 1000 women, Sawatsky, Dawson, and Lalumière (2015) found that most victims who subsequently dated their perpetrators already had a sexual or romantic relationship with them prior to the rape event; in other words, rape events that involved intercourse were more likely to occur when there was already a relationship between victims and perpetrators, and future dating was simply a continuation of that relationship in most cases. Yet, in the very small group of victims who had no prior sexual or romantic relationship with the perpetrators, the occurrence of penetration was predictive of future dating. Is it possible, then, that penetration triggers a relationship? Is there another third variable that could explain this association? Can sexual aggression function as a way to increase reproductive success for men by

not only increasing number of sexual partners, but also by initiating a relationship? These are controversial but very interesting questions that are worth pursuing. When discussing this kind of research, it is important to remind the audience that whatever explanation is found to be the most promising, the blame and responsibility of the crime under study remains entirely on the shoulders of the perpetrators.

When Dr. Lalumière isn't working in his Sex, Crime, and Evolution Research Laboratory with his students, he is busy teaching courses on forensic psychology, psychopathology, research methods, and evolutionary psychology. What he loves most about teaching is "interacting with smart students, helping them become critical thinkers." In his spare time, Dr. Lalumière enjoys hiking and fly-fishing in various parts of the world.

What's next for Dr. Lalumière? Certainly more fishing trips, but more importantly, he will continue to have a profound impact on our understanding of sexuality and criminality.

and behavioural characteristics, such as superficial charm, grandiosity, manipulation and lying, absence of remorse, inability to feel empathy, impulsivity, risk-taking behaviour, irresponsibility, and living a parasitic lifestyle (see Chapter 11 for an in-depth discussion).

A group of evolutionary forensic theorists (Harris, Lalumière, Mishra, and Quinsey) have hypothesized that the pathway to psychopathy can also be explained using an evolutionary framework—specifically, the principle of frequency dependent selection. Before defining frequency dependent selection, it is necessary to understand polymorphisms. In biological terms, when two or more forms of a discrete character exist (e.g., eye colour—blue eyes, brown eyes, green eyes; blood types—A, B, AB, O), the contrasting forms are called morphs. One way that natural selection maintains diversity in a population is through frequency dependent selection, which states that the reproductive success of a particular morph relative to another morph (hence its ultimate survival) depends on its frequency (or, more accurately, its *phenotypic* expression) in a given population (Campbell et al. 1999). If it becomes too common, its phenotypic expression will no longer be adaptive because its success is dependent on its rarity in comparison to its sister morph(s). The Theory in the Real World feature explores an illustrative example involving the "sneaker" salmon.

What Do a Psychopath and "Sneaker" Salmon Have in Common?

Most of us are familiar (maybe not!) with the life of a typical Pacific male salmon. They are born, leave their birthplace (a fresh-water stream), and swim into the open sea, only to eventually return (swimming upstream) to spawn and die. But the battle doesn't end there. Once the male salmon arrives home, he has to compete with other males to convince a female that he is a worthy candidate to fertilize her eggs.

Female salmon are extremely selective, with experimental conditions revealing that 90 percent of eggs will be fertilized by one or two males—generally the biggest and reddest ones who guard the best territory, which has better water flow/gravel conditions. Scientists have discovered that there are two pathways to fertilization. The first is exhibited by the vast majority of male salmon—the direct "look at me, I'm worthy of your eggs!" approach. The second pathway is extremely rare but still manages to be effective. A type of male salmon affectionately known as a "sneaker" uses it. He lies in wait, hidden from the legitimate courtship ritual, and once the female releases her eggs and makes them available to the target male salmon—Mr. Big and Red—the sneaker sneaks in and fertilizes as many eggs as he can until Mr. Big and Red extricates him.

Unlike typical Pacific salmon, which spend about 18 months away from home, some varieties of sneaker only leave the stream for 6 months or, in some cases, not at all. While sneakers are small and would not be able to compete physically with Mr. Big and Red to win the affections of a typical female, the sneaker fertilization strategy is a successful alternative—even if he only manages to fertilize a few eggs relative to the massive fertilization efforts of Mr. Big and Red.

The obvious question is why natural selection has allowed the sneaker to live. Biologists have calculated that the total expected payoff for each strategy—personal survival multiplied by the number of fertilized eggs—is about equal for Mr. Big and Red (fertilizes a lot of eggs but has a high probability of being killed in the open sea) and the sneaker (fertilizes only a few eggs but has a much lower probability of dying because he either doesn't make it to the open sea or only remains for a short time). Thus neither strategy produces any reproductive advantage, allowing the balanced polymorphism to exist (Palumbi 2002).

So what do you think? Are psychopaths the human equivalent of sneakers in the salmon world?

Lalumière and colleagues argue that psychopathic behaviour is a morph that has arisen as a direct result of frequency dependent selection. It is easy to see how "cheater" strategies (e.g., "have sex with me and I will protect you;" "let me have some of your food and next time I will share with you") would enhance one's reproductive success in an ancestral environment if, *and only if*, a small minority of individuals engaged in such tactics (e.g., 1 out of 100). As the number of cheaters increases, so does the probability that non-cheaters will find out and thus nullify the cheaters' success. Similarly, cheater strategies require a substantial pool of honest, trusting, cooperative individuals to manipulate in order to be successful (Lalumière et al. 2005; Quinsey et al. 2004).

Two lines of evidence have been presented in support of psychopathy as an adaptive life history strategy. The first involves the mere existence of "psychopathic-like" behaviour in the animal world (as exemplified in the Theory in the Real World box). The second line of evidence is somewhat indirect. Proponents of this perspective (see Harris, Rice, and Lalumière 2001; Quinsey et al. 2004) cite evidence illustrating that psychopaths are not competitively disadvantaged in a reproductive sense (Lalumière, Harris, and Rice 2001). So if there is nothing "wrong" with psychopaths, yet they still adopt a high mating effort/risk taking/criminal lifestyle, it can be inferred that their particular life history strategy must have been adaptive, evolutionarily speaking. This is still a controversial theory and requires further empirical investigation.

Homicide

In 1988, Daly and Wilson presented one of the first seminal accounts of homicide from an evolutionary perspective. They used evolution to understand various forms of homicide—spousal, blood-relative, casual acquaintance, revenge killings, and so forth. For the purposes of illustration, we will describe Daly and Wilson's evolutionary account of homicide between male strangers or male acquaintances.

Despite media reports, most homicides occur as the result of altercations arising from arguments, insults, or rivalries between male acquaintances. Usually, the men involved are unmarried and unemployed. Daly and Wilson cite numerous examples to support this position, ranging from anecdotal accounts from contemporary hunter-and-gatherer societies to large-scale quantitative studies dating back to Wolfgang's (1958) classic treatise on homicide. In his study, Wolfgang classified a large number of homicides as "altercations of relatively trivial origin; insult, curse, jostling, etc." (p. 125, as cited in Daly and Wilson 1988).

Daly and Wilson argue that a man's reputation depends largely on his ability to maintain a credible threat of violence. Evidence was based on various historical accounts (e.g., duels often led to status enhancement among prominent men in America) and anthropological accounts such as this quote from a Dani tribesman from New Guinea: "A man without valor is kepu—a worthless man, a man-who-has-not-killed" (Matthiessen 1962, as cited in Daly and Wilson 1988: 131).

Daly and Wilson claim that the apparent "trivial" nature of homicide motives may not be trivial after all, suggesting that homicide perpetrators are actually responding to perceived reputational or status threats. The researchers argue that failure to restore one's reputation in an ancestral environment would have resulted in dire consequences from a reproductive fitness standpoint for two reasons. First, responding with violence would prevent current and future exploitations of one's resources—territory, shelter, food, and so forth. Second, it would also signal prospective mates to a strong provider for herself and her future children, thereby enhancing her reproductive fitness.

It is important to underscore that Daly and Wilson do not necessarily argue that the act of killing has been naturally selected for, but rather that the broader spectrum of violence and aggression has been selected for, which at times can "go too far" and result

Genghis Khan

in death. Their argument posits that homicide is an evolutionary byproduct of the more encompassing, evolved mechanism of violence and aggression that occurs in response to environmental cues or threats to status/reputation. This position stands in stark contrast to an alternative evolutionary account of homicide that argues that natural selection has selected for the act of homicide in and of itself (see Duntley and Buss 2008). In sum, it is therefore argued that violence, aggression, and homicide exist today because in an ancestral environment they enhanced reproductive fitness, particularly among men.

Interestingly, a recent study involving Genghis Khan (Zerjal et al. 2003) provides vivid evidence in support of the hypothesis that violence, status, and power can dramatically enhance one's reproductive fitness. Genghis Khan (c. 1162–1227) and his male descendants established the largest land empire in history, spanning east and southwest Asia and parts of central Europe. Historical accounts indicate that Khan and his descendants were extremely violent (slaughtering conquered populations, raping women) but were simultaneously excellent progenitors of their genes, keeping multiple wives and concubines as a direct result of war conquests (Turnbull 2004).

Zerjal et al. (2003) examined the Y chromosomes of 2123 men from across Asia. Interestingly, 8 percent had Y chromosomes that were virtually identical, indicating a common forefather. It is estimated that 16 million men across Asia—from the Sea of Japan to Afghanistan—possess this particular Y chromosome. Although it is impossible to conclude with 100 percent certainty that Genghis Khan was the originator of this chromosome, researchers are reasonably confident that it most likely belonged to his paternal grandfather. It is estimated that the average man who lived at the time of Genghis Khan would have 20 direct descendants alive today—a far cry from Khan's 16 million!

Female-Perpetrated Crime

There is one universally accepted fact about crime. Men commit more crime, particularly more violent and serious crime, than women, irrespective of the disciplinary orientation of the researcher, the study methodology, or the timeframe of investigation (Blanchette and Brown 2006). While a number of evolutionary theorists are beginning to understand why females are simply less criminal than males (Daly and Wilson 1988; Quinsey et al. 2004; Walsh and Beaver 2008), the explanations put forth by Anne Campbell (Campbell 1995, 1999, 2002; Campbell and Cross 2012; Campbell, Muncer, and Bibel 2001) have been the most influential. Anne Campbell and other evolutionary theorists posit that risky behaviours were naturally selected for in the environment of evolutionary adaptation because they enhanced survival and consequently reproductive success under certain environmental pressures: specifically, resource scarcity. Campbell's perspective is succinctly described as follows:

> We argue that resource scarcity [e.g., food, money, shelter] drives both property and violent offending in women. Property offenses reflect women's attempts to provision themselves [directly] while violence reflects female–female competition for provisioning males [indirect source of resources]. Evolutionary pressure (the critical importance of maternal survival to females' reproductive success) [dependency of offspring on mother for survival] resulted in females' lower threshold for fear, relative to males, when faced with the same level of objective physical danger. This adaptation inhibits women's involvement in crime, makes them more likely to be involved in property rather than violent crimes and, when direct confrontation is inevitable, causes them to use low-risk or indirect tactics [e.g., verbal aggression]. (Campbell et al. 2001: 481)

Campbell (2002) further argues that poverty (the immediate cause of resource scarcity) is a necessary precursor to female crime. However, it is not necessarily sufficient. Individual differences in fear thresholds among women explain why some poverty-stricken females resort to crime while others do not. Campbell recognizes the importance of a number of direct and indirect factors that mediate the relationship between poverty and crime. These factors operate at both the macro (e.g., overcrowding) and individual levels (e.g., poor parenting) and are derived from existing criminological theories such as social learning theory, social control theory, and life course perspectives (see Chapter 3).

We can also understand Campbell's thinking in the context of life history theory—particularly by examining the costs and rewards associated with mating effort versus parental investment and whether they should, or do, differ between men and women. In fact, the rewards and costs associated with mating effort and parental investment are different for men and women. Further, it is these very differences that evolutionists use to explain why women commit less crime, particularly less serious forms of crime, than men. These differences are captured by the term **reproductive fitness variance**. In short, women's fitness variance is restricted in comparison to men's. Over the course of her life, it is impossible for a woman to produce more offspring than a man could. In other words, the number of offspring a woman can actually produce and take care of during her lifespan is relatively small compared to her male counterparts. Not only does she carry a finite number of eggs, it also takes considerable time and resources to raise one child (e.g., nine months gestation; lengthy lactation period, particularly in ancestral times before the advent of bottle feeding). It also takes time before she is physically able to conceive another child following birth. Hence, a woman's reproductive fitness potential is restricted.

In contrast, these limitations do not exist for men. In theory, men can produce significantly more children and with little effort (i.e., the time it takes to ejaculate, technically speaking, is all that is needed to produce a child). The male reproductive fitness potential (variance) is considerably wider—he may have no children or could have several hundred (recall Genghis Khan). Herein lies one reason why men commit more crime than women. In an ancestral environment, the cost/benefit ratio favoured high mating effort over parental investment (on average) for men, whereas it favoured high parental investment for women. On average, men who focused more of their energy on finding and maintaining sexual partners versus parental investment were more successful in propagating their genetic material. Conversely, women who were more selective about mates (pairing up with someone who would keep them and their children alive) and devoted more time to protecting their offspring were, on average, more successful in propagating their genetic material. Natural selection favoured evolved psychological mechanisms that supported high mating in men and high parental investment in women. For women, the costs of engaging in high mating effort and consequent risk-taking and aggressive behaviours simply weren't worth the risk of dying and not being able to ensure the survival of offspring. However, offspring survival wasn't nearly as dependent on the father's life. There is considerable evidence that men invest more energy in mating effort than women and that women are more partial to parental investment (Low 2000; Schmitt 2005). This statement is based on averages; it doesn't mean that men never invest in their children or that women never exhibit high mating effort. If you find this explanation particularly offensive, remember the natural fallacy described earlier.

FUTURE DIRECTIONS

THE STUDY OF CRIMINAL BEHAVIOUR THROUGH THE LENS OF EVOLUTIONARY AND biological perspectives is rapidly increasing. Moreover, disciplines such as criminology that historically have either ignored or vehemently attacked biological or evolutionary approaches are now slowly starting to recognize the strengths of these perspectives. Moreover, we are starting to gain a better appreciation of the complexity underlying criminal behaviour. A single, magic bullet theory simply does not exist. However, future scholars will continue to develop interdisciplinary theories of crime that actively integrate biological and evolutionary perspectives alongside social learning perspectives. Lastly, it is an exciting time in the field of molecular genetics—a field that is increasingly one step closer to understanding the actual mechanisms through which genes and the environment interact to produce infinite variations in human behaviour.

SUMMARY

1. There are multiple pathways to crime. In this chapter, we have focused on evolutionary and biological explanations. Multiple pathways also exist within each perspective, including a host of biological factors such as genetics, neurochemistry, hormones, psychophysiology, and others. Evolutionary perspectives are complex, and evolution is not a monolithic theory but is comprised of a series of micro evolutionary theories (e.g., life history theory, frequency dependent selection). We have only scratched the surface in this chapter.

2. Despite popular belief, biological and evolutionary explanations of crime underscore the importance of the environment. Environmental insults (e.g., a mother who drinks during pregnancy) change the biological makeup of an individual such that he or she is now predisposed to a future criminal lifestyle. Evolutionary mechanisms were shaped by the environment, albeit a distant one. Evolution itself has shaped our minds such that they adapt and change to current environmental cues. The theory of evolution has more in common with environmental theories such as social learning (discussed in Chapter 3) than one might think. The only difference is that evolution focuses on the learning environment of the entire species whereas social learning theories focus on the learning environment of an individual.

3. It is a myth that evolutionary accounts of crime contradict traditional theories. Evolutionary perspectives simply focus on providing ultimate explanations, while traditional criminological theories focus on more proximate explanations. The perspectives tend to complement rather than contradict one another. When theories do diverge, it indicates that one perspective is incorrect.

4. This chapter has shown that research unequivocally supports the influence of genetics on criminality. It has also demonstrated that the path to crime is complex and that a number of biological subsystems interact with one another to increase risk of future criminality, with the environment greatly influencing whether certain biological predispositions will manifest.

5. Evolution is uncontested in scientific circles. However, evolutionary psychology, in particular evolutionary forensic psychology, is in its infancy.

6. The link between evolutionary and biological explanations of crime is a natural one. In the evolution section, we focused on psychological mechanisms that have evolved in response to ancestral selection pressures. This does not negate the existence of evolved biological mechanisms such as those reviewed in the first part of the chapter.

Discussion Questions

1. Identify your favourite explanation of crime. Now put it to the test. What kind of a grade does it get with respect to the criteria reviewed at the beginning of this chapter

(what makes a strong theory)? What challenges did you face while you were doing this task? What additional information would have made your task easier?

2. Does society hold a more deterministic view of biological/evolutionary explanations of crime versus sociological explanations (i.e., if the cause is in your genes, we can't fix it, but if the cause is in the environment we can)? If so, how can we change current thinking?

3. What is the implication of the MAOA findings for females? Recall that the MAOA is X-linked. Does this mean that females might have built-in resiliency against aggression and crime? If so, why?

4. Based on evolutionary principles, what predictions would you make about how human behaviour will change over the next 1000 generations? What are the selection pressures in contemporary society? How are they shaping our species' collective future reproductive success?

Chapter 3
Theories of Crime: Learning and Environment

Aaron was 22 years old when he was convicted of murder and sentenced to time in a federal penitentiary. Reflecting on his life, one could wonder how he got himself into the situation he was in. Like many people, Aaron was raised in a single-parent home by his mother, who had to work extra shifts to support him and his two older brothers (his father was in prison for armed robbery). Aaron's family was not poor, though, and he felt he had all he needed growing up in what he called "a typical middle-class neighbourhood." Aaron was a bright boy and remembers enjoying school, at least initially. Problems began when Aaron was around 10 years old. During the evenings, his mother would work, and he would hang out with his brothers and their friends. The types of crimes he initially committed were minor, mostly consisting of vandalism "committed just for fun" and stealing from local stores, often in response to challenges from the older boys. Soon, however, Aaron was throwing rocks off bridges at passing cars, stealing stereos from vehicles, and getting into fights with other kids at school. Throughout his teens, Aaron started spending less time at school and more time at the arcade. His mother would frequently be called to his school to discuss his behaviour. As he got older, fights at school turned into fights on the street, and Aaron quickly gained a reputation among his friends as someone who "liked to knock one off." He would frequently get into fights while under the influence of alcohol. Aaron's reputation eventually caught up with him when he started a fight one night at a local bar because someone had embarrassed his friends. Sadly, things went too far. After moving the fight outside, one of Aaron's friends passed him a knife, which he used to kill his 20-year-old opponent.

Learning Objectives

1   Describe the primary differences between psychodynamic, learning, and social learning theories of crime.

2   Identify the key principles of psychodynamic theories and explain how these principles relate to our understanding of criminal behaviour.

3   Describe the major predictors of crime from the perspective of "control" theories, such as Gottfredson and Hirschi's general theory of crime.

4 Describe the principles of classical and operant conditioning.

5 Identify the key elements of Sutherland's differential association theory and Akers' social learning theory of crime.

6 Explain the personal, interpersonal, and community-reinforcement theory of crime proposed by Andrews and Bonta.

INTRODUCTION

As you saw in the previous chapter, psychologists have attempted to explain why people get involved in crime in a few different ways. In explaining Aaron's behaviour, for example, biological theories of crime—while not discounting the importance of social factors—would tend to focus on the impact of physiological, biochemical, neurological, and/or genetic factors. Biological theorists might stress the fact that criminality seems to run in Aaron's family, indicating a genetic basis to his behaviour. Evolutionary theories of crime, on the other hand, focus on explanations of how crime can be thought of as adaptive behaviour, developed as a means to survive in both our ancestral and present-day environments. To an evolutionary psychologist, the murder committed by Aaron may be viewed primarily as a means for him to achieve status among male competitors, which will ultimately influence his reproductive success either because his fighting makes him more attractive to females or because murder helps defeat rival males.

In this chapter, we will continue to explore how psychologists attempt to explain criminal behaviour, focusing on theories that emphasize learning and the environment. We will look at how variables such as a lack of parental supervision, the presence of pro-criminal role models, and positive reinforcement from friends for committing antisocial acts affect the lives of people like Aaron. We will present three general perspectives on crime—psychodynamic, learning, and social learning perspectives—and discuss specific theories that fall into each of these categories. In reviewing these theories, we will describe their key components, discuss how they differ from one another and how they are similar, evaluate the degree to which the theories are supported by empirical evidence, and examine some of the criticisms that are raised in relation to each theory.

CONTEXT

Sigmund Freud (1856–1939) is well known for his theories of the unconscious mind, the defence mechanisms he proposed, and the various therapeutic techniques he endorsed, such as free association and dream interpretation. Oddly, given his vast interests, Freud had relatively little to say about crime or criminal behaviour (Freud 1901). This is not to say, however, that Freud's perspective on human behaviour is irrelevant to our understanding of crime. Indeed, a number of theories of crime proposed throughout the 1900s have drawn on principles that Freud and his colleagues proposed. As we discuss later in this chapter, some of these theories, such as John Bowlby's theory of maternal deprivation, have largely fallen out of favour since they were first proposed. Other theories, such as the "control" theories proposed by Travis Hirschi and his colleagues, represent some of the best-validated theories of crime.

A common criticism of Freudian thinking is its focus on inner drives or conflicts that lead individuals to behave in a particular way. One can reasonably ask, how do we test whether unobservable mechanisms and processes are influencing our behaviour? Historically, these criticisms influenced the development of another approach to understanding human behaviour; a perspective referred to as **behaviourism**. Behaviourism focuses on the study of observable processes (Skinner 1953), and many theories of crime have their roots in behaviourism. These theories often focus on how criminal behaviour is learned (and how hypotheses about such learning can be tested). While the specific factors focused on in each theory vary, these theories generally propose that criminal behaviour is learned in the same way that non-criminal behaviour is learned. Like theories of crime that are based on Freudian principles, some learning theories of crime have not withstood the test of time. However, other learning theories, such as Aker's social learning theory, have received a great deal of support. Currently, learning theories are having a significant influence on the development of strategies for managing criminal behaviour, as you will see throughout this chapter and the rest of the book.

DEFINITIONS

Throughout this chapter we will focus on psychodynamic theories, learning theories, and social learning theories of crime. **Psychodynamic theories** of crime, as the name implies, focus on the internal (often unconscious) psychological forces that influence human behaviour. Many of these theories are rooted in Freudian thinking. These theories often focus on factors that influence personality development, how personality development influences our ability to resolve intra-psychic conflicts, and how these conflicts impact our behaviour (including antisocial behaviour). According to this perspective, experiences occurring early in childhood, such as separation from one's mother, are thought to have a profound effect on personality development and thus, how people behave. **Learning theories**, which are rooted in the behaviouristic tradition, take a different approach to understanding crime. These theories of crime focus on how information is encoded, processed, and retained in the process of learning to become criminal. These theories often propose specific conditions that promote (or inhibit) learning and they describe various forms of learning. **Social learning theories**, for example, focus on one particular form of learning; that is, learning that takes place by observing others being reinforced or punished for their prosocial and antisocial behaviour.

WHY DO WE CARE?

As discussed in Chapter 2, theories are important for a variety of reasons. Theories of crime can be used to organize complex ideas, establish hypotheses to test, and ultimately lead to research findings that can benefit society. For example, a particular theory of crime may lead a researcher to predict that exposure to a specific risk factor will increase the chance that a young person will get involved in a delinquent lifestyle. Researchers can then test this hypothesis and, if they find support for it, they might be able to develop an intervention program to minimize the impact of the risk factor. Thus, a theory might aid researchers in identifying important risk factors and in addressing those factors. A theory might also allow a researcher to understand why an intervention worked, or how an intervention could be improved if it did not have the intended effect.

Biological and evolutionary theories of crime can result in useful explanations of crime and potentially lead to research that has applied value. However, it is sometimes difficult to understand what can be done about crime (or the people committing it) if people are genetically predisposed to criminal behaviour; or, worse yet, destined to commit crime as a result of their evolutionary history. The research that was reviewed in the previous chapter highlighted the fact that criminal behaviour is rarely determined exclusively by one's biology. That being said, to the degree that crime is biologically determined, identifying appropriate targets for treatment can sometimes prove challenging.

In part, the value associated with the theories discussed in this chapter is that they provide alternative explanations of how crime develops that are less dependent on biological and evolutionary processes; which is not to say that these theories ignore biology or evolution. These alternative explanations of crime focus on factors that are theoretically linked to criminal behaviour, but many of the factors focused on in psychodynamic, learning, and social learning theories of crime are arguably more amenable to change and thus, potentially good targets for intervention programs. For example, learning theories of crime place great importance on the consequences associated with behaviour (i.e., whether people receive reinforcement or punishment for behaving antisocially). These factors can be manipulated with relative ease to determine if they have their desired impact (i.e., reducing antisocial behaviour). In light of this, it should not come as a surprise that many interventions currently being used with offenders are based on the theories discussed in this chapter.

METHODOLOGY

As is the case when one sets out to test a biological theory of crime, researchers that study the sorts of theories described in this chapter also use diverse research methods. **Cross-sectional research** designs are very common. Using this methodology, researchers examine different groups of individuals (e.g., criminals versus non-criminals) to determine if certain risk factors are associated with one group more than the other. If that is the case, the factor under examination is often said to be *associated* with criminality (it is not possible using this design to conclude that the factor being examined *causes* criminality). **Longitudinal research** is also common in this area. Using this methodology, researchers follow groups of individuals to examine how their behaviour develops or changes over time (e.g., does exposure to a risk factor in youth lead to criminal activity as an adult?). Finally, meta-analysis is becoming a common methodology used to test the theories discussed in this chapter, just as it has been used to test biological theories of crime. Once a number of studies exist that have examined the same variables (for example, the relationship between some potential risk factor and criminality), meta-analytic techniques can be applied to those studies to determine what the overall, or average, relationship is between these variables.

PSYCHODYNAMIC THEORIES

WE WILL BEGIN OUR DISCUSSION OF THEORIES OF CRIME BY REVIEWING PSYCHODYNAMIC theories. Before we do that, however, let us first turn our attention to a few basic psychodynamic concepts that are potentially relevant for understanding why people become involved in criminal activity.

Basic Psychodynamic Principles: The Id, Ego, and Superego

From a psychodynamic perspective, humans are thought to be inherently antisocial, driven by pleasure-seeking and destructive impulses (Blackburn 1995). According to this perspective, crime generally occurs when these (often unconscious) impulses are not adequately controlled. This is thought to happen when internal psychic forces tasked with the job of regulating such impulses fail to develop as they should, typically due to traumatic childhood experiences.

As an example of how a psychoanalyst might explain the emergence of criminal behaviour, consider the work of the late David Abrahamsen (1903–2002), a well-known forensic psychiatrist, psychoanalyst, and author of many books, including an interesting in-depth analysis of the crimes of serial killer David Berkowitz (a.k.a. Son of Sam) (Abrahamsen 1985). Like many other psychiatrists of his time, Abrahamsen's general perspective on crime and its development was psychodynamic. Consider the following passage from his book *The Murdering Mind* (Abrahamsen 1973), a detailed account of his involvement with Tiger, the murderer of a young girl:

> Having examined hundreds of people who have killed . . . I have found that homicide usually does not originate because of a clearly defined impulse to kill, but is released by the intensity of internal conflicts . . . In examining those who have committed murder, I have found one common characteristic . . . all the murderers were intensely tormented. Deep down, they felt beset, trapped in an intense conflict growing out of the struggle between their sexual and self-preserving feelings on the one hand and

their external surrounding on the other . . . It is these inner drives which shape the aggressive thrust that in a certain situation may trigger murderous impulses that result in violent acting out to the point of murder.

The conflict I refer to is due to serious traumatic situations, primarily experienced in the earliest childhood . . . When as children we feel hurt by people's rejection or criticism, we either give vent to it or push away from our mind our real resentment until we "forget" about them. They become unconscious. When we continue to repress and it becomes a pattern of behaviour, without finding any outward expression or release, these hateful emotions accumulate within us. If we are unable to curb these hostile feelings, our ego-protecting defences crumble and murderous acting-out impulses emerge. (pp. 9–10)

References to "inner drives," "traumatic situations," and "protecting defences" are commonplace in psychodynamic explanations of crime, but where exactly do psychoanalysts believe these "sexual and self-serving feelings" come from? What experiences "in the earliest childhood" are important, and what internal forces are meant to "curb" the potentially dangerous impulses that supposedly reside within us? To answer these questions, Freud and his followers relied on a set of psychic structures thought to develop throughout childhood and adolescence to form a dynamic personality system (Freud 1923).

Psychoanalysts believe that pleasure-seeking and destructive impulses originate in the **id**, part of an individual's personality that is present at birth and represents unconscious, primitive, and instinctual desires (Blackburn 1995). The id is thought to be governed by the **pleasure principle**: it seeks immediate pleasure with little consideration of the undesirable consequences that may result if an impulse is acted upon. These potentially destructive forces are believed to be controlled in one of two ways (Blackburn 1995). First, psychoanalysts believe that the activity of the id is opposed by the next personality structure to develop, the **ego**, which attempts to mediate between one's primal needs and society's demands. The ego is guided by the **reality principle**: its development coincides with the emergence of reality-oriented thinking and it allows the id to function in socially acceptable ways by suppressing the id's impulses until appropriate situations arise (e.g., by allowing for the delay of gratification). Second, in challenging id drives, the ego is guided by the **superego**, the last of the three personality systems to develop according to psychoanalysts. The superego represents the internalization of group standards, typically conveyed to the child through parental care and discipline, and it acts as a moral regulator. The superego is thought to consist of two sub-systems: the **conscience**, which allows an individual to distinguish between right and wrong and forces the ego to inhibit id pursuits that are out of line with one's morals, and the **ego-ideal**, which represents the socially accepted standards to which we all aspire (Blackburn 1995).

Problems that result in superego formation, which are generally thought to stem from a failure to identify with prosocial parental figures, are of particular interest to those attempting to develop explanations of crime. In fact, psychoanalysts have proposed three main sources of criminal behaviour, each relating to inadequate superego formation. The three sources relate to the development of a harsh, weak, or deviant superego (Blackburn 1995).

The individual who commits crime as a result of a *harsh superego* is sometimes referred to as a **neurotic criminal** (Meloy and Gacono 1997). The existence of a harsh superego is assumed to lead to pathological levels of unconscious guilt (typically over unresolved infantile desires) and criminal behaviour is meant to subconsciously invite punishment in an attempt to resolve this guilt. David, the offender described in the Theory in the Real World box, is an example of a neurotic criminal. Individuals who commit crime because of a *weak superego* are commonly associated with the psychopathic personality (Millon, Simonsen, and Birket-Smith 2002). Possessing a superego that fails to sufficiently regulate the instinctual needs of the id, this type of individual is typically "egocentric, impulsive, guiltless, and unempathic" (Blackburn 1995: 114). Many violent offenders are often assumed to commit crimes due to a weak or underdeveloped superego. The third type of criminal commits crime as a result of a *deviant superego*. As Blackburn (1995) explains, for these individuals, superego standards have developed, but those standards are thought to reflect **deviant identification** (i.e., identification with a deviant role model). This could occur, for example, when criminal parents have a good relationship with their son and the son grows up to mirror his parents' criminality; in this case, the child's delinquent behaviour "reflects an absence of guilt, but not the abnormality of psychic structures" (Blackburn 1995: 115).

Psychodynamic Theories of Crime

While these general categories of criminal types are useful, they provide inadequate information about the actual causes of crime, other than the fact that problems with superego development may play an important role. In an attempt to better understand what causes crime, at least from a psychodynamic perspective, we now turn our attention to a discussion of various theories of crime that relate to this perspective.

Bowlby's Theory of Maternal Deprivation The **theory of maternal deprivation**, which was developed and tested by the British child psychiatrist John Bowlby (1907–1990), draws heavily on the psychodynamic perspective and was a popular theory for how juvenile delinquency develops. Consistent with psychodynamic thinking, Bowlby's view was that young children require consistent and continuous maternal care in order for them to develop normally (Bowlby 1989). According to Bowlby, disruption to the mother–child relationship can have many harmful and potentially irreversible long-term effects, especially in relation to the child's ability to establish meaningful prosocial relationships. Lacking such abilities, the child will not develop the means to control his conduct (i.e., destructive impulses) and will be more likely to exhibit antisocial patterns of behaviour (Bowlby 1989).

Bowlby had some empirical data to support his view. For example, in a study of 44 juvenile delinquents, who were matched to a control group of non-delinquents, Bowlby (1944) found a significantly higher level of maternal deprivation in the delinquent group (39 percent) compared to the non-delinquents (5 percent). However, his research

David, an Example of a Neurotic Criminal

Freud (1916) believed that many criminals are motivated by a sense of guilt and a need to deal with this guilt by being punished through legal sanctions. Today, psychologists generally accept that neurotic criminals of this kind are very rare, although some appear to exist. David, a patient/criminal presented by Meloy and Gacono (1997), arguably fits the bill. Meloy and Gacono's description of David may provide a glimpse inside the mind of the neurotic criminal.

David is described as a 42-year-old Caucasian male, born and raised in a Greek Roman Catholic middle-class family. David had two older brothers. His mother was a housewife and his father was a store manager until his death from a heart attack when David was 31. David's early life was one of turmoil, filled with fear, unhappiness, and confusion, and while he was never physically or sexually abused as a child, he clearly had a poor relationship with his father. Indeed, as David recalls, "I had no warm times with [my father]. He told me what a shit I am. He'd scream, holler like a madman" (Meloy and Gacono 1997: 290). David described his mother as emotionally withdrawn and stated that she would often justify or rationalize his father's behaviour. Despite these issues, there were no signs of significant behavioural or medical problems in David's childhood, and no history of criminality, alcoholism, or psychiatric illness in his family history.

David married while in college and subsequently had three sons. However, after seven years of marriage, he divorced his first wife and began dating another woman. It was at this time that David started gambling. Gradually, more and more of David's time was spent gambling, which he viewed as an escape from his father—an environment where he could finally make his own choices instead of following his father's. When his father died, David said he became reckless, affirming his "father's opinion that I would f--- up without him here" (Meloy and Gacono, 1997: 290). While David regularly won when he gambled, he was borrowing larger and larger sums of money, and three years after he started gambling he owed approximately $600 000 to various individuals.

David sought treatment from a psychiatrist at this time, but was not hospitalized until he was arrested and charged with conspiracy to obtain, distribute, manufacture, and possess illegal drugs. Speaking of these crimes, David says, "Most compulsive gamblers will [commit crimes] . . . The meth manufacturing was part of my self-destruction. I knew I was being surveilled by the police five weeks before I did the lab" (Meloy and Gacono 1997: 290). In other words, despite knowing the police were on to him—even watching him—David continued to commit crimes. From a psychoanalytic perspective, this was probably done because the crimes David committed brought on the punishment he unconsciously felt he deserved (from disappointing his father).

David pled guilty to three non-violent crimes, including theft and tax evasion, and was sentenced to five years in prison. He was released to a halfway house after seven months and successfully completed his parole two years later.

has been challenged, both on methodological and empirical grounds (Feldman 1977). Methodologically, Bowlby's studies have been criticized for everything from the unrepresentative nature of his delinquent sample to poor control group matching (Morgan 1975). Empirically, Bowlby's results do not appear to hold up, especially in studies where large sample sizes are relied on (e.g., Hirschi 2002; Nye 1982). Even Bowlby himself didn't always find strong evidence for the role of maternal deprivation in explaining delinquency (e.g., Bowlby et al. 1956). What now seems clear is that maternal deprivation is not a critical factor to a child's healthy development (i.e., a paternal figure can provide adequate care), that any damage caused by early deprivation is not necessarily irreversible, and that the theory over-predicts juvenile delinquency given that many individuals who experience maternal deprivation do not get involved in crime (Rutter 1981).

Unravelling Juvenile Delinquency: The Work of Glueck and Glueck

Despite the criticisms of Bowlby's theory, family discord in general does seem to be associated with delinquent behaviour and this variable is included in several theories of crime that have received more support than Bowlby's theory (e.g., Andrews and Bonta 2010; Glueck and Gleuck 1950; Hirschi 1969). The work of Glueck and Glueck (1950) is one such example, though what this Harvard husband-and-wife team proposed was less a formal theory of crime and more a summary of their empirical findings. That being said, the Gluecks were heavily influenced by psychodynamic thinking (Andrews and Bonta 2010) and often spoke of such things as "mental conflict," "tensions between repressed and forgotten emotional experiences and more recent experiences," and "divergent instinctual energy propulsions" (Glueck and Glueck 1950: 15).

Keystone Pictures USA ZUMA Press/Newscom

Sheldon Glueck (1896–1980) and his wife Eleanor Glueck (1898–1972) were American criminologists who undertook extensive studies of juvenile delinquency. They were particularly interested in discovering the causes of delinquency and in predicting the likelihood of delinquent behaviour.

According to Sampson and Laub (1995), the primary interests of the Gluecks were discovering the causes of crime and assessing the effectiveness of correctional treatment in controlling criminal behaviour. One of the approaches they adopted to examine these issues, which is described in their book *Unravelling Juvenile Delinquency*, was to conduct cross-sectional research comparing the lives of juvenile delinquents with non-juveniles (Glueck and Glueck 1950). The ambitious study described in this book was based on 500 delinquent boys selected from the Massachusetts correctional system and 500 non-delinquent boys from Boston public schools, matched on age, race, type of neighbourhood, and intelligence (the Gluecks also conducted longitudinal research on the delinquent boys included in this study by following up with them at different points in time; Glueck and Glueck 1968). The Gluecks took a multidisciplinary approach to examining delinquency; for each boy, a wealth of information was collected, including social, psychological, and biological information, in addition to information about the boys' family lives, school performance, and work experiences. Not only were the boys interviewed, so were their parents and teachers.

Based on their findings, the Gleucks were able to provide a portrait of the delinquent. In summarizing their findings, they describe these individuals in the following way (note the psychodynamic tone to much of their description):

> The delinquents, far more than the non-delinquents, are of the essentially mesomor-phic [strong and muscular], energetic type, with tendencies to restless and uninhibited expression of instinctual-affective energy and to direct and concrete, rather than symbolic and abstract, intellectual expression. It is evidently difficult for them to develop the high degree of flexibility of adaptation, self-management, self-control, and sublimation of primitive tendencies and self-centred desires demanded by the complex and confused culture of the times. (Glueck and Glueck 1950: 278)

To a large extent, the Gluecks attributed the differences between delinquents and non-delinquents to parenting factors, the primary source for superego development. The Gluecks' findings clearly indicated a marked difference between these groups across a range of parenting variables (Glueck and Glueck 1950). For example, among the parents of the delinquents, there was a greater incidence of emotional disturbances, mental retardation, alcoholism, and criminality. Parents of the delinquent boys were also less educated, less likely to stay together, and less ambitious. Furthermore, the parents of the delinquents showed greater carelessness in the supervision of their children and often appeared neglectful. Finally, a greater proportion of delinquent families were found to lack cohesiveness, warmth, and respect for the integrity of family members, and fewer of the delinquents were affectionately attached to their parents, especially their fathers. Viewing these findings through a psychodynamic lens, the Gluecks stated that "the development of a mentally hygienic and properly oriented superego (conscience) must have been greatly hampered by the kind of parental ideals, attitudes, temperaments, and behavior found to play such a major role on the family stage of the delinquents" (Glueck and Glueck 1950: 281).

Drawing on these types of findings, the Gluecks proposed a "tentative causal formula" that could, in their view, be used to predict who would become engaged in juvenile delinquency. They believed that by drawing on their physical, temperamental, attitudinal, psychological, and socio-cultural data they could make accurate predictions, from a very young age, about the likelihood of children getting involved in crime. Unsurprisingly, such claims were met with resistance, and researchers quickly proceeded to show that the claims being made by the Gluecks were exaggerated (e.g., Reiss 1951). In addition, the work of the Gluecks has been challenged on methodological grounds (Sampson and Laub 1995). For example, the Gluecks have been heavily criticized for not carefully examining issues related to causal ordering (i.e., whether the factors they highlighted preceded delinquency or were the result of delinquency) as well as for inappropriate use of statistical techniques and procedures (e.g., Hirschi and Selvin 1967).

Despite the criticisms levelled against their research, the Gluecks' work is still regarded as a piece of classic research in the field of criminology; research of a scope that is unlikely to be seen again (Sampson and Laub 1995). In fact, much recent research, which does not suffer from the same methodological limitations, provides support for many of the important variables associated with criminal involvement that were highlighted by the Gleucks, especially variables related to peers, family, and school (e.g., Andrews and Bonta 2010; Loeber and Stouthamer-Loeber 1986). Most notable is the research by Sampson and Laub (1995), who have painstakingly re-analyzed much of the Gluecks' original data. The Gluecks' research was also instrumental in the development of other psychodynamically oriented theories of crime, such as those proposed by Travis Hirschi and his colleagues.

Hirschi's Control Theories Although not traditionally considered psychodynamic theories, it has been argued that Hirschi's control theories contain important psychodynamic themes (Andrews and Bonta 2010). For example, like the Gluecks, Hirschi (1969; 2002) views all humans as having the potential to exhibit antisocial behaviour and he incorporated into his theories of crime ideas about superego- and ego-type mechanisms that play a central role in controlling one's antisocial impulses. Although Hirschi does not appear to rely on Freudian thinking to the same extent that the Gluecks did (Andrews and Bonta 2010), the major question that he considers when attempting to understand crime is a classic psychodynamic one: it is not why people violate the law, but rather why more people don't violate the law. According to Hirschi's **social control theory**, or social bond theory, the reason why people don't violate the law is because of social controls, or "the bond of the individual to society" (Hirschi 2002: 16). Specifically, Hirschi presented four interrelated social bonds that are collectively thought to promote socialization and conformity: attachment, commitment, involvement, and belief.

Courtesy of Travis Hirschi

Travis Hirschi (1935–) proposed social control theory to explain why people conform to societal rules. Later, he and Gottfredson proposed their general theory of crime.

According to Hirschi (2002), "delinquent acts result when an individual's bond to society is weak or broken" (p. 16).

The first bond, **attachment**, refers to attachment and interest in others, most importantly parents, friends, and teachers. Hirschi (2002) believed that one's acceptance of and abidance with social norms and ideals depend on attachments to other human beings (particularly the quality of such attachments). One does not commit crime, Hirschi suggests, partly because one does not wish to jeopardize these valued relationships. In psychodynamic terms, attachment represents the ego-ideal. The second bond, **commitment**, refers to the time, energy, and effort placed in conventional behaviour (e.g., getting an education). As argued by Hirschi, people who have an investment in conventional pursuits run a heightened risk of losing that investment if they become involved in crime. Commitment serves the same theoretical value as the ego, according to Hirschi. The third bond, **involvement**, refers to the time and energy one spends taking part in activities that are in line with the conventional interests of society (e.g., school). Hirschi argues that heavy involvement in conventional activities limits the time that is available to participate in criminal pursuits. Lastly, **belief** refers to one's conviction to the view that people should obey common rules. This entails a respect for a societal value system, including a respect for the law and institutions that enforce the law. If such beliefs are weak, involvement in crime is assumed to be more likely. This bond has clear parallels with the conscience part of the superego.

Following the strategy adopted by the Gluecks, Hirschi (1969) tested his social control theory by conducting a study of delinquents and non-delinquents using a cross-sectional design described in his book *Causes of Delinquency*. Like the Gluecks, Hirschi collected a wide range of data on an impressively large sample of adolescents—4077 in all (3605 were boys), some of whom were delinquent and some of whom were not. Hirschi's analysis largely supported the core concepts of social control theory (and, for that matter, the major findings of the Gluecks; Andrews and Bonta 2010), and it has become one of the most frequently discussed and tested theories in criminology (Akers and Sellers 2004).

That being said, recent research suggests that Hirschi's theory might need to be re-assessed, at least to some extent (Bureind and Bartusch 2005). With respect to peer attachment, for instance, Hirschi believed that its presence or absence was important, not whether the peers were involved in delinquent acts (i.e., even for youths who were attached to delinquent peers, the stronger the attachment, the less likely the individual was to be delinquent). This is no longer thought to be the case. Now, attachment to peers is thought to lead to conformity only when the peers are not delinquent (Andrews and Bonta 2010). Causal ordering is also important to consider, given that some research shows that delinquent behaviour can precede weak bonds (e.g., delinquency may precede weak attachment to school; Liska and Reed 1985). In addition, some bonds (e.g., attachment) seem to be more important than others (Agnew 1991), different bonds appear to be more or less important at different ages (LaGrange and White 1985), and the explanatory power of certain social bonds appears to vary across genders (Rosenbaum and Lasley 1990).

In 1990, Hirschi, along with his colleague Michael Gottfredson, proposed a more refined and parsimonious control theory (Gottfredson and Hirschi 1990). Instead of focusing on the indirect controlling effects of social bonds, as Hirschi's (1969) original theory did, Gottfredson and Hirschi's **general theory of crime** argues that self-control, internalized early in life, is the primary determinant of crime. That being said, Gottfredson and Hirschi believed that crime is not an inevitable consequence for those who lack self-control; opportunities to commit crime are also crucially important. Thus, low self-control in the presence of criminal opportunities is assumed to explain an individual's propensity to commit crimes. Still, given their view that most offences are easy to commit, requiring "little in the way of effort, planning, preparation or skill" (Gottfredson and Hirschi 1990: 16–17), and that opportunities for crime are readily available, Gottfredson and Hirschi argued that, over time, people with low self-control will inevitably become more deeply involved in a criminal lifestyle.

Gottfredson and Hirschi's (1990) theory of crime is referred to as a general theory of crime because they believe that it can account for all crime in addition to a range of other behaviours that have been deemed "analogous" to criminal behaviour (e.g., alcohol, drug, and tobacco use). What is common about these crimes and other analogous behaviours? According to Gottfredson and Hirschi, they are all "short lived, immediately gratifying, easy, simple, and exciting" (p. 14), and therefore are appealing to those who are unable to resist temptations of the moment, those who are insensitive to the needs of others, and those who are unable to consider the potential long-term negative consequences of their own behaviour; in short, to people who can be characterized as low in self-control.

Consistent with a psychodynamic perspective, and the work of the Gluecks, Gottfredson and Hirschi (1990) believe that the level of self-control a person possesses depends on the quality of parenting in their early years. Specifically, Gottfredson and Hirschi's general theory of crime emphasizes effective monitoring of children's behaviour, recognition of deviant behaviour when it occurs, and consistent and proportionate punishment of rule violations. According to their theory, children whose parents care about them, monitor them, and discipline them appropriately will likely develop the self-control that is needed to behave in a prosocial manner. Such children will be "more capable of delaying gratification, more sensitive to the interests and desires of others, more independent, more willing to place restraints on his activities, and more unlikely to use force or violence to attain his ends" (Gottfredson and Hirschi 1990: 97). Children without such an upbringing will tend to be "impulsive, insensitive, physical (as opposed to mental), risk-taking, short-sighted, and nonverbal" (Gottfredson and Hirschi 1990: 90); thus explaining the increased likelihood of these individuals giving in to the temptations presented by crime. While the general theory of crime does recognize other sources of socialization, such as schools, Gottfredson and Hirschi believe that the role of these other sources in influencing one's level of self-control is limited given that self-control is assumed to be established very early in life and remain stable throughout the lifespan.

In terms of support, Gottfredson and Hirschi (1990) present a wealth of data about the correlates of crime and delinquency, and their theory (despite being proposed relatively recently) has generated an enormous amount of interest and attention from other researchers (Goode 2008). Most of the subsequent research provides at least partial support for the predictions put forward by Gottfredson and Hirschi. For example, there seems to be a link between low self-control and crime, and this link appears to exist across a variety of cultures (e.g., Hessing et al. 2001). In addition, meta-analytic research supports the view that there is a relationship between self-control and crime, even when self-control is defined using a broad range of behavioural and attitudinal measures and applied to a broad range of samples (e.g., community members vs. offenders, young vs. old, etc.; Pratt and Cullen 2000). However, Pratt and Cullen's meta-analysis also clearly showed that, while self-control is an important predictor of criminal behaviour, it is not the sole cause of crime, given that it only accounted for approximately 19 percent of the variance in criminal behaviour (as we discuss below, social learning variables were also found to be important predictors of crime). In looking at the role of parenting, self-control, and delinquency, Perrone et al. (2004) also found partial support for the general theory of crime. Based on a random sample of over 15 000 youths, they found that parental efficacy (basically the mother's attachment to the child) was a significant predictor of the youth's level of self-control, which is consistent with the view of Gottfredson and Hirschi. However, self-control only partially mediated the relationship between parental efficacy and delinquency, indicating that a valid theory of crime needs to account for more than just self-control.

Despite the fact that the general theory of crime is reasonably well supported, several criticisms exist. Perhaps the most commonly raised concerns have to do with the concept of self-control. For example, Akers (1991) views the general theory of crime as tautological, based largely on circular reasoning. According to him, defining self-control as the failure to refrain from crime, and then proposing self-control as a cause of crime, makes it impossible to falsify the hypothesis that self-control is the primary determinant of crime. Why do people commit deviant acts, one might ask? Because they lack self-control. How do we know they lack self-control? Because they're committing deviant acts! To avoid this tautological problem, Akers argues that operational measures of self-control must be developed that are separate from measures of deviant acts or a propensity toward committing such acts. According to Akers, at least, this issue has not been adequately resolved (however, see Grasmick, Tittle, Bursik, and Arneklev 1993).

In addition, Gottfredson and Hirschi's (1990) argument that self-control is fixed at a very young age and stable throughout the lifespan has been the target of much criticism. Gottfredson and Hirschi's argument is not that criminal involvement won't decline with age, which is a consistent empirical finding, but that between-individual differences in self-control will remain stable over time and be unaffected by social (or other) factors (i.e., if Person A is lower in self-control at Time 1 compared to Person B, they will be consistently lower in self-control, and thus always more likely than Person B to be involved in crime given equal opportunities; Lilly, Cullen, and Ball 2006). Yet studies have consistently demonstrated that other factors, beyond parental socialization processes, can "redirect offenders into a pathway to conformity" (Lilly et al. 2006: 109). This has led some researchers to conclude that the general theory of crime is overly simplistic, ignoring the reality that "change is as much a part of criminal careers as stability" (Lilly et al. 2006: 319; see also Buker 2011). Indeed, some studies have shown that self-control is malleable enough that it can be improved through targeted intervention, and that these interventions can help reduce delinquency (e.g., Piquero, Jennings, and Farrington 2010).

In addition to potential problems with the concept of self-control, the theory has also been criticised for not dealing with important questions around opportunities for crime (Schulz 2006), which is another crucial aspect of the theory. For example, as Goode (2008) points out, many questions remain unanswered. We do not yet fully understand what the relationship is between self-control and criminal opportunities. Are they independent or related in some meaningful way? Is it possible that individuals with low self-control are more likely to perceive criminal opportunities where high self-control people do not? Furthermore, does the lifestyle of individuals with low self-control open up more criminal opportunities?

LEARNING THEORIES AND CRIME

AN IMPORTANT APPROACH IN PSYCHOLOGY SEES OFFENDING, LIKE ALL BEHAVIOUR, as something that is learned. Learning in this case refers to "a change in pre-existing behaviour or mental processes that occurs as a result of experience" (Cassel and Bernstein 2001: 85). This emphasis on learning is what distinguishes learning theories of crime from psychodynamic theories of crime. For example, you will recall that control theories assume that "we would all be deviant if only we dared" (Thornberry 1996: 224). Learning theories of crime, on the other hand, assume that there is no natural, or inherent, impulse to act antisocially (Thornberry 1996). Instead, criminal behaviour must be learned, just as we learn to exhibit non-deviant behaviour. Although not really theories of crime per se, two general forms of learning—based on classical conditioning and operant conditioning—are very important to our understanding of criminal behaviour and its potential causes. Furthermore, both forms of learning have been incorporated into more formal theories of crime, which will be discussed throughout the remainder of this chapter.

Classical Conditioning

The principles of **classical conditioning** originated with the work of Ivan Pavlov (1849–1936), a Russian physiologist. In the early 1900s, Pavlov was studying the digestive system of dogs and was intrigued by his observation that dogs deprived of food began to salivate when his assistants walked into the room. Pavlov's laboratory dogs, which already salivated when presented with food, had come to associate the food with the lab assistants. When Pavlov observed the dogs, what he was seeing was a conditioned response to the people they associated with meal delivery. In classical conditioning terms, the **unconditioned stimulus** (UCS—food) elicited an **unconditioned response** (UCR—salivation). By repeatedly pairing the UCS with a lab assistant, this previously neutral stimulus (the lab assistant) became associated with the UCS and took on the power of a **conditioned stimulus** (CS). After repeated pairings, the CS, even when presented in isolation (without food), began to elicit a response—salivation—which is termed the **conditioned response** (CR).

Through his investigations, Pavlov showed that this interpretation of his observations was correct. After repeatedly pairing the delivery of food (UCS) with a tone, Pavlov found that the dogs began to salivate (CR) when the tone (CS) was presented without the food. Interestingly, when the tone was repeatedly sounded in the absence of food, in a process of **extinction**, it gradually lost its stimulus quality; the dogs salivated initially when the tone was presented, but this eventually stopped.

Master Pavlov is a bit strange these days:
For some reason,
he rings a bell before serving us dinner...

The principles of classical conditioning were first established by Ivan Pavlov in experiments conducted with dogs.

The principles of classical conditioning are now well established, and it has been known for some time that they operate in both animals and humans. Introductory psychology textbooks are often filled with interesting demonstrations of classical conditioning in people. Perhaps the most commonly presented example, although it is not always presented in an accurate fashion (Harris 1979), is that of Watson and Rayner's (1920) study of 11-month-old "Little Albert," who was conditioned to fear a harmless white rat (something that Albert did not fear at the outset of the experiment). By repeatedly pairing the rat with a loud noise, a conditioned response to the rat (fear) was established and was found to generalize to other similar (e.g., furry) stimuli (a process known as **stimulus generalization**). Many more recent examples exist, and classical conditioning is now assumed to be a powerful way of shaping many aspects of human behaviour (e.g., see Webb 1999 for an interesting application of classical conditioning to the field of consumer marketing, where products are often paired with popular celebrities, for example, in an attempt to influence our buying behaviour). For an illustration of how classical conditioning can be used to influence the expression of antisocial behaviour, specifically sexually deviant behaviour, see the Theory in the Real World box.

Eysenck's Biosocial Theory of Crime While it may seem a stretch to generalize from studies of dogs to potentially violent criminals, the principles of classical conditioning are built into some popular theories of criminal behaviour. Perhaps nowhere is this more obvious than in Eysenck's (1977) **biosocial theory of crime** (Raine 1997). Eysenck (1916–1997) argued that crime can largely be explained by individual differences in the functioning of the nervous system, which impacts the degree to which people learn from

Forms of Aversive Conditioning in the Treatment of Sex Offenders

Some view the development of sexually deviant fantasies/behaviours as the result, at least in part, of classical conditioning (e.g., the pairing of sexual arousal with an early deviant experience or object) (Laws and Marshall 1990; McGuire, Carlisle, and Young 1965; Storms 1981). Given this, treatment approaches have been developed for sex offenders that attempt to decrease sexual arousal to deviant objects (e.g., children) through conditioning procedures. In one common approach called **aversive conditioning**, the client is exposed to an unpleasant stimulus while experiencing sexual arousal, the goal being to create an aversion to the source of the arousal. In this context, several methods of aversive conditioning are available.

Using *covert aversive conditioning*, the goal is to have the offender pair an imagined aversive consequence with his deviant fantasies or behaviour in order to eliminate such fantasies or behaviour. A standard technique, described by Maletzky (1991), consists of having the offender listen to a story that contains the following three parts: (1) the offender's preferred deviant stimulus and a buildup of sexual arousal (e.g., a child molestation); (2) an aversive consequence that causes intense disgust, pain, or humiliation (e.g., imagining that they are vomiting while carrying out the offence); and (3) release from the adverse consequence by reversing the activity (e.g., removing the imaginary aversive consequence and encouraging relaxation).

Overt aversive conditioning techniques have the same goal as covert techniques, but actual (rather than imagined) aversive stimuli are presented during or immediately after the deviant stimulus. The deviant stimulus may involve slides, videos, or movies depicting the deviant experience or object. The aversive stimuli may be electric shocks, foul odors, nausea-inducing drugs, or even shame (e.g., by having the offender act out the deviant behaviour in front of observers).

Once the deviant arousal has been eliminated, it is often necessary to create non-deviant arousal to appropriate stimuli and *arousal reconditioning* is used for this purpose. According to Maletzky (1991), the goal of arousal reconditioning is to weaken deviant sexual arousal and simultaneously strengthen appropriate arousal. One method is called masturbatory satiation, which might involve an offender masturbating to consenting adult pornography. Just after ejaculation, when sex drive is assumed to be lowest, he continues masturbating but the offender switches to pornography involving sex between a man and a child. He does this for 30 minutes. The rationale of this method is that it causes the deviant fantasy to become conditioned to low sex drive as well as to excessive masturbation—an aversive stimulus—while the "normal" fantasy becomes conditioned to the pleasure of ejaculation.

environmental stimuli such as parental discipline. Eysenck also believed that differences in nervous system functioning shape one's personality and behaviour, and he made predictions about personality differences between antisocial and prosocial individuals (we will just focus on the conditioning aspect of his theory here).

Specifically, Eysenck believed that criminals and other antisocial individuals are deficient with respect to classical conditioning, or conditionability, a process he thought was important in the socialization or conscience-building process (Eysenck 1977). As Raine (1997) argues in his discussion of Eysenck's views on classical conditioning and crime:

> . . . the crucial mechanism that stops most of us from committing criminal and antisocial acts is the concept of conscience; a well-developed conscience is what holds many of us back from not stealing even in those situations when we are almost certain of getting away with the theft undetected. Eysenck argues that what we call "conscience" is, in effect, a set of classically-conditioned emotional responses. The greater the individual's ability to develop and form classically-conditioned emotional responses, the greater the conscience development, and the less likely will be the probability of becoming antisocial . . .
>
> Taking the scenario of a small child stealing a cookie (CS) from the kitchen, punishment by the parent (scolding or physical punishment—UCS) elicits an unconditioned response (UCR) whereby the child is upset and feels uncomfortable. After a number of similar "learning trials," the sight of the cookie (or even the thought of stealing the cookie) will elicit an uncomfortable feeling in the child (conditioned response—CR) which acts to avert the child from enacting the "theft." Similar "conditioned emotional responses" developed relatively early in life in varying situations combine, in Eysenck's view, to represent what we call "conscience."
>
> In this analysis, socialized individuals develop a feeling of uneasiness at even contemplating a criminal act (robbery, assault) presumably because such thoughts elicit representations or "unconscious" memories of punishment early in life for milder but related misdemeanors (theft, behaving aggressively). (pp. 123–124)

It is fair to say that there is a reasonable amount of research supporting the predictions made by Eysenck. Indeed, with respect to the prediction that antisocial individuals will condition less effectively than prosocial individuals, several reviews of the research have found that, generally speaking, this is true (e.g., Hare 1978; Passingham 1972; Raine 1997). According to Raine, most of the research conducted in this area uses skin conductance to assess conditionability. Using this technique, a UCS (e.g., an electric shock) and CS (e.g., a tone) are repeatedly paired together, and the CR (i.e., skin conductance) is then measured when the CS is presented in isolation. Research of this type shows that problems with conditionability are generally more pronounced in people with antisocial inclinations (e.g., psychopaths). What is less clear is how conditionability relates to the socialization process (Hollin 1989).

Despite some supportive evidence, there has certainly been much criticism levelled against Eysenck's theory of crime (e.g., Taylor, Walton, and Young 1973). Many of these criticisms relate to the predictions (not dealt with here) that Eysenck made regarding personality differences between antisocial and prosocial individuals, some of which are not supported by empirical research (see Hollin 1989 for a review). However, criticisms have also been brought against Eysenck's ideas about classical conditioning and crime. Many of these challenges are philosophical in nature and question the view that behaviour is as rule-governed and deterministic as Eysenck makes out, or that individuals are simple passive receptors of the conditioning process (e.g., Taylor et al. 1973). Other challenges are based on empirical grounds and relate to the fact that not all studies demonstrate conditioning deficits in antisocial individuals (Passingham 1972), and to the fact that strong evidence linking conditionability to the socialization process is currently lacking (Raine and Venables 1981).

Operant Conditioning

While Eysenck viewed the conscience as a set of conditioned fear responses, the relationship between learning and criminal behaviour can be conceptualized in other ways as well. For example, in addition to the associative learning that takes place in classical conditioning, behavioural psychologists have proposed another form of learning, one that is based on principles of **operant conditioning** (Skinner 1953). While operant conditioning principles have been used to intervene with offenders for a long time, we know of few theories of crime that focus exclusively on these principles. In this section, we will discuss the underlying principles of operant conditioning given that they play a crucial role in many criminal justice interventions, and we will briefly examine how they have been incorporated into some theories of crime. This discussion will continue into the next section, where we examine accounts of criminal behaviour in social learning terms; a perspective that draws heavily on Skinner's operant conditioning principles.

Principles of Operant Conditioning Harvard psychologist B.F. Skinner (1904–1990) is primarily credited with establishing the principles of operant conditioning (Skinner 1953). Basically, this approach to understanding human behaviour, including criminal behaviour, assumes that the emergence, maintenance, and cessation of behaviour is determined largely by its environmental consequences (Skinner 1953). Most commonly, four contexts (or contingencies) of operant conditioning are discussed, as illustrated in Table 3.1.

Specifically, **positive reinforcement** occurs when a behaviour is followed by a pleasant stimulus that increases the frequency of that behaviour. **Negative reinforcement** occurs when a behaviour is followed by the removal of an aversive stimulus, thereby increasing that behaviour. **Positive punishment** occurs when a behaviour is followed by an aversive stimulus, resulting in a decrease in that behaviour. Finally, **negative punishment** occurs when a behaviour is followed by the removal of a pleasant stimulus, resulting in a decrease in that behaviour. Note that the labels "positive" and "negative" are not being used in the popular sense to mean "good" and "bad"; offenders may see nothing "good" about positive punishment. Instead, "positive" and "negative" refer to either the addition or subtraction of a stimulus to/from the environment following a behaviour (either naturally or through manual means). Also note that the processes of reinforcement and punishment are defined solely in terms of their behavioural outcome and can be situation and/or person specific. In other words, a stimulus is not a "reinforcer" or a

Table 3.1 Different Types of Reinforcement and Punishment (and Their Associated Behavioural Outcomes)

		Stimulus	
		Added	**Subtracted**
	Pleasant	Positive reinforcement (behaviour increases)	Negative punishment (behaviour decreases)
Stimulus valence	Aversive	Positive punishment (behaviour decreases)	Negative reinforcement (behaviour increases)

"punisher" unless it increases (in the case of reinforcement) or decreases (in the case of punishment) the preceding behaviour, and what might be reinforcing or punishing for one situation (or for one person) might not be for another.

It is also important to appreciate that the effectiveness of the above strategies for either increasing or decreasing the likelihood of a behaviour depends on a wide range of factors (Andrews and Bonta 2010). Three factors in particular are important. First, immediacy is important in that the sooner the reinforcement (or punishment) follows the targeted behaviour, the more likely that behaviour will be to increase (or decrease) (Moffit 1983). Why is delayed reinforcement or punishment not as effective? Because delays increase the likelihood that some behaviour other than the one of interest becomes the target of the reinforcement or punishment (Skinner 1953). Second, consistency is a crucial variable to consider (Moffit 1983). Essentially, the more often the consequence follows the targeted behaviour, the more effective the consequence will be (however, in the case of reinforcement, intermittent schedules of reinforcement, where the consequence only occasionally follows the behaviour, can produce behaviours that are very resistant to extinction; Andrews and Bonta 2010). Finally, the intensity of the consequence is an important factor that partly determines how effective the consequence will be in increasing or decreasing behaviour (Moffit 1983). As a general rule, the stronger the consequence, the more effective it will be (Andrews and Bonta 2010).

Application of Operant Conditioning Principles to Criminal Behaviour

Within the field of criminal justice research, the principles of operant conditioning have typically been drawn on to develop strategies for intervening with offenders. Indeed, it is a fairly easy task to think of criminal justice interventions that fall nicely into each of the cells in Table 3.1. The use of token economies in prisons or psychiatric facilities, for example, where prisoners/patients earn points for good behaviour, which can then be exchanged for desired items (e.g., cigarettes), is an obvious instance of positive reinforcement. Similarly, we are all familiar with the use of positive punishment in our criminal justice system, such as when a fine or prison sentence is handed down by a judge in an attempt to decrease undesirable behaviour. It is also common to see the factors listed above (specifically lack of immediacy, consistency, and maximum intensity) called on to explain real-world failings of criminal justice strategies, especially the ineffective use of punishment to deter crime (e.g., Andrews and Bonta 2010).

What is less common is the direct application of operant conditioning principles to an understanding of how criminal behaviour patterns emerge. Few theories of crime rely exclusively on these principles, although some come pretty close. The theory proposed by Jeffery (1965) is one example. Jeffery proposed simply that whether someone commits crime depends on whether the individual has been reinforced for similar behaviour in the past. Specifically, he believed that what matters most is whether the reinforcing stimuli associated with previous criminal behaviour (e.g., the value of stolen goods in the case of burglary) outweighs the aversive stimuli associated with that behaviour (e.g., legal sanctions). Jeffery's differential reinforcement theory states that "A criminal act occurs in an environment in which in the past the actor has been reinforced for behaving in this manner, and the aversive consequences attached to the behaviour have been of such a nature that they do not control or prevent the response" (Jeffery 1965: 295). Thus, if an offender experiences only reinforcing stimuli when committing burglaries, the criminal behaviour is likely to continue. If, on the other hand, legal sanctions (or some other negative consequence) are consistently experienced, the aversive consequence is likely to deter the act.

Operant conditioning principles are also featured in more recent theories of crime (e.g., Wilson and Hernstein 1985), and the principles play a central role in social learning theories of crime, which will be discussed next. These social learning theories were proposed in part to deal with the primary criticisms of theories based on operant and/or classical conditioning principles, which include the fact that these theories underemphasize: (1) the role of internal (i.e., cognitive) processes in the learning of criminal behaviour and (2) the important role that social context plays in the learning process, in particular learning that occurs by observing others.

Social Learning Theories and Crime

While psychodynamic theories have undoubtedly contributed to our understanding of crime and have highlighted the crucial role that the childhood socialization process plays in the development of criminal behaviour, they do not adequately deal with how people learn to become criminal. Learning theories of crime, which are based heavily on the principles of classical and/or operant conditioning, fill in some of the gaps left by psychodynamic theories. As argued above, learning theories suggest that people learn to commit crime in the same way they learn any other behaviour—through processes of associative learning and/or by experiencing the environmental consequences of their behaviour. While learning theories contribute to our understanding of criminal behaviour and form the basis of successful intervention strategies for tackling crime, they also have several weaknesses—most notably an under-emphasis on learning in social settings. In this section we will focus on social learning theories of crime. Many of these theories are based on an important theory of crime, proposed in the mid-1900s, referred to as differential association theory.

Sutherland's Differential Association Theory Differential association theory was first proposed by Edwin Sutherland (1883–1950) (Sutherland 1947). Unlike many theorists before him, Sutherland discounted "internal" causes of crime (such as those suggested in psychodynamic theories, like the Gluecks') and believed instead that crime could be explained by learning in social contexts through interaction and communication. In particular, Sutherland proposed that the nature of one's conduct, including the likelihood of committing crime, is influenced by the norms present in the particular groups to which one belongs; norms that can include attitudes that are favourable towards following the law or its violation. According to differential association theory, it is the balance between contact with prosocial attitudes on the one hand and antisocial attitudes on the other that influence behaviour.

Differential association theory can be summarized in nine testable postulates put forth by Sutherland (1947):

1. Criminal behaviour is learned.

2. Criminal behaviour is learned in interaction with other persons in a process of communication.

3. The principal part of the learning of criminal behaviour occurs within intimate personal groups.

4. When criminal behaviour is learned, the learning includes: (a) techniques of committing the crime . . . and (b) the specific direction of motives, drives, rationalizations, and attitudes.

5. The specific direction of motives and drives is learned from definitions of the legal code as favourable or unfavourable.

6. A person becomes delinquent because of an excess of definitions favourable to violations of the law over definitions unfavourable to violations of the law.

7. Differential associations vary in frequency, duration, priority, and intensity.

8. The process of learning criminal behaviour by association within criminal and anti-criminal patterns involves mechanisms that are involved in any other learning.

9. Though criminal behaviour is an expression of general needs and values, it is not explained by those general needs and values since non-criminal behaviour is an expression of the same needs and values. (pp. 6–8)

As indicated above, the heart of Sutherland's differential association theory is postulates 6 and 8, but postulate 7 is also very important. To be clear, postulate 7 says that the impact of criminal and anti-criminal definitions can be affected by: (1) how often one interacts with the group(s) exhibiting these definitions (frequency); (2) the length of exposure to particular definitions (duration); (3) how early in life one encounters the definitions (priority); and (4) the prestige or status of the group members holding the definitions (intensity) (Akers and Jensen 2006). Put simply, to the extent that these four conditions are favourable to violations of the law (i.e., high frequency of contact, for a long duration, beginning early in one's life, with high-status members), the more likely it is that a person will become involved in an antisocial or criminal lifestyle.

Differential association theory has had a significant impact on the field of criminology (Gaylord and Galliher 1988) and a significant influence on other theories of crime, including the theories that will be discussed in the remainder of this chapter. It has also received a reasonable amount of empirical support (e.g., Andrews 1980; Johnson 1979; Matsueda 1982). Perhaps the strongest support comes from research demonstrating that some of its core concepts—the importance of antisocial attitudes and antisocial associates, in particular—are important predictors of crime (Andrews and Bonta 2010). These variables have emerged as two of the most powerful predictors of crime and are included in some of the most effective modern-day assessment tools for predicting reoffending (Andrews and Bonta 2010).

In terms of criticisms that have been levelled against the theory of differential association, the most common, and potentially the most serious, relates to Sutherland's concept of "definitions." It was never clear what Sutherland meant by definitions that are favourable or unfavourable to violations of the law. Even more contentious, Sutherland provided no guidelines on how to operationalize the ratio of definitions favourable to violations of the law over definitions unfavourable to law violations (Akers 1998). Some have argued that, in practice, it would be extremely difficult if not impossible to quantify these values (e.g., Glaser 1956), and even Sutherland (1947) himself recognized the problems inherent in this endeavour. Similar arguments can be made in reference to the measurement of factors that influence the impact of differential associations. For example, how does one measure the prestige or status of group members, or the frequency or duration of contact with them? Equally problematic is the fact that Sutherland neglected to specify how the learning process operates (Burgess and Akers 1966). Because Sutherland proposed that criminal behaviour is learned the same way other behaviours are learned (postulate 8), it was logical to seek insight into the learning mechanisms within behavioural psychology. This is exactly what Robert Burgess and Ronald Akers did. We briefly discuss their differential association-reinforcement theory next, but focus more thoroughly on Akers' social learning theory of crime, which was an extension of this theory.

Akers' Social Learning Theory In an attempt to overcome some of the limitations of Sutherland's differential association theory, several theorists developed versions of differential association theory that emphasized the learning process. The **differential association-reinforcement theory** proposed by Burgess and Akers (1966) is one such example. Essentially, Burgess and Akers combined Skinner's (1953) ideas on operant conditioning with Sutherland's (1947) ideas of differential association, and by so doing made differential association theory more appealing and testable. A crucial part of Burgess and Akers' work was their reformulation of Sutherland's original nine propositions in terms of reinforcement theory. The key proposition in the Burgess and Akers reformulation was that criminal behaviour is learned through a process of operant conditioning. Differential association-reinforcement theory received little attention when it was first proposed and Burgess eventually turned his attention to other matters. Akers, however, re-worked the theory, and in 1973 presented his social learning theory of crime in the book *Deviant Behavior: A Social Learning Approach.*

Like Gottfredson and Hirschi's theory, Akers' social learning theory is a general theory of crime (i.e., it is intended to explain all crime). As such, it goes beyond a model of learning based on direct environmental consequences of behaviour. While Akers' theory includes an emphasis on the operant conditioning principles outlined by Skinner (1953), it also draws heavily on the work of social learning theorists, such as Albert Bandura (e.g., Bandura 1973). Social learning theorists, while acknowledging the obvious importance

Ron Akers (1939–) proposed the popular and well-validated social learning theory of crime.

Courtesy of Ron Akers

of classical and operant conditioning, drew attention to another form of learning that can influence behaviour: learning by watching others (i.e., **observational learning**) and by vicariously experiencing the consequences of other people's behaviour (i.e., **vicarious conditioning**) (Bandura 1977).

Thus, according to social learning theories, not only can criminal behaviour be learned through a history of associative learning or by being personally reinforced for criminal behaviour, it can also be learned by watching others being reinforced for their antisocial behaviour and then imitating the rewarded behaviour. The primary role models that can influence behaviour are assumed to include parents, peers, and the media. Interestingly, the mass media played no role in Sutherland's (1947) differential association theory, but its importance in shaping behaviour, including antisocial behaviour, is generally well-accepted today (see the In the Media feature). In contrast to the learning that takes place in classical and operant conditioning, the learning that takes place through vicarious conditioning depends heavily on active cognitive processes. In essence, vicarious conditioning depends on "what we think about what we see and hear" (Cassel and Bernstein 2001: 103): when a youngster sees and hears a parent being rewarded for dishonest or unlawful behaviour, they process that information, remember it, and reason that it is not only okay to mimic their parents' actions, but it is potentially beneficial to do so.

According to Akers's social learning theory, crime is learned primarily through group interactions, by way of operant and vicarious conditioning. More specifically, the likelihood of someone exhibiting criminal behaviour (and continuing to exhibit that behavior) depends on how the behaviour, relative to alternative behaviours, has been reinforced and punished in the person's past (and continues to be reinforced or punished in the person's present) (Akers, Krohn, Lanza-Kaduce, and Radosevish 1979). In other

The Impact of Video Game Violence on Antisocial Behaviour

In 1999, Eric Harris and Dylan Klebold shot 12 students and a teacher at Columbine High School before killing themselves. Both individuals played the online game *Doom*, and reportedly referred to the game in a pre-recorded video (Simpson and Blevins 1999). In 2007, Seung-Hui Cho, a 23-year-old Virginia Tech student, killed 32 people at that university. He was a big fan of violent video games, particularly *Counterstrike* (Benedetti 2007). In 2011, Anders Breivik killed 77 people in Oslo, making him Norway's worst mass-murderer. He was also an avid player of violent video games, with one report stating that he had "used his video game *Call of Duty* to train for mass murder" (Jaccarino 2013).

Oberhaeuser/Caro/Alamy

Recent research suggests exposure to violent video games can increase the likelihood of antisocial behaviour.

We've all read them—headlines blaming various forms of media violence for serious acts of antisocial behaviour. Based on the news stories described above (and countless others we're sure you've also seen), it appears that the news media would have us believe that much of the violence in society can be attributed, at least in part, to the violent media that today's children and adolescents are exposed to, especially violent video games. Even "experts" who appear in the media passionately argue that exposure to violent video games contributes in a significant way to tragedies such as the Virginia Tech shootings. As budding psychologists, it is important to be skeptical of such claims and rely as much as possible on what research tells us about this issue (while also understanding that research is typically far from perfect). So what does the research say? What role do violent video games play in the types of tragedies discussed above?

As is typical in much of psychology, the answer is more complicated than we would probably like. Below is a summary of what research says, as presented by some leading experts in the field:

- Several meta-analyses (a meta-analysis uses statistical techniques to aggregate the findings from numerous primary studies) have examined the relationship between violent video game exposure and various measures related to aggression. While not all meta-analyses indicate that violent video game exposure is harmful, most of the recent, high-quality studies do. That is, it appears that the more a person is exposed to violent video games, the more likely that person will be to exhibit aggressive outcomes (Anderson et al. 2010).
- One such meta-analysis conducted by Anderson et al. (2010) suggests that violent

video game exposure is positively related to aggressive behaviour, cognition, and affect, and negatively related to empathy and pro-social behaviour. These results are stable across different types of studies. For example, effect sizes reflecting the relationship between violent video game exposure and aggressive behaviour were +.21 and +.26 for experimental studies and cross-sectional studies, respectively, where values approaching +1.00 represent extremely strong positive effects.

■ Violent video game exposure does not appear to just impact aggressive outcomes in the short-term. Anderson et al.'s (2010) meta-analysis found that longitudinal studies also indicate that violent video game exposure is a risk factor for long-term outcomes related to aggressive behaviour, cognition, and affect.

■ These sorts of findings also appear to be relatively stable across different cultures. For example, significant effects were reported by Anderson et al. (2010) for aggressive behaviour, cognition, and affect in both Western and Eastern cultures (with some evidence suggesting that the results are slightly stronger in Eastern studies). Variables such as gender and age also don't appear to significantly moderate the relationship between violent video game exposure and aggressive outcomes (though older participants have rarely been studied). Collectively, these findings suggest that the harmful effects of violent video game exposure are quite robust.

■ Interestingly, variables that have been specifically examined in experimental studies also don't appear to moderate the relationship between violent video game exposure and aggressive outcomes. For example, Anderson et al. (2010) found no evidence of a moderator effect for player perspective (first person vs. third person), player role (hero vs. criminal), target (human vs. non-human), or the duration of time spent playing the video game.

words, "Behaviour (whether deviant or conforming) results from greater reinforcement, on balance, over punishing contingencies for the same behaviour and the reinforcing-punishing contingencies on alternative behavior" (Akers et al. 1979: 638). In addition, through interactions with significant groups in their lives, people learn to define particular behaviours as "good" or "bad"; the more a person defines a criminal behaviour as "good", the more likely that person is to exhibit that behaviour. Particularly important groups include friendship circles, families, schools, and churches. According to research that has examined social learning theory, these are the groups that most often provide individuals with their major sources of reinforcement and punishment, expose them to behavioural role models, and influence whether certain behaviours are considered desirable or undesirable (Akers et al. 1979). In sum then, according to Akers's social learning theory, "...deviant behavior can be expected to the extent that it has been differentially reinforced over alternative behavior (conforming or other deviant behavior) and is defined as desirable or justified" (Akers et al. 1979: 638).

A review of the research reveals both direct and indirect evidence in support of Akers' social learning theory as it has been discussed here. The indirect evidence largely comes from studies examining the effectiveness of rehabilitation and treatment programs that are based on social learning principles. As you will see in other chapters, compared to alternative approaches, these programs have been shown to have a significantly greater impact on reducing crime (e.g., Cullen, Wright, Gendreau, and Andrews 2003). More direct evidence in support of social learning comes from research that shows the importance of variables derived from the theory in explaining criminal activity. For example, studies that have directly compared social learning theory to other theories usually show that social learning variables account for a larger proportion of the variance in dependent variables such as delinquency and other deviant behaviour (Akers 2009). In addition, a meta-analysis of 140 studies showed consistent support for the theory (Pratt et al. 2006, cited by Lilly et al. 2006), while another meta-analysis showed that social learning variables (e.g., antisocial attitudes and peers) were at least as promising as other variables (e.g., Gottfredson and Hirschi's 1990 construct of self-control) in accounting for variations in criminal involvement (Pratt and Cullen 2000). Empirical support for this theory appears to hold across nations and cultures (e.g., Kandel and Adler 1982; Kim and Goto 2003; Lopez, Redondo, and Martin 1989).

In terms of criticisms, social learning theory has been challenged just as all of the theories that came before it have. For example, just as the issue of causal ordering was raised in relation to the work of the Gluecks, Akers' social learning theory has often been criticized for not paying enough attention to the temporal sequence of its primary variables, most notably differential peer association and crime. Specifically, rather than delinquent associations causing delinquency, some have argued that it might be the case that delinquency actually causes delinquent associations (e.g., Gottfredson and Hirschi 1990). Another common argument is that social learning theory places too much weight on antisocial peer associations while ignoring other potentially important sources of reinforcement for antisocial behaviour. This criticism is fuelled by the fact that peer association is often the only variable studied in many tests of the social learning approach. However, this is somewhat of an unfair criticism. While antisocial peer associations are undoubtedly front and centre in Akers' theory, other sources of influence are clearly incorporated, most notably the family (Sellers and Akers 2005). Despite criticisms that have been raised about social learning theories of crime, variables emerging from these theories are frequently used to explain various forms of crime behaviour, such as gang behaviour, as indicated in the Hot Topics box.

Andrews and Bonta's Personal, Interpersonal, and Community-Reinforcement Theory

The final theory that we will discuss is the personal, interpersonal, and community-reinforcement theory of crime (**PIC–R**) developed by Don Andrews (1941–2010) and Jim Bonta, both well-respected Canadian psychologists (see the Canadian Researcher Profile feature for a profile of Don Andrews). Outlined in their important book *The Psychology of Criminal Conduct*, this theory fits within a general personality and social psychological framework and is heavily influenced by a behavioural and cognitive social learning perspective (Andrews and Bonta 2010). The theory is a driving force behind much recent research and many offender treatment approaches being implemented worldwide (Ward, Melser, and Yates 2007).

Youth Gangs in Canada

Canadians often think of youth gangs as a problem that exists south of the border. We frequently hear of gang shootings occurring in places like Los Angeles or Detroit. However, gang violence is increasingly being reported closer to home, and police agencies (and other community organizations) now dedicate substantial resources to curb gang problems in most Canadian cities. Indeed, estimates from 2002 suggest that there are more than 400 youth gangs that are active in Canada, with approximately 7000 members (this number has likely increased since 2002) (Public Safety Canada 2007a). Certain cities (such as Toronto, Winnipeg, and Regina) are particularly affected, but cities that have been traditionally thought of as "safe" are also encountering gang activity. For example, recent statistics indicate that Ottawa is experiencing a spike in gang-related shootings, which has resulted in more police officers being dedicated to the city's Guns and Gangs Unit in an attempt to get the gang problem under control (Trinh 2015).

Given these statistics, police agencies and academic researchers are attempting to identify the primary risk factors associated with gang membership. They are also trying to determine effective exit strategies to help individuals get out of gangs. Many of the risk factors (and exit strategies) that have been identified are consistent with the sorts of theories discussed in this chapter, such as social control theory and social learning theory. For example, Howell (2005) groups risk factors into five categories: individual characteristics, peer group, school, family, and community. Risk factors falling within these categories include:

■ Desire for group rewards such as status, identity, and companions
■ High commitment to, or interactions with, delinquent peers
■ Low attachment to school

■ Low educational aspirations
■ Lack of adult and parental role models
■ Exposure to family violence or neglect
■ Exposure to gangs, crime, and/or poverty in the community
■ Cultural norms supporting gang behaviour

Research suggests that the more of these risk factors a youth exhibits, the more likely they will be to get involved with gangs. Exhibiting risk factors from multiple categories also seems to significantly elevate one's risk level (Wyrick and Howell 2004).

Unsurprisingly, many of the exit strategies being proposed attempt to address these risk factors. Consistent with theories discussed in this chapter, some of the more promising exit strategies focus on these elements (Hastings, Dunbar, and Bania 2011):

■ Protecting the youth (and their family) against the risks and consequences of leaving the gang
■ Treating individual issues (e.g., mental health, substance abuse, aggression) and promoting positive change (e.g., with respect to antisocial attitudes)
■ Peer mentoring to share similar experiences, validate each other's challenges, and learn from others who have chosen to exit gangs
■ Providing access to education and to legitimate training and employment opportunities
■ Encouraging positive relationships with prosocial individuals, including the improvement of familial dynamics and processes

Strategies that adopt a multi-dimensional approach (i.e., targeting numerous risk factors in a meaningful way) are likely to be the most effective in preparing youth to exit gang life (Hastings et al. 2011).

Box 3.1

Canadian Researcher Profile Dr. Don Andrews

As an undergraduate student at Carleton University in the early 1960s, Dr. Don Andrews recalled touring the Kingston Penitentiary and the Kingston Mental Hospital. He hated the prison, saying "I would rather be a hospital patient than a prison worker!" As fate would have it, Dr. Andrews completed a summer internship in one of the departments of the Kingston Pen in 1963. He continued to work there for two years, gaining an appreciation for the complex histories of the inmates and the primitiveness of psychological assessment tools. Dr. Andrews often credited these experiences as fuelling his interest in the assessment and treatment of offenders.

After completing a Master's degree at Carleton and a Ph.D. at Queen's University, Dr. Andrews took a full-time position as a psychologist at the Rideau Correctional Centre and a part-time position at Carleton University. In 1970, Dr. Andrews

Courtesy of Dr. Don Andrews

switched the amount of time he spent at Rideau and Carleton, becoming a full-time faculty member at Carleton University. There he started on a path of trying to understand criminal behaviour, especially how it could be predicted and how it could be changed. Much of what he learned can be found in his classic book, *The Psychology of Criminal Conduct* (co-authored with Dr. Jim Bonta). This text breathed new life into psychological theorizing on criminality. In it, Dr. Andrews argues convincingly for a paradigm shift in the field of criminology by demonstrating that general personality and cognitive social learning differences among individuals do a better job of explaining criminal conduct than the more popular theories of class differences.

Dr. Andrews was a pioneer in the development of offender assessment instruments that identify key variables that, when targeted in treatment, will lead to behavioural change. Two of Dr. Andrews' instruments widely in use today are the Level of Service Inventory family of instruments (developed with Drs. Jim Bonta, Robert Hoge, and Stephen Wormith) and the Correctional Program Assessment Inventory (developed with Dr. Paul Gendreau). These instruments facilitate application of principles of effective treatment that reflect the knowledge base of prediction and treatment.

Dr. Andrews' contribution to the field of forensic psychology has been recognized with numerous awards and distinctions, including the Margaret Mead Award for Humanitarian Contributions from the International Community Corrections Association and the Career Contributions Award from the Criminal Justice Section of the Canadian Psychological Association.

Dr. Andrews' love for research was always evidenced in his teaching. He wanted students

The PIC–R is a truly integrated theory of criminal behaviour, using knowledge from both the biological and social sciences to explain crime. The theory emphasizes many different potential paths into crime and draws on key components from the various perspectives on crime (and its causes) discussed in this chapter (Andrews and Bonta 2010). For example, the theory incorporates ideas on the role of socialization in the development of antisocial attitudes, self-control in resisting temptations in the immediate situation, classical and operant conditioning in shaping criminal and non-criminal behaviour, and observational learning, especially in the context of peer groups, as a way of picking up on the many rewards and costs that can be associated with crime (Andrews and Bonta 2010).

True to its roots in behavioural psychology, behaviour, including criminal behaviour, is assumed to be under the control of both antecedent and consequent events in the PIC–R theory (Andrews and Bonta 2010). In other words, criminal behaviour is thought to be determined both by events (antecedents) that precede the behaviour (e.g., encouragement by peers to commit a criminal act may increase the likelihood of a crime being committed) and by events (consequences) that follow the behaviour (e.g., increased status among peers following the commission of a crime may increase the probability of crimes being committed in the future). According to the theory, antecedent and consequent events are believed to gain control over one's behaviour primarily by signalling various rewards and costs for different classes of behaviour (Andrews and Bonta 2006). As discussed in our review of operant conditioning, these rewards and costs can be either additive or subtractive.

In line with a cognitive social learning perspective, the controlling properties of antecedent and consequent events are assumed to be acquired from multiple sources. In the PIC–R model, four sources are viewed as particularly important: the individual (i.e., personally mediated events, e.g., rewarding oneself after evaluating the impact of a criminal act); other people (i.e., interpersonally mediated events, e.g., approval from one's peer group for exhibiting antisocial behaviour); the act itself (i.e., non-mediated events, e.g., experiencing the arousal of getting away with a crime); and other aspects of the situation (Andrews and Bonta 2010).

The PIC–R theory also reserves important roles for the major predictors of crime that have been identified through empirical research, specifically antisocial attitudes, antisocial associates, a history of antisocial behaviour, and having an antisocial personality (see Andrews and Bonta 2010 for a review of the relevant research). For example, antisocial attitudes or, more precisely, the existence of prosocial versus antisocial cognitions, are assumed to determine the direction of personally mediated control and whether personally mediated control favours criminal instead of non-criminal choices (Andrews and Bonta 2010).

Socio-economic factors, such as social class, also play a role in the PIC–R theory, though not the same role as in traditional criminological theories of crime. Specifically, in the PIC–R theory, these factors do not directly explain individual differences in criminal conduct, a view supported by numerous meta-analytic studies (Andrews and Bonta 2010). Instead, they act as background contextual conditions, believed to influence behaviour by establishing the fundamental reward and cost contingencies that are in effect within various social settings and communities.

Like Akers' social learning theory, much of the support for the PIC–R theory comes indirectly, from evaluations of offender treatment (rehabilitation) programs based on principles derived from the theory (some of these are described more thoroughly in other chapters). A very impressive body of research now exists demonstrating that these programs are among the most effective when the goal of treatment is to reduce the risk of an offender committing further crime (e.g., Andrews and Bonta 2010; Andrews, Zinger, Hoge, Bonta, Gendreau, and Cullen 1990; Dowden and Andrews 1999; 2000). Of course, because PIC–R theory is based largely on components of other theories, research evidence supporting the value of those theories can also be treated as evidence in support of PIC–R. Thus, consistent support for modern control (Gottfredson and Hirschi 1990) and social learning (Akers 2009) theories of crime clearly provide substantial backing for many aspects of PIC–R theory (e.g., the important roles of socialization, self-control, observational learning, etc.). The very limited role of socio-economic factors in PIC–R theory is also supported by empirical research, despite what many criminological texts say about their role in predicting crime (e.g., Gendreau, Little, and Goggin 1996; Simourd and Andrews 1994; Tittle, Villimez, and Smith 1978).

However, despite signs that the PIC–R theory may provide a valuable framework, especially for guiding the construction of offender treatment programs, it, like each of the other theories, has come under fire from critics. Again, because PIC–R draws on components from other theories of crime, not only does evidence supporting those theories come into play when evaluating its validity, so do criticisms levelled against those theories. These criticisms have been discussed throughout the chapter and will not be reiterated here. Criticisms that are more specific to the PIC–R theory of crime include the views that the link between the theory and its principles of effective correctional treatment is arguably weak; the relationship between the risk factors embedded in the theory, most notably antisocial attitudes, antisocial associates, a history of antisocial behaviour, and antisocial personality, is vague; and it is unclear how exactly these various risk factors operate and how they result in specific criminal actions (e.g., sex offences) being exhibited in specific settings (Ward, Melser, and Yates 2007).

FUTURE DIRECTIONS

THE THEORIES DISCUSSED IN THIS CHAPTER CLEARLY COMPLEMENT ONE ANOTHER. For example, learning theories of crime fill an important gap in psychodynamic theories by specifying possible learning mechanisms that can result in the emergence of criminal behaviour. Likewise, the focus on vicarious conditioning in social learning theories emphasizes a mode of learning that is ignored in learning theories that focus on classical and operant conditioning. Future research will likely explore how the theories discussed in this chapter can be further integrated with other theories (including those discussed in Chapter 2), much like what we see being done with the PIC-R. It may be that each theory has something to offer, and that by merging these elements into a fully integrated theory, we will be better able to understand criminality. Arguably, compared to the biological and evolutionary theories discussed in Chapter 2, the theories of crime focused on in this chapter are more clinically relevant. Future research will continue to explore how these theories can be used to create practical (and effective) methods for intervening with offenders in order to manage their behaviour and reduce their likelihood of reoffending. In the next chapter, we will discuss in more detail how one moves from theoretical accounts of crime to strategies for intervention at various stages of the criminal justice system.

SUMMARY

1. In explaining the causes of crime, psychodynamic theories emphasize the inability of internal psychic forces to control antisocial impulses; learning theories emphasize the role of associative learning and stress the importance of environmental factors in shaping criminal behaviour; and social learning theories emphasize the role of vicarious conditioning in the crime acquisition process, focusing on the cognitive mechanisms that facilitate learning in social settings.

2. Psychodynamic theories of crime are based on several key principles, including the existence of internal psychic forces (such as the id, ego, and superego) that are supposed to develop through a series of stages and control the antisocial impulses that are assumed to be an inherent part of human nature. Sometimes these internal psychic forces do not develop normally because of traumatic childhood experiences (often centring on problematic parenting practices).

3. Many psychodynamic theories of crime can be thought of as control theories in that they emphasize factors that control people's behaviour and prevent them from committing crime. Two of the most popular control theories are: (1) Hirschi's social control theory, which suggests that people don't commit crime because of the bonds they have with society, including attachments to significant others, commitment to conventional behaviour, involvement in conventional pursuits, and belief in common rule systems; and (2) Gottfredson and Hirschi's general theory of crime, which suggests that people don't commit crime because they possess a high degree of self-control, gained largely as a result of effective parenting practices.

4. Classical conditioning is a form of learning that takes place when an unconditioned stimulus (e.g., food) that produces an unconditioned response (e.g., salivation) is paired with a neutral stimulus (e.g., a tone) such that, over time, a conditioned response (e.g., salivation) is reproduced using only the previously neutral stimulus (now referred to as the conditioned stimulus). Operant conditioning, on the other hand, is a form of learning that takes place by experiencing environmental consequences caused by behaviour (e.g., reinforcement and punishment).

5. Sutherland's differential association theory emphasizes that criminal behaviour is learned when we interact with others (especially those who are important to us) and get exposed to a higher proportion of antisocial rather than prosocial attitudes. Akers' social learning theory builds on differential association theory by explicitly addressing the mechanisms by which we learn to commit crime. His theory emphasizes the role of operant conditioning in the crime acquisition process (whereby people learn to commit crime as a result of a personal history of being reinforced for that activity) but also includes the role of vicarious conditioning (whereby people learn to commit crime by observing that activity being reinforced in other people, especially intimate personal groups).

6. Andrews and Bonta's PIC–R theory of crime is influenced by a behavioural and cognitive social learning perspective. The theory emphasizes many different potential paths into crime, and crime is thought to be determined both by events that precede the behaviour and by events that follow it. These events are believed to gain control over one's behaviour primarily by signalling various rewards and costs for different classes of behaviour, which can be either additive or subtractive. The controlling properties of antecedent and consequent events are assumed to be acquired from multiple sources, including the individual, other people, the act itself, and other aspects of the situation.

Discussion Questions

1. Do you think it's possible to develop a general theory of crime that not only explains the causes of all crime, but also the causes of other antisocial or deviant behaviours? Why or why not?

2. As part of your practicum at an outpatient clinic, you have been assigned to work with a psychiatrist who has a patient with a serious foot fetish. The psychiatrist is interested in using aversive conditioning in an attempt to eliminate the fetish and asks for your opinion of how the treatment should be delivered. What you would suggest?

3. We discussed some ways in which operant conditioning principles are implemented in an attempt to reduce crime (or institutional misconduct). Think of other interventions that exist in our criminal justice system. Determine whether they are examples of positive reinforcement, negative reinforcement, positive punishment, or negative punishment.

4. You are a summer intern at Correctional Service Canada and are tasked with the job of coming up with a new treatment program for offenders based on Akers' social learning theory of crime. Describe what this program would look like (e.g., what would you target in treatment?) and explain your decisions.

Chapter 4
Canadian Corrections in Practice

John, age 28, is before the courts for an armed robbery charge. He robbed a convenience store late at night and threatened the lone store clerk with a knife. John admitted he was high on drugs and needed money for more drugs. This is not his first involvement with the courts. He served time in secure custody as a youth and in numerous provincial jails for property crimes (theft, break and enter, drug possession) and a couple of serious assaults. He dropped out of high school prior to completing Grade 10 and has infrequently held odd jobs, although neither situation appears to cause him much concern. Presentence reports describe a fairly chaotic childhood and family situation, with both family and friends being predominantly antisocial. Perhaps not surprisingly, he also has a long history of drug and alcohol abuse and multiple brief relationships.

The Crown is asking for a 48-month sentence, noting his prior criminal history and stressing the need for deterrence. His defence attorney is trying to convince the Crown that John's history is due to his poor family background and lack of stable employment. While John is reluctant to plead guilty, he wonders if the Crown would offer a lower sentence in a plea bargain. He recalls that the last time he was before this particular judge, he was warned not to return with new charges or he would suffer serious consequences.

What would be a reasonable sentence for John? Do you think a longer sentence would deter him from committing more crimes in the future? Should deterrence be the only reason for deciding on a particular sentence? Should the victim have a say on sentencing and on parole release?

Learning Objectives

1 Understand the role and importance of empirical findings and theory to inform *how* correctional practice works.

2 Understand the contribution of Canadian researchers to evidence-based correctional practice.

3 Review selected approaches to assessment and treatment to better understand *why* such approaches are popular in Canadian corrections and elsewhere.

4   Describe a typical experience for a sentenced offender.

5   Review contemporary challenges in order to understand future directions for corrections research.

INTRODUCTION

THE PURPOSE OF THIS CHAPTER IS TO DESCRIBE CONTEMPORARY CORRECTIONAL practice in Canada. Essentially, this chapter is about *what* is done in corrections and *why*. Underscoring correctional practice is an interplay between theory and evidence. New theories and research are used to analyze and guide real-world practices, a method often referred to as **evidence-based practice**.

This chapter explores contemporary practices across a range of correctional and criminal justice activities in order to more clearly illustrate the issues, challenges, and present-day approaches to corrections. Beginning with a review of the research on punishment models and deterrence (mainly in terms of sentencing), we will consider the evidence for its effectiveness in reducing reoffending. We will then examine the philosophy and evidence behind **restorative justice**, which has recently seen increasing interest. Discussions will also review the development of correctional programming efforts in support of **offender rehabilitation**, with emphasis on the current debate surrounding recent research regarding challenges to a risk-based model of understanding offender change.

Specific applications such as **custody classification** will be reviewed in some detail, as this is an important correctional activity that is often overlooked. Custody classification is the process of assigning a security level to incarcerated offenders and in Canada also typically considers treatment issues and the development of a **correctional treatment plan** to manage the offender throughout his or her sentence. Hence, theory is embedded within the information considered in custody classification and the process is more broadly referred to as **offender classification**. Offenders with different numbers and severities of criminal risk factors may warrant assignment to different security levels or custody placements and to different correctional programs in order to better manage their risk of escape, institutional adjustment problems, and reoffending. This chapter will more fully describe the central importance initial offender assessment has on numerous key decisions made regarding offenders throughout their sentence. Our review of theory and practice then moves to **risk assessment** and **risk management** for general recidivism. Subsequent chapters will provide details regarding risk assessment for specific offender subgroups using additional specialized risk measures.

The goal of this chapter is to highlight Canadian contributions to best practice and to illustrate how theory is embedded within such practice, even if it is refined through empirical research. Finally, this chapter will include a review of recent research regarding crime desistance and comment on how this research might be incorporated into current practice. The chapter concludes with commentary on emerging issues—understanding offender change and the process of crime desistance.

CONTEXT

Criminal justice issues are of great concern to Canadians and public opinion regarding corrections and parole is modest at best. Recent changes to legislation underscore this concern. Bill C-10 (formerly known as the *Safe Streets and Communities Act*) was passed on December 5, 2011, and encompasses several different pieces of legislation. Key aspects of the bill relate to increased victim rights, mandatory minimum sentences, and fewer conditional sentences. Sensational media coverage certainly invokes strong opinions regarding crime and criminals. Indeed, recent public opinion surveys note that Canadians feel sentencing is too lenient (Roberts, Crutcher and Verbrugge 2007). It appears ideology polarizes Canadians' views regarding how to enhance public safety.

WHY DO WE CARE?

There are generally two sides to the debate over what is needed to reduce crime and make Canada safer—greater rehabilitation or greater punishment. While both camps have their champions, in psychology we emphasize the importance of evidence to guide our actions. Specifically, what is the evidence that unbridled rehabilitation or punishment will yield better correctional outcomes (i.e., lower crime rates, lower recidivism)? Do *all* offenders respond equally to **rehabilitative programs**? Does programming actually make some offenders worse? Do *all* offenders require more severe punishment (i.e., longer sentences) in order to "get it"? The safety of Canadians depends on the answers to these questions. Chapters 2 and 3 reviewed a variety of theories posited to explain criminal behaviour. These theories have evolved over time, often integrating constructs from earlier viewpoints. Psychobiological and evolutionary explanations are less well developed in terms of practice, but social learning theories (especially those with a heavy cognitive component) appear to be the most empirically supported and are arguably the most relevant to correctional intervention. Evidence-based practices are constantly being developed and adjusted according to new research that applies these theories.

WHAT HAPPENS WHEN SOMEONE GOES TO PRISON?

Recall the story of Bill from the beginning of this chapter. What would happen to him after his arrest?

> Following Bill's arrest, it is unlikely he would have seen a justice of the peace for bail given the seriousness of his crime. Some accused individuals receive bail and await trial in the community under court sanctions (e.g., promise to appear, police reporting, keeping the peace, not using illicit substances, and non-association requirements), but many do not get bail and stay in jail (remand) until they are either found not guilty and released or found guilty and sentenced. Hence, Bill would have spent time on remand awaiting trial. During his intake at the jail, he would have been interviewed

Sensational Cases, Media, and Reality

It is impossible to read a newspaper without finding a sensationalized account of some aspect of the criminal justice system: egregious crimes, lenient sentences, or baffling parole decisions. In addition, popular television shows like *Criminal Minds* depict serial murderers on the loose, which is wildly inaccurate considering that most convicted murders in Canada are serving a life sentence and there are very few known serial killers in Canada. Against such a backdrop, it is understandable that the public has strong views regarding crime and what to do about it. As well, different strategies to address crime are often highly politicized, with different political parties promoting markedly different solutions to this complex issue. Unfortunately, the media portrayal of crime and criminals doesn't closely reflect reality and this disconnect undermines research, public policy, and the effectiveness of correctional practice.[1]

by corrections and health-care staff regarding possible security concerns that would affect his placement within the jail (i.e., incompatibles, risk of escape, gang affiliation) or evidence of health concerns warranting further assessment and intervention (i.e., requiring urgent physical care, mental health concerns, and risk of self-harm).

Suppose that after five months on remand, Bill ends up accepting a plea bargain (it has been estimated that almost 90 percent of cases are resolved through plea bargaining rather than trial) and receives a sentence of 36 months. Within a month or less he would be transferred to a reception prison, where he would be reviewed by staff for custodial and health concerns, as occurred previously at the jail. Any relevant concerns are referred to key staff in order to mitigate any institutional adjustment issues. Mental health concerns would be referred to psychiatric nurses and psychologists for further assessment and intervention. Overall, the intake process takes about 6 weeks. During this time, Bill would be interviewed by various staff who contribute to the development of a custody classification and correctional plan. The former is a risk assessment that determines Bill's level of security (minimum, medium, or maximum) and the latter is a review of his criminogenic needs (e.g., substance abuse, antisocial attitudes, education, and employment) and subsequent programming requirements. A static risk assessment to determine risk to public safety is also completed and used to determine dosage of programming (higher dosage programming is required for higher risk individuals). Finally, Bill would be provided an offender handbook and guidelines regarding his rights, such as eligibility dates regarding discretionary (i.e., day or full parole) and legislative release (i.e., Statutory Release and Warrant Expiry).

If Bill is initially sent to a medium or maximum security prison (which is likely given his sentence, crime, and criminal history) then after a year his parole officer will re-assess his suitability for transfer to reduced security using a standardized risk

---

[1] The *Toronto Star* series on prisons and crime published in 2008 is a notable exception.

Table 4.1 A Day in the Life of a Prison Inmate (Medium or Maximum Security)

06:45 Inmates are counted—must be up and dressed

07:00 Breakfast

08:00 Go to program, work, or back to the cell

11:45 Return to cell for inmate count and lunch

13:00 Go to program, work, or back to the cell

16:30 Return to cell for inmate count and then supper

18:00 Go to recreation, cultural events, self-help groups

22:30 Night inmate count

23:00 Lock-up

Source: Public Safety Canada (2005).

measure (Security Reclassification Scale). He will be regularly seen by his parole officer, who will monitor his progress on his Correctional Plan, including programming that targets his criminogenic needs. The parole officer will also write a report, should Bill apply for parole. Depending on Bill's conduct and his parole officer's report, Bill might be granted day parole—an early release opportunity where he would reside in a halfway house for three to six months prior to returning to the community in private accommodation (most likely on statutory release). While on day parole, Bill would be expected to avoid criminal peers and illicit drugs, seek and maintain employment, and complete aftercare or maintenance programming to maintain gains achieved while in prison. Finally, at his expiration of his sentence, Bill will be back in the community and no longer have conditions to follow on supervision. Approximately 20 to 30 percent of offenders fail to successfully complete their community supervision without committing a technical violation (failure to meet a condition of release) or a new crime (Public Safety Canada 2014).

As is apparent from this illustration, assessments of risk, criminogenic needs, and offender change occur at numerous points during Bill's sentence. This chapter will examine the specific risk assessment instruments that are used for different purposes (i.e., custody classification, risk of recidivism). Table 4.1 provides an example of a typical day for a medium- or maximum-security prison inmate.

ASSESSMENT APPROACHES AND EFFECTIVENESS

Risk Assessment

Risk assessment is pervasive throughout the criminal justice system and Canadian researchers have made major contributions to the development and validation of various risk assessment approaches. This chapter introduces several methods of categorizing risk assessment approaches and illustrates key decision points where risk assessment is used within the criminal justice system. Central to the selection of a particular risk approach are its accuracy (as a standalone instrument and relative to or in combination with others) and its costs (purchase price, time to complete, and training or credentialing requirements). Some clinicians might also consider the source of information in terms of whether the assessment is based on static file information or on more nuanced and dynamic factors, such as interviews. When reviewing different risk assessment instruments it is also important to consider the type of offender/outcome. It is important to utilize specific instruments for specific outcomes (e.g., sexual violence, intimate partner violence).

One popular model proposed by Bonta (1996) to better understand risk assessment approaches describes different generations presented in the evolution of risk assessment (see Table 4.2). Bonta's model categorizes assessments into four generations. The first generation is unstructured professional judgment. The second generation is actuarial analysis (typically of static factors). The third generation is actuarial analysis of both static and dynamic factors. Finally, the fourth generation is a comprehensive guide from intake to case closure and includes both static and dynamic factors. An important contribution of this model is the emphasis on risk assessment to inform intervention. While intuitively appealing, popular **structured professional judgment (SPJ)** instruments (e.g., HCR-20, SARA) do not readily fit within Bonta's model. SPJ utilizes empirically-derived factors but does not weight them according to their prediction of recidivism. Regardless, the accuracy of SPJ rivals that of second- and third-generation approaches (Hanson 2009). SPJ, third-, and fourth-generation risk assessment approaches are preferred by many over second-generation (actuarial) approaches because they identify potential treatment targets (Andrews and Bonta 2010). However, Harris, Rice, Quinsey, and Cormier (2015) remain staunch advocates of second-generation risk instruments, citing their slightly superior predictive accuracy and ongoing concerns regarding unbridled clinician discretion.

Hanson and Morton-Bourgon (2009) have proposed a five-category classification of risk tools that considers both the source of the risk factors and the method used to arrive at a risk estimate. *Empirical actuarial* tools use explicit risk items pre-selected based on empirical evidence and then combined such that scores yield expected recidivism rates. *Mechanical* tools have explicit items and methods (not empirical) for combining items into a total score but this score is not linked to recidivism probabilities; essentially they are risk scales that have not been validated. *Adjusted actuarial* tools permit a clinician to override scores from an actuarial and mechanical tool based on unspecified additional risk factors. *Structured professional judgment* tools utilize a structured list of risk factors derived from the literature but clinicians have discretion regarding how to combine scores and to assign levels of risk. *Unstructured* tools do not have the risk factors or methods for combining scores specified in advance. This latter method is considered the least predictive (Hanson and Morton-Bourgon 2009).

Table 4.2 Predictors of General Recidivism

Static	Dynamic
• Prior convictions/incarcerations (within 5 years)*	• Antisocial attitudes and/or peers
• Prior supervision failure	• Instability (employment, family, financial, leisure)
• Early onset of antisociality	• Current substance abuse
• Young age (< age 24)*	• Resistance to treatment/supervision
• Number of criminal associations	• Mood problems (anxiety, depression)
• History of alcohol abuse	
• School failure	

*Prell (2013).

Source: Adapted from Mills, Kroner, and Morgan (2011).

General Recidivism Prediction

Important static and dynamic predictors of criminal conduct (i.e., general recidivism) are summarized and presented in Table 4.2. As noted earlier, other chapters will review risk assessment for unique sub-populations (i.e., Aboriginal offenders, mentally disordered offenders, women offenders) and distinct offender outcomes (violent, sexual, and intimate partner violent recidivism). These predictors, especially dynamic factors, form the basis for treatment targets in correctional interventions.

Common Risk Instruments

While a plethora of valid risk scales exist (Desmarais and Singh 2013), within Canada there are only a handful of accepted general recidivism risk scales. Within the federal system, the most common is the Statistical Information on Recidivism—Revised 1 (SIR-R1), but it is not applied to Aboriginal or female offenders for policy reasons, despite evidence regarding its predictive accuracy (Nafekh and Motiuk 2002). For these cases, Correctional Services Canada (CSC) uses the Static Factor Analysis in lieu of the SIR-R1. Provincial jurisdictions invariably use a variant of the Level of Service Inventory—Revised (LSI-R) (Wormith, Ferguson, and Bonta 2013), a highly regarded risk/need assessment. Common risk scales used in Canada and their predictive accuracy are presented in Table 4.3.

Key Decision Points Using Risk Assessment

Pre-Trial Even prior to an individual being adjudicated and found guilty of a crime, risk assessment is a major consideration. Given marked public safety concerns, the courts need to decide who can be granted bail and be released prior to trial, and who must remain in jail awaiting trial. Underscoring this decision is the fact that procedural fairness is the

Table 4.3 Predictive Accuracy (Any Return to Prison) of General Recidivism Scales

Risk Instrument	Type	n	AUC
Statistical Information on Recidivism—Revised 1 (SIR-R1)	static	6881	.745
Static Factors Assessment (SFA) total	static	8768	.603
Static Factors Assessment (SFA) criminal history	satic	8768	.717
Static Factors Assessment (SFA) offense severity	static	8768	.551
Level of Service Inventory—Revised (LIS-R)	static/dynamic	5846	.719
Level of Service Inventory—Ontario Revision (LSI-OR)	static/dynamic	26 450	.758
Manitoba Risk/Need (non-Aboriginal)	static/dynamic	513	.709
Manitoba Risk/Need (Aboriginal)	static/dynamic	390	.684

Sources: Nafekh and Motiuk (2002); Helmus and Forrester (2014); Gendreau, Goggin, and Smith (2002); Hogg (2011); Bonta, LaPrairie, and Wallace-Capretta (1997).

cornerstone of a criminal justice system that supports the guarantees of our legal system: individuals must be considered innocent until proven guilty. Increasingly, especially in the United States, the field is applying risk assessment approaches to pre-trial decisions (Mamalian 2011). Hence, for pre-trial, such factors as prior convictions (especially for serious crimes and failure to appear) and employment and substance abuse problems are most often considered by judges, but decisions are based mainly on professional judgement rather than demonstrated validity (VanNostrand and Keebler 2009). For this reason, researchers are developing pre-trial statistical risk scales in an effort to increase transparency and accuracy in pre-trial decisions.

Custody Classification Another key time for utilizing risk assessment is at an individual's admission to a prison. During intake, corrections staff use risk assessments to determine the appropriate security placement for the offender and to develop a correction plan that outlines interventions intended to mitigate offender risk upon their release. This is commonly referred to as custody classification. Most provincial jurisdictions use risk and need assessments for both purposes, while CSC separates the two assessments.

Canadian corrections are world leaders in the area of offender classification. The applied and theoretical work by Don Andrews and his colleagues Jim Bonta and Steve Wormith in the development of the Level of Service Inventory (LSI) and its various derivatives is highly regarded internationally. Indeed, this research forms the core of offender classification in many countries (especially the United States) and is incorporated into all Canadian provincial corrections.

The initial part of **offender classification** is an intake assessment. Typically, the initial screening is completed by correctional staff who follow a standardized set of questions regarding current mental state, outstanding charges, incompatibles (identifying other offenders with whom the newly admitted offender may have problems), and prior incarceration history. This is followed by an orientation regarding the rules and regulations of the jail or prison, how to access information, and the availability of resources such as parole officers, social workers, psychologists, chaplaincy, and elders. Most correctional agencies have an offender handbook that is provided to newly admitted offenders. Newly admitted offenders are also seen by health care to determine if there are any ongoing health concerns. If mental health concerns are noted, the offender may be seen by a forensic nurse, psychologist, or psychiatrist, depending on the setting. All correctional systems screen for suicide risk at intake, given that it is a time of increased risk (Wichmann, Serin and Motiuk 2000). Suicide risk is covered in greater detail in Chapter 10.

CSC uses an Offender Intake Assessment (OIA) that was validated on the federal offender population and is similar in construction to the original LSI but is more expansive (Motiuk 1997). The OIA has undergone revisions since its inception in 1994. Items were revised so that they are more dynamic; consultations with staff have been conducted; and statistical analyses have been completed to confirm the improved predictive validity of the newer items (Brown and Motiuk 2005). The current intake assessment approach is referred to as Dynamic Factor Identification Analysis (Brown and Motiuk 2005) and is intended to inform case planning.

Specific to custody classification, it is important to note that concerns by such groups as the Office of the Correctional Investigator has challenged CSC to develop classification scales that are dynamic and can change over the duration of the offenders' sentence (i.e., Security Reclassification Scale) and are responsive to gender and ethnicity (i.e., Security Reclassification Scale for Women).

Assessment Domains in Offender Classification

CSC's **Custody Rating Scale** (CRS; Luciani 2001) considers three main factors for custody placement: 1) Institutional Adjustment, 2) Escape Risk, and 3) Public Safety Rating. These are combined to yield an overall custody placement of minimum, medium, or maximum security. This initial rating is done at intake and is revised following 12 months of incarceration. At that time, the index (i.e., current) crime is weighted less and factors such as program completion are now included. Cut-off scores are related to custody classification but, as in most classification schemes, there is provision for **professional override** whereby the parole officer can choose to recommend something disparate from the empirically validated scoring. There is some evidence that overrides diminish the accuracy of the assessment procedure (Motiuk, Luciani, Serin, and Vuong 2001).

Impact of Offender Classification

Over an eight-year period, an evaluation of the CRS demonstrated that concordance (staff recommendation and score on the CRS) increased from 63 percent to 77 percent.

Alex, aged 29, has been convicted of three counts of armed robbery and received a five-year sentence. This is his first federal sentence but he has more than 10 prior property offences relating to substance use and has been convicted twice of failure to appear. He also has committed two serious assaults while intoxicated. He has no outstanding charges and reports being motivated for treatment. He is married with a young son and he expects visits from his family while incarcerated. He feels it is time for him to change his life. He plans to begin his own roofing business upon release. He is asking to go to a minimum security facility to be closer to his family. There was a knife involved in the robberies but he states that he is non-violent. He states that the robberies were to get money to provide for his new family, although the pre-sentence report suggests that needing money for drugs may also have been a motive. He noted that he had a fight in the county jail when others hassled him while he was on remand. Nonetheless, he reports he can be in regular population. He has never been seen by a mental health professional.

Questions

What are Alex's major criminogenic needs? What is his escape risk? What is his institutional adjustment risk? What is his public safety risk? What security level would you recommend?

Moreover, the number of offenders placed in minimum security during this period went from 12 percent to 37.5 percent, while the escape rate fell from 13.1 percent to 4.5 percent. This indicates that implementation of the CRS led to more offenders being safely placed in minimum security with lower rates of escape. Not only does this yield cost savings (it costs approximately $15 000 less per year to incarcerate someone at minimum than medium security) it also meets the requirement set out by the **Corrections and Conditional Release Act** (CCRA) of implementing least restrictive level of custody.

Tendency to over-classify offenders has also been reported in provincial jurisdictions (Wormith, Hogg, and Guzzo 2012). As a result, custody classification instruments are preferred over unstructured clinical judgment.

Pre-Release It should be apparent that prior to release, decision makers will be particularly concerned about the individual's risk to public safety. Indeed, perhaps nowhere is the issue of risk assessment more germane than regarding pre-release decisions. Release can be discretionary, as in parole, or legislated as in statutory release (in the federal system). As well, a provision of the *Corrections and Conditional Release Act* (1992) authorizes individuals who are likely to commit a new violent offence or a serious drug offence to be detained until the end of their sentence. The main purpose of this provision is to improve the safety of society by keeping the most dangerous offenders in custody. Clearly, application of a valid risk appraisal for such decisions is paramount.

Both federal and provincial corrections agencies have developed specific criteria relating to offense severity that require specialized psychological risk assessments to be conducted for use by release decision makers (i.e., parole boards).

Understandably, parole boards are important consumers of risk assessments; surveys of parole board members (Caplan 2007) indicate that risk is a considerable concern in granting release. Common factors considered by parole authorities include current crime, criminal history, institutional behaviour, sentence length, offender mental status, correctional program performance, and victim information. Recently, the Parole Board of Canada (PBC) has adopted a Structured Parole Decision Making Framework (Serin, Gobeil, and Sutton 2009) as a policy requirement in an effort to improve decision accuracy and reflect transparent and accountable decisions (see Figure 4.1). The Framework is grounded by a statistical risk estimate and requires decision makers to systematically review empirically relevant predictors prior to reaching a decision.

Research has demonstrated slight improvements in decision accuracy (4 to 6 percent) while attending to the public's concern for transparency and accountability (Serin, Chadwick, and Lloyd, forthcoming). Certainly in the U.S., parole authorities have received considerable scrutiny and criticism (Petersilia 2001; Campbell 2008). Such concerns have gone well beyond issues regarding the occurrence of community failures to also include parole-board member selection criteria and the need for transparency in decision making (Paparozzi and Caplan 2009). Nonetheless, parole is enjoying a sort of renaissance (Burke and Tonry 2006) and PBC is highly regarded in the international paroling community.

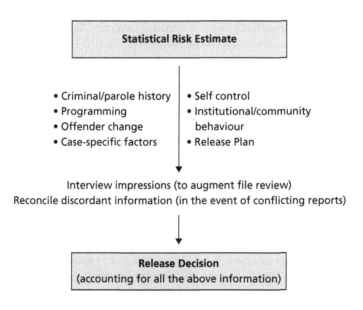

Figure 4.1 Structured Parole Decision-Making Framework

Source: Serin, Gobeil, and Sutton (2009).

Upon release, the vast majority of offenders will complete some form of community supervision prior to the expiration of their sentence. Again, community supervision is informed by risk assessment, whereby cases of higher risk are typically required to follow more supervisory conditions and are seen more frequently by probation/parole officers (Taxman 2012).

Community Supervision and Dynamic Risk

Risk assessment is obviously critical when supervising offenders in the community. Presumably, parole and probation officers assess *changes* in risk over time and intervene accordingly to manage risk. Hence, central to effective supervision is the inclusion of valid dynamic risk assessments (Douglas and Skeem 2005) that can provide differential case planning and real-time changes in risk management. Kraemer, Kazdin, Offord, Kessler, Jensen, and Kupfer's (1997) definition of a dynamic risk factor is important in that it requires directionality and causality. They suggest for a dynamic risk factor to be causal, it must be demonstrated that it can be changed either inadvertently (e.g., due to aging) or through intervention; its presence increases the offender's probability of recidivism; and that change in risk precedes the outcome. This means a minimum of two assessments are required to demonstrate the importance of dynamic risk measures. Two studies have illustrated that risk factors do change over time and the importance of dynamic risk (Brown, St. Amand, and Zamble 2009; Ullrich and Coid 2011). Also, a relatively new dynamic risk measure, the Service Planning Instrument (SPI; Orbis Partners 2003) is a stand-alone comprehensive measure of risk, needs, and strengths that shows considerable promise. Recent research ($n = 3656$) has demonstrated good predictive accuracy for male ($n = 2962$; AUC $= .77$) female ($n = 694$; AUC $= .77$), Aboriginal ($n = 635$; AUC $= .75$), and non-Aboriginal offenders ($n = 3021$; AUC $= .76$) (Jones et al. 2015).

Further, an ongoing program of research at Carleton University relates to the validation of the Dynamic Risk Assessment of Offender Reentry (DRAOR; Serin 2007), a measure of stable and acute dynamic risk and protective factors. Recent research from New Zealand and the U.S. suggests the measure has utility in that it predicts client outcomes at acceptable levels (AUC $\sim .70$) even when controlling for static risk (Hanby 2013), it works with female offenders (Yesberg et al. 2015), and the timing of the assessment relates to improved prediction where more proximal assessment is more predictive (Lloyd, Hanson, and Serin 2015). Protective factors also appear to yield incremental predictive validity (Serin, Chadwick, and Lloyd forthcoming). Research is ongoing to determine how a dynamic risk measure such as the DRAOR might inform and enhance community supervision.

USING THE LAW TO CHANGE CRIMINAL BEHAVIOUR

GIVEN THE AVAILABLE EVIDENCE THAT CORRECTIONS STAFF USING VALIDATED RISK instruments can identify offenders' risk for reoffending, this next section considers how such risk might be managed. In particular, we review the approaches or strategies intended to change criminal behaviour. These approaches are not preventative—they are applied to individuals already in conflict with the courts. With the exception of sentencing, which is intended to have a general deterrence effect (i.e., an individual will avoid criminal conduct based on sanctions imposed on others), these approaches are essentially tertiary prevention (Gendreau and Andrews 1991) that targets adjudicated offenders with the objective of reducing rates of recidivism. (Primary prevention aims to prevent crime from occurring; secondary prevention aims to reduce the impact of crime that has occurred; tertiary prevention aims to reduce the impact of ongoing criminal behaviour.)

Purposes of Sentencing

According to section 718 of the Canadian Criminal Code, the fundamental purposes of sentencing are to ensure respect for the law and the maintenance of a just, peaceful, and safe society. The expectation is that this is achieved through the imposition of sanctions on individuals. Other key purposes of sentencing include

- denouncing unlawful conduct,
- removing offenders from society,
- assisting in rehabilitation of offenders,
- providing reparation to victims, and
- promoting a sense of responsibility in offenders.

As noted previously, the most obvious goal of sentencing is to change the criminal behaviour of individuals who come into contact with the courts. However, amendments to the CCRA through Bill C-10 emphasize public safety as the paramount concern for the criminal justice system. Through the means of both **specific deterrence** and **general deterrence**, the expectation is that **sanctions** by the courts will reduce the criminal behaviour of both the specific individual and the general population, respectively. Recent public opinion surveys suggest decreased support for the traditional purposes of deterrence and incapacitation (Roberts, Crutcher, and Verbrugge 2007).

Deterrence

An important issue in crime deterrence relates to distinguishing between the *purpose* and the *impact* of a sentence. While the latter is perhaps of greatest concern in the context of correctional psychology, the former is worth reviewing to develop an appreciation of the complex challenges facing the courts. Consider Bill's sentencing for his armed robbery, discussed in the chapter opening. If punishment and deterrence are the sole concerns, then a longer sentence would be preferable. This might also find favour with many Canadians, especially those intolerant of crime and criminals. Most importantly, a longer sentence would have the most merit if it could be demonstrated that it reduced Bill's likelihood of future crime.

Consistent with the issue of ideology, it can be proposed that there are underlying assumptions with each of the punishment and rehabilitation extremes. The punishment extreme can be described as "hard," although some may choose the word realistic. Increasingly, the term "offender accountability" is used with reference to criminal justice interventions (Public Safety Canada 2015b). The evidence for this get-tough approach is not compelling, in part because punishment is rarely applied consistently or immediately within the criminal justice system (Gendreau 1996; McGuire 2004).

As we consider how punishment affects practice, it is worth noting that sentencing and sanctions reflect the major themes of *retribution*, *incapacitation*, and *deterrence*. **Retribution** asserts that society has the right, when harmed, to harm the offender. This harm or punishment should correspond to the crime (an eye for an eye). From an administration of justice perspective, such retribution is not necessarily intended to address issues at the individual level. Essentially, the commission of a crime warrants social retribution. **Incapacitation** is the application of crime control by making offenders unable to commit crimes by incarcerating them. In terms of reducing future crimes, since the vast majority of offenders do not die in prison but return to their community, this may have limited impact. Indeed, Tarling (1993) presents data consistent with the viewpoint that incapacitation is an expensive method for reducing crime. Lastly, **deterrence** is the application of punishment to influence behaviour.

Given the popularity of viewpoints emphasizing deterrence, researchers have investigated the effectiveness of its application. McGuire (2004) provides a detailed explanation of deterrence to which interested readers are referred. For instance, he notes that deterrence is measured across four dimensions: *certainty* (likelihood of legal punishment), *celerity* (the amount of time that elapses between an offence being committed and an official sanction being imposed), *severity* (magnitude of the punishment), and *scope* (the relationship between types of crimes in statutes and types of punishments). More specifically, Gendreau (1996) and McGuire (2004) both note that for punishment to be maximally effective, it must be first unavoidable, which is not the case in the criminal justice system. Second, its application should be immediately following the target behaviour; again, not the case in the criminal justice system. Third, it should be severe. Finally, even when these conditions are met, it is necessary to ensure the individual being punished cannot meet their goals through some alternative manner. It should be readily apparent that these dimensions are rarely applied in a systematic manner within the criminal justice system, which potentially diminishes the effectiveness of punishment to change behaviour. For instance, offenders often report committing crimes for which they were not caught. Discrepancies between police-reported crime and arrests confirm this (see discussion of the crime funnel in Chapter 1). Further, there are often long delays between arrest and conviction, resulting in the contentious two-for-one rule (one day on remand equals two days of a sentence, if found guilty). Previously this credit was applied almost automatically, but with the passing of Bill C-25 it is now under judicial discretion in Canada.

This short discussion about punishment is a good introduction for our review of examples where correctional practice (i.e., getting tougher on crime) might decrease crime. Again, the interested reader is referred to McGuire (2004) and French and Gendreau (2003) for a fuller description of this research. To illustrate the issue, we will briefly review the evidence for the effectiveness of deterrence in criminal justice applications. The evidence comes from six areas: 1) sentencing in terms of crime statistics, 2) the relationship between imprisonment and crime rates, 3) the effects of enhanced punishers, 4) meta-analytic reviews of outcome studies, 5) self-report surveys, and 6) research on the death penalty. Of note is that these studies are not uniquely Canadian and as such there may be debate regarding the generalizability of the findings.

A meta-analysis completed by Gendreau, Goggin, and Cullen (1999) examined the impact of sentencing on recidivism. This analysis reviewed 222 studies that examined a total of 336 052 cases. Compared to those who served longer (average 30-month) versus shorter (17-month) terms, those with longer sentences had a 2–3 percent *increase* in recidivism. Similarly, those incarcerated for an average of 10.5 months (103 studies) had a 7 percent *increase* in recidivism compared to those given community sanctions.

Thus, general deterrence does not appear to reduce crime. If specific deterrence is effective, there should be some association between the activity of the courts for targeted crimes and the amount of that crime. This does not appear to be the case. For example, Martin, Annan, and Forst (1993) considered fines versus short jail sentences and noted there was no effect on rates of drinking and driving. Moreover, Weisburd and Chayet (1995) found no differences in crime rates when considering while collar crimes (prison versus no prison with a 10-year follow-up on 742 offenders). Such findings suggest that simply getting tougher on certain types of crimes may not diminish the rates of these crimes.

Another deterrence strategy has been described as "punishing smarter." In this approach, enhanced punishers such as boot camps, shock incarceration, electronic surveillance, curfews, and intensive supervision are applied. Various studies have disputed the effectiveness of this newer brand of deterrence. In an informative summary of the utility of enhanced punishers, Gendreau et al. (2001) reviewed 135 outcome studies and reported a mean effect size of approximately zero. These findings are presented in Table 4.4. A positive value means increased recidivism. Interestingly, only fines and restitution resulted in a decrease in recidivism, albeit very slight!

The next area where we consider the effect of deterrence relates to self-report surveys of offenders. In a study of teenagers involved in shoplifting, Klemke (1982) interviewed juvenile offenders after their arrest and followed up several months later. Experiencing an arrest had little impact on the teens' subsequent criminal behaviour. Moreover, findings from the Denver Youth Survey (Huizinga et al. 2003), a longitudinal study of youth at risk, indicated that the majority of offenders, whatever their level of seriousness, were not arrested at all. As well, the more serious offenders were rarely arrested for their most serious offences (remember the issue of *certainty*).

Perhaps the ultimate deterrent is the use of the death penalty. Among the 71 countries that still retain its use, "the most common political justification is that it has a unique general deterrent capacity to save further innocent lives or significantly reduce other capital offences" (Hood 2002: 209). In his 40-year review for the United Nations,

Table 4.4 Effects of Sanctions on Recidivism

Type of Sanction	Sample Size	Average Effect Size
Supervision program	19 404	.00
Arrest	7779	.01
Fine	7162	−.04
Restitution	8715	−.02
Boot camp	6831	.00
Shock incarceration	1891	.07
Drug testing	419	.05
Electronic monitoring	1414	.05

Source: Gendreau et al. (2001).

Hood compared countries that were abolitionist, retentionist, or applied the death penalty with a moratorium, and found no difference in the frequency of capital crimes. Further, comparisons between neighbouring states with and without capital punishment found no difference in capital crime rates. In Texas, arguably the state with the highest use of capital punishment, no relationship was found between the execution rate and the murder rate: higher execution rates did not yield a lower murder rate. It would seem that the commission of crimes, including capital offences, is not influenced by punishment and deterrence.

Explanations of why punishment is not effective include perceived risk of (non) arrest (Foglia 1997) and the fact that criminal behaviour is dominated by "here and now" thinking (Andrews and Bonta 2006, 2010). Prior to committing an offence, most individuals are preoccupied with the implementation of the act, rather than deliberating upon the consequences should they be caught (McGuire 2002). Despite this, there remains interest by sociologists and criminologists in rational choice as an explanation for why individuals commit crimes (Baker and Piquero 2010; Matsueda, Kreager, and Huizinga 2006), although this perspective is not without its critics (Doob and Cesaroni 2004). Moreover, efforts to verify a **rational choice model** for various types of crimes have found mixed support (Carmichael and Piquero 2004).

Given that sentencing and deterrence appear to be less than effective in changing criminal behaviour, we are then left to explore alternative, more effective approaches. A utilitarian model suggests that people engage in criminal behaviour because crime pays. Therefore, to reduce crime, the cost of committing crime must increase. Andrews and Bonta (2006, 2010) and others (McGuire 2004) question if such a model applies equally to all offenders. They also refine this model and assert that criminality can be decreased when the rewards for crime are reduced while the costs for crime are increased *and* when the rewards for prosocial behaviour are increased while the costs for prosocial behaviour are decreased. Gendreau (1996) asserts that in order to change criminal behaviour, each single punishment should be balanced by the use of four rewards. It is worth noting that for several decades the United States has focused mainly on increasing individual costs to crime as a deterrent but in recent years has shifted its emphasis to **evidence-based practice**, in which empirical research is used to inform how to assess and intervene with offenders (Aos, Miller, and Drake 2006; National Institute of Corrections 2009; Taxman et al. 2004).

Paradoxically, the rehabilitative approach that focuses on increasing rewards for pro-social behaviour of offenders, and which was championed in Canada and later exported to the United States and internationally (Andrews and Bonta 2010), now appears to be consistently losing ground in Canada despite empirical evidence that rehabilitation is more effective at reducing crime than is punishment (French and Gendreau 2003).

From our review of sentencing, simply focusing on increasing the costs for criminal behaviour will be insufficient. Think again of Bill's case; even though the judge gave him a warning after his previous crime, he did not consider it when he committed his most recent crime. He impulsively sought money for more drugs and did not think about the inherent risks of such behaviour. It appears that multiple efforts are required to change offender behaviour and to decrease crime. It is also clear that different elements of the criminal justice system (courts, probation, prisons, and parole) may have different foci despite an agreed-upon goal of crime reduction. Notwithstanding the role of expert witnesses in the courts (where the interplay between psychology and the courts is less influential), psychology has a much more significant role in informing clinical practice in prisons and community corrections. Beyond a cost–benefit consideration, how might we conceptualize offender change?

USING CORRECTIONAL PSYCHOLOGY TO CHANGE CRIMINAL BEHAVIOUR

Model for Offender Change

There is substantial debate regarding how changes in contingencies (or the cost–benefits of crime) occur and whether individuals change incrementally (in small gains over time) or spontaneously with a sort of "aha" moment. In reality, there are likely multiple influences that inform the transition of an individual from being an active offender to one desisting criminal behaviour. According a social learning model, change in cognitions is fundamental to change in behaviour. Moreover, to varying degrees, client characteristics (age, motivation level, whether they self-identify as active criminal), staff characteristics (quality of working relationships, interpersonal style, experience), staff skills, client life changes (impact of addictions, mental health issues, etc.), and social capital (employment, prosocial peers, community supports) all influence offender change. This section will expand on some of these issues, beginning with a transition model of offender change, represented in Figure 4.2.

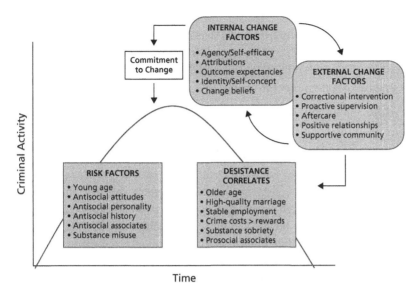

Figure 4.2 Conceptual Model of Offender Transition

Source: Serin and Lloyd (2009); Serin, Lloyd, and Hanby (2010).

It is important to appreciate that the factors that initiate criminal behaviour may be somewhat distinct from those that maintain it. At an earlier age, antisocial peers have a strong influence on criminal involvement, as do impulsivity and lifestyle instability. Over time, more engrained antisocial attitudes sustain criminality. Substance use and employment difficulties also provide a situational context for continued criminality. In trying to understand **crime desistance**, lifestyle stability in the form of older age and meaningful, quality relationships and employment become salient. Social support for change, referred to as social capital, begins to be considered (Farrall 2004). Again, changes in thinking, as reflected in agency, cost–benefit considerations, and expectations regarding the merits of crime versus desistance become important in changing criminal behaviour. While some researchers highlight the importance of protective factors in understanding desistance (de Vries Robbé, de Vogel, and Douglas 2013; Lösel and Farrington 2012), this remains a hotly debated topic, as some consider such factors as the obverse of risk factors (Rice and Harris 2005).

This untested transition model recognizes the major risk factors from Chapter 1 as being essential for the acquisition of crime, in addition to age. Notably, Blumstein and Cohen (1987) report that crimes are largely committed by individuals during their adolescent and early adult years, but criminal behaviour usually ceases between the ages of 30 and 40 (vanMastrigt and Farrington 2009). Indeed, offenders comprise a heterogeneous group (Piquero et al. 2001) and it has been shown that aggregate age–crime data conceal the distinct trajectories of widely different offenders (Barnett, Blumstein, and Farrington

1987). Still, as many as 70 percent of offenders follow some approximation of the age–crime curve, with only a small percentage of offenders maintaining criminal activity well into adulthood (Piquero et al. 2001). However, while age is important, it cannot fully explain crime cessation. Research underlying the model asserts that desistance from crime is a process that involves a commitment to change that precedes internal mechanisms and external events. Essentially the model bridges the risk and need literature with the crime desistance literature.

However, the timing, duration, and complexity of change pathways will undoubtedly vary by individual. For some offenders, the internal change factors are most potent, as evidenced by the fact that not all successful desisters complete correctional programs or receive community supervision. For other offenders, involvement in correctional program results in increased knowledge and skills, as well as changed cognitions, which leads to cessation of crime. If the field can better understand and identify the mechanisms underlying successful change, these could be incorporated into clinical practice to enhance client outcomes. See the Hot Topics feature for more discussion of our understanding of crime desistance.

While the model shown in Figure 4.2 may provide some hints regarding factors important in understanding offender change, there is no universal approach to facilitating

Hot Topics

What Exactly Is Crime Desistance?

Crime desistance, or the cessation of crime, is an area of increasing interest to researchers and clinicians who struggle with bridging theory and practice. A consistent finding in criminal behaviour research is that the aggregate level of crime peaks in the late teen years and early twenties and rapidly declines thereafter. That is, research shows that criminal behaviour is largely an attribute of youth. Rates of criminal activity drop sharply around age 30 and decline to nearly insignificant numbers later in the life course (Farrington and West 1993; Hoffman and Beck 1984). It appears, then, that offenders will eventually desist from criminal activity if given time (Sampson and Laub 2005).

Most researchers uphold that desistance is best understood as a process (see Maruna 2001; McNeill 2004 for specifics). So, while desistance is often defined dichotomously as the absence of criminal activity, current theory recognizes that

richer, more detailed data arises from conceptualizing desistance as an active, ongoing process of change and growth rather than a distinct, instantaneous event (Burnett and McNeill 2005; Maruna 2001). Recently, a transition model of offender change has been proposed (Serin, Lloyd, and Hanby 2010) that asserts that psychological mechanisms (i.e., propensities) moderate the change from an individual's self-perception of being an offender to being a citizen. These propensities could be a belief that one can change, an expectation that change requires effort, and so on. As well, a commitment to change one's goals, beliefs, and expectations is considered to be a prerequisite to eventual crime desistance (Ward and Marshall 2007). Such change drives crime desistance. Other factors, such as getting older, becoming involved in a stable relationship, maintaining stable employment, and securing prosocial friends, combine such that the costs of crime increase. Andrews and Bonta (2006) assert that this change in contingencies underlies crime desistance. That is, the rewards for proso-cial behaviour increase and are greater than the rewards for criminal behaviour.

In some respects, crime desistance research describes the factors present in successful desis-tance but it does not reflect an active intervention model. In considering the transition model in Fig-ure 4.2, it is clear that certain factors (e.g., older age, stable employment, quality marriage, sobri-ety, and prosocial associates) are associated with improved offender outcomes. Unfortunately, it is difficult to discern what levels and combinations of these factors predict eventual success. Do these factors function equally for offenders with different criminal risk profiles? Are desistance pathways similar for violent and non-violent offenders? Unfortunately, the relevant research is correlational, not causal, so we cannot say that all released offenders who get married and have a job will necessarily desist from crime. Indeed, unless criminals change the way they think, crime desistance seems unlikely.

Maruna (2010) nicely summarized the factors that offenders have reported as being important in their crime desistance and these are reflected in Figure 4.2. It is important to note that much of the research on desistance has used small samples and qualitative designs, and has been mainly conducted on property offenders. As well, much of this research has evolved out of dissatisfaction with current preoccupation with risk factors, which has excluded strength-based approaches and de-emphasized protective fac-tors (McNeil and Weaver 2010). Nonetheless it is an important area in that it recognizes that offenders do change and there are specific fac-tors that potentially forecast client success. In the U.K., there is an increasing movement to give a greater voice to offenders in their efforts to desist from crime using blogs and online videos (for example, see http://blogs.iriss.org.uk/discovering-desistance/). The assessment of desistance factors and the integration of this work into intervention, however, has not been incorporated into main-stream corrections.

such change, although the approach with the greatest empirical support reflects a social learning perspective (Cullen 2012). Central to these different approaches is identifying and understanding what *drives* change—internal mechanisms or external events? LeBel et al. (2008) have referred to this as a chicken-and-egg issue. One approach is more ancillary, such as providing social capital to offenders, with the expectation that this will either initiate change or support preliminary change. A somewhat more direct approach is a strength-based approach, such as restorative justice. The most common direct strategy is a tertiary approach that targets criminogenic needs, changes criminal thinking, and improves offenders' knowledge and skills in key areas. This type of approach is explored in more detail later in this chapter.

Restorative Justice

Although a universally accepted definition has yet to be established, a major tenet of **restorative justice** (RJ) is that it puts the emphasis on the wrong done to a person as well as on the wrong done to the community. It recognizes that crime is both a violation of relationships between specific people and an offence against society (Zehr 2002). Restorative justice is but one way to respond to a criminal act and to influence offender change.

RJ is a systematic response to wrongdoing that emphasizes healing the wounds of victims, offenders, and communities caused or revealed by criminal behaviour. RJ is seen as a viable third alternative to the traditional rehabilitation versus retribution debate (Zehr 1990) and is unique in that it attends to the needs of both victims and offenders. Restorative justice emphasizes the accountability of the offender and recognition of the harm they have caused to the victim and society at large.

Restorative justice programs involve the voluntary participation of the victim of the crime, the offender, and ideally members of the community in discussions. The goal is to "restore" the relationship, fix the damage that has been done, and prevent further crimes from occurring. Restorative justice requires wrongdoers to recognize the harm they have caused, to accept responsibility for their actions, and to be actively involved in improving the situation. Wrongdoers must make reparation to victims, themselves, and the community. RJ initiatives can occur at different entry points and via different agents: police at pre-charge; the Crown at post-charge; the courts at pre-sentence; corrections at post-sentence; and parole at pre-revocation (Latimer, Dowden, and Muise 2005). Encouragingly, recent Canadian public opinion surveys indicate strong support for restorative sentencing objectives to promote a sense of responsibility in offenders and secure reparation for crime victims (Roberts, Crutcher, and Verbrugge 2007).

Types of restorative justice approaches include the following.

1. **Victim–offender mediation**: Increasingly, this is described as conferencing (Amstutz and Zehr 1998) because mediation implies parties who are on somewhat equal ground seeking a settlement. This is not the case with victims and offenders, where one party has usually clearly wronged another. This conferencing has also been referred to as circles, consistent with Aboriginal culture (see Chapter 12) and has been used in sentencing and parole decision-making.

2. **Victim assistance**: Various criminal justice departments provide victim services. The courts, correctional agencies, and parole boards all provide information and services to victims. Much of this work involves helping victims understand their legal rights regarding representation and notification, and assisting them if they choose to provide information to decision makers regarding their experiences. The Public Safety website provides detailed information on provincial and federal assistance (www.publicsafety.gc.ca).

3. **Ex-offender assistance**: In some respects, victim assistance has overshadowed a long history of the National Volunteer Association (www.csc-scc.gc.ca/volunteers/003008-2003-eng.shtml) and its community agencies such as the Elizabeth Fry Society, the St. Leonard's Society, and others providing support and assistance to offenders. This work often begins while offenders are incarcerated and continues, through an after-care model, to include assistance with reintegration into the community. Similar to

recent work in the Unites States called offender **re-entry** (Travis, Solomon, and Wahl 2001), this assistance involves rehabilitative programming (e.g., addictions), support in returning to a community that may have changed markedly during the time of the offender's incarceration, and assistance with accommodation and employment.

4. **Restitution**: This involves financial compensation to the victim by the offender for loss related to their victimization. The courts typically assign the amount of compensation, however in RJ models all parties are involved in discussions. The compensation can include direct or tangible costs (i.e., repairing a broken door) and indirect or intangible costs (i.e., suffering).

5. **Community service**: Sometimes as an alternative to incarceration, and perhaps as part of a probation order, an offender is required to complete some sort of community service (i.e., provide labour for community projects) to make amends.

Both federal and provincial corrections provide services to victims, including notification regarding perpetrators' release, as does the Parole Board of Canada. Moreover, Correctional Service Canada has a Restorative Justice portfolio (www.csc-scc.gc.ca/restorative-justice/index-eng.shtml) and has an annual award in recognition of individuals who contribute to restorative issues in Canada. On April 23, 2015, the Government of Canada passed in Parliament the *Canadian Victims Bill of Rights* (CVBR), known as Bill C-32, which establishes statutory rights for victims at the federal level for the first time in Canadian history. Under the CVBR, victims of crime will have the right to information, protection, and participation, and the right to seek restitution—rights which are aimed at providing victims with more options for meaningful participation in the Canadian criminal justice system. The CVBR has important implications for the Parole Board of Canada (PBC), which in 2013–2014 had 22 323 contacts with 7500 registered victims and coordinated 264 presentations by victims at 142 hearings (Parole Board Canada 2014).

Does Restorative Justice Work?

To answer this question, it is necessary to clarify what is meant by "work." The gold standard of effectiveness is the reduction of future crime, as evidenced by lowered recidivism rates for offenders who participate in RJ initiatives. As noted earlier, however, RJ is *voluntary*. This means that there may be a selection bias (i.e., only motivated or less-serious offenders participate) (Latimer, Dowden, and Muise 2005). Moreover, not all RJ approaches are comparable; much of the evaluation research has been limited to victim–offender mediation approaches. Finally, one wonders how realistic it may be for a pre-trial intervention to reduce reoffending post-release if the RJ approach has not been reinforced over the time of the offender's incarceration or period of community supervision.

There are predominantly two approaches to evaluation research in restorative justice. One involves the evaluation of a specific program (Bonta, Wallace-Capretta, and Rooney 1998; Rugge, Bonta, Wallace-Capretta 2005) or a few distinct programs, as in study from the United Kingdom (Shapland et al. 2008). Another preferred strategy is to aggregate across all identified studies using meta-analysis, as done by Latimer, Dowden, and Muise (2005). In the study by Bonta, Wallace-Capretta, and Rooney (1998), despite lower recidivism rates for those offenders who completed the restorative program, only 10.3 percent of victims agreed to meet the offender, although 78.6 percent of victims submitted victim impact statements. Restitution was ordered by the courts in just over half of the cases. In a later study by Rugge, Bonta, Wallace-Capretta (2005) the major finding was that client satisfaction increased for those who participated in the Collaborative Justice Project. As well, there was a small reduction in recidivism over a three-year follow-up period. The study from the United Kingdom compared indirect mediation (in which information was passed by the mediator between the victim and offender), direct mediation (a meeting between victim and offender with a mediator present), and conferencing (a meeting with critic/third party and offender present as well). Based on a two-year follow-up summed over all three restorative justice schemes, those offenders who participated in restorative justice projects committed statistically fewer offences compared to a control group. Some qualitative analyses from this work suggested that reoffending was diminished when offenders realized the harm they caused and were somewhat reflective about their crimes. The authors also attempted to determine the costs and benefits of mediation-type RJ programs and implied that they are cost-effective.

Although some meta-analytic reviews are available within an overall evaluation of offender programming (Aos, Miller, and Drake 2006; Smith, Gendreau, and Swartz 2009), the meta-analysis completed by Latimer, Dowden, and Muise (2005) is the most comprehensive on the topic of the effectiveness of RJ models. It evaluated 22 unique studies for 35 individual programs (8 conferencing, 27 victim–offender mediation), and generated 66 effect sizes. The programs generally target male (94 percent), young (74 percent) offenders. Their conclusions are presented in Table 4.5.

It would appear that restorative justice programs, across a range of dependent measures, show positive effects. The greatest effect relates to restitution compliance and the weakest effect relates to recidivism. The findings are encouraging and suggest that in some cases, RJ approaches may be an effective alternative to incarceration and could

Table 4.5 Effectiveness of Restorative Justice Programs

Dependent Measure	Mean Effect Size (Standard Deviation)	95% Confidence Interval
Victim Satisfaction	.19 (.18)	.08 to .30
Offender Satisfaction	.17* (.13)	N/A
Restitution Compliance	.33 (.24)	−.02 to .63
Recidivism	.07 (.13)	.02 to 12

Note: *Outlier removed.

Source: Latimer, Dowden, and Muise (2005).

complement correctional programming (Latimer, Dowden, and Muise 2005). While RJ is not a common intervention with in the criminal justice system, it continues to be prominent as a mediation strategy, as evidence by its adoption for addressing concerns in the Dalhousie University Dental School incident where misogynistic comments were made through social media. The next section considers the evolution of rehabilitative (i.e., correctional) programs and the evidence regarding their effectiveness in reducing reoffending.

Offender Rehabilitation

Correctional programming has witnessed a marked evolution over the past three decades. This evolution has moved researchers from views of pessimism regarding the efficacy of direct intervention with offenders to reduce their future reoffending, to one of modest optimism. The seminal work in this area has been completed by Don Andrews and his colleagues. Indeed, Andrews, Zinger, Hoge, Bonta, Gendreau, and Cullen (1990) provided the first evidence regarding what became the "What Works" model. A goal of this chapter is to describe what appears to work with offenders to reduce reoffending. Other chapters will provide more specific information regarding programming for specific types of offenders (e.g., violent offenders, women offenders, Aboriginal offenders, sexual offenders, juvenile offenders). The current approach to offender rehabilitation is described as evidence-based practice (Serin 2005). However, it is important to realize that despite increased evidence regarding the effectiveness of these correctional programs (Aos, Miller, and Drake 2006; Smith, Gendreau, and Swartz 2009), social and political confidence in offender rehabilitation in Canada remains modest (Latimer and Desjardins 2007).

Most authors in the area of offender rehabilitation refer to Martinson's (1974) pessimistic review of the extant outcome data and conclusions regarding the ineffectiveness of rehabilitation as a "watershed event"(McGuire 2004). Martinson (1974) stated the results "give us very little reason to hope that we have in fact found a sure way of reducing recidivism through rehabilitation." He concluded "education at its best, or psychotherapy at its best, cannot overcome, or even appreciably reduce, the powerful tendency for offenders to continue in criminal behavior" (p. 47). Rebuttals from prominent scholars (e.g., Palmer 1975) as well as Martinson's (1979) re-analysis of his data and Gendreau and Ross' (1979) compilation of more favourable studies were unsuccessful in stemming the anti-rehabilitation (i.e., punishment) wave. It is perhaps not surprising, then, that advocates of offender treatment refer to this period as the "dark ages" in offender rehabilitation. Encouragingly Martinson, (1979) later recanted, noting that some interventions were beneficial, others were not, and some were downright harmful. The balance of this section will describe beneficial interventions, coined as "appropriate human service delivery" by Andrews and Bonta (2006).

It is particularly important to have an historical context in order to appreciate *how* offender programming has changed due to empirical evidence (Cullen 2012). Three decades ago, initial efforts at counselling were conducted mainly by psychologists, although chaplains also counselled offenders. Perhaps because correctional and forensic psychology was in its infancy, the treatment targets in the 1970s were often related to attenuating psychological symptoms (e.g., anxiety, self-esteem, depression) because this was consistent with psychologists' training. It was expected that improved psychological functioning would yield reduced reoffending. Until 2010, psychologists provided clinical oversight for high intensity programs. Most recently, programming within Correctional Service Canada utilizes para-professionals (parole and program staff who have a B.A. degree and specialized training). Psychologists in both federal and provincial corrections are now part of more formal mental health teams and their roles include risk assessment, crisis intervention, and some individual counselling.

The use of para-professionals to provide structured, skills-based correctional programming to offenders is facilitated by rigorous selection and training, as well as the development of standardized program curricula. In this manner, programming is more didactic than experiential, but the most effective programming includes role playing to ensure skill development. In community corrections (with the exception of specialized individual counselling by psychologists), most rehabilitation programming and aftercare is also provided by non-psychologists. The majority of these programs, whether prison-based or in the community, strive to deliver services consistent with an evidence-based model and follow a standardized program model that targets criminogenic needs. Nonetheless, there remains considerable variability regarding staff skills, program intensity, and degree of oversight. As we will see later in this chapter, these factors greatly influence the effectiveness of correctional programming.

Self-help groups and therapeutic communities are becoming less popular in Canada given the improved efficacy of skills-based programs that focus on criminogenic needs (Motiuk and Serin 1991; Taxman et al. 2004). Also, off-the-shelf skills-based programs are becoming increasingly more available (Multi-Health Systems 2005; National Institute of Corrections 2012) for a variety of treatment targets (i.e., anger, criminal thinking, problem solving, and substance abuse) and populations (i.e., juveniles, adults, women). Essentially, the current approach to correctional programming is to target motivation and reduce criminogenic needs using a cognitive-behavioural model that helps offenders understand high-risk situations and improve their prosocial skills. Substantial published research across multiple countries and correctional agencies has demonstrated that such correctional programming reduces reoffending (Andrews, Zinger, et al. 1990; French and Gendreau 2003; Lösel 1995; McGuire 1995, 2002). Arguably, rehabilitation programs are a critical strategy utilized by correctional agencies to reduce recidivism, thereby enhancing public safety. This is particularly important in federal corrections, where offenders are convicted for more serious crimes and receive longer sentences, thereby raising increased concern regarding their safe return to the community at the end of their sentence.

What Does an Effective Program Look Like?

Risk Based on the research by Andrews and others, the preferred contemporary approach to correctional programming has three main principles, typically referred to as **risk, need, and responsivity (RNR)** (Andrews and Bonta 2006, 2010). Risk refers to the requirement to provide higher intensity programming to higher risk offenders. This refers to the issue of program dosage. Increased dosage can mean more frequent sessions (i.e., every day versus once weekly), a longer program (i.e., three months versus six weeks), or a combination of increased program frequency/length to meet an acceptable level of intervention. There are two aspects of risk that are important to consider. First, providing programming to lower risk offenders may actually increase risk of reoffending (Andrews and Bonta 2006; Lloyd, Hanby, and Serin 2014). It appears that lower risk offenders (with presumably fewer antisocial attitudes) adopt more antisocial attitudes (e.g., lower motivation, denial, rationalization, antisocial views) when they associate with higher risk offenders during program sessions. Second, some minimum dosage is required in order for change to occur, but risk may moderate the relationship between dosage and recidivism (Makarios, Sperber, and Latessa 2014). At present, high intensity programs in CSC are typically about 250 hours, while some programs in New Zealand are almost 300 hours. Of particular note is a study by Bourgon and Armstrong (2005), in which they demonstrated that about 200 hours of correctional programming yields improved effect sizes (higher effect sizes equate to decreases in recidivism).

In summary, an effective program must be of sufficient intensity and target higher risk cases. At one point, it was assumed that program intensity was linearly related to risk, such that the highest risk cases warranted to greatest programming. There is now recognition that there may be a small group of very-high-risk offenders who may not fully benefit from programming (or for whom programming is insufficient to reduce risk). Certain sensational serial sex-offender and murder cases would likely be examples of this group. Overall, meta-analyses indicate that targeting higher risk offenders significantly increases risk reduction in comparison to targeting low risk offenders (Gendreau, French, and Taylor 2002).

Criminogenic Need As noted earlier, from the mid-1970s the issue of treatment targets has evolved from a focus on psychological symptoms to a focus on factors related to crime. Table 4.6 summarizes correlational data regarding these factors, illustrating why **criminogenic needs** have become a mainstay of offender assessment by correctional staff

Table 4.6 Types of Need and their Relationship to Criminal Behaviour

Criminogenic (r)		Non-criminogenic (r)	
Procriminal attitudes	(.21)	Self-esteem	(−.02)
Criminal associates	(.21)	Vague emotional feelings	(.08)
Antisocial personality	(.22)	Physical training	(.08)
Family/Marital concerns	(.18)	Fear of punishment	(−.05)
School/Employment concerns	(.15)	Conventional ambition	(.08)
Substance use	(.11)		

Source: Andrews and Bonta (2006).

(parole officers and psychologists). As described earlier, Canadian correctional agencies apply assessment procedures when an offender is admitted in order to determine the presence and severity of their criminogenic needs. Targeting criminogenic need has been shown to yield greater reductions in recidivism, while targeting non-criminogenic need can actually *increase* recidivism (Andrews and Bonta 2010). Most importantly, targeting multiple criminogenic needs is especially important and yields markedly higher effect sizes since most offenders have more than a single factor to address in order to improve their success upon release (Gendreau, French, and Taylor 2002).

Responsivity The responsivity principle states that the mode and style of treatment must be matched to the learning style and abilities of the offender. There are two types of responsivity: general and specific. The former relates to this issue of matching offenders to programming that is cognitive-behavioural and based on adult learning principles. While meta-analyses of treatment approaches indicate that the type of treatment is perhaps less important than the therapeutic relationship or certain client factors (Lambert 1992), offenders are adult learners and respond best to program models that are cognitive-behavioural (see Chapter 3) and skills-based. Indeed, programs that are behavioural are more than three times as effective in reducing reoffending than non-behavioural interventions (e.g., insight oriented) (Andrews 1994). This supports the principle of **general responsivity**. The issue of **specific responsivity** acknowledges that offenders differ significantly in their motivation and potential readiness for intervention. As well, other factors such as intelligence, age, gender, ethnicity/race, and language are all seen to be potential barriers to successful participation in programming. Further, staff have specific styles that may not universally apply to all offenders. Specific responsivity is the understanding of the need to match staff style to the offender's circumstance.

Taken together, the principles of risk, need, and responsivity reflect a model for offender programming. Research consistently demonstrates reductions in reoffending when these principles are applied. These findings are represented in Figure 4.3. Importantly, the most recent meta-analysis with respect to offender programming indicates that when *all* these principles are adhered to, there is an overall reduction in recidivism of 28 percent (Smith, Gendreau, and Swartz 2009). It is also worth noting that program effects appear to vary slightly by type of program. That is, some program domains (e.g., substance abuse) yield greater effects than other program domains (e.g., domestic violence) (Drake, Aos, and Miller 2009). The You Be the Therapist features provides a case study where you can consider an offender's programming requirements.

Describing a Correctional Program

Information on CSC's website (www.csc-scc.gc.ca) provides a description of a **correctional program** that is consistent with other sources (McGuire 2001). CSC notes that "a Correctional Program is a structured intervention that addresses the factors directly linked to offenders' criminal behaviour" (Correctional Service Canada 2009b). Moreover, the *Corrections and Conditional Release Act* (1992) specifies the legal framework

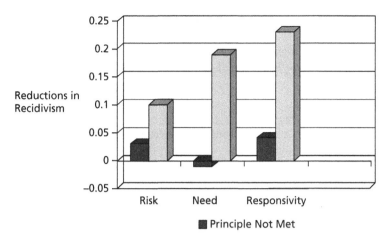

Figure 4.3 Empirical Evidence for Risk, Need, and Responsivity Principles

Source: Andrews and Bonta (2006).

Box 4.2

You Be the Therapist

Recall the case of Alex from earlier in the chapter: Alex, aged 29, has been convicted of three counts of armed robbery and received a five-year sentence. This is his first federal sentence but he has more than 10 prior property offences relating to substance use and has been convicted twice of failure to appear. He also has committed two serious assaults while intoxicated. He has no outstanding charges and reports being motivated for treatment. He is married with a young son and he expects visits from his family while incarcerated. He feels it is time for him to change his life. He plans to begin his own roofing business upon release. He is asking to go to a minimum security facility to be closer to his family. There was a knife involved in the robberies but he states that he is non-violent. He states that the robberies were to get money to provide for his new family, although the pre-sentence report suggests that needing money for drugs may also have been a motive. He noted that he had a fight in the county jail when others hassled him while he was on remand. Nonetheless, he reports he can be in regular population. He has never been seen by a mental health professional.

Questions
How motivated is Alex for treatment? What program(s) might be suitable for him? What program dosage would be appropriate? Should Alex take programming prior to release? If Alex does well in programming, do you think he would be a good parole candidate?

for rehabilitative programs: "The purpose of the correctional system is to assist the rehabilitation of offenders and their reintegration into the community as law-abiding citizens through the provision of programs in penitentiaries and in the community" (Correctional Service Canada 2009b). As well, CSC describes the components and principles of such programs.

> Correctional programs must:
> a. be based on theory and supporting research (empirically-based model of change);
> b. target criminogenic factors;
> c. address the diverse needs of women, Aboriginal, and other groups of offenders with special requirements;
> d. be skills-oriented;
> e. take into account the particular characteristics of offenders to help ensure that they derive maximum benefit (responsivity);
> f. address the particular risk and need profiles of offenders through their scope, intensity, duration, and type of group setting (program intensity);
> g. ensure a continuum of care between institutions and the community (continuity of care);
> h. include a detailed program description;
> i. include a plan for monitoring and evaluation; and
> j. be delivered:
> - using proven treatment methods,
> - in the least restrictive environment possible consistent with staff, offender, and public safety, and
> - according to approved standards (Correctional Service Canada 2009b).

It should be apparent that correctional programs are very specific activities that are clearly described in standardized manuals and delivered by highly trained staff, such that criminal risk is potentially reduced.

Sample Program Content

While programming for specialized populations is described in other chapters, a general program focuses on problem-solving and criminal attitudes, as these seem to be primary reasons for engaging in criminal behaviour. The initial cognitive-based program was called Cognitive Skills or Reasoning and Rehabilitation (Tong and Farrington 2006; Robinson and Porporino 2001). The most recent iteration of this program model is Thinking for a Change 3.1 (T4C; National Institute of Corrections 2012), created by the National Institute of Corrections (NIC) in the U.S. Thinking for a Change (T4C) is a non-proprietary, integrated, cognitive-behaviour change program for offenders that includes cognitive restructuring, social skills development, and development of problem solving skills. The NIC offers T4C offender program materials and a curriculum for training program facilitators. T4C is designed for delivery to small groups in 25 lessons and can be expanded on to meet the needs of specific participant groups. It is used in prisons, jails, community corrections, probation, and parole supervision settings with participants including adults and juveniles, males and females.

A similar Canadian example is the Counter-Point program. While this program has recently been revised, its purpose and goals remain relevant and are illustrative of how theory informs the practice of correctional programming.

According to Yessine and Kroner (2004), the primary goal of the Counter-Point program is to reduce reoffending by providing the participants with the skills necessary to identify, challenge, and enhance their willingness to alter antisocial attitudes and develop more prosocial attitudes. Additional objectives include promoting access to pro-social people and activities, identifying high-risk situations, and developing the necessary resources to prevent future criminal activity. Offenders participate in 25 sessions, which are divided into three processes: intake, intervention, and closures. Utilizing **motivational interviewing** techniques, the intake process consists of three individual sessions that entail orientation, assessment, and goal setting. The intervention process contains six modules that are introduced sequentially over 20 two-hour group sessions, which can be delivered from one to three times a week. The modules are

- Setting the context for change (two sessions)
- Identifying support for change (two sessions)
- Identifying pro-criminal attitudes, values, and beliefs (seven sessions)
- Altering pro-criminal sentiments (three sessions)
- Prosocial problem-solving (two sessions)
- Maintaining change (four sessions)

The closure process is comprised of two individual sessions, which are used to review the progress report and, together with a **parole officer** (PO), the relapse prevention plan of each participant. To facilitate attitudinal and behavioural change and increase participants' personal responsibility and accountability, Counter-Point is based on a social learning perspective and applies cognitive-behavioural principles and methods. For example, the program teaches self-monitoring, self-management, perspective-taking, and generic problem-solving skills, and features interactive presentation and practice, sequential and structured learning, prosocial modelling, role play, rehearsal, and effective reinforcement and disapproval. Program integrity is maintained through ongoing process evaluations and standardized manuals. Furthermore, program entry and participation guidelines are clearly outlined, and **correctional program officers** (CPOs) who are experienced in working with correctional clients have access to clinical support and guidance and receive training in the principles of effective intervention and professional conduct.

Statistically controlling for criminogenic need, risk, and prior program participation, offenders who completed Counter-Point showed a 24 percent reduction in the risk of being suspended, a 38 percent reduction in risk of being revoked, and a 33 percent reduction in risk of committing a new offence compared to offenders who failed to complete the intervention or were not exposed in any way to the program content.

To summarize, programs are mandated by the CSC mission and the *Corrections and Conditional Release Act* (1992). Their major goal is to reduce recidivism but they also help with population management (offenders who participate in programs are more likely to receive earlier release). Programs also assist in institutional management, in that offenders who participate in programs are less likely to be involved in institutional misconducts (French and Gendreau 2003). Finally, programs provide an opportunity to better understand an individual offender's case-specific risk factors, thereby enhancing risk management.

Program Evaluation and Accreditation

Following the principles of evidence-based practice, most correctional agencies endeavour to evaluate their correctional programs. Typically, programs that fail to demonstrate efficacy are terminated while the features of effective programs are expanded. The recent development of the Integrated Correction Program Model (ICPM) combines various program materials and processes to yield a new, integrated model (Correctional Service Canada 2015a). This new model essentially merges interventions for substance abuse, problem solving, and violence. There are distinct versions of the ICPM for Aboriginal and sexual offenders.

This high-intensity, multi-target program targets men who have been assessed as having a high risk to reoffend. The ICPM consists of 97 group and individual sessions (each two to two-and-a-half hours long) and is designed to teach offenders skills that help reduce their risky and harmful behaviours by helping them change their attitudes and beliefs. They learn goal-setting, problem solving, and self-management skills, and develop interpersonal, communication, and coping skills. To date, there are no published evaluations of ICPM, but CSC is expanding the model across the country after positive internal reviews.

Correctional jurisdictions continue to evolve their correctional programs, but the principles of RNR appear to be the most empirically supported over the past two decades (Cullen 2012). As well, Polaschek (2012) provides an insightful and cogent critique of the current state of RNR and its theoretical underpinning to programming, affirming its continued utility and relevance.

Given the resource implications of delivering programs (i.e., staff selection and training, curriculum development, validation, quality assurance) and their importance to correctional goals (i.e., reduced recidivism for program participants), correctional jurisdictions are both interested in and obliged to evaluate their programs. This is especially the case with recent reductions in correctional budgets. Goals of evaluations include ensuring that: 1) the programs are delivered in a manner consistent with policy; 2) the programs reflect a contemporary community standard; and 3) the programs yield reductions in reoffending. Some agencies have set up accreditation panels to assist in evaluations and to incorporate the opinions of external researchers. National Offender Management Services in the U.K. continues to use this model, whereas CSC previously had a formal accreditation panel. The panel was disbanded before the implementation of the ICPM. The ICPM was reviewed by external academic experts prior to its initial pilot.

If a program fails to meet accreditation and/or fails to reduce reoffending, its chances of survival are very slight. Correctional program staff constantly reviews programs and considers revisions to enhance such goals as offender engagement, offender retention, responsivity concerns, improved release rates, and improved release outcomes.

In an effort to more systematically consider the issue of program integrity, Don Andrews and Paul Gendreau developed the Correctional Program Assessment Inventory (CPAI-2000). Total scores on the CPAI-2000 (meaning higher quality programs) are related to higher program effectiveness in terms of lower recidivism (Lowenkamp, Latessa, and Smith 2006). In fact, the CPAI rivals standard risk assessments in terms of its relationship to recidivism (Andrews and Bonta 2006).

Program Effectiveness

It has been noted that the Canadian public is less than confident in the effectiveness of correctional interventions. Table 4.7 presents a summary of CSC's programs and their

Table 4.7 Evaluation of CSC Correctional Programs

Program	Discretionary Release*	Reduction in Readmission	Reduction for Any Offence	Reduction for Violent Offence
Substance abuse—high intensity	4.5x	45%	45%	63%
Substance abuse—moderate intensity	1.4x	18%	26%	46%
Violence prevention—high intensity	3.1x	29%	41%	52%
Family violence prevention—high intensity	3.0x	27%	ns**	ns
Family violence prevention—moderate intensity	1.7x	26%	36%	57%
Community maintenance	—	29%	40%	56%
Sex offender program—moderate intensity	ns	31%	ns	ns

*Values in this column indicate how many times more likely offenders were to obtain discretionary release.
**ns = not significant.

Source: Nafekh et al. (2009).

Table 4.8 Effect Sizes for Various Interventions

Intervention	Effect Size (*r*)
Psychotherapy overall (Smith and Glass 1977)	.32
Bypass surgery (cited in McGuire 2002)	.15
Aspirin for myocardial infarction (Steering Committee of the Physicians' Health Study Research Group 1988)	.03
AZT for AIDS (Barnes 1986)	.23
Appropriate service (RNR)—corrections (Smith, Gendreau, and Swartz 2009)	.29
Source: Marshall and McGuire (2003).	

impact on release rates and failure (any readmission, new offence, and new violent offence (Nafekh et al. 2009)). The results are quite encouraging. As the table illustrates, offenders who completed programs were up to four times more likely (in the case of high intensity substance abuse programs) to be released on some form of discretionary release and were much less likely to fail following their release. Of note, offenders who dropped out of programs had increased risk of failure upon release (Olver, Stockdale, and Wormith 2011). For contrast, Table 4.8 provides a comparison of effect sizes for various interventions, including medical and correctional approaches.

Despite a low level of public confidence, appropriate service (i.e., RNR) yields quite acceptable effect sizes in terms of reduced reoffending in offenders who completed the programs.

Core Correctional Practice

The concept of **core correctional practice** refers to a combination of interaction styles and techniques that correctional staff can use to more effectively interact with offenders and manage behaviour. Over the past decade there has been an explosion of interest in applying RNR principles to community corrections. Following Dowden and Andrews' (2004) meta-analytic review of effective staff skills in community supervision, agencies have been moving away from a strict supervision model to one where probation staff are expected to be agents of change (Bourgon, Gutierrez and Ashton, 2011). Current evidence indicates that staff who treat offenders fairly but firmly are more effective in changing offender behaviour than staff who are overly authoritative or rehabilitative (Skeem and Manchak 2008). Various authors have summarized the characteristics of effective staff:

- Empathic (reflects awareness and concern for others)
- Directive (active, leads discussions, set goals)
- Fair (balances the rights of all parties)

Box 4.3

Canadian Researcher Profile Dr. Paul Gendreau

Dr. Paul Gendreau was appointed the Order of Canada in 2007 in recognition that he has made seminal contributions to correctional theory and practice that have had an impact on criminal justice systems around the world. A psychologist and professor emeritus at the University of New Brunswick, he has used evidence-based research to develop rehabilitation programs for offenders. A highly sought-after consultant and advisor, he has shared his broad knowledge with government agencies, private sector organizations and universities across North America and in England, Australasia, and Jamaica. He has also earned accolades as an educator who has influenced a generation of criminology and psychology students and inspired them to become leaders in their field.

Courtesy of Dr. Paul Gendreau

Indeed, Dr. Gendreau has had a profound influence on correctional research and practice in Canada and internationally.

Since graduating from the University of Ottawa and Queen's University (where he claimed he majored in golf and basketball, respectively!), he has remained an influential and engaging pioneer in the area of corrections research and practice. A colourful speaker who is not shy about expressing his opinion, he has influenced practitioners and administrators alike regarding correctional policy. Less well-known facts about Dr. Gendreau are that he was a food critic for *Where to Eat in Canada* for 16 years, he is an ardent musician but a compulsive golfer, and he went to high school with Paul Anka and university with Alex Trebek.

Dr. Gendreau remains an active researcher, focusing on the prediction and treatment of criminal behaviour, the effects of prison life, alternatives to null hypothesis testing for data analysis, and assessing the quality of offender treatment programs with the CPAI-2000. He and his students continue his tradition of research excellence, most recently through meta-analysis to clarify and refine our understanding of effective corrections, while challenging what he refers to as "correctional quackery." Most importantly, underlying his more than three decades of research is his goal to help people. He believes that when the criminal justice system functions in a more humane fashion, the client and public are better served.

- Respectful (doesn't talk down to offenders)
- Reinforcing (supports and encourages positive efforts and accomplishments)
- Good communicator (has good interpersonal and verbal skills)

Broadly, staff who reflect these characteristics will have improved outcomes (Dowden and Andrews 2004; Liebling 2006; Marshall, Serran, Fernandez, Mulloy, Mann, and

Thornton 2003; Skeem, Eno Louden, Polaschek, and Camp 2007), including more disclosure in interviews, improved engagement in programs, offender acceptance of responsibility for their criminal behaviour, improved program participation and completion, better adherence to group rules, fewer prison misconducts, favourable response to supervision, and reduced reoffending.

In addition to the characteristics above, specific skills are required for effective community supervision. These include grounding client sessions with risk assessments; utilizing behavioural analysis of the client's criminal behaviour; using authority, disapproval, and reinforcement effectively; and implementing active listening, role clarification, effective feedback, and prosocial modelling (Robinson et al. 2012). Many probation officers also receive training in motivational interviewing (Walters, Clark, Gingerich, and Meltzer 2007) to enhance client engagement. Notably, research in the U.S. has found that the quality of the working relationship between client and probation officer (POs) predicts client outcome, even when client risk level is controlled for (Kennealy et al. 2012). This research highlights the need for POs to have strong relationship skills and be able to structure their sessions to ensure antisocial thinking is targeted (Bonta et al. 2008; Bonta et al. 2011). The model for research in this area has been to train probation officers regarding core correctional practice and then audiotape subsequent sessions with clients to ensure competence (Bonta et al. 2011; Lowenkamp et al. 2012). Research assistants then analyze the audiotapes to confirm if POs are applying their skills in an appropriate manner. This is a resource intensive process, but findings indicate that this approach significantly reduces (up to 13 percent) client failure on community supervision (Chadwick, DeWolf, and Serin 2015).

FUTURE DIRECTIONS

While the field can point to moderately accurate risk measures and moderately effective interventions, there remain areas for potential gains. Refining risk appraisals to include acute dynamic factors and protective or strength factors is increasingly of interest, as this could potentially inform real-time changes in case planning and risk management and identify differential trajectories for offender outcomes. A recent focus on staff attributes and skills is also becoming increasingly important, as it is evident that staff–client interactions are fundamental to client success or failure.

From this brief review it should be apparent that theory continues to inform practice and that challenges in practice continue to advance theory in a kind of symbiotic relationship. This notion of using research to inform practice underpins the scientist–practitioner model (Douglas, Cox, and Webster 1999). Specifically, it asserts that practice must be informed by the empirical literature and that clinicians must constantly strive to inform and improve practice. Indeed, delivery of effective practice is an ethical requirement of professional psychology (Canadian Psychological Association 2000).

Canadian social scientists are world leaders in corrections theory and practice who continue to make important contributions to correctional issues with a commitment to balancing rehabilitation with public safety.

SUMMARY

1. Effective correctional practice must be informed by theory and evidence.

2. Punishment and deterrence leads to increases in crime and incarceration, not decreases.

3. Offender change and crime desistance is influenced by an increase in rewards for prosocial behaviour. The factors that inform crime desistance may be different than those that inform crime acquisition.

4. For some offenders, restorative justice approaches are a viable alternative to getting tough on crime.

5. Using standardized classification measures yields lower levels of custody and lower rates of escape but the application of risk assessment must consider ethnicity and gender.

6. Provincial and federal corrections utilize standardized assessment approaches at intake and throughout an offender's sentence and supervision to target criminogenic needs and develop a correctional plan.

7. Correctional programming that is cognitive-behavioural and skills-based is most likely to result in decreases in reoffending.

8. Effective correctional programming reflects the principles of risk, need, and responsivity.

9. Staff skills are fundamental to effective corrections.

10. Research regarding dynamic risk is increasingly utilized to inform risk management of offenders.

Discussion Questions

1. What is the legislative backdrop to custody classification? What are some challenges to current approaches to custody classification?

2. If punishment seems to yield the least reduction in reoffending, why is it so popular?

3. Which principle of correctional programming (risk, need, responsivity) seems most critical?

4. What are the implications of having callous and authoritarian staff delivering programs to offenders?

Chapter 5
Adolescent Offenders

Jackson was born to a teenage mother. By the time he was five years old he had lived in six different homes due to his mother's inability to pay the bills and alcohol abuse. Once Jackson started kindergarten, his behaviour caught the attention of his teacher and school personnel. Jackson would often act out and be aggressive towards the other children in his class. If Jackson wasn't punching other children for their toys, he was damaging school property or throwing temper tantrums. His behaviour didn't change when he entered elementary school—in fact, it intensified, and by the time he was 12, he was being truant from school, playing with fire, and bullying both boys and girls. At age 14, Jackson brought weapons to high school and sexually coerced females. The police were called several times throughout his childhood, unfortunately to no avail in changing his behaviour. Not knowing how best to keep Jackson and other students safe, the school referred Jackson to a psychologist for assessment.

After interviewing Jackson, his family, and his teachers, and directly observing interactions between Jackson and his friends and family, Jackson's psychologist diagnosed him with conduct disorder, a precursor to antisocial personality disorder often found in adult offenders. However, not all youths diagnosed with conduct disorder go on to become adult offenders. Will Jackson?

Learning Objectives

1 Describe the history of juvenile justice in Canada.

2 Differentiate between the theories that explain juvenile offending.

3 Describe the risk and protective factors associated with juvenile offending.

4 Identify the psychiatric diagnoses and their trajectories relevant to juvenile offenders.

5 Describe the tools used to assess juvenile offenders.

6 Distinguish between primary, secondary, and tertiary interventions for children, youth, and juvenile offenders.

INTRODUCTION

ADOLESCENT CRIME IS OFTEN CONTROVERSIAL AND RAISES A NUMBER OF QUESTIONS for the criminal justice system and the larger community. For example, are adolescents that commit crime aware of the consequences of their behaviour? Should they be held accountable to the same degree as adults? Is treatment best left to prisons or other alternatives? You may assume that "anyone" who commits an act that is found in the Canadian *Criminal Code* will be charged and prosecuted. This is not the case, however. Children under the age of 12 are not charged, even when they commit violent acts such as murder. Professionals such as social workers, psychologists, and even police officers may intervene but the goal is to provide appropriate intervention or treatment so that these acts do not continue. In order to be processed through Canada's criminal justice system, an offender must be a minimum of 12. Prior to this age, children's behaviour is governed by the *Child and Family Services Act*. The Media Spotlight box describes a Canadian case involving two children, one a victim and the other a killer.

Once a child is 12, they are assumed to be in sufficient control of their behaviour such that acts committed against the Canadian *Criminal Code* will be pursued by the justice system. However, Canada does recognize that youth between the ages of 12 and 18

Media Spotlight

When a Child Kills a Child

In 2013, six-year-old Lee Bonneau was playing with some dogs outside the community centre where his foster mother was playing bingo. He was no longer there when his foster mother went to look for him. Following a 90-minute search, he was found behind the community centre on the Kahkewistahaw First Nation reserve in Saskatchewan. Lee had endured serious head trauma. He was rushed to the hospital where he was pronounced dead. The RCMP apprehended a 10-year-old boy at the scene of the crime who was believed to be responsible for the murder. The two boys did not know each other previously and no one else was believed to be involved in the crime.

The child (known as L.T. under a publication ban) responsible was known to have a history of violent behavioural problems. L.T. could not be charged under the *Criminal Code* or the *Youth Criminal Justice Act* because he did not meet the minimum age requirement (i.e., 12 years old) to be held criminally responsible for his actions. Instead, Child and Family Services will work with the Yorkton Tribal Council to provide the services deemed necessary. L.T. was in foster care living just outside of the reserve land at the time of the crime. Immediately following the crime, L.T. was classified as "in need of protection" (a term used when caregivers cannot provide the necessary care to a child) and became the responsibility of the "State." He is now under the care of the province and will remain closely supervised by social workers until he is 16, and possibly until he is 21 years old. If L.T. is not able to care for himself once he is 16 years of age, Saskatchewan's *Mental Health Act* may be applied to determine what additional steps may need to be taken.
Source: CBC News (2014, 2015).

are developmentally different than adults (over 18). The *Youth Criminal Justice Act* and outlines provisions for younger "offenders," including direction on how youth committing *Criminal Code* offences should be "processed." This chapter will examine the history of juvenile justice in Canada; the development of adolescent offending; and prevention, intervention, and treatment strategies for adolescent offenders.

CONTEXT
The History of Youth Justice in Canada

Prior to the nineteenth century in Canada, children and youth who committed criminal acts were treated similarly to adult offenders. No provisions or accommodations for age or developmental stage were made when it came to charging, sentencing, or incarceration. Adolescents were not even exempted from the death penalty.

In 1908, Canada enacted the *Juvenile Delinquents Act* (JDA) to recognize the special circumstances inherent with adolescent offenders. This legislation applied to individuals between the ages of 7 and 16 (although in some jurisdictions the upper limit was 18). These juveniles were termed "delinquents" rather than offenders and were seen to commit acts of delinquency (e.g., truancy) rather than criminal offences. A separate court was designed for delinquents and parents were encouraged to take part in the proceedings, which were more informal than was customary in adult court. Sanctions included adjournment without penalty, fines, probation, mandatory attendance in an industrial school to learn a skill or trade, and foster care. Delinquents who committed serious and violent acts could be transferred to adult court. Although the enactment of the JDA was a positive first step in juvenile justice, criticisms included the informality of youth court denying youth their rights, such as the right to legal representation and the right to appeal; that judges could impose open-ended sentences; and the broad definition of delinquency that included acts that were *not* illegal for adults.

In 1984, the *Young Offenders Act* (YOA) replaced the JDA. The YOA recognized that adolescent offenders were cognitively different than adults and that consequently their level of accountability and the sanctions for their behaviour should be more commensurate with their developmental stage. The act also recognized that the community had a right to be protected from adolescent offenders while granting these adolescents their rights as stated in the *Canadian Charter of Rights and Freedoms* (R.S.C. 1985: c. Y-1, s. 3).

With the YOA came an increase in the minimum age at which an individual could be charged with a criminal offence, from 7 years old to 12 (and up to 18). Child and Family Services would intervene with anyone under 12 who engaged in behaviour that violated the Canadian *Criminal Code*. Youth court judgments, with the possibility of a transfer to adult court, continued. However, in order to be transferred, an adolescent had to be at least 14 years old (R.S.C 1985: c. Y-1, s. 16).

The YOA also allowed youth cases to be diverted. **Diversion** is a decision not to prosecute a young offender but rather have them undergo an educational or community service program. A young offender would have to plead guilty for diversion to be possible

(R.S.C 1985: c. Y-1, s. 4). Other dispositions available for young offenders included absolute discharge (i.e., the young offender received no sentence other than a guilty verdict), a fine, compensation for loss or damaged property, restitution to the victim, a prohibition order (i.e., no weapons), community service, probation, and custody. Custody could be open (placing the youth in a community residential facility, group home, or childcare facility) or secure (incarceration in a prison facility) (R.S.C 1985: c. Y-1, s. 20).

The YOA was amended a number of times. In 1986, Bill C-106 section 16 was introduced to combat the problem of adolescents pleading guilty to avoid transfer to adult court. Youth court would be required to consider whether the Crown or defence would like to make an application to transfer. In 1995, Bill C-37 changed section 16 once again. If charged with murder, manslaughter, or aggravated sexual assault, 16- and 17-year-olds would automatically be tried in adult court. However, on application, these cases could stay in youth court if the youth court felt the objectives of rehabilitation and public protection could be reconciled. Youth sentencing also changed under Bill C-37: for first-degree murder, a ten-year maximum sentence with a six-year maximum to be served incarcerated was available. For second-degree murder, a seven-year maximum with a four-year maximum to be served incarcerated was available.

As can be seen by the number of amendments regarding transfers to adult court, the perception was that adolescent offenders received relatively short or light sentences even when committing seriously violent crimes. Moreover, the way the YOA was written allowed for discrepancies in the factors leading to transfer to adult court and how cases were handled. There also was issue with the overuse of incarceration. Canada has the highest incarceration rate for youth in the Western world, including the United States.

On April 1, 2003, the *Youth Criminal Justice Act* (YCJA) replaced the YOA. Part of the intent of the YCJA is to keep adolescent offenders out of court and out of custody. The three main objectives of the YCJA are:

1. To prevent youth crime
2. To provide meaningful consequences and encourage responsibility of behaviour
3. To improve rehabilitation and reintegration of youth into the community

As a first step when coming into contact with antisocial youth, police are to consider community options and less serious alternatives before bringing adolescents to the attention of youth court (*Youth Criminal Justice Act* 2002: s. 7). These alternatives are called **extrajudicial measures** and include giving a warning or making a referral for treatment (with the consent of the adolescent) (*Youth Criminal Justice Act* 2002: s. 10). Once an adolescent is charged, however, they can no longer be transferred to adult court under the YCJA. Rather, if an adolescent defendant is found guilty the judge can impose an adult sentence as long as the defendant is at least 14 years old (may be set at 15 or 16 depending on jurisdiction). An adult sentence cannot be applied unless the Crown notifies the youth court that it will be seeking an adult sentence (*Youth Criminal Justice Act* 2002: s. 61). A key issue in determining sentencing is that the sentence must be proportionate to the seriousness of the offence (*Youth Criminal Justice Act* 2002: s. 38(2)(c)).

Table 5.1 Overview of Key Changes to Canada's Adolescent Offending Legislation

Prior to JDA	Juvenile Delinquents Act (JDA), 1908	Young Offenders Act (YOA), 1984	Youth Criminal Justice Act (YCJA), 2003
No legislation for youth	Minimum age set to 7 years	Minimum age set to 12 years	Less serious and less violent crime kept out of court
Youth treated as adults	Separate court for children/youth	Youth not as accountable as adults	Increased extrajudicial measures
Adult sentences imposed	Parents encouraged to participate	Young offenders have rights	Greater focus on prevention and reintegration into the community
Sentences served with adults	Increased sanctions	Public has the right to be protected	No transfers to adult court
	Judicial discretion		Judge can impose adult sentences
			Victims are recognized

Expanded sentencing options also are provided for under the YCJA. Judges can give a reprimand (i.e., lecture or warning to the adolescent), an intensive support and supervision order, an attendance order (i.e., adolescent must attend a specific program), a deferred custody and supervision order (i.e., adolescent can serve sentence in the community as long as imposed conditions are met), and an intensive rehabilitative custody and supervision order (i.e., adolescent in custody receives intensive services and supervision) (*Youth Criminal Justice Act* 2002: s. 42).

The YCJA also considers the victims of adolescent offenders. Victims are to be informed of court proceedings and given an opportunity to participate. They also have the right to access youth court records and participate in community-based dispositions (*Youth Criminal Justice Act* 2002: s. 3). Table 5.1 provides an overview of the historical changes in adolescent justice in Canada.

WHY DO WE CARE?

Youth Crime Rates-

Approximately 48 000 cases were completed in Canada's youth courts for the 2011–2012 year (Dauvergne 2013). This number of cases represents an almost 10 percent decrease (or 5300 fewer cases) from the previous year, and the 2011–2012 rate was the lowest ever seen since these data were first collected by Statistics Canada in 1991–1992. In fact, almost

Table 5.2 Decreases in Offences by Youth in 2011–2012 Compared to 2010–2011

Property Crime Cases	Amount of Decrease
Theft	–17%
Break and enter	–15%
Violent Crime Cases	
Major assault	–15%
Criminal harassment	–14%
Other Cases	
Impaired driving	–21%
Administration of justice offences	–8%
Offences against the YCJA	–5%

Source: Dauvergne (2013).

every category of offense for youth decreased in 2011–2012. See Table 5.2 for a list of offences and their associated decrease.

Many other types of cases (specifically, attempted murder, major assault, common assault, theft, break and enter, fraud, mischief, failure to appear, breach of probation, unlawfully at large, and impaired driving) were also recorded at the lowest rates since the data were first collected in 1991–1992 (Dauvergne 2013).

Cases that were on the rise in youth court included drug offenses, with possession of drugs increasing 7 percent, and other types of drug crime such as trafficking, production, and exporting/importing increasing by 2 percent from the previous year (Dauvergne 2013). There was also one more homicide and six more sexual offence cases in 2011–2012 than in 2010–2011 (Dauvergne 2013).

It is important to note that most youth court cases involve older adolescents between 16 and 17 years old. As you will read later on in this chapter, this age range has a higher rate of offending compared to younger children. In 2011–2012, 61 percent of cases involved 16- and 17-year-old defendants, whereas only 39 percent involved 12- to 15-year-old defendants (Dauvergne 2013).

Of course, not all youth crime goes through the court system. Often adolescents will be diverted from the criminal justice system and no crime is recorded for first time offenses. Thus, we need to be cautious in our interpretation of the data, since diversion and other practices may give an inaccurate impression that crimes aren't occurring or have dramatically dropped.

Youth Sentences

There are three possible outcomes in youth court. These potential outcomes are illustrated in Table 5.3.

Table 5.3 Possible Outcomes in Youth Court	
Guilty	The youth defendant either pleads guilty or is found guilty by the court
Stayed proceedings	The charges against the adolescent defendant can be suspended up to one year, withdrawn, dismissed, or discharged because proceedings were interrupted or stopped (i.e., insufficient evidence or adolescent defendant is referred to an extrajudicial measures program)
Acquital	The adolescent defendant is found not guilty

Source: Dauvergne (2013).

More than half (57 percent) of the youth court cases in 2011–2012 resulted in a guilty finding. Approximately 42 percent of cases were stayed, withdrawn, dismissed, or discharged, and about 1 percent were acquitted. In less than 1 percent of the cases the adolescent defendant was found not criminally responsible or **unfit to stand trial** (see Chapter 10 for more on what these terms mean).

Variation in court decisions can be found across provinces and territories. For example, in Ontario and Nunavut, 50 percent of youth court cases resulted in a guilty finding, in contrast to New Brunswick where 79 percent of youth court cases had guilty findings. One explanation for the variation has to do with pre-charge screening practices. Crown prosecutors (rather than police) decide whether to proceed with a youth case in New Brunswick, Quebec, and British Columbia, hence different criteria may be used or the thresholds to meet those criteria may differ. As well, how extrajudicial measures are used may differ and influence court decisions across the country.

In 2011–2012, as was the case in previous years, **probation** was the most common sentence imposed on youth in 58 percent of the youth court cases found guilty. Probation requires youth to serve their sentence in the community while meeting certain conditions, such as not associating with certain peers and/or reporting to a probation officer. The median length of probation was 365 days (or 1 year) in 2011–2012 (Dauvergne 2013).

A **community service order** (where youth must perform unpaid work) was imposed in 25 percent of guilty youth cases. This order can be associated with cases involving "other drug offences" such as drug trafficking and drug possession. In 15 percent of guilty youth cases, a custody disposition that required the youth to be detained in a correctional facility or youth justice centre was imposed. This type of sentence is the most severe and is reserved for the most serious crimes committed by adolescents such as attempted murder and homicide. The duration of custody sentences are relatively short (3 months or less). Fewer than 2 percent of youth court guilty cases resulted in custody sentences of over a year. See Table 5.4 for the median length of custody sentences as a function of crime.

Table 5.4 Median Length of Custody Sentences as a Function of Crime	
Homicide	730 days
Attempted Murder	240 days
Sexual Assault	176 days
Source: Brennan (2012).	

There has been a drop in the number of youth sentenced to custody since the implementation of the YCJA in 2003. Custody sentences were applied in around 24 percent of cases in the 1990s and 29 percent in the early 2000s, but in 2011–2012 only 15 percent of youth cases resulted in a custody sentence (Dauvergne 2013).

The YCJA also introduced deferred custody and supervision as an alternative to a custody sentence. In this alternative, the youth serves his/her sentence in the community with a strict set of conditions. If the conditions are violated, the adolescent is sent to custody for the remainder of the sentence. Approximately 5 percent of youth cases have had deferred custody and supervision sentences imposed since 2003 (Dauvergne 2013).

Impact on Canadians

A major concern for policy makers and society is that youth who commit crime will go on to commit further crime into adulthood. If youth could be prevented from committing crime in the first place, or if those youth that do become involved in the criminal justice system could be "redirected" so that further crime is reduced or eliminated, a positive long-term impact would be seen both on the adolescent and larger society. Although it has been argued that Canada lags behind other countries when estimating the cost that can be saved by diverting young people from crime (Department of Public Safety, as cited in Thompson 2013), it is estimated that diverting a 14-year-old high-risk adolescent from a life of crime could save society between $2.6 to $5.3 million (Thompson 2013). Even if these estimates are high, it is safe to conclude that diverting criminal adolescents from committing further crime would be of significant benefit to society from a cost savings approach (at a minimum).

DEFINITIONS

Two trajectories can be seen with adolescent offenders; child-onset versus adolescent-onset (Moffitt 1993). For **child-onset adolescent offenders**, behavioural problems start very early in childhood. These adolescents often have histories that include behavioural problems dating back to daycare and preschool. As babies, they were difficult to soothe with problematic temperaments and were aggressive with other children, physically hitting them and throwing temper tantrums. In contrast, **adolescent-onset**

adolescent offenders begin to show behavioural problems in their teen years. These adolescents may engage in antisocial acts such as truancy, theft, and vandalism. Often the adage of "boys will be boys" is used to describe this group. These two trajectories make different predictions about the likelihood of engaging in adult offending.

When examining the trajectory to adult offending, age of onset is a critical factor. A clear pattern has been found linking early onset of antisocial behaviour to more serious and persistent antisocial behaviour later in life (e.g., Fergusson and Woodward 2000; Loeber and Farrington 2000). In addition, those with a childhood onset also may have a number of other challenges, including attention deficit hyperactivity disorder, learning disabilities, and academic difficulties (Hinshaw, Lahey, and Hart 1993). The childhood-onset trajectory is a less frequent occurrence, affecting about 3 to 5 percent of the general population (Moffitt 1993). It is important to remember that most young children with behavioural difficulties do *not* go on to become adult offenders.

The adolescent-onset pattern occurs in about 70 percent of the general population (Moffitt 1993). Many adolescents rebel against authority and engage in antisocial acts during adolescence, but these behaviours are few and limited. Although it is more common for adolescent-onset youth to desist antisocial behaviour in early adulthood than for those with a childhood onset, some continue to engage in antisocial acts in adulthood (Moffitt, Caspi, Harrington and Milne 2002). Recently, some have argued that certain types of behaviour (i.e., physical aggression vs. non-aggressive rule-breaking) are a stronger predictor of later antisocial behaviour than age of onset (Burt, Donnellan, Iacono and McGue 2011). It is also important to consider that some adolescent offenders experience substance abuse issues that may then play into adult offending if the substance abuse problems are not managed.

Brame, Nagin, and Tremblay (2001) followed a group of boys with high levels of aggression in Montreal from the time they entered kindergarten through to their late teens. The researchers found that the overall level of aggression decreased as the boys got older, regardless of how high it was when the participants were youngsters. For a small proportion of the boys, their levels of aggression continued into their teens. However, for a much larger proportion, little or no aggression was reported in the teen years. Thus, for a small group of youngsters with high levels of aggression, these levels will continue into later years.

METHODOLOGY

IN ORDER TO UNDERSTAND THE TRAJECTORY OF OFFENDING, SEVERAL METHODOLOGIES ARE possible but perhaps the most common is the longitudinal study or a prospective study where a large group of participants are followed for several years. For example, the study described above by Brame, Nagin, and Tremblay (2001) identified a group of boys with the characteristic of interest (i.e., aggression) and then followed up with them at several time points to assess their levels of aggression to determine its trajectory. In a study like this one, often the same set of measures is used throughout the period of study. For example, the same behaviour checklist could be used each year for 20 years.

Another methodology is considered retrospective in time, where a group currently exhibiting the behaviour (i.e., offending) is examined by looking back in time to assess various characteristics that researchers may deem important and associated with the key variable of interest.

In terms of examining the effectiveness of treatment programs or interventions, a pre-post test may be used, in which participants are measured before and after the treatment/intervention to determine if the treatment was effective. A follow-up study could then be performed to determine if treatments/interventions have a long-lasting impact.

When discussing offending, a recidivism study could be performed, in which adolescent offenders are followed up with after the commission of a particular crime. This group of offenders could be followed to examine whether they repeat their crime or behaviour.

THEORIES OF ADOLESCENT OFFENDING

A NUMBER OF THEORIES HAVE BEEN PROPOSED TO EXPLAIN WHY SOME ADOLESCENTS OFFEND. Below are descriptions of some common theories in the current literature on adolescent offending.

Biological Theories

A number of genetic and physiological differences exist between adolescents who engage in antisocial behaviour and those who do not. Genetic studies have found that fathers who engage in antisocial behaviour are more likely to have children (a stronger link for sons than daughters) who also engage in antisocial behaviour (Frick et al. 1992). Twin and adoption studies further support this conclusion. Specifically, children who have an antisocial biological father are more likely to engage in antisocial behaviour, even when raised apart from the father, suggesting that environment is not the only influence on behaviour (Cadoret and Cain 1980; Jarey and Stewart 1985). Moreover, the interaction between genetics and environment may be critical.

Along this line, researchers have investigated the brain region responsible for planning and inhibiting behaviour—the frontal lobe—to explain why some adolescents engage in antisocial acts. Moffitt and Henry (1989) found that antisocial adolescents have less frontal lobe inhibition than adolescents who do not engage in antisocial behaviour. Thus, the likelihood that these adolescents will act impulsively is increased, making it more likely that they will make poor behavioural choices. Also, Wadsworth (1976) found that antisocial adolescents have slower heart rates than non-antisocial adolescents, suggesting a higher threshold for excitability and emotionality.

A number of physiological and genetic differences may exist between adolescents that offend and those that do not. These physiological and genetic differences may predispose adolescents to antisocial behaviour and their environment may further influence criminal behaviour.

Cognitive Theories

Kenneth Dodge and his colleagues proposed a model of conduct-disordered behaviour that focuses on the thought processes that occur in social interactions (Crick and Dodge 1994; Dodge 2000). The model begins with thought processes that start when individuals pay attention to and interpret social and emotional cues in their environment. They then consider potential responses to the cues. Finally, a response is chosen and performed. Conduct-disordered adolescents demonstrate cognitive deficits and distortions (Fontaine, Burks, and Dodge 2002), often attending to fewer cues and misattributing hostile intent to ambiguous situations. Moreover, conduct-disordered adolescents demonstrate limited problem-solving skills, thus they generate few solutions to problems and often their solutions are aggressive in nature. Cognitive deficits are likely to be present in early childhood and may contribute to child-onset conduct disorder (Coy et al. 2001).

Dodge and his colleagues also distinguished between two types of aggressive behaviour—reactive aggression and proactive aggression (Dodge 1991; Schwartz et al. 1998). **Reactive aggression** is an emotionally aggressive response to a perceived threat or frustration. In contrast, **proactive aggression** is aggression directed at achieving a goal or receiving positive reinforcers (e.g., money, goods). Referring to Dodge's model, deficiencies in cognitive processes occur at different points for reactive and proactive aggression. Reactively aggressive adolescents are likely to demonstrate deficiencies early in the cognitive process, such as focusing on only a few social cues and misattributing hostile intent to ambiguous situations. Proactively aggressive adolescents are likely to have deficiencies in generating alternate responses and often choose an aggressive response. Furthermore, reactive and proactive aggressors tend to have different trajectories: reactive aggressors tend to have an earlier onset of problems than proactive aggressors (Dodge et al. 1997).

Social Theories

Bandura's (1965) social learning theory suggests that children learn their behaviour from observing others. Children are more likely to imitate behaviour that receives positive reinforcement than behaviour that receives negative reinforcement or punishment. As children develop, numerous models are available to imitate, including parents, siblings, peers, and media personalities. Studies have found that children who are highly aggressive and engage in antisocial behaviour have often witnessed parents, siblings, or grandparents engaging in similar behaviour (Farrington 1995; Waschbusch 2002). This is a pattern of intergenerational aggression, in which one aggressive generation produces the next (Glueck and Glueck 1968; Huesmann et al. 1984).

Consistent with this view is Patterson's (1982) coercive family process model, which posits aggressive behaviour among youth develops from imitation of parents and reinforcement. Other aspects of Patterson's model include the role of inadequate parental supervision and inconsistent disciplining of children. The combination of these factors increases the likelihood of adolescents behaving in antisocial ways (see also Huizinga, Esbensen, and Weiher 1991). Adolescents who witness interparental violence are found to be at risk for aggression themselves (Moretti, Obsuth, Odgers, and Reebye 2006). More specifically, this study assessed males and females between the ages of 13 and 18. Females who had witnessed their mothers' aggressive behaviour toward partners were significantly more aggressive toward friends. This pattern also was found for males who had witnessed their fathers being aggressive toward their partners: they were more likely to be aggressive toward friends. Both females and males who had witnessed parental violence were more likely to be aggressive with their romantic partners.

Perhaps the learning of aggression not only occurs through watching role models but via television and video games. Watching extremely violent television and movies in which actors are rewarded for aggression also increases children's likelihood of acting aggressively (Bushman and Anderson 2001). Aggressive videogames present a forum for adolescents to be reinforced for their aggression, which may increase their likelihood of acting aggressively in real life (Anderson and Dill 2000). Moreover, some data indicate a link between violent video exposure and aggressive behaviour to brain processes believed to be associated with desensitization to real-world violence (Bartholow, Bushman, and Sestir 2006). In contrast, a study by Adaci and Willoughby (2011) examined playing violent and non-violent video games and found that it was the *competition* in the games that influenced aggressive behaviour more so than the degree of violence. This reversal in the association between violent video game exposure and aggression has been found in other studies as well, casting doubts on the associations found several years ago. For example, Ferguson, San Miguel, Garza, and Jerabeck (2012) conducted a three-year longitudinal study of adolescents and found that exposure to video game violence was *not* related to negative outcomes. Rather, the best predictors of aggressive behaviour were depression, antisocial personality traits, exposure to family violence, and peer influences.

FACTORS ASSOCIATED WITH CRIMINAL CONDUCT AMONG ADOLESCENT OFFENDERS

THE TERM RISK FACTOR REFERS TO A VARIABLE THAT, IF PRESENT, POSES AN INCREASED likelihood of an undesirable outcome such as delinquency or antisocial behaviour (Kazdin et al. 1997). The presence of several criminological risk factors increases an adolescent's likelihood of offending (Hawkins et al. 1998). Rarely will one risk factor be sufficient to lead to offending, nor does the presence of numerous risk factors guarantee an adolescent will become an offender. When several risk factors are present, however, they may interact and have a multiplicative influence, thereby compounding the likelihood of offending. For example, Herrenkohl et al. (2000) found that a 10-year-old who is exposed to six or more risk factors is 10 times more likely to commit a violent act by age 18 than a 10-year-old exposed to only one risk factor. Risk factors occur across various domains: individual, familial, school, peer, and community. These domains are described in more detail below.

Individual Factors A number of prenatal complications can predispose a fetus to behavioural problems in childhood and potential adolescent offending. Mednick and Kandel (1988) suggest that offenders are more likely to have had delivery/birth complications compared to non-offenders. However, even before delivery, a mother's use of drugs, alcohol, and cigarette smoking during pregnancy increases the fetus' risk for later behavioural difficulties (Cohen et al. 2002).

Once a child is born, their own temperament can present a risk factor for later delinquency. For example, Farrington (1995) found that children who are difficult to soothe can be at risk for later behavioural difficulties. Hyperactivity, attention problems, impulsivity, and risk-taking have been associated with later adolescent offending (Hawkins et al. 1998). Substance abuse, especially starting at a young age (before the teen years), has received substantial support as a risk factor for adolescent offending (Elliott, Huizinga, and Ageton 1985). Low verbal intelligence and delayed language development also have been associated with behavioural problems (Seguin et al. 1995). Perhaps the strongest predictor of adolescent offending is the presence of aggressive behaviour before the age of 13. However, it is important to note that not all aggressive youth offend—why some do and others do not remains a question for researchers to answer.

Familial Factors A number of parental factors are risk factors for later antisocial behaviour. Researchers have found that poor parental supervision, low parental involvement, parental conflict, and parental aggression are related to later antisocial behaviour (Dekovic 1999; Carson and Butcher 1992; Farrington 1995; Hoge, Andrews, and Leschied 1996; Kumpfer and Alvarado 2003; Monahan et al. 2001; Melton et al. 1997; National Crime Prevention Council 1995, 1997; Patterson, Reid, and Dishion 1998; Rutter 1990). Child abuse, neglect, and maltreatment are also risk factors for behavioural difficulties. Abuse factors may pose a greater risk to boys, who may respond by acting aggressively and later engaging in spousal abuse (Fergusson and Lynskey 1997; Health Canada 2003; Loos and Alexander 1997). (See Chapter 13 for more on gender differences.) Widom (1989) found that abused or neglected children were 38 percent more likely to be arrested for a violent offence than children who had not been abused or neglected.

Lack of secure attachment to parents, parental loss, and divorce are risk factors for later behavioural problems (Amato and Keith 1991; Cummings, Davies, and Campbell 2000; Fagot and Kavanagh 1990). Other risk factors for delinquency include low socioeconomic status, large family size, and parental mental health problems (Frick 1994; Patterson, Reid, and Dishion 1998; Waschbusch 2002). Parents who are heavy drinkers increase the likelihood that their children will act in antisocial ways, possibly because when parents drink, they are unable to provide adequate parenting and supervision (Lahey, Waldman, and McBurnett 1989).

School Factors A number of school-related risk factors, such as poor academic performance (particularly in elementary school); low commitment to school; and low educational aspirations have been found to be associated with delinquent behaviour (Blum, Ireland, and Blum 2003; Hinshaw 1992). Truancy or not attending school is also a risk factor. For example, Farrington (1989) found that high truancy rates between the ages of

12 and 14 are related to adolescent offending that extends into adulthood. How academic difficulties are handled can be a risk factor as well. For example, suspension and expulsion may *not* reduce delinquent behaviour.

Peer Factors Risk factors related to peers are perhaps the most important during adolescence, when the peer group reigns paramount over family influences. A consistent relationship exists between associating with delinquent peers and engaging in delinquent behaviour. This association is true even at a very young age. Young children who play with aggressive peers at an early age are at risk for behavioural problems (Fergusson and Horwood 1998; Laird et al. 2001). Lipsey and Derzon (1998) found that 12- to 14-year-olds who associated with delinquent peers were more likely to engage in delinquency. McCord et al. (2001) found that peer approval of delinquent behaviour, allegiance to delinquent peers, time spent with delinquent peers, and peer pressure for delinquency are also associated with adolescent antisocial behaviour (see also Moffitt 1993). Taking this risk factor one step further, gang membership is more predictive of antisocial behaviour than associating with delinquent peers (Hill et al. 1999). Peer influence may compound when parents are uninvolved with their children. Farrington (1989) found that the presence of delinquent siblings acts much like the presence of delinquent peers in that it is predictive of violent juvenile offending.

As mentioned above, gang membership is more predictive of antisocial behaviour than associating with delinquent peers (Hill et al. 1999). Sometimes adolescents will be drawn to gangs for their peer socialization and then become a gang member. The National Crime Prevention Centre (NCPC) of Public Safety Canada is the federal organization responsible for providing direction on how to deal with the problem of youth gangs in Canada. There are three key elements to a youth gang:

1. The individuals involved must identify themselves as a group (they may have a group name, group colours, etc.).
2. Other people see the members as a distinct group.
3. Group members commit "delinquent" acts, often imposing on the rights of others in the community.

Public Safety Canada (2007b) has identified seven key risk factors for involvement in gangs:

- Negative influence in the adolescent's life
- Limited attachment to the community
- Reliance on antisocial peers to a great degree
- Poor parental supervision
- Substance abuse, both drugs and alcohol
- Poor academic achievement and employment possibilities
- Need for recognition and belonging

Although anyone can be a gang member, gangs are often comprised of individuals from socially disadvantaged communities and those that suffer great inequality. In Canada, the largest proportions of youth gang members are African-Canadian (at 25 percent), Aboriginal (at 21 percent), and Caucasian (at 18 percent). An overwhelming proportion of gang members are male (approximately 94 percent; Astwood 2002). However, there is an increasing trend in female Aboriginal gang membership in Western Canada. A Canadian police survey conducted in 2002 estimated that there were approximately 434 youth gangs in Canada with a total membership slightly over 7000. The provinces with most gangs and gang membership (in terms of absolute numbers, not taking population into account) were Ontario, Saskatchewan, and British Columbia (Public Safety Canada 2007a).

Erickson and Butters (2006) examined the relationship between gangs, guns, and drugs in Toronto and Montreal. A total of 904 male high school students, school dropouts, and young offenders were interviewed. The researchers found that as gang presence in schools increased, so did the number of guns and amount of drugs. Of the study participants, almost 19 percent of the boys aged 14 to 17 in Toronto and 15 percent in Montreal had brought a gun to school. The study also found that dropouts who sold drugs were more likely to be engaged in gun violence than dropouts who did not sell drugs.

Overall, social disapproval and rejection are likely to occur with aggressive children and adolescents (Coie, Belding, and Underwood 1988; Ebata, Peterson, and Conger 1990; Rutter 1990), and rejected, aggressive children are at risk for behavioural problems (Parker and Asher 1987; Rudolph and Asher 2000). Adolescents who are socially isolated or withdrawn (e.g., have low involvement in traditional, structured social activities) are at increased risk for engaging in antisocial behaviour.

Community Factors Where a child is raised can be a risk factor for adolescent offending. Just as parental income (i.e., lower socio-economic status) is a familial risk factor, so is living in a low-income neighbourhood (Farrington 1989; Henry et al. 1996). Assault when committing a felony or robbery was twice as common among adolescents raised in low-income/subsidized neighbourhoods than adolescents raised in middle-class areas (Hawkins et al. 2000).

Lower-income neighbourhoods also give rise to the opportunity to witness violence. Farrell and Bruce (1997) found that exposure to community violence is related to adolescent offending. Thus, disadvantaged neighbourhoods provide an opportunity to learn delinquent behaviour, associate with delinquent peers, and possibly have delinquent behaviour reinforced. Brewer et al. (1995) found that having access to weapons also increases the risk for violence.

What Do Canadian Youth Report?

The Department of Justice Canada conducted a study to examine the factors related to self-reported delinquency between the ages of 12 and 15 using data from the *National Longitudinal Survey of Children and Youth* (Latimer et al. 2003). Slightly less than 40 percent of youth reported engaging in at least one antisocial act in the 12-month period prior to the survey. This percentage translated into more than 540 000 youth across Canada reporting that they had committed at least one delinquent act in the previous year. It is important to note that the majority of these acts would be considered minor offences. The five main correlates of delinquency for male and female youth were: 1) inconsistent and inadequate parenting, 2) history of victimization, 3) antisocial peer involvement, 4) negative school attachment, and 5) aggression. These correlates are consistent with the risk factors described above.

PROTECTIVE FACTORS

ALTHOUGH CHILDREN MAY EXPERIENCE SIMILAR ENVIRONMENTS AND SETS OF RISK FACTORS, their responses and outcomes vary, with some children prevailing and prospering and others encountering a number of difficulties and negative outcomes. A child who has multiple risk factors but can overcome them and prevail has been termed **resilient**. Resilience is described as the ability to overcome stress and adversity (Winfield 1994).

It has been suggested that resilient children may have "protective" factors that allow them to persevere in the face of adversity. The notion of protective factors was introduced in the early 1980s (Garmezy 1985). Garmezy (1991) identified a number of areas where protectiveness can be present: genetic variables, personality dispositions, supportive family environments, and community supports. There is some debate over the definition of protective factors and how they work. Many agree, however, that they help improve or sustain some part of an individual's life (Leadbeater et al. 1999). We define **protective factors** as variables or factors that, if present, decrease the likelihood of a negative outcome (such as antisocial behaviour and adolescent offending) or increase the likelihood of a positive outcome (DeMatteo and Marczyk 2005). Rutter (1990) identifies four ways that protective factors are effective:

1. They reduce negative outcomes by changing the level of the child's exposure to a risk factor.
2. They change the negative chain reaction following exposure to risk.
3. They help develop and maintain self-esteem and self-efficacy.
4. They avail opportunities to children they would not otherwise have.

As with risk factors, protective factors occur across various domains: individual, familial, school, peer, and community. These domains are described in more detail below.

Individual Factors Factors that reside within an individual can serve to protect against acting in antisocial ways. For example, Carson and Butcher (1992) found that intelligence and a commitment to education serve as protective factors for adolescents at risk for antisocial behaviour (see also Hoge and Andrews 1996; Kandel et al. 1988). Individuals who focus schoolwork often have less time available to engage in antisocial behaviour.

Vance (2001) found that exceptional social skills; child competencies; and confident perceptions, values, attitudes, and beliefs can serve to protect a child from engaging in adolescent offending. Research from twin studies suggests that social support may have a heritable component that is influenced by personality. For example, likeable children may respond to good role models in a positive manner, thus promoting a positive and continuing relationship.

Perhaps one of the strongest protective individual factors is having an intolerant attitude toward antisocial behaviour (Department of Health and Human Services 2001). This may also reflect a commitment to social norms and a rejection of antisocial behaviour. An intolerant attitude may decrease the likelihood that a youth will associate with antisocial peers, hence further reducing the likelihood of antisocial behaviour.

Being female and a perception that peers disapprove of antisocial behaviour have also been identified as protective factors by the U.S. Department of Health and Human Services (2001).

Other protective factors include sociability, positive temperament, the ability to seek social support, and acting in a reflective (not impulsive) manner. Resilient adolescents typically utilize flexible coping strategies. Having a sense of control over one's environment may be associated with a decreased risk for antisocial behaviour. The acquisition of various skill sets such as problem solving, conflict resolution, anger management, and critical thinking also are seen as protective factors. The presence of certain internalizing disorders, such as nervousness and anxiety, may have a modest negative correlation with juvenile offending (Hawkins et al. 2000; Mitchell and Rosa 1979).

Familial Factors Protective familial factors are the positive qualities of parents and home environment (Carson and Butcher 1992; Kumpfer and Alvarado 2003; Melton et al. 1997; Thornberry, Huizinga, and Loeber 1995). For example, having a supportive relationship with an adult protects a child against engaging in antisocial behaviour (Werner 2000). This protective factor is generally effective regardless of whether the adult caregiver is a parent, teacher, or volunteer in a mentoring program such as Big Brothers Big Sisters. High levels of parental supervision and secure parent–child attachment are also protective factors. Providing clear and consistent norms for behaviour can reduce the likelihood that youth will engage in antisocial behaviour. Intriguingly, Kramer-Kuhn (2013) found that although positive parental messages and good family function were related to lower levels of aggression overall, these family factors did not protect adolescents with higher levels of risk.

School Factors Commitment to school and achieving academically is a protective factor for children at risk for juvenile offending (e.g., Carson and Butcher 1992; Department of Health and Human Services 2001; Hoge and Andrews 1996; Kandel et al. 1988). Children who are committed to school may be less likely to commit antisocial acts for fear of reducing their academic potential (Jessor et al. 1995). Participating in structured extracurricular activities, such as team sports and academic clubs, also protects against adolescent offending (Jessor et al. 1995). Extracurricular activities allow less time for antisocial acts and may foster a sense of achievement in children.

Peer Factors Vance (2001) reported that peer groups can have a strong effect on child outcomes. Associating with deviant peers is a risk factor for antisocial behaviour. The converse is a protective factor; that is, associating with prosocial children protects against antisocial behaviour (Fergusson and Horwood 1998). Some researchers have found that associating with peers who disapprove of antisocial behaviour is protective against performing antisocial acts (Hawkins et al. 2000).

Community Factors There is little research in the area of "community" protective factors. A strong community infrastructure that may provide opportunities for adolescents to engage in organized activities helps to reduce the likelihood that children will engage in antisocial behaviour. Social cohesion is also associated with lower levels of violence among adolescents (Sampson, Raudenbush, and Earls 1997). Riina, Martin, and Brooks-Gunn (2014) examined whether neighbourhood cohesion was a protective factor for children who experienced parent-child physical aggression. The study considered children aged 3–15 years and found that living in a highly cohesive neighbourhood was helpful for internalizing behaviour for children 11 and older.

Now that you know about risk and protective factors, examine the You be the Assessor box and consider what factors may be critical in designing a treatment plan for the youth in question.

Although we have devoted an entire chapter to gender differences and crime (Chapter 13), at this stage it is important to highlight the research on gender differences conducted by a key Canadian researcher, Dr. Tracey Skilling. Dr. Skilling studies gender

---

Box 5.1

You Be the Assessor

Randy Rolland was always a very "energetic" boy. His grandmother, who took over Randy's care when his mother passed away from a drug overdose, tried her best to be patient with Randy but as she noted on several occasions, "he has always been getting into one thing or another." Randy and his grandmother lived in government-assisted housing. Often Randy would come home with a few dollars in his pocket but his grandmother was never quite sure where it came from. There was a high crime rate in the neighbourhood and drugs were often sold in the area. When he was about 10 years old, Randy started being truant from school and hanging out with older boys who belonged to a gang. His grandmother would get calls from the school at least a few times a week about Randy's absence or behaviour. One night when Randy didn't come home from school, his grandmother called the police. The police found Randy under the town bridge selling drugs.

Questions

Imagine you are a psychologist dealing with Randy's case. What risk factors does Randy have? Does Randy have any protective factors? What predictions would you make, if any, for Randy's likelihood of future offending?

differences and aggression among youth and how aggression for males and females differ as they age. For example, Quinsey, Skilling, Lalumière, and Craig (2004a) stated that sex differences in aggression occur with consistency and frequency and are seen by around age six for boys and girls. Sex differences in aggression seem reduced for boys and girls when girls enter puberty. Violent crimes are more likely to be committed by both males and females between 14 and 24 years of age. Although, for females the onset appears to occur two years earlier than males. The researchers also found that males are more likely to commit more serious violent behaviour. See the Researcher Profiles box to learn more about Dr. Skilling and her research.

When developing prevention, intervention, and treatment programs, it may be important to consider both risk and protective factors across stages of development and gender such that targeted programs may be more efficient and cost-effective. An assessment is often the start of identifying the needs and appropriate programs for children and adolescents.

Box 5.2

Canadian Researcher Profile Dr. Tracey Skilling

Dr. Tracey Skilling started her research career as a graduate student at the University of Waterloo where she completed her Master's in Applied Science degree and then moved to Queen's University to complete her Ph.D. Her dissertation focused on the assessment of persistent antisociality across the lifespan. Upon graduating with her Ph.D., Dr. Skilling became a Research Fellow at the Mental Health Centre in Penetanguishene in Ontario. Currently, Dr. Skilling is a psychologist at the Centre for Addiction and Mental Health in Toronto, Ontario.

Her current research interests include examining the impact of mental health issues and treatment programming on outcomes for justice-involved youth and examining the similarities and differences between boys and girls. Dr. Skilling notes that she started in the field of youth justice research looking at the development of psychopathy in youth and its relevance for risk assessment, but after working clinically with these youth, she became more and more interested in the relationship between mental health issues and criminal outcomes in this population. One of the things that keeps Dr. Skilling interested in this area of research is that it is still in its infancy, particularly with respect to understanding how mental health issues are related to criminal behaviour in youth. She also is very interested in pathways into and out of crime for girls; Dr. Skilling states, "the fact that there is still so much to learn keeps me excited about this research."

One of Dr. Skilling's favourite studies was conducted with her first graduate student, Tracey Vieira (Vieira, Skilling, and Peterson-Badali 2009). Dr. Skilling notes that the reason it stands out for her is that it is one of the first studies to look at the impact of meeting the criminogenic needs of justice-involved youth at the individual level. The study clearly showed that targeting the right needs (i.e., matching treatments to a youth's specific individual criminogenic needs) can have a big impact on decreasing recidivism in youth. However, the results from this study also showed

Box 5.2   (Continued)

Courtesy of Dr. Tracy Skilling

that we are not doing a very good job at meeting those needs. This latter point had a big impact on Dr. Skilling's research, causing her to focus her researching on better understanding what happens to youth with mental health needs in the youth justice system.

When Dr. Skilling is not conducting research she is clinically assessing youth for the court. The clinic Dr. Skilling works in assesses youth in order to understand their mental health needs, their cognitive and academic functioning, and their risk to reoffend. These assessments are then used to inform sentencing and plan for treatment. Overall, Dr. Skilling believes that the *Youth Criminal Justice Act* has been working fairly well over the past decade, however she is concerned about some of the changes in Bill C-10. More specifically, Dr. Skilling states that "there is no evidence that harsher punishments lead to decreases in reoffending and I am concerned that youth who engage in violent offenses will receive less intervention and more punishment, ultimately leading to worse outcomes."

ASSESSMENT APPROACHES AND EFFECTIVENESS
Assessing the Under-12-Year-Old

For children under 12, behavioural problems are usually first identified at school, where the child's disruptive behaviour is a challenge to the teacher. Often parents are notified that the school is unable to manage their child's behaviour, which may include arguing, fighting, bullying, excessive talking, and possibly poor school performance. A psychological assessment may be recommended by the school and/or parents. Prior to the assessment, a clinician (e.g., psychologist, psychiatrist) must obtain two levels of consent: that of parents or guardians, and that of the child or adolescent him- or herself. It is not uncommon to interview the child and parent individually and together. Teachers may be asked to provide information on school performance and behaviour. To get a more complete picture of the issues, the clinician may want to observe the child at home and/ or at school. Tools used to assess the child include standardized tests such as intelligence tests and academic achievement tests, checklists to identify symptomology, play sessions, and structured interviews to assess for psychiatric diagnoses.

Broadly, children's emotional and behavioural difficulties can be categorized as **internalizing** or **externalizing problems** (Rutter 1990). Internalizing problems are emotional difficulties such as anxiety, depression, and obsessions. Externalizing problems are behavioural difficulties such as delinquency, fighting, bullying, lying, and destructive behaviour. It is the externalizing problems that can develop into more persistent and serious antisocial acts and receive the attention of parents, teachers, and the criminal justice system. Externalizing problems have been considered more difficult to treat and more likely to have long-term persistence (Ebata, Peterson, and Conger 1990; Robins 1986). Externalizing disorders have been known to be quite stable, though symptoms often peak in teenage years and decrease in the late 20s (Rutter 1995). Males are more likely to have externalizing difficulties than females, with a ratio of about 10:1 (Barkley 1997; Rutter 1990).

To assess externalizing problems, multiple informants are necessary because the child or adolescent may not be aware of their behaviour or the influence it has on others (McMahon 1994). As mentioned above, parents, teachers, and peers may be interviewed or asked to rate the child or adolescent. It is also important that behaviour be viewed within a developmental context. For example, rebelling against rules set by parents may be normative for adolescents but worrisome if younger children are oppositional and continually refuse to comply with parents' requests. The duration, severity, and frequency of troublesome behaviours should be measured.

Three childhood psychiatric diagnoses that occur with some frequency in juvenile offenders are **attention deficit hyperactivity disorder** (ADHD), **oppositional defiant disorder** (ODD), and **conduct disorder** (CD). ADHD is described as an inattention and restlessness (APA 2013). Some examples of features associated with ADHD include: does not appear to listen when spoken to, has difficulty in organization, loses items, fidgets, and talks excessively. To qualify for an ADHD diagnosis, a number of symptoms must be present, occur in two or more settings, and persist for at least six months. When making an ADHD diagnosis, it is important to consider the age of the child. In young children, many of the symptoms of ADHD are part of normal development and behaviour.

ODD is defined as a "pattern of negativistic, hostile, and defiant behaviour" (APA 2013). Some examples of features associated with ODD include: loses temper, deliberately annoys others, and is vindictive. Approximately 40 percent of children with ODD develop CD (Loeber et al. 1992). CD is a repetitive and persistent pattern of behaviour in children and youth whereby the rights of others or basic social rules are violated. These behaviour patterns are usually displayed at home, school, and in social situations. If a child with ODD qualifies for a CD diagnosis, an ODD diagnosis is not used. Some examples of features associated with CD include: initiates physical fights, is physically cruel to animals, sets fires, lies for gain, and is truant before 13 years of age. Approximately 50 percent of children who meet the criteria for CD go on to receive diagnoses of antisocial personality disorder in adulthood (APA 2013; Loeber and Farrington 2000).

An adolescent vandalizing a city wall.

Rates of Behaviour Disorders in Children

According to Public Health Agency of Canada (2009), almost 15 percent of children aged 2 to 5 years experience high levels of emotional and/or anxiety problems; almost 7 percent exhibit high levels of hyperactivity and/or inattention; and approximately 14 percent exhibit high levels of physical aggression and oppositional or conduct disorders. Researchers have found that behavioural disorders commonly occur together. For example, 20 to 50 percent of children with ADHD also have symptoms consistent with CD or ODD (Offord, Lipman, and Duku 2001). Elia, Ambrosini, and Berrettini (2008) found that approximately 40 percent of 6- to 18-year-olds with ADHD also had ODD.

Internalizing problems such as depression may be more severe in children with CD (Marriage, Fine, Moretti, and Haley 1986). Also, Arredondo and Butler (1994) found ODD and CD co-occurred with a mood disorder; more specifically, 27 percent of the studied adolescents with oppositional defiant disorder and 76 percent with CD also met the diagnosis of a mood disorder.

Assessing the Adolescent

Once an adolescent's antisocial behaviour receives the attention of the courts, a court-ordered assessment may be issued. In such cases, the adolescent need not provide consent/assent. The courts must determine the risk a particular adolescent has to reoffend. In other words, would having the juvenile in the community pose a risk to others? Does the juvenile have the potential to change in a positive manner? Juveniles are assessed so that resources can be used effectively and the risk to the community is reduced.

The instruments used to assess an adolescent offender's risk generally include a "checklist" where items are scored on a scale, the points are summed, and a cut-off value is set for either detaining or releasing the adolescent. Risk assessment instruments collect information about a set of factors, both static (factors that cannot change, such as age of first arrest) and dynamic (factors that can change, such as antisocial attitudes). Interviews with the adolescent as well as case files and histories may be used to complete a risk assessment. A total risk score is then obtained. Generally, the notion is that the more relevant risk factors are present, the more likely it is that the adolescent will reoffend. A number of professionals (front-line staff in institutions, probation staff, credentialed professionals) may be responsible for conducting the risk assessment.

The task of identifying risk factors for adolescent offenders who will reoffend is different than for adults (Mulvey 2005). For example, history of behaviour often is considered in the risk assessment of adult offenders. This may be limited and ambiguous for adolescent offenders. They simply do not have the years behind them to examine. Child and adolescent behaviour may be more influenced by context than enduring character. Children and adolescents may display behaviour that is adaptive to the environment they are in rather than the behaviour being a demonstration of their character across all situations (Masten and Coatsworth 1998). A child who is disruptive in one school may not be disruptive in another, so interpreting a behaviour problem may be inaccurate. Children and adolescents experience more change developmentally and in character than adults. It is a challenge to separate developmental issues from persistent personality and character for the prediction of future offending. Some researchers argue further that risk assessment may differ between adolescent boys and girls (Odgers, Moretti, and Reppucci 2005). Below are a list of risk assessment tools used with adolescent offenders in Canada.

Risk Assessment Tools Used with Adolescent Offenders in Canada

Hannah-Moffat and Maurutto (2003) provide a useful summary of assessment tools for adolescents, which is the basis of the descriptions below.

Adolescent Chemical Dependency Inventory (ACDI)—Corrections Version II This instrument is designed for 14- to 17-year-olds to screen for substance (alcohol and other drugs) use and abuse, overall adjustment, and issues for troubled youth. Adolescent offenders respond to 140 items that break down into seven scales: truthfulness, violence, adjustment, distress, alcohol, drugs, and stress and coping abilities.

Criminal Sentiments Scale (CSS) This 41-item self-report questionnaire uses five-point scales to assess key dimensions of criminal sentiments, such as antisocial attitudes, values, and beliefs that may play a role in the maintenance of antisocial behaviour. The offender reports on attitudes toward the law, courts, police, tolerance for law violations, and identification with other criminals.

HCR-20 The HCR-20 takes its name from the three scales it assesses—historical, clinical, and risk management—and from the number of items. It examines risk and violence broadly, including risk factors from the past, present, and future. The scale consists of ten historical factors, five clinical items to reflect current factors related to violence, and five risk-management items that focus on situational post-assessment factors that may aggravate or mitigate risk.

Level of Service Inventory—Ontario Revised (LSI-OR)
The LSI-OR is a standardized instrument used by the Ontario Ministry of Community Safety and Correctional Services with offenders aged 16 years and older. It is used to assess risk of recidivism, need for correctional programs to reduce recidivism, and factors related to the likelihood the offender will respond to treatment.

Offender Risk Assessment and Management System (ORAMS)
ORAMS is a set of tools developed by Manitoba Corrections to assess the different risks offenders pose. Two scales can be used with juvenile offenders: Inmate Security Assessment and Primary Risk Assessment.

Inmate Security Assessment (ISA)—Young Offenders
The objective of the ISA is to obtain information to assess a juvenile offender's threat to him- or herself and others in an institution. Dangerous behaviour includes suicide, assault on other inmates or staff, and escape risk. This scale is completed for security reasons once an offender has been admitted into an institution and also informs decisions relating to institutional placement or transfer.

Primary Risk Assessment (PRA)—Young Offenders
This scale is a modified version of the Youthful Offender—Level of Service Inventory (YO-LSI) described below. It is used to predict a juvenile offender's risk to reoffend in any type of offence (as opposed to specific types of offences such as sexual assault). This information is then used to determine the degree and type of supervision needed and to assist in the formulation of a case plan.

Pride in Delinquency Scale (PID)
The PID is a 10-item self-report scale used to assess a juvenile offender's comfort level (i.e., pride versus shame) in getting involved in specific criminal behaviour. It is used to complement the CSS measure.

Structured Assessment of Violence Risk in Youth (SAVRY)
The SAVRY is used to make assessments and recommendations about the nature and degree of risk that a juvenile may pose for future violence. Twenty-four risk factors and six protective factors are considered (Borum, Bartel, and Forth 2002).

Youth Level of Service/Case Management Inventory (YLS/CMI)
This is a standardized instrument including a 42-item checklist for use by professional workers in

assessing risk of future violence, need for correctional programs to reduce future violence, and responsivity factors that impact case plan goals. A detailed survey of youth risk and needs factors is produced that can be used to create a case plan. The instrument contains seven sections: 1) assessment of risk and need, 2) summary of risk/need factors, 3) assessment of other needs/special considerations, 4) assessment of the client's general risk/need level, 5) contact level, 6) case management plan, and 7) case management review (Hoge and Andrews 2002).

Youthful Offender—Level of Service Inventory (YO-LSI) The YO-LSI is a risk/needs assessment instrument used to classify and assess a juvenile offender's overall risk level and to identify and target areas of criminogenic need. The YO-LSI consists of 82 static and dynamic predictors of criminal risk/needs that are grouped into seven categories: criminal history, substance abuse, educational/employment problems, family problems, peer relation problems, accommodation problems, and psychological factors.

TREATMENT APPROACHES AND EFFECTIVENESS

TREATMENT OF ADOLESCENT OFFENDING CAN OCCUR AT THREE LEVELS; PRIMARY, SECONDARY, and tertiary (DeMatteo and Marczyk 2005; Flannery and Williams 1999; Mulvey, Arthur, and Reppucci 1993). **Primary intervention strategies** are implemented prior to any violence occurring with the goal of decreasing the likelihood that violence will occur later on (i.e., prevention). **Secondary intervention strategies** attempt to reduce the frequency of violence (i.e., intervention). **Tertiary intervention strategies** attempt to prevent violence from reoccurring (i.e., treatment).

Primary Intervention Strategies

At the primary level of intervention, the goal is to identify groups (of children) that have numerous risk factors for engaging in antisocial behaviour later on. The belief is that if the needs of these children are addressed early, before violence has occurred, then the likelihood that they will go on to become adolescent offenders is reduced. Because "groups" (rather than specific individuals) are targeted, often these intervention strategies occur at broad levels such as in the family, at school, and in the community (Mulvey et al. 1993). Examples of primary intervention approaches include family-oriented strategies, school-oriented strategies, and community-wide strategies.

Family-Oriented Strategies Targeting the family may be an effective means of preventing adolescent offending, given that family can pose a number of risk factors (Kumpfer and Alvarado 2003). According to Mulvey et al. (1993), family-based intervention efforts can generally be classified as either parent-focused or family-supportive. **Parent-focused interventions** are directed at assisting parents to recognize warning signs for later adolescent violence and/or training parents to effectively manage any behavioural problems that arise. **Family-supportive interventions** connect at-risk families to various support services (e.g., child care, counselling, medical assistance) that may be available in their community.

An example of a family-oriented strategy is a popular parent-education program known as The Incredible Years Parenting Program, a 12-week training program that starts with building a strong emotional bond between parent(s) and child, and then teaches parents how to set behavioural expectations for their children, monitor children's behaviour, reinforce positive behaviour, provide consequences for inappropriate behaviour, and develop and use effective communication skills (Webster-Stratton 1992). Videos are used to demonstrate parenting techniques and enhance parent learning. Although parent-focused approaches have shown some success in the shorter term, the most common research finding is that parents of high-risk children tend to discontinue the training at rates that may exceed 50 percent (Mulvey et al. 1993). With such high attrition rates, particularly among families with the greatest need for these services, it is unlikely that parent-focused approaches are a reliable mechanism for preventing youth violence. Parenting programs usually are not "stand alone" and are part of more comprehensive programs that may involve a child component, school component, and/ or community program.

School-Oriented Strategies Given the amount of time children spend in school and the number of difficulties that can arise there, school is a common environment for primary prevention strategies. School-based prevention programs include preschool programs (e.g., Project Head Start, which incorporates The Incredible Years Parenting Program); social skills training for children, which may include cognitive behavioural therapy; and broad-based social interventions designed to alter the school environment (Mulvey et al. 1993; Loeber and Farrington 1998a). Project Head Start is designed for children from low socio-economic backgrounds. A number of social services are provided to these children and families (e.g., nutrition, structured activities, academic tutoring, and medical services) to reduce disadvantages that may interfere with learning. Preschool programs can produce some positive outcomes in the short term; however, the positive effects in reducing antisocial behaviour over the long term are questionable (Mulvey et al. 1993; Loeber and Farrington 1998a).

A different in-school program from the more "traditional" school programs that focus on reading, writing, and arithmetic, is known as Scared Straight. The program was developed in the United States during the 1970s to "scare" at-risk children from choosing a life of crime. The program involves actual inmates making aggressive presentations about life behind bars. Discussions of sexual assault are included, as is a visit to a prison (Finckenauer 1982). Contrary to a 1979 documentary on the Scared Straight program that reported 94 percent of 16- and 17-year-olds who took part were law-abiding for three months following participation (Finckenauer 1982) a meta-analysis reports a different conclusion. In a systematic review by Petrosino (2000), Scared Straight-type programs produced a 1 to 28 percent *increase* in crime (see also Petrosino, Turpin-Petrosino, and Buehler 2003; Petrosino et al. 2013).

A number of countries have implemented Scared Straight and other "kids visit prison" programs: Day in Prison in Australia (O'Malley, Coventry, and Walters 1993) and Day Visits in the United Kingdom (Lloyd 1995), for example. The program has also been tried in Canada (O'Malley, Coventry, and Walters 1993). Despite the evidence of their inefficacy, Scared Straight–type programs remain in use.

It is not uncommon to recommend a social skills program to children showing some early signs of interpersonal and behavioural difficulties. Social skills training may involve a structured program with a limited number of sessions (e.g., 12), teaching alternative methods for conflict resolution, adjusting social perceptions (recall that a cognitive approach suggests that aggressive children may interpret ambiguous situations aggressively; e.g., Lochman, Whidby, and FitzGerald 2000), managing anger, and developing empathy. Cognitive behavioural therapy usually is a component of social skills programs. The cognitive behavioural component focuses on children's thought processes and social interactions. Concrete strategies for handling interpersonal conflict are outlined, which children practice through role-playing and modelling with others in the class. Program evaluations have suggested that social skills training with cognitive behaviour therapy can be beneficial in the short term, although long-term follow-up suggests that the effects on reducing antisocial behaviour may be small (e.g., Denham and Almeida 1987). Larger effects may be obtained if social skills programs are combined with others such as parent education (Webster-Stratton and Hammond 1997).

Dodge and Godwin (2013) examined the Fast Track program, which is the largest and longest-lasting funded program in the U.S. for primary intervention. Fast Track is an intervention that addresses social-cognitive processes via social-skills training, parent training, school programming, peer mentoring, and tutoring. In this study, 891 high-risk children (69 percent male and 31 percent female) in kindergarten were assigned to either the intervention or a control group. The children in the Fast Track program showed a lower antisocial behaviour score after Grade 9 compared to the children in the control group. The three key factors that showed the greatest impact on reducing antisocial behaviour later on were reducing hostile attribution biases, increasing positive response options to interpersonal problems, and devaluing aggression. Policy makers and program developers may want to focus on these processes at an early age in order to reduce antisocial behaviour later in life.

Community-Wide Strategies Community approaches include providing structured community activities for children and increasing a community's cohesion. Few community-based programs exist for children under 12 who are at risk for future juvenile offending. One such program developed in Canada in 1985 is known as the SNAP Under 12 Outreach Project (SNAP ORP).

The SNAP ORP is a standardized 12-week outpatient program with five key components:

1. The SNAP Children's Club—a structured group that teaches children a cognitive-behavioural self-control and problem-solving technique called SNAP (Stop Now And Plan) (Earlscourt Child and Family Centre 2001a)

2. A concurrent SNAP parenting group that teaches parents effective child management strategies (Earlscourt Child and Family Centre 2001b)

3. One-on-one family counselling based on SNAP Parenting

4. Individual befriending for children who are not connected with positive structured activities in their community and require additional support

5. Academic tutoring to assist children who are not performing at an age-appropriate grade level

Recently, the SNAP ORP's effectiveness was assessed in Toronto by Augimeri, Farrington, Koegl, and Day (2007). Sixteen pairs of children were matched on age, sex, and severity of delinquency (e.g., theft, fighting, severe defiance at home, vandalism, assault, arson, trespassing, and public mischief) and then randomly assigned to the ORP or to a control program that received a less-intensive version of ORP (i.e., arts and crafts and cooperative game activities). Data were collected at five intervals: Time 1 (pretreatment); Time 2 (post-treatment—at least three months after Time 1); Time 3 (three months after Time 2); Time 4 (six months after Time 3); and Time 5 (six months after Time 4). A national criminal record search was conducted between each participant's twelfth and eighteenth birthday. Results indicated a significant decrease in externalizing behaviours for children in the ORP group compared to those in the control program. These gains were sustained over the one-year follow-up period. Although children in the ORP group had fewer official contacts with the criminal justice system between the ages of 12 and 18 than the control group, this difference was not significant. Multifaceted interventions with cognitive behavioural skills training along with parent training may have produced positive effects for children under 12 displaying antisocial behaviours.

In a subsequent study (with a different sample), the number of cognitive-behaviour therapy sessions was once again compared with later convictions and more cognitive-behviour therapy sessions appeared to be associated with fewer convictions (Koegl et al. 2008). The association was larger for girls than boys, and for older children (i.e., 10–11 year olds) possibly because these groups were more cognitively advanced.

Secondary Intervention Strategies

Secondary intervention strategies are directed at adolescents who have either had contact with the police or criminal justice system or have demonstrated behavioural problems at school. The goal of these strategies is to provide social and clinical services so that adolescents do not go on to commit serious violence. Many of the same approaches used in primary intervention strategies are used here. One of the main differences is the "target" (i.e., which children are involved in the program) rather than the content of the intervention. Common secondary intervention strategies include diversion programs, alternative and vocational education, family therapy, and skills training (see Mulvey et al. 1993).

Diversion programs "divert" adolescent offenders from the youth justice system into community- or school-based treatment programs. The belief is that the justice system may cause more harm than good in reducing offending. Intervention and treatment in the community may be more successful at reducing the likelihood that the adolescent will escalate their offending. Alternative and vocational education programs offer the option of mainstream schooling. Family therapy and skills-training programs incorporate the adolescent and family. Diversion and certain school-, family-, and community-based interventions have shown some success at reducing antisocial behaviour in youth (e.g., Davidson and Redner 1988; Kazdin 1996).

One particular secondary intervention program that has undergone considerable evaluation is Multisystemic Therapy (MST). MST examines a child across the contexts or "systems" in which they live—family, peers, school, neighbourhood, and community (Henggeler and Borduin 1990; Henggeler, Melton, and Smith 1992; Henggeler, Schoenwald, and Pickrel 1995; Henggeler et al. 1998). MST has been implemented in various parts of Canada and the United States. In one study to evaluate its effectiveness, a four-year randomized study was conducted across four Ontario communities: London, Mississauga, Simcoe County, and Ottawa (Leschied and Cunningham 2002). Approximately 200 families received MST from 1997 to 2001. During the same time period, another 200 families (acting as the comparison group) were asked to access the services that were available through their local youth justice and social service organizations. These services included probation and specialized programs. All families underwent psychological testing at the start of the study and then again at the end. The psychological testing included measures to assess family functioning, caregiver depression, the youths' social skills, pro-criminal attitudes, and behavioural problems. Based on this assessment, the youth and families in the MST group were provided services and had access to a case manager 24 hours a day, 7 days a week. Areas that may be targeted in MST treatment include family communication, parent management, and cognitive-behavioural issues. All youth were followed for three years following the end of treatment (until 2004). Overall, MST was *not* found to be more effective than the typical services available in Ontario. For example, after the three-year follow-up, 68 percent of the participants in the MST group had at least one conviction, compared to 67 percent of those in the "comparison" group. The average number of days to reconviction for the MST group was about 283, compared to 310 for the control group (this difference was not statistically significant). It is important to note, however, that MST may have benefitted youths and their families on factors that were not measured. Interestingly, some studies evaluating MST in the United States have found it more effective than incarceration, individual counselling, and probation (Henggeler et al. 1998; Henggeler, Melton, and Smith 1992; Henggeler, Schoenwald, and Pickrel 1995).

In a recent meta-analysis examining the effectiveness of MST, some small positive treatment effects (e.g., on delinquency and substance use) were found but a number of factors moderated the effectiveness of MST (e.g., age of participant, type of offending; van der Stouwe et al. 2014). Overall, MST seemed most effective for adolescents under the age of 15 with serious problems. For older adolescents, treatment that is focused on peer relationships and school risk and protective factors may be beneficial.

Tertiary Intervention Strategies

Tertiary intervention strategies are aimed at adolescents who have engaged in criminal acts and who may have already been processed through formal court proceedings (Flannery and Williams 1999). As such, these intervention efforts are actually more "treatment" rather than prevention, and the recipients are often chronic and serious adolescent offenders. The goal of tertiary intervention strategies is to minimize the impact of existing risk factors and foster the development of protective factors, which may reduce the likelihood that the at-risk adolescent will engage in future offending.

Tertiary intervention strategies include inpatient treatment (i.e., institutional, residential) and community-based treatment (Mulvey et al. 1993). The approach can be one of retribution or rehabilitation. For those who favour retribution, they believe that adolescents should be held accountable for their actions, punished accordingly, and separated from society. Treatment for these adolescents should be provided in an institutional setting (e.g., youth detention centre). In contrast, those who favour rehabilitation believe that treatment based in the community is a more effective way to reduce the likelihood of reoffending. One meta-analysis reported that shorter stays (rather than longer stays) in institutional settings and greater involvement with community services are more effective for violent adolescents (Wooldredge 1988).

Box 5.3

You Be the Therapist

Steven Blondo had been in foster care since the age of 2 to 12 years at which time an uncle came forward to take care of him. In exchange, Steven would have to work part-time in the family restaurant after school. The transition to his new home was challenging. Steven was defiant with his aunt and uncle and often did not go to school and would not show up at the restaurant to take his evening shift setting up and clearing tables. He resented having to work to contribute to his new home. On several occasions his uncle saw Steven on the security footage taking money out of the till, and some of the servers noticed he would pocket tips if money was left on the tables he was clearing.

Steven's aunt and uncle were open to attending parenting workshops on how to manage his behaviour. However, Steven often chose not to participate in the youth section of the program so his aunt and uncle often did not stay to complete the programing. Instead of Steven's behaviour getting better, it kept getting worse. At 15, Steven often was abusive to the family cat and now at 16 Steven has been caught setting fires. At the end of his shift one Saturday night, Steven set a fire in the restaurant's kitchen after it closed. Steven was charged with arson.

Questions

Imagine you are a psychologist dealing with Steven's case. What treatment programing would you recommend for Steven to reduce the likelihood he will engage in criminal activity in the future? Do you have any suggestions for his aunt and uncle?

GUIDING PRINCIPLES AND RECOMMENDATIONS FOR REDUCING ANTISOCIAL BEHAVIOUR

MOST WOULD AGREE THAT THE SOONER THE PREVENTION OR INTERVENTION, THE GREATER the likelihood of success. Programs that target both the family and child in the context of school and community are most likely to have positive effects, reducing offending in the short and long term. Although these comprehensive, multipronged programs are most promising, they pose a number of challenges given the availability of services, the coordination of those services, and the commitment of participants and service providers. Also important to take into account are the two types of adolescent offenders: life-course persistent and adolescent limited. Different interventions are needed for each. More comprehensive and extensive programs should be directed toward life-course persistent juveniles. School-based prevention programs are more successful for adolescent limited juveniles. Risk and protective factors should be considered for each child when deciding on appropriate programs. Overall, reducing antisocial behaviour in the long term requires an extensive approach.

FUTURE DIRECTIONS

A RELATIVELY NEW TYPE OF AGGRESSION OCCURRING AMONG ADOLESCENTS INVOLVES THE Internet. Both Sarah Todd and Rehtaeh Parsons were bullied and harassed via the Internet to the point that they committed suicide. Legislation to prosecute those involved with these cybercrimes remains a work in progress. However, current legislation around child exploitation and child pornography is being applied when an adolescent transmits illicit images of other youngsters. See the Hot Topics box for a case of sexting with an adolescent victim and offender.

Hot Topics

Sexting Teen Found Guilty of Child Pornography

A controversial case of cyber bullying recently occurred in Victoria, B.C. A teenaged couple broke up, but the boyfriend still had explicit photos that his ex-girlfriend had sent him while dating. The boy met a new girlfriend and showed her his ex-girlfriend's photos and texts. The new girlfriend then distributed the photos and sent out thousands (yes, thousands) of explicit text messages. This 17-year-old female was found guilty of distributing child pornography and was convicted of possessing child pornography and uttering threats. She was found guilty because the sexting messages and images she distributed involved a teen who was 16 at the time. The conviction for uttering threats stemmed from the girl's use of texting and Facebook to threaten the ex-girlfriend with physical harm. She also threatened via text message to harm the ex-girlfriend's unborn child. The Youth Court Judge in the case noted that the images in question were within the scope of what is considered child pornography.

This case is not over, however. The defence counsel, Christopher Mackie said he was planning to argue against the conviction on constitutional grounds. Mackie claimed that it is "unconstitutional to charge youths who engage in sexting with child-pornography offences because the process of sending erotic images by wireless devices is currently lawful for adults." This attempt to overturn the conviction is in stark contrast to the federal government's movement to strengthen Canada's cyberbullying laws to reduce the spread of intimate photos.

Source: Meissner (2014).

SUMMARY

1. The first Canadian legislation to address juvenile offending was the *Juvenile Delinquents Act* (JDA) in 1908. In 1984, the *Young Offender's Act* (YOA) replaced the JDA and made several major changes to juvenile justice. The YOA underwent several amendments and was finally replaced with the *Youth Criminal Justice Act* (YCJA) in 2003.

2. Biological theories focus on genetic and physiological differences between adolescent offenders and those who do not behave antisocially. Cognitive theories propose a model of antisocial behaviour that focuses on thought processes that occur in social interactions. Social theories are based in social learning theory, which proposes that children learn behaviour from observing others and through reinforcement contingencies.

3. A risk factor is a variable or factor that, if present, increases the likelihood of an undesirable outcome such as antisocial behaviour. Risk factors occur across various domains that include individual (e.g., difficult temperament), familial (e.g., low parental involvement), school (e.g., low commitment to school), peer (e.g., associating with antisocial peers), and community (e.g., low-income neighbourhood) factors. A protective factor is a variable or factor that, if present, decreases the likelihood of an undesirable outcome such as antisocial behaviour. Protective factors occur across various domains that include individual (e.g., intelligence), familial (e.g., supportive relationship with parent), school (e.g., commitment to school), peer (e.g., associating

with peers who disapprove of antisocial behaviour), and community (e.g., strong community infrastructure) factors.

4. There are three common disorders diagnosed in adolescent offenders: attention deficit hyperactivity disorder (ADHD), oppositional defiant disorder (ODD), and conduct disorder (CD). Children/adolescents diagnosed with CD are at greatest risk for adolescent offending. CD is a precursor to adult antisocial personality disorder.

5. The instruments used to assess an adolescent offender's risk generally involve a "checklist" in which items are scored on a scale, the points are summed, and a cut-off value is set for either detaining or releasing the adolescent. These instruments collect information about a set of factors (both static and dynamic) related to reoffending, such as number of prior arrests, use of a weapon, and presence of a drug problem.

6. Primary intervention strategies are implemented prior to any violence occurring with the goal of decreasing the likelihood that violence will occur later on. Secondary intervention strategies attempt to reduce the frequency of violence. Tertiary intervention strategies attempt to prevent violence from reoccurring.

Discussion Questions

1. Your neighbour, Mrs. Kane, asks if you can babysit her five-year-old son Johnny. You have known Johnny since he was born—most neighbours know Johnny because of his "lively" behaviour. While you are babysitting, you notice that Johnny has a number of risk factors for adolescent offending. Make a list of protective factors that Mrs. Kane may be able to implement to reduce the likelihood that Johnny will engage in antisocial behaviour when he is older.

2. You want to become a psychologist focusing on children and adolescents who display externalizing disorders. Describe the three most common psychiatric diagnoses for children displaying disruptive behaviours. What are the core features of each diagnosis? Which diagnoses co-occur?

3. As part of your summer vacation, you decide to volunteer at the local Boys and Girls Club, which offers at-risk children a number of programs to reduce the likelihood that they will behave antisocially. You have been tasked with developing a social-skills program for 8-to 12-year-olds. Outline an eight-week program.

4. Design a study that will allow you to examine the effectiveness of the program you developed in question three. Test whether your program reduces antisocial behaviour in the short and long terms.

Chapter 6
Economically Motivated Offenders

DVDs, iPods, clothes—there wasn't anything Sam "Sticky Fingers" couldn't get at a substantially marked-down price. Sam would enlist a friend and they'd make their way to the mall, each armed with a cell phone. Once Sam found the store he wanted, he would go in as any other "customer," with his "friend" serving as the lookout via cell phone. Sam would "browse" while his friend stood outside the store watching the employees, relaying information to Sam via phone. Sam wouldn't be bothered by store employees when they saw he was on the phone. The friend would inform Sam when the workers weren't watching and Sam would pick up whatever he needed. Sam wore larger clothes with big pockets and even sometimes a knapsack for "storage." Once he had his cache, he would casually walk out of the store.

Sam was committing the theft of shoplifting. Although his target was not personal and he did not use violence to commit his crime, his behaviour was a criminal offence. Economic offending is associated with a large financial cost on society and the criminal justice system. Should the justice system treat economic offenders differently than other types of offenders?

Learning Objectives

1   Describe the various types of economically-motivated crimes.

2   Differentiate between theft and fraud.

3   Contrast characteristics of prostitutes versus their clients.

4   Describe characteristics of organized crime groups.

5   Describe factors associated with different types of economic crime.

6   Describe intervention methods associated with different types of economic crime.

INTRODUCTION

A NUMBER OF CRIMES ARE COMMITTED WITH THE PURPOSE OF ECONOMIC GAIN. ALTHOUGH Canada may have a "tough on crime" position, which is evidenced in higher incarceration rates compared to other countries, this notion seems to apply to violent offending rather than economically motivated offending. In fact, on an international scale, Canada is viewed as "soft" on white-collar crime, with few prosecutions and even fewer convictions.

This chapter focuses on crimes that occur with a primary goal of financial profit. We will examine various types of economic crime and their offenders. Violence may or may not occur during the commission of these crimes. If violence does occur, it is most often when the financial gain is in jeopardy. We also will discuss the role of drugs as a commodity to be sold for financial gain.

CONTEXT

HISTORICALLY, THE STUDY OF ECONOMICALLY MOTIVATED CRIME WAS RESTRICTED TO white-collar criminals. Sutherland (1949) is typically credited as one of the first scholars to draw attention to this area of study. In sum, Sutherland (1949) viewed white-collar criminals as high status and respectable, often male, highly educated, and in upper-management positions. Following the work of Sutherland in the 1940s, a further distinction was made to recognize corporate crime that occurs with the support of an organization and occupational crime committed by an individual offender (Clinard and Quinney 1967). Occupational fraudsters were thought to be primarily middle class (Weisburd, Wheeler, Waring, and Bode 1991). Today, the study of white-collar crime has evolved to encompass a broad class of economically-motivated crimes ranging from an individual who steals $20 from a cash register to highly elaborate criminal organizations making millions of dollars from the drug and sex trades.

DEFINITIONS

THE CRIMES DESCRIBED IN THIS CHAPTER ARE INDEED VERY DIFFERENT. HOWEVER, EACH IS characterized by one defining feature—the motivation to make money. Although there are many definitions of economic crime, for the purposes of this chapter we define **economic crime** as criminal offences in which the primary motivation is economic gain (e.g., Freeman 1996).

It will become clear throughout the chapter that economic crime can generally be classified into two broad categories: individual and group crimes. Many economic crimes (white-collar crime, theft, property crime, fraud, prostitution, drug dealing) can be perpetrated by a lone offender or by large organizations such as gangs, criminal organizations, or "legitimate" business corporations.

WHY DO WE CARE?

ECONOMICALLY MOTIVATED CRIMES, SUCH AS CORPORATE WHITE-COLLAR CRIME, CAN CAUSE far greater financial harm and personal injury (sometimes death) than "traditional" crimes such as assault. The total cost of white-collar crime in Canada is difficult to determine. However, using information from the Federal Bureau of Investigation, white-collar crime is estimated to cost the United States more than US$300 billion annually (Cornell University Law School 2015).

According to the 2014 *Global Economic Crime Survey* (PricewaterhouseCoopers 2015), 36 percent of Canadian organizations surveyed reported being the victim of one or more economic crimes. The top four reported forms of economic crimes were: 1) asset misappropriation (58 percent; e.g., employees stealing cash/assets), 2) procurement fraud (33 percent; e.g., unlawful bidding processes), 3) accounting fraud (22 percent), and cybercrime (22 percent; e.g., spreading viruses, hacking, phishing). The survey also revealed that a sizeable number of Canadian organizations were the victims of bribery/corruption, competition laws/anti-trust violations, illegal insider trading, money laundering, espionage, intellectual property theft, and mortgage/tax fraud. It should be noted that for most economic crime (including white-collar crime), male offenders outnumber female offenders. Prostitution is one exception to this trend and is discussed later in this chapter.

Human pain and suffering is the unfortunate outcome of crime in general. However, the human pain and suffering experienced by victims forced into the sex trade, by those who become severely addicted to illegal drugs, or by innocent bystanders hit by stray bullets in the midst of gang wars is particularly distressing. Similarly, victims of identity theft may spend years attempting to recover from the aftermath of having their identities stolen. Society as a whole pays for economically motivated crime—insurance premiums increase, as do our credit card and banking fees.

METHODOLOGY

NOT SURPRISINGLY, A VARIETY OF RESEARCH METHODS HAVE BEEN USED TO STUDY economically motivated crime. Some research approaches rely on large-scale surveys of corporations to understand the nature and extent of economically motivated crime from the perspective of the victim. Other approaches involve surveying or interviewing the perpetrators of economically motivated crime.

CATEGORIES OF ECONOMICALLY MOTIVATED CRIME

White-Collar Crime

Edwin H. Sutherland coined the term "white-collar crime" during the 1939 presidential address to the American Sociological Society as "crime committed by a person of respectability and high social status in the course of his occupation" (Sutherland 1949). This definition has evolved over time. A more contemporary definition can be seen in Green's *Occupational Crime Typology* (1997):

> Organizational crime—a corporation or agency profits from law-violating behaviour (e.g., bribing pubic officials, Chief Financial Officer falsifies tax record with Board of Director's consent).

Professional crime—law-violating behaviours by professionals such as lawyers, physicians, psychologists, etc. (e.g., a doctor bills for seeing eight patients when he only saw four).

State-authority crime—law-violating behaviours by those with legal authority (e.g., bribes taken by public officials, police brutality, torture of individuals in custody).

Individual crime—law-violating behaviours by individuals (e.g., stealing supplies from an employer, not reporting full income to Revenue Canada).

Some researchers simply view white-collar crime along two dimensions: occupational or corporate. **Occupational crimes** are offences committed against businesses and government by perpetrators with a "higher" social status. These offences include expense account fraud and tax evasion. See the Media Spotlight box for a look at suspended Senator Mike Duffy over allegations of expense account fraud against the Canadian government.

Corporate crimes are offences committed by organizations to advance their own interests. Corporate crime offences include **price fixing** (e.g., companies that all sell the same product decide on a price, preventing price variability for the consumer) and the payment of kickbacks to manufacturers or retailers (who use the organization's product). The distinction between occupational and corporate crime can be thought of as crime focused on individuals versus crime focused on organizations (Holtfreter 2005).

Media Spotlight

Former Senator Mike Duffy Goes to Court

Former Senator Mike Duffy has been charged with 31 counts of fraud, breach of trust, and bribery related to expenses he claimed as a senator and later repaid with money provided by Prime Minister Harper's former Chief of Staff, Nigel Wright. A number of allegations (e.g., claiming housing expenses for a home that he may not have been living in) have been made and the case is currently before the court. Part of the Crown's case against Duffy includes an allegation that Duffy billed $698 in expenses for a trip he took with his wife to a dog show in Peterborough, Ontario, in July 2010 to buy a Kerry blue terrier. Duffy claims he and his wife travelled to Peterborough in July 2010 on "public business to meet with local officials to discuss broadcasting issues." According to the Crown, Duffy's personal diary notes that he and his wife drove to Peterborough on July 2nd and spent the night at a Super 8 motel and had coffee with Dean Del Mastro (a Tory MP at the time) and his wife the next morning.

There seems to be some question as to Duffy's "business" in Peterborough. Was he there to buy a dog? Or maybe he took in a dog show after his "Senate business"? In any event, this is one example of a number of questionable expenses claimed by Duffy. It is anticipated that this case may be before the courts for several months.

Source: Gollom (2015).

Profiling the White-Collar Criminal Holtfreter (2005) provides the following review of the literature examining some of the common characteristics of offenders of "white-collar" crime:

> Age, Race, and Gender: Unlike "traditional" offenders, the common white-collar offender is a White male, approximately 40-years-old (Wheeler, Weisburd, Waring, and Bode 1988). In contrast, the common street offender is described as a Black male, approximately 30-years-old (U.S. statistics). Male offenders seem to outnumber female offenders when it comes to white-collar crime. Historically, women tended to occupy lower level positions such as clerical positions compared to males who tended to have higher level positions making it more likely that males would be in a position to commit white-collar or economically motivated crime.

> Education: White-collar criminals tend to have greater educational attainment compared to other types of offenders (Benson and Moore 1992). Once again, higher level corporate positions require a particular level of education whereas, more traditional offenders may have histories of low academic achievement and be high school dropouts.

> Position: Often white-collar criminals will have knowledge and be involved in the financial aspects of the organization that would facilitate occupational crime such as embezzlement. An individual's position in the organization facilitates the types of white-collar crimes possible to commit. Those in managerial or executive positions may have greater opportunities to commit white-collar crime. (pp. 355–356)

In a study by Holtfreter (2005), 1142 occupational fraud cases were examined to differentiate between individual offender characteristics and organizational victim characteristics. Three types of occupational fraud were assessed: asset misappropriation, corruption, and fraudulent statements. The results found that individuals who made fraudulent statements tended to be "high status." In comparison, those involved in asset misappropriation or corruption were considered "middle-class" offenders. The organizations that were victimized for corruption tended to be large profit-generating corporations. Asset misappropriation was committed more often in smaller organizations compared to larger organizations. Fraudulent statements were primarily made in smaller organizations.

Blickle, Schlegel, Fassbender, and Klein (2006) surveyed 76 prisoners convicted of white-collar crime in Germany and 150 managers working in various companies. Some significant differences were found between the two groups: white-collar criminals were more hedonistic (i.e., more supportive of the pursuit of pleasure and life enjoyment) and had a greater likelihood of giving in to temptation when they had the opportunity to make money illegally. The criminals also had stronger narcissistic tendencies and less behavioural self-control than the managers. Somewhat surprisingly, white-collar criminals were more conscientious. The researchers speculated that the criminals were high-level executives who would require conscientiousness to obtain the education and training necessary to achieve their level of employment. In another study, Collins and Schmidt (1993) found that white-collar criminals have lower integrity than non-criminals. Other differentiating traits of white-collar criminals included irresponsibility, lack of dependability, and disregard for rules and social norms.

Profiling Victims of White-Collar Crime Common characteristics of victims of white-collar crime are also outlined by Holtfreter (2005):

> *Organizational Type:* A study by Smigel (1956) found that there was a positive association between the size and level of bureaucracy of the organization and the willingness to approve of stealing from that organization. Corporations with large bureaucracies can receive little sympathy from the public, often perceived as making large profits (Smigel and Ross 1970).

> *Organizational Size:* Very generally, larger organizations are associated with greater crime than smaller organizations (Gricar 1983). A number of factors have been found to interact with organizational size however, including decentralization and level of control (Hill et al. 1992).

> *Internal Controls:* Organizations that have greater internal controls, such as audits and anonymous reporting systems, are less likely to be victimized. Furthermore, if these controls then result in the dismissal of guilty employees, less victimization will occur (Trevino and Victor 1992, p. 356–367).

Public Perceptions of White-Collar Crime In a national telephone survey to assess the public's view of white-collar crime versus street crime, Holtfreter, Van Slyke, Bratton, and Gertz (2008) examined responses from 402 U.S. citizens. A large proportion of respondents wanted white-collar criminals punished as harshly as or more harshly than violent criminals. This finding is contradictory to earlier research, possibly due to the recent media attention on a number of high-profile white-collar crime cases (e.g., Bernie Madoff, Conrad Black, and Martha Stewart). Respondents also wanted greater government resources allocated to combat white-collar crime. Along similar lines, Schoepfer, Carmichael, and Piquero (2007) found that U.S. citizens perceived street criminals as more likely to be apprehended and sentenced more severely than white-collar criminals. These researchers also found that the public felt that those who commit robbery should be punished similarly to those who commit fraud.

Theft

Economic crime generally is synonymous with the notion of stealing; that is, taking something that belongs to someone else. The *Criminal Code* of Canada (section 322) states that "every one commits theft who fraudulently and without colour of right takes, or fraudulently and without colour of right converts to his use or to the use of another person, anything, whether animate or inanimate, with intent." There is a demarcation at $5000 when deciding on the punishment for a crime. Theft over $5000 is an indictable offence with a maximum punishment of 10 years imprisonment. Theft under $5000 is considered a hybrid offence, meaning it can be treated either as an indictable offence or a less serious summary conviction. This decision is made by the Crown's office prosecuting the case. If theft under $5000 is prosecuted as an indictable offence, the maximum penalty is imprisonment for not more than two years. As a summary conviction, the maximum penalty is six months imprisonment, a fine of $2000, or both.

A common type of theft, as described in the opening vignette, is shoplifting. It is not a specific criminal offence, but simply a theft categorized by the value of the merchandise stolen under the Canadian *Criminal Code*. It incorporates both low-value and high-value items.

Property Crime

According to Employment and Social Development Canada (2015), property crime can be categorized in one of two ways:

- Theft of personal property such as wallets, credit cards, or money
- Household crime that includes breaking and entering, vandalism, theft of cars or car parts, and theft of household property

Employment and Social Development Canada (2015) also indicates that victimization rates of personal property crimes increased from 75 incidents per 1000 people in 1999 to 108 incidents per 1000 people in 2009. Household property crime victimization also increased from 218 incidents per 1000 households to 237 incidents from 1999 to 2009.

Fraud

Under section 380 of the *Criminal Code* of Canada, fraud is divided into two categories: fraud under $5000 and fraud over $5000. Fraud occurs when deceit or fraudulent means are used to deprive someone of property, money, valuable security, or services. Many thefts can also be fraud, and it is sometimes up to the police to decide whether to lay a fraud charge or a theft charge against an offender. Consider the scenario in which a person switches price tags at a store, attaching the price tag of a lower-priced good to a more expensive item. This is really an example of theft, but police may choose to lay a fraud charge because the person technically paid for something. In other words, the price paid was illegitimate, so the fraud is the difference between the actual value and the price paid. A critical element in fraud is that the offender uses deception to take something that does not belong to them.

Identity Theft: A Special Case of Fraud In January 2010, Senate Bill S-4 became law, which created a number of new offences under the Canadian *Criminal Code* and identified aspects of identity theft that were not already covered by existing provisions. Below are definitions of some of these offences with a focus on the "preparatory stages of identity theft by making it an offence to obtain, possess, transfer or sell the identity documents of another person" (RCMP 2015c).

The RCMP provides the following definitions and relevant offences to identity theft (2015c):

> **Identity Crime:** *a generic term used to describe all forms of illicit conduct (unlawful activity) involving identity including but not limited to identity theft and identity fraud.*
>
> **Identity Theft**: *is defined as obtaining and possessing identity information with the intent to use the information deceptively, dishonestly or fraudulently in the commission of a crime.*
>
> *Under Criminal Code Section 402.2 (1) Everyone commits an offence who knowingly obtains or possesses another person's identity information in circumstances giving rise to a reasonable inference that the information is intended to be used to commit an indictable offence that includes fraud, deceit or falsehood as an element of the offence.*
>
> **Identity Fraud**: *is the actual deceptive use of the identity information of another person (living or dead) in connection with various frauds (e.g., personating another person and the misuse of debit card or credit card data).*
>
> *Criminal Code Section 403.(1) Everyone commits an offence who fraudulently personates another person, living or dead, with intent to gain advantage for themselves or another person; with intent to obtain any property or an interest in any property; with intent to cause disadvantage to the person being personated or another person; or with intent to avoid arrest or prosecution or to obstruct, pervert or defeat the course of justice.*
>
> **Trafficking in identity information**: *Criminal Code Section 402.2 (2) Everyone commits an offence who transmits, makes available, distributes, sells or offers for sale another person's identity information, or has it in their possession for any of those purposes, knowing that or being reckless as to whether the information will be used to commit an indictable offence that includes fraud, deceit or falsehood as an element of the offence.*
>
> **Identity document**: *In the broadest sense, an identity document can be any document that identifies a person or that contains identity information. Parliament has created a specific criminal offence in relation to a list of the most common types of official identity documents.*
>
> *Criminal Code Section 56.1 (3) "identity document" means a Social Insurance Number card, a driver's license, a health insurance card, a birth certificate, a death certificate, a passport as defined in subsection 57(5), a document that simplifies the process of entry into Canada, a certificate of citizenship, a document indicating immigration status in Canada, a certificate of Indian status or an employee identity card that bears the employee's photograph and signature, or any similar document, issued or purported to be issued by a department or agency of the federal government or of a provincial or foreign government.*
>
> **Breeder document**: *a genuine document used to confirm one's identity when applying for other genuine documents. A birth certificate is a good example of a breeder document. Once altered, counterfeited or illegally obtained, a breeder document can be used to apply for other genuine ID documents or cards.*
>
> **Identity information**: *Criminal Code Section 402.1 "identity information" means any information — including biological or physiological information — of a type that is*

commonly used alone or in combination with other information to identify or purport to identify an individual, including a fingerprint, voice print, retina image, iris image, DNA profile, name, address, date of birth, written signature, electronic signature, digital signature, user name, credit card number, debit card number, financial institution account number, passport number, Social Insurance Number, health insurance number, driver's license number or password.

In addition to identity fraud, a number of other types of fraud are possible. These include:

1. Advance fee fraud: Fraud that requires a payment before delivery of service

2. Online auction fraud: Fraud that occurs through online purchasing (e.g., non-delivery of goods and services, non-payment for goods delivered)

3. Investment fraud: Fraud that occurs with investments impacting a person or company (e.g., insider trading)

4. Counterfeit: Fraud associated with counterfeit currency or payment cards (e.g., currency counterfeiting)

5. Home renovation fraud: Fraud associated with home and property renovation services or sale (e.g., real estate fraud)

6. Health fraud: Fraud associated with healthcare or services, including insurance

7. Fraudulent bankruptcy: Fraud associated with personal or corporate bankruptcy claims (e.g., concealment of assets)

8. Corruption/bribery: Any misuse of power and position by a public or non-government official (e.g., bribery of a public official) (Canadian Anti-Fraud Centre 2015)

Cybercrime

Foreign Affairs, Trade and Development Canada (2015) defines cybercrime as a "criminal offence involving a computer as the object of the crime (hacking, phishing, spamming), or as the tool used to commit a material component of the offence (child pornography, hate crimes, computer fraud). Criminals can also use computers for communication and document or data storage." The RCMP breaks cybercrime into two categories:

- **Technology as target**—criminal offences targeting computers and other information technologies, such as those involving the unauthorized use of computers, or mischief in relation to data

- **Technology as instrument**—criminal offences where the Internet and information technologies are instrumental in the commission of a crime, such as those involving fraud, identity theft, intellectual property infringements, money laundering, drug trafficking, human trafficking, organized crime activities, child sexual exploitation, or cyber bullying (RCMP 2015b)

Table 6.1 Cybercrime by Category

Technology as Target	Technology as Instrument
Mass marketing fraud	Hacking for criminal purposes
Money laundering	Criminal botnet operations
Identity theft	Malware threats
Child exploitation	Distributed denial of service
Intellectual property infringements	
Internet-based drug trafficking	

Source: RCMP (2015b).

See Table 6.1 for examples of these cybercrime categories

Cyberbullying According to the RCMP, "Cyberbullying involves the use of communication technologies such as the Internet, social networking sites, websites, email, text messaging, and instant messaging to repeatedly intimidate or harass others" (2015a).

The following acts constitute cyberbullying:

- Sending mean or threatening emails or text/instant messages
- Posting embarrassing photos of someone online
- Creating a website to make fun of others
- Pretending to be someone by using their name
- Tricking someone into revealing personal or embarrassing information and sending it to others

The intensity of cyberbullying can occur due to the inability of victims to escape the bullying. It can follow a victim 24 hours a day, 7 days a week, unlike traditional bullying that may be limited to certain locations (e.g., at school).

Dr. Debra Pepler, a leading Canadian researcher, has focused on understanding bullying and cyberbullying for over 25 years. Recently, Pepler participated in a Canadian study that examined cyberbullying in a 1-year longitudinal data set from the *Health Behavior in School-Aged Children Study* conducted by the World Health Organization (Cappadocia, Craig, and Pepler 2013). Almost 2000 adolescents were studied in order to better understand the prevalence, stability, and risk factors related with cyberbullying, cybervictimization, and simultaneous cyberbullying and cybervictimization. Increased antisocial behaviour and having fewer prosocial peers were identified as risk factors for cyberbullying. Transitioning into high school, traditional victimization, and depression were risk factors for cybervictimization. Traditional victimization also was related to both cyberbullying and cybervictimization co-occurring. See the Researcher Profile to learn more about Dr. Pepler.

Box 6.1

Canadian Researcher Profile Dr. Debra Pepler

Dr. Debra Pepler started her academic career with the completion of her PhD in children's play and creativity from the University of Waterloo in 1979. Over 35 years, Dr. Pepler has continued her research with a focus on children's aggression and victimization, children in families at risk (substance using women and their young children), adolescents with substance use and mental health problems, and on how healthy relationships promote healthy development. She is currently conducting research with the Canadian Red Cross Walking the Prevention Circle program on healing within Aboriginal communities.

Dr. Pepler is a co-lead with PREVNet (Promoting Relationships and Eliminating Violence Network), which is funded by the federal government's Networks of Centres of Excellence. In this network, Dr. Pepler works with 63 partner organizations (national youth-serving organizations, governments, and corporations) to prevent bullying and promote healthy relationships by providing knowledge and resources on these issues. Dr. Pepler states, "I have learned so much from our partners through the process [...] this is the most exciting and gratifying research activity of my career."

Since Dr. Pepler was trained in observational research, she decided to do a study in which she would videotape children behaving naturally. She found the challenge was to get not only the picture, but the sound. Dr. Pepler recalled that, "after my job interview at York University when I wore a remote microphone, the light went on! I could put a microphone on the children and capture their interactions." This is probably the research that Dr. Pepler is best known for, and she continues to move back to observational research whenever an exciting question arises. Dr. Pepler noted how exciting this research was and how it launched the bullying research program, stating "We learned and saw what no one had seen before. It opened so many doors to more questions."

Given Dr. Pepler's expertise in bullying and cyberbullying, it is not surprising that she was one of two experts consulting on the Rehtaeh Parsons case, in which Dr. Pepler noted that cyberbullying and sexual assault caused Parsons unfathomable distress to the point that her parents and teachers could not stabilize her and she tragically took her own life.

Dr. Pepler also worked with the Ontario Government to develop the *Safe Schools Act*. Although she realizes that governments are accountable and must keep citizens safe, when Dr. Pepler reflects back on this legislation, she regrets that it is generally punitive, rather than specifying the necessary education and remediation to help young people learn better ways of interacting.

Courtesy of Dr. Debra Pepler

Box 6.1   (Continued)

When Dr. Pepler talks to the public, she challenges us to compare how we support children and youth who make mistakes in reading or math and how we treat children who have behaviour problems—behavioural skills are much more challenging to learn. It is difficult for children and youth who make mistakes in social interactions. Pepler states "rather than having skills broken down and taught, we relegate these students to the edges of a classroom, the principal's office, the couch at home, or the street corner This is one of the processes that leads youth onto a pathway to crime."

Dr. Pepler continues her work at York University, where she is a Distinguished Research Professor. If she isn't in front of computer screen, you may find her playing squash, tennis, or skiing, to name a few possibilities. Dr. Pepler finds it critical to have balance for both mind and body.

According to the RCMP, the following acts are considered illegal in Canada:

- Threats of death or serious bodily harm—whether done face to face, online, over the phone, or through text messaging

- Criminal harassment—repeated tormenting online, with texts, phone calls, and/or emails causing the other person to fear for their safety

- Distribution of intimate images without consent—sharing naked or sexual pictures of another person without their consent (also known as "revenge porn") (RCMP 2015a)

As an example, the Hot Topics box in Chapter 5 described a case involving cyberbullying among adolescents.

Prostitution

Providing sexual services in exchange for money is broadly known as **prostitution**. This "exchange" requires a buyer and a seller, who may be heterosexual or homosexual. Female sellers and male buyers constitute the most common form of prostitution, with male homosexual exchanges occurring less frequently. Very little information exists regarding lesbian prostitution.

In 2014, Bill C-36 was brought in to amend the *Criminal Code* of Canada after the Supreme Court of Canada ruled that parts of the *Criminal Code* were unconstitutional because they put sex workers in danger. The *Protection of Exploited Persons and Communities Act* was introduced and passed. This Act criminalizes buying sex (rather than the selling of sex), profiting from the sale of sex, and third-party advertising for the sale of sex.

You can now communicate with the intention of selling sex in some instances. You cannot sell sex in locations where those under 18 are reasonably expected to be (e.g., schools, playgrounds, day cares). However, it is illegal to *buy* sexual services or communicate with the intention of buying sex. This crime is punishable with up to five years in jail and fines that begin at $500 and increase as the number of offences increase. Fines double if the attempt to purchase sex is conducted anywhere children may be present.

The Male Client As stated above, research tends to focus on the "male client" in sex trades. Xantidis and McCabe (2000) examined the characteristics and motivations of men seeking the services of female sex workers. In this study, 66 clients and 60 non-clients completed a questionnaire assessing sex roles, social–sexual effectiveness, and sensation-seeking behaviour. In terms of demographics, the clients and non-clients were similar in age, education, marital status, and occupation. Clients were significantly less likely to subscribe to a feminine sex-role orientation, had lower social–sexual effectiveness, and had higher sensation-seeking behaviours. In terms of motivation to visit sex workers, the client group appeared to partition into two separate groups: one group had low social–sexual effectiveness and seemed motivated to visit sex workers because they desired interpersonal intimacy, and the other had a high level of sensation seeking and seemed motivated to visit sex workers because they wanted novelty and variety in sexual encounters.

In a similar study, Sawyer, Metz, Hinds, and Brucker (2001) examined the attitudes towards prostitution of 140 males aged 19 to 66 years who had used prostitutes. Younger and less educated males (when compared to men who were older and more educated) were more likely to believe in inaccurate myths about prostitution and less likely to support the decriminalization of prostitution. Approximately 33 percent of men had who used a prostitute reported they enjoyed sexual relations with the prostitute. Fifty-seven percent reported that they tried to stop using prostitutes. Approximately a third of the participants reported being arrested for using prostitutes. Overall, the study suggests that men who engage in the use of prostitution are a mixed group with varying backgrounds and motivations for seeking to purchase sexual services.

The Pimp A "pimp" controls prostitutes, arranges customers for them, and takes part of the prostitute's earnings. Pimps may start as male clients, then become an intimate partner, and end as a controlling pimp (Karandikar and Próspero 2010). In a study that compared women controlled by pimps to those not controlled by pimps, Norton-Hawk (2004) questioned 50 jailed prostitutes, of which 40 percent had been controlled by a pimp. Table 6.2 lists characteristics associated with prostitutes controlled by pimps. If we

Table 6.2 Characteristics of Prostitutes Controlled by Pimps

- Single (not in a relationship)
- Did not complete high school
- Non-Caucasian
- Never held legitimate employment
- Dysfunctional family background
- Younger age for first sexual activity
- Younger age for use of illegal drugs
- More likely to experience violence from customers

Source: Norton-Hawk (2004).

Young Female Pimps, Pimping Even Younger Victims

In June 2012, Kailey Oliver-Machado was arrested at the age of 15 along with two other females aged 15 and 16 (the other two cannot be named under the *Youth Criminal Justice Act*) and charged with procurement for the purpose of prostitution, human trafficking, making child pornography, sexual assault, child luring, uttering threats, and unlawful confinement. Machado pled not guilty (the other two girls pled guilty) but was found guilty and given an adult sentence of six and a half years in prison. Machado was accused of orchestrating a prostitution ring in which she lured young female victims (ranging in age from 13 to 17 years old) to engage in sexual acts with older men. According to a news report, over the course of a few months, the victims would be "lured over to the Machado's house for sleepovers, then they would be drugged, photographed naked, beaten, their cellphones taken, and they would be dragged into a car and taken to a 'john's' house and forced to perform sex" (CTVnews.ca 2014).

Source: CTVnews.ca (2014).

consider these characteristics as "risk factors," it may be helpful to target the factors to reduce pimp-controlled prostitution.

A recent case made headlines across the country due to the gender and age of the pimps: three girls under 18 years of age. The Hot Topics box discusses this case.

Organized Crime

A "criminal organization" is defined in section 467.1 of the *Criminal Code* as a group that "1) is composed of three or more persons in or outside Canada; and 2) has as one of its main purposes or activities the facilitation or commission of one or more serious offences that, if committed, would likely result in the direct or indirect receipt of material benefit, including financial benefit, by the group or by any of the persons who constitute the group." This definition does not include a group of individuals who come together randomly to commit a single offence. Organized crime and gangs have existed in Canada for over 150 years. *R. v. Lindsay* (2005) was the first time Canadian courts recognized a group—namely, the Hells Angels—as a "criminal organization." Courts also have declared "street gangs" to be criminal organizations (*Aurélius c. R.* 2007).

Extent of Organized Crime in Canada The Canadian Security Intelligence Service (CSIS) estimated that there were approximately 900 organized crime groups in Canada in 2008. In 2011, CSIS identified 729 crime groups in Canada (Standing Committee on Justice and Human Rights 2012). Differences in these numbers may represent changes in the criminal marketplace, effective law enforcement, and the research methods used. Table 6.3 provides a sample of the various types of organized crime groups in Canada.

Table 6.3 Types of Organized Crime Groups in Canada

- Outlaw motorcycle gangs
- Asian-based groups
- Italian-based (or traditional) groups
- Aboriginal-based groups
- Eastern European-based groups
- Street gangs
- Columbian groups
- Latino groups
- Haitian groups
- Lebanese groups
- South American groups
- Japanese (Yakuza) organizations
- Quebecois groups
- Indo-Canadian groups
- Nigerian groups
- Jamaican groups
- Somali organizations

Source: Criminal Intelligence Service Canada (2014).

Gang membership in Canada is very real and very fluid. Gang-related crime can span various geographic regions with a variety of crimes. In a recent CBC news report Kwong (2015) gave a startling overview of the prevalence of gangs across Canada. In Atlantic Canada, the Bacchus Outlaw Motorcycle club is in charge of the drug trade. The Red Scorpions battle with the United Nations in western Canada. The White Boy Posse spans Edmonton and Saskatchewan, and in Ottawa, the Crips are prominent. North Preston's Finest is a gang from Halifax that has now expanded to Toronto with a focus on sex trafficking. The "856 Gang" from the Yukon and Northwest Territories is now in Yellowknife with drugs and guns. Perhaps the largest organization in Canada is the Hells Angels, which runs across Canada with about 450 members, the majority in Ontario (150), Quebec (100), and British Columbia (100) (Kwong 2015).

Between 2003 and 2012, Saskatoon averaged two gang-related murders a year, which is more than double the per capita rates in Montreal, Toronto, and Calgary. However, Abbotsford-Mission in B.C.'s Fraser Valley is now the gang-murder capital of Canada, averaging more than one gang murder per 100 000 population a year between 2003 and 2012. Stats Canada reported Vancouver as having the highest number of gang murders (18) in 2013. Montreal came in second with 16 murders, and Toronto was third with 14 murders, while Winnipeg had 4 and Edmonton had 3 murders.

Criminal Intelligence Service Canada (CISC) identified the following as cornerstones to organized crime in Canada:

1. The British Columbia lower mainland, southern Ontario, and greater Montreal contain both the largest concentrations of criminal groups and the most active criminal markets. The illegal drug trade remains the largest criminal market in terms of extent, scope, and the degree of involvement by most organized crime networks.

2. Any impact that law enforcement has in disbanding organized crime networks is short-lived. These organizations can quickly regroup in response to consumer demand.

3. Most organized crime networks have international affiliations, ensuring that the supply and distribution chains for several commodities remain strong. In addition,

strategically located areas on the Canada/United States border provide significant opportunities for the movement of illegal commodities and/or people without requiring large or sophisticated operations.

4. Organized crime groups infiltrate and exploit legitimate businesses, laundering money, facilitating criminal activity (i.e., through import and export companies), co-mingling licit and illicit goods, and further protecting organized crime networks from legal action. (CISC 2008)

How do Organized Crime Networks Operate? Criminal organizations use a number of methods to increase profitability, expand power bases, and protect against criminal charges. Some crime groups have a hierarchy and a core membership, but more often these groups are fluid, working competitively or collaboratively among various networks. According to CISC, the following methods are used to gain a competitive advantage in the criminal marketplace:

- **Violence and Intimidation:** Violence and intimidation are used both externally against criminal rivals and internally to maintain discipline. Lower-level criminal groups may pose a more immediate and direct public safety threat through acts of violence that are often carried out in public places. These groups are largely but not entirely composed of street gangs, some of which have committed assaults or shootings in public places across the country. In some instances, intimidation is used against individuals and their communities to silence witnesses to crimes.

- **Critical Skills:** Organized crime groups use and manipulate individuals or organizations with critical skills that are necessary to facilitate certain crimes (i.e., securities fraud, counterfeiting, mortgage fraud, etc.). Skilled outsiders are either recruited or coerced into provision of these services. For instance, organized crime groups often exploit financial professionals such as accountants, bank representatives, and lawyers to facilitate fraud or the movement of money through different stages of the money-laundering process.

- **Money Laundering:** Lower-level criminal groups conduct simpler money-laundering processes, including the use of cash-intensive businesses (e.g., restaurants), casinos, currency exchanges, and the purchase of luxury goods. Higher-level criminal groups insulate themselves through more complex methods such as real estate ventures and off-shore investment opportunities that exploit weaknesses in the global financial regulatory and reporting systems. Criminal groups also use both legitimate and shell companies to launder money, which allows for the co-mingling of funds, provides the appearance of legitimacy, and insulates groups from detection. (CISC 2008)

Organized Crime and the Sex Trade

The United Nations Office on Drugs and Crime (UNODC) created the Protocol to Prevent, Suppress and Punish Trafficking in Persons (also called the Trafficking Persons Protocol), which defines **human trafficking** as:

recruitment, transportation, transfer, harbouring or receipt of persons, by means of threat or use of force or other forms of coercion, of abduction, of fraud, of deception, of the abuse of power or of a position of vulnerability or of the giving or receiving of payments or benefits to achieve the consent of a person having control over another person, for the purpose of exploitation. Exploitation shall include, at a minimum, the exploitation of the prostitution of others or other forms of sexual exploitation, forced labour or services, slavery or practices similar to slavery, servitude or the removal of organs. (UNODC 2015)

The Human Trafficking Protocol also outlines three specific elements of human trafficking, which are described in Table 6.4.

Trafficked females are often sexually exploited and frequently lured by individuals known to them or their families with promises of jobs as waitresses, nannies, or cleaners, then forced into sex work or exploited while working. Women risk abuse and exploitation as prostitutes for up to 18 hours a day, 7 days a week, until they repay so-called travel debts to regain their passports from their captors/employers.

The trafficking of women and adolescents is increasingly recognized as one of the world's fastest-growing crimes and a significant violation of human rights. The RCMP estimates that 800 people are trafficked into Canada each year. However, data from other non-governmental agencies put this figure closer to an astounding 16 000 people. On an international scale, some sources suggest that there are approximately four *million* girls and women sold for prostitution, slavery, or forced marriage *every year* (Barnett and Béchard 2011).

Bill C-49 (sections 279.01–279.04 of the *Criminal Code*) created three new indictable criminal offences to specifically address trafficking in persons:

- Section 279.01 prohibits anyone from recruiting, transporting, transferring, receiving, holding, concealing, or harbouring a person, or exercising control or influence over the movements of a person for the purpose of exploiting or facilitating the exploitation of that person. The maximum penalty for trafficking involving the kidnapping, aggravated assault, aggravated sexual assault, or death of an individual is life in prison.

- Section 279.02 prohibits anyone from receiving a financial or other material benefit for the purpose of committing or facilitating the trafficking of a person, with a maximum penalty of 10 years.

Table 6.4 Elements of Human Trafficking

1. **The act** (*what* is done)—e.g., recruitment, transportation, transfer, habouring, receipt of persons

2. **The means** (*how* it is done)—e.g., threat or use of force, coercion, abduction, fraud, deception, abuse of power or vulnerability, or giving payments or benefits to a person in control of the victim

3. **The purpose** (*why* it is done)—e.g., exploitation, which includes exploiting the prostitution of others, sexual exploitation, forced labour, slavery or similar practices, and the removal of organs

Source: United Nations Office on Drugs and Crime (2015).

■ Section 279.03 prohibits the withholding or destruction of documents such as a victim's travel documents or documents establishing their identity for the purpose of committing or facilitating the trafficking of that person, with a maximum penalty of 5 years.

Under this federal legislation, charges were laid against an acupuncture centre in 2005. The defendant was charged with bringing women into Canada under false pretences and forcing them into prostitution.

The changes to the *Criminal Code* also allow for charges against Canadians who go to other countries seeking child prostitution (known as **sex tourism**). The first such charge occurred in 2004 against a British Columbia man who travelled to Cambodia for child prostitution. A married father, he filmed himself having sex with young children (the oldest was a 12-year-old girl). He was charged with sexual interference, sexual touching, and soliciting the services of a girl under the age of 18 (Associated Press 2005). Law-enforcement agencies can also charge tour operators or travel agents who arrange for such services (Canadian Security Intelligence Service 2012). The B.C. man initially pled not guilty, arguing that Canada could not lawfully prosecute citizens for behaviour they engaged in in other countries. In 2005, he changed his plea to guilty of 10 counts of sexual assault and received a 10-year prison sentence (CBC News 2012).

An in-depth study was conducted by Wohlbod, LeMay and Harrison-Baird (2014) to examine the nature and scope of trafficking in Ottawa. Three roundtables were conducted and an online survey was administered with 34 community stakeholders. Interviews were also conducted with 27 key informants (3 self-identified survivors, 1 former human trafficker, and 23 frontline workers currently supporting trafficked persons), and focus groups and interviews were done with 90 youth and 10 self-identified sex worker. An online survey conducted with 104 people who had bought sex. Overall, 140 local victims of human trafficking (for purposes of sexual exploitation) were identified. Ninety percent were Canadian and local. The victims were predominately young women (ranging from 12 to 25 years old, with an average age of 16) being victimized in private informal settings. Victims were typically groomed over many months and restrained by subtle psychological control mechanisms (threat of force, deception, paying a person who controlled the victim) rather than through brute force. One victim recalled the following:

> I never felt socially accepted as a teenager because I was 'different' than the rest of the girls, when J. [trafficker] came along he not only gave me lots of attention and love but he also made me feel included and accepted for who I was—that made it 'easy' for him to pull me in and keep me. For a while it felt like home. (Local Survivor, quoted in Wohlbod et al. 2014, p. 15.)

A number of mechanisms are used to maintain control. Traffickers may use blackmail (e.g., threaten to send pornographic images to family and friends), psychological control (e.g., threaten one's family), create or strengthen a pre-existing chemical dependency (e.g., giving victims drugs and alcohol), or employ a complex "grooming" process in which they first create an illusion of being in a loving relationship. The victim then feels that they owe the trafficker something, which leads to a gradual process of exploitation (e.g., having sex with the trafficker's "friend" as a favour, eventually building into more exploitative situations such as attending a party where the victim is gang-raped and filmed). The victim then experiences low self-worth, accepts the circumstances she finds herself in, and feels she deserves it and cannot get out.

Sex workers tend to transition in and out of trafficking situations—sometimes working outside of trafficking, sometimes not. It is important to note that the sex trade does not always equate with human trafficking.

Wohlbod et al. made several recommendations in their study, including:

1. Improving public awareness

2. Providing better outreach and intervention for victims

3. Providing better housing/protection for victims (e.g., dedicated human trafficking shelters) (Wohlbod et al. 2014)

Organized Crime and the Drug Trade

Generally operated by organized crime groups, the drug trade generates greater profits than any other trafficked commodity. Requests to deliver drugs, however, occur at an individual level (Vale and Kennedy 2004). Drugs may be hidden in luggage, in personal belongings, or swallowed or stuffed into body cavities. Harper and Murphy (2000) undertook an analysis of 1715 adult drug traffickers caught smuggling drugs into Heathrow airport between 1991 and 1997. They found that the majority were male (72 percent) and the most common method of smuggling was to hide it in luggage (32 percent).

Street value is used when estimating the revenue potential of drugs seized by law-enforcement agencies. In 2006, drug seizures in Canada were estimated at $2.3 billion. China was the largest single source of drugs seized between 2007 and 2012, most of which were substances often referred to as "date rape" drugs (McKie 2013). In 2015, a drug bust in Chilliwack, B.C. resulted in the seizure of drugs worth over $5 million and involved a variety of drugs including cocaine, crystal methamphetamine, and marijuana (*Chilliwack Progress* 2015).

Money generated from drug sales is typically laundered. **Money laundering** is the process whereby money received through illegal activity is disguised to mask where it came from. Money from drug deals can be laundered by wiring it in small amounts to off-shore accounts or using legitimate businesses (such as restaurants) that produce large amounts of cash to combine legitimate and illegitimate funds.

Organized Crime and Fraud

Organized crime groups are often extensively involved in fraud. Riley (1998) compiled a useful summary of organized crime fraud activities:

> ■ **Mass Marketing Fraud** Organized crime groups in Canada target Canadians and consumers in other countries, including the United States and Australia. Top

mass-marketing fraud schemes include prize/sweepstakes/lottery and gift schemes, Internet auctions, and vacation giveaways. Canadian mass-marketing fraud grosses over $500 million annually. Canadians are also targeted by foreign fraudsters from approximately 105 countries.

■ **Mortgage Fraud** Organized crime groups operate a number of schemes involving fraudulent mortgage applications that contain false information about the prospective buyer or property through the use of false appraisals and employment records. Organized groups may recruit family members to submit fraudulent mortgage applications to avoid detection.

■ **Payment Card Fraud** Information is transferred from point-of-sale terminals to vehicles nearby and almost instantly transferred to "card factories" (locations where payment cards are manufactured illegally), which can be located anywhere in the world. This presents a lucrative market for organized crime.

■ **Contraband Tobacco** Illegal cigarettes are primarily supplied by organized crime groups based in Ontario and Quebec. It is estimated that approximately 22 percent of the cigarettes smoked in Canada are illegal. Of these, some are legitimately manufactured, smuggled, and illicitly sold through Aboriginal reserves.

■ **Intellectual Property Rights Crime** Ever been tempted to buy a fake designer bag or watch? Organized crime groups are involved in the illegal import of counterfeit goods into Canada, mainly from China. Sometimes these fakes are difficult to detect and make their way into the legitimate market without the supplier or customer knowing. Counterfeit goods are sold on the Internet and through classified ad sites.

■ **Vehicle-Related Crime** Primarily in Toronto and Montreal, organized crime groups are involved in the theft of vehicles. Thieves then change the VIN numbers once the vehicles are obtained. These cars can be exported or disassembled and the parts resold. Few vehicles are exported internationally. Some organized crime groups are also involved in staging collisions for insurance fraud.

■ **Identity Theft and Fraud** This area is highly profitable for organized crime groups with low potential for detection. Not all identity theft and fraud is committed by organized groups, however; some fraud is committed by individuals.

Group Types in Organized Crime and Street Gangs

Mellor, MacRae, and Pauls, and Hornick (2005) developed a gang typology that included gang activities, gang organization, motivation to join gangs, recruitment strategies, and exit strategies (see Table 6.5 for a summary).

Kelly and Caputo (2005) conducted a police survey on gang activity and found that street gangs tend to provide distribution networks for the drug trade, to control territory, and to collect debts. Although some street gangs do run their operations, such

Table 6.5 Mellor, MacRae, Pauls, and Hornick's Gang Typology

Type A
Group of Friends—a group that does not engage in antisocial acts.

Type B
Spontaneous Criminal Activity Group/Gangs—can be large and social in nature. Members are generally prosocial, and the criminal activity that does occur is spontaneous or situation-motivated, such as shoplifting, theft, bullying, swarming, and gratuitous violence. These groups tend to be fluid, with no permanent leadership or hierarchy. Individuals could be members of multiple groups/gangs without negative consequences. They typically are not connected to organized crime groups. Weapon use is limited but can include knives, bats, homemade weapons, and handguns. In addition to being a fashion statement, members may join for other reasons: protection from others, belief that gang membership is "normal," gaining a sense of belonging and recognition, and a lack of legitimate alternative activities or associations. Recruitment is usually based within existing social networks where friends come together, and in other cases protection is offered. Members tend to leave the group/gang as they mature or change their peer group.

Type C
Purposive Group/Gangs—these groups/gangs usually form for the main purpose of committing a specific offence. Size is dependent on the purpose of the group and can disappear after that purpose is fulfilled. Crimes include property offences, home invasion, drug trafficking, procurement, extortion, robbery, hate crimes, and vigilante-type assaults. These gangs tend to be more structured than Type B groups, with a small, male-dominated membership and few if any links to criminal business organizations. Members may join to fulfill survival or emotional needs, engage in thrill-seeking, alleviate boredom, or take part in retribution. Recruitment can be done within existing social groups that tend to be short-lived, but police intervention by arrest or diversion can result in the group dissolving.

Type D
Youth Street Gangs—organized to carry out money-making criminal activity or organized violence against other gangs. Members can be identified through gang-specific clothing, tattoos, or jewellery and mark their territory with gang graffiti. Activities tend to be planned and organized. Youth street gangs have been known to commit a wide variety of offences including harassment, vehicle theft, drug trafficking, weapons procurement, prostitution, intimidation, extortion, robbery, assault, and homicide. These gangs usually have a hierarchy and may or may not have connections to organized crime groups. They tend to have moderate levels of leadership and a code of conduct is often imposed. There can also be affiliate members associated with these gangs who are not fully initiated and are not aware of all operations but may receive protection and have access to drugs and weapons. The core members generally have full membership status and offer complete loyalty and devotion to the gang. Some of the motivations for joining this type of gang include money, power, protection, a lack of legitimate alternatives, and social acceptance. Recruitment can be done by friends or family, or by taking in disenfranchised youth. Some members are coerced to join while in prison.

Table 6.5 (Continued)

Initiations are usually directed by the leaders and may involve committing certain offences, being beaten, or for females, having intercourse with all male members. Some gangs may even require proof of criminality. These gangs are typically the most difficult to leave but members may have the opportunity of being "beaten out," which involves a severe assault. Those who choose to leave usually require multifaceted exit strategies with help from the police, community groups, and family.

Type E

Structured Criminal Organizations—these organizations tend to be highly structured and sophisticated business operations that may operate internationally. To maintain a low profile and distance from criminal acts, these groups tend to use street-level groups to carry out many aspects of their business. They have been known to use children under 12 to spy, commit break and enter, act as couriers, and to engage in child pornography.

Source: Mellor, MacRae, Pauls, and Hornick (2005), cited in Hemmati (2006).

Igor Mojzes/Fotolia

An adolescent street gang member.

as marijuana grow operations, fraud operations (credit and debit cards), and prostitution rings.

Many street gangs seem to have connections to organized crime groups to varying degrees. Organized crime groups use street gangs to mark their territory. A key component to all street gangs appears to be their involvement with drugs and violence around the drugs.

As of November 2011, 10 percent of Correctional Service Canada's inmate population was known to be affiliated with a criminal organization or gang (2293 out of 23 021 offenders). Of these inmates, 39 percent were street-gang affiliated, 26 percent were Aboriginal-gang affiliated, 17 percent were motorcycle-gang affiliated, 8 percent were affiliated with traditional organized crime, 3 percent were Asian-gang affiliated, and 7 percent were indicated as "other" (Grekul and LaBoucane-Benson 2006).

THEORIES OF ECONOMICALLY-MOTIVATED CRIME

General theories of crime and theories associated with other specific types of crime (discussed in previous chapters) can also be applied to economically motivated offenders. Below are some specific theories that are commonly applied to the economic crimes described in this chapter.

Explaining Property and Theft

A common theory used to explain economically motivated property crime is the routine activity theory (Cohen and Felson 1979). The routine activity theory has three components: availability of suitable targets, absence of guardians, and motivated behaviour. This theory is applicable to property crimes (e.g., Wilcox, Madensen, and Tillyer 2007). For example, in the case of a robbery, an offender identifies an empty home as a suitable target with the absence of guardians and financial strain might be a motivator behind the offending behaviour.

Explaining Fraud

The **fraud triangle** (Cressey 1973) is an explanation of fraud that has three facets that form the triangle: 1) opportunity to commit fraud, 2) pressure to commit fraud, and 3) rationalization of the fraud. Figure 6.1 illustrates this relationship. The perceived pressure is the motive for the offender to commit the crime. Once the offender believes that he or she is able to commit the crime without being caught (i.e., has an opportunity), the act will be carried out (Dorminey, Fleming, Kranacher, and Riley 2012). Lastly, the offender rationalizes that his or her behaviour is morally acceptable due to the situation he or she is currently in (e.g., financial strain).

Wolfe and Hermanson (2004) proposed a fraud *diamond*, which considers four elements of fraud. As in Cressey's model, fraud is considered more likely to occur when someone has pressure or incentive to commit fraud, when weak controls are in place that allow for opportunity, and when the person can rationalize the behaviour (which is an attitudinal component). Wolfe and Hermanson's fourth factor concerns "capability." That is, the person must have the traits and abilities to commit the fraud. In order to be "capable" one must be

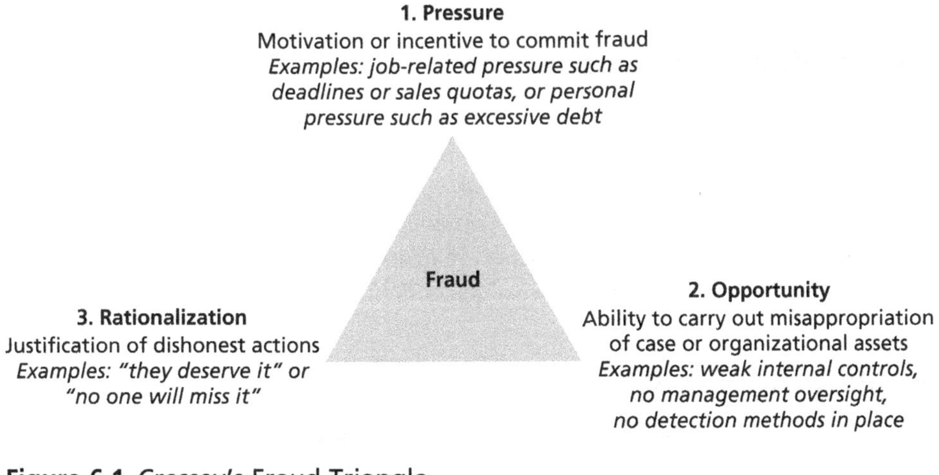

1. Pressure
Motivation or incentive to commit fraud
Examples: job-related pressure such as deadlines or sales quotas, or personal pressure such as excessive debt

Fraud

3. Rationalization
Justification of dishonest actions
Examples: "they deserve it" or "no one will miss it"

2. Opportunity
Ability to carry out misappropriation of case or organizational assets
Examples: weak internal controls, no management oversight, no detection methods in place

Figure 6.1 Cressey's Fraud Triangle

Source: Based on Cressey (1973).

in the right position to commit the fraud, be intelligent, immune to stress, have a narcissist personality (i.e., egotistic, grandiose), be deceptive, and have strong coercive skills.

Explaining Cybercrime

A theory that is helpful in explaining cybercrime is rational choice theory (Cornish and Clarke 1986). Rational choice theory posits that offenders weigh the costs and benefits of the crime in question prior to committing it. Wada, Longe, and Danquah (2012) suggest that this theory can also extend to cybercrime criminals. For example, cyber criminals may perceive electronic mechanisms such as firewalls, user identification regulations, and/or surveillance technology as risks to a crime that might deter them from committing it. Therefore, if such security measures are in place, the offender might perceived a high risk of getting caught, the cost of which might outweigh any benefits. However, if there are relatively few security measures, a cybercriminal may perceive a reduced likelihood of being caught and thus proceed with their crime (i.e., the benefits are believed to outweigh the costs).

Explaining Prostitution

While there is no set theory that explains why offenders become involved in economically motivated prostitution, one could argue that social strain theory may provide an explanation. Social strain theory proposes that society has predetermined, set goals, but does not offer the ability to achieve these goals to every person in society (Merton 1938). People who are in need of money may turn to prostitution in order to acquire income so they can achieve societal goals. Agnew (2006) also proposed that individuals may engage in prostitution to achieve monetary goals, since they may feel that it is the only option to overcome the stress and strain experienced in their lives.

Explaining the Drug Trade

Walters (2002) suggests that social strain theory also can be applied to offenders in the drug trade. The basic premise of social strain theory is that when there are opportunities for economic advancement, one will do whatever it takes to generate income. Because of this, offenders may seek out drug-trade opportunities to generate quick and easy profits to lessen the financial strain they experience. Similarly, Agnew (2006) considers that the selling of drugs may be an avenue a person takes to help achieve monetary goals.

Explaining Gangs

Interactional theory (Thornberry 1987; Thornberry and Krohn 2001) is a common theory used to help explain gangs. Interactional theory suggests that positive bonds with society must first be weakened before a person engages with a gang. This breakdown of positive bonds then leads to delinquent behaviour and the seeking out of peers who engage in similar behaviour. Decker, Melde, and Pyrooz (2012) discuss two different theoretical approaches to gangs and gang violence. The first is a structural control perspective, which posits that gangs are a product of weakened systems of social control. The second perspective is structural adaptation whereby gangs are created in response to environmental conditions. Once gang members are initiated, they are in an environment that promotes and fosters their delinquency. Gangs then work as a unit to achieve any economic goals they may have.

FACTORS ASSOCIATED WITH CRIMINAL CONDUCT AMONG ECONOMICALLY-MOTIVATED OFFENDERS

Property Crime

A common factor associated with criminal conduct among property offenders is substance abuse (Baron 2013). Offenders will typically commit a property crime in order to support their habit. Homelessness is also a factor associated with criminal conduct (Baron 2013). A homeless person may feel the need to commit a property crime in order to get food and/or shelter. Moreover, Howsen and Jarrell (1987) discuss how the poverty level and unemployment can motivate an individual to commit property crime.

Fraud and White-Collar Crime

Sutherland (1949, 1983) originally classified white-collar crime offenders as male, of high status, and highly educated. However, more recent research (e.g., Holtfreter 2005) found that some types of fraud are actually committed by persons of middle-class status. One factor found to be associated with criminal conduct among economically motivated fraud offenders is low self-control (Holtfreter, Reisig, Piquero, and Piquero 2010). Low self-control partially explained different types of fraud such as credit card fraud, academic fraud, and driver's license fraud.

Cybercrime

Low self-control among offenders has also been associated with cybercriminals (Hinduja 2006). Cybercriminals may believe that since they are not committing a person-to-person crime, there are relatively few risks of being caught. This, in turn, encourages them to offend. Most advanced cybercriminals also are highly educated and have an in-depth set of technological skills. Some cybercriminals may have an inflated level of confidence from being behind a computer screen while offending (Kshetri 2010).

Prostitution

A woman who has lived on the street and turns to prostitution for economically motivated reasons (e.g., needing money) may also have drug use problems (Daly 1994). Daly also suggests that these street women may have run away from home, had abusive house-holds, and/or were drawn by the excitement of the street. Other factors associated with criminal conduct among prostitution offenders include mental health issues such as low self-esteem.

Drug Trade

A common factor associated with criminal conduct among drug trade offenders is unem-ployment, which can lead an individual to create a goal to achieve financial success (Baron 2013). In order to meet this goal, the offender then sells drugs to make a quick and easy profit. Similar to property offenders, drug trade offenders also are commonly engaged in substance abuse. Violence is also typically associated with economically motivated drug trade offenders (Kuziemko and Levitt 2004). Violence can stem from a number of things such as disagreements on pricing, retaliations, or punishment for poor quality drugs.

Gangs

Similar to the other crimes, drug use is a common factor associated with criminal conduct among economically motivated gang offenders; gang members both use and deal drugs to make a profit (Fagan 1989). The possession of weapons is also a common element of gang crime (e.g., Bjerregaard and Lizotte 1995). Gang offenders typically carry weapons for both protection and possibly to use in the case of a threat. Melde, Taylor, and Esbensen (2009) reported that gang members also have reduced levels of fear; this reduced fear could, in turn, lead to other offending behaviours. Violence is prevalent in economically motivated gang offenders. Gang offenders typically have low levels of education (Klemp-North 2007).

ASSESSMENT APPROACHES AND EFFECTIVENESS
Property Crimes and Fraud

The Virginia Sentencing Commission created an assessment approach that is often used for offenders who commit a fraud or a property crime offence (such as larceny). This approach assesses an offender's likelihood of reoffending and classifies them based on their relative risk of future offences (Farrar-Owens 2012). Scores are used to determine if an offender should be incarcerated. Individual factors such as offender characteristics, prior arrest record, prior incarcerations, and prior felony convictions are all examined. Recommendations for an offender's diversion are based on a point total (Ostrom et al. 2002). This instrument has been successful in predicting risk; offenders who have been assessed with this instrument and received higher scores did have higher recidivism rates. Similarly, offenders who were recommended for diversion using this tool had a lower rate of recidivism (compared to those offenders who were not recommended).

Cybercrime

There is no general assessment approach to cybercrime as a whole. Cybercrime in itself covers a number of activities, which makes overall assessment difficult. When considering cybercrime of a sexual nature, for example, a clinical assessment tool for sexual offending that is also useful in assessing risk for online offenders may be useful. Although online sex offenders have not been included in the validation of the Risk Matrix 2000/Sex (RM2000/S) assessment tool (Thornton et al. 2003), the RM2000/S does include "being a non-contact offender" and "not knowing the victim" as aggravating factors; both of these factors are prevalent in online sexual offending. Similarly, the STABLE 2007 and ACUTE 2007 (Hanson, Harris, Scott, and Helmus 2007) assess trait characteristics that are also common in Internet offenders and these assessment tools can be useful in examining the level of risk that an online sexual offender presents (Elliott and Beech 2009).

Prostitution

The Vermont Assessment of Sex Offender Risk-2 (VASOR-2) is designed to assess risk among adult males who have been convicted of a qualifying sex offence (McGrath, Hoke, and Lasher 2013). This assessment consists of a 12-item reoffence risk scale and a 4-item severity factors checklist. Although this scale cannot be used for an offender convicted solely for prostitution, it can be used when a prostitution offence is committed in addition to contact sex offences such as sexual assault. The VASOR-2 can also be used to asses non-contact sex offences, such as exhibitionism, in addition to prostitution (McGrath, Hoke, and Lasher 2013). The VASOR-2 reoffence risk scale has been shown to have moderate accuracy in predicting recidivism.

Drug Trade

The Level of Service Inventory-Revised (LSI-R; Andrews and Bonta 1995) is an assessment tool that contains 54 items and covers different criminogenic domains such as criminal history, education/employment, alcohol and drug use, and emotional health. For those convicted of involvement in the drug trade, the LSI-R has been shown to be effective in predicting whether an offender will return to prison for similar drug trade offences. An offender's LSI-R scores are considered when making decisions involving sentencing, discretionary release opportunities, and/or parole eligibility (Iowa Department of Human Rights 2011).

Gangs

An assessment approach for gangs can be characterized as an approach for group-based violence (Cook 2014). This type of risk assessment can be applied to an individual who identifies with a larger group. The Multi-Level Guidelines approach is another way to assess group-based violence. This approach is a form of structured, professional-judgment

Box 6.2

You Be the Assessor

Amir Haybe was 10 when he moved into one a housing complex with his mother and younger sister. It was a high-density neighbourhood with large apartment buildings. Most residents were one-parent families that often included two or more children, many on social assistance. Although there was some ethnic diversity in the "hood," many were first generation Canadians. Drugs were sold and bought in the alleyways between buildings and sometimes in parking lots and on school grounds. It was not uncommon to see teens or younger children with knives and sometimes guns.

Now 13 years old, Amir resents that his mother has to work two low-paying jobs and still can't afford much. He knows that he could quickly make a lot of money by selling drugs, but the local drug business belongs to the Black Eagles. Amir decides to start the initiation process into the Black Eagles and before long is given his first "job" picking up some drugs at the Buffalo/Niagara Falls border. As he is waiting for his pick-up just outside the Niagara Falls city limits, he is arrested by the RCMP.

Questions

What factors might the RCMP want to assess to determine Amir's risk of continuing his gang-related behaviour? Develop an assessment tool that targets the behaviours that are critical to Amir's continued association with the Black Eagles.

risk assessment. It consists of 20 risk factors broken down into four categories: individual, individual-group, group, and group-societal. Factors that are examined include violent behaviour, group-based identity, group violence, and intergroup threat. This assessment is still relatively new. However, professionals that have utilized this assessment reported these guidelines to be useful and helpful for assessing group-based violence (Cook 2014).

As you can see, assessment approaches for economically motivated offenders is diverse and complex. Often, different aspects of the offence need to be considered to provide a comprehensive assessment. This may require the incorporation of several tools or risk assessment instruments. The You Be the Assessor box offers an opportunity to try your hand at assessment.

TREATMENT APPROACHES AND EFFECTIVENESS

GIVEN THE DIVERSITY OF ECONOMICALLY-MOTIVATED OFFENDERS, THERE ARE A MULTITUDE of intervention strategies ranging from systematic legislative attempts to prevent white-collar crime to individualized treatment programs targeting individual offenders.

White-Collar Crime Legislation

In 2003, the National White-Collar Crime Centre of Canada (NW4C) was incorporated under the *Canada Corporations Act* in order to prevent and respond to economic crime

Table 6.6 Legislation Prohibiting White-Collar Crime

Competition Act (1986): Prohibits advertising sales when prices have not been lowered, claiming a product can do something it cannot, and selling used cars as new cars
Food and Drugs Act (1985): Prohibits selling contaminated food and/or drugs
Hazardous Products Act (1985): Prohibits selling dangerous items
Immigration Act (2008): Prohibits bribing an immigration officer
Income Tax Act (2007): Prohibits tax evasion

by linking national and international systems through the Canadian Anti-Fraud Centre. There are a number of acts dealing with various forms of economically motivated crime, as outlined in Table 6.6.

White-collar criminals tend to work for the institution they are stealing from. This theft may be ongoing due to lack of detection, or the organization may prefer not to report it to avoid publicity. White-collar criminals may be fired and/or requested to pay back the equivalent of what they stole. Federal, provincial, and municipal laws prohibit various corporate crimes. Typically, government inspectors are responsible for the enforcement of corporate offences and tend to have less authority to investigate than police.

Property Crime Interventions

The Alternatives, Attitudes, and Associates Program is a commonly used treatment program for offenders who commit property crime (Correctional Service Canada 2014a; John Howard Society of Southeastern New Brunswick 2013). This program is geared towards offenders who have been identified as needing interventions in criminal attitude, values, and beliefs. A common goal is to teach goal-setting and problem-solving techniques. Offenders are taught self-management, emotion, and attitude skills. Additionally, the program emphasizes the importance of positive relationships and self-management. Typically, the program consists of 26 group sessions that vary in duration; most commonly the sessions last between two-and-a-half to three hours.

Fraud Interventions

A common program for an offender who commits an economic crime such as fraud is an all-day group session (Ascend Counseling 2015). The goal is to examine and challenge the motivation behind the crime. Moreover, the personal, legal, and societal consequences are discussed. Factors related to why offenders commit these types of crime are also examined. Offenders in this program discuss the potential risks and rewards of future crimes to help deter them from reoffending. For example, the impact of future crime is discussed in relation to legal, career, family, and personal impacts.

Cybercrime Interventions

There is no general treatment program for cybercriminals as a whole; however, treatment programs may be available for the specific type of offence committed. For example, the Lucy Faithful Foundation in the U.K. (a registered a child protection charity, see http://lucyfaithfull.org) has developed a program geared towards offenders who view online child pornography. This program allows offenders to discuss what they have done, the implications their actions have on both themselves and the children, and how they can prevent it from happening again. Offenders in this program are confronted with trying to figure out why they looked at the pictures and whether they do or do not have a sexual attraction to children. Offenders are taught to understand that the people in the pictures they are looking at and/or sharing are human beings that have rights and feelings. The program typically runs for 10 weeks with sessions lasting two-and-a-half hours. To date, it is unclear whether such a program is effective. Sexual offenders and related treatment approaches are covered in more detail in Chapter 12.

Prostitution Interventions

Women working in the sex trade may experience violence, substance abuse, physical and mental health issues, and homelessness. In order to address these issues, a group of Victoria, B.C., sex-trade workers formed an organization called PEERS (Prostitutes Empowerment Education and Resource Society) in 1995 (Rabinovitch and Strega 2004). PEERS is based on four principles:

1. Choice: PEERS supports both women who want to get out of the sex trade and those who want to continue working within it. PEERS focuses on providing sex-trade workers with concrete, practical, and accessible help without judgment.

2. Capacity building: PEERS recognizes the strengths of sex workers (e.g., communication and interpersonal skills, adaptability, ability to work under pressure, experience with difficult clients, and the ability to negotiate) and works to build on these skills through employee therapy, counselling, and chemical dependency treatment.

3. Harm reduction: A variety of programs are provide for people who are actively in addiction and working regularly in the trade.

4. Trust: Peer-led services are organized, in which sex-trade workers design and deliver their own services.

Through PEERS and organizations like it, sex-trade workers may become empowered to make choices in their best interests. Some workers will choose to remain in the profession and others may choose to leave it and enter mainstream employment. See if you can assess what types of intervention may be helpful in the scenario described in the You Be the Therapist box.

Box 6.3

You Be the Therapist

Flower Adams ran away when she was 10 years old. She slept in bus shelters and pan-handled for change. It didn't take long for Bad Boy Brown (B.B. for short) to notice her. B.B. took a keen interest in Flower and offered to look after her. Within a few weeks Flower was living in an apartment with some other "friends" of B.B. Soon thereafter, these friends introduced Flower to drugs and alcohol. B.B. would come by every couple of days to check on his "girls," but told Flower she was special to him and he wanted her to be his girlfriend. Being B.B.'s girlfriend made Flower feel important and she would do anything to keep B.B.

One night, B.B. asked Flower if she could do him a favour. He needed a pretty young girl to "dance" at his club. Flower was scared that if she said no, she would be back on the street, so she agreed. At first Flower was a background dancer

for the girls that took centre stage to strip. After a couple of weeks, it was Flower's turn to take centre stage. B.B. gave her cocaine before her show. Flower began stripping in two shows a night. She became popular with the men that frequented the club and they started asking for private time with her. B.B. told Flower that he needed her to do this. Reluctantly, Flower did two to three private shows a night. B.B. was pimping her out. She had to have sex with these men, who would then pay B.B. Flower wanted out but didn't know what to do. She had virtually no money of her own and nowhere to go.

Questions

What would you recommend to Flower? How might Flower get out of this life of stripping and prostitution?

Drug Trade Interventions

Offenders who have been convicted of low-level drug trade offences to sustain their own habit can attend a drug treatment court (DTC; Rideauwood Addiction and Family Services 2015; Toronto Drug Treatment Court 2015). The first phase in DTC is the dependency assessment, in which the individual's drug use history, consequences of drug use, and social support are examined. This is also the first step in developing the individual's treatment plan. The offender then goes through orientation and stabilization, which consists of group sessions that discuss the norms of DTC. Prior to intensive treatment, individuals go to three two-hour support group sessions for four to eight weeks to work on discontinuing drug use and developing links to community resources. Once the intensive treatment plan is set in place, individuals attend two-hour group sessions four times a week for three weeks. This is where the individuals are taught to recognize their triggers, understand functions of drug use, and learn how to develop positive coping mechanisms. After intensive treatment is complete, individuals attend group sessions bi-weekly for three more months. Therapy is also used to help offenders learn to overcome their behaviours. The goal is for the offender to be more inclined to make better decisions and fewer mistakes.

Gang Interventions

Gang intervention is an incredibly complex issue. The Little Village Gang Violence Reduction Project (GVRP; Spergel 2007) was a community-wide program designed to reduce serious violence in Chicago's gang-ridden Little Village neighbourhood. The goals of the program were to reduce the high level of serious gang violence at the individual and aggregate level. The program takes an integrated, community-wide approach that includes law enforcement, social welfare agencies, and grassroots organizations all working together in a team-oriented manner. The programs five core principles are:

1. Community mobilization—community leaders and residents are involved
2. Social intervention—multidisciplinary teams provide outreach to at-risk and current gang members and provide an array of services
3. Provision of academic, economic, and social opportunities
4. Gang suppression—gang-involved youth are held accountable for their actions
5. Facilitating organizational change and development—support is provided to the community to solve the gang problem

The comparison groups in the Little Village project were predominately male Latinos. A total of 493 youth fully participated in the program, 90 youth received some programming, and 208 youth did not participate. Arrest levels during the 4.5 years preceding program were compared with levels during the 4.5 years the program was in place and study results were mixed. Overall arrest rates did not differ across groups and no differences were observed in property-related crime. However, some evidence for reductions in violence-related arrests was found. Due to these mixed results, the program is no longer in operation. The lack of success may have been due to program implementation problems and unsuccessful community mobilization. Some components may actually have increased gang cohesiveness (e.g., having rival gangs play softball). Finally, none of the programming targeted criminal thinking or the cognitive distortions held by gang members (Spergel 2007).

FUTURE DIRECTIONS

ECONOMICALLY MOTIVATED OFFENDERS ARE A DIVERSE GROUP CROSSING SOCIO-ECONOMICAL lines, education levels, and ethnicities. It is difficult to develop assessment and treatment for this diverse group. Comprehensive assessment and treatment requires a multi-faceted approach. A rapidly growing area of concern within this diverse group involves the use of the Internet. Economically motivated crime is increasingly committed using online technology, often crossing provincial and international borders. Local, national, and international criminal justice organizations will need to work together to develop adequate approaches to dealing with modern crime.

SUMMARY

1. White-collar crime is categorized into occupational crime and corporate crime. Occupational crimes are offences committed against businesses and government, generally by those with a "higher" social status. Examples include expense account fraud and tax evasion. In contrast, corporate crimes are committed by organizations to advance their own interests. Corporate crime offences include price fixing. The distinction between occupational and corporate crime can be thought of as occupational crime being committed by individuals and corporate crime being committed by organizations.

2. Theft is the notion of "stealing." That is, taking something that belongs to someone else. Theft is covered in section 322 of the Canadian *Criminal Code*. There is a demarcation line at $5000 when deciding on punishment for theft. Fraud occurs when deceit or fraudulent means are used to deprive someone of property, money, valuable security, or services. The *Criminal Code* defines fraud in section 380. Similar to theft, fraud offences are categorized in the justice system as fraud under $5000 or fraud over $5000. Many thefts also can be frauds and it is sometimes up to the police to decide whether to charge an offender with fraud or theft.

3. Compared to non-prostitute youth, adolescent prostitutes are more frequently classified as runaways and use a wider variety of drugs, whereas the non-prostitute youth tend to experience more childhood physical abuse. Although adolescent prostitutes often have a number of issues (e.g., abuse, poor family relations, low self-esteem), these variables are also present in adolescents who are not prostitutes. Prostitution clients are significantly less likely to subscribe to a feminine sex role orientation, have lower social–sexual effectiveness, and have higher sensation-seeking tendencies.

4. A "criminal organization" is defined in section 467.1 of the *Criminal Code* as a group that is: 1) composed of three or more persons in or outside of Canada; and 2) has as one of its main purposes or activities the facilitation or commission of one or more serious offences that, if committed, would likely result in the direct or indirect receipt of material benefit, including financial benefit, by the group or by any of the persons who constitute the group.

5. Organized crime groups engage in fraud (including mass-marketing fraud and intellectual property rights crime), the sex trade (including prostitution and human trafficking), and the drug trade (including the importation and distribution of a variety of drugs such a marijuana and cocaine).

Discussion Questions

1. During your summer job at a large manufacturing company, you notice that the supply cabinet has many of the office supplies (e.g., paper, pens, Post-it notes, binders, etc.)

you will need when you go back to school in September. You decide to take a few things each week, believing that such a large corporation won't notice the items as missing. Debate whether your actions constitute white-collar crime or theft.

2. You volunteer at an after-school drop-in program for teens aged 13 to 16. Many of the teens have difficult home lives. List factors that should be targeted to reduce the likelihood that these teens will run away and become prostitutes.

3. Debate whether the legalization of drugs would reduce drug trafficking.

4. After being declined for a credit card, you contact your bank to better understand why your application was rejected. It soon becomes clear that someone has stolen your identity, obtained and used numerous credit cards in your name, and defaulted on the debts. What are some strategies to prevent this from happening to others?

Chapter 7
Substance Abusing Offenders

Sam had never really been in trouble with the police before. He wasn't exactly a straight-A student but his grades were ok, and he had never been suspended from school. His dad died when he was 15. He and his mom had to move to a new neighbourhood and his mom had to take on a second job at night to make ends meet. Sam had a lot of unstructured, free time on his hands. His mom wasn't around much to supervise his whereabouts. He met a group of different friends in his new neighbourhood. His new peer group just "hung out," listened to music, smoked pot, drank lots of beer and whisky, and occasionally dabbled in harder drugs like crack cocaine. Some of Sam's new acquaintances had also been arrested previously for some pretty serious crimes like break-and-enters and robbery. While Sam was no stranger to the occasional joint or binge-drinking incident, he had never tried anything harder before. Eventfully, curiosity and peer pressure got the best of him and he finally tried crack for the first time, and then a second time. Then he couldn't stop. However, he wasn't working, and his allowance certainly wasn't sufficient to support his new habit. One night, Sam and his buddies ran out of booze and drugs. Collectively, they had less than five dollars. In the spur of the moment, they decided to rob the corner store down the street, thinking it would be an easy way to get some cash for more drugs and alcohol. A few of the guys had previously gotten away with robbing this particular corner store. Sam and his buddies were arrested for robbery. Sam is currently serving a one-year sentence in a youth custody facility.

Learning Objectives

1   Describe the nature and prevalence of substance abuse within criminal populations.

2   Describe prominent theories of substance abuse.

3   Review key theories linking substance abuse and crime.

4   Describe risk factors leading to crime among substance users.

5   Illustrate the complex relationship between substance abuse and crime.

6   Describe how substance abuse is assessed within correctional populations.

7   Describe and evaluate justice-based intervention for substance abusers.

INTRODUCTION

The opening vignette demonstrates just one possible pathway through which drugs can lead to criminal justice involvement. Thus far in the textbook we have learned that substance abuse is a risk factor for criminal conduct. Recall that Andrews and Bonta (2010) have identified substance abuse as one of the Central Eight risk factors (see Chapter 1) for criminal behaviour. As well, in Chapter 6 we were briefly introduced to the drug trade and how the drug trade is a defining feature of organized crime. We now examine more closely how an individual's substance use may either directly or indirectly lead to criminal justice involvement.

We begin the chapter by providing some historical context about substance abuse and crime. Then we devote time to defining the term "drug," followed by a review of prominent definitions used in the literature to describe when the use of substances becomes a problem. We also discuss the research illustrating the astonishingly high number of offenders who were either intoxicated at the time of their crime, or who would be assessed as having a substance abuse problem by any definition or measure after the fact. Next, we delve into prominent theories of substance abuse itself and examine perspectives that have tried to explain the substance use/crime relationship. We also talk about the risk factors leading to criminal conduct among substance abusers, as well as some promising protective factors. Finally, we explore how substance abuse is commonly assessed and treated in correctional settings.

CONTEXT

Substance use and abuse is prevalent in all societies (Durrant and Thakker 2003). Moreover, substance use has been around for a very, very long time. Chemical analysis of Stone Age pottery jugs provides strong evidence that alcoholic beverages have been around since 10 000 B.C., first emerging in the Middle East (Patrick 1952). As well, the use of marijuana for medicinal purposes dates back to approximately 2800 B.C. in ancient China (Abel 1980). However, it was Lombroso, the father of criminology (see Chapter 2) who was one of the first criminological scholars to observe a link between alcohol consumption and crime.

Our understanding of substance abuse and how it impacts individuals, families, and societies has proliferated exponentially since the first Alcoholics Anonymous program was established in Akron, Ohio in 1935 (Alcoholics Anonymous 2015). The 1970s in particular gave birth to the medical or disease model of addictions with the pivotal discovery regarding the role of dopamine in drug addictions (Nutt, Lingford-Huges, Erritzoe, and Stokes 2015). Although the disease model of addictions remains endorsed by prominent figures (e.g., Nora Volkow, Director of the National Institute on Drug Abuse (NIDA 2014)), it has received strong opposition from equally reputable sources; namely a Canadian neuroscientist, Marc Lewis (2015).

Countless studies have examined the nature and prevalence of substance abuse within criminal populations. As well, there are numerous assessment methods and treatment options available to offenders, ranging from motivational interviewing and cognitive behavioural treatments to pharmacological interventions such as methadone maintenance programs.

Further, these treatment programs are offered to offenders in prison once they have been formally convicted and processed through the regular court system. However, substance-abusing offenders are increasingly being diverted out of the regular court system and into specialized drug courts that deal exclusively with substance-abusing offenders. We will learn more about treatment approaches currently available to offenders later on in the chapter.

DEFINITIONS

The Oxford dictionary defines a drug as a substance that impacts the body in a physiological sense once ingested. Interestingly however, the Oxford dictionary categorizes drug use as illegal if drugs are consumed for their stimulant effects. (Oxford Dictionary, n.d.). Thus, while drugs can be classified as legal ("licit") or illegal ("illicit"), they have one feature in common—all drugs impact our mind and body physiologically. As well, both legal and illegal drugs can be further described as synthetic or natural. While humans manufacture synthetic drugs, natural drugs, are (as you would expect) found in nature (e.g., marijuana). However, sometimes the distinction is not so clear. More often than not, "natural" illegal drugs are laced with other additives that may be synthetic. Lastly, although we may not typically think of alcohol, caffeine, or cigarettes as drugs because of their legal status, they are drugs nonetheless. See Table 7.1 for an overview of various drugs and their classifications.

The use of marijuana for recreational purposes is illegal in Canada. However, it is estimated that 10 to 15 percent of all adults, and 20 to 30 percent of young adults

---

Table 7.1 Drug Categories

Legal Drugs	Illegal Drugs (grown, manufactured, or some combination thereof)
Alcohol	Cocaine and crack
Tobacco/cigarettes	Magic mushrooms
Caffeine/energy drinks	Heroin (opioids)
Inhalants (e.g., glue, fuel, paints)	Marijuana (cannabis), hash and hash oil[1]
Prescription Drugs	**Illegal Drugs (synthetic)**
Anabolic steroids	Meth (methamphetamine)
Painkillers (e.g., morphine, oxycodone/ oxycontin, codeine)	Ecstasy (MDMA)
Stimulants (e.g., Ritalin, Adderall)	Acid (LSD)
Tranquilizers/Barbiturates (e.g., Valium, Xanax, Ativan)	GHB (gammahydroxybutyrate)
	PCP (phencyclidine)
	Ketamine
	Bath salts (synthetic cathinones)
	Spice (synthetic Cannabinoids)

[1] In Canada, marijuana use is legal when prescribed by a physician for medicinal purposes (see the Media Spotlight for further discussion).

Source: Adapted from RCMP (2015d).

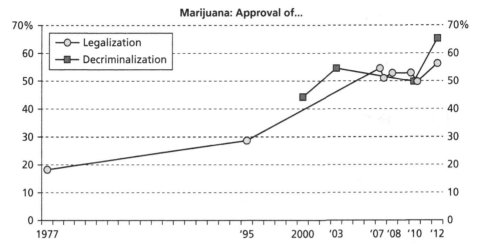

Marijuana: Approval of...

Figure 7.1 data showing two lines — Legalization (open circles) and Decriminalization (filled squares) — plotted from 1977 to '12, with percent approval on both vertical axes (0% to 70%).

Figure 7.1 Canadian Public Support for Marijuana Use Over Time

Source: Grenier (2013)

currently use marijuana recreationally (Health Canada 2014). Further, there is growing public support for both the decriminalization and legalization of marijuana (Grenier 2013), as illustrated in Figure 7.1. Although marijuana for medicinal purposes is now legal in Canada, this has not always been the case. See the Media Spotlight box for some background on the legalization of marijuana for medical use in Canada.

Media Spotlight

When Marijuana Use Is Legal

Mr. Green/Shutterstock

Growing Marijuana Plants

Owen Smith worked for the Cannabis Buyers Club of Canada. Part of Mr. Smith's duties involved the production of edible marijuana products for medicinal purposes. In December 2009, Smith was arrested and charged for producing baked goods containing marijuana—a direct violation of the *Controlled Drug and Substance Act*. Notably, at the time of his arrest, the production of dried marijuana leaves for medicinal purposes was indeed legal as per the *Marihuana Medical Access Regulations* (MMAR; Government of Canada 2013), the production of editable forms of marijuana was not. Mr. Smith's case eventually made its way to the Supreme Court of Canada. In June of 2015 the Supreme Court of Canada ruled that the regulations set out in the MMAR were unconstitutional and Mr. Smith was acquitted of all charges (*R. v. Smith* 2015).

Although cannabis (marijuana) has been used for medicinal purposes for over 4000 years in some cultures, its medicinal use in Canada has only been legal for less than 20. Health Canada provides access to marijuana for individuals identified by physicians as experiencing medical symptoms that could be therapeutically improved by the use of medical marijuana. Medical use is currently regulated by the *Marihuana for Medicine Purposes Regulations* (MMPR) (Government of Canada 2013). It is estimated that there are 37 000 Canadian adults currently approved to use marijuana for medicinal purposes, and that this number will grow to almost 500 000 people by 2024 (*Globe and Mail* 2013). As well, there are currently 26 licensed producers of medicinal marijuana across Canada— the vast majority can be found in Ontario (14) and British Columbia (6) (Health Canada 2015a).

The timeline below outlines how legalization of medicinal marijuana developed in Canada since 1999 (Canadian Press 2014; Health Canada 2015b).

- 1999: Courts allow two Canadian medical patients to use marijuana.
- 2000: Courts rule Canadians have a constitutional right to use marijuana for medical purposes.
- July 2001: Health Canada implements the *Marihuana Medical Access Regulations* (MMAR), making Canada the first country in the world to allow citizens to legally access marijuana for medicinal purposes.
- September 2002: Recommendations are put forth to amend the MMAR to establish new

rules regarding eligibility, production, and distribution of medicinal marijuana.

- August 2003: Health Canada distributes the first batch of medicinal marijuana. Consumers are unsatisfied with the quality.
- December 2003: Amendments are made to the MMAR.
- May 2004: The second batch of medicinal marijuana is distributed.
- November 2004: The third batch is released, with more changes.
- February 2005: The *Income Tax Act* allows medicinal marijuana expenses as an eligible medical tax credit.
- March 2005: The fourth batch of medicinal marijuana, with greater potency, is distributed.
- June 2013: *Marihuana for Medicine Purposes Regulations* (MMPR) comes into force, shifting medical marijuana access rules from home-grown production to licensed commercial producers. As well, physicians (rather than the government) are now responsible for authorizing patient use of medical cannabis based on broader criteria (if the patient will therapeutically benefit from the use of cannabis). The MMPR only authorizes the use of dried marijuana leaves or a vaporized format; oral ingestion (e.g., food or capsules) is prohibited.
- March 2014: *Marihuana Medical Access Regulations* (MMAR) are officially repealed.
- March 2014: The Federal Court grants a temporary injunction allowing for continued use of home-grown marijuana for medicinal purposes pending legal arguments.
- June 2015: In *R. v. Smith*, the Supreme Court of Canada rules that the MMPR laws prohibiting the oral ingestion of cannabis are unconstitutional.
- Present day: Government is appealing the *R v. Smith* decision.

Popular culture and scientific literature are replete with terms such as alcoholism, addiction, substance abuse, substance misuse, binge drinking, and substance abuse disorder. While there are some nuanced differences between these terms, they do have one common underlying feature—the ingestion of the substance in question causes some degree of harm to the individual and those around him or her. See Table 7.2 for some

Table 7.2 Definitions of Substance Abuse and Healthy Alcoholic Drinking

- **National Institute on Drug Abuse (NIDA):** "Addiction is defined as a chronic, relapsing brain disease that is characterized by compulsive drug seeking and use, despite harmful consequences" (2014:1).
- **World Health Organization:** "Substance abuse refers to the harmful or hazardous use of psychoactive substances, including alcohol and illicit drugs. Psychoactive substance use can lead to dependence syndrome—a cluster of behavioural, cognitive, and physiological phenomena that develop after repeated substance use and that typically include a strong desire to take the drug, difficulties in controlling its use, persisting in its use despite harmful consequences, a higher priority given to drug use than to other activities and obligations, increased tolerance, and sometimes a physical withdrawal state" (2015).
- **American Psychiatric Association:** The Diagnostic and Statistical Manual of Mental Disorders, Fifth Edition (DSM-5; American Psychiatric Association, 2013 has 10 separate substance abuse-related categories such as alcohol-related disorders, cannabis-related disorders, hallucinogen-related disorders, and inhalant-related disorders. The DSM-5 actually has 10 separate substance abuse-related categories, such as alcohol-related disorders, cannabis-related disorders, hallucinogen-related disorders, and inhalant-related disorders. Also, the DSM-5 purposely does not use the word "addiction." The APA argues that the term "substance abuse disorder" is more neutral and encompasses the full spectrum of related problems from mild to severe. Notably, the term "addiction" is still used in some circles to denote severe forms of substance abuse problems.
- **Centre for Addiction and Mental Health (CAMH):** Binge drinking is defined as having many drinks on one occasion: five or more drinks if you are male, four or more if you are female (CAMH 2008). However, both Health Canada and the World Health Organization define heavy drinking as binge drinking that occurs at least once per month over the course of a year.
- **Canadian Centre on Substance Abuse (CCSA):** In 2011, the CCSA published Canada's first set of low-risk alcohol drinking guidelines. These guidelines recommend that men have no more than 15 drinks per week, and women no more than 10. The guidelines further state that men should have no more than 3 drinks per occasion, whereas women should have no more than 2 drinks per occasion. However, for special occasions, the amounts can be increased to 4 and 3 for men and women respectively (CCSA 2013).

currently recognized definitions in scientific literature. Importantly, the table also provides Canada's recommended healthy drinking guidelines.

WHY DO WE CARE?

The last systematic analysis of the economic costs associated with substance abuse in Canada was published in 2006. According to this study, the cost to arrest, prosecute, and sentence offenders for illicit drug use and trafficking approached 8.2 billion dollars in 2002 (Rehm et al., 2006). Official crime statistics tell a similar story—a significant amount of crime is linked to substance abuse; so much so, that a causal relationship is often inferred with little debate. In 2013, 2.1 million incidents were reported to police, of which 5 percent (or 1 in 20) had as the most serious crime—a crime(s) against the *Controlled Drugs and Substances Act* (CDSA) (Statistics Canada 2014b), albeit, cannabis possession accounts for 54 percent of all police-reported drug offences (Cotter, Greenland, and Karam 2015). Interestingly, although the crime rate has decreased by 50 percent since 1991, the rate of police-reported drug offences has actually increased by 52 percent.

Research has also revealed more nuanced results. For example, we know that next to administration of justice offences (e.g., breach of probation, failure to appear in court), driving while impaired is the number-one crime prosecuted in the court system (Public Safety Canada 2015a). The link between violence and alcohol is overwhelming. In 2013, almost 75 percent of Canadians accused of homicide were under the influence of alcohol, drugs, or another intoxicating substance at the time of the offence (Cotter et al. 2015). Similarly, 29 percent of physical assaults and 27 percent of weapons-related crimes co-occurred with drug-related offences (Cotter et al. 2015). Not to mention, a staggering number of incarcerated inmates were under the influence of illegal drugs or alcohol during the crime that lead to their incarceration (Johnson 2004; Kouyoumdjian et al. 2014).

The prevalence of substance abuse among incarcerated populations is astonishing. While only 2 percent of Canadians reported using an illicit drug other than cannabis within the last year (Government of Canada 2015a), 63 percent of offenders reported using alcohol or drugs on the day of the crime that brought them to federal custody (Ternes and Johnson 2011). Moreover, 77 percent of female offenders within the federal correctional system have been assessed as having some issue with substances, and 55 percent have been identified as having moderate to severe substance abuse needs (MacDonald 2014). The prevalence of substance abuse among Aboriginal offenders is equally high. Eighty-two percent of Aboriginal offenders have been identified as having a substance abuse need upon admission to the federal correctional system (Correctional Service Canada 2013b).

Given these exceedingly high prevalence rates, it may seem a forgone conclusion that substance abuse must be causally linked to crime. However, as we will soon see, the relationship is more complex. More often than not, other criminal risk factors often co-exist alongside substance abuse that catapult an individual from a begin drug addict to becoming a multi-talented criminal.

METHODOLOGY

Researchers who study substance abuse, as well as the substance abuse/crime link have used virtually every possible method available. Neuroscientists have used animal studies and human brain scans to learn how drugs alter brain chemistry. Twin and adoption studies dominate in attempts to unravel the contributions of nature and nurture to the development of substance abuse. Psychologists have even studied the effects of alcohol on the brain under controlled conditions in laboratory settings. Criminologists and correctional researchers have interviewed substance users, analyzed official crime statistics, administered countless surveys, and synthesized substance abuse treatment outcome studies. As a result, the research evidence reviewed in the next section is rather eclectic.

THEORIES OF SUBSTANCE ABUSE

The theoretical landscape that attempts to explain substance abuse problems is vast and complex. As well, the reasons why someone initially develops a substance abuse problem are sometimes different from why they *continue* to abuse drugs. Also, as we shall see, while some people may be genetically predisposed to drug use, it doesn't necessarily mean that they will inevitably develop a substance abuse problem. Like most other domains of human behaviour, scientists are still trying to unravel the nature/nurture relationship in the field of substance abuse.

In this section we briefly review three overarching theories aimed at understanding why people develop and maintain drug addictions (Lewis 2015). First, we start at the level of the brain and try to understand how drugs alter the neurochemistry of our brains—this is typically known as the disease model. Then we will explore a social learning perspective and a self-medication model.

The Brain and Addictions—The Disease Model

The **dopamine** theory of reward and addictions is perhaps the longest-standing theory for why people become addicted to substances (Nutt et al. 2015). It is also strongly endorsed by leading experts in the field such as Nora Volkow, Director of the National Institute on Substance Abuse (NIDA) in the United States. In sum, the theory argues that drugs stimulate the dopamine neurotransmitter system in the brain, which in turn causes direct pleasurable or euphoric sensations—a "high." It is also important to note that dopamine is pivotal for motivating and driving goal-directed behaviour (Lewis 2015). Thus, individuals are motivated to continue using drugs because of the rewarding or positive reinforcing effects that dopamine activation has on the brain. Moreover, this perspective underscores how the brain physically changes in response to repeated drug use—namely in the areas of judgment, decision making, learning, memory, and behaviour control (National Institute on Drug Abuse 2014). Although the dopamine theory of reward and addictions is firmly grounded in neurochemistry, it also actively integrates some of the most basic tenets of

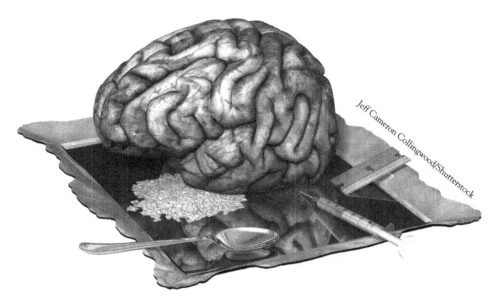

The disease model of addiction: drug addiction is a brain addiction.

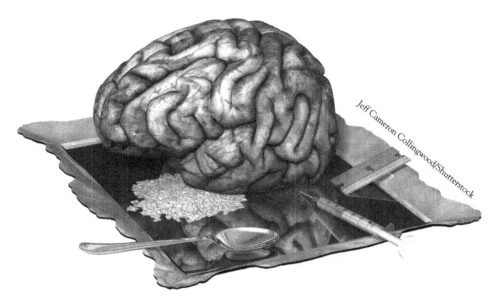

Jeff Cameron Collingwood/Shutterstock

psychology—motivation and positive reinforcement. Thus, other researchers refer to the dopamine theory of reward and addictions as a biopsychological theory of addictions (see DeMatteo, Filone, and Davis 2015). However, Marc Lewis, a former-addict-turned-neuroscientist (also a Canadian), still refers to this model as the disease model.

Nutt et al. (2015) have cogently criticized the universality of the dopamine theory of addictions for a few key reasons. First, not all drugs actually alter the brain's dopamine neurotransmitter system. While there is evidence that stimulants, such as cocaine, activate the brain's dopamine system, there is no clear evidence that cannabis, ketamine, or opiates do so. Further, the evidence appears to be mixed regarding the effects of alcohol and cigarettes on the dopamine system.

Second, Nutt et al. challenge the basic assumption underlying the dopamine theory of addiction—that dopamine release is the key causal mechanism that directly causes drug addiction due to dopamine's euphoric effects. Alternatively, Nutt et al. point to existing research showing that there may be an alternative pathway: that dopamine release leads to increased impulsivity, which in turn leads to addiction. In fact there is increasing evidence that the various dopamine mechanisms that have historically only been used to explain substance-related addictions may also help explain other disorders characterized by impulsivity such as attention deficit hyperactivity disorder (ADHD) and pathological gambling (Reeves et al. 2012; Trifilieff and Martinez 2014).

Genetics and Substance Abuse Researchers have spent considerable time examining the link between genetics and crime and have used twin and adoption studies to help tease out the relative contributions of genetics and the environment. Evidence from twin and adoption studies have consistently shown that genetics plays at least a moderate (and sometimes a strong) role in explaining substance use. Kendler (2001) reported that the heritability estimates for sedative, stimulant, cocaine, and opiate use range from 60 to 80 percent. The heritability estimates for alcoholism among males are lower, but still substantial, at 50 to 60 percent (Kendler et al. 1994; Prescott et al. 2005). However, the alcoholism heritability findings among females are mixed. Kendler et al. found evidence for stronger heritability effect among females, while Prescott et al. reported environmental factors to be more important among females.

The genetics research also tells us that there are potentially many more genetically inherited factors that may make someone more susceptible to developing a substance-related addiction. For example, other inherited behavioural, temperamental, and personality traits may either increase the risk for developing an addiction, or reduce the risk for developing an addiction (protective factors). Quinn and Fromme (2010) reported that traits of alienation, anger, interaction anxiety, and lower self-regulation predicted adolescent drug use. Also, some research has shown how several genes that control the sensitivity to acute intoxication and alcohol withdrawal are protective against alcoholism (Hinckers et al. 2006; Pihl 2009). Having higher dopamine receptor availability may protect against alcohol abuse among genetically high-risk individuals (Volkow et al. 2006).

The Social Learning or "Choice" Model

According to Lewis (2015), the **social learning** perspective underscores individual choice. The basic tenet of this perspective is that addiction is a choice. More importantly, it is a *rational* choice in which individuals opt for short-term rewards in exchange for the long-term consequences of drug abuse. However, a common criticism levied against this model is that it panders to the earliest perspectives that viewed addicts as indulgent, weak individuals with no will power. This model seems to explain why individuals may start and eventfully stop substance abuse, while the disease model explains its maintenance (Lewis 2015). The social learning model also emphasizes a number of broader contextual factors such as poverty and social isolation. Importantly, Lewis (2015) has recast the traditional social learning perspective of addictions with a "choice" model. Or, more generously, Lewis equates social learning with choice.

The Self-Medication Model

Lewis argues that this model is rooted in psychology, sociology, and medicine. Essentially this theory argues that individuals start using drugs to cope with stress and related negative outcomes associated with trauma and abuse. Psychoactive drugs do relieve anxiety and stop rumination in the short term. But as Lewis so eloquently illustrates, these drugs eventfully become the source of the problem rather than the solution. In most cases, mood and anxiety problems will occur before the onset of substance abuse, suggesting that individuals self-medicate with alcohol or drugs to temporarily diminish their anxiety (Lewis 2015).

A variety of sources support the self-medication theory. However, much of this support comes from research on female offenders (see Chapter 13). The "feminist pathways" perspective on female criminal conduct posits that a number of girls are pushed out of their homes due to abuse and choose to self-medicate to deal with the anxiety and depression associated with early traumas, which in turn may lead to criminal justice involvement. The self-medication model is also consistent with the fact that so many individuals—men and women alike—suffer from co-occurring addictions and internalizing mental health disorders. For example, a recent study reported that women participating in methadone maintenance treatment had a substantial number of mental health issues including depression (63 percent), anxiety (62 percent), and panic disorder (32 percent). Many had also experienced physical (81 percent), mental (74 percent), and sexual (67 percent) trauma (MacSwain, Cheverie, Farrell MacDonald, and Johnson 2014).

In sum, Lewis explicitly advocates for a new conceptualization of addictions—one that views addictions as a learned behaviour rather than a disease of the mind. Lewis is not arguing against the disease model of addiction, but is advocating for a more integrated perspective that will empower individuals with addictions. This in turn will encourage individuals to believe that they are not powerless against their "disease" and have the power to take control of their lives once again.

THEORIES EXPLAINING THE SUBTANCE ABUSE/ CRIME LINK

ONE OF THE PREVAILING PERSPECTIVES USED TO ACCOUNT FOR WHY SUBSTANCE ABUSE leads to crime is that the addiction comes first and crime follows in order to feed the addiction. The You Be the Assessor box illustrates this approach. The overwhelming prevalence of substance abuse among offender populations has led many scholars and laypeople to assume that crime and substance abuse are directly and causally related (DeMatteo, Filone, and Davis 2015). However, it should come as no surprise that the relationship is more complex and definitely not always causal. An alternate perspective proposes that substance abuse is merely an extension of an already deviant lifestyle. Moreover, there are a myriad of additional risk factors interacting with substance abuse in complex ways that ultimately culminate in criminal conduct (Sinha and Easton 1999). McMurran's (2012) theory of the alcohol–violence relationship is a classic example of the latter perspective.

In brief, McMurran argues that the relationship between alcohol consumption and violence depends on a variety of factors related to the person, the context, the nature of the alcohol consumption, and the situation. First, is the person predisposed toward aggression, irrespective of the amount of alcohol consumed? Second, what is the degree

You Be the Assessor

Sarah Jacobs has spent most of her adult life living in crack houses and cheap motels. As a child, she ran away from home to escape repeated sexual abuse at the hands of her stepfather. Her biological mother turned a blind eye to what was happening and told Sarah that she needed to "either shut-up or get out." She chose to get out. Sarah left her home when she was 15 and never looked back.

At the height of her addiction, Sarah spent weeks scoring and smoking crack. By the time Sarah turned 45 she had accrued 35 convictions for prostitution and theft-related crimes. Her life was drugs, guns, and pimps. All of Sarah's crimes were motivated by her need to support her drug habit, which cost her upwards of $300 a day.

Sarah did try to quit a few times. She was sick of her life. At times she felt so hopeless she secretly wished the next hit would kill her. However, the benefits of continued drug use simply outweighed the costs. Physiologically, her withdrawal symptoms were unbearable. But they were nothing compared to the emotional distress that came with being straight. In Sarah's own words, "I was in love that drug... it made all my worries disappear... it numbed the pain, the disappointment about the past and future."

All of Sarah's relationships were abusive. In her teens, it was her pimp that first introduced her to cannabis, then acid, and then crack. Sarah never wanted to use any of these drugs but she felt she had no choice. Or did she? At age 45, Sarah is currently serving a 3-year sentence for trafficking cocaine, possession of proceeds of a crime, and aggravated assault.

Questions

How would you explain Sarah's drug addiction using the disease, self-medication, and/or social learning models? If you were Sarah's therapist, what kind of counselling, medical support, and/or behavioural therapy do you think would help her? If Sarah beats her drug addiction, would that also mean she wouldn't commit any more crimes? Does Sarah have other treatment targets that need to be addressed? Can you speculate what her correctional treatment plan might look like?

and speed of intoxication? Third, what is the context—who is the individual drinking with and where? Interestingly, about 50 percent of substance abusers use substances in the presence of others (Wakeman et al. 2009). Lastly, has the individual encountered provocation? See Figure 7.2 for a visual representation of McMurran's model.

McMurran (2013) appropriately cautions that despite the clear link between alcohol and crime, the nature of its influence is unclear. That is, does alcohol cause crime directly through diminished inhibitory control or increased cognitive impairment? If so, then substance abuse is an important treatment target. If, however, alcohol is mediated by another factor such as personality or social cues, then such an influence may not be addressed by a program that simply addresses an addiction problem, at least for offenders.

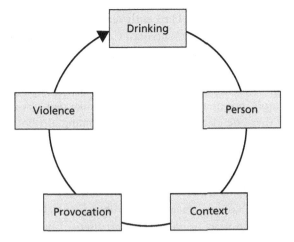

Figure 7.2 A Model for Understanding the Alcohol–Violence Relationship

Source: Adapted from McMurran (2013).

FACTORS ASSOCIATED WITH CRIME AMONG SUBSTANCE ABUSING INDIVIDUALS

ANDREWS AND BONTA (2010) CATEGORIZE SUBSTANCE ABUSE AS A MODERATE RISK FACTOR for criminal conduct. This is further supported by meta-analytic evidence illustrating that treating substance abuse reduces criminal recidivism (Dowden and Andrews 2000). Many studies have established that substance abuse is predictive of future crime in both males and females (e.g., Dowden and Brown 2002). However, researchers rarely ask the question, "when does substance use or abuse actually increase the odds that someone will also engage in criminal conduct?" There are two plausible answers to this question that depend on: 1) the nature of the drug and the type of crime we are interested in examining, and 2) how many additional criminal risk factors are present.

Type of Drug by Type of Crime: An Interaction Effect?

There appears to be growing evidence for the hypothesis that whether or not substance use translates into criminal conduct (above and beyond the illegal drug use itself) depends on two factors: the nature of the drug involve and the type of crime we are interested in predicting.

As discussed previously, alcohol use is linked more with interpersonal conflicts such as assault and homicide, whereas illicit drug use is linked with instrumental violence such as robbery (Goldstein 1985; Kunic and Grant 2007; Pernanen, Cousineau, Brochu, and

Sun 2002). Ternes and Johnson (2011) recently reaffirmed these finding, at least in part. In a study involving 10 845 federally sentenced Canadian male offenders, 82 percent of the sample reported committing an instrumental crime (e.g., theft, robbery, drug-related) whilst under the influence of an illicit drug. In contrast, only 31 percent of the offenders who were under the influence of a drug also admitted to committing expressive forms of violence such as assault, sexual assault, or murder. Unlike past research, the researchers in this study found that offenders who reported consuming alcohol on the day of their offence(s) were equally likely to report committing either expressive or instrumental type crimes (53 percent vs. 51 percent, respectively).

Another study involving women suggests that the use of "harder" drugs in particular is linked to financially-motivated crime. Miller and Neaigus (2002) examined the life histories of 28 drug-abusing women from low-income neighbourhoods in New York City. The women were 18 years or older and were users of heroin (79 percent), crack (43 percent), or cocaine (21 percent). Of interest to the researchers was how the women financed their drug use. Most reported engaging in illegal activities to acquire money and/or drugs. Seventy-five percent reported working in the drug trade, 68 percent stole, and 68 percent worked in street-based prostitution. In addition, 79 percent of the women had sex partners who would provide financial compensation and/or other benefits (i.e., drug supply). Eighty-nine percent of the women had been arrested for drug offences. Overall, the vast majority of the respondents financed their illegal drug use by illegal means.

Presence of Additional Risk Factors

An additional area of research in this field has also considered how substance abuse may or may not interact with other criminogenic risk factors to enhance the likelihood of future crime. McMurran's model discussed above is a perfect illustration of this approach. Recall that McMurran's model posits that alcohol use in and of itself is not a sufficient causal factor in the prediction of violence. Rather, it depends on the level of intoxication, the context (is there provocation?), and the person (does this person have a tendency to respond with attributions of hostile intent, regardless of whether or not he/she is intoxicated?).

Alternatively, another way to think about this perspective is as follows. How likely is your best friend—lets call him Robert—to end up in a police cruiser when he is intoxicated or stoned? Is the answer "highly unlikely"? If so, why? Possibly because Robert has never broken a law in his life, he respects the police, wouldn't hurt a fly, has no criminal friends to encourage him in the moment, and he has a strong sense of what is right and wrong. Thus, no matter how cognitively impaired or behaviourally inhibited Robert may be due to his extreme level of intoxication, there is virtually no chance of him committing a crime.

Alternatively, let's consider Frank. All of Frank's friends are criminal. Frank has been in and out of jail over the last five years, firmly believes that "laws are made to be broken," and has a hard time controlling his temper even when he is sober. So, what are the odds that Frank will end up in a police cruiser after a night of hard drinking? The odds are substantially higher. Why? Because Frank possesses a number of additional risk factors that already elevate his risk to commit crime. Being intoxicated or stoned exacerbates this pre-existing risk by impairing Frank's judgment and lowering his behavioural inhibitions even further.

Protective Factors

The role of protective factors in the realm of crime and substance abuse has not received much attention. However, there is speculation that several genes may be involved in promoting sensitivity to acute intoxication and alcohol withdrawal. In turn, these genes are thought to protect against alcoholism (Hinckers et al. 2006; Pihl 2009). Moreover, as stated earlier, higher dopamine receptor availability may insulate individuals who are genetically as risk for developing alcoholism (Volkow et al. 2006). Lastly, some research suggests that the presence of self-regulation protects individuals against risky drinking and risky sexual behaviour (Quinn and Fromme 2010).

ASSESSMENT APPROACHES AND EFFECTIVENESS

STRONG ASSESSMENT IS THE CORNERSTONE OF EFFECTIVE CORRECTIONAL INTERVENTION. Not surprisingly, the same principle applies in the context of substance abuse. Before we can treat substance abuse among offenders, we must know the nature and extent of the problem. The assessment process however, can serve many objectives simultaneously. It can: 1) provide initial screening to determine if a more comprehensive and perhaps more costly assessment is required, 2) help motivate clients to enter into a treatment program, 3) describe the nature and extent of the problem to help focus treatment planning, and 4) help evaluate treatment process and change outcomes (Donovan 2013).

There are an extensive number of validated substance abuse assessment tools readily available to therapists. For example, Donovan (2013) lists upwards of 160 different assessment tools! Some of Donovan's tools are strictly for screening purposes, while others are more specialized in examining the severity of dependency, the nature and extent of cravings, whether or not there is a formal diagnosis (these are typically interview-based measures as opposed to self-reports), relapse risk, and barriers to treatment.

Correctional Service Canada (CSC) provides standardized assessments of offenders to ensure that the same measures are used across the country. These assessments facilitate decisions about the best programming and treatment for each offender. The Computerized Assessment of Substance Abuse (CASA) was implemented in 2002 to assess its utility with offenders. This assessment tool was pilot-tested on 907 male offenders who were admitted into federal custody between 2002 and 2004 (Kunic and Grant 2007). The CASA measures seven components of substance abuse: 1) alcohol, 2) drug abuse severity, 3) patterns of use, 4) links to criminal behaviour, 5) parental substance abuse, 6) previous participation in programs, and 7) treatment readiness. Severity of substance abuse is also assessed using the Alcohol Dependence Scale (ADS; Skinner and Allen 1982), the Drug Abuse Screening Test (DAST; Skinner 1982), and the Problems Related to Drinking Scale (PRD).

The pilot program results indicated that 5 percent of the offenders had a severe substance abuse problem, 16 percent had a substantial problem, 15 percent had a moderate problem, 32 percent had a low-level problem, and 31 percent had no substance abuse problems. The most commonly used drugs during the 12 months prior to the offenders' arrests were cannabinoids (52 percent), cocaine (26 percent), and opioids (13 percent). The CASA was found to accurately differentiate between levels of abuse among offenders. Compared to offenders with lower severity levels, offenders with higher severity levels on the ADS and DAST were strongly associated with substance use and impairment at the time they committed their offence.

Dr. John Weekes is a psychologist who has studied substance abuse problems with offenders and is an advocate for measures used by CSC; namely, the CASA, the ADS, and the DAST. The Canadian Researcher Profile discusses Dr. Weekes and his research.

Canadian Researcher Profile Dr. John Weekes

Dr. John Weekes is a leading researcher in substance abuse issues, having worked almost exclusively in this area since 1993. His research in the criminal justice system spans over three decades. He has explored the nature and dynamics of offenders' use of alcohol and other drugs, the relationship between substance abuse and criminal behaviour, offender motivation and readiness for treatment, and the effectiveness of substance abuse intervention programs for individuals involved in the criminal justice system. Dr. Weekes gets excited when he hears about issues that can be informed by research. Fortunately for the criminal justice system, he is driven to find answers.

Dr. Weekes subscribes to social psychological explanations for criminal conduct, not surprising given his training as a cognitive-social psychologist. Over the years, he has undertaken extensive research examinations of the Alcohol Dependence Scale and the Drug Abuse Screening Test. These instruments are an integral part of the Computerized Assessment of Substance Abuse

Box 7.2   (Continued)

instrument used by the Correctional Service of Canada. Dr. Weekes states that he is continually impressed by the accuracy of these instruments in identifying offender alcohol and drug use. "They are brief, behaviourally-oriented measures that really capture problematic substance use."

In terms of training future researchers interested in forensic psychology and criminal behaviour, Dr. Weekes believes Canada has been at the cutting edge of criminal justice research since the late 1980s and thinks that expanding the number of related academic programs in Canada will benefit future generations of forensic researchers and practitioners. He has been an enthusiastic and active member of Carleton University's adjunct faculty in Psychology since 1994. He enjoys teaching both introductory psychology and an upper year class in addiction, in which he imparts his enthusiasm and excitement about forensic psychology to students. He actively encourages students' questions, comments, and class participation. Dr. Weekes has supervised dozens of undergraduate and graduate students who have gone on to professional

careers in psychology and he is deeply committed to teaching and training future generations of forensic psychologists.

Dr. Weekes has served as a consultant and advisor on substance abuse and drug strategy issues to numerous correctional jurisdictions and agencies. These include organizations such as the Volunteers of America, the Royal Norwegian Ministry of Justice and the Police, the Swedish Prison and Probation Service, the Irish Prison Service, and the National Offender Management Service for England and Wales, to name a few.

Dr. Weekes relaxes with his favourite pastime, aviation. He received his private pilot's license at age 17 and he has been building and flying model airplanes since the age of 8. When not working, he can be found in his workshop or out at the field flying his many models. He is the president of a model club and is active on a national level promoting model aviation in Canada. He and his wife Helen, who is a registered nurse, live in Ottawa. Their son is a research mathematician and their daughter is a graduate student specializing in women's reproductive health research.

The CASA has been extensively studied within CSC since the original pilot study in 2006. For example, the Women's CASA (W-CASA) was first piloted in 2010 and has been fully implemented since 2011 (as cited in MacDonald 2014). However, a report explicitly describing the pilot study and validation process is not available yet. Ternes, Johnson, and Weekes (2011) re-validated the CASA with a sample of 10 845 federally sentenced male offenders. The results were again encouraging. Specifically, the results illustrated that the majority of offenders responded reliably (e.g., were aware they had a problem and did not try to hide it). CSC has also examined male offender satisfaction with the CASA (MacDonald, Mullins, and Ternes (2011). In general, this study revealed that offenders are generally satisfied with the CASA and also showed that the assessment can be completed on a computer. However, the most important role of the CASA is to match offenders to the appropriate intensity level of substance abuse treatment. This will be discussed shortly in the context of what treatment programs the CSC offers for offenders.

TREATMENT APPROACHES AND EFFECTIVENESS
Legislation

In Canada, there are two main pieces of legislation governing alcohol and drug related crimes: the *Criminal Code* (2015), and *Controlled Drugs and Substance Act* (2015). While the *Controlled Drugs and Substance Act* deals with crimes related to the possession, production, trafficking, and importation of illicit drugs, the *Criminal Code* deals with crimes related to impaired driving and public intoxication. In addition to systemic laws seeking to combat illicit drug use, the Canadian government has gone one step further. In 2007 the government launched a National Anti-Drug Strategy (NADS; Government of Canada 2015b). Spearheaded by Justice Canada and in collaboration with Public Safety Canada and Health Canada, the NADS seeks to reduce illicit drug production and distribution, prevent illicit drug use, and treat those with illicit drug addictions.

Canada's policies aim to combat illicit drugs through both legal sanctions and treatment methods. We'll now take a closer look at some of the more common methods for treating alcohol and drug abuse problems among criminal populations. In general, substance abuse treatment initiatives can be divided as follows: methadone maintenance programs, therapeutic communities, counselling boot camps, cognitive-behavioural models, and motivational interviewing. Notably, some of these programs, or combinations thereof, are either offered within the prison system or through **drug treatment courts** (see the Hot Topics box for a discussion of drug treatment courts).

Drug Treatment Courts

In 1998, Toronto was the first city in Canada to enact a drug court. In 2001, another drug court was established in Vancouver. Four other cities have since followed suit: Edmonton, Winnipeg, Ottawa, and Regina (Department of Justice 2015) Approximately $3.6 million is spent on drug courts in Canada annually (Treasury Board of Canada Secretariat 2015).

Drug treatment courts are intended to provide an alternative to the traditional justice system under the following circumstances:

- The accused committed a crime motivated by substance abuse. For example, a drug addict may commit theft in order to use the money generated to purchase drugs to feed his or her habit.
- The crime was non-violent and not related to drug trafficking.
- The accused pleads guilty in a traditional court of law.
- The Crown prosecutor supports the alternative drug treatment court.

Drug courts have the following objectives:

- Reduce crime committed as a result of drug dependency through court-monitored treatment and community service support for offenders.
- Reduce the cost of substance abuse on the Canadian economy.

Offenders in the drug-court system participate in a structured outpatient program where they attend both individual and group counselling sessions, receive appropriate medical attention, and are tested randomly for drugs. Offenders make regular court appearances, where a judge reviews their progress and can either impose sanctions (ranging from verbal reprimands to expulsion from the program) or provide rewards (ranging from verbal praise to fewer court appearances). Staff associated with drug courts coordinate with community partners to address offenders' needs, such as housing and employment. Once an offender has conquered his or her addiction, criminal charges are either stayed (i.e., suspended or postponed) or the offender receives a non-custodial sentence (i.e., house arrest). If unsuccessful, an offender will be sentenced as part of the regular court process.

The Canadian government remains committed to the operation of drug courts. However, the evidence that drug courts actually reduce future criminal reoffending is equivocal. It is also painfully clear that there are very few methodologically rigorous evaluations of drug courts in existence (see the Hot Topics box for further discussion).

Hot Topics

Do Drug Treatment Courts Work?

Gutierrez and Bourgon (2009) have conducted one of the most comprehensive examinations of the effectiveness of drug courts. The authors conducted a meta-analytic review of 96 studies that evaluated drug treatment courts. Notably, the authors derived their studies from three previous meta-analytic reviews of drug treatment courts.

This important meta-analysis presented some interesting findings. Surprisingly, 81 percent of the studies (n = 71) had to be rejected due to poor methodological rigour, and the remaining 25 studies were rated either "weak" (23) or "good" (2) in terms of methodological quality; no studies received a "strong" ranking. Overall, based on the aggregated 25 studies, the average reduction in criminal recidivism was 8 percent. However, when the researchers focused their analyses on the two studies classified as "good," the average reductions in recidivism fell to 4 percent.

The researchers also coded to what extent each study adhered to the principles of risk, need, and responsivity (RNR). Unfortunately, only 14 of the 25 coded studied adhered to one or two RNR principles. No study adhered to all three principles. The authors did report on the extent to which drug treatment courts may have impacted other important domains such as reduced substance abuse, better quality of life, and improved housing. When assessing recidivism, the study's recidivism outcome was binary in nature—offenders either recidivated or did not. The authors did not evaluate if there was simply reduced criminal justice involvement along a continuum. These later outcome variables are extremely important to consider, given that drug courts are largely aligned with the principles of harm reduction that recognize the importance of relative versus absolute improvements.

Overall, Gutierrez and Bourgon's findings indicate that yes, drug courts do yield a mild reduction in recidivism (4 to 8 percent). However, the reductions could be substantially higher if drug treatment courts adhered to the principles of risk, need, and responsivity.

A Typical Corrections-Based Substance Abuse Treatment Program

Substance abuse treatment programs are staples within the correctional environment. By the late 1990s virtually every federal prison offered some kind of substance abuse treatment programming for offenders (Federal Bureau of Prisons 2012). The situation in Canada is equally impressive, particularly within Correctional Service Canada. Before we review the nature and extent of substance abuse programming within CSC, it will be helpful to review common approaches to treating substance abuse in general. The best corrections-based substance abuse programs have adopted an integrative approach using multiple methods.

Methadone Maintenance Programs Methadone was discovered in Germany as a substitute to morphine during World War II. In 1963, a Canadian researcher by the name of Dr. Robert Halliday established the first methadone maintenance treatment (MMT) program in British Columbia. Dr. Halliday's program was the first of its kind in the world. In brief, MMTs are designed to treat opioid dependency.

Users may develop an opiate-related dependency to illicit opiates (heroin) as well as prescription-based opiates that have been prescribed for pain relief (such as morphine or oxycontin). There is some evidence that incarcerated women who participate in MMTs are more likely to have abused prescription-based opioids rather than heroin (MacSwain, Cheverie, Farrell MacDonald, and Johnson 2014). Methadone is a long lasting, synthetic opioid that is administered orally. It is also important to note that while some clients may remain on methadone until the opiate dependence is relieved, others may remain on methadone indefinitely (College of Physicians and Surgeons Ontario 2011).

In essence, MMTs work by:

- Suppressing opioid withdrawal symptoms, which include insomnia, violent yawning, weakness, nausea, vomiting, diarrhea, chills, fever, muscle spasms, and abdominal pain
- Reducing cravings for opioids
- Preventing the intoxication that typically accompanies opioid use (e.g., sedation or euphoria)
- Blocking the euphoric or sedative effects of other opioids, such as heroin (Francis, Black, Johnson, and Payette *n.d.*)

Notably, methadone is not the only synthetic opioid used to treat opioid addictions. Other synthetic opioids, such as buprenorphine and buprenorphine combined with naloxone (naloxone prevents misuse), are also currently in use (Volkow 2014).

Do Corrections-Based Methadone Maintenance Programs Work?

Research illustrates that the medication-assisted treatment of opioid addiction incurs many benefits. It reduces heroin-related overdoses, decreases drug use, minimizes infectious disease transmission, and ultimately reduces criminal conduct (Volkow 2014). Thus, when we consider all of the potential treatment benefits to individual users, their families, and society at large, it is perhaps not too surprising to learn that the cost of heroin addiction in Canada is close to five billion dollars (Schechter and Kendall 2011).

Rigorous evaluations of methadone maintenance programs in correctional populations are lacking. However, results from three Canadian studies are encouraging. For example, Cheverie, MacSwain, Farrell MacDonald, and Johnson (2014) compared institutional outcomes before and after MMT programs for 1508 offenders who were enrolled in a methadone maintenance program between 2003 and 2008. The authors concluded that program participation: 1) decreased overall drug use (including opioids) during incarceration, 2) increased participation in and completion of other correctional programs, and 3) reduced serious disciplinary charges and admissions to segregation. The importance of continuing MMT in the community cannot be overstated. MacSwain, Farrell MacDonald, and Cheverie (2014) illustrated that offenders who participated in MMT in an institution and continued whilst in the community were less likely to return to custody following release.

Methadone maintenance treatment programs are not without controversy or risk (Fischer 2000; Schechter and Kendall 2011). Methadone can be lethal if combined with alcohol or other sedatives such as benzodiazepines (Zador and Sunjic 2000). In any event, MMT is not meant to be offered in isolation. It ideally involves a multidisciplinary team of experts ranging from physicians and nurses to social workers, psychologists, case managers, and peer support workers. It should also be used in conjunction with other therapies such as motivational interviewing and cognitive behaviourism (College of Physicians and Surgeons Ontario 2011).

Motivational Interviewing Motivational interviewing (MI) is rooted in client-centered therapy. It emphasizes clinical empathy and explicit support for client autonomy. Specifically, it is the counsellor's job to discuss collaboratively (in a non-judgmental manner) with the client whether change would be worth making, rather than trying to explicitly convince the client that change is desirable (Moyers and Glynn 2013). Thus, motivational interviewing is a form of talk therapy designed to motivate clients to change because they *want* to, not because they *have* to. It has been applied in many settings including hospitals, college campuses, and prisons. The You Be the Therapist box illustrates how motivational interviewing works in practice.

Does Motivational Interviewing Work? In general, there is support for motivational interviewing either as a stand-alone interview technique or in combination with other methods. The empirical support extends well beyond the substance abuse domain and into other realms such as diet and exercise and HIV medication adherence (Moyers and Glynn 2013). However, MI does seem to be most effective for alcohol use disorders and less so for nicotine, marijuana, and other drugs (Lundahl et al. 2010;

Box 7.3

You Be the Therapist

Fred is a third-year university student. Every weekend, Fred goes out with his friends and has several beers, to the point that he usually vomits before the night is over. Afterwards, Fred typically doesn't remember what happened the night before. Fred got into a fight last weekend and needed 20 stitches for a gash above his left eye. The next day, Fred went to university counselling services on the urging of his girlfriend. The counsellor (trained in motivational interviewing) used the following motivational interviewing approach with Fred:

■ **Listen reflectively** (without judgment or interpretation, only mirroring what Fred says):
  • Fred: "I don't know what all the fuss is about. It wasn't a big cut; I am good as new now."
  • Therapist: "If I understand, you are telling me that the gash on your forehead wasn't a big deal, right?"

■ **Provide feedback** (with permission and without judgment):
  • Fred: "I don't remember what happened that night. We were at Fat Tuesday's and the next thing I knew, I was in the back of a police cruiser being taken to the hospital."
  • Therapist: "Can I share the police report with you?"

■ **Elicit client's own motivation for change** (this is the bread and butter of MI!):
  • Fred: "I don't see why I should change my drinking, everybody else is just like me."
  • Therapist: "Ok. Well let's explore this further. What do you think some of the *potential* benefits might be to changing; what are some of the potential cons of not changing?

■ **Enhance self-efficacy** (identify strengths and accomplishments):
  • Fred: "At least I showed up today."
  • Therapist: "Yes, you did. Who or what can help get you to come back next week to meet with me?"

■ **Reinforce positive self-talk**:
  • Fred: "I could try hanging out with my girlfriend who doesn't like to drink much."
  • Therapist: "That sounds like a great suggestion."

Questions

Think of someone in your life that you would like to encourage to change. Perhaps they need to exercise more, drink less, etc. How would you use the basic tenets of motivational interviewing to help this person realize that they want to change for themselves (not because you want them to)?

Source: Adapted from Community Care of North Carolina (2013).

Vasilaki, Hosier, and Cox 2006). The effectiveness of MI alone in a correctional setting is less well known. While MI is an integral part of most correctional-based substance abuse programs, treatment outcome studies have not been able to tease out the independent effects (if any) for MI.

McMurran (2009) conducted a systematic review of studies examining the effectiveness of MI among offender populations. She found 19 studies in total that examined the effectiveness of MI among substance abusing offenders, impaired drivers, intimate partner violence perpetrators, and general offenders. McMurran concluded that MI can reduce treatment drop-outs, enhance motivation to change, and reduce reoffending. However, there was considerable variability across the studies.

Large-Scale Evaluations of Prison-Based Substance Abuse Programs

Mitchell, Wilson, and Mackenzie (2006) conducted one of the most comprehensive meta-analytic reviews of corrections-based substance abuse programming to date. In sum, the researchers found evidence that some types of drug treatment programs reduce recidivism. However, the study concluded that the methodological rigour of the reviewed studies was regrettably poor. In this meta-analytic study:

- Four types of programs were reviewed: therapeutic communities (TC's), counselling, boot camps, and narcotic maintenance programs
- 61 studies were reviewed (52 American, 3 Canadian)
- Overall criminal recidivism rates for the treated groups were lower (28 percent) than the comparison groups (35 percent)
- No differences were observed in terms of drug relapse
- Narcotic maintenance programs and boot camps did not impact criminal recidivism
- Therapeutic communities and counselling programs accounted for the observed reductions in recidivism

Substance Abusing Programming within Correctional Service Canada (CSC)

Correctional Service Canada (CSC) provides national substance abuse programs that constitute a component of a larger drug strategy to combat abuse and related difficulties. The National Substance Abuse Program (NSAP) is designed to help offenders alter their substance problems and criminal behaviour. The techniques employed in the program are directed at helping offenders better manage the situations that may trigger relapse into crime and/or substance abuse. The NSAP does not work from a one-size-fits-all approach. Rather, the NSAP is tailored to meet the diverse needs of the federal offender population. There are four main types of NSAP: a high intensity NSAP (NSAP-H), a moderate intensity NSAP (NSAP-M), a pre-release NSAP, and a community NSAP. NSAPs have also been created specifically for female and Aboriginal offenders (CSC 2014b).

NSAP is based on an integrated theoretical model that posits substance abuse problems occur for many reasons but can be explained by the principles of learning to some degree. It is believed that substance abuse is poor coping with ongoing challenges in life. Behaviour is begun and maintained by previous learning experiences, including peer modelling, reinforcement, cognitive expectations or beliefs, and biological factors. This model treats substance abuse as a learned behaviour that can be changed into more positive behaviour and provides offenders with better coping mechanisms to daily stressors.

Using an offender's CASA information, offenders are referred to the appropriate level of intensity of NSAP. It is important to note that in order for an offender to be referred to NSAP, their substance abuse must have been directly involved in their current offence. Offenders scoring within the substantial to severe range using CASA are referred to the "high" level NSAP. Offenders scoring in the moderate to substantial range using CASA are referred to the "moderate" NSAP, and those scoring in the low range are deemed not to require any substance abuse programming.

Does NSAP Work? To date, Correctional Service Canada has comprehensively evaluated both the high-intensity NSAP and the moderate-intensity NSAP. Based on a sample of 2382 male offenders who participated in NSAP-H (to some degree) between 2004 and 2009, Doherty, Ternes, and Matheson (2014) made the following conclusions:

- NSAP-H non-completers were twice as likely to be involved in serious institutional misconducts versus NSAP-H completers
- Offenders who had been assigned to NSAP-H but did not participate in NSAP-H were 49 percent more likely to commit serious institutional misconducts versus NSAP-H program completers
- During a two-year post-release follow-up,
  - NSAP-H non-completers were 34 percent more likely to be returned to prison than NSAP-H completers
  - Offenders who were assigned to NSAP-H but did not participate in NSAP-H were 13 percent more likely to be readmitted to prison than NSAP-H program completers

The evaluation of the moderate-intensity version of NSAP was not as promising. Specifically, NSAP-M did not appear to reduce institutional misconducts nor reduce return to custody (Ternes, Doherty, and Matheson 2014).

FUTURE DIRECTIONS

THE FIELD OF SUBSTANCE ABUSE RESEARCH IS HIGHLY DEVELOPED BUT THERE IS ALWAYS room for improvement. In particular, stronger theoretical integration is required, along with the implementation of methodologically rigorous designs that tell us exactly what elements of treatment are working and for whom. More research regarding the complex needs of substance abusers with co-occurring needs such as traumatic brain injury, foetal alcohol syndrome, and mental illness is required. A greater focus is also needed on understanding a broader range of protective factors among high-risk individuals.

SUMMARY

1. Compared to the general population, substance abuse is astonishingly high among offender populations. Not only do a significant number of offenders admit to using alcohol or drugs at the time of their offence, they also evidence moderate to severe substance abuse disorders. Canada, like most developed countries, invests considerable resources into combating drug problems. Although marijuana is an illegal drug in Canada, it can be taken legally for medical reasons. However, the legal use of medical marijuana is heavily regulated in Canada and is ever evolving.

2. There are three general classes of substance abuse theories: the disease or medical model, the social learning/choice model, and the self-medication model. Each perspective is amply supported in the literature. However, the strongest perspective is the one that integrates elements from all three theories whilst simultaneously yielding the greatest dividends in the real world.

3. Theories that link crime to substance abuse are less developed. However, there are generally two perspectives. One perspective is that addiction comes first and ultimately drives criminal conduct. Thus, according to this perspective, if you treat the addiction, you treat the "criminality." In contrast, the second perspective argues that addiction is merely part of a pattern of antisociality. It posits that a criminal lifestyle and criminal thinking come first, followed by addiction. Thus, adherence to this model necessitates a more holistic approach to intervention—both the addiction and the criminal risk factors must be treated simultaneously. CSC has adopted this latter approach.

4. There are hundreds of substance abuse assessment tools available to therapists. Some are merely screening tools, others are meant to provide in-depth assessment of the exact nature of the problem to better inform treatment planning and help motivate the client. Correctional Service Canada relies heavily on a self-report computerized assessment tool known as the CASA.

5. Substance abuse programming is well established in correctional environments. For example, CSC offers some of the most developed and diverse programming options in the world. Sample correctional programs include methadone maintenance programs, motivational interviewing techniques, and drug treatment courts. However, most substance abuse programs are highly integrated and rely on multiple components and approaches to yield the best outcomes.

6. Rigorous methodological evaluations of substance abuse programs are lacking. Nonetheless, we do know that drug treatment courts reduce recidivism by 4 to 8 percent. We also know that motivational interviewing can be successful, particularly for alcohol disorders. There appears to be mixed evidence for the success of methadone maintenance programs offered to correctional samples. Lastly, while CSC's high-intensity substance abuse program yielded promising findings, its moderate-intensity version was less promising.

Discussion Questions

1. What model best explains drug addiction—the disease model, the choice model, or the self-medication model?

2. Should the government continue to fund drug treatment courts? Discuss the pros and cons of these courts.

3. Should methadone maintenance programs be maintained across the country?

4. What are the best evidence-based substance abuse programs for offenders?

Chapter 8
Violent Offending: General Violence and Homicide

STEVEN: A PERSISTENTLY VIOLENT OFFENDER

Steven Smith is 36 years old. He is a fourth-time federal offender currently serving a three-year sentence at Collins Bay Penitentiary in Kingston, Ontario. Shortly after his release from his last term of incarceration, he went on a crime spree, in which he threatened to kill a man who refused to lend him money, used counterfeit money at a convenience store, broke a window at his ex-girlfriend's house by throwing rocks at it (and was found to be in possession of a knife and a toy gun at the time), and threatened to kill a woman. After he was taken into custody for these offences he threatened and assaulted several correctional officers and offenders at various jails and prisons.

Learning Objectives

1   Review the scope and characteristics of violent offending as well as consequences for victims.

2   Summarize some of the major theories of aggression.

3   Understand important methodological issues in research investigating the causes of violence and the effectiveness of treatment programs aimed at reducing violence.

4   Identify some of the key assessment instruments used to estimate risk of violent recidivism and discuss their predictive accuracy.

5   Describe the effectiveness of treatment in reducing violent recidivism.

INTRODUCTION

MUCH OF THE THEORY AND RESEARCH PRESENTED IN PREVIOUS CHAPTERS GENERALLY applies to violent behaviour. In this chapter we will focus more specifically on violence. We will define some key terms and then review the prevalence and characteristics of violence in Canada. We will briefly discuss multiple murder (e.g., serial murder), violent hate crimes, and violent terrorism. We will also present some models that aim to explain violent behaviour and discuss methodological considerations for research on violence, major approaches to risk assessment, some established risk-assessment instruments, and research on the predictive accuracy of these instruments. Finally, treatment programs for violent offenders and research on their effectiveness will be reviewed.

CONTEXT

Aversion to violence and concern about violence seem to have been increasing for decades—if not centuries—in many parts of the world (Pinker 2011). There have also been dramatic advances in research and practice, particularly in the area of violence risk assessment. Most of us still know less than we think we know about the causes of violence and how to reduce violence, but we are learning more all the time. In this chapter, we will try to heed and model the wise advice to maintain a clear distinction between speculation/hypotheses and evidence (Harris and Rice 2015).

DEFINITIONS
Reactive versus Instrumental Violence

Violence can take different forms, serve different purposes, and have different motives. One major distinction that is receiving increasing research attention is between **reactive violence**, which is an impulsive reaction to some real or perceived provocation or threat, and **instrumental violence**, which is premeditated and aimed at achieving some secondary goal (e.g., Feshbach 1964). A classic example of reactive violence would be a man who comes home early from work to find his wife in bed with another man, flies into a rage, and assaults the other man. The husband is extremely angry, there is little (if any) forethought and planning, the assault is in response to perceived provocation, and the primary goal is to physically harm the other man. Contrast this with the following example of instrumental violence. A man plans to rob another man leaving a bank. He demands the victim's wallet. The victim refuses and the robber pushes him against a wall and punches him a few times, again ordering him to hand over the wallet. Injured and scared, the victim now gives him the wallet. Once the robber has the wallet, he leaves the victim alone. You can see that in this example, the aggressor is not provoked by the victim or particularly angry, there is some degree of planning, and the primary goal is to get money; physically harming the victim is a means to an end rather than the main goal.

A number of other terms are generally synonymous with reactive and instrumental violence (e.g., Ramírez and Andreu 2006). Reactive violence has also been referred to as affective, impulsive, and hostile violence. Instrumental violence is generally similar to predatory, premeditated, or proactive violence. Although there are some subtle differences between these terms, they generally reflect the distinctions noted above.

Homicide

Four types of homicide are identified in the Canadian *Criminal Code*: **first-degree murder**, second-degree murder, infanticide, and manslaughter. Murder is first degree when it is planned and deliberate. However, even when not planned and deliberate, murder is also first degree in certain circumstances; for example, if the victim is a peace officer (e.g., police officer) or if the death is caused while committing or attempting to commit terrorist activity. Second-degree murder is simply defined as murder that is not first degree. Infanticide is defined in section 233 of the *Criminal Code* as follows: "A female person commits infanticide when by a willful act or omission she causes the death of her newly-born child, if at the time of the act or omission she is not fully recovered from the effects of giving birth to the child and by reason thereof or of the effect of lactation consequent on the birth of the child her mind is then disturbed." Homicide that would otherwise be considered murder can be reduced to manslaughter if it was committed during the heat of passion or caused by sudden provocation that would overwhelm one's self-control. Homicide is also manslaughter if death results from criminal negligence.

Multiple Murder: Definitions and Characteristics Multiple murder is usually defined as killing three or more victims. Multiple murders can be divided into mass murder, spree murder, and serial murder. **Mass murder** occurs in a single location with no "cooling-off period" between murders. Some Canadian mass murderers are Mark Lepine, who fatally shot 14 women and then killed himself at Montreal's École Polytechnique in 1989; Valery Fabrikant, who fatally shot four fellow professors at Concordia University in 1992; Pierre Lebrun, who in 1999 fatally shot four employees and subsequently killed himself at the head office of Ottawa-Carleton Transpo, where he had formerly worked; and Matthew de Grood, who allegedly fatally stabbed five fellow University of Calgary students at a party in 2014. **Spree murder** is killing three or more victims at two or more locations, again with no cooling-off period between murders. A recent Canadian spree murderer is Justin Bourque, who killed three RCMP officers in Moncton in 2014. **Serial murder** involves three or more victims but differs from other multiple murders in that there is a cooling-off period between murders and the murders usually occur in different locations. Some high-profile Canadian serial killers are Clifford Olson, who murdered eight girls and three boys aged 9 to 18 in the early 1980s in British Columbia; Paul Bernardo and Karla Homolka, who killed three teenage girls in the early 1990s in St. Catharines, Ontario; and, more recently, Robert Pickton, who murdered several women in Port Coquitlam, British Columbia (see the Media Spotlight box).

Fox and Levin (1998) created one of the more comprehensive typologies of mass and serial murder, reflecting five categories of motivation: power, revenge, loyalty, terror, and profit (see Table 8.1).

Terrorism

Not all terrorism involves violence against a person. Threats and acts of violence are classified as terrorism according to the Canadian *Criminal Code* if they are:

> ...committed (a) in whole or in part for a political, religious or ideological purpose, objective or cause, and (b) in whole or in part with the intention of intimidating the

Table 8.1 Fox and Levin's Typology of Serial and Mass Murder

Motivations for Multiple Murder	Type of Multiple Murder	
	Serial Murder	Mass Murder
Power	Inspired by sadistic fantasies, a man tortures and kills a series of strangers to satisfy his need for control and dominance.	A pseudo-commando, dressed in battle fatigues and armed with a semiautomatic turns a shopping mall into a "war zone."
Revenge	Grossly mistreated as a child, a man avenges his past by slaying women who remind him of his mother.	After being fired from his job, a gunman returns to the worksite and opens fire on his former boss and coworkers.
Loyalty	A team of killers turn murder into a ritual for proving their dedication and commitment to one another.	A depressed husband/father kills his entire family and himself to remove them from their miserable existence to a better life in the hereafter.
Profit	A woman poisons to death a series of husbands in order to collect on their life insurance.	A band of armed robbers executes the employees of a store to eliminate all witnesses to their crime.
Terror	A profoundly paranoid man commits a series of bombings to warn the world of impending doom.	A group of antigovernment extremists blows up a train to send a political message.

Source: Fox and Levin (1998, p. 444).

Media Spotlight

Robert Pickton

Robert William Pickton was born on October 26, 1949. He lived and worked on his pig farm in Port Coquitlam, British Columbia. Pickton was charged with the murders of 26 women, most of whom were prostitutes. Pickton picked up the women from Vancouver's Downtown East-side, about a half-hour drive from his farm, and brought them back to the trailer in which he lived. The women were killed on the farm and police later found the remains of some of their bodies and personal effects. Pickton's trial dealt with six murder charges, for which he was eventually convicted of six counts of second-degree murder and sentenced to life with eligibility for parole after 25 years. Pickton's appeals of the verdicts were dismissed by the British Columbia Court of Appeal in 2009 and by the Supreme Court of Canada in 2010.

ANDY CLARK/Corbis

Below are some key dates in the case:

Sept. 1998: Vancouver police set up team that reviews files of women missing from city's Downtown Eastside as far back as 1971.

Feb. 5, 2002: RCMP officers, accompanied by members of the missing women joint task force, enter property in suburban Port Coquitlam on firearms warrant.

Feb. 6, 2002: Task force officers use their own warrant to begin searching pig farm for clues in missing women case.

Feb. 22, 2002: Robert Pickton, who owns the property with his brother and sister, is charged with two counts of first-degree murder—Sereena Abotsway and Mona Wilson.

April 2, 2002: Crown announces three more first-degree murder charges against Pickton—Diane Rock, Jacqueline McDonell, and Heather Bottomley.

April 9, 2002: Sixth murder charge laid against Pickton—Andrea Joesbury.

May 22, 2002: Pickton charged with first-degree murder of Brenda Wolfe.

June 6, 2002: Police begin excavating Pickton properties with help of archeologists.

Sept. 19, 2002: Pickton charged with four more murders—Georgina Papin, Helen Hallmark, Patricia Johnson, and Jennifer Furminger.

Oct. 2, 2002: Pickton charged with murders of Heather Chinnock, Tanya Holyk, Sherry Irving, and Inga Hall.

Jan. 13, 2003: Preliminary hearing begins in provincial court in Port Coquitlam.

July 23, 2003: Judge David Stone commits Pickton for trial on 15 counts of first-degree murder.

Nov. 18, 2003: Investigators wrap up mass excavation and search of Pickton farm.

Feb. 20, 2004: B.C. government reports investigation costs will likely run up to $70 million and that the money has been set aside in the provincial budget.

May 2005: Crown lays 12 more first-degree murder charges.

June 2005: Pre-trial hearings begin in B.C. Supreme Court in New Westminster under a publication ban.

October 2005: Pre-trial hearings end.

Jan. 30, 2006: Voir dire portion of Pickton trial begins in B.C. Supreme Court.

March 2006: Judge quashes murder count involving unidentified woman.

Aug. 9, 2006: Judge decides to sever charges to prevent unreasonable burden on jury.

Sept. 8, 2006: Crown decides to proceed on six counts first, with other 20 counts to be tried at a later date.

Dec. 9, 2006: Jury selection begins.

Dec. 12, 2006: Jury selected.

Jan. 22, 2007: Crown opens case against Pickton on six charges of first-degree murder.

Aug. 13, 2007: Crown closes case after calling 98 witnesses.

Oct. 16, 2007: Defence closes case after calling 30 witnesses.

Nov. 19, 2007: Final arguments begin.

Nov. 30, 2007: Jury begins deliberations.

Dec. 9, 2007: Jury finds Pickton guilty of six counts of second-degree murder.

Source: Canadian Press (2007).

public, or a segment of the public, with regard to its security, including its economic security, or compelling a person, a government or a domestic or an international organization to do or to refrain from doing any act, whether the public or the person, government or organization is inside or outside Canada.

Hate Crimes

As with terrorism, not all hate crimes involve violence against a person, but threats and acts of violence would generally be classified as hate crimes if they are motivated by hostility towards the victim's race, ethnicity, language, religion, sexual orientation, and so on.

WHY DO WE CARE?
Scope of Violence

Violent crime accounted for approximately one in five (21 percent) of the criminal incidents reported to police via the **Uniform Crime Reporting (UCR) Survey** in Canada in 2014 (Boyce 2015). A total of 369 359 violent incidents were reported, for a rate of 1039 incidents per 100 000 people (Boyce 2015). Generally, violence has been decreasing over the last few decades (for a comprehensive review and explanation, see Pinker 2011). Figure 8.1 shows the Canadian homicide rate since 1984, which illustrates this decreasing trend.

Offence Characteristics

Men are much more likely to commit violent offences, but the rates of violent victimization among men and women are quite similar (e.g., Gannon and Mihorean 2005; Perrault

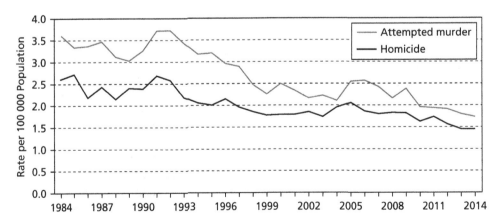

Figure 8.1 Attempted Murder and Homicide, Police-Reported Rates, Canada, 1984 to 2014

Source: Boyce (2015, p. 14), based on data from the Uniform Crime Reporting Survey.

and Brennan 2010). However, differences between the victimization of men and women become apparent when the type of violence is taken into consideration. For example, men are more likely to experience non-sexual violence than women, whereas women are more likely to experience sexual violence. Violent crimes are slightly more likely to be committed by someone known to the victim (e.g., a friend or acquaintance) than by a stranger. Some characteristics associated with higher rates of violent victimization are being young, being single, being Aboriginal, often going out in the evening, and living in a city.

Impact on Victims

Violence causes physical and emotional harm. Approximately one in five violent crimes cause physical injury to victims (Gannon and Mihorean 2005; Perrault and Brennan 2010). Approximately one quarter of victims of violent crimes typically report that the crime caused them to have difficulty functioning in their everyday activities.

THEORIES OF VIOLENT OFFENDING

Social Learning Theory

Social learning theory (Bandura 1973) holds, as the name suggests, that aggression is learned (see Chapter 3 for more details). The main tenet is quite simple and parsimonious: aggression is more likely to occur when it is expected to be more rewarding than non-aggressive alternatives. As Bandura (1973, p. 2) noted:

> Concern over the adverse consequences of aggression obscures the fact that such behavior often has functional value for the user. Indeed, there is a property unique to aggression that generally creates conditions fostering its occurrence. Unlike other social behaviors that cannot be effective without some reciprocity acceptable to the participants, aggression does not require willing responsiveness from others for its success. One can injure and destroy to self-advantage regardless of whether the victim likes it or not. By aggressive behavior, or dominance through physical and verbal force, individuals can obtain valued resources, change rules to fit their own wishes, gain control over and extract subservience from others, eliminate conditions that adversely affect their well-being, and remove barriers that block or delay attainment of desired goals. Thus, behavior that is punishing for the victim can, at least on a short-term basis, be rewarding for the aggressor.

How is aggression learned? As stated above, expected outcomes influence the likelihood and extent of aggressive behaviour. In operant conditioning, behaviour is shaped by its consequences; that is, reinforcement or punishment. Reinforcement increases the likelihood that a given behaviour will occur, whereas punishment decreases the likelihood of its occurrence. For example, a young child wants another child's toy, but the other child does not want to share it. The child pushes the other child out of the way and takes the toy. Aggression is rewarded by obtaining the toy (positive reinforcement). Alternately, instead of getting the toy, the child's aggression may result in a scolding from his or her mother (positive punishment). Consider the child who is being made fun of by other children but is able to silence them by punching one of them. In this case, aggression is rewarded by the removal of some aversive state (negative reinforcement). Alternately, instead of silencing his harassers, the child's aggression may earn him or her exclusion from that day's fun field trip by a teacher who observed the child's behaviour (negative punishment).

Adding to the familiar concept of operant conditioning, Bandura (1973) argued that people learn not only from direct experience, but also from observing the behaviour of others and the outcomes of others' behaviour. Observing others receiving various rewards for their aggression would increase the likelihood that one would engage in similar forms of aggression. In contrast, observing others receiving punishment for their aggression would decrease the likelihood that one would engage in similar forms of aggression. The self is also an important source of reinforcement. Self-reinforcement refers to the influence of self-administered rewards or punishments for aggression. If self-evaluation following aggression is positive, aggression will be more likely than if self-evaluation is negative. For example, following aggression, one person may feel powerful, assertive, and generally quite pleased, whereas another person may be racked with guilt and self-contempt. These reinforcement influences on aggressive behaviour are mediated by cognition, such as one's attention, perception, memory, and resulting expectancies regarding reinforcement.

General Aggression Model

The General Aggression Model (GAM) (Anderson and Bushman 2002) is an integration of a number of smaller, more specific theories of aggressive behaviour. Shown in Figure 8.2, the GAM describes the processes involved in any one episode among an ongoing series of episodes of a social encounter. The main components are inputs from the person and situation, the routes (cognitive, affective, and arousal states) that mediate the influence of inputs, and the appraisal and decision processes that lead to a particular action in the episode. The outcome influences the social encounter, which then provides inputs in the next episode.

Person inputs, such as traits, gender, beliefs, attitudes, values, long-term goals, and behavioural scripts, refer to relatively stable characteristics that individuals bring to any given situation and can predispose one toward or against aggression. Situation inputs can also influence aggression in a given episode. Such factors include aggressive cues, provocation, frustration, pain and discomfort, drugs, and incentives.

The routes through which person and situation inputs influence aggression are cognitive, affective, and arousal states. Cognitive states include hostile thoughts and behavioural scripts. Affective states include mood and emotion as well as expressive motor responses. Arousal can influence aggression in a number of ways. For example, high levels of physiological arousal preceding a provocation can be mislabelled as anger, thereby increasing aggressive behaviour. Note that cognition, affect, and arousal are all interconnected in the GAM and each may influence the other. For example, hostile

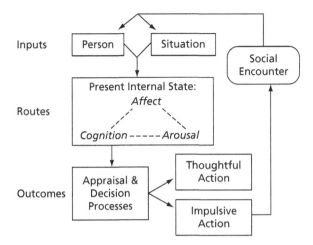

Figure 8.2 The General Aggression Model

Source: Anderson and Bushman (2002).

thoughts (cognition) may increase feelings of anger (affect). Some of the variables may seem to overlap between inputs and routes; for example, scripts are listed as both a person factor and a cognitive state. However, scripts as a person factor refer to a relatively stable characteristic (i.e., the presence and level of activation of such a script typical of a given person), whereas scripts as a cognitive state refer to the degree to which a particular behavioural script is activated in a particular situation.

Evolutionary Psychological Perspective

As you will recall from Chapter 2, in our ancestral environments certain physiological, psychological, and behavioural characteristics were associated with increased reproductive success (i.e., having a relatively high number of children who in turn have a relatively high number of children, and so on) (Lalumière, Harris, Quinsey, and Rice 2005). To the extent that such characteristics are heritable, the genes responsible for them would be passed on to subsequent generations more so than genes that are responsible for characteristics associated with reproductive failure.

Building on research and theory on general antisocial behaviour (e.g., Harris, Rice, and Lalumière 2001; Moffitt 1993; Quinsey, Skilling, Lalumière, and Craig 2004), Lalumière et al. (2005) propose that most violent people fall into one of three groups: young men, competitively disadvantaged men, or psychopaths. Adolescent and young men typically have relatively few resources and low status, which puts them at a competitive disadvantage relative to other males with whom they are competing for resources and mates. Through violence and general risk taking, these young men may be able to increase their status, resources, and/or access to more and better mates. However, as they move into adulthood and begin to acquire legitimately gained resources and status, the costs of violence begin to outweigh the benefits, so they switch from short-term, high-risk strategies to more long-term, lower-risk strategies. Therefore, the violent behaviour of this group is limited to adolescence and young adulthood. This is the most common type of violent offender.

This desistance with adulthood, however, does not occur for the competitively disadvantaged men. Their violent behaviour is life-course persistent. The ability to compete for resources and status in prosocial ways is impaired by early neurodevelopmental insults, such as obstetrical complications and low IQ. Because men in this group do not have the skills or abilities to achieve status and resources in prosocial ways, they maintain their high-risk approach into adulthood. The final group, psychopaths, are also life-course-persistent. In contrast to the competitively disadvantaged men, psychopaths are not competitively disadvantaged but select short-term, high-risk strategies as an alternate approach. Competitively disadvantaged men and psychopaths are thought to make up a relatively small proportion of violent individuals.

METHODOLOGY

CONDUCTING INFORMATIVE TESTS OF HYPOTHESES ABOUT THE CAUSES OF VIOLENCE OR THE effects of interventions on violence first requires a clear and precise conceptualization of the constructs of interest (e.g., attitudes towards violence). Once we have a clear definition of the constructs, only rigorous methodology and replication permit strong conclusions about the extent to which a given factor plays a causal role in violent behaviour, or an intervention reduces violent behaviour. The validity (or truth) of the inferences (or conclusions) we can draw from evidence has been organized into four main types (Shadish, Cook, and Campbell 2002):

- *Internal validity:* To what extent does the evidence reflect a causal relationship between the variables as measured or manipulated?
- *Construct validity:* To what extent do the people, places, and variables as measured or manipulated represent the presumed constructs?
- *External validity:* To what extent does the causal relationship generalize to other people, places, and variables?
- *Statistical conclusion validity:* To what extent do the results accurately reflect the statistical significance or strength of association between variables?

For every study, there are at least some threats to validity that limit the inferences one can draw from the evidence. Shadish and colleagues (2002) describe threats to validity as "reasons why we can be partly or completely wrong when we make an inference about covariance [statistical conclusion validity], about causation [internal validity], about constructs [construct validity], or about whether the causal relationship holds over variations in persons, settings, treatments, and outcomes [external validity]" (p. 39). Methodologically rigorous studies minimize the number and plausibility of threats to validity, thereby permitting stronger inferences.

Some approaches that have been used or could be used in research on violence are:

- Description of a case or sample, but no comparisons or associations examined
- Cross-sectional/retrospective observational/correlational
- Single-wave longitudinal observational/correlational or quasi-experiment
- Multi-wave (the factor was assessed at two or more time points) longitudinal observational/correlational or quasi-experiment
- Randomized experiment

With the exception of the first approach, all of the approaches listed above examine the degree of association between presumed causal variables and presumed effects. We briefly define some design terms here (for more information, see Shadish et al. 2002). In cross-sectional and retrospective designs, the main variables of interest are measured at the same time, whereas in longitudinal designs the presumed causal variable is measured before the presumed effect occurs and is measured. Single-wave longitudinal studies measure the presumed causal variable once, whereas multi-wave longitudinal studies measure the presumed causal variable on two or more separate occasions. In observational (also referred to as correlational) designs, the presumed causal variable cannot be manipulated. In quasi-experimental designs, the presumed causal variable could have been manipulated but participants are nevertheless not randomly assigned to different levels of the presumed causal variable. In randomized experiments, participants are randomly assigned to different levels of the presumed causal variable.

FACTORS ASSOCIATED WITH VIOLENCE

TO ILLUSTRATE SOME OF THE METHODOLOGICAL ISSUES RAISED ABOVE, WE WILL REVIEW some of the available research on the relationship between various factors and violent behaviour, describe their methodology and results, and consider the conclusions supported by the evidence.

Polaschek et al. (2009) reviewed transcripts of interviews with incarcerated violent offenders in New Zealand about their experiences, thoughts, feelings, decisions, and behaviours prior to, during, and after their violent offences. Polaschek et al. organized offenders' statements into four main themes thought to represent underlying beliefs about violence. Each theme is presented below along with offender statements that Polaschek et al. identified as exemplary of each theme:

Normalization of violence

- "Yeah, I got a beating, but it wasn't anything"
- "My son was getting into fights at school. So I taught both sons to box after school, so they could defend themselves. I didn't want my sons looking like [cowards] or being walking [sic] over by every Tom, Dick, or Harry. Everyone needs respect."
- "she wouldn't listen to me unless I hit her first"

- "how else was I going to get through to him that schoolwork was important"
- "I told him this would happen if he didn't pay up in time."

I am the law

- "People come to me with their problems because they know they can rely on me to sort them out"
- "My niece phoned me up. Her partner had been hitting her. She'd been asking me what she should do. I said "just throw him out" but she said, "I can't, it's my baby's father." So me and him had a fight. I went a bit overboard, my niece got really mad at me. She called the police. I was really hurt that she did that, after she asked for my help"

Beat or be beaten

- "I thought I was a gangsta, one bad dude, I could do anything I want and no one could stop me. . . . Don't ever get smart on me, like you're thinking bad things about me 'cause I beat you up. If you aren't cool, don't even talk to me... Used to go to town on Friday nights just to have a fight. If I wasn't beating someone up I was getting beaten up. I loved it, chance to prove myself."
- "He was trying it on: if I hadn't sorted it then, it would just have got worse"
- "I am still [angry] at the guys who [stole my drug supply]. It is bad for me. If I get ripped off, people will think that they can get away with it. It has got to stop"
- "I was about 20 when I started to go hard. I learned in jail that if I don't do violence this [derogatory person term] is going to walk all over me. I don't like hurting people, but what choice have I got?"

I get out of control

- "I know once on the streets I'm going to get into [violence], it just can't be helped"
- "All of a sudden I go on a rage"
- "I really lost it. I really laid into him"
- "I was planning on doing things differently but once I got going, just see red, nothing else matters"
- "I only meant to hurt him a bit. But once I started . . . my friends had to pull me off him. That's how it is sometimes with me"

What can we conclude about the causes of violence from a study like this? No association between variables or difference between groups is examined, so this evidence does not support any conclusions about the extent to which these beliefs are associated with, predict, or cause violent behaviour. However, studies like this make a valuable contribution to the literature by providing some exposure to what individual violent offenders say and by generating hypotheses. Qualitative studies like this are an ideal starting point for research on violence.

In another study Polaschek, Collie, and Walkey (2004) examined the relationship between beliefs about violence and violent offending in a cross-sectional study. Scores on a self-report measure of beliefs about violence were compared between a group of offenders incarcerated for violent offences and a group of offenders with no record of violent offences. Some examples of items on the self-report measure are "If somebody insults me or my family I feel better if I beat them up;" "Fighting between men is normal;" and "If a person hits you, you have to hit them back." The violent offenders reported markedly stronger agreement with beliefs like these than did the non-violent offenders. What can we conclude about the causes of violence from a study like this? We can conclude that there was an association between beliefs and violent offending, but the evidence does not address whether beliefs predict or play a causal role in violent offending.

Lansford et al. (2007) examined the relationship between childhood physical abuse and violent behaviour in a longitudinal study. Childhood physical abuse—measured through interviews with mothers when their children were young—was associated with a higher likelihood of violent offending in childhood or adolescence—as measured by official court records. This association between childhood abuse and violent offending remained statistically significant even after statistically controlling for a number of plausible alternative causal variables: socioeconomic status, single-parent status, family stress, maternal social support, child exposure to violence, child temperament, and child health.

What can we conclude about the causes of violence from a study like this? The longitudinal design combined with statistical control of plausible alternative causal variables permits tentative conclusions about a causal link between childhood physical abuse and later violent offending. However, without random assignment we can never rule out the possibility that the observed results may be due to some other factor instead of childhood abuse. Of course it would not be desirable or possible to randomly assign children to experience physical abuse, but this does not give us a free pass to jump to causal conclusions. Instead, the strongest conclusion we can hope for is that there very likely is a causal link, assuming an association is consistently demonstrated by sophisticated non-experimental longitudinal studies that statistically control for the most plausible alternative causal variables.

DeWall, Baumeister, Stillman, and Gailliot (2007) tested the effects of low self-control on aggressive behaviour in four randomized experiments. In the first experiment, female and male undergraduate students were asked to write an essay and then randomly assigned to the self-control depletion condition (restrain themselves from eating a donut for five minutes) or the non-depleting condition (restrain themselves from eating a radish for five minutes). Participants were then given negative feedback on their essay (e.g., "this is one of the worst essays I've ever read"), ostensibly from a fellow participant who strongly dislikes spicy food. Participants were then asked to prepare a snack for their fellow participant with three chips and hot sauce. Participants who restrained themselves from eating the donut put more hot sauce on the chips for their fellow participant than did participants who restrained themselves from eating the radish. The finding that participants whose self-control was depleted responded to provocation with greater aggression was replicated in three other experiments with university students (also mostly female) using a variety of self-control manipulations (e.g., doing tasks that require inhibition of intuitive or habitual responding, or are otherwise attention-demanding) and aggression variables (intensity and duration of noise blasts, negative recommendation for a competitive research assistant position, and self-reported likelihood of smashing a beer bottle over the head of a person who has provoked the participant).

What can we conclude about the causes of violence from a study like this? We can be very confident that depleted self-control (as manipulated) caused greater aggressive behaviour (as measured) (internal validity). However, we cannot be as certain about how well the manipulations reflect real self-control deficits or how well the aggression variables reflect real violent behaviour (construct validity). There is also some uncertainty about the extent to which the observed association would be found with other samples (e.g., non-students, criminals), other self-control variables (e.g., different manipulations or measures), and other aggression variables (e.g., arrest for violent offences) (external validity).

The point of this brief review is not to disparage the contributions of our fellow researchers. As illustrated above, validity is a matter of degree and every study has weaknesses. In spite of any methodological weaknesses, past research on violent behaviour is important, valuable, and useful. Furthermore, different approaches to research often have complementary strengths and weaknesses (e.g., trade-off between internal validity and construct or external validity). When the evidence from these complementary studies is considered together, it is sometimes possible to draw stronger conclusions than would be supported by any one type of study. For example, the evidence for the association between self-control and violence converges across randomized experiments like DeWall et al.'s (2007) and cross-sectional and longitudinal non-experimental studies examining variables more obviously representative of real violent behaviour (e.g., Henry, Caspi, Moffitt, and Silva 1996; Longshore and Turner 1998). Taken together, this body of evidence really does suggest that low self-control plays a causal role in violent behaviour. The take-home message is that the degree of methodological rigour limits the strength of the conclusions that can be drawn from the available evidence. Recognizing and acknowledging this permits more accurate interpretation and synthesis of evidence and identifies important gaps in knowledge to address with future research. Luckily, there are a number of people, like Dr. Mark Olver, who are committed to conducting rigorous research on violent offenders (see the Canadian Researcher Profile).

ASSESSMENT APPROACHES AND EFFECTIVENESS
Recidivism Rates

Compared to general criminal recidivism, violent recidivism is less frequent. For example, in a meta-analysis of recidivism of mentally disordered offenders, Bonta, Law, and Hanson (1998) found an average violent recidivism rate of 24.5 percent and a general recidivism rate of 45.8 percent over a mean follow-up period of 4.8 years. A similar rate of violent recidivism was reported for non-mentally disordered offenders in a meta-analysis by Campbell, French, and Gendreau (2009), with 21.73 percent over a follow-up period of approximately 2 to 5 years. Although most violent offenders do not violently recidivate, it is possible to identify subgroups with relatively high rates of violent recidivism.

Box 8.1

Canadian Researcher Profile Dr. Mark Olver

Dr. Mark Olver, University of Saskatchewan

Dr. Mark Olver

Dr. Mark Olver is an Associate Professor in the Department of Psychology at the University of Saskatchewan. Dr. Olver completed a BA, MA, and Ph.D. in Psychology at the University of Saskatchewan. For his Ph.D. thesis, which was supervised by Dr. Stephen Wong, Dr. Olver developed and validated a sexual offender risk assessment and treatment planning tool called the Violence Risk Scale—Sexual Offender version (VRS-SO). Dr. Olver's first professional employment after completing his Ph.D. was as a Psychologist on the Young Offender Team with the Saskatoon Health Region, and he also conducted Parole Board of Canada psychological assessments at Correctional Service Canada's Regional Psychiatric Centre.

Dr. Olver is internationally recognized and widely respected for his research and training in sexual, violent, and psychopathic offender risk assessment, treatment, and change evaluation. He has authored dozens of publications, many of them in high-impact scientific journals. His current clinical work has primarily involved supervising sexual offender assessments and Parole Board of Canada psychological risk assessments at the Regional Psychiatric Centre in Saskatoon.

One of the reasons Dr. Olver's research is so impactful may be his integration of statistical sophistication with in-depth knowledge of general clinical psychology literature and more specialized forensic psychology literature. When asked about the main methodological approaches he uses in his research, Dr. Olver said "I do a lot of archival research, in part because the files I utilize are very detailed and comprehensive, which enable coding a vast range of variables. I examine recidivism as an outcome variable in much of my research and employ a lot of correlational and quasi-experimental designs to examine the associations between risk, treatment participation, change, and outcome." In terms of future directions for his research, Dr. Olver said "I think incorporating protective factors into the assessment of risk and evaluation of change is important. One of my doctoral students found protective factors to be incremental in a sample of treated violent offenders and I am curious to see if this is the case in sexual offenders."

When asked which of his studies is his favourite, Dr. Olver identified two articles published in the prestigious journals *Psychological Assessment* and the *Journal of Consulting and Clinical Psychology*: "It would have to be a tie between two papers. Our 2007 paper (Olver, Wong, Nicholaichuk, and Gordon) because it is essentially the inaugural VRS-SO article and is an early study demonstrating the association between risk change and recidivism. It was also in writing this and analyzing the data that we stumbled across the manner in which pretreatment risk confounds the relationship of risk change to recidivism and how vital it is to control for baseline risk in these

Box 8.1   (Continued)

sorts of analyses. The tying paper would be our recent 2014 paper (Olver, Nicholaichuk, Kingston, and Wong) because this is essentially a prospective replication of our 2007 paper on a large multisite sample of treated Canadian sexual offenders."

In terms of the main approaches he uses in his clinical work, Dr. Olver said "I like to think of myself as being integrative with a foundation in cognitive behavioural therapy and interpersonal approaches. The expanded risk-need-responsivity model invariably plays a major role in my approach to case conceptualization and bridging the link between assessment and treatment."

When asked what keeps him interested in his areas of research and clinical work, Dr. Olver said, "Forensic psychological research and practice are never dull. The fields I work in have made tremendous strides and it is gratifying to be part of a development to contribute to new knowledge and to apply this in my practice to help offenders move onto better lives and to contribute to a mission of reduced violent victimization."

In terms of teaching, Dr. Olver said, "I enjoy teaching forensic psychology, but as a clinical psychologist on staff in the psychology department, I am required in other roles such as teaching graduate courses in assessment. I am also a bit of a dabbler and enjoy new learning challenges—this past year I co-developed and co-taught a graduate course on the Historical and Philosophical Foundations of Psychology with a departmental colleague."

Dr. Olver said the following about how we should be training our future researchers and clinicians interested in the psychology of criminal behaviour: "I think we have some great applied forensic psychology programs in Canada, whether they stress research or also involve clinical training. I firmly believe that skills are best taught by 'doing' and that an integration of specialized coursework, research, mentorship, and field training are vital."

When asked if there is any legislation or policy he would like to see changed to improve the criminal justice system, Dr. Olver said "Yes—mandatory minimum sentences are an unfortunate drain on taxpayer dollars and involve taking a gratuitously punitive stance toward offenders. In 2012, my colleagues and I drafted a response to the omnibus crime bill (Bill C-10) submitted to the Senate Standing Committee on Legal and Constitutional Affairs presenting evidence to support a rehabilitative and evidence-informed approach to reduce criminal behaviour."

Dr. Olver likes to stay physically active (running, biking, and weights) and has a passion for guitar. Those of us who have heard him play can vouch for his impressive guitar chops!

Approaches

Approaches to risk assessment can be categorized in a number of ways. Four key categories are described here: unstructured clinical judgment, empirical actuarial, mechanical, and structured professional judgment (Hanson and Morton-Bourgon 2009). **Unstructured clinical judgment** involves arriving at an estimate of risk based on the assessor's own idiosyncratic decisions about what factors to consider and how to combine those factors. In contrast, the empirical actuarial and mechanical instruments both follow explicit rules about what factors to consider and how to combine those factors to arrive at a final estimate of risk. However, two characteristics distinguish empirical actuarial from mechanical. For **empirical actuarial** instruments, 1) the selection and combination of items are derived from their observed statistical relationship with recidivism; and 2) tables linking scores to expected recidivism rates are provided. For **mechanical** instruments, the selection and combination of items are derived from theory or reviews of the empirical literature and no tables are provided. **Structured professional judgment** incorporates features of both unstructured clinical judgment and the actuarial approach; there are explicit guidelines for which factors to consider (although additional factors may also be considered), but the combination of those factors is left up to the discretion of the assessor.

Instruments

Violence Risk Appraisal Guide-Revised (VRAG-R)
The Violence Risk Appraisal Guide—Revised (VRAG-R) (Rice, Harris, and Lang 2013) is an empirical actuarial risk-assessment instrument designed to estimate risk for violent recidivism. The VRAG-R consists of 12 static predictors of violent recidivism. The correlation between each VRAG-R item and violent recidivism is shown in Table 8.2. VRAG-R items are summed to compute total scores, which can be grouped into nine risk categories (or bins). Higher scores and categories indicate greater risk of violent recidivism. The inter-rater reliability of the VRAG-R was very high (intraclass correlation between raters = .99). Sadly, Marnie Rice died in August, 2015, and Grant Harris died less than a year earlier in October, 2014 – they were two of the most important researchers in the area of violent behaviour.

Table 8.2 VRAG-R Items and Their Correlations with Violent Recidivism

VRAG-R Item	r
Antisociality (Facet 4 of Psychopathy Checklist-Revised)	.38
Prior admissions to correctional institutions	.31
Failure on prior conditional release	.30
Elementary school maladjustment	.30
Conduct disorder	.30
Nonviolent criminal history score	.29
Young age at index offence	.27
Violent criminal history score	.24
History of alcohol or drug problems	.22
Sexual offending history	.19
Did not live with both biological parents to age 16	.19
Never married	.12

Source: Adapted from Rice et al. (2013).

HCR-20 Violence Risk Assessment Scheme The HCR-20 (Webster, Douglas, Eaves, and Hart 1997) is a structured professional judgment instrument designed to assess risk for violence. It consists of ten historical items, five clinical items, and five risk management items. The historical items, which are static and reflect the past, include previous violence, young age at first violent incident, relationship instability, employment problems, major mental illness, psychopathy, early maladjustment, personality disorder, and prior supervision failure. The clinical items, which are dynamic and reflect current functioning, include lack of insight, negative attitudes, active symptoms of major mental illness, impulsivity, and unresponsive to treatment. The risk management items, which concern future circumstances that may be encountered in the institution or community that could increase or decrease risk, include feasibility of plans, exposure to destabilizers, lack of personal support, noncompliance with remediation attempts, and stress.

The HCR-20 items were selected based on a review of factors related to violence in the empirical literature and based on clinical experience. Each item is scored on a three-point scale: zero indicates that the particular factor is not present, one indicates the factor may be present, and two indicates the factor is present. Although subscale and total scores are computed by summing the appropriate items, Webster and colleagues (1997) recommend that evaluators use their professional judgment to arrive at a final risk estimate of low, moderate, or high. Unlike the VRAG-R, then, risk level would be determined primarily by consideration of the salience and relevance of each of the 20 items for the individual being assessed as well as any other information thought to be relevant. Subscale and total scores (i.e., summing the items) has yielded high levels of inter-rater reliability. For example, Douglas, Yeomans, and Boer (2005) found intraclass correlations between raters of .90 for the historical scale, .81 for the clinical scale, .91 for the risk management scale, and .93 for the total score. However, when structured professional judgment was used to arrive at a final risk estimate (i.e., not necessarily simply summing the scores across the 20 items), the inter-rater agreement was not as impressive: intraclass correlation = .41. Version 3 of the HCR-20 was recently published (Douglas, Hart, Webster, and Belfrage 2013).

Self-Appraisal Questionnaire (SAQ) The Self-Appraisal Questionnaire (SAQ) (Loza 2005) is a self-report empirical actuarial risk-assessment instrument developed to estimate risk of violent and non-violent recidivism (Loza, Dhaliwal, Kroner, and Loza-Fanous 2000). Initially, the SAQ consisted of 67 self-report items designed to tap a variety of factors theoretically and empirically linked to recidivism. From an initial pool of 100 items, 67 were retained through consultation with correctional staff and examination of correlations between items within each subscale and frequency of responses to each item. These items were grouped into six subscales:

1. Criminal Tendencies (CT): 27 items. Sample item: "I have carefully planned a crime before." Assesses antisocial attitudes, beliefs, behaviours, and feelings.

2. Antisocial Personality Problems (AP): 5 items. Sample item: "Since the age of 15, I have been described by others as manipulative." Assesses antisocial personality characteristics.

3. **Conduct Problems (CP):** 18 items. Sample item: "I have spent time at a group home, a juvenile facility/training school/reformatory." Assesses childhood behavioural problems.

4. **Criminal History (CH):** 6 items. Sample item: "My criminal involvement has been getting worse." Assesses past criminal behaviour.

5. **Alcohol/Drug Abuse (AD):** 8 items. Sample item: "I would not have served time if it was not for my alcohol or drug habit." Assesses substance abuse.

6. **Antisocial Associates (AS):** 3 items. Sample item: "One reason for my involvement with crime is my friends or acquaintances." Assesses association with antisocial peers.

Subscale scores are calculated by summing the appropriate items and a total score is calculated by summing all items in the six subscales noted above. Higher subscale and total scores indicate higher risk for violent and non-violent recidivism.

The SAQ demonstrated good test-retest reliability over one week: $r = .95$ for the total score, .69 for CT, .71 for AP, .95 for CP, .78 for CH, .93 for AD, and .85 for AS subscales. Most of the subscale scores showed adequate internal consistency, as measured by Cronbach's alpha: $\alpha = .78$ for CT, .58 for AP, .87 for CP, .68 for CH, .76 for AD, and .42 for AS. The SAQ subscales demonstrated expected correlations with similar constructs assessed by other measures. For example, self-reported Antisocial Personality Problems (AP) was correlated with the PCL-R ($r = .36$). In addition, the SAQ was significantly correlated with number of past violent offences ($r = .32$). The SAQ was also correlated with validated risk assessment instruments and the PCL-R, which are scored by an assessor and require file reviews, interviews, or both—see Table 8.3.

Table 8.3 Correlations between SAQ and Other Risk Studies

Measure	SIR	LSI-R	PCL-R	VRAG
SAQ total	−.61	.70	.54	.67
SAQ subscales				
Criminal tendencies	−.31	.31	.25	.34
Antisocial personality problems	−.42	.42	.36	.46
Conduct problems	−.56	.65	.54	.68
Criminal history	−.66	.62	.53	.57
Alcohol/drugs	−.31	.53	.27	.23
Associates	−.24	.40	.31	.45

Note: All correlations are statistically significant (p < .05). SIR = Statistical Information on Recidivism (lower scores reflect higher risk); LSI-R = Level of Service Inventory Revised; PCL-R = Psychopathy Checklist Revised; VRAG = Violence Risk Appraisal Guide.

Source: Adapted from Loza et al. (2000).

The SAQ was designed to be an efficient and informative risk assessment instrument. It is efficient because offenders complete it themselves. Most offenders can complete it in 15 to 20 minutes. It does not require assessors to conduct extensive file reviews or interviews like most other risk-assessment instruments do. It is informative in that it addresses theoretically relevant domains and over half the items are potentially dynamic. Thus, not only does the SAQ indicate risk of recidivism, it may also provide information relevant to the planning of treatment and supervision because it suggests areas of criminogenic need that could potentially be treated or otherwise managed.

Would you use self-report measures to estimate risk for violent recidivism? Many people would probably say no. Why? Usually this has to do with skepticism about the accuracy of offenders' self-reports. Offenders are often considered unreliable sources of information, especially when the information they provide will be used to make decisions that impact them, such as whether to grant conditional release or to move them to lower security facilities. So one major concern is whether they will respond deceptively to make themselves appear lower risk or just better in general. Inaccurate reports could also stem from lack of insight; that is, misrepresentation of themselves due to lack of awareness rather than intentional deceptiveness. Despite these concerns, the available evidence suggests that the SAQ can predict violent recidivism as well as more typical risk-assessment instruments.

Violent Extremist Risk Assessment (VERA) The VERA (Pressman, 2009) is a structured professional judgement guide for estimating risk for violent terrorist acts. The VERA consists of five sections:

1. Attitude/Mental Perspective

   ■ Sample items: attachment to ideology justifying violence; high levels of anger, frustration, persecution.

2. Contextual

   ■ Sample items: user of extremist websites; direct contact with violent extremists.

3. Historical

   ■ Sample items: early exposure to violence in home; state-sponsored military or paramilitary training.

4. Protective

   ■ Sample items: rejection of violence to obtain goals; interest in constructive political involvement.

5. Demographic

   ■ Sample items: male; young age.

The assessor rates each item as low, medium, or high, and determines an estimate of risk. The predictive accuracy of the VERA has not yet been evaluated. As Pressman (2009) has stated, the VERA should be used only for research purposes until sufficient evidence has demonstrated that it can estimate risk for terrorism-related violence with a reasonable degree of accuracy.

Box 8.2

You Be the Assessor

Imagine you are a clinical forensic psychologist conducting a risk assessment on Steven Smith, who was described at the beginning of the chapter. Recall that Steven is 36 years old and currently in prison for a series of violent and non-violent offences. In addition to his index offences, Steven has a long history of criminal behaviour, including violence. Not counting his index offences, he has 32 adult and 4 youth convictions. The most serious of these were assaults, weapons offences, armed robbery, and break and enters. Also on his record are numerous thefts, escapes from custody, failures to comply with release conditions (e.g., bail, probation), and failures to appear in court. His past prison sentences were also marked by threats and assaults on correctional officers and inmates; not surprisingly, he has spent a great deal of time in segregation (separated from other offenders).

Steven grew up in a small town in Ontario. His biological father, who also has a criminal history, left his mother before he was born. He was raised by his biological mother and his alcohol-abusing stepfather, who threw Steven out of the family home when he was 11 years old because of his stealing and other disruptive behaviour. Steven was subsequently placed in a series of group and foster homes, but was removed from each of them as a result of his unmanageable behaviour. At age 16, he robbed two variety stores at knifepoint.

Steven has spent most of his adult life incarcerated and has little in the way of educational or vocational skills or experience. He is impulsive, easily frustrated, and has difficulty focusing his attention. He has worked a total of six months and one week in his entire life. Most of his jobs lasted for only a short time and ended with him being fired (e.g., for sleeping on the job). When not in prison, Steven lives on the street, relies on social assistance, or is taken in for brief periods of time by various women. However, he has never been married and never lived with the same woman for more than a few months. All his friends and associates are involved in crime. Steven's financial situation is chronically poor. He has a history of abusing alcohol and drugs; he is often drunk or high during his criminal offences. Steven holds deeply entrenched antisocial attitudes. Although he says he wants to stop being violent, he perceives violence to be rewarding for him in many ways. He says that being aggressive gets him women and money, and generally facilitates his needs. "If I'm going to be a nice guy, people will start egging me on and saying I'm scared and I gotta prove myself."

Steven is eligible for parole. Use the information provided above to address the following risk assessment questions.

Questions

What is Steven's risk of violent reoffending if released (percent chance; low, moderate, or high)? What factor makes you most concerned that Steven will violently reoffend if released? What factor makes you most confident that Steven will not violently reoffend if released? Would you recommend Steven be released on parole? Why or why not? If paroled, what conditions would you recommend (e.g., restrictions on activities and movement, requirements for meeting with parole officer and psychologist, etc.)?

The You Be the Assessor box provides an opportunity to try your hand at risk assessment, perhaps by considering some of the evidence regarding risk factors for violence discussed above.

Accuracy

The primary concern with violence risk assessment instruments is the extent to which they are accurate. Obviously, it is important that such instruments are relatively accurate at predicting violent recidivism if they are to be used to make decisions about release and other offender management issues. So which risk-assessment instrument best predicts violent recidivism? Rice et al. (2013) found that the VRAG-R predicted violent recidivism with a high degree of accuracy ($r = .44$; AUC = .76). A number of researchers have examined the accuracy of various instruments. In a recent meta-analysis, Campbell, French, and Gendreau (2009) summarized the findings from these studies. Measures examined included those designed specifically to estimate the risk of violent recidivism, such as the original VRAG (Harris, Rice, and Quinsey 1993) and HCR-20, as well as measures designed to estimate risk of general recidivism (i.e., violent or non-violent), such as the Level of Service Inventory—Revised (LSI-R) (Andrews and Bonta 1995) and the Statistical Information on Recidivism scale (SIR) (Nuffield 1982). In addition, the PCL-R was examined. Although the PCL-R was not designed to estimate risk of recidivism, it is an important predictor of violent recidivism and is addressed in many risk assessments. The effect size used by the researchers was the average correlation coefficient weighted by sample size. As shown in Table 8.4, the SAQ and VRAG were among the best predictors of violent recidivism. The SAQ performed significantly better than the LSI, PCL, SIR, and HCR-20. The VRAG performed significantly better than the SIR and HCR-20.

Although Campbell et al. (2009) did not examine the accuracy of unstructured clinical judgment, it has been found to be less accurate at predicting violent recidivism than actuarial approaches in a number of meta-analyses (Bonta, Law, and Hanson 1998; Hanson and Morton-Bourgon 2009; Mossman 1994).

Table 8.4 Average Correlation (Weighted by Sample Size) between Risk-Assessment Measures and Violent Recidivism

Measure	k	N	r	95% CI
SAQ	8	1094	.37	.31 to .43
VRAG	14	2082	.32	.28 to .36
LSI/LSI-R	19	4361	.28	.25 to .31
PCL/PCL-R	24	4757	.27	.24 to .30
SIR	17	5618	.22	.19 to .25
HCR-20	11	1395	.22	.17 to .27

Note: k = number of effect sizes; N = number of subjects; CI = confidence interval around the average correlation.

Source: Adapted from Campbell, French, and Gendreau (2009).

TREATMENT APPROACHES AND EFFECTIVENESS

A NUMBER OF TREATMENT PROGRAMS HAVE BEEN DEVELOPED TO REDUCE VIOLENT recidivism. Some of these programs are designed to develop effective management of emotions (such as anger) that may play a role in violence, whereas others are more general in focus. The Hot Topics box presents a description of the correctional programs for violent offenders in Canadian federal penitentiaries.

Hot Topics

Correctional Service Canada (CSC) Correctional Programs for Violent Offenders

Our colleagues at Correctional Service Canada (CSC) provided the following "insider's view" of some of the approaches and techniques used in their correctional programs for violent offenders:

Grounded in a cognitive-behavioural approach to treatment, CSC has traditionally operated within a "multi-correctional program model," offering a large number of correctional programs (e.g., family violence programs, substance abuse programs, life skills programs, aggression, sex offending, programs targeting associates and attitudes, etc.) to offenders in order to target their criminogenic needs and ultimately reduce the likelihood of reoffending. As part of this multi-program model, the Service delivered a total of thirty-one national correctional programs to offenders, including seven distinctive correctional programs for Aboriginal offenders. Although for most of these programs it has been demonstrated that offenders who participate in the program have lower rates of reoffending than offenders who do not participate, the multi program model continued to present operational challenges for the Service that negatively impacted on enrollment and completion rates, particularly among male offenders. These

challenges were further compounded by the growing needs of a changing offender profile, as well as ongoing financial and human resource pressures.

In response to these challenges, CSC introduced the Integrated Correctional Program Model (ICPM) in all institutions and community sites in the Pacific and Atlantic regions beginning in January 2010 and January 2011, respectively. In June 2013, CSC's Executive Committee approved the national expansion of the Integrated Correctional Program Model into all men's institutions and community sites, which will occur over the next 3.5 years. The model was designed by combining the most effective aspects of existing interventions with the most promising innovations in the area of correctional programming and is applied through the span of an offender's sentence. The ICPM is an innovative and holistic approach to correctional programs, designed to enhance program efficiencies, program effectiveness, and public safety results. The ICPM consists of three distinct program streams for offenders: a multi-target program, an Aboriginal multi-target program, and a multi-target sex offender program, all of which include an institutional and community maintenance component. The ICPM also includes an Adapted Program in order to better support the needs of those offenders experiencing cognitive challenges who may otherwise be unable to successfully participate in the programming model. While these three distinct program streams allow continuing to target the needs and risks presented by specific offender populations, the multi-target nature of the program streams also allows to more holistically address the individual needs and risks of offenders. As most offenders enter CSC custody with needs in more than one domain, it is anticipated that the integrated, multi-target nature of ICPM programs will enhance offenders' understanding of the interplay among their multiple personal risk factors, as well as their understanding of how the same skill sets can be used to effectively manage them. More specifically, this approach helps them learn to apply the same skills to manage all of their harmful relationships, thoughts, emotions, and behaviours. As different offenders show different criminal behaviour, instead of focusing on separate behaviour, the ICPM focuses on the common deficits or general criminogenic needs that have been identified as important risk factors for all criminal behaviour.

The ICPM is guided by the risk-needs-responsivity (RNR) model [described in previous chapters] and the Good Lives Model (GLM) principles across three domains: program objectives (approach goals [goods promotion] and avoidance goals [risk management]), program content (assessment and intervention), and program delivery. For example, CSC provides correctional programs of differing intensity

levels—moderate or high—within each of the principal program areas. High intensity programs are longer than moderate intensity programs in duration and generally provide offenders with more skills and opportunities for skills rehearsal. The Correctional Program Officers (CPO) work collaboratively with offenders to take stock, consider what has gone wrong, and identify their risk factors, needs, and goals. They then try to reduce the risk to reoffend by developing cognitive and behavioural strategies to facilitate prosocial alternatives to offending; that is, to identify and achieve their goals and meet their needs in ways that are not only more acceptable to society than offending, but are also more effective and rewarding for the offender. There are three distinct program primers (short-term preparatory programs) within ICPM for each of the three streams: multi-target, Aboriginal, and sex offender. The primer takes place either at reception or at the offender's placement institution. Following the offender's participation in the ICPM primer, the offender is referred to a main program with supplementary motivational components as required, and follow-up institutional and community maintenance programs, which provide a sufficient level of intervention without requiring delays in safe release dates. Including the time spent in maintenance programs, high-risk and moderate-risk offenders would spend an average of 300 hours and 190 hours, respectively.

Some of the ICPM targets relevant for general violence and family violence are problem solving, goal setting, cognitive restructuring, emotion management, and self-regulation, on which they will work all the way through the correctional program continuum. For example, time is spent examining and countering thinking that supports violence, such as "violence works," "I need violence for respect and status," "I can't control myself," victim-blaming, minimizing harm, and hostile attribution bias. One approach to challenging such thinking is called CPR (Consequences, Personal standards, and Reality check):

Consequences: The offender is invited to think about what could be the consequences if he keeps thinking this way, what is likely to happen to him or to people around him.

Personal standards: The offender is invited to think about the person he wants to be and see if his thinking aligns with what he is striving for (what he wants to achieve).

Reality check: The offender is invited to evaluate if there are facts to support his thinking, if there is any other way to consider the situation (other possible explanations). The offender is then invited to come up with a more realistic and nuanced thought, called a "counter" which will likely start with "I would prefer if…," "It would be nice if…," etc.

Learning to solve problems without resorting to violence is another important target. One approach to examining and improving problem solving is called FOCUS:

F: Find the facts and deal with the feelings.

O: What are your options?

C: What are the consequences of your options?

U: Use a plan.

S: Stand back and evaluate: Did your plan work and/or what else do you need to do?

All individuals who deliver correctional programs must be trained in the correctional program area that they are delivering. This training includes a review of program content, program implementation structure, program policy, the process of assessing offender progress, and reporting on offender performance. Correctional program officers must undergo a thorough evaluation of their key program delivery competencies, as demonstrated throughout the training period. As part of the initial training evaluation, the certified program trainer will recommend whether the candidate is suitable or unsuitable for program delivery, and outline any special conditions that must be met before the CPO can deliver the program. The standardization of the initial training evaluation and scoring system helps to ensure that all staff members involved in correctional program delivery are evaluated objectively and consistently across the country. They also undergo a quality review process to ensure program integrity and compliance with policy. Those who meet all of the identified requirements are then certified within the program area in which they have been trained.

Effectiveness

There are a number of ways to address questions about the effectiveness of treatment for violent offenders. However, the most important issue regarding effectiveness is the extent to which treatment reduces violent recidivism. Studies addressing this issue typically compare the recidivism rates of offenders who receive the treatment to those who do not. There have been surprisingly few well-controlled evaluations of the effectiveness of these programs (Jolliffe and Farrington 2007; Polaschek and Collie 2004). Dowden and Andrews (2000) conducted a meta-analysis of studies on treatment and violent recidivism that included 52 comparisons from a total of 35 studies of any programs (broadly defined to include treatment as well as sanctions) for male offenders, most of whom were adults. The effect size used in their meta-analysis was the phi coefficient (a correlation coefficient for the relationship between two dichotomous variables; in this case, treatment versus comparison group and violent recidivism versus no violent recidivism). By convention, a correlation of around .10 is considered small, .30 is considered medium, and .50 is considered large (Cohen 1988). The average correlation for any treatment was .12 ($p < .05$), which reflects violent recidivism rates about 12 percentage points lower among treated groups than comparison groups. This was significantly higher than the correlation between sanctions (e.g., prison) and violent recidivism (−.01). Thus, treatment was associated with significantly lower violent recidivism rates, whereas sanctions were not.

Programs can vary widely in terms of who is treated, what is treated, and how treatment is delivered. Here we are referring to the principles of effective correctional treatment: the risk, need, and responsivity principles discussed in Chapter 4 (Andrews, Bonta, and Hoge 1990). Dowden and Andrews (2000) also examined whether reductions in violent recidivism for treated versus comparison groups would be greater when programs adhered to these principles than when they did not. Their findings were generally supportive of the importance of these principles for maximizing the effectiveness of treatment. Concerning the risk principle, effects were larger (though not significantly so) for programs directed at higher-risk offenders ($r = .09$) than for programs directed at low-risk offenders ($r = .04$). With regard to the need principle, effects were significantly larger for programs focusing primarily on criminogenic needs ($r = .20$) than for those focusing primarily on non-criminogenic needs ($r = .00$). For the responsivity principle, effects were significantly larger for behavioural or cognitive-behavioural programs ($r = .19$) than for other approaches to treatment ($r = .01$). In addition, the greater number of principles to which programs adhered, the greater the association between treatment and lower violent recidivism. Specifically, for sanctions and treatment that did not adhere to any of the three principles, the average effect was .01; for treatment following only one of the three principles the average effect was .07; for treatment following any two of the three principles the average effect was .15; and for treatment following all three of the principles the average effect was .20. Thus, just as with general offending, treatments that follow the principles of effective corrections are associated with larger reductions in violent recidivism than treatments that do not follow these principles.

Although the outcome examined by Dowden and Andrews (2000) was violent recidivism, their meta-analysis included studies not only on violent offenders in programs designed to reduce non-sexual violence, but also on other offenders (e.g., sex offenders, mixed groups of offenders) and programs (e.g., sex offender, family violence, general crime). It is very encouraging that these programs reduced violent recidivism despite the breadth of participants and focus, but how well do programs with the explicit aim of reducing violent recidivism perform with general violent offenders? Jolliffe and Farrington

(2007) addressed this issue in a recent meta-analysis on the effectiveness of general violence programs with generally violent offenders. They only included studies a) on generally violent (e.g., not primarily family violence or sex offending) adult male offenders, b) with relatively strong methodology (e.g., random assignment to treatment and comparison condition; matching of treatment and comparison subjects on a risk-relevant variable), c) with at least 25 offenders in both the treated and comparison groups, and d) published between 1975 and 2007. Jolliffe and Farrington (2007) found eight studies that met their criteria and that included the outcome of violent recidivism. The effect they used in their meta-analysis is Cohen's d. By convention, a d of around 0.20 is considered small, 0.50 is considered medium, and 0.80 is considered large (Cohen 1988). In this meta-analysis, a d of 0.00 would indicate no difference between treated and comparison groups in their rates of violent recidivism. A d greater than zero would reflect lower rates of violent recidivism in the treated groups than in the comparison groups, whereas a d less than zero would reflect higher rates of violent recidivism in the treated groups than in the comparison groups.

The effect sizes, both for the individual studies and the average of these studies, are shown in Figure 8.3. Looking at the effects for the individual studies in the meta-analysis, you can see that most found lower rates of violent recidivism in the treated group than in the comparison group; six of the eight effects are above zero. However, these individual effects reached statistical significance ($p < .05$) in only two studies. Overall, a small significant average effect size was found; mean d between 0.13 and 0.16 depending on whether the effects were calculated using a fixed effect or random effect model. Thus, treatment for violent offenders is associated, on average, with lower rates of violent recidivism.

Jolliffe and Farrington (2007) also examined some potential moderators of treatment effectiveness, such as the features of the treatments and research designs. With regard to treatment features, they determined whether a given program included each of the following elements: a) addressed offenders' anger (anger control); b) included cognitive-behavioural

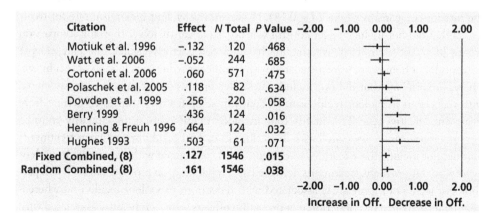

Citation	Effect	N Total	P Value
Motiuk et al. 1996	−.132	120	.468
Watt et al. 2006	−.052	244	.685
Cortoni et al. 2006	.060	571	.475
Polaschek et al. 2005	.118	82	.634
Dowden et al. 1999	.256	220	.058
Berry 1999	.436	124	.016
Henning & Freuh 1996	.464	124	.032
Hughes 1993	.503	61	.071
Fixed Combined, (8)	.127	1546	.015
Random Combined, (8)	.161	1546	.038

−2.00   −1.00   0.00   1.00   2.00
Increase in Off. Decrease in Off.

Figure 8.3 Effect Sizes (Cohen's *d*) for Treatment and Violent Recidivism

Source: Jolliffe and Farrington (2007).

Table 8.5 Effect Sizes for Violent Recidivism by Program or Study
Features

Feature	k	Mean d	Feature	k	Mean d
Anger control	6	0.14*	No anger control	2	0.08
Cognitive skills	7	0.16*	No cognitive skills	1	−0.05
Moral training	3	0.06	No moral training	5	0.15*
Role play	6	0.19*	No role play	2	−0.08
Empathy training	3	−0.05	No empathy training	5	0.20*
Relapse prevention	5	0.18*	No relapse prevention	3	−0.01
Offender homework	3	0.37*	No offender homework	5	0.07
Rehabilitation professional	5	0.10	Correctional officer	3	0.15*
High quality studies	5	0.08	Low quality studies	3	0.37*
Intention to treat	3	0.07	Completers	5	0.22*

Note: k = number of studies; * $p < .05$.

Source: Adapted from Jolliffe and Farrington (2007).

skills training (cognitive skills); c) included training about morals (moral training); d) used role-playing for training (role play); e) addressed empathy (empathy); f) included relapse prevention planning (relapse prevention); and g) included rehearsal of skills or training between treatment sessions (homework). As illustrated in Table 8.5, some of these features were associated with observed reductions in violent recidivism. More specifically, the violent recidivism rate for treatments that included anger control was significantly lower than the rate for comparison groups ($d = 0.14$). However, the violent recidivism rate for treatments that did not include anger control was not significantly lower than for comparison groups ($d = 0.08$). Similarly, treatments that included cognitive skills, role play, relapse prevention, or homework were associated with significant reductions in violent recidivism, whereas treatments that did not include these elements were not significantly associated with reductions in violent recidivism. In contrast, some features seemed to detract from treatment effectiveness. Treatments that included moral training or empathy training were not significantly associated with reductions in violent recidivism, whereas treatments that did not include these features were significantly associated with reductions in violent recidivism. Surprisingly, treatments delivered by a rehabilitation professional such as a psychologist were not significantly associated with reductions in violent recidivism, whereas treatments delivered by correctional or probation officers were significantly associated with reductions in violent recidivism!

Note, however, that just because one effect reached statistical significance and the other did not, it does not necessarily mean that the two effects are significantly different from each other. For example, the effect for treatments including cognitive skills (d = 0.16) was not significantly higher than the effect for treatments not including cognitive skills (d = −0.05). Similarly, effects did not significantly differ as a function of the presence or absence of anger control, moral training, and relapse prevention. Nor did they differ between programs delivered by rehabilitation professionals or correctional/probation officers. However, the difference between effect sizes was statistically significant for role play, empathy training, and homework.

You may now be ready to conclude that these treatments generally do reduce violent recidivism. Violent recidivism rates are on average lower among treated offenders than comparison groups. These differences may be small, but they are significant, and better treatments (e.g., those adhering to principles of effective treatment, those including role play to practice and develop new skills) show larger differences between the treated and comparison groups. What else do you need to know? There are some important methodological issues to take into consideration before drawing any conclusions from the available findings. Although Jolliffe and Farrington (2007) included only studies that met a minimal standard of methodological rigour, there was still variability in the quality of these studies. Two key issues in these sorts of studies are random assignment and attrition. The most rigorous tests of causal relationships are true experiments, which, in this case, would involve randomly assigning violent offenders to a treatment group or a comparison group (e.g., no-treatment control group or treatment as usual). Offenders would then be followed up after a few years in the community to determine whether they had violently reoffended. One could be fairly confident that any observed difference in violent recidivism between treated and comparison groups was caused by the treatment.

But what should be done with offenders who were assigned to the treatment group but did not complete their treatment? Attrition presents a real challenge to researchers and non-completion rates can be fairly high among violence programs (over 30 percent in some studies; e.g., Cortoni, Nunes, and Latendresse 2006). On one hand, it seems reasonable to exclude non-completers from the treatment group and compare the recidivism rate for the completers against the rate for the untreated offenders. Exclusion of the non-completers can introduce bias, however. Non-completion of treatment is associated with increased violent recidivism (Cortoni et al. 2006) and non-completers are generally more antisocial than completers (Nunes and Cortoni 2006; Nunes, Cortoni, and Serin 2010). Although it is easy to identify and exclude non-completers in the treated group, it is not possible to identify those in the untreated group who would not have completed treatment had it been offered. Thus we would expect lower rates of violent recidivism among treatment completers compared to untreated offenders even if treatment had no effect at all. The most conservative way to deal with attrition, then, is to retain all offenders who had been assigned to treatment (whether they actually completed it or not) in analytic comparisons with the untreated group. This approach is sometimes referred to as "intention to treat."

Jolliffe and Farrington (2007) found that studies of higher methodological quality generally yielded smaller effect sizes than studies of lower quality (r = −.64). Ratings of methodological quality generally reflected the degree to which a study was a relatively accurate and unbiased test of the effectiveness of treatment. Among other things, these ratings considered the issues mentioned above: assignment to groups, non-equivalence of treated and comparison groups, and attrition. As shown in the last two rows of Table 8.5, treatment was not associated with significant reductions in violent recidivism in studies of high methodological quality or studies that did intention-to-treat analyses. However, treatment was associated with significant reductions in violent recidivism in studies of lower methodological quality or studies that only compared completers to comparison groups. The difference between these effect sizes was statistically significant for methodological quality (0.08 vs. 0.37, $p < .05$), but not for intention to treat (0.07 vs. 0.22, non-significant).

As Jolliffe and Farrington (2007) point out, the finding that methodological quality is negatively correlated with effect size makes it "difficult to ascertain the extent to which the interventions with large effect sizes are effective because of their superior type or method of treatment or because their effects were artificially increased by biased methods" (p. 10). To address this issue, Jolliffe and Farrington (2007) re-analyzed the program features presented in Table 8.5, but this time statistically controlled for the study feature of methodological quality. In these multivariate analyses, none of the program features emerged as significant moderators of treatment effectiveness. That is, program features such as role play and homework that were associated with greater effectiveness in the univariate analyses described above were no longer significantly related to observed reductions in violent recidivism after methodological quality was taken into account. Given the small number of studies in this meta-analysis, it would be premature to draw any strong conclusions. Based on the available evidence, it remains unclear whether the lower rates of violent recidivism associated with treatment actually demonstrate that treatment is effective or are more parsimoniously attributed to methodological shortcomings (Dowden and Andrews 2000; Jolliffe and Farrington 2007; Quinsey, Harris et al. 2006).

Now that we have examined some approaches to treatment of violent offenders, try applying these discussions in the You Be the Therapist box.

Box 8.3

You Be the Therapist

Imagine Steven Smith (described in the chapter opening and the You Be the Assessor box) has just begun his current sentence and it is your job to provide treatment that will reduce his risk for violent reoffending.

Questions

What would you target in treatment? How would you target it? How would you monitor Steven's progress (i.e., how do you determine the extent to which Steven has improved in the area targeted)? How would you try to increase and maintain Steven's investment and commitment to treatment? Do you think any treatment could be effective at reducing Steven's risk of violent reoffending?

FUTURE DIRECTIONS

WE NEED MORE CONCLUSIVE EVIDENCE ABOUT THE CAUSES OF VIOLENCE. SUCH EVIDENCE will improve the accuracy of assessments and the effectiveness of interventions, and, ultimately, reduce violence. As noted above, stronger methodology will produce more conclusive evidence both about the causes of violence and about the effectiveness of interventions aimed at reducing violence.

SUMMARY

1. Violence is relatively rare in Canada. The rate of violent crime has generally decreased since the early 1990s.

2. Reactive violence is an impulsive reaction to some real or perceived provocation or threat, whereas instrumental violence is premeditated and ultimately aimed at achieving some secondary goal. Reactive and instrumental aggression may be best viewed as opposite ends of a continuum along which acts of violence can fall.

3. Four key approaches to risk assessment are unstructured clinical judgment, empirical actuarial, mechanical, and structured professional judgment. Actuarial risk-assessment instruments (e.g., VRAG) are more accurate in predicting violent recidivism than unstructured clinical judgment.

4. Researchers generally find lower violent recidivism rates among treated compared to untreated offenders, and programs that follow the general principles of effective corrections appear to be more effective than programs that do not. Although these findings are very encouraging, debate continues about whether the lower rates of violent recidivism associated with treatment actually demonstrate that it is effective because the research methodology used in most studies leaves the results open to alternate interpretations.

Discussion Questions

1. What explains the drop in violent crime rates over the last few decades?

2. Given that static factors are such robust predictors of long-term violent recidivism, is incapacitation a more realistic goal than rehabilitation with very high-risk offenders?

3. Evidence indicates that the SAQ, a self-report risk-assessment instrument, can predict violent recidivism as accurately as instruments based on extensive file reviews, such as the VRAG. Should correctional agencies and assessors start using the SAQ instead of other more resource-demanding instruments?

4. Although studies of poorer methodological quality have found that treatment is associated with significant reductions in violent recidivism, studies of better methodological quality have not. How should these findings be interpreted?

Chapter 9
Intimate Partner Violence

Susan was 21 when she married her college sweetheart, Matthew, an officer in the Canadian Armed Forces. Prior to his deployment to Afghanistan, Matthew occasionally yelled at Susan about her excessive spending and her failure to keep the children quiet. When they first married, he called her names and threatened to use violence, which escalated to slapping her several times and once shoving her down the front steps of the house. Despite the verbal and physical abuse, Susan never called the police or told her family or friends due to her fear of what would happen to her, her husband, and her children.

Shortly after Matthew returned from overseas, the military transferred him, Susan, and their two children Michael (ten) and Natalie (seven), from their on-base home in Petawawa to an off-base home in Alberta. Susan hoped that moving to a new location would bring a fresh start. However, the verbal and physical abuse resumed once the family had settled into their new home. While in Alberta, Matthew continued to limit the amount of money Susan was allowed to spend. One evening Mathew and Susan again argued about money but this time it escalated to Mathew punching Susan in the face, throwing her on the ground, and choking her. The next morning she went to a medical clinic to get treatment for a fractured wrist. The physician who examined Susan suspected domestic abuse but she denied the allegation. Susan felt partly to blame and believed that if she could change her behaviour Matthew would be happier and stop the abuse.

Learning Objectives

1   Distinguish between different types of abuse and understand the prevalence of intimate partner abuse.

2   Describe the consequences of abuse.

3   Outline how social learning theory has been used to explain intimate violence.

4   Explain the ecological model of family violence as it relates to risk factors for intimate partner violence.

5   Describe the effectiveness of treatment programs for intimate violence.

6   List the different typologies of male batterers.

INTRODUCTION

IDEALLY, A RELATIONSHIP IS A PLACE WHERE SOMEONE CAN FEEL LOVED, SECURE, and safe. However, within some relationships, there is abuse, fear, and a lack of emotional bonds that can lead to violence. The occurrence and aftermath of this violence can have devastating short- and long-term effects. In some cases, children who witness violence become abusers themselves and the cycle passes from generation to generation. As in the opening vignette, it is not unusual for victims of abuse to initially blame themselves. Victims will often attempt to change their behaviour to avoid triggering an abusive episode, but the abuse usually continues and even escalates.

Why study intimate partner violence? First, it is the most prevalent form of violence in society. Second, it is distinct from other types of violence since the victims and perpetrators know each other and there is often an ongoing relationship prior to, during, and after a violent episode.

Although violence occurs between other family members (siblings, child and parent) this chapter focuses on violence occurring between intimate partners either living together or not (including violence that occurs within dating relationships.) Estimates of the magnitude of intimate partner violence vary depending on the sample, type, and severity of violence and the method of data collection. What is clear, however, is that intimate partner violence is likely the most common form of violence.

CONTEXT

INTIMATE PARTNER VIOLENCE OCCURS BETWEEN INTIMATE PARTNERS WHO ARE living together, separated, or dating. Spousal violence is more specific and refers to violence between same-sex couples who are legally married, common-law, separated, or divorced. For much of history, intimate partner violence had a quasi-legitimacy, due primarily to cultural and religious attitudes that effectively placed women in subservient roles within the family. Only in the recent past have attitudes toward the issue changed. The women's liberation movement and the growth of feminism led women to question the long-standing acceptance of family violence. Not until the 1980s did major changes take place in Canadian law dealing with intimate partner violence. In approximately the same time period, it also become a major research area.

Defining intimate partner violence is controversial. Should all abuse in the context of a relationship be included or only more serious forms of abuse? How intimate partner violence is defined has a considerable impact on the reported rates. Unfortunately, no consensus exists for a definition, although most current definitions of intimate partner violence include non-violent abuse (such as emotional or financial abuse) and sexual abuse. Differential rates of abuse can be the result of differences in who is sampled and what is counted.

When examining the frequency of violence, it is important to clarify the distinction between prevalence and incidence. **Prevalence** refers to the *total* number of people who have experienced violence in a specified time period, whereas **incidence** is the number of *new* cases identified or reported at a given point in time, usually one year. When reporting

Table 9.1 Types of Intimate Partner Violence

Types of Abuse	Characteristics	Examples
Psychological/emotional	The infliction of mental distress	Insulting, swearing, yelling, threatening, mocking, ignoring, isolating, or excluding the person from meaningful activities
Physical	The infliction of pain or injury	Beating, punching, burning, pushing, kicking, hitting with hand or object, stabbing, choking, force-feeding, or restraint
Financial/material	The illegal or improper exploitation and/or use of funds or resources	Misusing power of attorney, tricking or threatening a person out of assets, cashing cheques without authorization, restricting access to bank accounts, or using a person's money for something it was not intended to be used for
Sexual	Any kind of unwanted sexual behaviour directed toward an adult	Showing of pornography, exposure of genitals, sexual harassment, exploitation through prostitution, or sexual assault

on the estimates of intimate partner violence, many factors will influence the prevalence and incidence figures.

DEFINITIONS

THE TYPES OF ABUSE THAT CAN OCCUR WITHIN INTIMATE RELATIONSHIPS ARE described in Table 9.1. Some forms of abuse are more common than others. Psychological abuse is often described by individuals as one of the most hurtful types of abuse. Financial abuse is most often studied in the context of elder abuse but can also occur within intimate relationships.

WHY DO WE CARE?

Prevalence and Nature of Intimate Partner Violence

How often do married or common-law couples engage in violence? Every five years, Statistics Canada conducts the General Social Survey on victimization experiences and includes questions about violence within spousal partners. The most recent Canadian survey was completed in November of 2015, but at the time of writing the data on spousal violence were not yet available. As a result, this chapter uses data from the 2009 survey (Brennan 2011).

In the 2009 survey, a modified version of the Conflict Tactics Scale (Straus 1979; see the Hot Topics box) was administered to a large sample (19 422) of men and women aged 15 years or older from across Canada. The scale was designed to measure psychological, physical, and sexual violence in spousal relationships, including threats and sexual assault over both the previous 12 months and the previous five years (questions about emotional and financial abuse were also asked). Respondents reported that in the year preceding the survey, 2 percent of male and female respondents had experienced physical and/or sexual assault. In the five years preceding the survey (2005 to 2009), 6 percent of male and female respondents reported having experienced physical and/or sexual assault (17 percent of respondents reported experiencing emotional or financial abuse).

Although both men and women experienced violence, women reported experiencing triple the amount of severe forms of violence (i.e., being choked, sexually assaulted, or threatened by a partner using a knife or gun), were more likely to experience repeated victimizations (57 percent of women versus 40 percent of men), and were more likely to have been injured (42 percent of women versus 18 percent of men). Younger people (aged 25 to 34 years) were three times more likely to experience intimate partner violence (IPV) as compared to older people (aged 45 years or older). Violence (in the previous five years) was more common for those respondents who identified as Aboriginal or as having physical or mental health problems, but was less common for immigrants. The highest rates of violence were reported by gays and lesbians (twice as high as compared to heterosexuals) and bisexuals (four times higher as compared to heterosexuals). The experience of IPV did not vary across income or educational level. Violence against women was more likely to be reported to the police (23 percent) than was violence against men (7 percent), a finding echoed in research discussed later in the chapter. The primary reason for respondents to report to the police was to have the violence stopped and to obtain police

Table 9.2 Spousal Violence in Different Groups over the Previous Five Years (Physical and/or Sexual Assault), as Reported in 2009

Group	Percent
Immigrant	4%
Female	6%
Male	6%
Physical and/or mental condition	8%
Aboriginal	10%
Gays and lesbians	12%
Bisexuals	24%
Source: Statistics Canada (2011).	

How to Measure Intimate Partner Violence: The Conflict Tactics Scale

In 1979, Murray Straus was interested in studying conflict in intimate relationships but needed some way to quantify the different forms of conflict resolution techniques. He developed the **Conflict Tactics Scale (CTS)** to assess how a person and their partner resolve conflict. The CTS consists of 18 items ranging from constructive problem-solving (e.g., discussing issues calmly) to verbal aggression (e.g., swearing or threatening to hit) and physical aggression (e.g., slapping or using a knife). Respondents indicate how often they have used different methods and how often they have experienced these acts. The CTS has been used in hundreds of studies in over 25 countries to measure intimate violence. Having a common measurement tool enables researchers to compare findings across studies. However, a number of limitations have been identified (see Archer 1999 and Dobash, Dobash, Wilson, and Daly 1992 for reviews). These limitations include a failure to assess for the context and purpose of violent acts (offensive versus defensive responses), few items measuring psychological aggression, no assessment of sexual aggression, and no assessment of the consequences of aggression (what types of injury occur). In response to these concerns, Straus, Hamby, Boney-McCoy, and Sugerman (1996) developed a more comprehensive version—the CTS-2, in which the following changes were made:

1. The physical aggression scale was expanded to include more acts (e.g., burned or scalded partner on purpose, slammed partner against wall).

2. The verbal aggression scale was renamed psychological aggression and additional items were added (e.g., did something to spite partner).
3. The reasoning scale was renamed negotiation and additional items were added (e.g., explained side of argument).
4. New scales were added to measure sexual aggression (e.g., I used threats to make my partner have sex) and physical injury (e.g., I had a broken bone from a fight with my partner).
5. A better description was developed of minor versus more serious forms of acts.
6. Items from each scale were interspersed to minimize response sets.

The CTS-2 contains 78 items and has become the dominant instrument for assessing violence among dating and cohabiting partners. Researchers have also begun to investigate whether couples agree with each other. Simpson and Christensen (2005) had 273 treatment-seeking couples complete the CTS-2. There were low to moderate levels of agreement, with both men and women reporting that their partner had committed more aggressive acts than they had committed. There was better agreement on specific objective acts (e.g., I slapped my partner) as compared to more general items (e.g., I did something to spite my partner). Some researchers have started to develop alternative methods to assess intimate violence, such as interviews or diary methods where participants record violent acts as they occur (Fals-Stewart, Birchler, and Kelley 2003).

protection. The primary reason for respondents not to report to the police was because they viewed it as a personal matter.

In 2013, the World Health Organization (WHO) reviewed research from 79 countries and concluded that "violence against women is pervasive globally" (p. 3). It found global lifetime prevalence of physical and/or sexual violence in intimate relationships to be 30 percent, however prevalence rates varied widely around the world. The highest lifetime prevalence rates were found in central sub-Saharan Africa (66 percent), South Asia (42 percent), and Andean Latin America (41 percent), and the lowest rates were found in East Asia (15 percent), Western Europe (19 percent) and North America (21 percent). In addition, findings showed that 38 percent of all murders of women were committed by their intimate partners. These survey results provide a clear indication that IPV remains a prevalent and ongoing societal concern.

Is there increased risk of engaging in IPV among people with a psychiatric disorder? A recent meta-analysis of 17 studies found that there was an increased risk of lifetime physical violence against a partner in men and women with a psychiatric disorder as compared to those without a psychiatric disorder (Oram et al. 2014). However, it was not clear from the studies reviewed whether the violence occurred when the person was actively experiencing psychiatric symptoms. In addition, the authors were not able to examine whether the violence perpetrated might have been due to substance use. It has been shown that much of the increased risk of general violence in mentally ill people is due to substance use (Van Dorn, Volavka, and Johnson 2012).

The International Dating Violence Study (Chan et al. 2008) used the Conflict Tactics Scale–2 to examine the prevalence of dating violence in 14 252 university students across 32 countries. Table 9.3 presents victimization reports of any physical aggression including minor violence (e.g., threw something to hurt partner, slapped, twisted partner's arm) to severe violence (e.g., choked partner, beat up partner, used a knife or gun on partner) over the previous 12 months in selected countries. Rates of being a victim of sexual coercion in selected countries were also reported. Sexual coercion included both minor acts (e.g., made my partner have sex without a condom, insisted on sex when my partner did not want to) to more severe acts (e.g., used force to make my partner have oral or anal sex, used threats to make my partner have sex). Although there were substantial variations across nations, it is important to note that even in Israel, the country with the lowest rate, 14 percent of students had been physically assaulted by a dating partner within the previous 12 months. In comparison to other countries, Canadian dating violence rates were in the lower half of the nations surveyed. However, about one in five Canadian university students reported having experienced physical assault by their dating partners in the previous 12 months. In contrast, the United States and Canada had relatively high rates of sexual coercion as compared to other countries.

Also in 2013, Statistics Canada (Beaupré 2015) provided information on the number of police-reported intimate partner and dating partner violence incidents across Canada. Statistics Canada has been examining the nature and extent of family violence since 1998. Their most recent survey also included information about dating violence. A total of 90 720 incidents were reported in 2013 (this rate has remained steady over the past five years). The survey showed that violence often does not end when a relationship ends—in 33 percent of cases the perpetrator was an ex-intimate or dating partner. The highest incidence of victimization was in younger people between the ages of 20 to 29. The data

Table 9.3 Victimization Rates of Physical Assault and Sexual Coercion in Dating Relationships in University Students over a 12-Month Period

Country	Any Assaults (%)	Severe Assaults (%)	Sexual Coercion (%)
Asia and Middle East			
China	27.2	7.8	15.4
India	35.5	13.7	18.6
Israel	13.9	4.9	21.4
Australia and New Zealand			
Australia	22.3	5.8	22.6
New Zealand	27.0	5.6	26.4
Europe			
Belgium	25.4	4.5	11.3
Germany	30.4	8.3	41.6
Greece	34.4	14.0	46.2
Netherlands	28.0	2.3	9.1
Portugal	14.4	2.8	24.4
Russia	27.3	7.1	25.6
Sweden	15.1	2.7	16.4
United Kingdom	32.1	7.5	24.2
Latin America			
Brazil	19.3	5.4	37.0
Mexico	39.1	10.2	21.4
North America			
Canada	22.2	7.3	28.4
United States	28.3	9.3	31.8

Source: Adapted from Chan et al. (2008).

likely underestimate the amount of violent offences, since most victims do not call the police. In addition, police data only include forms of intimate partner violence that are chargeable under the Canadian *Criminal Code* (most forms of psychological and financial abuse are excluded). Similar to other violent crimes, there regional differences are evident. Police-reported rates of intimate partner violence are highest in Saskatchewan and Alberta (635.0 and 512.7 victims per 100 000 population, respectively) and lowest in Ontario and PEI (231.8 and 239.0 victims per 100 000 population, respectively).

A victim of intimate partner violence.

However, in Nunavut the rate is six times higher than in Saskatchewan (3995.4 per 100 000 population). These differences may be due to the differing number of risk factors across the provinces and territories: social isolation, younger couples, higher levels of unemployment, higher rates of alcohol consumption, more common-law marriages, lack of resources for victims, and the proportion of Aboriginals. Females are the most likely victims of police-reported intimate partner violence across all provinces and territories, with 80 percent of the victims being female. Charges were laid in 74 percent of the incidents against female victims and in 64 percent of incidents against male victims.

Police forces recognize that intimate partner violence is a continuing problem that requires a serious response. Unfortunately, the majority of women who are abused by their partner do not call the police. A study by Akers and Kaukinen (2009), using data from the Canadian General Social Survey from 1999, examined which demographic and incidence-related variables were related to police-reporting decisions. Married women were less likely to report violence to the police. This finding may be due to the stronger financial and emotional ties a married woman has to her spouse. In contrast, women with children living at home who witness their abuse were more likely to contact the police. Minority women were more likely than Caucasian women to report spousal violence. The likelihood of reporting increased with age, but in older samples this effect was reduced. Women were also more likely to call the police if they were injured or if a weapon was involved. If the abuser was drinking during the incident or if he also destroyed property, the victim was more likely to report the abuse. Police officers responding to calls of

Should Cultural Background Be an Excuse for IPV?

In 2015, the court of appeal in Ontario overturned the 18-month sentence given to an Iranian man for repetitive violence towards his wife and children. The offender often beat his wife and children by hitting and punching them and would sexually assault his wife three to four times a month. The family immigrated to Canada from Iran in 2009 and according to the victim the abuse started in Iran and continued when they immigrated to Canada. The victim did not report the abuse because she felt ashamed and was not sure the police in Canada would do anything since this type of violence was common in Iran. The police were notified when one of the sons told his teacher about the abuse. The sentencing judge stated that this "suggests a significant cultural gap between what is not accepted in this country, and what is accepted in her native country." The court of appeal overturned the 18-month sentence and replaced it was a 4-year sentence. The three appeal court judges stated in their decision the following:

> "Cultural differences do not excuse or mitigate criminal conduct. To hold otherwise undermines the equality of all individuals before and under the law, a crucial Charter value… This is of particular significance in the context of domestic violence. All women in Canada are entitled to the same level of protection from abusers. The need to strongly denounce domestic violence is in no way diminished when that conduct is the product of cultural beliefs that render women acceptable targets of male violence."

It is clear from this ruling that cultural factors should not be used a mitigating factor when determining sentence length.

Source: *R. v. H.E.* (2015).

domestic violence need to be aware of who is likely to contact them (and, potentially, who is not likely to contact them despite the presence of abuse). With this information, they can better respond with sensitivity and care. See the Media Spotlight box for a discussion of whether cultural background should be a mitigating factor for engaging in IPV.

Male Victims of Intimate Violence

Historically, domestic violence has been conceptualized as male violence against female partners, and this form of violence has been the focus of research and public policy. However, intimate violence is not solely the province of men acting against women. Women also initiate violence and, according to some studies, engage in more minor violence than men (Archer 2002). In a large study, Williams and Frieze (2005) analyzed the occurrence of violence in 3519 couples and found that the most frequently occurring type of violence was mutual and mild violence followed by mutual severe violence. This pattern indicates that, at least for some forms of intimate violence, the long-held belief that males are the primary instigators is false (Carney, Buttell, and Dutton 2007). Recent evidence indicates that it is possible to identify personality and behavioural features in 15-year-old girls that will predict their use of violence in dating relationships at age 21 regardless of whether their male partner uses violence (Moffitt, Caspi, Rutter, and Silva 2001). Mutuality of violence is also found in dating relationships. In a large international study of dating violence among university students in 32 countries, Straus (2008) reported that a slightly higher percentage of women engage in minor violence (e.g., slapping, throwing something at a partner that could hurt) and that equal rates of serious violence occur for men and women.

Gender biases in which men are disadvantaged exist in several other contexts. A long-standing belief associated with intimate violence is that due to differences in physical size and strength, women are most likely to suffer serious injuries compared to men. However, several studies (e.g., Carney et al 2007; Felson and Cares 2005) have shown that while it is true that women are more likely to be injured than men as a consequence of intimate violence, the incidence of men being injured by women is surprisingly high. A gender bias is also present in police responses to domestic violence. G. R. Brown (2004) found that when the female partner was injured, the male was charged in 91 percent of the cases; however, when the male was injured, the female was charged only 60 percent of the time. When no injury occurred, the female was charged in 13 percent of cases as compared to 52 percent of cases for males. The way courts treat men and women charged with domestic violence also appears to differ. Charges against women are more likely to be dropped by prosecutors and, if charged, women are less likely to be found guilty. Brown (2004) reported that in severe injury cases, 71 percent of men and 22 percent of women defendants were found guilty. A major factor for why such a low percentage of women are found guilty was that male victims were often not willing to testify.

Follingstad, Helff, Binford, Runge, and White (2004) found that the gender bias even extends to psychologists. They presented two scenarios to a large sample of clinicians (N = 449, 56 percent male, median age 52). The scenarios provided a context and description of psychologically abusive behaviours. Critically, Follingstad et al. reversed the gender of the protagonists in the scenarios. Results showed that the same behaviour was rated more abusive and severe when it was carried out by a male than when carried out by a female. Moreover, this bias was not affected by the context of the scenario (i.e., frequency, intent, perception of recipient) nor by the gender of the psychologist. Specific items rated more abusive if performed by a man included "made to account for whereabouts at all times," "would not allow to look at members of same sex," "threatened to have committed to an institution," and "made derogatory comments."

Almost all prevention and intervention programs target men who abuse their partners. It is essential that violence by women be recognized and that robust efforts implemented to end assaults by women.

CONSEQUENCES OF INTIMATE PARTNER VIOLENCE

THERE IS CONSIDERABLE RESEARCH ON THE PREVALENCE AND NATURE OF SPOUSAL and dating violence globally. However, there has been less research examining the outcomes of experiencing this form of violence. The negative consequences can be a result of physical trauma, psychological trauma and stress, or fear and lack of control. Multiple adverse health outcomes for both victims and their children have been identified, including physical, sexual and reproductive, and mental health disorders (WHO 2013). The following consequences have been identified:

- Physical trauma: Physical injuries can lead to permanent disabilities. Spousal violence resulted in 42 percent of women reporting physical injuries.

- Sexual health: Refusal of men who engage in violence to use contraceptives leads to higher rates of HIV, sexually transmitted diseases, and unwanted pregnancies in victims of spousal violence.

- Reproductive health: Violence during pregnancy increases the likelihood of having a miscarriage, stillbirth, premature delivery, and low-birth-weight babies.

- Mental health: Violence leads to higher rates of depression, post-traumatic stress disorder, sleep and eating disorders, problem drinking, and suicide attempts.

- Physical health: A wide range of physical health problems can result including headaches, back pain, gastrointestinal disorders, and fibromyalgia.

- Social and economic costs: Women who experience violence often suffer isolation, inability to work, loss of wages, and limited ability to care for themselves and their children.

- Impact on children: Children who grow up in families where there is violence may have emotional and behavioural problems. They are also more likely to engage in violence as adolescents and adults.

The WHO (2013) demonstrated that violence against women is a major contributing factor to physical and mental health problems, causes harm to observing children, and limits victims' participation in society.

Typologies of Female Victims

Little research has been done to develop typologies of battered women. Roberts and Roberts (2005) developed a typology that classified victims into five levels based on duration and severity of abuse using interviews with 501 battered women.

The features of the Level 1 (short-term) group include:

- Mild to moderate intensity violence
- One to three violent incidents
- Less than one year in the dating relationship
- Leaving the relationship shortly after the onset of violence
- Middle class with secondary or higher education
- Presence of caring support system

Features of the Level 2 (intermediate) group include:

- Moderate to severe intensity violence
- Three to fifteen incidents

- Cohabitating or recently married for several months to two years
- Leaves when the violence escalates
- Middle class
- Presence of caring support system

Features of the Level 3 (intermittent long-term) group include:

- Severe intensity violence with long periods without violence
- Four to thirty incidents
- Married with children
- Leaves when children are grown up
- Middle to upper class, reliant on husband's resources
- No alternative support systems

Features of the Level 4 (chronic and predictable) group include:

- Severe and frequent violence including use of weapons, forced sexual acts, and death threats; serious injuries sustained
- Several hundred violent acts
- Married with children
- Violence precipitated by substance abuse
- Abuse continues until husband is arrested, hospitalized, or dies
- Lower to middle class

Features of the Level 5 (homicidal) group include:

- Severe and frequent violence
- Hundreds of severe violent acts
- Long-term marriage or separated
- Lower class with limited education
- Abuse ends when woman kills her partner
- Suffers from depression, suicidal ideation, post-traumatic stress disorder, and battered woman's syndrome

Roberts and Roberts' typology provides an initial step toward understanding types of battered women. However, additional research is needed to replicate this typology. Categorizing women this way serves more than an academic purpose. Roberts (2007) has proposed that intervention be geared toward different types of battered women based on typology. For example, Level 1 or Level 2 women may benefit from crisis intervention, brief psychotherapy, support groups, and restraining orders. In contrast, Level 3 and Level 4 types who have experienced more severe violence over longer periods will likely need more intensive psychotherapy.

Triggers for Violence

What triggers a man to engage in physical violence? (This question is framed in terms of male violence against a female partner because much of the existing research has focused on male-initiated violence.) When battered women are asked about what triggers violent incidents, their answers have included:

- Not obeying or arguing with the man
- Not having food ready on time
- Not caring adequately for the children or home
- Questioning the man about money or girlfriends
- Going somewhere without the man's permission
- The man suspecting the woman of infidelity
- Refusing the man sex

Certainly, none of the above are acceptable reasons for anyone to use violence. Nonetheless, it is important to understand what constitutes a trigger in order to challenge these beliefs in treatment programs. In some countries, men perceive themselves as "owners" of their wives and children and feel that it is justified to use force in certain circumstances. For example, in Egypt, 57 percent of urban women and 81 percent of rural women agree that a man is justified in beating his wife if she refuses to have sex with him. In New Zealand, the majority of men believe that under no circumstances should you physically abuse a woman, although 5 percent agree that physical force would be justified if the man came home and found his wife in bed with another man.

A World Health Organization (2005) study asked women under which circumstances a man would be justified in beating his wife. The reasons most commonly given were not completing housework, refusing to have sex, disobeying her husband, or being unfaithful. Across all countries, the most widely accepted justification for violence was female infidelity, ranging from 6 percent in Serbia to 80 percent in Ethiopia. Women were also asked if they believed a woman has the right to refuse sex if she is ill, if her husband is drunk, if her husband is mistreating her, or if she does not want to have sex. The most acceptable reason to refuse sex was illness, and the least acceptable reason was if she did not want to have sex. In some countries, such as Ethiopia and Tanzania, about 20 percent of women felt they did not have the right to refuse sex under any conditions. In a large survey of 5238 adults in the United States, Simon et al. (2001) found that 98 percent of men did not think it was "ok to hit your wife to keep her in line" (p. 118). In addition, participants were more accepting of women hitting men as compared to men hitting women. To date there have been no published studies measuring Canadian beliefs about intimate partner violence.

Victims' Response to Abuse

The options available to a person determine how they respond to an abusive event. One person might leave immediately, whereas another might stay in an abusive relationship.

While one person will tell others about the abuse, another will remain silent. In most cases, leaving an abusive relationship is an extended process, with many women leaving then returning several times before deciding to permanently end the relationship (Shurman and Rodriguez 2006). In addition, victims often seek help from a variety of sources—both legal and extralegal—in their efforts to address the violence in their lives (Cattaneo et al. 2007). Researchers have found that the following factors can keep an abused woman in a relationship:

- Fear of retribution
- Lack of economic support
- Concern for children
- Emotional dependence
- Lack of support from friends and family
- Hope that the man will change
- Fear of being socially ostracized (in developing countries)

Abuse does not necessarily end when the abusive relationship ends. Ending a relationship may subsequently initiate unwanted behaviour by the ex-partner (such as stalking) in a bid to re-start the relationship using intimidation. This type of behaviour can lead to tragic consequences. A significant portion of intimate partner homicides occur when a woman makes the decision to leave her abusive mate. Between 1997 and 2006 in Canada, there were 766 spousal homicides, with 616 being female and 150 being men (Li 2008). Sixteen percent of the female homicides occurred when the woman was separated from her partner.

What types of support do survivors of abuse find most helpful? What barriers do women encounter when seeking help? Most clinicians and researchers agree that seeking help will lessen the long-term impact of battering (Coker et al. 2002). Most battered women seek help first from friends and family and some may then seek help from more formal supports (e.g., police, domestic violence shelters). In a study assessing the help-seeking behaviour of women who had experienced violence (92 percent had experienced intimate partner violence), Postmus, Severson, Berry, and Yoo (2009) found that the options women used were not necessarily what they considered the most helpful. The top five resources used were emotional support from friends or family (75 percent, ranked helpfulness = 12), professional counselling (64 percent, ranked helpfulness = 13), medication for emotional problems (54 percent, ranked helpfulness = 15), welfare (51 percent, ranked helpfulness = 4), and support group or self-help (50 percent, ranked helpfulness = 16). However, only welfare was rated as one of the top five in terms of helpfulness: subsidized day care (ranked 1), religious or spiritual counselling (2), subsidized housing (3), welfare (4), and educational support (5). Women also indicated the barriers to using resources, with the top five being: "I wanted to handle the problem myself" (82 percent), "I thought the problem would go away" (70 percent), "I was unsure about where to go or whom to see" (59 percent), "I didn't think treatment would work" (54 percent), and "I was concerned about how much money it would cost" (48 percent). This study suggests that although battered women need emotional support, they also need more tangible support (e.g., housing, financial, child care) that will provide them with the resources necessary to obtain self-sufficiency.

METHODOLOGY

Studying Intimate Violence in the Lab

How do you study intimate violence in a laboratory? Dutton and Browning (1988) conducted one of the first analogue lab studies to examine the influence of abandonment themes in groups of violent men. They presented video or audio clips of a woman telling her husband she was joining a women's consciousness-raising group and was spending the weekend with a group of women in another city. The researchers tested three groups of men: men who had engaged in intimate partner violence, generally violent men, and non-violent men. Men who had engaged in intimate partner violence reported much higher rates of anxiety and anger after hearing the clips.

In another analogue study, Costa and Babcock (2008) used an anger induction task to measure articulated cognitive thoughts of intimately violent and non-violent men. In this study, the men were asked to imagine two scenarios. First they overheard their female partner flirting with another man. Then they were asked to imagine their female partner criticizing them (e.g., about job performance, performance in bed, their friends and family, and intelligence) to a female friend. After each scenario, the subjects were asked to verbalize how it made them feel. The researchers found no group differences in men's verbalizations after the first scenario but found that intimately violent men were more likely to express anger during the criticism scenario and non-violent men were more likely to express sadness.

THEORIES OF INTIMATE VIOLENCE

Several theories have been proposed to account for intimate violence. This section focuses on two of these theories: patriarchal theory and social learning theory. Patriarchal theory assumes a long-standing set of cultural beliefs and values that support the idea that the male dominance of women contributes to the domestic assault of women by men (e.g., Dobash and Dobash 1979; Ellis 1989; Straus 1977). Often associated with sociology and feminism, the theory was first described in the 1970s. Dobash and Dobash (1979) stated: "the seeds of wife beating lie in the subordination of females and in their subjection to male authority and control" (p. 33). **Patriarchal theory** is somewhat challenging to evaluate directly because it is hard to show a causal link between patriarchal attitudes and intimate violence. A correlational study by Yllo and Straus (1990) showed that degree of patriarchal attitude was positively correlated with rate of intimate violence. Yllo and Straus compared spousal abuse rates in the United States by identifying the degree to which each state was characterized by patriarchal structure. States with higher levels of patriarchal attitudes (as measured by male-dominant norms) had much higher rates of spousal assault than states with less patriarchal attitudes.

Patriarchal theory has been criticized because it provides an incomplete explanation of intimate violence and cannot predict which individuals will engage in it. Dutton (1995) argues that additional variables are necessary to account for intimate violence, including community (e.g., work, peers), family (e.g., communication level between couple), and individual characteristics (e.g., coping skills, empathy). Thus, if two men grow up to have the same cultural values, comparable social support, and similar levels of conflict with their partners, one man may respond with violence and the other may not. Dutton and Corvo (2007) provide a cogent review of the lack of scientific evidence for patriarchy being a key factor in explaining intimate violence.

An alternative account of intimate violence is **social learning theory** (see Chapter 3). The theory was originally proposed by Bandura (1973) to explain aggression and was extended by Dutton (1995) to account for intimate violence. It has three major elements related to aggression: origins, instigators, and regulators. A key feature of social learning theory is how individuals acquire new behaviours, especially aggression. A prominent mechanism for learning new behaviours is observational learning, in which an individual models a behaviour that they observe. Bandura (1973) proposed that observational learning could occur in three contexts: family of origin, the subculture in which a person lives, and the media. Consistent with social learning theory, men who engage in intimate violence are more likely to have witnessed parental violence than men who do not engage in intimate violence (Kalmuss 1984; Straus, Gelles, and Steinmetz 1980). It is important to note that not all behaviour that is observed will be repeated by the observer. Bandura (1973) argues that for a behaviour to be acquired, it must have functional value for the observer. Like operant conditioning, behaviour that is rewarded increases the likelihood that it will be repeated, whereas behaviour that is punished decreases its likelihood of being repeated.

Social learning also states that acquired behaviours are only manifested if an appropriate event in the environment, called an **instigator**, acts as a stimulus. Dutton (1995) proposed three categories of instigators in intimate violence: aversive instigators, incentive instigators, and delusional instigators. Aversive instigators are stimuli that the individual attempts to avoid. They produce emotional arousal, and how a person labels that emotional arousal will affect how they react. Male batterers have a predisposition to interpret a wide variety of emotional states as anger. Gondolf (1985) describes this tendency as the "emotional funnel system" (p. 41). Incentive instigators are stimuli that are perceived as rewards for engaging in aggression. When individuals believe they can satisfy their needs by using aggression, they may decide to be violent. Delusional instigators are associated with bizarre belief systems, such as delusional jealousy, in which an individual erroneously believes their partner to be unfaithful, potentially resulting in aggression.

An additional concept in social learning theory includes the assumption that behaviour is regulated by the outcomes it generates (similar to the concept of reinforcement that underlies operant conditioning). **Regulators** include external punishment and self-punishment. External punishments are exogenous forms of punishment, such as when a person is arrested for engaging in violence. Self-punishment is an internal reaction to the consequences of one's behaviour that is akin to "having a conscience," such as when a person feels remorse for engaging in violent behaviour. According to social learning theory, the likelihood of intimate violence should be reduced if the consequences for violence are exceeded by incentives for engaging in non-violent behaviour and if alternatives are provided to attenuate the effect of any instigators.

FACTORS ASSOCIATED WITH INTIMATE PARTNER VIOLENCE

THE ECOLOGICAL MODEL OF FAMILY VIOLENCE (DAHLBERG AND KRUG 2002) PROVIDES a useful way to conceptualize the interaction among risk factors related to violence in intimate relationships. As illustrated in Figure 9.1, the model focuses on the relationship between multiple levels of influence in understanding violence, including individual, relationship, community, and societal factors. At the individual level, biological, and personal history characteristics of the abuser and victim need to be considered. Such factors often include age, substance use, and history of abuse.

At the relationship level, a person's closest social circle of peers, partners, and family members may contribute to an increased risk. Important factors may include level of stress or exposure to violence. The community level incorporates places such as schools and neighbourhoods that are associated with becoming a victim or perpetrator of family violence, as well as factors such as poverty, social isolation, and community disorganization. The societal level includes broad societal factors in which violence is supported or discouraged, including social norms, cultural beliefs, and police and government policies.

Like all violence, a combination of individual, situational, social, and community factors cause intimate violence. Table 9.4 summarizes the range of risk factors that have been identified. Much research has focused on the individual characteristics of men who abuse.

Young age and low income have consistently been found to be associated with an increased likelihood of a man committing physical violence against a partner (Kantor, Jasinski, and Aldarondo 1994). Exposure to parental violence as a child is a historical risk factor that has been related to domestic violence. For example, Mitchell and Finkelhor

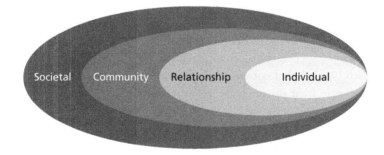

Figure 9.1 Ecological Model of Family Violence

Source: Dahlberg and Krug (2002).

Table 9.4 Risk Factors for Intimate Violence

Individual	Relationship	Community	Society
Young age	Relationship conflict	Weak sanctions	Traditional gender norms
Alcohol use problems	Dominance imbalance	Poverty	Social norms supportive of violence
Personality disorders	Economic stress	Low social capital	
Depression			
Fear of rejection			
Childhood exposure to violence			
Anger and hostility			

(2001) found a more than 100 percent increase in the risk for spousal violence if the perpetrator had been exposed to violence as a child. The Hot Topics box further explores this relationship. There are also psychological, relationship, community, and societal risk factors that have been found to contribute to the perpetration of intimate violence.

Are there specific risk factors for abuse that occur during pregnancy? James, Brody, and Hamilton (2013) conducted a meta-analytic study and found that two of the strongest predictors for abuse during pregnancy were lower educational level and a past history of abuse.

Hot Topics

Overlapping Violence: Child Abuse and Intimate Partner Violence

How often does intimate partner violence and child abuse occur in the same families? Researchers have examined this issue using two different approaches. The first is to look for evidence of spousal violence in families where child abuse has occurred. For example, Hangen (1994) examined all child protection cases in Massachusetts over a seven-month period and found evidence of spousal violence in 33 percent of the cases. The second approach is to look for evidence of child abuse in cases of spousal violence. Some of these studies have asked mothers in women's shelters about whether their children were also victimized, whereas other studies have surveyed battered women. Studies from women's shelters have reported between 40 percent (Suh and Abel 1990) and 60 percent (Hughes 1988) of children also experienced abuse. According to results from a survey of 775 battered women with children, 70 percent of women reported that their partners also physically abused their children (Bowker, Arbitell, and McFerron 1988). In a study of intact families with children between the ages of 3 and 7, 45 percent of families reported partner aggression and aggression towards a child in the past year (Smith Slep and O'Leary 2005).

These studies provide evidence for a robust overlap between partner violence and child abuse and provide evidence that if there is one type of violence identified in a home, other family members might also be a risk for victimization. Recent research has also identified a link between animal abuse and co-occurring child abuse and partner violence (DeGue and DiLillo 2009). In a study of 860 university students, 60 percent of those who witnessed or perpetrated animal abuse as a child also reported being a victim of child abuse or witnessing parental violence.

ASSESSMENT APPROACHES AND EFFECTIVENESS

NUMEROUS METHODS OF RISK ASSESSMENT ARE CURRENTLY IN USE (SEE CHAPTER 4). Many of the risk factors described earlier in Table 9.4 are included in risk-assessment measures. There is empirical support for both actuarial and structured professional judgment methods in the prediction of future intimate violence. However, in contrast to research measuring the validity of risk measures for general violence and sexual violence, the field of IPV risk assessment has lagged behind these other areas (Bowen 2011). An actuarial instrument developed in Ontario to predict future intimate violence is the **Domestic Violence Risk Appraisal Guide (DVRAG)** (Hilton et al. 2008). The DVRAG is an empirically derived 14-item measure designed to predict spousal assault recidivism in male spousal assault offenders. It consists of individually weighted items from the Ontario Domestic Assault Risk Assessment (ODARA) (Hilton et al. 2004), a scale designed to be used by frontline police officers, and scores on the Hare Psychopathy Checklist–Revised (PCL-R) (Hare 2003). (See the Canadian Researcher Profile box for a profile of Dr. Zoe Hilton.) Scores on the DVRAG can range from –10 to +41, and are divided into seven risk categories or bins. Each risk bin has a probability of spousal assault recidivism within five years ranging from 14 percent (bin 1) to 100 percent (bin 7). Only 3 percent of the scale development sample was included in bin 7. Whether or not the recidivism rates linked to each bin will replicate in other samples remains to be studied. The items in the DVRAG include:

- Number of prior domestic incidents
- Number of prior non-domestic incidents
- Prior correctional sentence (30 days or more)
- Failure on prior conditional release
- Threat to harm or kill at the index incident
- Confinement at the index incident
- Victim concern
- Number of children

- Victim's number of biological children from previous partner
- Violence against others
- Substance abuse score
- Assault on victim when pregnant
- Number of barriers to victim support
- Hare PCL-R score

Box 9.1

Canadian Researcher Profile Dr. Zoe Hilton

Courtesy of Dr. Zoe Hilton

The research of Dr. Zoe Hilton provides an excellent example of how empirical research can be translated into use in the real-world. Dr. Hilton has contributed greatly to the development of risk assessment measures to assess the likelihood of future violence in intimate relationships. She has a diverse educational background,

completing her bachelor's degree in Psychology at the University of Southampton and her master's degree in Criminology at Cambridge University in the United Kingdom. Dr. Hilton completed her Ph.D. in Psychology at the University of Toronto, focusing on domestic violence. Her Ph.D. supervisor was Dr. Christopher Webster, who is well known for his work in the area of risk assessment and the use of structured professional judgment. Currently, Dr. Hilton is a senior research scientist at Waypoint Centre for Mental Health Care and an Associate Professor of Psychiatry at the University of Toronto. Her primary research is on domestic violence with an emphasis on risk assessment and criminal justice. She also studies how research can inform clinical practice and policy decision-making.

When asked how she became interested in studying domestic violence Dr. Hilton stated:

> When I was studying criminology, violence against women was receiving a lot of public attention, partly because of some shocking footage of the police response. I saw a British TV documentary that highlighted the progressive initiatives taken by the London, Ontario police service and that inspired me to do a research project on the effectiveness of police responses to domestic violence.

Box 9.1   (Continued)

Dr. Hilton has continued to conduct research in domestic violence in hopes that criminal justice policy can be improved if informed by empirical research. She finds collaborating with other colleagues and developing new research partnerships keeps her motivated, excited, and interested in research.

Her primary work involves archival research using data from police reports and criminal justice records, and clinical assessment using samples of male domestic violent offenders in the community or in institutions. Dr. Hilton is the senior author of the Ontario Domestic Assault Risk Assessment (ODARA), an assessment measure used to predict the likelihood of future domestic violence. One of her favourite studies was a validation study of the ODARA that examined the effects of sampling methods on reoffending rates between samples.

Dr. Hilton has been a consultant to police and correctional services on how to implement and interpret risk assessment measures. She is concerned with the public's perceptions of people with mental illness. She hopes that the 2014 *Not Criminally Responsible Reform Act*, which emphasizes security over treatment, and the identification of high-risk patients will be carefully evaluated. She believes that this is a great time for forensic psychology given the number of keen and bright students wanting to study in this area. She thinks students need a strong education in scientific method and encourages students not to be scared by statistics.

Dr. Hilton enjoys teaching professionals about risk assessment and enjoys seeing them figure out how they will apply what they have learned to their work. She acknowledges the role of her husband Brad, who has been a great supporter of her career.

The **Spousal Assault Risk Assessment (SARA)** (Kropp, Hart, Webster, and Eaves 1999) was designed to assess the risk for spousal assault in male offenders. The SARA uses the structured professional judgment approach to risk assessment and was developed by a group of researchers in British Columbia. The evaluator conducts a comprehensive assessment and refers to a list of risk factors, each having a specific coding criteria and a demonstrated relationship with spousal assault recidivism based on the existing professional and empirical literature. The SARA consists of 20 risk factors: 10 general violence risk factors and 10 spousal violence risk factors. Users code each of the items on a three-point scale, indicating the presence of any case-specific risk factors, designating any "critical" risk factors (those that are particularly salient to the degree of risk), and making a summary risk judgment of low, moderate, or high risk for future spousal violence. Some researchers have summed the risk factors together to create a total risk score. The items in the SARA include:

- Past assault of family members
- Past assault of strangers or acquaintances
- Past violation of conditional release
- Recent relationship problems
- Recent employment problems

- Victim of or witness to family violence as a youth
- Recent substance abuse problems
- Recent suicidal or homicidal ideation
- Recent psychopathic or manic symptoms
- Personality disorder with anger, impulsivity, or behavioural instability
- Past physical assault
- Past sexual assault/sexual jealousy
- Past use of weapons and/or credible threats of death
- Recent escalation in frequency or severity of spousal assault
- Past violation of "no contact" orders
- Extreme minimization or denial of spousal assault history
- Attitudes supportive of spousal assault
- Severe and/or sexual assault during index offence
- Use of weapons and/or credible threats of death during index offence
- Violation of "no contact" order during index offence

In a meta-analysis of 18 studies, Hanson, Helmus, and Bourgon (2007) investigated the effectiveness of different approaches and measures used to assess the risk of recidivism in male spousal assault offenders. The researchers compared measures that were designed specifically to predict spousal assault (average weighted d of .40), measures designed to predict general or violent recidivism (average weighted d of .54), and general assessments of risk provided by the female victims (average weighted d of .36). Helmus and Bourgon (2011) recently included four additional studies that assessed the predictive validity of the SARA and transformed results from Hanson, Helmus, and Bourgon's 2007 study from Cohen's d to AUCs. The results for the SARA, DVRAG, ODARA, and victim judgment are presented in Table 9.5. Although only based on a limited number of studies, the DVRAG and the ODARA appear to be the most accurate. In addition, there was little

Table 9.5 Predictive Accuracy for Spousal Assault Recidivism Across Measures

Measure	AUC	Number of Studies	Sample Size
SARA—total score	.63	8	2174
SARA—risk judgment	.64	4	890
ODARA	.66	2	446
DVRAG	.70	1	346
Victim judgment	.60	2	2179

Source: Adapted from Hanson, Helmus, and Bourgon (2007) and Helmus and Bourgon (2011).

difference in predictive accuracy between the SARA summary risk judgment and studies that summed the 20 risk factors into a numerical total score. Additional research will need to be conducted to determine if spousal-specific risk measures are more accurate than other risk measures designed to assess for violence in general. In addition, it is not known whether these risk measures designed with samples of males will be equally predictive in females who engage in IPV.

TREATMENT APPROACHES AND EFFECTIVENESS

Many intervention programs have been developed to target men who engage in intimate violence. One of the most widely used programs is the Duluth Domestic Abuse Intervention Project (DAIP), often referred to as the **Duluth model**, which originated in 1981 in Duluth, Minnesota. The goal of this program, like other treatments, is to prevent future violence. However, in contrast to more multifaceted treatment programs, it focuses on men's use of power and control. The Duluth model focuses on changing patriarchal beliefs, however some programs tend to be judgmental and use shaming to accomplish this change. A very high drop-out rate (75 percent) has been observed in some programs using the Duluth model.

Despite its widespread adoption, the Duluth model has been criticized on several grounds. For example, Dutton and Corvo argue that "the Duluth model, and its underlying ideological assumptions, is incompatible with progressive social theory and policy" (Dutton and Corvo 2007, 477). There is ongoing debate in the literature concerning the model's effectiveness. Dutton and Corvo (2006) summarize the literature evaluating this model as having "negligible success in reducing or eliminating violence among perpetrators" (p. 462).

The other most common type of treatment program for male batterers is based on social learning models of violence and uses cognitive-behavioural techniques. These programs are multifaceted, targeting a range of different risk factors with the goal of helping participants understand their motivations for engaging in violence and focus on alternative skills and behaviours to form non-abusive positive relationships. These programs often include both individual and group counselling. One example of such a program is Correctional Service Canada's Family Violence Prevention Program. Consistent with the risk principle of effective correctional programming (see Chapter 4), there is a shorter program targeting moderate risk offenders (Moderate Intensity) and a longer, high-intensity program (High Intensity) designed to target offenders who are at high risk to engage in future intimate violence. Approximately 40 percent of male federal offenders and 15 percent of female federal offenders have a history of violence against their intimate partners (Gabora, Stewart, Lilley, and Allegri 2007; Robinson and Taylor 1995). This program targets a range of factors, including:

■ Motivation for change
■ Attitudes and beliefs that condone the use of violence
■ Management of emotion skills relating to jealously, anger, and fear of relationship loss

- Development of communication skills
- Coping strategies to deal with criticism
- Relapse prevention plans to avoid and manage high-risk situations
- Identification of social support networks to assist in maintaining healthy relationships

Stewart, Gabora, Kropp, and Lee (2008) recently evaluated the effectiveness of these programs in a sample of 572 male Canadian federal offenders who participated in either the moderate- or high-intensity program. In contrast to community-based programs, the attrition rate was relatively low, with only 18 percent of offenders dropping out of the high-intensity program and 14 percent of offenders dropping out of the moderate-intensity program. Comparing pre- and post-treatment characteristics, offenders had lower levels of jealously, fewer negative attitudes about relationships, better relapse prevention skills, and increased empathy. A sample of 160 treated offenders was compared to a combined sample of 86 drop-out/untreated offenders using a six-month follow-up. Only 4 percent of treated offenders were charged with a spousal-related offence compared to 13 percent of the untreated group. Whether the program effects continue with longer follow-up periods or using partner reports remains to be evaluated.

The largest evaluation of treatment effectiveness done to date was by Dunfond (2000), who compared a cognitive-behavioural group, a couples therapy group, and a non-treatment control group in a sample of U.S. Navy personnel. Based on victims' reports, neither the cognitive-behavioural treatment nor the couples therapy had a significant impact on spousal assault recidivism in a one-year follow-up. What was unusual about this sample was the atypically low rates of recidivism, even in the untreated group (4 percent). The participants in this study were all employed and had a high stake in conformity. Thus any intervention, including arrest and identification by the authorities, may have been sufficient to deter these men from committing future violence.

To date, two meta-analyses has been conducted to compare outcomes for different types of treatment for male batterers. Babcock, Green, and Robie (2004) examined 22 studies to test the relative effectiveness of the Duluth model, cognitive-behavioural therapy, and other types of interventions on police- and victim-reported recidivism. There were no differences in the effectiveness of the different types of treatment, and overall treatment had "a minimal impact on reducing recidivism beyond the effect of being arrested" (p. 1023). Feder and Wilson (2005) examined 10 studies that measured the effectiveness of court-mandated treatment and also concluded that there were "modest" beneficial effects when using official police reports as outcome. However, when using victim reports there were no positive effects for treatment.

Treatment: Which Treatment for Whom?

In order to better understand the motivations and characteristics of men who engage in intimate violence and to develop more targeted interventions, researchers have developed typologies (or categories) of male batterers. The typology that has received the most attention was developed by Holtzworth-Munroe and Stuart (1994), who identified three types of male batterers based on the severity and frequency of violence, generality of violence, and psychopathological features.

The **family-only batterer** type displays the following characteristics:

- Engages in the lowest levels of intimate violence
- Is infrequently violent outside the home and rarely engages in other criminal acts
- Does not show much psychopathology
- Has few risk factors (i.e., witnessing violence as a child, poor relationship skills)
- Aggression is triggered by stress

The **generally violent/antisocial batterer** type has the following features:

- Engages in moderate to high levels of intimate violence
- Is frequently violent outside the home and engages in other criminal acts
- Has antisocial and psychopathic personality features
- Has substance abuse problems
- Has problems with impulsivity and many violence-supportive beliefs
- Attachment style best described as dismissive

The **dysphoric-borderline batterer** type is characterized by:

- Engages in moderate to severe levels of intimate violence
- Usually focuses violence on female partners
- High rates of mood disorders
- Has borderline personality features such as instability, jealously, and fear of rejection
- Experienced childhood abuse
- Attachment style best described as preoccupied

Holtzworth-Munroe and Stuart's typology has been replicated by several studies (Holtzworth-Munroe et al. 2003; White and Gondolf 2000). Dixon and Browne (2003) reported that on average, offenders were classified as 50 percent family-only type, 30 percent generally violent/antisocial type, and 20 percent dysphoric-borderline type.

Several other typologies of male batterers have been proposed that focus on behavioural, psychological, or physiological characteristics. Most of these alternative typologies classify batterers into two or three groups. For example, Gondolf (1988), using data from 6000 battered women, created a three-tier typology based on the severity and generalizability of violence. The Type I or sociopath (accounting for about 10 percent of batterers) engages in the most severe levels of violence in and outside the home. Type II or antisocial (accounting for about 30 to 40 percent of batterers) is primarily violent within the home and is less likely to have a criminal record. The Type III or typical (accounting for 50 to 60 percent of batterers) engages in less severe violence, engages in violence within the home, and is least likely to have a criminal record. Using a psychological perspective, Hamberger and Hastings (1994) identified three types of male batterers: the low-risk non-pathological, who engages in family-only violence; the passive aggressive–dependent type with attachment and psychopathological problems; and the antisocial type, who engages in high levels of violence in and outside the home.

Working from a physiological perspective, Gottman and colleagues (1995) used the heart rate of male batterers at rest and during conflict to categorize batterers into groups. Type 1 abusers or the "cobra group" (accounting for 20 percent of the sample) showed a decreased heart rate as they became verbally abusive. Type 1 abusers engaged in high rates of severe violence in and outside the home. Type II or the "pitbull group" (accounting for 80 percent of the sample) showed an increased heart rate as they became verbally abusive. Type II abusers were more insecure and emotionally dependent, and primarily engaged in violence inside the home. Other researchers have suggested two subtypes of IPV: characterological violence and situational violence (Kelly and Johnson 2008). These subtypes parallel the typologies by Gottman. Characterlogical violence occurs when the male is attempting to dominate or control his partner. The perpetrator generally lacks remorse and insight, blames his partner for the violence, and the violence is often one-sided. Situational violence occurs during a conflict, partners are remorseful, and the violence is often reciprocal.

Box 9.2

You Be the Therapist

Jay and Kumiko have been married for 4 years. They both state they are in love with each other but report things need to change. Jay sometimes feels jealous about the time Kumiko spends with her coworkers at happy hour. Jay agrees he spends many hours at pubs with his friends watching sports but says his friends are all guys. Kumiko works in an office with men and women, and Jay is well aware that one of the men often flirts with Kumiko. They have had confrontations about this more than once. Kumiko also confronts Jay about the amount that he drinks, especially on weekends. While confrontations such as these do not happen very often, they get heated quickly when they do. Jay and Kumiko both get upset, yelling at first, and sometimes throwing things or hitting each other. These confrontations often occur when Jay comes home drunk or when Kumiko comes home late

after spending time with her co-workers. Eventually, things calm back down and the couple reaches some sort of temporary resolution. They report feelings of remorse and find reconciliation through apologizing and blame sharing. Neither feels necessarily bullied by the other, but both want to find a way out of this cycle in which they feel trapped. They report some insight into their conflicts: that sometimes they do not know how else to solve their problems. Jay is not violent at work and has two criminal convictions: one for driving while impaired and one for possession of stolen property.

Questions

What type of male batterer is Jay? Are they a characterlogically or situationally violent couple? What risk factors for violence are present? What type of intervention would you recommend for this couple?

Couples therapy for intimate partner violence.

The plethora of typologies has led to criticism of the methodology used in this area. In a critique of the male batterer literature, Chiffriller, Hennessy, and Zappone (2006) point out the methodological deficits of the existing research, including a lack of control groups, inconsistent terminology, and poor measurement of constructs. The You Be the Therapist box provides an opportunity to apply some of these discussions about typologies and risk factors for violence.

FUTURE DIRECTIONS

RESEARCHERS AND THE PUBLIC ARE RECOGNIZING THE NEED TO UNDERSTAND AND prevent IPV and there has been increasing research in this area. However, IPV is still far too common. Research measuring the prevalence of IPV in different types of relationships has been neglected. In addition, the predictive validity of IPV risk-assessment measures has lagged behind measures in other areas such a general violence and sexual violence.

In particular, further research is needed to determine how different types of male batterers respond to various treatments, what risk factors are associated with each type of batterer, and whether different causal mechanisms exist for each type. For example, Friend, Cleary Bradley, Thatcher, and Gottman (2011) have proposed that different types of treatment are needed for those who engage in characterological violence as compared to situational violence. Several researchers have also suggested that couples therapy should be avoided for characterologically violent couples since it is ineffective and puts the victim at risk (Cleary Bradley and Gottman 2012; Stare and Fernando 2014). Instead, perpetrators should be given individual therapy. However, couples therapy may be effective for situationally violent couples. Clearly Bradley and Gottman (2012) found that a group couples-based psychoeducational intervention program was effective at fostering healthy relationships and reducing future violence. Finally, almost all prevention and intervention programs target men who abuse their partners. It is essential that violence by women be recognized and robust efforts be implemented to end assaults by women.

The WHO (2013) survey of the global prevalence of IPV concluded: "The findings send a powerful message that violence against women is not a small problem that only occurs in some pockets of society, but rather is a global public health problem of epidemic proportions, requiring urgent action" (p. 3). IPV is a serious health concern that needs to be taken seriously by all sectors of society including health-care providers, police, and governments. Legal and policy guidelines need to be strengthened to address the underlying causes in order to prevent violence against both men and women. The best possible outcome is to prevent violence, but when it does occur we need empirically informed interventions that target specific risk factors for those individuals who engage in this form of violence.

SUMMARY

1. Intimate partner violence can be classified into the following types: physical abuse, sexual abuse, financial abuse, and emotional abuse. The prevalence rates of intimate partner violence are difficult to estimate accurately since the abuse often occurs in private. However, there is evidence that partner violence is a pervasive global problem!

2. Multiple adverse health outcomes for both intimate partner violence victims and their children that have been identified, including physical, sexual/reproductive, and mental health disorders.

3. The two prominent theories of intimate violence place emphasis on society versus the individual. Patriarchal theory focuses on long-standing cultural beliefs and values that support male dominance over women. In contrast, social learning theory focuses on the observational learning of new behaviours, different types of instigators, and the regulators that increase or decrease the probability of intimate violence.

4. The ecological model of family violence focuses on the relationship between multiple levels of influence in understanding intimate partner violence, including individual, relationship, community, and societal factors. Risk factors associated with each of these levels have been identified for intimate violence and risk-assessment measures have been developed to predict future intimate partner violence.

5. The two most common treatments for male batterers are the Duluth model, which focuses on power and control, and cognitive-behavioural treatments. Meta-analysis

of male batterer treatment programs have found no differences in effectiveness across treatment types and show relatively small treatment effect.

6. Typologies of male batterers have been proposed, with most identifying three main types: family-only, generally violent/antisocial, and dysphoric/borderline.

Discussion Questions

1. Both men and women engage in dating violence. Do they do so for the same reasons? What are the motives for engaging in dating violence? Do you think there are any gender-specific motivations?

2. A new shelter for battered women has opened in your city. What factors might encourage or discourage abused women from using this resource?

3. You are interested in conducting a study to determine if the typologies that have been identified for male batterers can also be applied to female batterers. Describe the methodology you would use and the variables you would measure.

4. You have been hired by the World Health Organization to identify the risk factors for IPV across different countries. Describe the study you would propose, focusing on what risk factors you would measure.

Chapter 10
Mentally Disordered Offenders

Michael is a 36-year-old male. After being found not criminally responsible for a minor assault on account of mental (bipolar) disorder, he was hospitalized for 30 months in a medium-security forensic hospital. He eventually enjoyed off-ward privileges without incident for eight months. Shortly thereafter, he was released by the Review Board and lived on a disability pension in a rooming house.

Michael is now before the court with a manslaughter charge. Following a minor argument in a bar, he assaulted another patron with a beer bottle and the person died at the scene. This is Michael's first formal contact with the criminal justice system, as he was diverted to a mental health court following his previous offence. He has been employed sporadically as a labourer and is now on a disability pension. He left high school after grade 10, in part due to poor grades and lack of motivation, and left home a year later. He has struggled with mental health symptoms since his mid-twenties. Early psychiatric reports indicate that he experiences extreme mood swings. At times of severe depression he has coped by using alcohol and street drugs (cannabis). These bouts of depression led to referrals to community mental health services and contact with psychiatry. During periods of hypomania his insight is poor, he refuses treatment, is noncompliant with prescribed medication, and avoids contact with his treatment team. His mental health issues have led to problems in relationships and employment. He has had several common-law relationships but is currently single.

Assessments completed following the manslaughter indicate that Michael had not slept for days prior to the incident, was agitated, reported racing thoughts, and was delusional, believing that others were monitoring his behaviour. This paranoia and his feelings of invulnerability were underlying aspects of the initial argument and subsequent assault. His situation has stabilized with medication and his psychiatric assessment indicates he was competent at the time of the crime and is fit to stand trial in that he knows right from wrong.

Is Michael responsible for his crime? Should it matter that he stabilized once on medication? Should he go to jail or be hospitalized again? What concerns might there be if he is admitted to jail? These are all issues will explore in this chapter.

Learning Objectives

1   Identify the most prevalent types of mental disorders in offenders.

2   Understand the prevalence, assessment, and management of mental disorders within the correctional environment.

3   Describe public and police attitudes towards mentally disordered offenders.

4   Describe the effectiveness of treatment approaches for mentally disordered offenders.

INTRODUCTION

THE ISSUE OF MENTALLY DISORDERED OFFENDERS HAS GAINED INCREASING prominence due to sensational media coverage of community incidents, key reports by government commissions (Kirby 2006) and watchdog groups (such as the Office of the Correctional Investigator), and public inquests in cases of tragic events. The purpose of this chapter is to define mentally disordered offenders using accepted psychiatric diagnostic guidelines in order to compare the prevalence of mental health concerns in incarcerated samples to community samples. Central to this review will be the assessment and management of mentally disordered offenders within a prison context, notably in terms of risk of self-harm and suicide. Regarding release and community supervision, a major discussion point will be balancing public concerns regarding the potential risks individuals with mental health needs pose in the community with the rights and needs of offenders. Underscoring this discussion will be the attitudes towards mentally disordered offenders, including those of the general public to key groups such as the police, who are increasingly in contact with people in crisis. This chapter will also highlight the specific risk scales validated for application with this population and will review strategies in place within the criminal justice system to address the unique needs of this specific subgroup of offenders.

Hence, important goals of this chapter are to describe the prevalence of mentally disordered offenders in the criminal justice system and to understand contemporary assessment and management approaches while dispelling common misconceptions regarding this group of offenders.

CONTEXT

THE DEINSTITUTIONALIZATION OF MENTALLY ILL PERSONS BEGAN IN THE 1950S with a movement to open doors and expose patients to the community through outings and visits home (History of Madness 2015). The 1960s and 1970s saw the closure of many inpatient beds and individuals were discharged into the community. However, the development of community mental health services progressed slower than the transfer of patients out of hospitals (Sealy and Whitehead 2004). Interestingly, in 1939 Lionel Penrose asserted there was an inverse relationship between the number of mental hospital beds and the number of prisoners. Loosely translated, with deinstitutionalization there was an expectation that more individuals with mental health needs would be incarcerated, although this is considered a somewhat simplistic explanation (Hartvig and Kjelsberg 2008).

Perhaps surprisingly to some readers, when an individuals who present with serious mental health issues come in conflict with the courts, they do not all end up in psychiatric hospitals. The courts (informed by psychiatric opinion) carefully review cases to determine whether individuals with apparent mental health symptoms should be diverted to the forensic mental health system. This is referred to as a fitness and criminal responsibility test. Not all such individuals are diverted to a hospital; some end up in prison despite displaying evidence of mental health concerns. This chapter examines this group of offenders.

DEFINITIONS

What is actually meant by *MENTAL DISORDER*? Are there degrees of mental disorder? Are all individuals who are mentally disordered insane? Who can make a diagnosis of mental disorder? These and other issues need to be carefully defined in order to dispel common misconceptions and to foster a reasoned understanding of mental illness.

Mental Disorders and the Diagnostic and Statistical Manual (DSM)

The concept of mental disorder presupposes that it is possible to discriminate between normal and abnormal behaviour. In North America the primary tool used to diagnose mental disorders is the **Diagnostic and Statistical Manual of Mental Disorders (DSM)**. The DSM was first published by the American Psychiatric Association (APA) in 1952 in order to facilitate the diagnosis of mental disorders and to collect statistical information about the prevalence of different types of mental disorders. Outside North America, the International Statistical Classification of Diseases (ICD), published by the World Health Organization, is used to classify mental disorders. The most recent iteration of the DSM is the DSM-V, published in 2013. Key changes in this version include harmonization between the DSM and the ICD and the dropping of a multi-axial description (noted below).

A mental disorder is a syndrome characterized by clinically significant disturbance in an individual's cognition, emotion regulation, or behaviour that reflects a dysfunction in the psychological, biological, or developmental processes underlying mental functioning. Mental disorders are usually associated with significant distress in social, occupational, or other important activities. An expected or culturally approved response to a common stressor or loss, such as the death of a loved one, is not a mental disorder. Socially deviant behaviour (e.g., political, religious, or sexual) and conflicts that are primarily between the individual and society are not mental disorders unless the deviance or conflict results from a dysfunction in the individual, as described above (APA 2013).

In 1980, the DSM-III introduced a multi-axial system designed to provide a more comprehensive description of the individual being assessed. The DSM-III organized diagnoses into five levels (axes) relating to different aspects of a disorder:

- Axis I: Clinical disorders including mood disorders, anxiety disorders, phobias, schizophrenia, bi-polar disorder, dissociative disorders, gender identity disorders, eating disorders, substance-related disorders and developmental and learning disorders

- Axis II: Mental retardation and personality disorders including avoidant, dependent, obsessive-compulsive, histrionic, antisocial, borderline, narcissistic, paranoid, schizoid, and schizotypal disorders.

- Axis III: General medical conditions that may be related to the mental disorder or that might influence the choice of medications for treating the disorder.

- Axis IV: Psychosocial or environmental factors contributing to disorders including family problems, educational problems, economic problems, or problems with the legal system.

- Axis V: Assessment of the patient's general level of functioning.

Although the DSM-V dropped the multi-axial system, the axial approach is still somewhat helpful from a criminal justice and criminal responsibility perspective. This is because it would be more common for individuals meeting an Axis I disorder to be diverted to the mental health system rather than go through the criminal justice system since these disorders relate to the individual's disconnection with reality, and hence, the ability to form intent. As well, the symptoms of Axis I disorders are more overt, meaning police, courts, and corrections staff would be more likely to detect such symptoms. Some authors refer to serious mental illness (SMI) or major mental illness (MMI), which refer to Axis I disorders. For Axis II disorders, symptoms disrupt interactions with others but do not impair one's ability to know right from wrong and to form intent. Unsurprisingly, offenders with Axis II diagnoses are quite common in correctional samples, as we will discuss later in the chapter.

Given that treatment recommendations, as well as payment by health-care providers, are often dependent on DSM classifications, a diagnostic system is of considerable importance. The value of a diagnostic system is that enables a diagnosis to act as a sort of specialized short hand for describing a cluster of symptoms, a preferred treatment approach, and a prognosis. Within a correctional environment, the focus tends to be more on symptoms rather than diagnoses, except perhaps at pretrial when psychiatric evidence is presented. Diagnoses are also reported at specialized treatment facilities that are combined prisons and accredited hospitals.

Earlier versions of DSM have met with a number of criticisms, including construct validity and reliability of the diagnostic categories and symptoms (Baca-Garcia et al. 2007; Kendell and Jabelnsky 2003) and these continue with DSM-V (Kapur, Phillips, and Insel 2012). It remains unclear why certain disorders are included and how the symptoms for each disorder were selected; although DSM diagnoses are defined by consensus, not empirical evidence. Hence, critics have argued that the DSM lacks a strong empirical basis. Moreover, as it has evolved, critics have argued that the DSM places an undue emphasis on the existence of symptoms, which in turn leads to a proliferation of disorders. Between the DSM-I and the DSM-IV there was a 280 percent increase in the number of disorders; the DSM-V adds additional diagnoses. Importantly, the DSM-V manual provides a cautionary statement regarding its forensic use in the context of the courts, the absence of treatment guidelines for any given disorder, and the possibility of psychiatric information being misunderstood. Some clinicians believe that the DSM should use a dimensional approach and should address level of impairment since the impact of a symptom will vary across individuals. Despite these criticisms, the DSM continues to be the default tool for diagnosing mental disorders in North America.

Notwithstanding these concerns, there is an obligation to identify individuals who engage in criminal acts but who have mental health concerns that may have influenced their criminal behaviour. This is not to imply that mental disorders necessarily *cause* crime, but it may be that the symptoms sufficiently impaired the individual to warrant due consideration by the courts. This impairment is considered at two key times during the criminal justice process—at the time of the alleged crime and at the time of the court proceeding. The former is a competency assessment and the latter is a fitness assessment. Figure 10.1

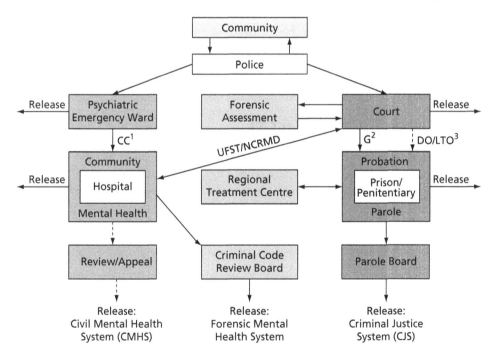

Figure 10.1 Assessments and Decisions Regarding Mentally Disordered Offenders in Conflict with the Courts

[1] Criminal Court

[2] General

[3] Dangerous offender/long-term offender

Source: Adapted from Webster (2003).

presents a flowchart of different kinds of assessments and decisions made regarding people involved in the criminal justice system. In cases where the police immediately consider the individual to be mentally disordered, they can take them directly to a psychiatric emergency department in a hospital. If concerns remain after examination by a psychiatrist, the accused can be involuntarily admitted to a psychiatric hospital under a civil commitment order. Such orders are typically related to a determination of risk of harm to self or others and are time limited. Alternatively, the accused can be arrested, taken to jail/court, and then referred for a forensic assessment (fitness and competence). Again, there are time limits (usually within 30 days) and then the court will determine next steps. If the assessment finds the person **unfit to stand trial (UFST)** or **not criminally responsible on account of mental disorder (NCRMD)**, they are transferred to a psychiatric hospital. If there are ongoing mental health concerns but the individual is found fit and competent, they proceed through the corrections system (either probation or prison depending on the court ruling). If mental health concerns arise while in prison, the individual can be transferred to a psychiatric hospital within the corrections system. Correctional Service Canada (CSC) has approximately 700 treatment beds in Treatment Units for mentally disordered offenders. For mentally disordered offenders within the corrections system, release is granted by the Parole Board or at expiration of sentence. For those in the mental health system, the release authority is a physician or criminal review board.

Unfit to Stand Trial (UFST)

If a person legitimately thought a judge was trying to poison them or thought that their lawyer worked for the devil and therefore refused to speak to him/her, would it be fair to make that person go forward with a trial? In Canada, if an accused is not able to participate in his or her defence on account of a mental disorder it is deemed unfair to try this person. According to Section 2 of the Canadian *Criminal Code*, an accused is unfit to stand trial (UFST) if he or she is:

> . . . unable on account of a mental disorder to conduct a defence at any stage of the proceedings before a verdict is rendered or to instruct counsel to do so, and in particular on account of mental disorder to:
>
> a) understand the nature or object of the proceedings;
> b) understand the possible consequences of the proceedings; or
> c) communicate with counsel.

In such cases, the accused would be diverted to the mental health system prior to sentencing and they would not enter the criminal justice system (although in many cases they could be housed in a jail on remand until the fitness assessment is completed and the court's decision rendered).

Not Criminally Responsible on Account of Mental Disorder (NCRMD)

In order to find a person guilty of a crime, ***mens rea*** (criminal intent) must be established. In other words, if there is no criminal intent then there is no crime. It is presumed that if you know what you are doing and subsequently choose to do it, you are culpable. However, if you are mentally disordered and do not understand the consequences of your actions then you should not be culpable for your actions. If a person fails this competency assessment, they may be diverted to the mental health system.

It is important to note that for our purposes, understanding mental disorder among offenders (i.e., individuals found guilty of a crime) will apply only to those who passed the UFST and NCRMD assessments. The UFST and NCRMD assessments are intended to be a safety net to protect mentally disordered individuals from falling into the criminal justice system.

WHY DO WE CARE?

FIRST, IT SHOULD BE CLEAR THAT SOME INDIVIDUALS WITH MENTAL HEALTH concerns will end up in jail. The extent to which prevalence rates increase, especially above that of the community, highlights the fact that mentally disordered offenders (MDOs) are a vulnerable population warranting increased consideration. As will be presented later, this population warrants specialized assessment approaches to ensure the safety and appropriate care of such individuals. However, as the Media Spotlight box highlights, this is a complicated and challenging issue. Once admitted to a jail, the corrections agency is responsible for the care and well-being of individuals assigned to their custody. Failure to meet community standards regarding care can potentially lead to harmful effects for staff and offenders, and possible litigation in the event of serious negative events.

The Effects of Deinstitutionalization on the Prison Population

In Canada, deinstitutionalization primarily occurred from 1960 to 1980. Health and Welfare Canada estimated that the number of inpatient beds in psychiatric hospitals decreased from 4 beds per 1000 population in 1964 to less than 1 bed per 1000 population in 1979 (Health and Welfare Canada 1990). The Conference Board of Canada (2012) estimated that lost market participation in Canada due to mental illness cost the nation and alarming $20.7 billion in 2012. This does not even include direct or indirect costs relating to criminal justice involvement by individuals with mental health needs. Interestingly, the rate for criminal incidents increased fairly steadily up until the early 1980s. At that point, it levelled off throughout the decade, then increase again in the early 1990s before declining steadily up to the present (Bunge, Johnson, and Baldé 2005).

Given this deinstitutionalization of mentally ill patients over 2 decades in Canada, it is possible that the resultant diminished access to health care and social support systems

How Should Mentally Disordered Offenders Be Treated?

Imagine a 21-year-old male relative has recently been diagnosed with schizophrenia. He had always been creative and a little eccentric in his mannerisms, but for the past several years you and other family members have noticed he has become more reclusive and distant. This is particularly noticeable at family gatherings. Contact with the family doctor has been unhelpful, in part because your relative prefers to smoke cannabis rather than take his medication, which he says makes him feel numb, suppresses his creativity, and makes him always tired. Finally, you start to notice he appears to hear voices and is often whispering when he doesn't think people can hear.

Now imagine your relative is at a shopping mall one day and gets into a public disturbance. The police are called and you get a telephone call saying he has been arrested. What are your expectations? How would you like the criminal justice system to interact with him?

led to these patients seeking such services in the criminal justice system. In comparison to community rates, offenders experience much greater mental health symptoms, consistent with Teplin's (1990) comment that jails have become "a repository of the severely mentally ill." However, as we consider the mental disorder–crime link, there is a possible tautology. People with antisocial personality engage in criminal behaviour. Prisoners have high rates of antisocial personality. Therefore, mental disorder is related to crime. This is referred to as the "criminalization of the mentally ill" (Brink et al. 2001). Disturbed public behaviour and relatively minor offences should lead to arrest and incarceration in jail. However, as noted below, high prevalence rates occur in prisons (Coté and Hodgins 1990; Motiuk and Porporino 1991), not just jails and remand centres. Brink, Doherty, and Boer (2001) concluded that such findings suggest that inadequate social policy and arrest bias alone fail to explain the high prevalence rates of mental disorders in prison populations.

Mental Disorder and Stigma

In 2001, the World Health Organization declared stigma as the "single most important barrier to overcome" regarding mental illness in that it is a major barrier to people seeking help (Mental Health Commission of Canada 2013). As such, **stigma** is primarily a problem of behaviours resulting in the unfair and inequitable treatment of people with a mental illness and their family members, likely due to misconceptions and misunderstanding about mental illness. A common misconception is that all mentally ill individuals are violent and unpredictable, as this is often depicted in media. Since causes of mental illness are unclear, some may worry the symptoms may be contagious; this would be a particular concern in a confined space like prison. At a minimum, most people are uncomfortable around individuals who are symptomatic and try to keep a safe distance away.

The Mental Health Commission of Canada (2013) noted media portrayals of mentally ill individuals are problematic. For instance, they found that 40 percent of Canadian newspaper articles negatively associated crime, violence, and danger with mental illness. Moreover, only 17 percent of articles included the voice of someone living with a mental illness; only 25 percent included the voice of an expert; only 19 percent of articles discussed treatment; and only 18 percent discussed recovery or rehabilitation. Considering such bias in news coverage, it is unsurprising that Canadians are uncomfortable, if not afraid, when interacting with mentally ill individuals.

Stigma occurs at individual, group, and agency levels. Self-stigma occurs when people with mental illness accept and agree with negative cultural stereotypes. They may feel ashamed, blameworthy, and try to conceal their illness from others. Public stigma encompasses the prejudicial attitudes and discriminatory behaviours expressed toward people with mental illness by members of the public. This relates to challenges such individuals face when attempting re-entry into the community after being in prison. Agency-level or structural stigma occurs at the level of institutions, policies, and laws. It creates situations in which people with mental illness are treated inequitably and unfairly, such as placement in segregation.

J. Brown (2004) completed an innovative review of Canadian male and female offenders returning to the community and noted a variety of barriers to success (e.g., regaining and finding family and community support, lack of work skills and low income, and stigma). He asserted these factors can have an impact on offenders' reintegration efforts, and the effects of multiple stigmas for some offenders may be particularly strong. Hence, the combined stigma of having both a mental illness and a criminal record may be particularly challenging and would likely impair successful transition to becoming a law abiding citizen.

Many people with mental illness who used to be housed in institutions are now trying to function in our communities. Police officers are becoming the frontline contact for many of these people, who are both victims of crime and offenders. As a result, some researchers have labelled the police as "street corner psychiatrists" (Teplin 1984). Police have considerable discretion in deciding how to manage a crisis and whether or not to arrest a person. When dealing with a mentally ill person they may decide to informally resolve the problem, to arrest the person, or to take the person to a hospital for evaluation.

Brink et al. (2011) summarized the current situation regarding the mentally ill and crime, noting:

> Most people with mental illness do not commit criminal acts; however, contact with the police is common among this population. The reasons people with mental illness interact with the police are complex, but are generally attributed to clinical risk factors, such as co-occurring substance use problems and treatment non-compliance, as well as social and systemic factors, such as improperly implemented deinstitutionalization policies, homelessness and poverty, community disorganization, poorly funded and fragmented community-based mental health and social services, hospital emergency room bed pressures, overly restrictive civil commitment criteria, intolerance of social disorder, and criminal law reforms.

Their review of the empirical literature concluded:

- 2 in 5 people with mental illness have been arrested in their lifetime.
- 3 in 10 people with mental illness have had the police involved in their care pathway.
- 1 in 7 referrals to emergency psychiatric inpatient services involve the police.
- 1 in 20 police dispatches or encounters involve people with mental health problems.
- Half of the interactions between the police and people with mental illness involve alleged criminal behaviour.
- 2 in 5 encounters between the police and people with mental illness involve situations that are unrelated to criminal conduct.
- The majority of interactions between the police and people with mental illness are initiated either by the police (~25 percent), the person with mental illness (~15 percent), or their family (~20 percent).
- People with mental illness are over-represented in police shooting, stun gun incidents, and fatalities.

However, the authors went beyond a simple literature review and included interviews and surveys with approximately 300 mentally ill persons to gain a more complete and contextual understanding of this important criminal justice and societal issue. Table 10.1 presents the reasons for police contact. For interview participants, the most common type of interaction involved being transported (e.g., to hospital or to jail) by a police officer. Almost two-thirds of survey participants also reported being transported to a hospital by the police. Interactions with the police that involved a mental health crisis were experienced by 35 percent of interviewees and 66 percent of survey respondents. Many of the participants (survey: 48 percent; interview: 64 percent) had an interaction with the police in relation to their alleged criminal behaviour. A large proportion of the survey and interview participants also reported requesting assistance as a victim of a crime (survey: 62 percent; interview: 55 percent), being stopped on the street by police (survey: 66 percent; interview: 68 percent), or interacting with police in a casual or informal situation (survey: 59 percent; interview: 75 percent).

In 2014 the Mental Health Commission of Canada sponsored a 3-day conference addressing the topic of the nexus between policing and mental illness. Key themes included understanding and managing crises, risk assessment and management, effective education and training, new models of community safety to include recovery models, promoting workplace mental health for police, and measuring outcomes (Mental Health Commission of Canada 2014). Key messages from this conference included:

- People with lived experience of mental illness should be included.
- Collaboration is essential.
- Collaboration requires information sharing.
- A sense of "procedural justice" is key.

Table 10.1 Reasons for Police Contact

Reason for Police Contact	Survey Participants (N = 244)		Interview Participants (N = 60)	
	n	Valid %	n	Valid %
Mental health crisis	156	65.5	21	35.0
Domestic dispute	97	40.8	32	53.3
Public disturbance	71	30.0	24	40.0
DUI or traffic violation	109	45.8	17	28.3
Committed a criminal offence	113	48.1	38	64.4
Committed a violent criminal offence	n/a	n/a	22	36.7
Requested assistance as a victim of crime	149	62.1	33	55.0
Requested assistance as a witness to a crime	103	43.3	21	35.0
Requested assistance to report a crime	129	54.2	25	41.7
Street stop	158	66.1	41	68.3
Served with a warrant	85	35.9	20	33.3
Casual or informal	142	59.4	45	75.0
Intoxicated or high	96	40.3	n/a	n/a
Attended a police public information session	60	25.6	na	n/a
Checked on my well-being	106	45.3	n/a	n/a
Transported (e.g., to hospital)	156	64.6	54	90.0

Source: Brink et al. (2011).

- Housing, peer support, and access to interdisciplinary support are hallmarks of successful programs.
- Police must have good mental health themselves.
- Removing stigma improves interactions and outcomes.
- The full continuum of resources needs to be engaged.

Cotton and Coleman (2010) note that traditional policing has been primarily reactive, while contemporary policing reflects a more proactive interventionist approach to prevent or minimize crime. Accordingly, as it relates to mental health issues, Cotton and Coleman (2008) have suggested that standard education and training for police forces should include:

- The understanding and identification of mental illnesses
- How to communicate with mentally ill persons

A police officer questioning a mentally ill person.

- How to use defusing and de-escalation techniques
- How to assess suicidality
- How to assess risk and dangerousness
- Issues related to stigma
- The role of the family with mentally ill persons
- How to access mental health services
- The provincial *Mental Health Act* (MHA)
- Issues related to the use of force with mentally ill persons

Encouragingly, the Brink et al. (2011) study with interviews and surveys of mentally ill persons in British Columbia suggest such training is having an impact. Thirty percent of participants indicated positive perceptions of police and 47 percent were somewhat or fully satisfied regarding their interactions with police. Moreover, following contact with police, the overwhelming majority felt better (65 percent), calmer (66 percent), respected (85 percent), and clearer about the situation (76 percent).

Overall, people with mental illness appear to have more frequent contact with police than the general community but not all contacts result in an arrest. The policing model in Canada informed by risk management and community collaboration seems to be influencing the manner in which police engage persons with mental disorders. Continued research is required to determine the extent to which these models improve outcomes.

Prevalence of Mental Disorders among Offenders

Various studies have reported on prevalence of various mental disorders among offenders using different diagnostic criteria. In the early 1990's CSC conducted a national survey on prisoners using the Diagnostic Interview Schedule (DIS), which provides ICD diagnoses (Motiuk and Porporino 1991). These studies involved interviewing volunteers from prison samples in order to determine if certain symptoms were present. The clustering and pervasiveness of the symptoms (lifetime, within the past year, within the past 2 months) were then used to assign individuals to diagnostic groups. Systematic selection, a modification of simple random sampling, was used as the method to select cases from regional listings with the intent to generate representative samples across regions and prison security levels. The total Mental Health Survey sample consisted of 2185 primarily Caucasian (85 percent) adult male inmates. Of the 9801 offenders targeted for sampling, 28.7 percent were actually selected, with an overall response rate of 68.5 percent. The results of this survey are presented in Table 10.2. As is apparent in the table, lifetime rates yield higher rates and the most serious mental disorders (sometimes referred to as major mental illness reflecting Axis I disorders) are more prevalent. More than 50 percent of incarcerated individuals met formal diagnostic criteria for antisocial personality, and more than 40 percent met diagnostic criteria for substance abuse disorders. This national study, the largest of its type in Canada, is now 20 years old. Current prevalence rates would be helpful to inform contemporary treatment planning and resource allocation (at a minimum). Encouragingly, in the past several years CSC has formed interdisciplinary mental health teams that function in each major institution. As well, each region has a

Table 10.2 National Federal Offender Prevalence Rates According to Diagnostic Interview Schedule

Disorder	Lifetime	Within 1 Year	Within 2 Weeks
Organic	0.1	n/a	n/a
Psychotic	7.7	5.0	3.6
Depressive	21.5	9.9	5.4
Anxiety	44.1	27.0	11.8
Psychosexual	21.1	n/a	n/a
Antisocial	56.9	n/a	n/a
Drug abuse/dependence	40.9	13.1	3.0
Alcohol abuse/dependence	47.2	9.8	0.5

Note: n/a = not available
Source: Motiuk and Porporino (1991).

treatment centre that is an accredited hospital and is reserved to provide acute care to mentally disordered offenders.

Coté and Hodgins (1990) also utilized the DIS with 1018 offenders in Quebec and reported similar rates for mental disorders (psychosis: 6.5 percent; bipolar: 6.8 percent; depression: 14.8 percent, drug abuse: 48.9 percent; antisocial personality: 61.5 percent; and alcohol abuse: 66.9 percent). As well, Hodgins and Coté (1992) examined co-morbidity (the co-occurrence of two or more disorders), noting that there were few forms of pure disorders—meaning offenders with severe mental disorders (schizophrenia, bipolar, and manor depression) commonly met the criteria for at least one other severe disorder, antisocial personality, or substance abuse/dependence. This finding may have important implications for intervention for MDOs. As noted in Chapter 4, the predominant treatment approach is to follow RNR principles to target criminogenic needs. The issue of intervention will be covered later in this chapter.

Of particular interest is determining whether prevalence rates vary as a function of the type of crime for which an offender is currently serving time. Motiuk and Porporino also examined this in their study (1991) and their findings are presented in Table 10.3. Unsurprisingly, robbery offenders were found most likely to be diagnosed with antisocial personality, but overall, there was no indication of specialization; each diagnostic category was represented in each crime category.

More recent studies support the evidence that there are high rates of mental disorders among Canadian prisoners relative to community samples. Brink, Doherty, and Boer (2001) completed diagnostic assessments using a more robust measure, the Structured Clinical Interview of DSM-IV (SCID) in a cohort of offenders newly admitted to the federal prison system (CSC) in British Columbia. With a Canadian sample, the SCID (a semi-structured interview) is the best available diagnostic tool for the assessment of

Table 10.3 Lifetime Prevalence Rates According to the Diagnostic Interview Schedule by Type of Offence

Disorder	Homicide (337)	Manslaughter (98)	Robbery (498)	Sex (103)	Drugs (105)	Other (1044)
Organic	.03	0.0	0.0	0.0	0.0	0.2
Psychotic	10.7	11.2	8.0	5.8	3.8	9.2
Depressive	29.1	30.6	19.3	36.9	12.4	21.1
Anxiety	41.3	46.9	44.6	47.6	29.5	45.2
Psychosexual	23.7	26.5	18.5	31.1	15.2	22.7
Antisocial	45.4	44.9	71.5	42.7	36.2	58.3
Drug abuse	30.0	36.7	54.6	22.3	36.2	41.7
Alcohol	46.1	46.9	51.0	36.9	29.5	50.3

Source: Motiuk and Porporino (1991).

Table 10.4 Prevalence Rates of DSM-IV (Axis I) Disorders among Male Federal Admissions (N = 202) Compared to a Community Male Sample

Disorder	Current (1 month) (n = 64)	Lifetime (n = 138)	Combined (n = 170)	% of Sample (84%)	Community
Mood disorders	8.4%	21.8%	61	30.2	7.1%
Schizophrenia/psychotic disorders	3.5%	5.0%	17	8.4	0.5%
Anxiety disorders	17.3%	1.0%	37	18.3%	8.7
Substance use disorders	5.9%	69.8%	153	75.7%	32.5
Adjustment disorders	4.0%	0%	8	4.0%	–

Source: Bland, Orn, and Newman (1988), cited in Brink, Doherty, and Boer (2001).

major Axis I disorders (Arboleda-Florez 1994). Despite being completed a decade later than these initial studies and using a more sensitive measure, prevalence rates were still comparable. Table 10.4 presents an adapted version of findings by Brink et al. The prevalence rate for schizophrenia/psychosis were low, but were still 10 times greater in the prison sample than the community. Mood and anxiety disorders were 4 times greater, while substance abuse disorders were slightly more than twice as prevalent in a prison compared to a community sample. Equally important, 68.3 percent of the prison sample was diagnosed with a mental disorder at some point in their lives, and 43.1 percent were diagnosed with a disorder other than substance abuse. Notably, anxiety and adjustment disorders were *higher* at the time of the assessment (when admitted to prison) than previously, which is the opposite trend to the other disorders. Given the prisoners had mainly been incarcerated for a month prior to their assessment interview, it is unsurprising that access to illicit substances was diminished, hence the current substance abuse prevalence rates were low (even lower than the community sample).

Thus far, we have studied the prevalence of mental disorders in select prison samples with findings that rates are high; the most serious disorders (previously referred to as Axis I) had rates lower than substance abuse and antisocial personality. What happens if we study an entire country rather than select samples? Denmark is one of few countries in the world with a national database that allows it to track its entire population to determine the prevalence of criminality. Hodgins, Mednick, Brennan, Schulsinger, and Engberg (1996) did a follow-up study of all Danes born between 1944 and 1947, a total of 358 180 individuals. They tracked individuals to determine if they were ever diagnosed with a mental disorder and then checked their criminal records. Table 10.5 presents Hodgins et al.'s findings across different types of mental disorders for any conviction and for violent convictions. In both men and women, the presence of a mental

Table 10.5 Percent of People Convicted of Any Crime or Violent Crime Across Different Types of Mental Disorder

Mental Disorder	Convicted of Any Crime		Convicted of Violent Crime	
	Male	Female	Male	Female
No mental disorder	6.1	2.1	1.5	.1
Major mental disorder	23.0	9.5	6.7	.9
Mental retardation	42.4	11.6	1.3	1.4
Drug abuse	46.2	23.7	13.0	1.6
Alcohol abuse	35.8	18.7	10.0	1.6
Antisocial personality disorder	32.4	13.6	10.8	1.3

Source: Hodgins et al. (1996).

disorder substantially increased the risk for criminality and violence. As concluded by Hodgins et al. (1996, p. 495) "It would be destructive for societies to allow the findings on the criminality of the mentally disordered and mentally retarded to be used to further stigmatize these individuals. Rather, these data can be used constructively to provide more adequate, appropriate, and humane care to individuals who, through no fault of their own, suffer from devastating disorders and at the same time to protect society." See the Canadian Researcher Profile box for more information on Dr. Sheilagh Hodgins and her research.

Since 1994, CSC has used a standardized intake assessment (Offender Intake Assessment, OIA) to examine mental health needs in federal offenders. Key factors considered include prior psychiatric diagnoses, admissions, and care. While CSC has recently developed a new mental health screening approach that is now considered confidential medical information, national data from 2008 are still available. Extrapolations from these data suggest there were approximately 239 women and 4018 men admitted in that year. Table 10.6 presents findings regarding mental health factors in the admission cohort from 2007–2008 and trends over time are presented in Figure 10.2. It is clear from Table 10.6 that there are gender differences, with women reporting double the rate of prior diagnoses and past psychiatric admissions than men. Women also had higher rates for previously being prescribed psychiatric medication and receiving outcome care. Extended over two years (the average federal sentence is more than three years), the number of offenders with mental health needs exceeds the capacity of hospital beds (approximately 700) in psychiatric treatment centres. It is for this reason that the treatment centres mainly provide acute care and the CSC has developed mental health teams (social workers, forensic psychiatric nurses, psychologists) to provide care in major institutions. Figure 10.2 presents evidence of increasing prevalence of mental health indicators over the decade for which standardized information was collected. However, as noted in Table 10.6, this figure obscures gender differences.

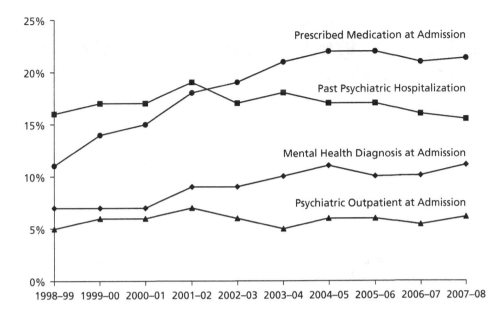

Figure 10.2 Percentage of Warrant of Committal Admissions with Mental Health Indicators

Source: Public Safety Canada (2009), Figure c10, p. 55, based on data from Correctional Service Canada.

Prevalence of Personality Disorders

In a study of 1396 male violent offenders in England, Roberts, Yang, Zhang, and Coid (2008) found a prevalence rate of 73 percent for any personality disorder. Table 10.7 presents the prevalence of personality disorders, with antisocial personality disorder and paranoid being the most prevalent, and dependent and histrionic the least common.

Table 10.6 Mental Health Indicators in a Federal Offender Intake Assessment Cohort 2007–2009

Mental Health Indicator at Time of Admission	Women		Men		Total	
	#	%	#	%	#	%
Prior diagnosis	52	21.8	394	10.4	446	11.1
Prescribed psychiatric medication	78	33.2	772	20.6	850	21.3
Past psychiatric hospitalization	72	30.1	547	14.5	619	15.5
Psychiatric outpatient care in past	21	8.7	225	5.9	246	6.1

Source: Public Safety Canada (2009).

Box 10.1

Canadian Researcher Profile Dr. Sheilagh Hodgins

Dr. Sheilagh Hodgins first became interested in psychology as a child. In school she observed some children having many problems. She wondered why no one helped these children with conduct problems. This interest in youth and adults with conduct problems and mental illness has been the focus of her clinical and research endeavours.

Dr. Hodgins completed her Ph.D. at McGill University. The research for her dissertation was carried out in a maximum security penitentiary, where she measured psychophysiological responses of psychopathic offenders in anticipation of an electric shock. Her first academic appointment was in the School of Social Work at the Université de Montréal. She then moved to the Psychology Department, and is currently in the Psychiatry Department. She is also a Professor at the Karolinksa Institute in Stockholm. She was named a fellow of the Royal Society of

Canada in 2009 and was awarded the Wolfson Merit Award by the Royal Society of the United Kingdom in 2004.

In Canada in the 1980s psychiatric hospitals were being shut down with the intention of providing care in the community for released patients and for newly ill patients. Dr. Hodgins realized that the public perceived persons with mental health problems as dangerous, despite there being no methodologically sound research that had determined whether or not severe mental illness impacted the risk of violent behaviour. Dr. Hodgins conducted the first large-scale epidemiological study to address this issue. Criminal and health records of a birth cohort of 15 000 Swedes were examined. Results showed that there was an increased risk for violence among persons with severe mental illness. Wanting to determine whether there was a specific mental illness associated with this increased violence, Dr. Hodgins conducted another study of a birth cohort that included 358 000 Danes. She found that individuals with schizophrenia were at an elevated risk for violence. These findings have now been replicated in many countries around the world.

Dr. Hodgins' research subsequently focused on identifying the factors that promote violent behaviour using a variety of methodologies. She recognized the importance of conducting longitudinal prospective studies in order to gain an understanding of the development of aggressive and antisocial behaviours. She also studies clinical samples of adults with schizophrenia to identify both distal and proximal factors associated with violent behaviour and to find humane treatments that prevent violence for people with schizophrenia.

Courtesy of Professor Sheilagh Hodgins, Institute of Psychiatry

Dr. Sheilagh Hodgins

Box 10.1 (Continued)

Dr. Hodgins attributes much of her success to fruitful collaborations with scientists in many different countries (United Kingdom, Canada, Sweden, Denmark, Finland, and Germany) who work in different disciplines (clinical psychiatry and psychology, neuroscience, genetics, epidemiology, statistics) and to many bright, insightful students who have pushed her to clarify existing knowledge.

Dr. Hodgins has continued to perform research on offenders with psychopathy and with antisocial personality disorder in an effort to understand the differences in aetiology and treatment responsiveness of these offenders with personality disorders as contrasted with those with schizophrenia. For example, with a Ph.D. student and several colleagues, she recently published a study showing that in middle childhood, boys with conduct problems and callous-unemotional traits display differences in brain structures linked to their personality and behavioural traits.

Currently, Dr. Hodgins' research focuses on understanding the abnormal neural development that characterizes individuals who display patterns of antisocial and aggressive behaviour using magnetic resonance imaging brain scans. Additionally, she studies the interactions between both negative and positive environmental factors and specific genotypes that affect neural development and thereby modify the risk of antisocial and aggressive behaviour.

When asked what keeps her interested in research, she responded "I see enormous progress in our understanding of antisocial behaviour. I find it fascinating to advance knowledge—really discover new things. But what is most gratifying is to see results used to help people."

Table 10.7 Prevalence Rates of Personality Disorders in Male and Female Offenders

Personality Disorder	Male Offenders	Female Offenders
Paranoid	22%	27%
Schizoid	7%	5%
Schizotypal	4%	4%
Antisocial	65%	43%
Borderline	18%	24%
Histrionic	1%	4%
Narcissistic	10%	10%
Avoidant	9%	14%
Dependent	1%	4%
Obsessive-compulsive	7%	15%

Source: Adapted from Roberts et al. (2008) and Warren et al. (2002).

Prisoners with personality disorder were more likely to report childhood conduct problems, adverse childhood experiences, and victimizations than those with no personality disorder. For comparison, a sample of 261 American maximum security female offenders (Warren et al. 2002) is also presented in Table 10.7. The prevalence rate in this sample for any personality disorder was 67 percent. The most common personality disorder in the female offenders were antisocial, paranoid, and borderline. The least common diagnoses were schizoid, schizotypal, and dependent.

Summarizing and integrating across mainly Canadian prison prevalence studies, some main themes emerge. These include:

■ There are meaningful gender differences, with women offenders having higher prevalence rates of mental health indicators.

■ Prevalence rates for mental disorders using different assessment approaches (DIS, SCID) are higher in prison samples than community samples.

■ Prevalence of major mental disorder (Axis I) is high, but rates of substance abuse and antisocial personality are especially higher in prison samples, indicating significant co-morbidity.

■ There appears to be no relation between type of disorder and type of crime.

■ When examining population data, there appears to be an increased likelihood of criminality in those individuals with mental disorders.

The following situations highlight why the criminal justice system "cares" about the issue of mental disorder.

■ Police have disproportionate contact with persons with mental illness.

■ Admission to jail is a high-risk time and may exacerbate mental health symptoms, potentially increasing an offender's risk of harming themselves or others.

■ The prevalence rates of mental diagnoses greatly exceed that of the community.

■ Placement of mentally disordered offenders may be challenging and problematic: deciding whether or not to segregate these offenders is an issue.

■ Correctional staff are not "care givers" per se and require specialized training to assess and manage individuals with mental health concerns. This increases training costs.

■ Other offenders may victimize vulnerable mentally disordered offenders.

■ Many mentally disordered offenders come to jail having stopped their medication. There are challenges in prescribing the correct medication in a timely manner, addressing costs of medication, and allowing time for symptoms to ameliorate.

METHODOLOGY

THE MOST COMMON METHODOLOGY FOR UNDERSTANDING MENTAL DISORDER AND crime has been prevalence studies using validated diagnostic approaches, mainly within offender samples. In some rare cases, population studies have been conducted that compared the criminal propensities of those with and without disorders. Studies examining co-occurring disorders have suggested that risk is exacerbated when multiple disorders are present, and that substance abuse and antisocial personality disorder are particularly salient in understanding criminal behaviour.

It should be apparent from the earlier section on prevalence rates of mental illness that there is slight variation across settings (community versus prison), between genders, and the assessment approaches utilized (DIS, SCID, etc.). More recent studies, both meta-analytic and large-scale follow-up studies, have examined the unique contribution of major mental disorders to future crime, controlling for common moderators that are highly prevalent and definitional (e.g., substance abuse and antisocial personality disorder—key components of the Central Eight risk factors).

In an important study to better understand risk assessment with mentally disordered offenders (MDOs), Bonta, Law and Hanson (1998) reviewed more than 100 studies with 64 unique samples to identify key factors related to general and violent reoffending. Figure 10.3 presents an overview of their findings. Their research indicated that, similar to findings from the VRAG, serious mental health indicators were actually protective while traditional criminogenic predictors functioned similarly for MDOs as for other correctional samples; most of the Central Eight were comparably predictive in this meta-analysis with MDO samples. Notably, contemporary risk-assessment instruments were the most predictive, highlighting once more that unstructured clinical opinion is unhelpful in distinguishing between successes and failures. The authors concluded that a case can be made to apply what is known about general offender risk assessment to the risk assessment of MDOs.

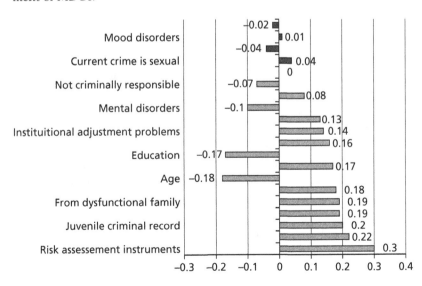

Figure 10.3 Risk Factors for Violent Recidivism

Source: Bonta, Law, and Hanson (1998).

THEORIES LINKING MENTAL DISORDER AND CRIME

INITIAL THEORIES PROPOSED THE CRIMINALIZATION OF THE MENTALLY ILL WAS DUE to deinstitutionalization (Teplin 1990), essentially suggesting MDOs ended up in jail and prison due to diminished community resources and a police response rather than a social work response. Recent research regarding the frequency and nature of police contacts with MDOs and satisfaction ratings suggest this is not the case (Brink et al. 2011). Prevalence studies have also indicated that prevalence rates for jails are not demonstrably higher than prisons, although the overlap among risk factors and co-morbidity of psychiatric (Axis I) and criminogenic (antisocial personality and substance abuse) diagnoses prompted Bonta, Blais and Wilson (2014) to argue for the application of a General Personality Cognitive Social Learning approach to intervention strategies. It is possible they view Axis I disorders as responsivity factors because Axis II disorders clearly reflect the Central Eight.

Symptoms of Mental Disorder that Increase Risk of Violence

Another approach to understanding the link between mental disorder and crime is to review specific symptoms that might influence the expression of criminal conduct. Three general areas are worth comment. In the area of substance abuse (see Chapter 7 for greater detail), MDOs may use substances to ameliorate symptoms (i.e., they self-medicate), which can lead to both diminished self-control and increased financial need. Hallmarks of antisocial personality disorder are criminal attitudes and thinking. In addition to these obvious symptoms, several studies have examined the risk factors for violence within samples of schizophrenics. Swanson and colleagues (2006) reported that minor violence (assault with no injury or weapon use) was related to co-occurring substance abuse and *acute* psychotic symptoms. Serious violence (assault with injury or with a lethal weapon, sexual assault) was related to *acute* positive psychotic symptoms (delusions and hallucinations), depressive symptoms, childhood conduct problems, and being victimized, while having negative psychotic symptoms (social withdrawal, blunted affect) was related to lower risk. It seems the presence and type of symptoms may be related to risk of criminal violence.

Delusions are one factor that increases the risk of violence in those with schizophrenia. Schizophrenics who experience what have been called **threat/control override (TCO) delusions** or command hallucinations are at an elevated risk. The other factor that increases the risk of violence in those with schizophrenia, discussed in an earlier section, is the combination of psychotic symptoms and substance abuse/dependence. According to the DSM-V, **delusions** are "fixed beliefs that are not amenable to change in light of conflicting evidence" (APA 2013, p. 87). Delusions can be categorized as either bizarre (e.g., aliens controlling your thoughts) or non-bizarre (e.g., you think the police are constantly watching you).

Link and Stueve defined TCO symptoms as "psychotic symptoms that cause a person to feel threatened or involve the intrusion of thoughts that can override self-controls"

(1994, p. 155). In their study they compared three TCO symptoms (How often have you felt that your mind was dominated by forces beyond your control? How often have you felt that thoughts were put into your head that were not your own? How often have you felt that there were people who wished to do you harm?) to other psychotic symptoms (e.g., How often have you felt you had special powers? How often have you felt your thoughts were taken away from you by some external force? How often have you felt you were possessed by a spirit or a devil?). In both a community and a psychiatric sample, only the three TCO symptoms were related to violence. In the majority of studies by Link and his colleagues (Link, Monahan, Stueve, and Cullen 1999; Link, Stueve, and Phelan 1998) and others (Hodgins, Hiscoke, and Freese 2003; Swanson et al. 1997), TCO symptoms were strongly related to violence. For example, Swanson et al. (1997) found that patients who exhibited TCO symptoms were twice as likely to become violent during a one-year follow-up period.

However, other studies have failed to find a relationship between TCO symptoms and violence (Skeem et al. 2006), finding that hostility, not TCO symptoms, predicted violence in a community sample of patients. One potential explanation for the discrepant findings has been proposed by Teasdale, Silver, and Monahan (2006). These authors found that men and women respond to TCO symptoms differently. Although the rates of threat delusions (17 percent vs. 11 percent) and control override delusions (18 percent vs. 16 percent) were similar in men and women, it was only in men that threat delusions were related to violence (in this study TCO symptoms were not related to violence in men). In the Skeem et al. (2006) study, almost 50 percent of the sample was female.

Many people with schizophrenia and delusional disorders experience auditory and visual hallucinations but these vary in content. For example, command hallucinations are auditory hallucinations. Between 30 to 50 percent of psychiatric inpatients report experiencing command hallucinations (Hersh and Borum 1998; Rogers, Gillis, Tuner, and Frise-Smith 1990). Some of these command hallucinations are nonviolent, others are related to self-injurious behaviour, and some relate to other-directed violence. For example, Lee, Chong, Chan, and Sathyadevan (2004) examined the content of auditory hallucinations in 100 patients with command hallucinations that were classified as either violent or nonviolent. The prevalence rate of command hallucinations was 53 percent, with 29 percent of these having violent content. When asked if they had complied with the command hallucination, 62 percent indicated they had, with most complying to a nonviolent command. However 18 percent complied to a self-harm command and 15 percent complied to a "harm others" command. Thus, patients were more likely to comply with non-violent than violent commands. Junginger (1995) examined the rates of compliance to command hallucinations and found that compliance was related to less dangerous commands and voice recognition. This line of research has unfortunately not been replicated in correctional samples to date. However, in summary, increased risk of violence in mentally disordered offenders is likely when the following are present:

- Active psychotic symptoms with a substance abuse disorder and a history of violence or current attitudes supportive of violence

- The presence of a delusional belief (TCO)
- Command hallucinations to commit violence

FACTORS ASSOCIATED WITH CRIMINAL CONDUCT AMONG MENTALLY DISORDERED OFFENDERS

Mental Disorder: Associations with Crime, Violence, and Recidivism

The Bonta et al. (1998) meta-analysis indicates that MDOs are similar to non-MDOs (regular offenders) in terms of risk factors, yet the prevalence research indicates much higher rates of mental illness in prison samples compared to the community. This raises the question, how does mental disorder relate to crime, violence, and recidivism? The extant research indicates that those with serious mental illnesses are responsible for a small portion (5 percent) of violent offences (Short, Thomas, Mullen, and Ogloff 2014). Nonetheless, meta-analytic studies indicate there is a relationship between these illnesses and violence (Bonta, Blais and Wilson 2014; Douglas, Guy, and Hart 2009); psychotic individuals are four to five times more likely to commit violent offences than others. A large Australian study with a cohort of 4168 people with schizophrenia examined violence over their lifespan, and found a matched control group had rates of 2.4 percent compared to 10 percent for those with the mental illness. Moreover, contrary to earlier concerns regarding the criminalization of mental illness, these effects are present even when controlling for moderating variables such as substance use (Short et al. 2014), but substance use exacerbates risk, as does antisocial personality disorder (Ogloff, Talevski, Lemphers, Wood, and Simmons 2015; Porporino and Motiuk, 1995).

Clearly, the presence of substance abuse and antisocial personality increase the risk of violence in MDOs. In an early Canadian study, Coté and Hodgins (1990) examined patterns of co-occurring disorders in a sample of 1018 prisoners in Quebec. First, they noted high rates of co-occurring disorders, with few pure forms of a severe mental disorder alone. Second, amongst their sample, when examining the chronology of diagnoses, half of the subjects with a diagnosis of schizophrenic disorder manifested this disorder before other secondary diagnoses (e.g., antisocial personality disorder and substance abuse). In contrast, antisocial personality disorder showed an early onset in 62 percent of their sample, while drug and alcohol abuse were primary in 22 percent and 30 percent, respectively. Unfortunately, while this study distinguishes between drug and alcohol abuse, it does not relate them to future reoffending.

What can we conclude from the current literature on serious mental disorder and violence?

- The majority of people with serious mental disorder do not engage in violence.
- The likelihood of committing violence is greater for people with a serious mental disorder than for those with no mental disorder.

- People with co-occurring antisocial personality disorders and substance abuse are at an elevated risk for violence.

- The causal mechanisms that are responsible for the link between mental disorder and violence are not clearly understood. It may be that it is not factors unique to the mental illness that lead to criminal behaviour, but rather factors associated with mental illness, such as poverty, substance use, unemployment, and homelessness (Junginger, Claypoole, Laygo, and Crisanti 2006).

Protective Factors

An important area that warrants increased attention relates to the management or reduction of risk through the presence of protective factors. Two new risk instruments for MDOs described in the assessment section below have incorporated protective factors into assessment: the Structured Assessment of Protective Factors for violence risk (SAPROF; de Vogel, de Ruiter, Bouman, and de Vries Robbé 2009) and the Short-Term Assessment of Risk and Treatability (START, Nicholls et al. 2006; Desmarais, Nicholls, Wilson, and Brink 2012). Initial comparisons suggest there is reasonable agreement regarding candidate protective factors (Serin, Chadwick, and Lloyd, 2015). Some reflect mental health issues (e.g., compliance with medication) and some reflect more general criminogenic factors (e.g., employment, positive social relationships) that are common in the crime desistance literature (see Chapter 4; Maruna 2010). While the presence of protective factors appear to be related to improved offender outcomes (de Vries Robbé, de Vogel, and de Spa 2011; Desmarais et al. 2012), how do they function? Do they buffer or reduce risk? Are they the opposite of risk factors and therefore invariant of risk, or are they independent of risk? Moreover, are there unique protective factors for MDOs compared to other offenders? This new area is an exciting adjunct to risk assessment and should further inform idiographic (i.e., case-specific) case planning and risk management of MDOs.

ASSESSMENT APPROACHES AND EFFECTIVENESS

Assessment of Mental Health Indicators

Given that prevalence studies have confirmed high rates of mental disorders in jail and prison populations, corrections agencies have put in place approaches to identify these persons at intake to prison. As noted earlier in the chapter, Correctional Service Canada has a standardized intake assessment of mental health indicators. Many correctional agencies utilize a mental health screening approach or triage, whereby if specific items are identified during an interview with a correctional officer, a referral is made to a mental health specialist. The Brief Jail Mental Health Screen (BJMHS; Osher, Scott, Steadman, and Robbins 2006) is a typical and popular screening instrument, given that others are longer (Brief Psychiatric Rating Scale, BPRS; Overall and Gorham 1962), are restricted in temporal scope to within the past week (Brief Symptom Inventory; Derogatis 1993),

Table 10.8 Brief Jail Mental Health Screen Items

1. Do you currently believe that someone can control your mind by putting thoughts into your head or taking thoughts out of your head?

2. Do you currently feel that other people know your thoughts and can read your mind?

3. Have you currently lost or gained as much as two pounds a week for several weeks without even trying?

4. Have you or your family or friends noticed that you are currently much more active than you usually are?

5. Do you currently feel like you have to talk or move more slowly than you usually do?

6. Have there currently been a few weeks when you felt like you were useless or sinful?

7. Have you ever been in a hospital for emotional or mental health problems?

8. Are you currently taking any medication prescribed for you by a physician for any emotional or mental health problems?

Source: Osher et al. (2006).

and/or are more expensive to implement. The Brief Jail Mental Health Screen (BJMHS) is brief, requiring only 2.5 minutes, and can be administered by non–mental-health staff. It also doubles as a screen for mental health symptoms and risk of suicide. The Referral Decision Scale (RDS; Teplin and Swartz 1989) is another popular measure in that it has 14 items reflecting schizophrenia, major depression, and bipolar disorder symptoms. However, concerns regarding its validity and utility in jail samples have limited its application (Hart, Roesch, Corrado, and Cox 1993; Rogers et al. 1995; Veysey et al. 1998). Osher, Scott, Steadman, and Robbins' (2006) research with 10 330 American jail detainees indicated 11.6 percent were referred for a more comprehensive assessment when using the BJMHS. The accuracy of the BJMHS is approximately 74 percent (comparing to SCID diagnoses), however, it missed about one-third of currently symptomatic women. An adapted version of the BJMHS is presented in Table 10.8. If two or more of items 1 through 6 are answered yes, *or* if items 7 or 8 are answered yes, the offender is referred to further assessment. A primary goal of the BJMHS is to identify suicide risk.

Once the screen is completed, then what? A Simon Fraser Research group has developed the Jail Screening Assessment Tool (JSAT; Nicholls et al. 2005). This interview-based structured professional judgement approach is a comprehensive integration of the extant mental health research that guides mental health professionals to conduct standardized assessments. These assessments inform cell placement and both short- and longer-term case planning and would follow from referrals by corrections staff (who use something like the BJMHS). Some sites may choose to use specific JSAT items as a screener assessment in the absence of a standardized and validated screening instrument. The JSAT content areas are presented in Table 10.9.

Table 10.9 Jail Screening Assessment Tool (JSAT) Domains

- Legal situation—current charges, previous incarceration history
- History of violence
- Prior mental health treatment
- Suicide/self-harm issues
- Management and placement recommendations regarding suicide risk
- Social background
- Substance use
- Mental health status—based on Brief Psychiatric Rating Scale

Source: Nicholls et al. (2005).

Since 2009, CSC has been using a new Computerized Mental Health Intake Screening System (CoMHISS). Recent findings suggest the following prevalence rates of mental health indicators:

- 62 percent of incoming female offenders required further mental-health evaluation.

- 50 percent of incoming male offenders required further evaluation; of these 28 percent had a confirmed mental diagnosis.

- There were no differences between Aboriginal and non-Aboriginal offenders.

- The most prevalent problems have been substance use disorders. However, over 40 percent of offenders met the criteria for a current diagnosis other than substance abuse or antisocial personality disorder.

- Rates of current mood disorders varied from 15 percent to 19 percent, and psychotic disorders varied from two percent to seven percent.

Assessment of Risk of Suicide

In jail and prisons, when an offender is assessed as having high risk for self-harm or suicide, they are typically placed on a watch in an isolation cell (sometimes in administrative segregation). Monitoring can be done one-on-one or via camera. A mental-health assessment is required before an offender can be taken off suicide watch. In an early but landmark study, Burtch and Ericson calculated that from 1959 to 1975, the suicide rate of inmates in Canadian penitentiaries was 95.9 suicides per 100 000 prisoners. This is substantially higher than the corresponding rate of 14.2 suicides per 100 000 in the general Canadian population. The Office of the Correctional Investigator (2014) noted that in the 20-year period from 1994/95 to 2013/14, a total of 211 federal inmates took their own lives. Suicide is the leading cause of unnatural death among federal inmates, accounting for about 20 percent of all deaths in custody in any given year.

Given that admission to prison is a time of increased risk of suicide and self-harming behaviour, many correctional agencies have standardized risk assessment approaches for suicidal and parasuicidal behaviour. Typically, a suicide assessment includes such items as:

- The offender may be suicidal.
- The offender has made a previous suicide attempt.
- The offender has undergone recent psychological/psychiatric intervention.
- The offender has experienced recent loss of a relative/spouse.
- The offender is presently experiencing major problems (i.e., legal).
- The offender is currently under influence of alcohol/drugs.
- The offender shows signs of depression.
- The offender has expressed suicidal ideation.
- The offender has a suicide plan.

Assessment of Risk of Future Criminal and Violent Behaviour

Similar to other sub-populations, there are specialized risk-assessment instruments for use with MDOs, including the Historical Clinical Risk Management-20, Version 3 (Douglas, Hart, Webster, and Belfrage 2013); the Short-Term Assessment of Risk and Treatability (START; Webster et al. 2009); and the Structured Assessment of Protective Factors for violence risk (SAPROF; de Vogel et al. 2009). All are structured professional judgement (SPJ) approaches for the assessment and management of violence risk. The SAPROF is a measure of protective factors and is intended to be used in concert with HCR-20^{V3}. All instruments are applied within correctional, forensic, and general or civil psychiatric settings, whether in the institution or in the community, and are applicable to adults aged 18 and above who may pose a risk for future violence. Training is essential prior to using any of these instruments clinically. The HCR-20^{V3} now has online training available.

HCR-20 The original version of the Historical Clinical Risk Management-20 (HCR-20) was developed in 1995. Version 2 was released in 1997, followed by Version 3 (HCR-20^{V3}) in 2013. An important aspect of the HCR-20 and its authors has been a quest to bridge the seemingly separate worlds of the prediction of violence and the clinical practice of assessment. Consistent with this goal has been a refinement of Version 3 to include greater elaboration of the process of SPJ as well as enhanced clarity of items and scoring, intended to improve both prediction and clinical utility.

In the paper that describes the new Version 3, Douglas et al. (2014) provide a particularly cogent description of SPJ, situating it against actuarial instruments such as the VRAG:

> SPJ measures typically include 20–30 risk factors chosen on the basis of a thorough review of the scientific literature, rather than based on the results of a single or small number of samples. This is done to enhance comprehensiveness of coverage in terms of risk factors, and to promote generalizability across settings and samples. The approach

helps evaluators and decision-makers identify risk factors that are present and relevant to the individual being evaluated; risk reduction and management strategies; and relative risk level. SPJ measures adopt non-algorithmic, non-numeric decision processes and risk estimates. They do so to avoid the pitfalls inherent in actuarial approaches, such as sample dependence, exclusion of potentially important risk factors, instability of precise probability estimates across samples, and the inherent difficulty in applying group-based probability estimates to individuals. (p. 94)

Strub, Douglas, and Nicholls (2014) provide initial validity data for a small sample of offenders ($n = 56$) and civil commitment psychiatric patients ($n = 50$), reporting findings comparable to earlier versions of the HCR-20. Predictive accuracy indices (e.g., AUC) exceed .70 for both samples for 4–6 week and 6–8 month timeframes. Moderation analyses indicated that gender was not predictive while summary risk rating (e.g., low, moderate, high) was predictive, adding incremental prediction over HCR-20^{V3} totals.

START The START measure incorporates 20 items that can be scored as either a risk or a strength factor. Items include areas to reflect social situation and relationships, mental state, substance use, impulse control, medication adherence, treatability, supports, insight, coping, and current plans. To date, the measure has demonstrated good interrater agreement in initial research with a sample of 137 forensic psychiatric patients ($ICC_2 = .87, p < .001$; Nicholls et al. 2006), as well as good predictive accuracy using strength total score and vulnerability total score for any aggression. The START violence risk estimate ($n = 119$) yielded good predictive validity for aggression in the 3 months following the START assessment, including any aggression (AUC = .80), verbal aggression (AUC = .78), physical aggression towards objects (AUC = .84), and physical aggression towards others (AUC = .85; Desmarais et al. 2012). On the strength of such findings, the START has been swiftly implemented and it is currently used in at least 10 countries. It appears to have become the preferred dynamic risk measure for use in forensic mental health settings.

SAPROF The Structured Assessment of Protective Factors for violence risk (SAPROF; de Vogel et al. 2009) was developed as a dynamic addition to the Historical Clinical Risk Management-20 (Webster et al. 1997). The instrument consists of 17 items, including 2 static factors and 15 protective factors, which are assessed to identify potential goals or targets for intervention. The SAPROF is designed to prospectively prevent recidivism by informing treatment rather than to be used as a prediction tool. In a retrospective validation, de Vries Robbé, de Vogel, and de Spa (2011) found that SAPROF total scores were able to significantly predict non-recidivism (defined as lack of violent offence) with stability over three follow up periods ($r_{pb} = -.35$ at 1 year, $r_{pb} = -.38$ at 2 years, and $r_{pb} = -.35$ at 3 years). Overall psychometric properties of the SAPROF appear sufficient (de Vries Robbé et al. 2011). Further, results have suggested that, when combined with a dynamic measure of risk, the inclusion of protective factors from the SAPROF improved the overall prediction of recidivism at both a three-year follow up and a long-term follow up (de Vries Robbé, de Vogel, and Douglas 2013). The SAPROF shows promise as

Box 10.2

You Be the Assessor

Mr. Robert Jones is 24 years old and has been charged with theft and assault. Following a minor argument in a bar, he assaulted another patron with a beer bottle and stole the person's wallet while fleeing the scene. Apparently he was a regular at the bar and was known to the staff. He was quickly arrested by police without incident. When arrested, he seemed somewhat confused, showed lability of mood, and appeared to be under the influence of street drugs. The next day he was remanded in court, awaiting legal aid, and was brought to jail by the police. At admission, the police report indicated that Robert appeared odd, was probably coming down from something, and told staff that he had nothing to live for. The police also noted marks on Robert's wrists that had not yet healed.

Questions

Imagine you are a correctional officer interviewing Robert as a new admission to your jail. What areas should you consider in your assessment of Mr. Jones? What are your major concerns? What are your likely next steps?

a structured assessment, but has only been utilized among forensic samples to date and is preferably used to augment the risk assessment by the HCR-20^{V3} (Douglas et al. 2013).

Overall, these approaches provide acceptable predictive accuracy (i.e., AUCs > .70) regarding new crime and new violent crime in MDOs. The protective or strength perspectives of the START and SAPROF represent recent innovations in risk assessment, although this research is in its infancy, warranting improved conceptual and empirical work (Serin, Chadwick, and Lloyd, 2015).

The You Be the Assessor box offers an opportunity to apply these discussions of assessment goals and methods.

TREATMENT APPROACHES AND EFFECTIVENESS

Diversion

The Criminal Code of Canada, Section 672, identifies a specific process for individuals with mental health conditions who are in conflict with the law. For example, mental health diversion programs are becoming popular, whereby offenders with mental illness are diverted pre-charge so that they can be assessed and receive treatment. Those who need support have access to physician referrals, emergency housing, and medication. As a result, more people with mental illness stay out of jail. In short, the identification of mental health needs requires a different approach by the criminal justice system. A benefit of the diversion model that it is cost-effective: court costs are reduced because there are fewer hearings involving judges, prosecutors, and lawyers; policing costs are lower because more people are assessed and supported before they get into crisis; and hospitalization costs are reduced because intervention typically occurs in outpatient settings.

Empirical evaluations are scarce, but a small but rigorous U.S. study used propensity-weighted Cox regression analysis to control for non-random assignment while also controlling for other potential confounding variables (demographic characteristics, clinical variables, and criminal history). After a 12-month follow-up, findings showed that participation in the mental health court program was associated with longer time without any new criminal charges or new charges for violent crimes. Successful completion of the mental health court program yielded maintenance of these gains following supervision by the mental health court (McNeil and Binder 2007).

Intervention

Apart from pharmacological intervention to manage acute symptoms (which is sometimes rejected by offenders due to side effects), little is known regarding correctional programming for MDOs. Knabb, Welsh, and Graham-Howard (2011) completed a systematic review of the literature regarding treatment approaches in correctional and psychiatric settings for offenders/patients with Axis I or Axis II diagnoses. They concluded that only five are empirically validated with MDO populations (i.e., behavioural therapy, cognitive-behavioural therapy, dialectical behaviour therapy, assertive community treatment, and therapeutic communities). However, they fail to endorse a particular approach, citing the need for randomized trials.

Cullen et al. (2012) completed a multi-site randomized control trial comparing a cognitive skills (RandR) program to "treatment as usual" (TAU) conditions in a forensic hospital setting. RandR (36 two-hour sessions delivered in a group) is a highly structured, manualized program that targets social problem-solving and thinking styles. While the numbers were small (RandR $n = 44$; TAU $n = 40$) and there was moderately high program attrition ($n = 21$), the treatment group demonstrated significantly lower levels of verbal aggression during treatment and after a 12-month follow-up. There were no group differences on incidents of violence or substance use, suggesting partial treatment success. These programs adapted delivery by considering mental disorder as a responsivity factor, yielding very high completion rates. For MDOs, it does seem that correctional programming can be effective but management of severe mental health symptoms is also a consideration.

A U.K. study (Rees-Jones, Gudjonsson, and Young 2012) across 10 hospitals also applied the RandR program within an MDO population using a quasi-experimental design. The treatment group ($n = 52$ of 67 completed) had improved self-reported change on violence attitudes and locus of control at a 3-month reassessment, compared to the waiting-list controls ($n = 54$). Effect sizes were significant but small.

Consistent with this interest in applying RandR to MDOs, in their recent meta-analysis Bonta, Blais, and Wilson (2014) made a compelling case for applying extant correctional programming approaches that follow a social learning model and incorporate the RNR principles. It may be that mental disorders function as responsivity factors, such that adapting the style of program delivery for MDOs will lead to effective correctional programs for this population. Skeem, Winter, Kennealy, Eno Louden, and Tatar (2014) compared offenders with mental illness (OMI; schizophrenia or other psychotic disorder, bipolar disorder, or major depression) and a matched sample of parolees (total $n = 221$) using one-year criminal justice outcomes using both the HCR-20 and the LSI-R. Psychiatric symptoms were moderately correlated with general risk factors for recidivism. The general risk factors predicted re-arrest and return to custody for OMIs and the unique psychiatric factors failed to improve on prediction. Hence, they are even more explicit in their comments after examining recidivism in offenders with mental illness (OMI). They state: "the relationship between mental illness and recidivism is largely indirect. If the goal is to reduce the recidivism for OMIs, then antisocial features must be explicitly assessed, acknowledged, and targeted in correctional treatment effort" (p. 221–221). Their conclusion is that OMIs require both psychiatric *and* correctional treatment.

Box 10.3

You Be the Therapist

Recall Michael's case from the beginning of the chapter. Michael has now served 12 months of a 6-year sentence for manslaughter. He killed a stranger in a bar with apparently minimal provocation. He had been infrequently seeing a community mental health worker, but was noncompliant with his medication, preferring to use cocaine and crystal meth. The police report indicated he had not slept for days, was agitated, reported racing thoughts, and was increasingly delusional, believing that others were monitoring his behaviour. This paranoia and his feelings of invulnerability were underlying aspects of the initial argument and subsequent assault.

Lets review some of the specifics of Michael's case. Michael has had fairly significant prior contact with the criminal justice system, with seven prior convictions (including theft, assaults, impaired driving, fail to appear, and breach probation) that resulted in brief periods of incarceration in remand and provincial jails. Given this history, there is some evidence of antisocial personality disorder. His employment has been mainly as a labourer and has been sporadic. He left high school after grade 10, in part due to poor grades and lack of motivation, leaving home

a year later. Since his mid-twenties he has struggled with mental health symptoms. Early psychiatric reports indicate that he has experienced extreme mood swings. At times of severe depression he has coped by using alcohol and street drugs. These bouts of depression led to referrals to community mental health and limited contact with psychiatry. At times of hypomania his insight is poor, he refuses treatment, is noncompliant with prescribed medication, and avoids contact with his treatment team. Both situations have led to problems in relationships and employment. He has had numerous common-law relationships but is currently single. His VRAG score places him in the moderate risk (4th lowest risk category) to violently reoffend within 10 years.

At admission, Michael became stabilized on a regimen of medication for his bipolar disorder. You now need to develop a treatment plan for him.

Questions

What are Michaels's treatment needs? Are they unique from other offenders? How would these be best addressed? Should he be followed by the mental health team?

Effective Treatment for MDOs

With accurate risk-assessment approaches available to clinicians working in corrections, a major goal will be to allocate resources (based on risk and diagnostic profile) to improve intervention and post-release outcomes for MDOs. The overlap among risk factors and co-morbidity of psychiatric (Axis I) and criminogenic (APD and substance abuse) diagnoses prompted Bonta, Blais, and Wilson (2014) to argue for the application of a General Personality Cognitive Social Learning approach to intervention strategies. It is possible they view Axis I disorders as responsivity factors because Axis II disorders clearly reflect the Central Eight.

If this is the case, then research is required that examines the sequencing or ordering of intervention and its impact on outcomes. It seems unlikely that an acutely psychotic offender could benefit greatly from a CBT program. Does this mean medication must precede correctional programming? Similarly, Ogloff et al. (2015) underscore the importance of addressing recovery from substance abuse if MDOs are to manage other symptoms. Does this mean criminal thinking is a secondary rather than primary treatment target for MDOs with co-occurring disorders? Further, given the complexity of these cases, what is the ideal dosage of intervention? Finally, medication compliance is often intermittent with MDOs, even when essential for symptom management. What is the availability of psychiatric community aftercare for this group of offenders? Should treatment compliance become a condition of release?

Despite the plethora of published studies on offender treatment, including several meta-analyses, little is actually known regarding correctional treatment of MDOs. In light of the prevalence of mental disorders and their relationship to crime and violence, research regarding effective treatment is essential. How protective factors are related to treatment is also important.

FUTURE DIRECTIONS

MDOs ARE A SUB-POPULATION OF OFFENDERS WITH NEEDS THAT, FOR THE MOST PART, ARE similar to other offenders but for whom sequencing of intervention and quality aftercare may be particularly critical. The course of these disorders may also uniquely influence crime desistance, but this is pure speculation at this point. Encouragingly, the SPJ risk assessment approach that is popular for this population should guide case-formulation, thereby leading to improved understanding of risk factors and treatment needs for MDOs. This in turn should lead to improved communication among disciplines/staff, which should enhance public safety and offender outcome.

SUMMARY

Mental disorder is highly stigmatized, although recent cooperation between community mental health, police, and the courts appears to be yielding positive results. Nonetheless, the prevalence of mental disorders is greater in correctional samples than the community, which leads to initial management concerns and challenges for support upon offender release. As well, the presence of mental disorder increases the risk of criminal behaviour and violence. There are specialized diagnostic approaches and risk-appraisal measures that identify co-occurring disorders (e.g., substance abuse and antisocial personality with psychosis or bipolar disorder) that inform both risk and treatment need. Advancement in risk assessment that includes protective factors is an encouraging trend but further research is required to better understand their unique contribution to MDO outcomes. Finally, there is limited empirical research regarding MDO-specific intervention but the proposal to adapt correctional programming for this group of offenders seems viable.

Discussion Questions

1. What are the more common co-occurring mental disorders and what implications do they suggest regarding risk of future criminal behaviour?

2. How are police changing their approach to dealing with mentally disordered persons who come in conflict with the law?

3. What are some of the primary considerations regarding the assessment of someone suspected of having a mental disorder upon admission to jail?

4. If you were asked to complete a risk assessment prior to the release of an MDO, what approach would you choose and why?

Chapter 11

Psychopathic Offenders

Earl Jenkins had an extensive history of criminal offending that began at the age of 13. He spent most of his life incarcerated or under supervision in the community. His criminal history was diverse, including 56 convictions for drug, violence, fraud, property, and driving offences. While in prison, he often started treatment programs but almost always dropped out of them. He stated that he was "not interested in changing" and liked himself the way he was. His most recent conviction was a seven-year sentence for manslaughter. While staying in a rooming house with an underage sex trade worker, he got into an altercation with a drug dealer. Jenkins pushed the dealer down the stairs and the man died as a result of injuries from the fall. When Earl was asked about how he felt about what happened he stated "The idiot pissed me off. I just pushed him, it is not fair that I was charged because he died." While incarcerated, Earl often got into altercations with prison staff and other inmates. Earl had a history of malingering psychotic symptoms and was repeatedly moved from prison into secure psychiatric facilities. Often he would stay at the psychiatric facility for a couple of months and then asked to be returned to prison, stating "there are too many crazies here." Earl was released on statutory release but was stabbed to death in another drug-related incident. He was 54 years old when he was killed.

Learning Objectives

1   Define psychopathy and distinguish between the labels used to describe psychopathy.

2   Describe the prevalence of psychopathy across different samples.

3   Outline the differences in assessment measures for psychopathic traits across ages.

4   Describe the link between psychopathy and violence in institutions and in the community.

5   Explain the main theories of psychopathy and recent genetic and biological research.

6   Describe the effectiveness of treatment programs for psychopathic children, youth, and adults.

INTRODUCTION

SHOULD PSYCHOPATHS BE HELD RESPONSIBLE FOR THEIR CRIMINAL ACTIONS? Psychopaths know that what they are doing is legally wrong, but may not have the capacity to understand it as "morally" wrong. Psychopaths commit a disproportionate amount of violence both in institutions and in the community, are more likely to reoffend than other offenders, and are resistant to treatment strategies. This chapter examines the nature and prevalence of psychopathy. After establishing what psychopathy is, we will examine psychopathy assessment measures, describe the role psychopathy plays in the criminal justice system, and identify treatment programs for psychopathic offenders.

CONTEXT

THE CONCEPT OF **PSYCHOPATHY** HAS EXISTED FOR WELL OVER A CENTURY. Psychopathy was one of the first personality disorders to be recognized by psychiatry (see Millon, Simonsen, Birket-Smith, and Davis 1998). It was first established by French psychiatrist Philippe Pinel, who in 1801 used the term *manie sans delire* ("madness without delusions") to describe patients who engaged in impulsive violent acts. In Britain, physician James Prichard coined the term *moral insanity* in 1883 to describe patients who committed illegal and immoral acts and knew what they were doing but did not care. Prichard also believed that the morally insane were prone to engaging in criminal acts, did not respond to punishment, and should be socially condemned.

In 1888, German psychiatrist Julius Koch introduced the term *psychopathic inferiority*. He was the first to describe psychopathy as a personality disorder and believed it was primarily biologically predetermined, rather than a function of one's environment. Koch's fellow German, Emil Kraepelin, was the first to suggest there may be different types of psychopathies. In 1907, he described different types of personality disorders, several of which share the features of current conceptualizations of psychopathy, including born criminals (individuals with no morals who lack remorse and engage in criminal acts), morbid liars (individuals who enjoy lying and deceiving others), and personality subtypes such as the spendthrifts (individuals who live beyond their means and rely on family or society for economic support) and vagabonds (individuals who live day-to-day, make few plans, and often take off on a whim).

One of the main problems with early conceptualizations of psychopathy was that it became a "wastebasket category" that included a variety of different mental and personality disorders (Hervé 2007; Whitlock 1982). In the nineteenth and early twentieth centuries, many antisocial individuals were called psychopaths but there was no clear description of what being a "psychopath" entailed.

In 1928, American psychologist George Partridge felt that the term *psychopathy* was being applied to many diverse disorders and wanted to replace the term with a more specific construct of **sociopathy** (Partridge 1930). Based on a review of 50 psychiatric patients that had been diagnosed as psychopaths, Partridge proposed three sociopathic

Table 11.1 Psychopathy: An Emerging Construct

Date	Name	Country	Term
1801	Philippe Pinel	France	*manie sans delire*
1812	Benjamin Rush	United States	moral derangement
1835	James Prichard	England	moral insanity
1888	Julius Koch	Germany	psychopathic inferiority
1907	Emil Kraepelin	Germany	psychopathies
1928	George Partridge	United States	sociopath
1941	Hervey Cleckley	United States	psychopath
1946	Benjamin Karpman	United States	psychopath
1947	David Henderson	Scotland	psychopath
1950	Kurt Schneider	Germany	psychopathies
1963	Silvano Arieti	Italy	psychopath
1964	Joan and William McCord	United States	psychopath
1980	Robert Hare	Canada	psychopath

subtypes: delinquent (most commonly male), inadequate (most commonly female), and emotionally unstable. Partridge proposed that the delinquent and inadequate subtypes were biologically predetermined, while the emotionally unstable were the product of early environmental factors (e.g., an abusive or chaotic upbringing).

In the mid-twentieth century, Benjamin Karpman and Silvano Arieti, both psycho-analysts, were also concerned with the ambiguous nature of the diagnosis of psychopathy. Their description of the psychopath mirrors contemporary views. They defined psychopathy as a personality disorder characterized by early onset of antisocial behaviours, a need for immediate gratification, a grandiose sense of self-worth, being impulsive and irresponsible, lacking anxiety or remorse over their actions, and being callous. In their views, psychopaths experienced only fleeting and shallow emotions, leading them to engage in impulsive and socially damaging acts (Arieti 1963; Karpman 1948). Table 11.1 summarizes the labels for psychopathy used over time.

DEFINITIONS

In 1941, Hervey Cleckley, an American psychiatrist, described a subgroup of patients as appearing normal yet lacking in remorse and empathy, who were impulsive, deceptive, and grandiose. Their normal appearance coupled with the presence of these aberrant behaviours led Cleckley to characterize such patients as having a "mask of sanity." Cleckley described 16 clinical features of psychopathy and considered a lack of emotional reaction to be central to the disorder (Cleckley 1941).

Following Cleckley's work and his early clinical descriptions, a substantial amount of research has focused on understanding how to evaluate the presence of psychopathy and on delineating its features and underlying causes. In the 1980s, Robert Hare, a researcher at the University of British Columbia, developed a rating scale for the assessment of psychopathic traits (Hare 1980). This scale measures a range of interpersonal, affective, behavioural, and antisocial features. This measure was later developed into the Hare Psychopathy Checklist—Revised (PCL-R) and has been used globally to assess for psychopathy (Hare 2003).

The term **psychopath** comes from the Greek *psyche* meaning "mind or soul" and *pathos* meaning "suffering or disease." *Psychopath* is sometimes confused with *psychosis*, but the two are not the same. Psychosis represents a serious mental disorder that is characterized by delusions (false thoughts), hallucinations (seeing or hearing things that are not there), and impaired contact with reality. The terms **sociopath** and *psychopath* are also sometimes used synonymously but refer to separate groups of individuals based on the etiology of their symptoms.

DSM: Changing Conceptualizations of Psychopathy

When diagnosing people for mental and personality disorders, psychologists and psychiatrists use the Diagnostic and Statistical Manual of Mental Disorders (DSM). The DSM has undergone several revisions since its introduction in 1952. The term *sociopath* was adopted in the first edition of the DSM and was defined as a chronically antisocial person who lacked loyalty to anything or anyone and was callous, lacking judgment, immature, and often able to rationalize their antisocial behaviours. Although the term was changed to *antisocial personality* in the DSM-II, it retained a focus on personality features. A big shift occurred in 1980 with the publication of the DSM-III; the term changed to Antisocial Personality Disorder (ASPD) and emphasis was placed on behavioural symptoms rather than personality traits. This change was intended to increase the reliability of clinical assessments by focusing on overt behavioural symptoms instead of personality symptoms, which are harder to measure. Since 1980, the diagnostic criteria have remained similar over subsequent revisions, including the most recent DSM-5, published in 2013. According to Section II of the DSM-5, to be diagnosed with ASPD you must be diagnosed with Conduct Disorder prior to age 15 and manifest three of seven adult symptoms.

The prevalence of ASPD in male offenders ranges from 24 percent (Coolidge, Marle, van Horn and Segal 2011) to 47 percent (Fazel and Danish 2002) to a high of 75 percent according to Motiuk and Porporino (1991). In a national study by Correctional Service Canada, Beaudette, Power, and Stewart (2015) reported a prevalence rate of 44 percent of ASPD in a sample of 1110 incoming male federal offenders.

One new feature of DSM-5 is the proposed "alternative DSM-5 model for personality disorders" (APA 2013, p. 761). The model for personality disorders focuses on a

Psychopaths: What the Media and Public Believe

Who comes to mind when you think of a psychopath? The first type of offender most people think of are serial killers. Although many serial killers have several psychopathic traits, the vast majority of psychopaths are not serial killers. In addition most psychopaths did not kill, and most killers are not psychopaths. Movies and television shows often portray psychopaths as serial killers. Think of Hannibal Lector in the movie *The Silence of the Lambs* or Dexter Morgan in the *Dexter* television series.

Smith, Edens, Clark and Rulsh (2014) asked 404 jury-eligible Texans "Who is the first person who comes to mind to you as a typical psychopath?" (p. 3). The most frequent response was a known serial killer or mass murderer (e.g., Ted Bundy, Jeffrey Dahmer), followed by a fictional killer (e.g., Hannibal Lector). In some cases respondents provided examples of someone they knew, such as an ex-spouse, or boss. Table 11.2 provides a summary of these findings.

In the news, some journalists mix up the term *psychopathy* with *psychosis* or *psychotic*. This confusion also extends to the public. In the Smith et al. (2014) study, participants were asked to rate symptoms on a scale of 1 to 7, with 1 meaning "not typical of a psychopath" and 7 meaning "very typical of a psychopath." The researchers included three psychotic symptoms in their list of symptoms. The five symptoms that were rated the highest (i.e., the most typical) were manipulative, lacks remorse, delusional beliefs, self-centered, and self-justifying. One of the psychotic symptoms (delusional beliefs) was rated the third highest, and the two other psychotic symptoms were rated as highly typical (peculiar behaviour and disturbed thinking).

What is clear is that researchers and clinicians need to do a better job at educating the public about what psychopathy *is* and what it is *not*.

Table 11.2 The Categories of Psychopaths People Report

Category	Percent Reported
Known serial killer/mass murderer	33.7%
No response	20.8%
Fictional killer	14.4%
Other	14.1%
Personalized response	9.2%
Political figure	4.0%
Known murderer (not serial killer)	3.0%
Entertainer/celebrity/athlete	1.0%

Source: Adapted from Smith et al. (2014).

dimensional approach and defines each personality disorder on a set of 25 personality traits that are categorized into 5 domains (negative affectivity, detachment, antagonism, disinhibition, and psychoticism). To be assessed as having ASPD, a person must exhibit manipulativeness, deceitfulness, hostility, and callousness (antagonism traits); and impulsivity, risk taking, and irresponsibility (disinhibition traits). To be assessed as psychopathic, a person must exhibit these ASPD traits as well as three psychopathic-specific traits: low anxiousness (from the negative affectivity domain), low withdrawal (from the detachment domain), and high attention-seeking (from the antagonism domain). It is not clear why the APA decided to select these specific traits as indicative of psychopathy.

Several studies have examined the overlap between the psychopathic-specific traits in the DSM-5 and other measures of psychopathy. For example, Strickland et al. (2013) compared the psychopathic-specific traits with the Triarchic Psychopathy Measure (TriPM) and found they were consistent regarding the components of meanness and disinhibition, but the TriPM also emphasized boldness. (The TriPM and other assessment measures are discussed later in this chapter.) Two studies have examined the incremental utility of the psychopathic-specific traits over ASPD traits to predict psychopathy scores. Few and colleagues (2015) concluded that although psychopathic-specific traits were more strongly related to psychopathy scores than ASPD traits, the three psychopathic-specific traits were only weakly associated with psychopathy scores. Results from these studies suggest that the psychopathic-specific traits in the DSM-5 are still not capturing the same traits that other psychopathy measures include.

WHY DO WE CARE?
Prevalence of Psychopathy

How common are psychopaths? The answer depends on where you look. In the general community, less than 1 percent score high on psychopathy measures (Coid, Yang, Ullrich, Roberts, and Hare 2009). In the study done by Coid and colleagues in the United Kingdom, 71 percent of the sample had no psychopathic traits. Although the prevalence of psychopathic traits was low in this sample, Coid and Yang (2011) reported that those scoring high on psychopathy were much more likely to engage in violence. Using a community sample in the United States, Hare and Neumann (2008) found that only 1.2 percent of their sample had scores in the "potential psychopathic" range.

There has been increasing interest in studying psychopaths in the corporate world. Babiak, Newmann, and Hare (2010) examined the prevalence of psychopathic traits in 203 upper-level managers. These professionals scored slightly higher on psychopathic traits as compared to the general community, but only eight professionals (4.9 percent) scored in the diagnostic range. You will find more individuals with psychopathic traits in prisons or forensic psychiatric hospitals. Approximately 10 to 25 percent of adult offenders can be classified as psychopaths (Hare 2003), with higher prevalence in male than female offenders (Beryl, Chou, and Völlm 2014).

The gender difference in psychopathy scores is found both in community and forensic samples. The largest study to examine the prevalence of psychopathic traits was done by Neumann, Schmitt, Carter, Embley, and Hare in 2012. In this study, 33 016 people (13 833 males and 19 183 females) from 58 countries completed a self-report psychopathy scale. Across the world, males had consistently higher psychopathy scores as compared to females, with lifestyle features (e.g., impulsivity and risk-taking) being the most common, and antisocial features (e.g., violence and arrest history) the least common.

Psychopaths may be a small group of individuals, but they exert an influence within society that is disproportionate to their numbers.

Survivors: The Impact of Being a Victim of a Psychopath

Psychopathic researchers have neglected studying those involved with psychopaths. Nearly all published research has focused on the psychopath and not their victims. It is not clear why the voices of survivors have been ignored. There is considerable research on the effects of criminal victimization, with some concluding it "is among one of the most stressful and potentially traumatizing human experiences" (Green and Pomeroy 2007, p. 63).

To date, one published study has explored the experiences of victims of psychopaths. Kirkman (2005) interviewed 20 females who had been involved for 6 months or longer with a man they described as being psychopathic (using the B-Scan measure). The participants were asked about their experiences within the relationship from the first time they met their male partners. The length of their relationships ranged from 10 months to 31 years (averaging about 14 years). The average age of the participants was 48 years old, and most were well-educated. All of the participants reported that their relationship had a negative impact on their health. In the women's descriptions of their relationships, eight themes became evident: talking the victim into victimization (e.g., many women were living with or married to man within weeks of first meeting), lying (e.g., the man lied about his history or created a false identity), economic abuse (e.g., majority of the men lived parasitically off the participant, expecting her to pay for all living expenses), emotional abuse/psychological torture (e.g., controlling her contact with others, taunting her about his infidelities, threatening to injure her children), multiple infidelities (e.g., one woman reported that her partner was sexually involved with six other women and each of them believed they were his sole partner), isolation and coercion (e.g., the man kept her isolated from family and friends), assault (e.g., 40 percent of participants reported being physically assaulted), and mistreatment of children (e.g., the participant's children were emotionally abused).

Brown and Leedom (2008) conducted an online survey of 75 women who reported being involved with a psychopath. All the women reported that they had been harmed in some way by the psychopath: 95 percent reported emotional harm, 71 percent reported financial harm, 67 percent reported harm in their careers, 51 percent reported physical harm, and 51 percent reported sexual harm. Brown and Leedom (2008) stated that "No matter how you try to explain it, psychopathy is a disorder that poisons everyone in the path of the psychopath and devastates the woman who tries to love him" (p. 5).

METHODOLOGY

Researchers are attempting to understand psychopathy from a wide range of different methodologies and perspectives. Much of the early research was conducted with adult male offenders, but new research is increasingly targeting males and females, student samples, community samples, adolescent and youth samples, and victims of psychopaths. One sample that has yet to be the focus of research is elderly psychopaths.

Studies have been conducted by a diverse group of researchers, including developmental researchers, personality researchers, cognitive researchers, social researchers, forensic researchers, criminologists, and neuroscientists. In 2006, Farrington stated "The time is ripe for Western countries to mount an ambitious coordinated program of research on psychopathy, focusing on international multidisciplinary collaboration and aiming to train a new generation of biopsychosocial researchers. Given the enormous social costs of psychopathy, the benefits of such a large-scale coordinated program of research should easily outweigh its costs. And, of course, a reduction in the number of psychopathic individuals and in the number of their victims would greatly increase the sum of human happiness." (p. 245). Although there has been much progress, there are still many questions yet to be answered about psychopathy.

THEORIES OF PSYCHOPATHY

Cleckley (1941) believed that the core deficit in psychopathy relates to a poverty of emotions, ". . . probably in the core of the psychopath's essential abnormality—perhaps in a lack of emotional components essential to real understanding" (p. 173). Several theories have been proposed relating to the notion of an affective deficit (Brook, Brieman, and Kosson 2013). The theory proposed by Cleckley can be described as a general emotional deficit. According to this theory, psychopaths have a general lack of ability to experience emotion and are therefore also not able to appreciate the emotional reactions of others. Brook et al. (2013) described their theory as a *specific emotional deficit theory*. Other researchers have focused on the inability of psychopaths to experience fear. Lykken (1995) termed this the *low-fear hypothesis* and believed that psychopaths are not responsive to punishment and are therefore not motivated to avoid antisocial behaviour because of the threat of punishment. Another specific emotional deficit theory is the violence inhibition mechanism theory (VIM; Blair 1995), which posits that psychopaths are specifically impaired in their ability to recognize sadness or distress in others. One consequence of this is that psychopaths do not inhibit their violent behaviour in response to others' emotions.

Cognitive Models

Another prominent theory of psychopathy focuses more on cognitive as opposed to emotional processes and was developed in research with adult offenders. Newman and his colleagues proposed that psychopaths have a response modulation deficit (Newman and Wallace 1993; for review, see Newman, Brinkley, Lorenz, Hiatt, and McCoon 2007). According to this theory, once psychopaths have focused their attention, they will fail to use information to modify their response. This deficit can help explain why psychopaths fail to learn to inhibit their behaviour (e.g., show poor passive-avoidance conditioning).

Developmental Models

Certainly, developmental psychologists have emphasized the importance of emotion in the development of conscience (Kochanska 1994; Blair, Jones, Clark, and Smith 1997). Figure 11.1 illustrates the importance of emotion in the development of conscience, as well as the key role of parents. Parents make salient the connection between misbehaviour and sanctions, elicit moral emotions such as empathy and guilt, and provide incentives for engaging in prosocial behaviour. For most children, when they engage in some transgression (e.g., hitting their younger sister), the victim elicits distress and the parents disapprove, causing negative emotions in the offender that lead to guilt and empathy. These feelings then result in the inhibition of future transgressions (the dashed line in the figure).

From an early age (as young as 30 months), healthy children learn to inhibit behaviours that have negative consequences to others (Kochanska, Murray, and Coy 1997). A

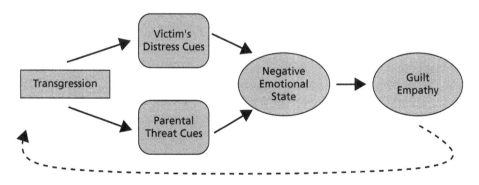

Figure 11.1 The Role of Emotions in the Development of Conscience

Source: Adapted from Kochanska (1993).

key component of socialization is developing the appropriate emotional response to distress in others based on cues from victims and parents. Research has shown that children and adults with psychopathic traits show reduced autonomic responses to the distress of others and reduced recognition of sad and fearful expressions (see Blair 2007 for a review). Therefore, without this emotional response, psychopaths will not learn to inhibit their behaviours.

Children with psychopathic traits, and callous/unemotional traits in particular, are less responsive to parental socialization practices (Oxford, Cavell, and Hughes 2003; Wootton, Frick, Shelton, and Silverthorn 1997), display less distress over actions that hurt others (Blair et al. 1997; Pardini, Lochman, and Frick 2003), and have a reduced emotional response to emotional stimuli (Blair, Colledge, Murray, and Mitchell 2001; Kimonis, Frick, Fazekas, and Loney 2006; Loney, Frick, Clements, Ellis, and Kerlin 2003) compared to children with other conduct problems. Frick and Marsee (2006) proposed two developmental models, one for the development of callous/unemotional traits and the other for impulsive conduct problems. The developmental model of callous/unemotional traits posits that youth are born with a predisposition to fearlessness or low behavioural inhibition that leads them to be insensitive to parental and social sanctions, show little arousal to the misfortune of others, and ignore the harmful effects of their behaviours. Over the course of development, this leads to a callous/unemotional interpersonal style, which ultimately leads them to engage in antisocial behaviours—in particular, instrumental aggression. The developmental model for impulse conduct problems involves inadequate socializing environments, low intelligence, and poor response inhibition, leading to a lack of planning and being susceptible to angry arousal. In turn, this leads the child to engage in unplanned antisocial acts, especially reactive aggression.

Genetics Models

To examine the role of genetics in psychopathy, several researchers have focused on comparing monozygotic (MZ; identical) twins to dizygotic (DZ; fraternal) twins. The rationale is that MZ twins share all their genes, whereas DZ twins share only 50 percent of their genes (see Chapter 2 for a discussion of twin studies). Twin studies have consistently found a large and significant heritable component to psychopathic traits in children (Fontaine, Rijsdijk, McCrory, and Viding 2010; Viding, Blair, Moffitt, and Plomin 2005), adolescents (Blonigen, Hicks, Krueger, Patrick, and Iacono 2005; Larsson, Andershed, and Lichtensetin 2006; Taylor, Loney, Bobadilla, Iacono, and McGue 2003), and adults (Blonigen, Hicks, Krueger, Patrick, and Iacono 2006). These studies indicate that for all aspects of psychopathic traits, there is moderate to strong genetic influence (see Table 11.3). For studies comparing males and females (Blonigen et al. 2006; Larsson et al. 2006), there was no evidence for sex differences. But a strong genetic contribution to psychopathic traits does not imply immutability; rather, it suggests that any interventions to attenuate negative developmental trajectories must be applied as early as possible.

Table 11.3 Heritability Estimates for Psychopathic Traits

Study	Sample (N, sex/age)	Callous/ Unemotional	Impulsive/ Antisocial
Viding et al. (2007)	3687 males and females, 7 years	67%	
Blonigen et al. (2005)	626 males and females, 17 years	45%	49%
Blonigen et al. (2006)	626 males and females, 24 years	42%	49%
Taylor et al. (2003)	398 males and females, 16 to 18 years	40%	40%
Larsson et al. (2006)	1100 males and females, 16 years	43%	56%
Fontaine et al. (2010)	9462 males and females, 7 to 12 years	78%	

Brain-Based Models

Are the brains of psychopaths different from others? Recently, neuroimaging techniques have been used to investigate if psychopaths have any structural or functional brain differences compared to non-psychopaths. A literature review by Weber, Habel, Amunts, and Schneider (2008) concluded that psychopaths have a reduction in prefrontal grey matter, less grey matter in the right superior temporal gyrus, less hippocampal volume, less amygdala volume, and an increase in callosal white matter. They argue that "psychopathy cannot be explained by one particular neurobiological theory or by one neurobiological substrate. Rather, the various brain abnormalities seem to involve a network, including prefrontal regions as well as temporo-limbic areas" (p. 23). Table 11.4 summarizes the brain areas found to be related to psychopathy by structural and functional neuroimaging studies.

Functional neuroimaging studies have reported reduced activation of the amygdala and anterior cingulate/ventromedial prefrontal cortex with psychopaths in emotional memory paradigms (Kiehl et al. 2001), aversive conditioning (Birbaumer et al. 2005), and emotional photos (Muller et al. 2003). In addition, some studies have implicated other areas in psychopathy, such as the superior temporal cortex and the dorsal anterior cingulated cortex (Kiehl 2006). Kiehl proposed a paralimbic model to explain the emotional processing deficits seen in psychopaths. Recently, Seara-Cardoso and Viding (2014) reviewed functional neuroimaging studies of adult high-risk samples (assessed using the PCL-R) and concluded "Although the direction of the findings is not entirely consistent across studies, overall, these studies seem to point to reduced response in regions typically associated with affective processing and increased activity in regions typically associated with cognitive control during processing of emotional and salient stimuli" (p. 7).

Table 11.4 Brain Areas Implicated in Psychopathy

Brain Region	Function	Outcome
Ventro-medial prefrontal cortex	• Decision making • Emotion regulation • Empathy • Moral judgment	• Poor planning/impulsivity • Poor anger control • Callous disregard for others • Antisocial behaviours
Corpus callosum	• Connectivity between hemispheres • Asymmetries of function	• Reduced lateralization of functions
Superior temporal gyrus	• Social judgment • Perspective-taking and moral judgment	• Misattribution of others' motives • Antisocial behaviours
Hippocampus	• Fear conditioning	• Failure to desist from punished behaviour
Amygdala	• Social-emotion judgments • Moral emotions	• Misperception of others' feelings • Antisocial behaviours
Anterior cingulate	• Inhibition	• Failure to control behaviour

Source: Adapted from Raine (2008) and Weber et al. (2008).

Although neuroimaging studies have provided insight into the areas of the brain implicated in psychopathy, in addition to providing tentative functional models of psychopathy, caution is required when interpreting such findings. Recently, Poldrack (2009) summarized several critical limitations of neuroimaging procedures when attempting to understand mental disorders. First, he warns that increased or decreased activation of particular brain regions should not be automatically equated with "better" or "abnormal" functioning. Second, researchers should not assume that because they see activation in an individual brain area, this area is solely responsible for a specific mental function. Poldrack provides an example to illustrate this point that is particularly relevant to accounts of psychopathy and the function of the amygdala: "The fact that the amygdala, for example, responds to threat does not mean that activity in this area signifies that a person is feeling threatened. That would be true only if threat were the only thing that activates the amygdala, and we know this is not the case."

If a psychopath suffers from brain impairments that predispose him to commit impulsive violence, should we hold him fully accountable for his behaviour? Some may argue that psychopathy should be considered a mitigating factor, while others have gone as far as to suggest psychopaths should not be found legally responsible (i.e., they should be found not criminally responsible on account of mental disorder (NCRMD)). Morse (2008) reviewed the literature on criminal responsibility and psychopathy and concluded that "severe psychopathy should be a basis for non-responsibility in appropriate cases because psychopathy deprives people of rational capacities that are fundamental for fair

The Psychopathic Brain in the Courtroom

Should psychopathy be a mitigating factor when sentencing an offender? In death penalty cases in the United States, the jury must weigh aggravating (circumstances about the offender or crime that heighten its seriousness, such as the vulnerability of the victim) and mitigating (circumstances about the offender or crime that would justify not giving a death sentence, such as mental illness) factors when deciding on a sentence of death versus life in prison.

Brian Dugan is a serial killer who between 1974 and 1985 raped seven and killed three girls and women (7-year-old Melissa Ackerman, 27-year-old Donna Schnorr, and 10-year-old Jeanine Nicarico). He was caught in 1985 and plead guilty to the murders of Ackerman and Schnorr in order to avoid the death penalty. At the time, he offered to admit his guilt in Nicarico's murder but prosecutors did not believe he was responsible since two other men (Rolando Cruz and Alejandro Hernandez) were already convicted and on death row for her murder.

Dugan was given a life sentence for the murders of Ackerman and Schnorr. Then in 1995, the state overturned the convictions of Cruz and Hernandez (who sued and received a 3.5 million settlement for their wrongful conviction). In 2002, DNA evidence linked Brian Dugan to the Nicarico murder and he was charged with the capital murder in 2005. On July 22, 2009 he plead guilty to the kidnapping, rape, and murder of Nicarico. The defense lawyers knew it was going to be a challenging case and turned to neuroscience. In September, 2009, the defense hired a neuroscientist and psychopathy researcher named Kent Kiehl to scan Dugan's brain. Kiehl also administered the PCL-R and gave Dugan a score of 38 out of 40

(an extremely high score). The defense lawyers hoped that Kiehl would be able to convince the jury that Dugan had deficits in certain brain regions and therefore should not be given the harshest sanction—the death sentence.

Kiehl was permitted to testify in the trial but the judge refused to allow him to show Dugan's brain scans after the prosecution argued that the brain scans might bias the jury. Prosecutors referenced a 2008 study by Skolnick Weisburg, Keil, Goodstein, Rawson, and Gray that examined the impact of neuroscience on non-experts and experts when making decisions about psychological phenomena. In this study, the non-experts found explanations that included irrelevant neuroscience information (such as brain scans showing different pattern of activation in specific brain region) more satisfying than explanations that did not, while the neuroscientists (experts) were not influenced by the inclusion of irrelevant neuroscience information. The researchers concluded "Given the results reported here, such evidence presented in a courtroom, a classroom, or a political debate, regardless of the scientific status or relevance of this evidence, could strongly sway opinion, beyond what the evidence can support (p. 477).

Can you guess what happened when the jury heard testimony about how psychopathic Dugan was and that he had decreased areas of activation in specific brain areas, as seen in other criminal psychopaths? After deliberating for 10 hours, the jury unanimously decided on the death penalty. However, since Illinois abolished the death penalty in 2011, Dugan's death sentence was commuted to a life sentence.

In 2014, Dugan gave his first interview to a reporter from the *Chicago Tribune* about his crimes. Dugan admitted he was a psychopath and that "he viewed his victims as objects, not as human beings." When asked why he let some of the victims live, he stated he only did so because he felt they would not be able to identify him. When Jeanine Nicarico's parents were contacted they stated "...there is nothing he could say—no words of sympathy, remorse or regret—that would hold any value for them." The couple said his motivation to speak publicly after all this time was "an effort to manipulate public opinion and the system for his own gain."

Sources: Gutowski and Mills (2014); Hughes (2010).

ascriptions of blame and punishment" (p. 212). Glenn, Laufer, and Raine (2013) have argued that the combined deficits (e.g., empathy deficits, deficits in processing punishment cues), found in psychopathic individuals impairs their decision-making ability when they commit criminal acts. In contrast, Vitacco, Erickson, and Lishner (2013) posit that psychopathic individuals do know what they are doing and that it is wrong, and that the brain abnormalities found in psychopaths are not sufficient to make a claim for a lack of criminal responsibility.

Brain differences alone are not sufficient to explain the emergence of psychopathy. Researchers are now looking for specific genes that may result in these brain abnormalities, which in turn lead to antisocial and violent behaviour. However, environment and socialization can influence gene expression. Thus, any explanation of the etiology of psychopathy will need to examine the interactions between genetic predispositions, neurobiological functioning, and developmental experiences.

ASSESSMENT APPROACHES AND EFFECTIVENESS

OVER THE PAST TWO DECADES, A VARIETY OF METHODS HAVE BEEN DEVELOPED TO assess for psychopathic traits in adults and youth. In rater-based assessments, either parents or teachers are asked to assess children for psychopathic features. Alternatively, clinicians can use information from interviews and related files to assess youth and adults for psychopathic traits. Another common method is self-report, in which an individual is given a questionnaire containing questions or statements that are linked to psychopathic characteristics.

Self-Report Methods

Using self-report to assess for psychopathic features has been criticized by some clinicians and researchers (Lilienfeld and Fowler 2006). First, psychopaths are often dishonest. Not only do they lie to obtain tangible benefits, they also engage in what has been called "duping delight" (i.e., lying for the sheer fun of it). For example, if the psychopath is placed in a situation in which creating a positive impression is desirable (e.g., applying for early release from prison), they may attempt to make themselves look good (e.g., pretend they are remorseful when they are not). Or, in a situation in which creating a negative impression is desirable (e.g., being evaluated for insanity), a psychopath may attempt to make themselves look worse than they are (e.g., pretend they are delusional when they are not). Second, psychopaths may not have sufficient insight to accurately assess their traits. They may not see themselves as others see them and might not be able to accurately report the impact of their behaviour on others. For example, they might not consider themselves as arrogant or grandiose even though other observers might. Finally, asking a person who has never experienced a specific emotion to report on its presence is problematic. Psychopaths may not understand the meaning of remorse (i.e., feeling negative emotions for the suffering caused to others) and may equate this with regret (i.e., feeling sorry for getting caught and the consequences for being caught).

Despite these concerns, self-report measures have several advantages. They are able to measure emotions or beliefs that are not easily observable by others (e.g., feelings of anxiety or hostile attributional style). In addition, self-reports are easy to administer, tend to be relatively quick, and are inexpensive. Many self-report scales include measures of response styles in order to detect invalid responding. Since individuals complete the questionnaires themselves, concern about inter-rater reliability is eliminated. Two self-report scales that have been used with adults are the Psychopathic Personality Inventory–Revised (PPI–R) (Lilienfeld and Widows 2005) and the Self-Report Psychopathy Scale (SRP-III) (Paulhus, Hemphill, and Hare forthcoming). More recently, Babiak and Hare (forthcoming) developed the Business-Scan (B-Scan), an instrument for rating psychopathy-related features in the business sphere. The B-Scan has a self-rating scale (B-Scan Self) component and the B-Scan 360 component, in which other members of the corporation rate their coworkers (e.g., supervisor, peers, subordinates).

The most common self-report scales in use today are outlined in the sections that follow.

Psychopathic Personality Inventory–Revised (PPI-R) (Lilienfeld and Widows 2005)

- 154-item self-report measure that uses a four-point rating format
- Designed to assess psychopathic traits in offender and community samples
- Validated for use in men and women aged 18 to 86 years
- Consists of eight content scales, two validity scales, and three factors of psychopathy (self-centred impulsivity, fearless dominance, and cold-heartedness)

Self-Report Psychopathy Scale (SRP-III) (Paulhus et al. forthcoming)

- 40-item self-report measure that uses a five-point rating format
- Designed to assess psychopathic traits in offender and community samples
- Validated for use in men and women aged 18 years or older
- Measures four factors of psychopathy (interpersonal manipulation, callous affect, erratic lifestyle, and criminal tendencies)

Triarchic Psychopathy Measure (TriPM) (Patrick, Fowles, and Krueger 2009)

■ 58-item self-report measure that uses a four-point rating format

■ Designed to assess psychopathic traits in community samples

■ Validated for use in men and women aged 18 years or older

■ Measures three factors of psychopathy (boldness, meanness, disinhibition)

Business Scan (B-Scan Self; B-Scan 360) (Babiak and Hare forthcoming)

■ 20-item self-rated measure that uses a five-point format (B-Scan Self)

■ 20-item other-rated measure that uses a five-point format (B-Scan 360)

■ Designed to asses psychopathic traits in corporate or management settings

■ Validated for use in men and woman aged 18 years or older

■ Measures four factors of psychopathy (manipulative/unethical, callous/insensitive, unreliable/unfocused, and intimidating/aggressive)

Rater-Based Methods

Rater-based instruments for assessing psychopathy require more resources to administer than self-report instruments. As formerly noted, an interview is required, plus evaluation of collateral information (e.g., police records). In addition, the reliability of the person doing the rating should be established in order to ensure consistent application of the instrument (i.e., inter-rater reliability). Rater-based instruments tend to be used most in forensic settings, where life-altering decisions about sentencing and risk of reoffending are required. The two most popular rater-based instruments for the assessment of psychopathy in adults are the Hare Psychopathy Checklist—Revised (PCL-R) (Hare 2003) and the Hare Psychopathy Checklist: Screening Version (PCL:SV) (Hart, Cox, and Hare 1995). The Hare PCL-R is considered by some to be the "gold standard" for assessing psychopathy (Fulero 1995) and has been adopted worldwide as the most reliable and valid measure.

Hare Psychopathy Checklist–Revised (PCL-R) (Hare 2003)

■ 20-item symptom-rating measure that uses a three-point scale

■ Designed to assess psychopathic traits in correctional and forensic psychiatric samples

■ Validated for men and women aged 18 years and older

■ Measures two factors of psychopathy (interpersonal/affective and social deviance) and four facets of psychopathy (interpersonal, affective, behavioural, and antisocial)

Hare Psychopathy Checklist: Screening Version (PCL:SV) (Hart et al. 1995)

■ 12-item symptom-rating measure that uses a three-point scale

■ Designed to assess psychopathic traits in the community and screen for psychopathic traits in forensic samples

Psychopaths in the Workplace

Until recently, researchers have studied psychopaths where they are most likely to find them—in prison. Relatively few studies have examined psychopathy in the business world. Heinze, Allen, Magai, and Ritzler (2010) suggest that this paucity of research may be due to the difficulty in obtaining access to participants (many businesses do not want to know how psychopathic their employees are) and to concerns about privacy and liability. Despite these challenges, the past decade has seen increasing research on the "corporate psychopath." Three studies that have investigated psychopathy in the workplace are described here.

Corporate Psychopathy: Talking the Walk (Babiak, Neumann, and Hare 2010)

Method: 203 corporate professionals were assessed for psychopathic traits using an 18-item PCL-R (revocation of conditional release and criminal versatility were not rated) and were assessed on key performance indicators.

Results: The prevalence of psychopathic traits in the corporate professionals was higher as compared to community samples. Professionals with more psychopathic traits were less likely to be team players, had poorer management skills, and poor performance appraisals, but were more creative, engaged in more strategic thinking, and had stronger communication skills than professionals with few psychopathic traits.

The Dark Side of Leadership (Mathieu, Neumann, Hare, and Babiak 2014)

Method: Two samples of employees (136 employees of a large financial company and 515 employees of a public service agency) rated their supervisors on the B-Scan 360 and completed self-report questionnaires on job satisfaction, psychological distress, and work-family conflict.

Results In both samples, when an employee reported more psychopathic traits in his or her supervisor, they also tended to report less job satisfaction and more psychological distress. B-Scan 360 scores were weakly related to work-family conflict but only in the public service company.

What Predicts Success in Finance? (Howe, Falkenbach, and Massey 2014)

Method: 55 employees at several financial institutions in New York completed a self-report psychopathy measure (PPI-R), an emotional IQ measure (to assess ability to perceive, use, and manage emotions), and a professional success measure (to assess annual income and corporate rank).

Results: Corporate participants had higher PPI-R total and fearless dominance scores as compared to a community sample. Fearless dominance scores were not related to emotional IQ, but higher self-centered impulsivity scores were related to lower emotional IQs. Fearless dominance scores were related to higher annual income and higher corporate rank.

Sources: Babiak, Neumann, and Hare (2010); Mathieu et al. (2014); Howe, Falkenbach, and Massey (2014).

- Validated for men and women aged 16 years and older
- Measures four factors of psychopathy (interpersonal, affective, behavioural, and antisocial)

The Dark Triad: Narcissism, Machiavellianism, and Psychopathy

In 2002, Paulhus and Williams coined the term "dark triad" to describe a group of three personality traits related to socially aversive behaviours: narcissism, Machiavellianism, and psychopathy. People scoring high on narcissism have a sense of entitlement and superiority over others, are arrogant, and are self-centred. People scoring high on Machiavellianism are cynical and manipulative, using others to satisfy their own self-interests. People scoring high on psychopathy are unemotional, manipulative, impulsive, risk-taking, and engage in illegal acts with no remorse or empathy. Although these personalities are associated with each other, they also have different correlates.

There is an increasing amount of research examining how distinct each of these personalities are in both community and student samples (Furnham, Richards, and Paulhus 2013). Much of this work has been done by Delroy Paulhus and his colleagues at the University of British Columbia. For example, as compared to the other personalities, Machiavellian students were found to be more likely to plagiarize essays (Williams, Nathanson, and Paulhus 2010) and to claim extra credits they did not earn in experiments (Furnham, Richards, and Paulhus 2013), and narcissistic students were found to be more likely to respond with aggression to ego insults (Jones and Paulhus 2010) and to believe they should receive high grades without studying (Turnipseed and Cohen 2014). Psychopathic students were more likely to cheat on exams (Nathanson, Paulhus, and Williams 2006), to bully others (Baughman et al. 2012), to poach mates from others (Jonason, Li, and Buss 2010), and were attracted to others with high psychopathy traits (Jonason, Lyons, and Blanchard 2015).

Recently, Book, Visser, and Volk (2015) have investigated what accounts for the overlap between these three constructs and have found that low levels of honesty and humility from the HEXACO personality model (Lee and Ashton 2004) appear to link the three traits of the dark triad.

Assessing Psychopathy in Youth

Until about a decade ago, relatively little attention was focused on the possibility of psychopathic traits being present in children or youth. Recently, however, a growing number of studies have been designed to shed light on the origins of psychopathy during childhood development. Similar to adult assessment, there are both self-report and rater-based assessments for use with children and adolescents. Measures of psychopathic traits in children and youth are described below.

Youth Psychopathic Traits Inventory (YPI) (Andershed, Kerr, Stattin, and Levander 2002)

- 50-item self-report measure that uses a four-point scale
- Designed to assess psychopathic traits in community adolescents
- Valid for boys and girls aged 12 to 18 years
- Measures three factors (grandiose/manipulative, callous/unemotional, and impulsive/irresponsible)

Antisocial Process Screening Device (APSD) (Frick and Hare 2001)

- 20-item symptom-rating measure that uses a three-point scale
- Designed to assess psychopathic-like traits in children using a parent or teacher as informant
- Valid for boys and girls aged 6 to 12 years
- Measures three factors (narcissism, impulsivity, and callous/unemotional)

Hare Psychopathy Checklist: Youth Version (PCL:YV) (Forth, Kosson, and Hare 2003)

- 20-item symptom-rating measure that uses a three-point scale
- Designed to assess psychopathic traits in juvenile justice samples
- Validated for boys and girls aged 12 to 18 years
- Measures four factors of psychopathy (interpersonal, affective, behavioural, and antisocial)

Assessing Psychopathic Traits in Youth: Concerns

> Juveniles who are branded as psychopaths are more likely to be viewed as incorrigible, less likely to receive rehabilitative dispositions, and more likely to be transferred to the criminal justice system to be tried as adults and face the possibility of adult sanctions. (Steinberg 2002: 36)

The quote above lists several negative outcomes that could result from youth being labelled as psychopathic. Ethical, professional, and practical concerns about the use (or misuse) of measures designed to assess psychopathy in youth have been raised by various authors (Edens, Skeem, Curise, and Cauffman 2001; Hart, Watt, and Vincent 2002; Seagrave and Grisso 2002; Zinger and Forth 1998). Their concerns have focused on three main issues:

1. Negative consequences (e.g., transfer to adult court, harsher sentences, denial of access to treatment) of labelling a youth a psychopath
2. The possibility that psychopathic traits are common features of normally developing youth
3. The stability of psychopathic traits from childhood to adolescence and on to adulthood

Table 11.5 Studies Examining the Effects of the Psychopathy (P) and Conduct Disorder (CD) Labels and Traits in Adolescents

Study	Sample	Manipulation	Higher Risk	Harsher Sanction	Less Treatment
Edens et al. (2003)	Undergraduates	P traits versus positive traits	—	Yes	Yes
Murrie et al. (2005)	Juvenile probation officers	P versus CD versus no disorder	No	No	No
Murrie et al. (2007)	Judges	P versus CD versus no disorder	No	No	No
Rockett et al. (2007)	Clinicians	P versus CD versus no disorder	Yes	—	No
Vidal and Skeem (2007)	Juvenile probation officers	Is a psychopath versus not a psychopath	Yes	Yes	Yes
Jones and Cauffman (2008)	Judges	Is a psychopath versus not a psychopath	Yes	Yes	Yes
Boccaccini et al. (2008)	Community	Is a psychopath versus P versus CD versus no disorder	Yes	Yes	No
Blais and Forth (2014)	Undergraduates	Is a psychopath versus P versus CD versus no disorder	Yes	Yes	No

Source: Adapted from Boccaccini et al. (2008).

To address the labelling concern, several studies have investigated the effects of different labels (e.g., psychopath, conduct disorder, non-disorder) or different traits (e.g., psychopathic versus no psychopathic traits) on mock juror decision making (see Table 11.5 for a summary of findings). These studies typically provided participants with a written description of a defendant and the violent crime committed. All participants received the same information, with the exception of the clinical assessment, which varied across participants. The studies used a variety of samples ranging from university students to juvenile justice judges. In general, the studies found that the labels of psychopathy and conduct disorder were equally associated with higher risk. Also, describing underlying traits had a stronger impact on decision making than using a label. The strongest influence on decision makers was having a history of antisocial behaviour. In some studies (Boccaccini et al. 2008; Murrie et al. 2005; 2007), participants recommended treatment more often for youth described as psychopathic than for other youth.

The studies also determined that wording matters: If a description is worded, "Michael meets the diagnostic criteria for psychopathy," there was little impact on decision making. However, if it was worded, "Michael is a psychopath," it was more likely for harsher sentences to be recommended.

Edens et al. (2001) raised another concern that "scores on measures of psychopathy arguably may be inflated by general characteristics of adolescence" (p. 59). Edens et al.'s argument is that during the normal course of development, many adolescents may engage in activities that could be classified as bordering on criminal, thus leading researchers to overestimate the level of psychopathic traits in adolescent samples. However, this argument is not supported by any data: high ratings of psychopathic traits are rare in community youth (80 percent of community males score very low on the PCL:YV) (Forth, Kosson, and Hare 2003).

A final concern has been the stability of psychopathic traits from childhood to adulthood. Adolescence is a period of substantial change in a person's biological, psychological, and social systems. Several studies have measured the stability of psychopathic traits. There are several ways to measure the stability of psychopathic traits. The most common is rank-order stability or relative stability, in which a person's psychopathy score would stay in the same relative place as compared to others in the sample (Andershed 2010). Studies using rank-order stability have found moderate to high levels of stability (Bergstrom, Forth, and Farrington 2016).

Another way of measuring stability is to assess the mean-level stability or absolute stability, which requires examining a sample's mean psychopathy score over time. Studies using mean-level stability have also found that the mean score remains stable across different periods (Forsman et al. 2008; Lynam et al. 2009). Harpur and Hare (1994) examined the average PCL-R factor scores across seven age cohorts (16–20, 21–25, 26–30, 31–35, 36–40, 41–45, and 46–70) in a sample of male offenders. Factor 1 scores (interpersonal and affective traits) remained stable across age, but factor 2 scores (lifestyle and antisocial traits) decreased as age increased. One limitation of this study is that it was cross-sectional in design (i.e., not longitudinal) and thus age effects cannot be separated from cohort effects.

The least common, but perhaps most important, method for measuring stability is individual-level stability. This type of stability measures whether the individual's psychopathic traits increase, decrease, or stay the same over time. In a study examining individual-level stability, Salihovic, Ozdemir, and Kerr (2014) assessed the stability of the YPI between the ages of 13 and 17 in a large sample of community youth (N = 1068). They found four distinct trajectories: low-decreasing, moderate-stable, moderate-decreasing, and high-decreasing. The most common pattern across the different initial levels of psychopathic traits (low, moderate, and high) was a decrease in these traits during adolescence. However, there was one group that had moderate levels of psychopathic traits at age 13 and remained stable throughout adolescence.

As can be seen in Table 11.6, studies have examined both childhood-to-adolescence stability and adolescence-to-adulthood stability. Some studies have used different

Table 11.6 Stability of Psychopathic Traits

Study	Age at First Assessment	Length of Follow-Up	Measure	Stability Analysis	Stability Strength
Dadds et al. (2005)	4–9	1 year	APSD	Rank-order	Large
Van Baardewijk et al. (2011)	9–2	1.5 years	YPI-CV[1]	Rank-order	Moderate to large
Barry et al. (2008)	9–12	2 years	APSD	Rank-order	Large
Frick et al. (2003)	8	4 years	APSD	Rank-order	Large
Lynam et al. (2009)	7	11 years	CPS[2]	Rank-order mean-level	Moderate to large
Muñoz and Frick (2008)	13	2 years	APSD	Rank-order	Moderate to large
Forsman et al. (2008)	16	3 years	YPI	Rank-order mean-level	Moderate to large
Salihovic et al. (2014)	13	4 years	YPI	Rank-order individual-level	Moderate to large
Lynam et al. (2008)	13	11 years	CPS PCL:SV	Rank-order	Moderate

[1]Youth Psychopathic Traits Inventory—Child Version.
[2]CPS = Child Psychopathy Scale.

follow-up periods, different methods to assess psychopathic traits, and different types of analyses, and their stability estimates range from moderate to large.

Research on the stability of psychopathic traits have found the following:

1. Psychopathic traits show moderate to high rank-order stability across the lifespan. This means that those who are rated the "highest" on psychopathic traits remain the highest, while those who are rated low on psychopathic traits stay low.

2. In longitudinal studies, higher stability is found in shorter as compared to longer follow-up periods.

3. Most change in psychopathic traits occurs during adolescence.

4. When change happens, it is towards decreasing psychopathic traits.

5. Research is needed to determine why in some individuals psychopathic traits are stable whereas in others they decrease.

RELATIONSHIP BETWEEN PSYCHOPATHY AND CRIME

RESEARCH HAS ESTABLISHED A STRONG LINK BETWEEN PSYCHOPATHIC TRAITS AND criminal and aggressive behaviour in adults, adolescents, and children. Psychopathic traits identify a distinct subgroup of people who begin their criminal careers at an early age (Hare 2003), persist in violence across the lifespan (Porter, Birt, and Boer 2001), engage in high-density offences (Brown and Forth 1997), and engage in both proactive/reactive and predatory/instrumental aggression (Blais, Solodukhin, and Forth 2014; Flight and Forth 2007).

Table 11.7 presents the results of two meta-analyses that compared the association between psychopathy and criminal behaviour in adolescents and adults. Edens, Campbell, and Weir (2007) conducted a meta-analysis of 13 studies of adolescents measured by the PCL:YV or a modified version of the PCL-R and the total number of incidents involving both verbal and physical aggression, and incidents involving physical aggression only. Guy, Edens, Anthony, and Douglas (2005) conducted a meta-analysis of 38 adult samples using the PCL-R or PCL:SV. The weighted mean effect sizes for the relation between the PCL:YV and the total number of incidents and number of aggressive incidents were

Table 11.7 Weighted Mean Effect Sizes for Hare PCL Scales and Institutional Misconduct in Youth and Adults from Two Meta-Analyses

Outcome and Score	Guy et al. (2005) Adults		Edens and Campbell (2007) Youth	
	ks & ns	$r_w s$	ks & ns	$r_w s$
Total				
Total Score	38 (5381)	.29	15 (1310)	.24
Factor 1 Score	25 (3219)	.21	− (1002)	.21
Factor 2 Score	25 (3219)	.27	− (1002)	.28
Aggression				
Total Score	31 (4483)	.23	14 (1188)	.25
Factor 1 Score	22 (2786)	.15	− (880)	.22
Factor 2 Score	22 (2786)	.20	− (880)	.34
Physical Violence				
Total Score	22 (3502)	.17	10 (1001)	.28
Factor 1 Score	16 (2129)	.14	− (775)	.24
Factor 2 Score	16 (2129)	.15	− (775)	.37

Source: Guy et al. (2005), Edens, Campbell, and Weir (2007).

Table 11.8 Weighted Mean Effect Sizes for Hare PCL Scales and Recidivism in Youth and Adults from Three Meta-Analyses

Recidivism and Score	Walters (2003ab) Primarily Adults		Leistico et al. (2008) Primarily Adults		Edens et al. (2007) Youth	
	ks & ns	r_ws	ks & ns	d_ws	ks & ns	r_ws
General Recidivism						
Total Score	33 (4870)	.26	62 (11 140)	.50	20 (2787)	.24
Factor 1 Score	26 (4360)	.15	29 (5439)	.37	15 (2157)	.18
Factor 2 Score	26 (4360)	.32	29 (5439)	.64	15 (2157)	.29
Violent Recidivism						
Total Score					14 (2067)	.25
Factor 1 Score	27 (6365)	.18			12 (1776)	.19
Factor 2 Score	27 (6356)	.26			12 (1776)	.26
Sexual Recidivism						
Total Score					4 (654)	.07
Factor 1 Score	5 (726)	.05			3 (437)	.03
Factor 2 Score	5 (726)	.08			3 (437)	.08

Source: Leistico et al. (2008), Edens et al. (2007), and Walters (2003a, 2003b).

similar to the effect sizes obtained for adult samples using the PCL-R or PCL:SV. A weighted mean effect size of .28 demonstrates a significant association between PCL:YV and institutional physical violence and is much stronger than that reported by Guy et al. (2005) with adult samples (.17). In adults, association between psychopathy and institutional misconduct was strongest for a total number of incidents and weakest for physical violence, whereas for adolescents the opposite pattern was obtained. Thus, youth with psychopathic traits are more likely to engage in overt aggression compared to their adult counterparts. For both adolescents and adults, Factor 2 (behavioural and antisocial features) consistently had greater predictive value than Factor 1 (interpersonal and affective features) across each of the three categories of institutional incidents.

What is the association between psychopathy and recidivism? Table 11.8 presents the effect sizes of three meta-analytic studies with primarily adult samples and one meta-analytic study focusing on youth. Leistico, Salekin, DeCoster, and Rogers (2008) found that age was not a significant moderator, indicating that the "relations between psychopathy and future antisocial conduct were consistent across differences in the average age of the samples" (p. 33). The results of these studies suggest that increased psychopathy scores in adults and youth are associated with increased general and violent recidivism but only weakly with sexual recidivism. However, a more recent meta-analysis by Hawes,

Boccaccini, and Murrie (2013) reported somewhat stronger effect sizes between total PCL-R ($d = .40$), Factor 2 ($d = .44$), and Facet 4 ($d = .40$) and sexual recidivism. The sexual offenders who were most likely to sexually reoffend were those who scored high on the PCL-R and who scored high on sexual deviance.

Why is there a link between psychopathy and crime/violence? Given the features of psychopathy, it is perhaps not surprising that a strong link exists. The features listed below illustrate why psychopaths engage in higher rates of criminal and violent behaviour.

- Psychopaths are sensation-seekers and risk takers. They put themselves in high-risk situations.
- Psychopaths are impulsive. They fail to consider alternatives to or consequences of crime or violence.
- Psychopaths are unemotional. They do not have the ability to appreciate the consequences of crime or violence.
- Psychopaths are suspicious. They perceive hostile intent in others.
- Psychopaths are selfish and arrogant. The want to have power and control over others.

TREATMENT APPROACHES AND EFFECTIVENESS

UNTIL RECENTLY, PSYCHOPATHY WAS ASSUMED TO BE LARGELY UNTREATABLE. This perspective can be traced to Cleckley's book on psychopathy, where he stated, "Over a period of many years I have remained discouraged about the effect of treatment on the psychopathy . . . I have seen some patients treated for years . . . The psychopaths continued to behave as they had behaved in the past" (1976: 454).

Most of the relatively few studies that have evaluated the effectiveness of treatment for psychopaths suggest that Cleckley's initial assessment was correct: psychopathic offenders respond poorly to treatment, display poor motivation, show little improvement, and have high drop-out rates (Barbaree 2005; Hare et al. 2000; Hobson, Shine, and Roberts 2000; Langton, Barbaree, Harkins, and Peacock 2006). Rice, Harris, and Cormier (1992) found that some treated psychopaths not only did not improve with treatment but engaged in more offending. However, more promising treatment outcomes have been observed in some recent studies. Olver and Wong (2009) examined the treatment responses of psychopathic sex offenders and found that those who dropped out of treatment were more likely to violently reoffend, whereas those who stayed in treatment showed positive treatment gains and had a reduced risk for both sexual and violent recidivism.

One of the challenges in treating psychopathic offenders is to keep them in treatment. Psychopathic offenders often have low motivation for treatment and are more likely to drop out of treatment (Olver, Stockdale, and Wormith 2011; Olver and Wong 2011). When examining psychopathy treatment using the Risk-Needs-Responsivity (RNR) model (see Chapter 4 for discussion of the RNR model), psychopathy has implications for the risk principle (they are high risk offenders), the need principle (they have many criminogenic needs to target), and the responsivity principle (they need different styles of treatment). Wong, Gordon, Bu, Lewis, and Olver (2012) have posited that treatment for adult offenders should be focused on the behavioural and lifestyle traits (e.g., impulsivity, poor behavioural controls, sensation-seeking, etc.) since these traits will likely be more amenable to treatment as compared to the interpersonal and affective traits.

Encouraging evidence also comes from a treatment program for high-risk violent adolescent offenders. Caldwell, Skeem, Salekin, and Van Rybroek (2006) treated violent youth with many psychopathic traits (mean PCL:YV score of 33) at the Mendota Juvenile Treatment Center. The treated group was compared to juveniles referred for assessment who returned to the juvenile correctional system without treatment (mean PCL:YV score of 32). In a two-year follow-up, the treated group's rate of violent recidivism was 21 percent, compared to the non-treated group's rate of 49 percent. The study illustrates that using cognitive-behavioural treatment can be effective for youth with psychopathic traits as long as it is sufficiently intense and sustained. Caldwell, McCormick, Wolfe, and Umstead (2012) reported a reduction in psychopathic traits and an improvement in institutional conduct in a sample of incarcerated adolescent offenders. This program provided immediate positive reinforcement, used a cognitive-behavioural approach that individualized the treatment for each offender, and included a skills training component.

Several proposals have been made about the treatment of psychopathy. Wallace and Newman (2004) suggest that an effective treatment program should include targeting deficits in response modulation. Blair (2006) has proposed that since psychopathy is associated with reduced activity in the amygdala and associated structures, treatment could include giving pharmacological agents that increase activity within the amygdala. Blair acknowledges that "Although pharmacological agents are likely to be necessary for the successful treatment of psychopathy, they are unlikely to be sufficient . . . such agents will need to be coupled with cognitive behaviour-based treatments designed to associate actions that hurt others with an emotional response to the victim's distress" (Blair 2006: 391).

Based on the research discussed, treatment of adult psychopaths should have the following characteristics:

1. Psychopaths should not be considered untreatable. Treatment should target potentially changeable factors linked to the psychopathic offenders' criminal behaviour.

2. Treatment programs should be high-intensity and cognitive-behavioural; incorporate relapse prevention; and target substance abuse, anger arousal, antisocial thinking, and cognitive distortions (Wong and Hare 2005).

3. Treatment providers should be familiar with the cognitive and emotional processing deficits.

4. Treatment programs need to target behaviours that interfere with treatment and develop methods to enhance psychopaths' motivations for treatment.

In a recent review of treatment of community youth with callous and unemotional (CU) traits, Hawes, Price, and Dadds (2014) addressed three questions: Are CU traits

Box 11.1

Researcher Profile Dr. Stephen Wong

After finishing his doctorate at Queen's University in Kingston, Ontario, Dr. Stephen Wong moved to Saskatchewan and worked as an entry-level staff psychologist at the Regional Psychiatric Centre (RPC) in Saskatoon. The RPC is a forensic hospital within Correctional Service Canada (CSC) and is affiliated with the University of Saskatchewan (U of S). It operates both as a forensic hospital and a research and teaching facility. The blend of research and clinical practice, including the assessment and treatment of violence-prone and personality-disordered offenders, together with graduate student supervision was an excellent fit for Dr. Wong's interests. He stayed at the RPC for the next 27 years until his retirement in 2008 as the Director of Research.

Dr. Wong was intrigued and fascinated by offenders with psychopathy and started a research program focusing on treatment of psychopathy shortly after arriving at the RPC. His interests in psychopathy took him to Dr. Hare's

Courtesy of Dr. Stephen Wong

lab at the University of British Columbia in 1982, and he came away with a mimeographed copy (in blue ink!!) of Hare's preliminary 22-item Psychopathy Checklist. Armed with this new tool, Wong implemented the first systematic survey of the prevalence and characteristics of psychopathic offenders within CSC in 1982–84. The development of the PCL-R led to rapid progress in both risk assessment and psychopathy research. The same cannot be said for the treatment of psychopathy, which was hampered by a strong headwind created by work suggesting that such treatment could be counterproductive or even harmful.

In the 1980s and 90s, Wong worked directly with offenders with antisocial personality disorder, delivering treatment on a daily basis. This front-line contact made him aware of the need for structured, evidence-based treatment programs (which were sorely lacking at the time), and sensitized him to the need for tools to assess violence risk and treatment changes. The emergence of the seminal work by Andrew, Bonta, Gendreau, and colleagues (culminating in the publication of the now-classical text *The Psychology of Criminal Conduct*, 1994) and the wide dissemination of the Risk/Need/Responsivity principles in their work provided Wong with a solid theoretical framework that guided his formulation of rehabilitation programs.

The rapid growth of forensic psychology at the University of Saskatchewan saw an influx of many talented graduate students interested in clinical and research work at the RPC. In collaboration with his graduate students, Wong developed a number of tools that are now used internationally to assess violence risk and measure treatment change. These include the Violence Risk Scale (VRS), the VRS—Sexual Offender Version (VRS:SO)

Box 11.1   (Continued)

and the VRS—Youth Version (VRS:YV), as well as the Violence Reduction Program. All were largely based on the theses and dissertation work of his graduate students. Wong then focused on bringing together the areas of offender risk assessment, psychopathy, and effective offender rehabilitation research (all of which are now well-supported by solid empirical evidence) to address risk-reduction treatment of psychopathy in offender populations.

Dr. Wong considers himself fortunate to have been in the right place at the right time to do what he enjoys doing. He said he owes an enormous debt of gratitude to his colleagues; his many talented graduate students for their commitment, hard work, and stimulating ideas; and the many offenders who volunteered to participate in numerous research projects. Dr. Wong continues to encourage students in forensic psychology today, stating "never under-estimate what you can achieve even when you are an undergraduate student feeling completely lost and overwhelmed with work ... you can, if you persevere, achieve great things."

Box 11.2

You Be the Therapist!

Kevin Mills is a 25-year-old from Vancouver. He is a first-time federal offender beginning a 4-year sentence for robbery and assault causing bodily harm. The related offence occurred in Toronto at the Gay Pride parade when he offered to sell drugs to a parade participant. Kevin and the victim went to a back alley where Kevin beat the victim and stole his wallet. At the time, Kevin was already on probation for a series of break-and-enter offences.

Kevin has been sentenced 12 times (7 times in youth court and 5 times in adult court) for a total of 17 convictions (10 in youth court and 7 in adult court) for assault, assault causing bodily harm, robbery, carrying a concealed weapon, theft under $5000, break and enter, drug possession, criminal harassment, failure to appear, and failure to comply with a probation order.

Kevin has violated probation on several occasions and is often hostile and aggressive with probation officers. When asked about the number of his undetected crimes, he stated he had broken into "lots" of homes. He claimed when he was younger he would wait until a homeowner was at home and then break into their house while they were sleeping. He refused to say if he currently does this and refused to be more specific about the number of times he has done this. When asked about his first violent offence, he described how at the age of 15, he and a friend would pick up out-of-town "Johns." He claimed his friend would agree to have sex with a man and drive to Stanly Park, where Kevin would be waiting in the bushes with a knife and rob the John. Kevin claimed they would often target men with U.S. license plates since these men would rarely contact the police.

In his descriptions, Kevin minimizes the harm he has done to his victims and often shifts the blame to the victims. He justified his assault of a former girlfriend by saying she "lipped off" at him. When asked about his break-and-enter crimes, he claimed the victims had insurance. When describing one break-and-enter victim he

Box 11.2 (Continued)

stated "The guy showed up in court wearing a turban. Then I did not feel so bad. The guy should feel honoured just to be in Canada."

Kevin has minimal employment history in the community. He has been fired from two jobs for getting into altercations with his boss and other employees. He last worked for his uncle's landscaping business. Kevin was often late for work, sometimes showed up intoxicated, and occasionally didn't show up at all. When his uncle confronted him about this behaviour, Kevin always had an excuse. When asked about his future goals he said "maybe I could get some girls working for me." When asked what he meant, he refused to elaborate. He then stated he believed he could easily get a job in computers. He acknowledges that he might need to get his high school diploma, but then stated that it was

unlikely he would get one because he had other plans. When asked what these plans involved, he smirked and said "that's not something you need to know."

At the prison intake psychological report, Kevin was described as hostile, arrogant, manipulative, impulsive, and remorseless. He was diagnosed with antisocial personality disorder and was described as scoring high on the PCL-R. He indicated he would be willing to participate in treatment programs but warned the interviewer he did not "have much use for psychologists."

Questions

What kind of intervention do you think Kevin needs? What should his treatment priorities be? What might be some of the challenges in treating Kevin?

related to poorer treatment outcomes? Do CU traits respond to family-based intervention? What are the best practices for treatment of youth with CU traits? The researchers concluded that CU traits are related to poorer treatment outcomes with higher rates of treatment dropout (Dadds et al. 2012; Kimonis et al. 2014) and less responsiveness to parent training programs and programs that include both a parent and child component (e.g., Manders et al. 2013). The researchers also wanted to know if family-based intervention programs could change CU traits. There have been four published studies that have used a randomized clinical treatment (RCT) design to examine change in CU traits. In RCT studies, youth are randomly assigned to either a standard intervention or the enhanced parent training intervention. CU traits are measured prior to treatment and post-treatment (sometimes at a later follow-up). The two studies that involved children (McDonald et al. 2011; Somech and Elizur 2012) reported that children whose parents received training showed a significant decrease in CU traits, while those assigned to standard interventions did not. The two studies that focused on adolescents found mixed effects. Butler, Baruch, Hickey, and Fonagy (2011) found that adolescents who received multi-systemic treatment (MST) showed a significant decrease in parent-reported APSD total scores (youth self-reported APSD scores did not change). In contrast, Manders et al. (2013) found no change in parent-reported CU traits in adolescents assigned to MST or standard intervention.

Finally, Hawes et al. (2014) provided some suggestions for which type of intervention might be most effective for children with CU traits. They suggest that social-learning-based parent training should be provided early in childhood. In addition, interventions should focus on positive reinforcement (not punishment) and on promoting warmth between the parent and child. Dadds and colleagues (2014) also describe a novel intervention designed to promote emotional engagement between the child and parent. In reciprocal eye-contact interventions, children and parents are encouraged to spend more time in shared eye contact with each other. This intervention would be done prior to more standardized parent skills training. Research is currently being conducted to determine whether this novel intervention is effective.

FUTURE DIRECTIONS

PSYCHOPATHY CONTINUES TO GAIN PROMINENCE AS A CRITICAL CONSTRUCT IN accounting for a substantial portion of criminal and aggressive behaviour. Like many other mental disorders, it is complex in terms of its etiology and treatment. Research over the past 30 years has led to many advances in measuring psychopathy, determining its biological and environmental origins, and treating it. Within the next several years, new research will provide further insights in the development and treatment of psychopaths.

Researchers have also started to examine the effects psychopaths have on others. This is much-needed research since victims of psychopaths have not yet been a focus of research in this field. Victims of psychopaths need to be heard so that appropriate support and intervention programs can be developed for them. However, the ultimate goal of psychopathy research is to understand what causes psychopathy in order to prevent the development of this disorder and thus avoid having any victims.

SUMMARY

1. Psychopathy is a personality disorder defined by a cluster of interpersonal, affective, and behavioural features. Psychopathy overlaps with symptoms from DSM-5 antisocial personality behaviour, but only moderately. Prevalence of psychopathy varies as a function of the sample studied, with incarcerated offenders having the highest prevalence and community samples having lowest prevalence.

2. There has been little research on victims of psychopaths. Researchers have found that psychopaths in the community can cause substantial emotional, financial, and physical harm. More research is needed to understand the short- and long-term impacts of being involved with a psychopath.

3. A variety of assessment measures have been developed to assess for psychopathic traits in children, adolescents, and adults, including the PCL, TriPM, PPI-R, SRP-III,

B-Scan, YPI, and APSD. A number of concerns have been raised about the measurement of psychopathic traits in youth. These include the issue of labelling a youth a psychopath, how stable psychopathic traits are from childhood to adulthood, and whether some psychopathic traits are normal in healthy adolescents.

4. Psychopathic traits are related to institutional misconduct and general and violent recidivism in both youth and adult offenders. The combination of high psychopathy scores and high deviant sexual arousal is most strongly predictive of sexual recidivism in sex offenders.

5. Developmental, biological, and cognitive theories have been used to explain the etiology of psychopathy. Recent neuroimaging studies have identified two areas of the brain in those with psychopathic characteristics that are of specific interest: the amygdala and the ventromedial prefrontal cortex.

6. Although adult psychopaths are resistant to treatment, recent research has reported some positive outcomes, especially for youth with psychopathic traits. Intervention programs that focus on positive reinforcement (not punishment) and on promoting warmth between the parent and child have reported positive outcomes with children with CU traits.

Discussion Questions

1. You have been hired by the World Health Organization to identify the prevalence of psychopathy across different countries. Describe the study you would propose, focusing on how you would measure psychopathy.

2. You are interested in conducting a study on how the media portrays crimes committed by psychopaths. Develop two hypotheses and describe the methodology you would use and what variables you would measure to test these hypotheses.

3. You want to know more about victims of psychopaths. Are there differential effects if the psychopath is a family member, an intimate partner, or a supervisor in the workplace? Describe the methodology you will use and what you would measure.

4. The CSC has proposed a new treatment program for psychopathic violent offenders. You have been hired to develop an evaluation of the program to see whether it is effective. Describe how you plan to do your evaluation.

Chapter 12
Sexual Offenders

A PEDOPHILIC CHILD MOLESTER

Arnold is a 24-year-old man currently serving a four-year sentence at Warkworth Institution (a medium-security federal penitentiary in Ontario) for sexual offences against two children who lived in his neighbourhood. The first victim was an eight-year-old boy who often rode his bicycle around the neighbourhood. Arnold spent hours in his garage with the door open so that he could see and talk to the boy when he rode by. The boy sometimes had trouble with his bicycle, and Arnold would fix it for him in his garage. The first time he simply fixed the bicycle, but eventually he began sexually offending against the boy. The offences occurred on two separate occasions roughly one month apart. The first time he touched the boy's genitals. The second time, he and the boy touched each other's genitals. The boy did not return to Arnold's house after that.

The second victim was a 10-year-old girl who delivered the newspaper to Arnold's house. Arnold would usually be in his garage when the girl arrived and he routinely spoke with her and invited her in for a drink and snack. Eventually, Arnold began sexually offending against the girl. The offences occurred on four separate occasions and escalated from touching to oral sex. Arnold gained compliance from his victims through psychological manipulation (e.g., befriending them, bribes) rather than physical coercion or threats of violence. The younger victim eventually told his mother about the abuse, the police were notified, and Arnold was arrested. Upon news of his arrest, the other victim came forward and Arnold was also charged for offending against her.

Learning Objectives

1 Understand the scope of sexual offending and consequences for victims.

2 Describe pedophilia.

3 Summarize some of the major theories explaining sexual offending.

4 Describe key research on factors associated with sexual offending.

5 Explain some of the key assessment instruments used to estimate risk of recidivism among sexual offenders.

6 Understand various approaches to the treatment and management of sexual offenders and the extent to which these approaches are effective at reducing sexual recidivism.

INTRODUCTION

Reading the opening vignette and considering sexual offences presented in the media raises a number of intriguing questions. How common is this sort of behaviour? What are the prototypical characteristics of sexual offenders? What are the causes of sexual offending? After being caught, do sexual offenders typically persist with sexual offending? What can be done to identify the most persistent sexual offenders and reduce their risk of sexual recidivism? We will address these and other questions in this chapter.

More specifically, we will consider the scope and characteristics of sexual offending in Canada. We will also describe pedophilic disorder, which is one of a set of psychiatric disorders called paraphilic disorders and particularly relevant to sexual offending. We will also review some key theories that attempt to explain why some people sexually offend. Research examining the association between sexual offending and some of the factors identified in theory will also be reviewed. We will then present a number of key sexual offender risk-assessment instruments and research on the predictive accuracy of these instruments. Finally, some of the major approaches to treatment for sexual offenders will be presented and research on the effectiveness of treatment will be reviewed.

CONTEXT

We have recently seen increased awareness of and attention to the problem of sexual aggression against women and children, likely at least partly influenced by feminist efforts (e.g., Brownmiller 1975). There have been a number of different approaches to studying sexual aggression, but one major distinction is between forensic/criminological research and lab-based research. Forensic/criminological research generally focuses on sexual offending in the context of the forensic or criminal justice system (e.g., sexual offences are operationally defined as official arrests, charges, or convictions; samples are often selected from forensic/criminal justice populations). Lab-based research, in contrast, generally focuses on sexual aggression and coercion in the context of the general community (e.g., operational definitions include a broad range of self-reported sexually coercive and aggressive behaviours, only some of which would unambiguously fit within legal definitions of sexual offences; samples are often selected from populations of university students and the general community that have not necessarily been involved with the forensic/criminal justice system). We see these approaches as providing complementary evidence and having different advantages and disadvantages, and accordingly we incorporate evidence from both approaches.

DEFINITIONS

Sexual offences comprise a wide range of sexual acts—with or without physical contact—involving people who do not or cannot provide informed consent (e.g., children, or someone who is unconscious). A **paraphilia**, as defined in the *Diagnostic and Statistical Manual of Mental Disorders* (DSM-5) (American Psychiatric Association 2013), is an "intense and persistent sexual interest other than sexual interest in genital stimulation or preparatory fondling with phenotypically normal, physically mature, consenting human partners" (p. 685). Not all paraphilic disorders involve illegal behaviour (e.g., fetishism, sexual masochism), but some can manifest as sexual offending. One of the most relevant paraphilic disorders for this chapter is pedophilic disorder.

Pedophilia generally refers to sexual attraction to children who have not yet begun puberty. It has been estimated that the prevalence of pedophilia in the general population is up to approximately 5 percent (Seto 2008). The specific diagnostic criteria for pedophilic disorder in the DSM-5 are:

(A) Over a period of at least 6 months, recurrent, intense sexually arousing fantasies, sexual urges, or behaviors involving sexual activity with a prepubescent child or children (generally age 13 years or younger).

(B) The individual has acted on these sexual urges, or the sexual urges or fantasies cause marked distress or interpersonal difficulty.

(C) The person is at least age 16 years and at least 5 years older than the child or children in Criterion A.

Note: Do not include an individual in late adolescence involved in an ongoing sexual relationship with a 12- or 13-year-old. (American Psychiatric Association 2013: 697)

Although the terms pedophile and child molester are often used interchangeably, they are not synonymous. It has been estimated that only about 50 percent of sexual offenders against prepubescent children are pedophiles (Seto 2008). Moreover, the DSM-5 makes a distinction between *paraphilias* and *paraphilic disorders*. Pedophilia—or *pedophilic sexual orientation*—refers to sexual attraction to children, but without any related illegal behaviour, distress, or interpersonal difficulties. As we will discuss later, sexual offending against children can be motivated by a number of factors besides a sexual preference for prepubescent children.

WHY DO WE CARE?

Scope of Sexual Offending

Before examining sexual offenders themselves, it is important to consider the scope of sexual offending. How many sexual offences are committed and how many people are victimized?

The Uniform Crime Reporting (UCR) Survey reports on the incidence of crimes reported to police in Canada in a given year and some of the characteristics of those crimes. The prevalence of various sexual offences for 2013 is presented in Table 12.1. These 2013 rates are lower than in 2003, with the exception of child pornography offences. The number of sexual offences actually committed is undoubtedly higher than the police-reported rates because many sexual offences are not reported to the police (e.g., Brennan and Taylor-Butts 2008), but the decrease in sexual offending over the

Table 12.1 UCR Survey Data for Sexual Offences Reported to Police in Canada in 2013

Offence	Number	Per 100 000 Population
Aggravated sexual assault (level 3)	137	0
Sexual assault with a weapon or causing bodily harm (level 2)	370	1
Sexual assault (level 1)	20 804	59
Sexual offences against children	4232	12
Child pornography	2668	8

Source: Boyce, Cotter, and Perrault (2014).

last three decades appears to be real and extend beyond Canada (e.g., Finkelhor and Jones 2008).

Surveys of the general public and police-reported crime also provide descriptive information about the typical characteristics of victims, offenders, and offences (e.g., Brennan and Taylor-Butts 2008; Cotter and Beaupré 2014). Women and girls are more likely to be victims of sexual offences than men and boys. As shown in Figure 12.1,

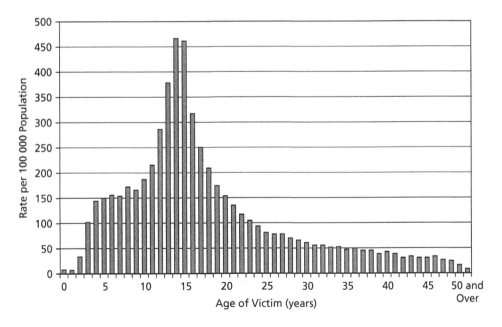

Figure 12.1 Victims of Police-Reported Sexual Offences, by Age, Canada

Source: Cotter and Beaupré (2014), Chart 5, p. 10. Based on data from Statistics Canada, Canadian Centre for Justice Statistics, Uniform Crime Reporting Survey.

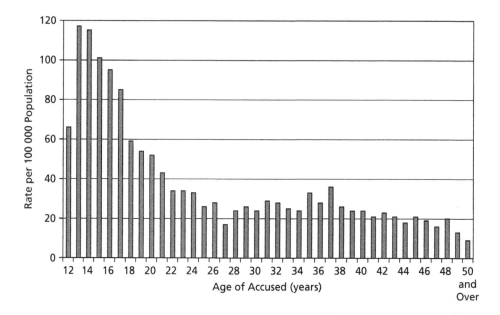

Figure 12.2 Persons Accused of Sexual Offences Against Children and Youth, by Age of Accused, Canada, 2012

Source: Cotter and Beaupré (2014), Chart 7, p. 13. Based on data from Statistics Canada, Canadian Centre for Justice Statistics, Uniform Crime Reporting Survey.

teenagers are at greatest risk for sexual victimization. Teenagers are also more likely than adults to commit sexual offences (see Figure 12.2), but the vast majority of offenders are male. The offender and victim often know each other (e.g., acquaintances, friends, family members) prior to the sexual offence in the majority of incidents. Children are most often victimized by family members, whereas adolescents and adults are most often victimized by acquaintances or friends. Sensational cases covered most heavily in the media are generally not representative of the majority of sexual offenders. See the Media Spotlight box for a particularly heinous recent Canadian case that received extensive media attention.

Consequences for Victims

Sexual victimization is associated with a number of short- and long-term negative outcomes, such as physical injury, sexually transmitted infection, unwanted pregnancy, embarrassment, shame, fear, anxiety, depression, relationship difficulties, and sexual dissatisfaction and dysfunction (Beitchman et al. 1992; Browne and Finkelhor 1986; Irish, Kobayashi, and Delahanty 2010; Paolucci, Genuis, and Violato 2001; Resick 1993).

The Double Life of Colonel Russell Williams

By all accounts, Colonel Russell Williams was an accomplished and respected leader in the Canadian military; well-educated, successful, married, and well-liked by his friends and co-workers. At the same time, however, he was committing sexually motivated break-ins at nearby homes to steal women's and girls' underwear, sexually assault women, and kill women. Although neither Williams nor his offences are typical of the majority of sexual offenders brought to the attention of the criminal justice system, this especially disturbing case received a lot of attention in the media. Below is a timeline of events from his recent offences to his convictions.

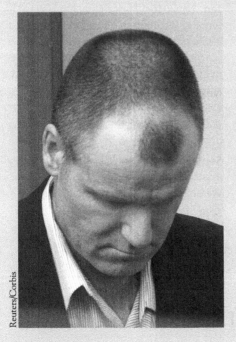

Reuters/Corbis

Colonel Russell Williams

Col. Russell Williams Timeline

Col. Russell Williams, former base commander of CFB Trenton, has been convicted of first-degree murder in the deaths of Jessica Lloyd, 27, and Cpl. Marie-France Comeau, 38.

Williams has also pleaded guilty to forcible confinement and the sexual assault of two other women in Tweed, Ont., a small community north of Belleville, as well as 82 counts of breaking and entering and attempted breaking and entering.

Here is a timeline of events in the case:

Oct. 20, 2010—A judge sentences Williams to two terms of life in prison with no chance of parole for 25 years for the first-degree murders. Williams is also sentenced to 10 years for each of his two sexual assaults, as well as one year for each of the other charges he faced.

Oct. 19, 2010—Following the reading of the agreed statement of facts, Williams is formally convicted of all charges against him.

Oct. 18, 2010—Williams pleads guilty to all charges against him, including two counts of first-degree murder, two counts each of sexual assault and forcible containment as well as 82 counts of breaking and entering and attempted breaking and entering.

Crown attorneys begin a two-day presentation of the agreed statement of facts, including photographs Williams took of himself and descriptions of the videos he took of the rapes and murders of Jessica Lloyd and Cpl. Marie-France Comeau.

Oct. 7, 2010—In Col. Russell Williams' first in-person appearance before a judge, his lawyer says Williams intends to plead guilty to the murder, sexual assault and breaking and entering charges against him at a later date. The hearing is adjourned until Oct. 18.

Aug. 26, 2010—Williams appears in court via video link and waives his right to a preliminary inquiry. His next appearance in Superior Court is scheduled for Oct. 7.

July 22, 2010—Williams makes a brief court appearance via video link in a Belleville, Ont., courtroom. The court agrees to reconvene on Aug. 26. Williams remains in custody at the Quinte Detention Centre in Napanee, near Belleville.

April 29, 2010—Williams is charged with 82 more offences in connection with break-ins in Ottawa, Belleville, and Tweed in Ontario. The new charges include:

- 61 counts of breaking and entering and theft
- 11 counts of attempted breaking and entering
- 10 counts of breaking and entering with intent to commit an indictable offence

April 5, 2010—Williams is placed under suicide watch at the Quinte Detention Centre after an apparent suicide attempt, according to a media report.

Feb. 18, 2010—Williams appears before a Belleville court via video link from the Quinte Detention Centre in Napanee. He is represented by Michael Edelson, a prominent Ottawa-based defence lawyer. On the same day, OPP confirm they have finished searching Williams' Ottawa home.

Feb. 16, 2010—OPP search Williams' home in Ottawa's Westboro neighbourhood.

Feb. 11, 2010—Sources tell CBC News Williams led police to the body of Jessica Lloyd.

Feb. 8, 2010—Police find the body of Jessica Lloyd off Cary Road in Tweed, Ont.

Feb. 7, 2010—Williams is arrested in Ottawa and charged with two counts of first-degree murder in the deaths of Jessica Lloyd and Cpl. Marie-France Comeau. He is also charged with two sexual assaults that happened in Tweed in September.

Jan. 28, 2010—Jessica Elizabeth Lloyd, 27, sends a text message to a family friend at 10:36 p.m. The next day she does not show up for work. Lloyd's family tells police it is out of character for her to be out of contact.

Nov. 25, 2009—Cpl. Marie France Comeau, 38, is found dead on Nov. 25, 2009, in her home in Brighton, Ont. The death is ruled a homicide.

Sept. 30, 2009—Another woman is sexually assaulted in her home on Cosy Cove Lane. Williams has a cottage on Cosy Cove Lane.

Sept. 17, 2009—A woman in Tweed, Ont., is tied up and sexually assaulted in her home.

Source: CBC News (2010).

THEORIES OF SEXUAL OFFENDING

Why do some people sexually offend against adults and children? A number of theories and models have attempted to address this question and explain why some people commit sexual offences (e.g., Finkelhor 1984; Hall and Hirschman 1991, 1992; Lalumière et al. 2005; Malamuth 2003; Marshall and Barbaree 1990; Seto 2008).

Together these theories and models identify four key factors thought to play a causal role in sexual offending: 1) deviant sexual interests involving attraction to children (e.g., pedophilia) or to sexual violence (e.g., sexual sadism); 2) disregard for the suffering or needs of others; 3) problems regulating negative emotions; and 4) social inadequacy. Theories vary in the extent to which they focus on each factor and on the precursors emphasized. Although there are some inconsistencies between the different theoretical perspectives, there is consensus that sexual offending is likely caused by multiple factors (not just one) and that different sets of causal factors may be involved for different sexual offenders.

Finkelhor's Four Factor Model

Finkelhor (1984) attempted to organize existing explanations of sexual offending against children into a multifactor framework, which reflects four underlying factors he identified in the literature. The first is **emotional congruence** and refers to a perceived "'fit' between the adult's emotional needs and the child's characteristics" (Finkelhor 1984: 38). An individual may find sexual contact with a child emotionally gratifying because he or she is psychologically immature and views him or herself as a child. In addition, some individuals may feel emotionally gratified by sexually offending against a child because they feel powerful and competent when doing so; for example, they may generally feel inadequate (e.g., low self-esteem, low social self-efficacy). Emotional congruence alone would not necessarily lead to sexual offending against children. What is also needed is some degree of sexual arousal to the prospect of sexual contact with a child, which is the second factor in this model. **Blockage** is the third factor and refers to the idea that some people may be blocked from meeting their sexual and emotional needs in prosocial ways (e.g., consenting sexual contact with adults). Blockage may occur because of social anxiety, social skills deficits, problems in a current romantic relationship, or repressive beliefs about sexual norms (e.g., against masturbation and extramarital affairs). The final factor, **disinhibition**, refers to the fact that inhibitions against sexual offending against children are either circumvented or are absent to allow one to commit the offence. Disinhibition may occur because of personality (e.g., impulse control deficits, lack of empathy), situational (e.g., intoxication, extreme stress), or cultural factors.

Evolutionary Explanation of Rape

Lalumière et al. (2005) have attempted to explain sexual assault from an evolutionary perspective. Evolutionary psychology was described in detail in Chapter 2, but briefly the idea is that in our ancestral environments, certain physiological, psychological, and behavioural characteristics were associated with increased reproductive success (i.e., having a relatively high number of children who in turn have a relatively high number of children, and so on). To the extent that such characteristics are heritable, the genes responsible for them would be passed on to subsequent generations more so than genes that are responsible for characteristics associated with reproductive failure. Thus today, we generally think and do what led to reproductive success in ancestral environments. Lalumière et al. argue "that rape is part of a general antisocial, aggressive, and risk-tolerant lifestyle and that very few rapists specialize in rape" (p. 184). Building on research and theory on general antisocial behaviour (e.g., Harrris, Rice, and Lalumière 2001; Moffitt 1993; Quinsey, Skilling, Lalumière, and Craig 2004), Lalumière et al. propose that most rapists fall into one of three groups: young men, competitively disadvantaged men, or psychopaths. Adolescent and young men typically have relatively few resources and low status, which puts them at a competitive disadvantage relative to other males with whom they are competing for mates. Through violence (including sexual coercion) and general risk taking, these young men may be able to increase their status, resources, and/or access to more and better mates. However, as they move into adulthood and begin to acquire legitimately gained resources and status, they switch from high mating effort (focus is on casual sex with many partners) to high parental investment (focus is on ensuring the health and well-being of one's children). So the sexual assaults and other antisocial behaviour of this group are limited to adolescence and young adulthood. This is the most common type of rapist.

This desistance with adulthood, however, does not occur for the competitively disadvantaged men. Their sexual coercion and other antisocial behaviour is life-course persistent. The ability to compete for resources and status in prosocial ways is impaired by early neurodevelopmental insults, such as obstetrical complications and low IQ. Because men in this group do not have the skills or abilities to achieve status and resources in prosocial ways, they maintain their high mating effort and antisocial approach into adulthood. The final group, psychopaths, are also life-course persistent. In contrast to the competitively disadvantaged men, psychopaths are not competitively disadvantaged but select high mating effort over parental investment as an alternate strategy. The competitively disadvantaged and psychopaths are thought to make up a small proportion of rapists. This quote from Lalumière and colleagues (2005) sums it up nicely: "Young men are involved in intense competition, competitively disadvantaged offenders are trying to make the best of a bad deal, and psychopaths are pursuing a finely tuned alternative strategy of defection and aggression" (p. 124).

Seto's Motivation–Facilitation Model of Child Sexual Offending

Dr. Michael Seto (2008), who is profiled in the Canadian Researcher Profile box, has put forth a comprehensive model of sexual offending against children. This model draws from a very broad literature of theory and research. It is somewhat similar to the model above in that there is an adolescence-limited path, a pedophilia path, and an antisociality path, which includes the sub-paths of competitive disadvantage and psychopathy. Basically, adolescence-limited sexual offenders against children are those who may be blocked from romantic relationships with peers because of lack of resources (e.g., unattractive, poor, weak) or poor social skills. These boys may occasionally sexually offend against a child.

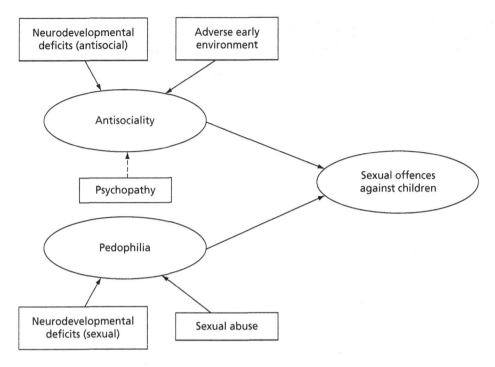

Figure 12.3 Seto's Motivation–Facilitation of Child Sexual Offending

Source: Seto (2008).

Some adolescence-limited offenders may also be pedophiles, motivated by their sexual interest in children. Two more persistent paths are presented in Figure 12.3. As proposed above for rape, persistent offending may be a manifestation of antisociality, stemming from enduring competitive disadvantage or psychopathy. Pedophilia would be another cause of sexual offending against children. Offending against children would be especially likely when both antisociality and pedophilia are present.

METHODOLOGY

How would you test the assertions of the theories and models we have just described? Empirically demonstrating that a given factor plays a causal role in sexual offending is more difficult than you might think. Referring back to our discussion about methodology and inferences in Chapter 7, the majority of published studies on sexual offending are descriptive or cross-sectional observational designs and most of the remainder are single-wave longitudinal observational designs. There are very few multi-wave longitudinal observational designs or randomized experiments. As such, most of the available evidence does not permit conclusions about the causes of sexual offending. The

Box 12.1

Canadian Researcher Profile Dr. Michael Seto

Dr. Michael Seto is the Forensic Research Director with the Royal Ottawa Health Care Group. He is also the Editor-In-Chief of *Sexual Abuse: A Journal of Research and Treatment*, as well as an Adjunct Professor at Carleton University, Ryerson University, the University of Ottawa, and the University of Toronto. Dr. Seto completed a B.Sc in psychology at the University of British Columbia and then moved to Kingston, Ontario, where he completed an M.A. and a Ph.D. in clinical psychology at Queen's University. His Ph.D. thesis supervisor was Dr. Vern Quinsey. Dr. Seto's first professional job after completing his Ph.D. was as a Research Scientist at the Clarke Institute of Psychiatry in Toronto, which later became part of the Centre for Addiction and Mental Health. He continued there until he moved to his current position.

Dr. Seto is internationally recognized as one of the leading authorities on pedophilia and sexual

Dr. Michael Seto

offending, with extensive research on the assessment, diagnosis, and treatment of pedophilia and sexual offenders against children. He has authored over 100 publications, many of them in high-impact scientific journals, such as *Psychological Bulletin and Journal of Abnormal Psychology*. He has also written two books that should be considered required reading for anyone working in this area: one on pedophilia and sexual offending against children (Seto 2008), and the other on Internet-facilitated sexual offending (Seto 2013).

One of the reasons that Dr. Seto's work is so influential is likely that he sees both the trees and the forest. He has conducted sophisticated original scientific research in which he demonstrates an impressive depth of knowledge about the literature and methodology in specific sub-areas, but he has developed and applied this same depth of knowledge in a wide range of specific sub-areas within the broader field of sexual offending. He also draws from more general and established research areas, such as sexuality, developmental psychology, and evolutionary psychology. In addition to this depth and breadth of research expertise and knowledge, he is also well-informed about clinical practice, legislation, and policy. He is one of a handful of people in the world who is able to critically review and synthesize the scientific literature across the entire field to provide informative, interesting, and balanced big-picture summaries of current knowledge to researchers, practitioners, policy makers, and the general public.

When asked which of his studies is his favourite, Dr. Seto identified his meta-analysis published in the prestigious journal *Psychological Bulletin* (Seto and Lalumière 2010):

> I think my favourite is the 2010 meta-analysis of studies comparing adolescent

Box 12.1 (Continued)

sex and non-sex offenders. The main findings revealed a pattern of both similarities and differences between the two offender groups, consistent with the idea that adolescent sex offenders resemble other adolescent offenders in many ways, with some exceptions. The exceptions support some hypotheses but are not consistent with others about adolescent sexual offending. It's well-cited after five years in publication and seems to be having an influence on the adolescent sexual offending field, which was our intention. A major reason I like it is that it took my co-author and I over five years to complete it, with a major job change and move for both of us and parental leave for me contributing to the time involved.

Dr. Seto collaborates extensively with researchers in Canada, the United States, Europe, and elsewhere, and he mentors students, junior colleagues, and clinical staff. When asked how we should

be training our future researchers and clinicians interested in the psychology of criminal behaviour, Dr. Seto said, "Using evidence-based training techniques to develop their understanding and ability to apply evidence-based policies and practices."

When asked where he sees his research going next, Dr. Seto said, "I am going to spend the next decade or so trying to make some progress in understanding the clinical and scientific puzzle of incest offending. What are the factors that contribute to this form of sexual offending? The two major risk dimensions that have been identified for sexual offending are antisociality (criminal tendencies) and atypical sexual interests (e.g., pedophilia). But incest offenders are typically low in both these dimensions. Many theories of incest cite the role of family factors such as dysfunctional relationship dynamics or spousal conflict, but there are surprisingly few studies testing these ideas."

Dr. Seto is also an avid fisherman: "I love fishing and would prefer to do that to almost anything else after work and my family."

point here, of course, is not to dismiss the work researchers have done in this area. It is difficult and sometimes impossible to do more rigorous studies on potential causes of sexual offending because of limited resources, limited access, or ethical/moral considerations. Even the ambiguous evidence presented in most studies still has value because it can be used to generate and refine hypotheses about causal relationships that can eventually be tested in series of increasingly rigorous and conclusive studies. The point is that we need to attend to methodology so that we can keep the strength of our conclusions in line with the strength of the evidence, and we can identify areas for improvement and work towards getting more conclusive evidence where possible. For example, even if ideal randomized experiments are not always possible, methodological rigor is a matter of degree and there is certainly room for improvement.

FACTORS ASSOCIATED WITH SEXUAL OFFENDING

IN THE BRIEF REVIEW OF THE AVAILABLE LITERATURE ON SOME POTENTIAL CAUSES of sexual offending, we have organized the available evidence in Table 12.2 based on methodological rigour and whether the evidence demonstrates that the factor

Table 12.2 Summary of Evidence Regarding Potential Causes of Sexual Offending

Variable	Associated	Predictive	Causal
Sexual interest in children	Yes	Yes	Untested
Sexual interest in rape	Yes	No	Untested
Antisocial orientation	Yes	Yes	Untested
Childhood sexual abuse	Yes	No	Untested
Cognition distortions/ rape myths	Yes	Maybe	Maybe not
Emotional congruence with children	Yes	Yes	Untested

Note: Associated = Evidence generally demonstrates that the factor, alone or in combination with other factors, directly or indirectly, is associated with the likelihood or amount of past, current, or future sexual offending.
Predictive = Evidence generally demonstrates that the factor, alone or in combination with other factors, directly or indirectly, is associated with the likelihood or amount of sexual offending in the future.
Causal = Evidence generally demonstrates that the factor, alone or in combination with other factors, directly or indirectly, leads at least some people to sexually offend.

is associated with sexual offending, predicts sexual offending, or plays a causal role in sexual offending.

Deviant Sexual Interests

The most established method for assessing deviant sexual interests is phallometric assessment or **penile plethysmography (PPG)**, which involves the physiological measurement of penile tumescence (erection) during the presentation of various stimuli, such as descriptions of sexual activity. Sexual attraction is usually inferred from the amount of arousal in response to deviant stimuli (e.g., stories about sexual abuse of a child, rape) relative to non-deviant stimuli (e.g., stories about consenting sex between adults).

Researchers and clinicians have also attempted to assess deviant sexual interests with a variety of other methods. Unobtrusively recorded viewing time has become one of the most commonly used methods for assessing sexual interest in children over the last two decades (McGrath et al. 2010). The basic viewing time procedure involves showing a series of pictures depicting girls, boys, women, or men (typically in swimsuits). Respondents may be asked to examine the pictures in preparation for questions they will be asked later, or asked to rate each picture on various attributes (e.g., level of physical attractiveness). Respondents are instructed to proceed to the next picture at their own pace, and are presumably unaware that the key dependent measure is the amount of time they spend looking at each picture. Self-report questionnaires have also been used to gather information about sexual thoughts, fantasies, or urges involving children or non-consenting adults (e.g., Banse, Schmidt, and Clarbour 2010; Laws, Hanson, Osborn, and Greenbaum 2000). Finally, sexual offence history information (any male child victims, more than one child victim, any victims aged 11 or younger, and any unrelated [non-familial] child victims) has also been used to assess sexual interest in children (Screening Scale for Pedophilic Interest; SSPI; Seto and Lalumière 2001).

With regard to the validity of these methods, viewing time and self-report measures are correlated with each other and with independent indicators of sexual interest in children, such as sexual offending against children, the SSPI, and PPG (e.g., Abel et al. 2004; Babchishin, Nunes, and Kessous 2014; Banse et al. 2010; Gress 2005; Harris et al. 1996; Letourneau 2002; Mokros et al. 2012; Schmidt et al. 2014). The SSPI is also correlated with PPG (Canales, Olver, and Wong 2009; Seto and Lalumière 2001; Seto, Harris, Rice, and Barbaree 2004; Seto, Murphy, Page, and Ennis 2003). Although viewing time, self-report, and the SSPI appear to be promising methods for assessing deviant sexual interests, the strength of the observed correlations with each other and with PPG suggests that these methods may not assess exactly the same thing. This presents some important and challenging questions for future research: Do these methods really assess deviant sexual interests or just something(s) correlated with deviant sexual interests? Does each method provide independent or redundant information about deviant sexual interests compared to PPG and other methods? Can these methods be used interchangeably and as substitutes for PPG?

Perhaps not surprisingly, one of the strongest and most consistent correlates and predictors of sexual offending is deviant sexual interests. On average, sexual offenders against children show greater sexual interest in children than do non-sexual offenders and non-offenders (e.g., Harris, Rice, Quinsey, and Chaplin 1996; Seto 2001; Seto and Lalumière 2010). Similarly, meta-analytic reviews indicate that, on average, rapists show greater sexual interest in rape than non-rapists (e.g., Lalumière and Quinsey 1994; Lalumière et al. 2003). Sexual interest in children is also one of the strongest predictors of sexual recidivism, but sexual interest in rape has not been found to consistently predict sexual recidivism (Hanson and Morton-Bourgon 2004). The available evidence is consistent with the seemingly obvious notion that sexual interest in children plays a causal role in sexual offending, but if falls short of demonstrating a causal relationship. The evidence is less clear regarding the role of sexual interest in rape.

General Antisociality

General antisociality in this context refers to personality and behavioural characteristics that are not specific to sexual offending. Some examples of general antisociality are non-sexual criminal behaviour, rule breaking, non-sexual aggressiveness, anger, hostility, impulsivity, antisocial personality disorder, and psychopathic traits. The available evidence generally indicates the following rank order of groups from most to least antisociality: non-sexual offenders and sexual offenders against adults are tied for most antisociality, sexual offenders against children are less antisocial than sexual offenders against adults and non-sexual offenders, and non-offenders are the least antisocial (e.g., Porter et al. 2000; Seto and Lalumière 2010; Whitaker et al. 2008). General antisociality is also one of the strongest predictors of sexual recidivism (Hanson and Morton-Bourgon 2004).

There is convincing evidence that deviant sexual interest and psychopathy interact in predicting sexual recidivism (e.g., Harris et al. 2003; Hawes, Boccaccini, and Murrie 2013; Olver and Wong 2006; Rice and Harris 1997). So although sexual deviance and psychopathy are generally associated with increased sexual recidivism on their own, sexual offenders with both characteristics are much more likely to sexually recidivate than sexual offenders with only one.

Although the available evidence does not demonstrate a causal relationship, it is consistent with the notion that general antisociality plays a causal role in sexual offending. It would be consistent with some theoretical assertions and intuition if antisocial features such as lower self-regulation, callousness, and a tendency to break formal rules increased the likelihood of sexual offending—especially when antisociality is accompanied by deviant sexual interests.

Childhood Sexual Abuse

Many theories posit that sexual victimization in childhood plays an important role in later sexual offending. Studies generally find an association between childhood sexual abuse and sexual offending. More specifically, sexual offenders have been found to have experienced more childhood sexual abuse than non-sexual offenders (i.e., people who have committed offences other than sexual offences) and non-offenders (i.e., people who have not committed any offences) (Jespersen, Lalumière, and Seto 2009; Seto and Lalumière 2010; Whitaker et al. 2008). Even when information beyond self-reports was used to document childhood sexual victimization, sexual offenders were still found to have higher rates of victimization than non-sexual offenders (Jespersen et al. 2009; Seto and Lalumière 2010). These analyses compared reports of abuse based on self-reports with information gained in part from other sources, such as reports from parents or from child protection agency files. Thus the higher rates cannot be accounted for simply by potential biases associated with self-report. For example, we might expect some sexual offenders to falsely report childhood sexual abuse after being caught for their offences in an attempt to gain sympathy or to excuse their offending (Hilton 1993).

There is also evidence that childhood sexual abuse is associated with sexual offending against children and pedophilia. Sexual offenders against children have higher rates of childhood sexual victimization than sexual offenders against adults (Jespersen et al. 2009; Nunes, Hermann, Malcom, and Lavoie 2013; Seto and Lalumière 2010; Whitaker et al. 2008). Sexual offenders who were sexually abused as children are more sexually interested in children than those who were not sexually abused, as measured by a wide range of indicators of pedophilia such as offending against many child victims, male child victims, younger victims, many prior sexual offences against children, pedophilia diagnosis, and phallometrically assessed preferential sexual arousal to children (e.g., Freund and Kuban 1994; Freund, Watson, and Dickey 1990; Lee, Jackson, Pattison, and Ward 2002; Nunes et al. 2013).

In contrast to the evidence summarized above, longitudinal studies on predictors of recidivism generally have not found that sexual offenders who were sexually abused as children are more likely to persist with their sexual offending than sexual offenders who were not sexually abused as children (Hanson and Morton-Bourgon 2004). It is not obvious how to reconcile the seemingly inconsistent results from these different approaches. At this point, the available evidence is consistent with at least two possible interpretations: 1) childhood sexual victimization may increase one's likelihood of sexually offending, but it may not increase one's likelihood of sexually reoffending after being caught, or 2) childhood sexual victimization may be just a correlate rather than a causal factor in sexual offending. More rigorous and creative research is needed to get a better sense of which of these or other interpretations may be correct.

Beliefs Regarding Sexual Offending

Beliefs regarding sexual offending are thought to play a causal role in sexual offending (e.g., Abel, Becker, and Cunningham-Rathner 1984; Gannon, Ward, and Collie 2007; Hall and Hirschman 1991, 1992; Malamuth 2003; Marshall and Barbaree 1990; Ward and Siegert 2002) and accordingly are considered in some sexual offender risk assessments (Olver, Wong, Nicholaichuk, and Gordon 2007) and are a major focus in most treatment programs in North America (McGrath et al. 2010). Considerable attention in research and practice has been directed to a vague set of beliefs referred to as cognitive distortions or **rape myths**, which have been conceptualized as beliefs that condone, justify, excuse, minimize, rationalize, or otherwise support sexual offending.

Empirically, sexually aggressive men—including sexual offenders—generally show greater endorsement of cognitive distortions and rape myths than men who are not sexually aggressive (e.g., Bumby 1996; Mann, Webster, Wakeling, and Marshall 2007; Murnen, Wright, and Kaluzny 2002; Whitaker et al. 2008), and cognitive distortions can predict sexual recidivism (Helmus, Hanson, Babchishin, and Mann 2013). There is also emerging evidence that evaluation of rape (e.g., rape is negative vs. positive) is associated with sexually aggressive behaviour, that evaluation of rape may be distinct from cognitive distortions regarding rape, and that both evaluation and cognitive distortions may be independently associated with sexually aggressive behaviour (Nunes, Hermann, and Ratcliffe 2014; Nunes, Hermann, White, Pettersen, and Bumby 2016).

Although there does seem to be an association between various beliefs and sexual offending, researchers have not yet tested whether such beliefs actually influence sexual offending. However, correlational studies have generally not found the expected link between change on measures of cognitive distortions and recidivism (Barnett et al. 2013; Beggs and Grace 2011; Hudson et al. 2002; Nunes et al. 2014; Wakeling, Beech, and Freemantle 2013). Although we cannot infer causation from correlation, the absence of correlation casts doubt on the possibility of causation. If cognitive distortions and other beliefs are in fact dynamic causal risk factors for sexual recidivism, they should not only be predictive of recidivism and be changeable, but changes in beliefs should be related to changes in risk for recidivism (Andrews and Bonta 2010; Douglas and Skeem 2005; Harris and Rice 2003; Kraemer et al. 1997; Quinsey, Harris, Rice, and Cormier 2006; Seto 2008). This is a very important area for future research— ideally randomized experiments—because treatment will be more effective at reducing recidivism if it targets causes of sexual offending in treatment rather than factors that do not play a causal role in sexual offending (need principle).

Emotional Congruence with Children

Partly consistent with Finkelhor's model, researchers have generally found that emotional congruence with children is associated with sexual offending against children. McPhail, Hermann, and Nunes (2013) conducted a meta-analysis to synthesize the available relevant evidence. Their findings generally indicate the following rank order of groups from most to least emotional congruence with children: 1) sexual offenders against unrelated children—especially boys; 2) non-offenders and non-sexual offenders; and 3) sexual offenders against exclusively related children. McPhail and colleagues also found that emotional congruence predicted greater likelihood of sexual recidivism for sexual offenders against children with unrelated victims, but not for those with exclusively related victims. Although the available evidence does not demonstrate a causal relationship, it is consistent with the notion that emotional congruence with children plays a causal role in sexual offending against unrelated and male children. McPhail and colleagues speculated about how emotional congruence might influence sexual offending if there is in fact a causal relationship: "Perhaps high [emotional congruence with children] facilitates access to potential extrafamilial victims through physical proximity, but low [emotional congruence with children] facilitates offending against intrafamilial victims by making the familial relation less salient and bypassing incest avoidance mechanisms" (2013, p. 746). It will take creative and resourceful researchers to figure out ways to further explore whether emotional congruence with children actually does influence sexual offending and, if so, how.

ASSESSMENT APPROACHES AND EFFECTIVENESS

Contrary to what most people in the general public believe (e.g., Levenson, Brannon, Fortney, and Baker 2007), arrest or conviction for a new sexual offence following an initial sexual offence conviction is relatively rare. A large-scale meta-analysis indicates that over an average follow-up period of five to six years, the observed recidivism rates are 13.7 percent for sexual recidivism, 14.0 percent for non-sexual violent recidivism, 25.0 percent for any violent recidivism (sexual or non-sexual violent recidivism), and 36.9 percent for any recidivism (sexual, non-sexual violent, or non-violent recidivism) (Hanson and Morton-Bourgon 2004). These rates surely underestimate the actual rates of sexual reoffending given that many sexual offences are not reported to the police (Brennan and Taylor-Butts 2008). Nevertheless, they have important implications for managing sexual offenders. For example, if the majority of sexual offenders do not persist in sexual offending, then it is only the persistent minority that require extreme measures such as intensive treatment and supervision or long-term incarceration to prevent their potential recidivism. But how can you know in advance who will persist and who will desist? Luckily, there has been a lot of rigorous research on sexual offender risk assessment to help identify offenders who pose the greatest risk.

Several instruments have been developed to assess risk of recidivism among sexual offenders, including Static-99 (Hanson and Thornton 1999; 2000), RRASOR (Hanson 1997), Risk Matrix-2000-Sexual (Thornton et al. 2003), Sexual Violence Risk-20 (SVR-20; Boer, Hart, Kropp, and Webster 1997), Violence Risk Scale: Sex Offender version (VRS:SO; Wong, Olver, Nicholaichuk, and Gordon 2003), Stable-2007 (Hanson, Harris, et al. 2007), and Acute-2007 (Hanson, Harris, et al. 2007). Approaches to risk assessment can be categorized in a number of ways. Four key categories are described here: unstructured clinical judgment, empirical actuarial, mechanical, and structured professional judgment (Hanson and Morton-Bourgon 2009). **Unstructured clinical judgment** involves arriving at an estimate of risk based on the assessor's own idiosyncratic decisions about what factors to consider and how to combine those factors. In contrast, the empirical actuarial and mechanical instruments both follow explicit rules about what factors to consider and how to combine those factors to arrive at a final estimate of risk. However, two characteristics distinguish empirical actuarial from mechanical. For **empirical actuarial** instruments, 1) the selection and combination of items are derived from their observed statistical relationship with recidivism; and 2) tables linking scores to expected recidivism rates are provided. For **mechanical** instruments, the selection and combination of items are derived from theory or reviews of the empirical literature and no recidivism tables are provided. **Structured professional judgment** incorporates features of both unstructured clinical judgment and the actuarial approach; there are explicit guidelines for which factors to consider (although additional factors may also be considered), but the combination of those factors is left up to the discretion of the assessor. Hanson and Morton-Bourgon's (2009) meta-analysis revealed that, on average, all approaches are significantly accurate in predicting sexual recidivism. However, unstructured clinical judgment is the least accurate and empirical actuarial and mechanical instruments are the most accurate. The predictive accuracy of structured professional judgment fell between actuarial and unstructured clinical judgment.

Static-99 The **Static-99** (Hanson and Thornton 2000) is an empirical actuarial risk-assessment instrument designed to estimate risk of sexual recidivism among adult sexual offenders. It consists of 10 static items. **Static** refers to items that cannot potentially be changed through intervention. The items include young age at the time of the assessment, absence of long-term cohabitation (two years or longer) with a romantic partner, current and prior convictions for non-sexual violent offences, prior sexual offences, prior sentencing dates (i.e., number of separate occasions on which an offender has been sentenced for one or more offences of any kind), presence of convictions for non-contact sexual offences (e.g., indecent exposure), any unrelated victims versus exclusively related victims, any stranger victims (i.e., offender did not know victim for at least 24 hours prior to offence) versus exclusively known victims, and any male victims versus exclusively female victims. Examples of victims that would be considered related are daughters, sons, spouses, siblings, nieces, and nephews. In addition, step-relations are counted as related if the step-relationship started at least two years prior to the offence. Scores for the 10 items are summed to calculate a total score, which can range from 0 to 12. Higher scores indicate higher risk of recidivism.

The Static-99 has repeatedly demonstrated good predictive validity; that is, research indicates that it is a good predictor of sexual recidivism. The Static-99 is the most widely used sexual offender risk-assessment instrument and has received by far the most research attention. A meta-analysis by Hanson and Morton-Bourgon (2009) examined the predictive accuracy of various sexual offender risk-assessment instruments. On average, across 63 studies and over 20 000 sexual offenders, the Static-99 is one of the most accurate tools available for estimating risk of sexual recidivism.

What About Dynamic Risk Factors?

Although instruments like the Static-99 are invaluable for estimating the likelihood of sexual recidivism, they do not provide any information about how to reduce or manage offenders' risk beyond limiting opportunities for recidivism through preventative supervision and incarceration for higher-risk offenders. This is clear from looking at the items. They are all static factors. A sexual offender's score on the Static-99 can decrease if he gets older or lives with a romantic partner for two years or more. The scores for almost all the remaining items, however, will stay the same or worsen; for example, if he commits additional offences. So as a treatment provider, the Static-99 does not tell you what areas to address in treatment to reduce the offender's risk of sexual recidivism. Similarly, assessors cannot determine with the Static-99 if offenders' risk has decreased over time; for example, from the start of their prison sentence to the time they become eligible for parole. This is where dynamic risk factors come in. **Dynamic risk factors** are factors than can change over time, with such change related to reduced criminal behaviour.

Research on dynamic risk factors has lagged behind work on static risk factors. It is much easier to extract static factors from archival data for groups of sexual offenders that have already spent considerable time in the community than to prospectively assess potential dynamic risk factors and follow up groups of sexual offenders. Given the low base rate of detected sexual recidivism, large sample sizes and long follow-up periods (around five years) are required to adequately test the relationship between a potential dynamic risk factor and sexual recidivism. In addition, demonstrating that a given variable is truly a dynamic risk factor for sexual recidivism requires more evidence than static risk factors. Specifically, to demonstrate that a variable is truly a dynamic risk factor, it must not only be able to change, but changes on that variable must be related to changes in risk (Douglas and Skeem 2005). The putative dynamic variable must also add incrementally to the predictive accuracy achieved with static risk factors (Seto 2008). In the absence of evidence that change is related to recidivism, the alternate, more parsimonious, explanation that these putative dynamic factors are simply manifestations of underlying static characteristics cannot be ruled out. Thus the mere possibility that a variable can change does not necessarily make it a dynamic risk factor in any meaningful sense (e.g., observing and effecting change on it may have no impact on likelihood of recidivism). Despite these enormous challenges, assessment instruments that include potential dynamic risk factors for sexual recidivism have been developed. Two are described below.

Violence Risk Scale—Sexual Offender Version (VRS-SO) The VRS-SO (Wong et al. 2003) is an assessor-rated instrument consisting of 7 static items and 17 dynamic risk items and is designed to estimate risk of sexual recidivism, identify treatment targets, and assess change on the dynamic factors. The static items are similar to those in the Static-99. The dynamic items are: 1) sexually deviant lifestyle (hobbies, interests, work, or relationships involving sexually deviant behaviours); 2) sexual compulsivity (high sex drive and frequent sexual behaviours and thoughts); 3) premeditation and victim-grooming in sex offence; 4) interpersonal and emotional antisocial personality features; 5) cognitive distortions; 6) interpersonal physical or verbal aggression; 7) over- or under-control of emotions related to sex offending; 8) poor understanding of factors causing sex offending and unwillingness to talk or think about his or her sex offending; 9) substance abuse; 10) lack or rejection of positive supports, services, and plans in the community; 11) released to high-risk situations; 12) presence of a pre-offence cycle of interpersonal, situational, and personal factors; 13) impulsivity; 14) negative attitude or poor compliance with community supervision; 15) negative attitude or poor compliance with sex offender treatment; 16) deviant sexual interests; and 17) intimacy deficits. For dynamic items that are rated as problematic for a particular offender, the extent to which the offender has accepted and attempted to remediate those problems is assessed prior to treatment and again after treatment (or at other key points, such as when being considered for parole). Offenders' scores on the dynamic factors can increase or decrease depending on the amount and direction of change in their acceptance and remediation efforts for each factor.

The available evidence indicates that the VRS-SO is a good predictor of sexual recidivism, the static and dynamic factor scores independently predict sexual recidivism, and change in the dynamic factor scores predict sexual recidivism (Beggs and Grace 2011; Olver et al. 2014; Olver et al. 2007). Change in the dynamic factor scores has been found to significantly predict sexual recidivism even after controlling for pre-treatment scores in one study (Olver et al. 2007) but generally not in other studies (Beggs and Grace 2011; Olver et al. 2014). Taken together, the results are encouraging, but additional high-quality research is needed to determine the extent to which the VRS-SO actually does assess truly dynamic causal risk factors for sexual recidivism as defined above.

Estimate of Risk of Adolescent Sexual Offense Recidivism (ERASOR) The ERASOR (Worling and Curwen 2001) is a structured professional judgement tool designed to assess risk of sexual recidivism among youth aged 12 to 18 years using a 25-item checklist. Each item is rated as *present, possibly or partially present, not present,* or *unknown.* The ERASOR consists of 9 static and 16 putatively dynamic risk items:

- Deviant sexual interests (younger children, violence, or both)
- Obsessive sexual interests/preoccupation with sexual thoughts
- Attitudes supportive of sexual offending

Box 12.2

You Be the Assessor

Imagine you are a clinical forensic psychologist conducting a risk assessment on Arnold, who was described at the beginning of the chapter. Recall that Arnold is 24 years old and currently in prison for sexual offences against an 8-year-old boy and a 10-year-old girl. In addition to these index sexual offence convictions (i.e., the current or most recent offences), Arnold has four prior sexual offence convictions. The first two were for sexual offences committed on numerous occasions when he was 16 against a 5-year-old boy in the foster home in which they both lived. He was sentenced to probation for these offences. When Arnold was 18, he exposed himself to an 8-year-old boy in the restroom of a local park. He asked the boy to come into the bathroom stall with him. The boy ran away and told a group of adults. Arnold pleaded guilty to this offence and was sentenced to three months in prison. At 20, he sexually abused a 6-year-old girl in the restroom of her elementary school. He exposed himself and fondled the girl. He pleaded guilty and was sentenced to a year in prison.

Arnold's childhood was difficult. His father left his mother when he was two years old and was not involved in raising him. Arnold was put into foster care at age four because of extreme neglect and physical abuse by his mother. He was repeatedly sexually abused while in foster care. Arnold left high school at age 17 and began working for minimum wage on an assembly line in a factory. He has never been married, lived with a romantic partner, or had a long-term romantic relationship. He has no adult friends and likes to spend most of his free

time with children. He has a sexual preference for prepubescent boys, as indicated by his self-report and physiological testing (penile plethysmography (PPG)). Compared to other offenders in the prison, he possesses relatively few psychopathic traits and does not have any major mental disorders (e.g., schizophrenia). By all accounts, Arnold is a model inmate. He is respectful of staff and cooperative with supervision, assessment, and treatment. He has been very motivated regarding treatment. In addition to other programs, he participated in a pre-treatment program for sexual offenders when he began his sentence and subsequently participated in a moderate-intensity sexual offender program and a maintenance sexual offender program. He successfully completed all programs. He is very remorseful and takes full responsibility for his offences.

Arnold is eligible for parole. Use the information provided above to address the following risk assessment questions.

Questions

What is Arnold's risk of sexually reoffending if released (percent chance; low, moderate, or high)? What is the one thing that makes you most concerned that Arnold will sexually reoffend if released? What is the one thing that makes you most confident that Arnold will not sexually reoffend if released? Would you recommend Arnold be released on parole? Why or why not? If paroled, what conditions would you recommend (e.g., restrictions on activities and movement, requirements for meeting with parole officer and psychologist, etc.)?

- Unwillingness to alter deviant sexual interests/attitudes
- Ever sexually assaulted two or more victims
- Prior adult sanctions for sexual assault(s)

- Threats of, or use of, violence/weapons during sexual offence
- Ever sexually assaulted a child
- Ever sexually assaulted a stranger
- Indiscriminate choice of victims
- Ever sexually assaulted a male victim (applicable only for male offenders)
- Diverse sexual-assault behaviours
- Antisocial interpersonal orientation
- Lack of intimate peer relationships/social isolation
- Negative peer associations and influences
- Interpersonal aggression
- Recent escalation in anger or negative affect
- Poor self-regulation of affect and behaviour
- High-stress family environment
- Problematic parent–offender relationships/parental rejection
- Parent(s) not supporting sexual-offence-specific assessment/treatment
- Environment supporting opportunities to reoffend sexually
- No development or practice of realistic prevention plans/strategies
- Incomplete sexual-offence-specific treatment

A recent meta-analysis indicates that the ERASOR is a good predictor of sexual recidivism (Viljoen, Mordell, and Beneteau 2012), but researchers have not yet examined whether the putatively dynamic risk factors meet the criteria outlined above for dynamic causal risk factors.

Consider the questions regarding sexual-offender risk assessment in the You Be the Assessor box. Try to apply information we have reviewed about risk assessment and factors associated with sexual offending.

TREATMENT APPROACHES AND EFFECTIVENESS

WE HAVE SEEN THAT SEXUAL RECIDIVISM RATES ARE GENERALLY LOW, BUT SOME characteristics are associated with increased rates of sexual recidivism, and by combining these characteristics into risk-assessment instruments it is possible to distinguish sexual offenders at the highest risk to sexually recidivate from those who are at lower risk. The community is especially concerned about the management of risk posed by sexual offenders. Horrific but infrequent sexual offences, often involving the abduction, sexual assault, and murder of children, understandably elicit fear and outrage from the public and demands for harsher penalties and closer monitoring of sexual offenders in the community (e.g., Levenson et al. 2007). The response from the criminal justice system is often to enact extraordinary measures specific to sexual offenders, such as community notification and sexual offender registries. **Community notification** involves informing the public that a sexual offender is being released to a particular city or neighbourhood. These notifications increasingly utilize the Internet to disseminate information about released sexual offenders. Although such notifications in Canada are reserved for offenders judged to be high risk and the information is limited (e.g., offender's name, photograph, and offence description), some states in the United States are less selective and provide more information, such as home addresses, telephone numbers, and employment locations (Petrunik, Murphy, and Fedoroff 2009). **Sex offender registries** require sexual offenders to register with the police upon release, check in regularly (e.g., once a year), and to maintain current information about their address (Murphy, Fedoroff, and Martineau 2009). In Canada, this information is accessible only by the police, but in some states, personal details about offenders are accessible by the public (Harris, Levenson, and Ackerman 2014; Murphy et al. 2009).

Despite much public support of extreme (and expensive) measures for sexual offenders (e.g., Levenson, Brannon, Fortney, and Baker 2007), the available evidence generally does not indicate that they achieve their intended goal of reducing recidivism (e.g., Freeman 2012; Sandler, Freeman, and Socia 2008; Zevitz 2006). In fact, public registries and community notification may have unintended negative effects on sexual offenders that may hinder their safe reintegration into the community, such as losing employment, being threatened or harassed by neighbours, having their property damaged, being forced to move from their residences, and being physically assaulted or injured (Lasher and McGrath 2012; Levenson, D'Amora, and Hern 2007).

Harsher prison sentencing is another common demand from the public (Levenson, Brannon, et al. 2007). Although incarcerating sexual offenders obviously limits opportunity for sexual offending while incarcerated, indefinite incarceration of all sexual offenders is not a realistic option. As discussed earlier, the majority of sexual offenders do not return to the criminal justice system for another sexual offence. Thus incarcerating all sexual offenders in the name of preventing sexual recidivism would be an unacceptable use of scarce resources and unfairly restrict the liberty of the majority of sexual offenders. Currently, most sexual offenders do not receive indefinite sentences and are released to the community at some point. Does incarceration deter sexual offenders from recidivating once they have been released? An intuitive expectation is that receiving a prison sentence, especially a long sentence, would deter an offender from sexually recidivating once released back into the community. Prisons are generally not the greatest places for sexual offenders and you would think the threat of returning to that environment would be enough to curb any behaviour. However, as with general criminal behaviour (Gendreau, Goggin, and Cullen 1999; Smith, Goggin, and Gendreau 2002) (see Chapter 4 for a full discussion), the available evidence generally does not support the effectiveness of prison as a deterrent of post-release sexual recidivism (Hanson and Bussière 1998; Nunes et al. 2007). Although incarceration does not seem to achieve the goal of specific deterrence, it is effective for incapacitating offenders who pose an unacceptably high risk of sexual recidivism.

So if incarceration and other punitive measures do not reduce reoffending among sexual offenders, what else can be done? Treatment designed to target putative dynamic risk factors is an obvious option. Treatment of sexual offenders varies widely and can take a number of different approaches.

Treatment Approaches

Pharmacological Treatment Pharmacological treatments generally reduce sex drive (e.g., desire, arousal). This is an obvious target given the sexual nature of offending and evidence that places **sexual deviancy** among the top predictors of sexual recidivism. A number of drugs have been used in this sort of treatment (Seto 2008). The most common are antiandrogens, selective serotonin reuptake inhibitors (SSRIs), and gonadotropin releasing hormone (GnRH) agonists. Antiandrogens like cyproterone acetate (CPA) and medroxyprogesterone acetate (MPA) reduce circulating testosterone. GnRH agonists like leuprolide acetate also reduce testosterone. SSRIs like buspirone, fluoxetine, and sertraline inhibit the binding of serotonin to receptors. A side effect of SSRIs is decreased sex drive, which makes them potentially useful for sexual offenders. Unfortunately, some of these medications have a number of unpleasant and sometimes serious side effects. For example, antiandrogens are associated with the development of breasts and osteoporosis in men.

Behavioural Treatment Behavioural treatments attempt to reduce deviant sexual interests and, sometimes, to increase appropriate sexual interests. Some examples are aversion, covert sensitization, and masturbatory satiation. Aversion involves pairing deviant sexual stimuli or thoughts with aversive stimuli, such as unpleasant odours or pain (Laws, Meyer, and Holmen 1978; Marshall 1971; Quinsey, Bergersen, and Steinman 1976). For example, a person may be presented with deviant stimuli such as pictures of children or stories about sexual offending, while an unpleasant odour or ammonia is inhaled. The goal is to decrease deviant interests by developing an association between deviant stimuli and unpleasant stimuli. Covert sensitization (Callahan and Leitenberg 1973) pairs negative thoughts (e.g., potential consequences of sexual offending, such as prison, loss of family and friends, etc.) with deviant stimuli. In masturbatory satiation (Marshall and Lippens 1977), the person masturbates to an appropriate fantasy (i.e., consenting sex with adult partners) until orgasm. A short time after orgasm, the person resumes masturbating but this time to a deviant fantasy (e.g., sexual abuse of children). During the refractory period following orgasm, genital stimulation is generally not arousing and is boring or unpleasant for most men. The goal here is to increase appropriate interests by pairing pleasant stimulation and orgasm with appropriate fantasies and to reduce deviant interests by pairing unpleasant stimulation with deviant fantasies.

Cognitive-Behavioural Therapy As the name suggests, **cognitive-behavioural therapy (CBT)** combines elements of cognitive and behavioural treatments to address psychological problems and abnormal behaviour. Some of the main targets in many cognitive-behavioural sex-offender programs include beliefs regarding sexual offending, victim empathy, social skills, and self-management. The dominant approach in CBT programs for sexual offenders for over two decades was **relapse prevention (RP)**. In this case, relapse would be a new sexual offence (i.e., recidivism). Generally, the focus in RP is on addressing putative dynamic risk factors, identifying situational risk factors (e.g., high-risk situation), and developing ways to avoid or otherwise cope with these situational risk factors, with the ultimate goal being to avoid recidivating (Pithers 1990; Pithers, Marques, Gibat, and Marlatt 1983). A number of limitations of RP were identified, such as the poor fit of the RP model for many sexual offenders and the negative tone (e.g., Marshall et al. 2005; Ward and Gannon 2006), and support for the RP model began to waiver in the late 1990s. The **Good Lives Model** (Ward and Gannon 2006) has since replaced RP as the dominant approach in sexual offender treatment. The Good Lives Model is more positive and collaborative than RP. In addition to focusing on the usual risk-management issues, the goal is to help offenders identify and achieve healthy goals that promote psychological well-being. This is expected to increase the motivation of offenders to participate and engage in treatment, as well as reduce their likelihood of reoffending because they learn how to achieve fundamental human needs through prosocial means rather than through offending.

Hot Topics

Correctional Service Canada Correctional Programs for Sexual Offenders

Our colleagues at Correctional Service Canada (CSC) provided the following "insider's view" of their correctional programs for sexual offenders:

Guided by the risk principle and the risk-need-responsivity (RNR) model more generally, CSC provides correctional programs of differing intensity levels (moderate and high) within each of the principal program areas, including programs for sex offenders. Higher intensity programs are longer than moderate intensity programs in duration and generally provide offenders with more skills and opportunities for skills rehearsal. As part of a consistent continuum of care throughout the correctional process, CSC also provides institutional and/or community maintenance programs, which contribute to increasing program dosage when needed. Therefore, including the time spent in maintenance programs, high-risk and moderate-risk sex offenders

would spend, in multi-target sex offender programming, an average of 300 hours and 190 hours respectively.

In addition, the programs adhere to the Good Lives Model (GLM) principles across three domains: program objectives (approach goals [goods promotion] and avoidance goals [risk management]), program content (assessment and intervention) and program delivery.

The Integrated Correctional Program Model (ICPM) (described in Chapter 8) has a distinct program stream for sexual offenders. It follows the same principles as the general ICPM and the Correctional Program Officers (CPOs) take the same collaborative approach to reducing risk. Some of the main program targets for sexual offenders are problem solving, goal setting, cognitive restructuring, emotion management, and general and sexual self-regulation, on which offenders will work all the way through the correctional program continuum. Programs aim to address different risk factors using various techniques (e.g., self-monitoring, goal setting, thought stopping, mindfulness, social skills, etc.), including the FOCUS and CPR approaches (discussed in Chapter 8).

Phallometric assessment of deviant sexual interests is done as part of the initial assessment for some sexual offenders at the beginning of their prison sentence. If necessary, behavioural techniques are taught in the program to help offenders manage their sexual arousal and impulses and to develop appropriate fantasies. Some of these techniques are self-monitoring, thought stopping, distraction, thinking of consequences, covert sensitization, directed masturbation, masturbatory satiation, and verbal satiation (some of these techniques are described elsewhere in this chapter).

Now that we have examined some approaches to treatment of sexual offenders, try applying this information in the You Be the Therapist box.

Effectiveness

Does sexual offender treatment work? The most important issue regarding effectiveness is the extent to which treatment reduces sexual recidivism. Studies addressing this issue typically compare the recidivism rates of offenders who received the treatment to those who did not. Although this sounds very straightforward, there are a number of major challenges. First, as you already know, sexual recidivism rates are quite low. If you were running a treatment program, you would need to follow up with a large number of participants for about five years. A bigger problem is finding an adequate comparison group. Ideally, a randomized experiment would be conducted in which offenders would be randomly assigned to the treatment group or a no-treatment control group. Then when you

Box 12.3

You Be the Therapist

Imagine Arnold (described in the You Be the Assessor box) has just begun his current sentence and it is your job to provide treatment that will reduce his risk for sexual reoffending.

Questions

What would you target in treatment? How would you target it? How would you monitor Arnold's progress (i.e., how do you determine the extent to which Arnold has improved in the area targeted)? How would you try to increase and maintain Arnold's investment and commitment to treatment? Do you think any treatment could be effective at reducing Arnold's risk of sexually reoffending?

compare the rates of recidivism, you could be reasonably confident that any observed difference between treated and untreated groups was caused by the treatment rather than pre-existing differences between the groups. However, the general public would probably be outraged if treatment was purposely withheld from a group of sexual offenders so that researchers could determine if they are more likely to sexually reoffend than a group of treated sexual offenders. Very few, if any, governmental agencies would be willing to conduct such an experiment. However, some researchers have argued that withholding treatment from some sexual offenders to permit a strong test of a treatment's effects on recidivism is not unethical because there is not yet convincing evidence that treatment actually reduces sexual recidivism (e.g., Seto et al. 2008).

So, random assignment to a treatment and no-treatment group is not realistic in most cases. What about just comparing treated offenders to those who refused treatment, did not complete treatment, or for whom treatment was not available? Currently, most convicted sexual offenders do participate in treatment and are actively encouraged to do so (although participation is ultimately voluntary). Thus it is difficult to find a sufficient number of untreated sexual offenders. Even if such a group could be found, it is likely that they would differ prior to treatment on important variables related to treatment success and recidivism. For example, some researchers have compared treatment completers to treatment dropouts to test the effectiveness of treatment. Why is this a problem? Dropping out of treatment is associated with increased sexual recidivism (Hanson et al. 2002) and dropouts are more antisocial than completers (Nunes and Cortoni 2008). Given that dropouts are higher risk than completers to begin with, we would expect higher rates of sexual recidivism among the dropouts than completers even if treatment had no effect at all. Some researchers have compared treated offenders to offenders from an earlier time period when treatment was not offered. Although this is a large improvement over comparing completers with dropouts, it is still vulnerable to the possibility that the recidivism rates may differ between cohorts for reasons other than treatment, such as changes in reporting and arrest rates for sexual offences over time (Hanson, Broom, and Stephenson 2004). In addition, the treatment group typically contains only those offenders who agreed to participate, whereas the untreated cohort contains offenders who would have agreed to treatment had it been offered as well as those who would have refused or dropped out; this is yet another potentially important source of non-equivalence between groups (Rice and Harris 2003).

These challenges leave the findings open to different interpretations, which is why knowledgeable experts considering the same studies disagree about whether treatment works and what constitutes credible evidence of treatment effectiveness (Hanson et al. 2002; Marshall and Marshall 2007, 2008; Rice and Harris 2003; Seto et al. 2008). Nevertheless, when the findings from studies of varying credibility are combined in meta-analyses, significantly lower rates of sexual recidivism are found for the treated group compared to the untreated group (Hanson et al. 2002; Lösel and Schmucker 2005). In the most comprehensive meta-analysis of sexual offender treatment outcome studies to date, Lösel and Schmucker reviewed 69 treatment studies ($N = 22\ 181$) and found significantly lower rates of sexual (11.1 percent for treated versus 17.5 percent for comparison group), violent

(6.6 percent for treated versus 11.8 percent for comparison group), and general (22.4 percent for treated versus 32.5 percent for comparison group) recidivism among treated sexual offenders compared to untreated sexual offenders. Hanson, Bourgon, Helmus, and Hodgson (2009) examined whether sexual offender treatment programs adhering to the principles of risk, need, and responsivity (Andrews, Bonta, and Hoge 1990; see Chapter 4) would perform better than those not following these principles of effective correctional treatment. Hanson et al.'s (2009) meta-analysis revealed findings consistent with the general offender treatment literature. Specifically, greater differences in sexual recidivism between treated and untreated groups were found for programs that adhered to a greater number of the principles. Despite these encouraging findings, debate continues about whether the lower rates of recidivism associated with sexual offender treatment actually demonstrate that treatment is effective or are more parsimoniously attributed to alternate explanations.

FUTURE DIRECTIONS

INCREASING INTEREST IN DYNAMIC RISK FACTORS FOR SEXUAL RECIDIVISM IN clinical assessment and treatment has encouraged more research on the causes of sexual offending. To that end, some priority areas are 1) refinement of the conceptualization and measurement of constructs thought to contribute to sexual offending; 2) more creative and rigorous approaches to testing causal hypotheses, such as randomized experiments or statistically controlling for important covariates; 3) more research on sexual aggression in the general public; and 4) better integration of forensic/criminological research and lab-based research. This fundamental research will facilitate more applied research on risk-assessment instruments and treatment programs, which in turn will lead to practice and policy that can more effectively and efficiently reduce sexual offending.

SUMMARY

1. A significant minority of the population are victims of sexual offences. The vast majority of sexual offences are committed by male offenders. Both sexual offending and victimization are more common among younger people. Offenders and victims know each other (e.g., acquaintances, friends, family members) prior to the sexual offence in the majority of incidents. Sexual victimization is associated with a number of negative emotional reactions as well as physical and psychological problems. Contrary to public opinion, there is little evidence that sexual offences are on the rise in Canada.

2. Some paraphilias, such as pedophilia, can manifest as sexual offending. However, paraphilia and sexual offending are not synonymous. For example, one can be a pedophile but never commit a sexual offence against a child and one can commit a sexual offence against a child but not be a pedophile.

3. There is considerable overlap and convergence in most theories and models of the initiation of sexual offending. A number of factors likely combine and interact to cause sexual offending. It is generally difficult to conduct conclusive research to test these theoretical hypotheses about the causes of sexual offending, but the available evidence has identified correlates and predictors, such as sexual interest in children, general antisociality, and emotional congruence with children.

4. Sexual recidivism rates are generally low; relatively few sexual offenders are charged with new sexual offences after their initial conviction. Subgroups of sexual offenders who have higher rates of recidivism can be identified with risk-assessment instruments.

5. Researchers generally find lower recidivism rates among treated compared to untreated sexual offenders. Programs that follow the general principles of effective corrections are associated with larger differences in recidivism between treated and untreated groups. Although these findings are very encouraging, debate continues about whether the lower rates of recidivism associated with sexual offender treatment actually demonstrate that it is effective because the research methodology used in most studies leaves the results open to alternate interpretations. More creative and innovative research will move us closer to resolving these and other important questions about sexual offenders.

Discussion Questions

1. Consider the research reviewed on factors associated with sexual offending against adults or children. Is it consistent with the theories and models discussed? What is the nature of the relationship between these variables and sexual offending? Do you think these factors play a causal role in sexual offending or are they just correlates or even consequences of it? If causal, do you think their influence is direct or indirect? If indirect, what intervening variables might be involved and how?

2. What criteria must a variable meet to be a truly dynamic risk factor for sexual recidivism? If you were conducting research in this area, how would you go about demonstrating that a given variable is in fact a dynamic risk factor?

3. Imagine you are a forensic psychologist doing a risk assessment of a sexual offender for his upcoming parole hearing. If you had to consider only two factors in your assessment, what would they be? What approach to risk assessment would you use? Which risk-assessment instrument would you use? If challenged, how would you justify your decisions about risk factors, approaches, and instruments?

4. Imagine you are involved in program development and research at CSC. Your current assignment is to design a new sexual offender treatment program and evaluate its effectiveness. Given the research reviewed in this chapter, what would your program look like? What would you target in treatment? How would you evaluate whether the program was effective?

Chapter 13
Female Offenders

SALLY AND THE SEX TRADE

After years of living with a crack-addicted mother and an abusive stepfather, Sally Johnson left home in search of a better life on the eve of her thirteenth birthday. Alone in a coffee shop one week later with less than $10 in her pocket, a man named Sam bought her a warm meal. He drove an expensive car, wore nice clothes, and showed Sally warmth and kindness. Within a few months, she was working for Sam, selling her body for sex. The lifestyle was not her choice, but she knew it would only anger Sam if she openly discussed her reluctance. She also knew she would be severely beaten if she did not comply. With a sense of helplessness, Sally wondered if it might be easier to simply end her own life. Sam bought her nice clothes, flowers, and expensive dinners, especially after their fights, which often ended with swollen eyes and bruises. The drugs he provided made her numb—a real benefit while she was working, but she had reached a point of needing the drugs to survive.

Sally's official criminal record included minor assaults, theft, and drug trafficking. She made no apologies and was even proud of her survival strategies, believing it was okay to steal to survive or physically hurt another person if it meant getting money. After fifteen years of bouncing in and out of youth custody facilities and provincial jails, Sally eventually landed in the federal correctional system. She is now serving a life sentence for second degree murder. At age 28, she is ready to change. She knows the road ahead will be difficult given her profile—an abusive and unstable family background, grade eight education, no formal job training, drug addiction, and unhealthy relationship choices. But for the first time in her life, she is optimistic and has found her voice. She honestly believes she can learn new skills, beat her drug addiction, and—most importantly—that she is worth the investment.

Learning Objectives

1 Explore the nature and types of crime committed by girls and women.

2 Highlight similarities and differences between female and male offenders in terms of theory, assessment, and treatment.

3   Compare and contrast the strengths and weaknesses associated with gender neutral and gender-informed risk-assessment approaches.

4   Describe what gender-informed treatment programs look like and determine whether these programs achieve their desired effects.

5   Describe criticisms levied by feminist scholars against the existing correctional literature as it relates to female offenders.

INTRODUCTION

As will be illustrated throughout this chapter, Sally typifies the kind of female who has come into contact with the law. However, there are many pathways to the criminal justice system and "one size" definitely does not fit all. While there are young women who initially turn to crime as a result of a maladaptive family upbringing, there are also girls and women who end up in the criminal justice system predominantly because of other factors such as substance abuse and criminal friends. Thus, not surprisingly, the factors that place girls and women at risk for future criminal conduct are multifaceted.

In this chapter, we begin by reviewing why scholars and correctional agencies have historically paid little attention to female offenders. Next, we explore the nature and types of crimes that females commit and explore whether the female violent crime rate has been increasing in recent years. We also discuss the similarities and differences between female and male offenders from both theoretical and practical perspectives. Gender-neutral and gender-informed risk-assessment approaches for girls and women will be presented as well as existing challenges and controversies surrounding their use. We review the need for gender-informed treatment, describe what some of these programs look like, and discuss whether they achieve their desired outcomes. Throughout the chapter, similarities and differences between youth female and adult female offenders, as well as male and female offenders, are highlighted as much as possible.

CONTEXT

Cesare Lombroso (1835–1909), an Italian physician and psychiatrist, was the first individual to study criminal behaviour using traditional scientific methods. Lombroso's *L'uomo Delinquente (Criminal Man)* was published in 1876 (Volume 1). Volumes 2 through 5 followed almost 20 years later but were not translated into English until 1911. Lombroso also wrote about female criminal behaviour. He published *La Donna Delinquente (The Female Offender)* in Italian in 1893 with his research assistant, Guglielmo Ferrero. It was first translated into English in 1895, but Rafter and Gibson published the most recent and most accurate translation in 2004.

Lombroso's account of female criminal conduct was unequivocally sexist and overly focused on biology and sexuality relative to his explanation of male criminal conduct. Nonetheless, he was the first individual to systematically study female offending using traditional scientific methods. Although a few post-Lombrosian researchers (e.g., Thomas 1923; Pollack 1950) continued to write about female criminality, like their predecessor, their explanations were inherently sexist—females committed crime because of faulty internal mechanisms of a biological and/or sexual nature. In stark contrast, the rest of the criminological world was focused on explaining male criminality. Moreover, criminological explanations of male crime emphasized external or environmental causes, including lower social class origins and structural inequality such as Merton's theory of social structure and anomie (1938). Typically, these theories either explicitly ignored female offenders (e.g., Hirschi 1969) or implicitly assumed through omission that the theories would generalize to girls and women.

It wasn't until 1975 that researchers again turned their attention to female offenders. But unlike their predecessors, these scholars—Rita Simon (author of *Women and Crime*, 1975) and Freda Adler (author of *Sisters in Crime*, 1975) were women. They sought to understand female criminality through the lens of **feminism**. Since the writings of Adler and Simon, scholarly interest in female criminal conduct has flourished, largely due to vocal feminist advocates who continually pose the question, "What about girls and women?"

DEFINITIONS

THE TERM *FEMALE OFFENDER* REQUIRES LITTLE EXPLANATION—IN SHORT, THE TERM female offender is reserved for girls (age 12 to 17) and women (18+) who have committed crime as outlined in the *Criminal Code* of Canada. It doesn't matter whether or not the justice system detected the crime, or how serious or minor the crime may have been. Lastly, as we learned in Chapter 5 (Adolescent Offenders), youth under the age of 12 are not subject to criminal prosecution in Canada. Thus, our definition precludes girls who have committed crimes under the age of 11.

WHY DO WE CARE?
Girls, Women, and Correctional Sanctions

According to the best available data, almost 21 000 Canadian youth were found guilty of one or more crimes and were admitted to custody or community services (e.g., probation) between April 1, 2013 and March 31, 2014. Importantly, female youth accounted for 23 percent of these admissions. It is noteworthy that these figures have remained relatively constant during the last five years (Statistics Canada 2015e).

Within the same timeframe, approximately 330 000 adults were found guilty of one or more crimes and were subsequently admitted to custody or community services. Similar to their youthful counterparts, women account for a relatively small proportion of sentenced adult offenders. Specifically, women accounted for 20 percent of community-related sentences such as probation, 13 percent of provincial custody admissions, and 6 percent of federal custody admissions (Statistics Canada 2015a, 2015b, 2015c).

There are two key messages to take away from this section. First, girls and women account for a small minority of admissions to correctional services in Canada. Second, the very fact that the male offender population eclipses the female offender population necessitates that we pay close attention to justice-involved girls and women. Otherwise, distinct gender differences will ultimately be overshadowed.

Prevalence and Nature of Female-Perpetrated Crime

In 2009, approximately 23 percent of people accused of a *Criminal Code* offence in Canada were female (Hotton Mahony 2011). The typical female offender in Canada has probably shoplifted small items, knowingly written a bad cheque, failed to appear in court, or committed a very minor assault that did not physically hurt the victim (Hotton Mahony 2011). Countless studies have repeatedly demonstrated that compared to boys and men, girls and women commit substantially less crime, particularly less violent and less serious crime (Belknap 2007; Blanchette and Brown 2006; Kong and AuCoin 2008). This fact holds true regardless of who published the study, or what methodological approach was adopted (Blanchette and Brown 2006).

It should come as no surprise that males also markedly outnumber females in all types of non-violent crimes in Canada. However, the size of this gender gap does vary as a function of the crime. For example, in the realm of property crimes, males commit 87 percent of break-and-enters and motor vehicle thefts. In contrast, females account for a greater share of theft and fraud related crimes (66 percent committed by males, 34 percent by females). However, there is one crime category that does not appear to discriminate on

Most female offenders commit non-violent property crimes such as fraud and theft.

the basis of gender—prostitution. In 2009, 3001 Canadians were accused of prostitution-related offenses, of whom 1351 were female (45 percent), and 1652 were male (55 percent) (Hotton Mahony 2011).

The gender gap in crime is even more pronounced in the context of violence. The most serious forms of violence—homicide, sexual assault, forcible confinement, robbery, and aggravated assaults—are, in essence, the purview of male offenders. In 2013, 452 individuals were accused of homicide in Canada. However, only 52 (or 11.5 percent) of the accused individuals were female. Once again, the key message is that female-perpetrated homicide is rare. Further, adolescent females who perpetrate homicide are even more rare. Only five girls (aged 12–17) were accused of homicide in Canada in 2013 (Statistics Canada 2014a). The official statistics also reveal a staggering gender disparity in sexual assault crimes. Female offenders accounted for a mere 2.4 percent of all sexual assault accusations in 2009 (Hotton Mahony 2011).

Interestingly, the gender gap in violent crime is less pronounced for less serious forms of violence. For example, while females accounted for 16 percent of all aggravated assaults in 2009, they accounted for a somewhat higher proportion of all minor assaults (25 percent). Similarly, when we define violent crime as making threatening or harassing phone calls, females account for a staggering 40 percent of all such violent crimes (Hotton Mahony 2011).

Unofficial data mirrors the official crime rate in some, but not all, respects. A self-report study of youth delinquency in Toronto revealed boys were twice as likely to report engaging in violent behaviour over their lifetime (30 percent) than girls (15 percent). However, the gender gap narrowed considerably when youth were asked about non-violent crimes against property (30 percent for boys versus 26 percent for girls) (Savoie 2007). A methodologically rigorous study conducted in New Zealand found similar trends. Terrie Moffitt and colleagues (Moffitt and Caspi 2001; Moffitt, Caspi, Rutter, and Silva 2001) examined the criminal trajectories of children (N = 1037, 52 percent male, 48 percent female) born in Dunedin, New Zealand, using a prospective cohort design. The study collected multiple sources of data at multiple time intervals from 91 percent of all children born between April 1972 and March 1973 in Dunedin (the study is ongoing). In sum, Moffitt and Caspi reported that the male-to-female ratio for individuals classified as "adolescent-limited" (i.e., criminal conduct begins during adolescence and is relatively minor and short-lived; see Chapter 6) was only 1.5:1. In contrast, the male-to-female ratio for individuals described as "life-course persistent" (i.e., antisocial conduct begins during childhood and is serious, diverse, and persistent) was considerably higher—10:1. In sum, the important take-home message is that official and unofficial reports confirm that males commit more crime than females and that the gender gap is particularly more pronounced in the realm of serious and violent offending.

Despite this evidence, a number of highly sensationalized cases have left the general public with the impression that female violence is out of control. On November 14, 1997, near Victoria, British Columbia, seven teenage girls (including Kelly Ellard, the primary offender who was 15 at the time) and one teenage boy swarmed, severely beat, and eventually drowned 14-year-old Reena Virk. On April 15, 2006, in Medicine Hat, Alberta, a 12-year-old girl and her 23-year-old boyfriend were charged (and eventually convicted) with murdering the girl's parents and her eight-year-old brother. The motivation for the crime allegedly stemmed from her parents' insistence that she end the relationship with her boyfriend. On March 20, 2009, a 17-year-old girl from Toronto was convicted of first-degree murder in the death of a 14-year-old girl. Prosecutors argued that she had counselled her teenage boyfriend to commit the homicide via instant text messaging; the alleged motivation was jealousy. The female offender was 15 at the time.

Females can and do commit acts of extreme violence. However, as discussed, these events are rare. We explore the question of whether females are becoming more violent in the Media Spotlight box.

Media Spotlight

Girls, Crime, and Violence: No Longer Sugar and Spice?

"Teen [15-year-old girl] guilty of 1st-degree murder in death of Stefanie Rengel, 14" (CBC News 2009)

"Medicine Hat man plotted with girlfriend [12 years old] to kill family" (CBC News 2008)

"Girl violence increasing in 'lethality,' experts say" (Proudfoot 2009)

See Jane hit: Why girls are growing more violent and what we can do about it (Gabarino 2007)

"Kailey Oliver-Machado, Ottawa teen [15 years old] prostitution ringleader gets 6½-year adult sentence" (CBC News 2014b)

Headlines and book titles such as these suggest that girls are becoming more violent and that the nature of their violence is becoming increasingly lethal. But is this really the case? Let's take a closer look at the evidence and determine if female violence is indeed on the rise.

In 2008, the Canadian Centre for Justice Statistics (CCJS) published a report entitled "Female Offenders in Canada," authored by Rebecca Kong and Kathy AuCoin. The report highlighted that "while still quite low compared to male youth, the rate of serious violent crime among female youth has more than doubled since 1986 growing from 60 per 100 000 to 132 per 100 000 in 2005" (Kong and AuCoin 2008). Kong and AuCoin's definition of serious violent crime was restricted to serious violence—manslaughter, attempted murder, sexual assault, major assault, or unlawfully causing bodily harm; discharging a firearm with intent; abduction of a person under 14; and robbery. On the surface, the results suggest that the serious violent crime rate (as measured by the number of individuals per 100 000 charged by police) increased for both genders, but that the increase for youthful females—120 percent from 1986 to 2005—outpaced that for youthful males (84 percent from 1986 to 2005). Similar yet more pronounced findings have also been reported in the United States (Synder and Sickmund 2006).

Three findings are immediately apparent. First, the "surge" in violent crime occurred primarily during the late 1980s and early 1990s. Specifically, from 1986 to 1993, the serious violent charge rate for females went from 60 per 100 000 people to 134 per 100 000, representing a 123 percent increase. Similarly, the corresponding male rate went from 352 per 100 000 people to 709 per 100 000, representing a smaller but still substantial increase of 101 percent. Second, with the exception of a few "blips," the serious violent crime rate for both genders has essentially stayed the same since 1993 and has actually declined since 2002. Lastly, regardless of the year, males were always charged with committing substantially more violent crime than females (e.g., 132 per 100 000 females charged in 2005 versus 649 per 100 000 males). So are girls becoming more violent? It depends on the starting point of your data (e.g., 1986 versus 1993).

The observed increase in female-perpetrated serious violent crime evidenced in official police data does not emerge when unofficial crime statistics are examined. American researchers (Steffensmeier, Schwartz, Zhong, and Ackerman 2005) conducted a sophisticated analytic comparison of official police arrest data obtained from the Uniform Crime Reports (UCR), with unofficial crime data from the National Crime Victimization Survey (NCVS) from 1980 to 2003. (As an aside, the NCVS is conducted annually and involves polling a large representative sample of American households about their experiences as victims of crime during the previous year, regardless of whether they had reported their experiences to the police.) Steffensmeier and colleagues reported that both the UCR and NCVS data revealed *no increase* in two of the most serious forms of violence—homicide and sexual assault. However, the UCR data did show a sharp increase in female-to-male arrests for criminal assault whereas the NCVS data did not. The authors argue that net-widening policy shifts such as zero-tolerance policies in public schools and mandatory arrests for domestic violence have artificially increased the likelihood of females being arrested for criminal assault. Thus it is argued that females are now being arrested for crimes that they weren't arrested for in the past and that these crimes involve physical attacks and/or threats of a marginal nature—a situation more characteristic of female- than male-perpetrated assault. In sum, Steffenesmeier et al. and various other prominent researchers (e.g., Chesney-Lind and Irwin 2008; Chesney-Lind and Paramore 2001; Doob and Sprott 1998; Gaarder and Belknap 2004; Holsinger, Belknap, and Sutherland 1999) have convincingly argued that girls are not becoming more violent, but changes in criminal justice practices and policies have artificially inflated female violence statistics.

Some researchers (Barron and Lacombe 2005; Luke 2008) have proposed the "moral panic hypothesis" as a means of explaining why society is seemingly so willing to believe that girls are becoming more violent. In brief, the hypothesis posits that rare yet highly sensationalized incidents of girl-perpetrated violence create panic or anxiety among the general populace. This panic leads to the belief that girls are "out of control" and need to be restrained using informal (e.g., suspensions for hurtful gossip at school) and formal mechanisms (e.g., more official policing). The moral panic hypothesis also argues that the underlying reason for mass societal anxiety is not because girls have become more violent, but because of the emergence of feminism: feminism has not only lead to greater equality in the workplace and increased "girl power," it has also eroded patriarchal norms and gender conformity, which in turn has allowed for the emergence of the "nasty girl."

Understanding the Context of Female-Perpetrated Crime

Not only do females commit less crime and less serious forms of crime than males, there is a long-standing hypothesis that the "offence gestalt"—the motivations, circumstances, and context of their crimes—differ markedly from that of their male counterparts (Steffensmeier and Allan 1996). Greenfeld and Snell (1999) examined the characteristics of all homicide offences that occurred between 1976 and 1997 in the United States—60 000 committed by females and 400 000 committed by males. Females were markedly more likely to have murdered an intimate partner or family member (60 percent) relative to their male counterparts (20 percent). In contrast, females were less likely to have murdered a stranger (1 in 14) versus males (1 in 4), but when females did commit non-familial homicide, there was some evidence that their motivations mirrored that of males—vindication and/or an attempt to restore personal integrity (Campbell 1984; Daly and Wilson 1988; Kruttschnitt 2001). When females murder an intimate partner, they often appear to do so in response to domestic violence, whereas males appear to be acting out of jealousy, infidelity, desertion, and control (Belknap 2001; Daly and Wilson 1988; Owen 2001).

Researchers have also tried to understand if there are different reasons for the commission of non-violent crimes by males and females. In short, this body of literature suggests that women commit property crime out of economic necessity (e.g., to feed and clothe children) (Belknap 2001; Campbell 2002; Carlen 1988; Chesney-Lind 1986; Gilfus 1992; Hunnicutt and Broidy 2004), and men commit property crime as a means of adventure and status enhancement (Campbell 2002). In sum, it would seem that there are both similarities and differences between males and females in the realm of offence gestalts and that women's violence appears to be more relational, directed against intimate partners.

METHODOLOGY
To Quantify or Qualify?

How do researchers study female offenders? In brief, there are two approaches: qualitative, which involves the analysis of words; and quantitative, which involves the analysis of numbers. For example, feminist pathways researchers often use qualitative interview techniques with incarcerated girls/women or self-identified sex-trade workers to understand female criminality. In doing so, they allow girls and women to tell their stories in their own voices. Conversely, applied correctional feminist researchers have relied on quantitative techniques such as meta-analyses and recidivism studies that do not necessarily involve interviews with girls and/or women. Historically, these approaches have not always yielded similar results. Contemporary thinking asserts that researchers should incorporate elements of both research strategies, an approach used by Dr. Kelley Blanchette, a prominent researcher in the field of women's corrections (see the Canadian Researcher Profile).

THEORIES OF FEMALE OFFENDING

FEMINIST CRITIQUES (E.G., BELKNAP 2001; COVINGTON AND BLOOM 2003; FEINMAN 1986; Leonard 1982; Morris 1987; Naffine 1987; Smart 1976, 1982) have underscored two crucial flaws in the study of female offenders. First, some feminist scholars have criticized early theories that predate the 1950's (e.g., Freud 1953; Lombroso and Ferrero 1895; Pollack 1950; Thomas 1923), for being sexist and inappropriately focused on female

Box 13.1

Canadian Researcher Profile Dr. Kelley Blanchette

Dr. Blanchette has published extensively in peer-reviewed and government journals. Her research has addressed a multitude of areas germane to women offenders, spanning the fields of risk assessment, security classification, and program development and evaluation. In 2007, she was the co-winner of the Significant Contribution Award from the Criminal Justice Section of the Canadian Psychological Association for her book *The Assessment and Treatment of Women Offenders: An Integrative Perspective.*

During her career, Dr. Blanchette was married and had two boys. She somehow finds time to supervise undergraduate and graduate students at Carleton University and is also an adjunct professor at Mount Royal University in Calgary. For fun, Dr. Blanchette is a recreational runner, attends book club meetings with friends, and is captain of a recreational volleyball team.

Dr. Blanchette worked for five years as Director General of the Women Offender Sector at Correctional Service Canada. This job represented a shift from researcher to correctional administrator, where she provided advice and leadership with regards to the development and implementation of policy and programming for the approximately 1000 female offenders under CSC's jurisdiction. Since April 2014, Dr. Blanchette has been working in the role of Director General, Mental Health. Given the extremely high prevalence of mental illness in prison populations, Dr. Blanchette will continue to have a profound effect on how Canada deals with federally sentenced women.

Courtesy of Dr. Kelley Blanchette

Dr. Kelley Blanchette

sexuality, biology, and psychology. In contrast, theories about male criminal conduct written before the 1950's emphasized factors outside of a male's control such as lower social class origins. Second, feminist scholars have aptly noted that the majority of traditional theories of criminal conduct have either ignored females completely or assumed generalizability across gender without female-specific empirical support.

As a result, female-centred theories have emerged in which gender is afforded preeminent status. Moreover, most female-centred theories posit that the onset, maintenance, and eventual desistence of female criminal conduct are different from that of their male counterparts (Steffensmeier and Allan 1996).

Feminist Pathways Perspective

A body of research collectively known as *feminist pathways research* (Belknap 2007) or more recently pathways theory (Belknap, 2015), emerged in the 1970s to explain female crime. Feminist pathways researchers use one-time qualitative interview techniques with incarcerated girls/women or self-identified sex-trade workers to ascertain pathways to delinquency. To date, 20 or more feminist pathways studies have concluded that aversive family environments (e.g., abuse) propel girls from their homes and schools and into the streets. This in turn leads to further victimization in the form of prostitution (forced or by "choice") and poor coping strategies such as drug use and "criminalized" survival strategies including robbery, fraud, and drug trafficking (Bloom, Owen, Rosenbaum, and Deschenes 2003; Chesney-Lind and Rodriguez 1983; Daly 1992, 1994; Gilfus 1992; Kruttschnitt 1996; Miller 1986; Owen 1998; Richie 1996; Silbert and Pines 1981; Simkins and Katz 2002). While this research underscores the pivotal role of childhood abuse and maltreatment, some feminist pathways researchers also highlight factors such as poor parental supervision, parental psychopathology (e.g., parental criminality, substance abuse), and economic marginalization (e.g., Arnold 1990; James and Meyerding 1977; Hunnicutt and Broidy 2004).

Although feminist pathways researchers have discovered much about female criminality, our understanding remains incomplete. Notwithstanding one British study (Carlen 1988) and a few Canadian studies (Fox and Sugar 1990; Shaw 1991), most feminist pathways research has been conducted on American samples and has used qualitative techniques. Researchers have not disaggregated data by age (girls versus women), thereby potentially masking potential developmental differences. Male comparison groups have also been noticeably absent, a methodological prerequisite in the quest for **gender specificity**. As others have noted (Blanchette and Brown 2006; Moretti, Odgers, and Jackson 2004; Odgers et al. 2007), a final limitation of the research is its emphasis of a unidimensional pathway to crime—the criminalized survivor pathway (see Daly 1992; Miller 1986 for exceptions)—that denies female heterogeneity in the form of multiple female offender pathways.

Personal, Interpersonal, and Community-Reinforcement (PIC–R) Theory

Recall from Chapter 3 that the PIC–R theory (Andrews and Bonta 2010) is a multidisciplinary perspective that integrates biological, sociological, cultural, familial, interpersonal, personal, and situational variables. Grounded heavily in social learning and self-control theory, PIC–R argues that individuals commit crime when the rewards for doing so exceed the costs. Various factors influence the balance of rewards and costs, ranging from rapidly changing factors found in the immediate situation (e.g., opportunity, intoxication) to background factors that tend to be more static or unchanging (e.g., political/economic/cultural influences). The theory organizes these factors along four dimensions: situational, personal, interpersonal, and community. Situational factors include opportunities/temptations, stressors (e.g., negative affect), facilitators (e.g., psychotic state), and disinhibitors (e.g., substance abuse). Personal factors include antisocial cognitions, history of antisocial behaviour, antisocial personality, and biological factors. Interpersonal factors include variables such as antisocial associates and family, and the community dimension encompasses factors such as living in a high-crime neighbourhood. Although each category differs as a function of temporal proximity to the immediate situation, each influences the chances that an individual will find him- or herself in a situation conducive to committing crime. Additionally, each category also determines whether an individual will develop an internal dialogue consistent with definitions favourable of criminal conduct (e.g., rewards exceed the costs) and consequently commit the criminal act.

PIC–R corresponds with sociological perspectives that suggest broad-based societal/structural factors are important, but only to the extent that they control the distribution of rewards and costs within a social system. Further, the theory is primarily concerned with explaining individual differences in criminal conduct. With this in mind, Andrews and Bonta (2010) identified which risk factors (derived from the empirical evidence) account for the greatest individual variation in criminal conduct.

Each risk factor has been assigned to one of three predictive accuracy levels. These **risk factors** were introduced in Chapter 1. The first and most powerful set includes: 1) antisocial cognitions (attitudes, beliefs, values that support criminal conduct); 2) antisocial associates; 3) a history of antisocial behaviour; and 4) antisocial personality (including indicators such as restless energy, adventurousness, impulsiveness, poor problem-solving skills, hostility, and callousness). Risk factors in the middle range include: 1) substance abuse; 2) marital/family factors; 3) poor school/employment achievement; and 4) inadequate leisure/recreation. Risk factors in the low range of predictive validity include: 1) lower-class origins; 2) low verbal intelligence; and 3) personal distress.

PIC–R is presented as a general theory that can account for individual differences in criminal conduct irrespective of gender, class, or ethnic origin. While gender is classified as a distal, personal variable that shapes both the person and the immediate situation, it is not central to the model. The applicability of PIC–R to female offenders has been both fully supported (Andrews and Bonta 2010) and challenged to some extent (Blanchette and Brown 2006). Ultimately, however, we need to carefully examine the evidence presented in the next section and use this evidence to form our own expert opinions about the merit of any theory of crime, be it PIC–R or the feminist pathways perspective.

FACTORS ASSOCIATED WITH FEMALE OFFENDING

SO FAR WE HAVE DESCRIBED THE PREVALENCE AND NATURE OF FEMALE CRIMINAL CONDUCT and highlighted contemporary theories used to explain why females engage in crime. In this section, we take a closer look at different risk factors proposed to be important in predicting female criminal conduct. As we shall see, although some of these risk factors are no different than those in other types of offending, some are indeed new. Can you tell the difference? We will also take a brief look at protective factors or strengths—factors that, in theory, reduce the risk of future reoffending, or at the very least are positive personal attributes that facilitate treatment engagement in some way.

Individual Risk Factors

Criminal History Criminal history is one of the strongest predictors of future criminal behaviour. Moreover, research indicates that individuals who 1) demonstrate general behavioural problems from an early age (e.g., truancy/expulsion from school, aggressive behaviour at home/school, stealing from parents), 2) commit crime frequently, and 3) evidence criminal versatility (i.e., commit a range of different crimes) are substantially more likely to commit future crime (Andrews and Bonta 2010; Gendreau, Goggin, and Smith 2002; Moffitt 1993).

Until recently, few researchers asked whether criminal history was an equally important predictor for female offenders. We know that female offenders on average are lower risk than their male counterparts (i.e., are less likely to criminally reoffend) (Brown and Motiuk 2005; Kong and AuCoin 2008; Public Safety Canada 2007). However, the evidence also indicates that criminal history variables predict equally well for both genders (Andrews et al. 2012; Hubbard and Pratt 2002; Green and Campbell 2006). But, more research is needed to address feminist concerns that a *"high risk"* female offender should not be equated with a high risk male offender, in part because females are less likely to reoffend violently.

Antisocial Personality and Impulsivity The construct of antisocial personality and impulsivity is multifaceted and complex. Some researchers equate it with psychopathy as measured by the Hare Psychopathy Checklist–Revised (PCL–R; Hare 2003). Others argue that antisocial personality/impulsivity should be operationalized more broadly (e.g., Andrews and Bonta 2010). Regardless, it is clear that psychopathy as measured by the PCL–R is a robust predictor of both general and violent recidivism among male offenders. In general, the research to date is mixed regarding its ability to predict recidivism among female offenders (Blanchette and Brown 2006; Coid, Yang, Ullrich, Roberts, et al. 2009; Edens, Campbell, and Weir 2007). For example, Stockdale, Olver and Wong (2010) found that the PCL measure was predictive of recidivism in adolescent female offenders, but not adult female offenders.

If we adopt Gottfredson and Hirschi's (1990) definition of antisocial personality as low self control—the tendency to pursue short-term, immediate gratification while ignoring long-term consequences—then the evidence suggests that antisociality is predictive of crime in both genders (Pratt and Cullen 2000). Despite evidence in favour of self-control theory, feminist scholars criticize this perspective for failing to assign a pre-eminent role to gender (e.g., Miller and Burack 1993).

Criminal Attitudes Criminal attitudes and/or antisocial cognitions are considered to be one of the "Central Eight" predictors of crime (Andrews and Bonta 2010). However, until recently, this conclusion has been based primarily on male or predominantly male samples. Research suggests that adult male offenders are more likely than their female counterparts to be identified as having a need in this domain (30 percent versus 14 percent) (Boe et al. 2003). Moreover, a growing body of research indicates that the global construct of criminal attitudes predicts crime equally well in both genders (Andrews et al.

2012; Brown and Motiuk 2005; Green and Campbell 2006; Rettinger and Andrews 2010; Van Voorhis, Wright, Salisbury, and Bauman 2010). However, it is important to note that some feminist scholars are strongly opposed to the inclusion of constructs like criminal attitudes and cognitions in treatment regimes. Why? It is argued that this practice only serves to individualize and pathologize female criminal conduct. Instead, we need to focus on the real problem—societal level crime-causing factors such as poverty, sexism, racism, and a system that wrongly criminalizes women's survival strategies (Pollack 2005).

Correctional programs that target criminal attitudes and cognitions in samples of female offenders have been associated with moderate reductions in criminal recidivism (Dowden and Andrews 1999). When Brown and Motiuk (2005) disaggregated the global construct of criminal attitudes, several gender differences emerged. Women who indicated that "marital/family holds no value" were more likely to recidivate than women who believed that marriage and family do have value. This indicator evidenced no relationship with recidivism for men. Research that continues to dissect the construct of criminal attitudes may find more important gender differences.

Poor Self-Efficacy/Poor Self-Esteem/Disempowerment Some correctional feminists argue that low self-esteem or poor self-efficacy (e.g., does not believe she can achieve a specific goal, like get a job) are important risk factors for female offenders (Bloom, Owen, and Covington 2003; Koons, Burrow, Morash, and Bynum 1997; Leeder 2004). In contrast, mainstream correctional researchers argue that self-esteem is not a risk factor for males nor females (Andrews and Bonta 2010). Although, mainstream correctional researchers do support the importance of enhancing specific forms of self-efficacy (e.g., increasing an offender's belief that she can acquire new prosocial skills through positive reinforcement and behavioural rehearsal) in correctional treatment (Gendreau, French, and Gionet 2004).

Quantitative research suggests that interventions that target self-esteem or those that are purely empowerment-based have no impact on reductions in recidivism (Dowden 2005; Dowden and Andrews 1999). However, more recently, VanVoorhis et al. (2010) found evidence that low self-esteem and low self-efficacy predicted criminal recidivism in a sample of women offenders. Perhaps the more interesting question is not whether future research will also find similar results but whether it would be more beneficial to recast self-esteem and related constructs as strengths rather than risk factors.

Poor Mental Health While most researchers agree that internalizing mental health problems such as anxiety, depression, and suicide attempts impact male and female offenders, there is debate about how these sorts of mental health problems (that in general do not predict criminal reoffending) should be incorporated into risk assessment and treatment planning (McCormick, Peterson-Badali, and Skilling 2015). Additionally, it is clear that female offenders are not only more likely to experience certain types of internalizing mental health problems (e.g., depression, self-injurious behaviour, suicide attempts), they are more likely to experience these issues co-morbidly (at the same time) than their male counterparts (Bloom, Owen, and Covington 2003; Johansson and Kempf-Leonard 2009; Johnson 2006; Wasserman, Mcreynolds, and Schwalbe 2010).

Traditionally, internalizing mental health variables have been conceptualized as responsivity factors—factors that can impede treatment rather than as risk factors and/or criminogenic needs (Andrews and Bonta 2010; Bonta, Blais and Wilson 2014). However, Van Voorhis, Salisbury, Wright, and Bauman (2008) found that depression and anxiety are predictive of crime in women. Again, more research is needed to clarify how certain mental health factors, like depression and anxiety, are either directly or indirectly related to criminal justice involvement and treatment outcomes. In any event, this is one area that feminist inspired researchers have championed.

Substance Abuse Researchers agree that substance abuse is a risk factor for all offenders—men, women, girls, and boys. Approximately 40 to 60 percent of female offenders have significant substance abuse problems (Boe et al. 2003; Brown and Motiuk 2005). Moreover, two meta-analyses have concluded that substance abuse predicts crime in both males and females (Dowden and Brown 2002; Green and Campbell 2006). Dowden and Brown's (2002) meta-analytic review revealed that, on average, a range of substance abuse risk factors (e.g., alcohol or drug problems, parental substance abuse) predicted future crime to the same degree in male and female offenders. However, more recently, evidence has emerged suggesting that substance abuse problems are more strongly related to criminal recidivism in females than males (Andrews et al. 2012)

Although substance abuse is relevant for both genders, irrespective of age, some gender differences have been noted. Dowden and Brown observed that the predictive strength of having a parent who abused substances was stronger for females than males. Similarly, research suggests that women maintain their drug use as a coping mechanism, whereas men do so because of peer pressure or pleasure (Inciardi, Lockwood, and Pottieger 1993). There is also some evidence that a woman's pathway to substance abuse differs from that of a man. Specifically, her substance abuse is likely to have already started before she commits any crime. In contrast, men are more likely to already be actively engaged in a criminal lifestyle before developing substance abuse problems (Johnson 2006).

Familial Risk Factors

Childhood Maltreatment Research indicates that girls and women are substantially more likely than boys and men to have experienced some form of childhood or adulthood maltreatment in the form of physical, sexual, or emotional abuse (23 to 85 percent for females; 6 to 14 percent for males) (Bloom et al. 2003; Harlow 1999; Task Force on Federally Sentenced Women 1990). Importantly, however, researchers have not conclusively determined if childhood maltreatment is in fact a **female-salient predictor** of future recidivism with some studies showing an effect (Green and Campbell 2006; Hubbard and Pratt 2002; Van Voorhis et al. 2008) and others not showing an effect (e.g., Andrews et al. 2008; Daigle, Cullen, and Wright 2007; Lowenkamp, Holsinger, and Latessa 2001). Thus, more research is needed to better under if the mechanisms through which childhood maltreatment may trigger criminal behaviour are indeed different for females. Regardless, it is clear that girls and women are more likely to have experienced childhood maltreatment and thus, at a very minimum, require trauma-informed services.

Negative Parental Factors In addition to childhood maltreatment, researchers agree that many different negative parental factors play a significant role in the onset and maintenance of crime in both genders. These factors include poor parental supervision, inconsistent or inappropriate use of discipline, parental substance abuse, and parental criminality (Piquero 2008; Thornberry and Krohn 2003; also see Chapter 5 for a general review). However, there is some speculation that girls may have a higher threshold before the cumulative effects of multiple risk factors take their toll. For example, it may be that while one or two risk factors are all that are needed to trigger behavioural problems in youthful boys, perhaps at least five risk factors are needed to trigger behavioural problems in youthful females. While intriguing, this hypothesis has yet to be confirmed (Hipwell and Loeber 2006). Also, there is some evidence that girls may be more negatively impacted by family conflict, in particular mother–daughter conflict (Hipwell and Loeber 2006). Interestingly, Dowden and Andrews' (1999) meta-analytic review of treatment programs targeting female offenders revealed that programs targeting family process variables yielded the largest reductions in recidivism (as did programs that targeted antisocial cognition). Thus, there is no doubt that poor family functioning is an important risk factor for youthful females.

Relational Risk Factors: Beyond Criminal Friends

Relationships with Criminal Friends Research shows that criminal friends is an important risk factor in both the onset of delinquency and the prediction of recidivism in both genders (Brown and Motiuk 2008; Hipwell and Loeber 2006; Hubbard and Pratt 2002). However, there is the belief that girls and women may be more likely to be influenced by criminal friends given that females experience more intimacy and loyalty in the context of relationships—regardless of whether the relationship is positive or negative (Hipwell and Loeber 2006). Importantly, we know that when treatment interventions target criminal peers, recidivism is less likely among female offenders (Dowden and Andrews 1999).

Negative Relationships with Intimate Partners A number of researchers have identified dysfunctional and negative relationships with intimate, criminal partners as problematic for women and girls (Bloom et al. 2003; Hipwell and Loeber 2006). Although further empirical validation is required, Benda's (2005) longitudinal study that examined a large number of boot-camp graduates in the United States revealed that women were more negatively impacted by criminally active romantic partners than their male counterparts. Similar conclusions have been reached in the adolescent literature (see Hipwell and Loeber 2006).

Community/Structural Risk Factors

Poor School Performance/Employment Difficulties Applied correctional feminists and gender neutral correctional researchers agree that inadequate schooling and employment difficulties are risk factors for both genders (Andrews and Bonta 2006; Bloom et al. 2003). Moreover, both genders appear to be lacking in education (52.6 percent of male offenders and 42.4 percent of female offenders have not completed Grade 10), and both genders evidence employment instability to the same degree (62.3 percent of male offenders; 54.5 percent of female offenders) (Brown and Motiuk 2005). There is some evidence that employment training opportunities are particularly beneficial to female offenders. Brown and Motiuk (2008) reported that while having participated in employment training programs in the past was a strong protective factor for female offenders upon release from prison, it had no protective influence for male offenders.

Poor Community Functioning Community functioning is a multidimensional construct that encompasses accommodation instability, criminogenic neighbourhoods, and poor use of leisure time. Several correctional feminist scholars have identified poor and unsafe housing as another risk factor for women (Bloom et al. 2003). Brown and Motiuk (2005) reported that 54 percent of women identified as having a considerable need in this domain were readmitted to prison over a one-year period versus only 17 percent of women who were identified as having an asset in this domain. However, similar readmission rates were also reported for their male offenders (23.8 percent rated "asset" returned to custody versus 55.9 percent rated "considerable need for improvement"). It would appear that community functioning is equally important for both genders; however, for women, the importance of unsafe housing merits inclusion.

Economic Marginalization and Patriarchy There is evidence that economic hardship may be a genuine female-salient risk factor (Andrews et al. 2008; Brown and Motiuk 2008; Farrington and Painter 2004; Holtfreter, Reisig and Morash 2004; Hunnicutt and Broidy 2004). A quantitative analysis conducted at the individual level demonstrated that poverty was related to self-reported re-arrest rates in a sample of female offenders (n = 134) in Oregon (Holtfreter et al. 2004). Using a methodologically rigorous design, Farrington and Painter (2004) reported that poverty indicators (e.g., low social class, low family income, poor housing) evidenced stronger predictive associations with criminal behaviour among a sample of sisters (n = 519) compared to their brothers (n = 494).

Assessing whether patriarchy—a social structure that values males over females and ultimately results in the oppression of girls and women—is directly related to crime is difficult. While some theorists argue that females internalize feelings of powerlessness and oppression that then lead to crime, others believe the general economic marginalization and oppression of females—via childhood abuse, domestic violence, and general inequality—are what force women and girls into crime (see Blanchette and Brown 2006 for a review).

Summary

In sum, a number of risk factors have been identified that predict both the onset and maintenance of delinquency and crime among girls and women. It is clear that many of these factors are equally important for both genders, and have long been hailed as "tried and true." However, now that we are actually looking for gender differences, interesting differences are starting to emerge. For example, family and substance abuse risk factors appear to be more important for females than for males. Regardless, the quest for determining whether or not females possess unique risk factors is only in its infancy.

PROTECTIVE FACTORS

As we learned in Chapters 4 and 5, the definition of what constitutes a protective factor is far from clear. Nonetheless, all researchers agree that "protective" factors are positive (e.g., youth has prosocial friends, prosocial hobbies, displays optimism) and that they either a) decrease the likelihood of recidivism among all offenders, regardless of risk level or b) have the potential to enhance treatment engagement. Interestingly, simply being female is a protective factor in and of itself (Moffitt and Caspi 2001; Department of Health and Human Services 2001). This is not surprising given that males account for the vast majority of crime, and that this gender gap is most pronounced at the far end of the crime severity scale—murder, sexual assault, aggravated assaults, armed robberies.

The more interesting question though is whether or not justice-involved females have different protective factors than justice-involved males. Very few studies have explicitly examined this question. Further, we really know very little about potential gender differences (if any) at the individual, peer, familial, or community level. However, Jones, Brown, Robinson, and Frey (2015) observed that male and female offenders do not differ in terms of the prevalence of protective factors. More interesting though, this study demonstrated that protective factors reduced recidivism in both low- and high-risk offenders, but the effects were slightly more pronounced among the high-risk offenders. These results were the same for both genders. As well, Leve and Chamberlain (2005) reported that just one positive friendship for a girl can buffer against high-risk behaviours.

ASSESSMENT APPROACHES AND EFFECTIVENESS

Predictions are made every day about whether someone will succeed in university, recover from depression, break rules while incarcerated, or commit a new crime upon release from prison. Three broad approaches have been used to make predictions about future crime committed inside or outside prison: 1) professional/clinical judgment; 2) structured professional judgment (SPJ); and 3) mathematical or statistically-based approaches.

Decision-makers who use professional judgment rely on their clinical expertise and professional discretion rather than an instrument to render decisions. Structured professional judgment methods tell decision makers which factors should be considered but still allow them to decide how those various factors should be combined and weighted to render a final classification decision (e.g., low, medium, or high risk). Mathematical and statistical approaches involve the use of instruments that not only indicate exactly which risk factors a decision maker must use, but also specify how these factors should be weighted and combined. Sometimes these approaches are called mechanical or actuarial methods. Each of the approaches results in a classification decision such as a prison security level or an estimate of the likelihood of recidivism.

Gender-Neutral Risk-Assessment Instruments

We use the term **gender-neutral** to describe risk-assessment devices that were originally crafted using samples comprised predominantly of male offenders and based on gender-neutral theories of crime but that are used on female offenders. Critics argue that "gender neutral" means "inherently male," hence these instruments are biased against females. Defenders respond that gender neutral means "it happens to work equally well with males and females." We will examine these conflicting perspectives.

Two of the most well-known and most researched risk-assessment tools are the Level of Service/Case Management Inventory (LS/CMI) (Andrews, Bonta, and Wormith 2004), used to assess adult offenders, and the Youth Level of Service/Case Management Inventory (YLS/CMI 2.0) (Hoge and Andrews 2011), used to assess youthful offenders. The LS/CMI and YLS/CMI 2.0 are risk/need-assessment protocols that measure eight risk factor domains: offence history, family circumstances or parenting, education or employment, peer relationships, substance abuse, leisure or recreation, personality or behaviour, and attitudes.

Table 13.1 illustrates the results of two recent meta-analytic reviews that examined the predictive ability of the Level of Service Inventory and its predecessors for males and females separately. Schwalbe (2008) focused specifically on the youth version, and Smith, Cullen, and Latessa (2009) focused on the adult version. Using the data presented in the first row of Table 13.1 (i.e., Schwalbe—girls), the results can be interpreted as follows. Four different correlation coefficients (i.e., see the column labelled "Number of Effect Sizes") were combined based on a total sample of 572 youthful female participants that yielded an average effect size of .35 (see column labelled "Average r with General Recidivism"). In this example, the 95 percent confidence interval ranged from .21 to .49. A 95 percent confidence interval simply means that we can be 95 percent sure (or confident) that the true average r value (or average effect size) ranges from .21 and .49. Because the confidence interval does not contain zero, we can safely conclude that the average r of .35 is statistically significant at the .05 level.

There are two important conclusions to take away from Table 13.1. First, although female-centred research is growing, there haven't been many studies devoted exclusively to female offenders, especially youthful females (see Olver, Stockdale, and Wormith (2009) for another meta-analytic review of risk assessment tools that disaggregated the

Table 13.1 Level of Service and Youth Level of Service/Case Management Inventory: The Predictive Meta-Analytic Evidence for Males and Females

Meta-Analysis	No. of Effect Sizes	No. of Participants	Average r with General Recidivism	95% Confidence Intervals
Schwalbe (2008)				
Girls	4	572	.35	.21–.49
Boys	5	2010	.31	not reported
Smith, Cullen, and Latessa (2009)				
All women	27	14 737	.35	.34–.37
Men versus women*				
Men	16	9250	.27	.25–.29
Women	16	33 616	.26	.24–.26

*Smith et al. also calculated the average r for a subset of studies that specifically collected data on both genders within the same study. It is argued that these approaches are methodologically more rigorous than studies based exclusively on one gender or the other.

Source: Schwalbe (2008); Smith, Culllen, and Latessa (2009).

results by gender). In the case of girls, while four effect sizes may seem like a lot, it is important to realize that an earlier meta-analysis examining the predictive validity of the LS/CMI and its various predecessors (e.g., the Level of Supervision Inventory–Revised; Andrews and Bonta 1995) for male offenders included 30 effect sizes based on 5846 offenders (Gendreau, Goggin, and Smith 2002). Second, the average effect sizes for both girls and women are comparable to what has been obtained for males, as evidenced in these meta-analyses and others (Gendreau et al. 2002; Olver et al. 2009). If we use predictive accuracy as our benchmark for considering whether inherently gender-neutral tools such as the LS/CMI can be used with females, the answer appears to be yes.

Criticisms of Gender-Neutral Instruments

One specific area that requires more attention is the extent to which the gendered pathway to crime impacts the validity of risk-assessment devices. Critics assert that tools such as the Level of Supervision Inventory–Revised (LSI–R, Andrews and Bonta 1995; the predecessor to the LS/CMI) are invalid for females primarily because they fail to take the hypothesized gendered pathway to crime into account (Covington 2003; Holtfreter and Morash 2003; see Hannah-Moffat 2004; Hardyman and Van Voorhis 2004; Holtfreter and Cupp 2007; Kendall 2004; and Maidment 2006 for additional criticisms). Relatedly, it is argued that gender-neutral tools such as the most recent versions of the YLS and LSI are missing key female specific risk/need factors such as financial stress, internalizing mental health symptomology, victimization histories, relationship dysfunction, and poor self-efficacy (VanVoorhis 2012). Reisig, Holtfreter, and Morash (2006) directly tested this concern by examining the predictive validity of the LSI–R in a sample of 235 American female offenders whom the researchers qualitatively classified into three groups: economically-motivated/male typical, gendered pathway, and unclassifiable. In sum, the LSI-R predicted recidivism for the "economically motivated" and "unclassifiable" group but not for the "gendered pathways" group.

It has also been argued that certain risk factors, while relevant to both genders, may be more important for females. There is ample evidence that family dysfunction, measured in a variety of ways such as poor parental supervision, inappropriate and inconsistent use of discipline, and abuse, contribute to criminal conduct in both genders (Green and Campbell 2006; Hubbard and Pratt 2002), but some researchers contend that girls have a lower (familial) risk threshold in that they are more vulnerable to family dysfunction. For example, let's assume we have a scale that measures family dysfunction, where a score of 1 represents no dysfunction and 10 represents extreme dysfunction. Now consider two youths—one female and one male—who both receive a score of 4 on this measure. If the familial risk threshold hypothesis is correct, the female youth (scored 4) would be considered at risk for future delinquency whereas her male counterpart (who also scored 4) would not. The male youth might hypothetically need to reach a higher threshold (such as a score of 6) before negative family dysfunction would elevate his criminal risk level. The evidence for this hypothesis is sparse and requires further validation (Hipwell and Loeber 2006). A reverse effect has been proposed in regards to criminal associates. It is hypothesized that the threshold is considerably less for boys than girls because girls have an internal protective mechanism (Mears, Ploeger, and Warr 1998).

Brown and Motiuk (2008) found that close to 45 percent of the yes/no risk indicators (e.g., drinks alcohol to excess, has impulsivity problems) that are part of the Correctional Service Canada's standardized intake assessment protocol were identified as either female-specific (predicted for women but not men) or female-salient (predicted for men and women but the magnitude of prediction was stronger for women). A number of male-specific and male-salient risk factors have also been identified. Benda (2005) also found evidence for gender specificity and salience. He reported that while being married was protective for men in that it reduced their chances of future reoffending, it was a risk factor for women. Similarly, Van Voorhis and colleagues (2010) have found that hypothesized female-specific need factors such as relationship dysfunction, parental stress, poor self-efficacy, and adult victimization predict criminal reoffending and prison misconducts among women offenders. Yet, such factors are not explicitly incorporated into the YLS or LS/CMI risk scoring algorithms. Thus, the evidence is mounting in support of gender-responsive methods.

Gender-Informed Risk Instrument

In response to criticisms, risk-assessment tools built from the ground up for girls and women are now emerging. Van Voorhis and colleagues (2008, 2010) developed the Women's Risk Need Assessment (WRNA) and a subsequent revision (the Revised

Table 13.2 Revised Women's Risk/Need Assessment Domains: Standalone Probation Version

Risk/Need Items:
- Criminal History
- Antisocial Friends
- Substance Abuse History
- Current Substance Abuse
- Depression
- Employment/Financial
- Housing Safety
- Anger
- Child Abuse
- Adult Abuse
- Parental Stress

Strength Items:
- Educational Assets
- Self-efficacy
- Family Support

Source: VanVoorhis, Bauman, and Brushett (2013a, 2013b).

WRNA) for convicted women either serving time in the community or in prison (Van-Voorhis, Bauman, and Brushett 2013a; 2013b). The WRNA measures gender-informed risk, need, and strength factors (see Table 13.2 for a list of revised WRNA domains). Importantly, shorter versions of the tool have also been developed for use in pre-trial settings (Van Voorhis and Gehring 2014) and to supplement existing gender neutral risk/ need tools such as the LSI/CMI. To date, the results are promising. The WRNA predicts prison misconducts and/or criminal recidivism (e.g., area under the curve (AUC) averaging .70). Importantly, the WRNA improves the predictive accuracy of the gender neutral LS/CMI among women offenders (Van Voorhis et al. 2013a; 2013b).

Canadian researchers have also developed two risk/need measures: one for girls—the Youth Assessment Screening Inventory for Girls (YASI-G) (Orbis Partners 2007c), and one for women—the Service Planning Inventory for Women (SPIn-W) (Orbis Partners 2007b). While predictive validity indices have yet to be investigated for the YASI-G, recently published findings in regards to the SPIn-W are very promising (Jones et al. 2015).

Blanchette and Taylor (2007) developed a gender-informed security reclassification tool specifically for **federally sentenced women** in Canada. This measure, the Security Reclassification Scale for Women (SRSW), is an actuarial tool designed to identify the most appropriate classification level for women that ensures placement in the least restrictive level of custody. This tool was designed with an initial pool of variables that were hypothesized to be salient for women, including child custody issues, family factors, self-injurious behaviour, and mental health factors. Additional variables include historical risk factors, program progress, motivation, and recent institutional behaviour.

The resultant SRSW has a range of 30, with higher scores suggesting higher security levels. It consists of nine items with reasonable reliability (see Table 13.3). Part of the validation process involved comparing the SRSW to clinical judgment (i.e., what security

Table 13.3 Security Reclassification Scale for Women

Security Reclassification Items

1. Correctional plan progress/motivation

2. Serious disciplinary convictions

3. Recorded incidents during review

4. Unlawfully at large from an unescorted temporary absence/work release or community supervision

5. Custody rating scale incident history

6. Pay grade

7. Segregation: danger to others during review

8. Number of successful ETAs during review

9. Regular prosocial family contact

Source: Blanchette and Taylor (2007).

level correctional workers would place a woman at based on structured professional judgment). The SRSW placed fewer women in maximum security and more women in minimum security than the professional judgment method. These findings demonstrate that this actuarial tool does not "over-classify" women relative to clinical judgment (i.e., it does not place more women at a higher security level than the professional judgment method). In fact, the SRSW does just the opposite—it "under-classifies" women by putting more in lower security settings when compared to the clinical judgment method.

Predictive accuracy rates for the raw SRSW score were high (AUC = .75) for the prediction of any institutional misconduct versus the clinical judgment method (AUC = .69). Upon revalidation, the tool demonstrates an acceptable AUC (.69) for the prediction of any institutional misconduct. The revalidation study again illustrated that professional decision-making actually works against women via over-classification (Gobèil and Blanchette 2007). Correctional Service Canada continues to research the SRSW with promising results (Thompson, McConnel and Paquin-Marseille (2013). See the Hot Topics box for more discussion about over-classification issues.

TREATMENT APPROACHES AND EFFECTIVENESS

Canadian Approaches

Until recently, most correctional treatment approaches for girls and women essentially mirrored male services or, conversely, promoted gender-stereotypes (e.g., hairdressing school) (Hannah-Moffat 2004). This has changed dramatically internationally as well as within Canada and the United States (see Bloom, Owen, and Covington 2003 for the American approach). In 1990, a Canadian Task Force Report titled "Creating Choices: Report of the Task Force on Federally Sentenced Women" generated five basic principles

Legal, Professional, and Ethical Issues: Are Women Being Over-Classified?

Classification instruments serve multiple functions. Not only do they assist correctional decision-makers in making security-level placements, they also assign offenders to risk probability levels. The outcome of these decisions can profoundly impact a person in terms of freedom of movement while in prison and when they are released. A number of feminist researchers have argued that classification and/or risk tools routinely applied to girls and women are inherently biased against females because they were originally developed on males (Brennan 1998; Farr 2000; Hardyman 2001; Hardyman and Van Voorhis 2004). The primary argument against these tools is that they over-classify for two primary reasons: 1) a high-risk female has a lower probability of recidivating (in general) compared to her high-risk male counterpart; and 2) a high-risk female is not the same as a high-risk male because she is substantially less likely to commit serious violent recidivism.

Evidence examining the over-classification hypothesis is inconclusive. Some research suggests that actuarial tools actually generate more liberal decisions in the sense that they are more favourable toward the offender (Austin 1983; Blanchette and Taylor 2007). However, given that we know girls and women rarely commit violence, the second component of the over-classification argument holds merit. More research is needed and developers of tools such as the LS/CMI are diligently investigating the issue. While it may appear that the solution is simple—adjust the cut-off scores such that a woman would require a much higher score than a man to be considered "high risk"—there may be serious ramifications that negatively impact subgroups of females such as Aboriginal women. Aboriginal offenders demonstrate higher rates of violence and recidivism relative to their non-Aboriginal counterparts (see Chapter 14). While the critics have raised important issues, potential solutions will require careful thought prior to implementation.

to guide programming for women: empowerment, meaningful and responsible choices, respect and dignity, supportive environment, and shared responsibility.

These principles remain in effect and continue to guide CSC. However, it is important to note that Canada's approach to corrections has not always been progressive and that we have advanced considerably since the first federal prison for women—The Prison for Women (P4W)—which opened its doors in Kingston, Ontario, in 1934. From the beginning, numerous investigations, commissions, and advocacy groups called for its closure. It was argued that the P4W was problematic because it was a maximum security environment that housed all women regardless of their security level, it forced women to be geographically separated from their families and support systems, the architecture of the building was inadequate, gender-informed programs were not provided, and culturally responsive programs for francophone and Aboriginal women were not available (CSC 2006)

Demolition of the stone security wall of the Prison for Women, March 10, 2008, Kingston, Ontario

In 1989, CSC established a Task Force on Federally Sentenced Women mandated to develop a comprehensive strategy for the treatment and management of federally sentenced women. Importantly, this Task Force was co-chaired by CSC and the Canadian Association of Elizabeth Fry Societies and included representation from diverse stakeholders including the government, correctional practitioners, Aboriginal organizations, and female offenders. The Task Force produced a report entitled, "Creating Choices" published in 1990. This lengthy report provided several recommendations aimed at improving the manner in which CSC manages women under its care. One of these recommendations included the closure of the P4W and the creation and subsequent opening of smaller, regional facilities and an Aboriginal healing lodge that could address the problems associated with the P4W.

Between 1995 and 2004, five new regional institutions and a healing lodge for women were opened across Canada. Unlike the P4W, these facilities embrace a community-living environment as recommended in "Creating Choices". Each facility is comprised of several stand-alone houses (up to 10 women live in each house) where the women are responsible for daily living needs such as cooking, cleaning, and laundry. Each house has a communal living area as well as a kitchen, dining area, bathroom, and laundry room. There is also a main building with offices for staff, program rooms, a health-care unit, and a visiting unit. Maximum security women are housed in secure units commensurate with traditional cells. These facilities can accommodate anywhere from 44 women (Okimaw Ohci Healing Lodge) to 150 (Edmonton Institution for

Women). The Okimaw Ohci Healing Lodge is located in Saskatchewan. Structurally and operationally, it is based on Aboriginal spirituality and traditions and can accommodate both minimum and medium security women.

Arbour's "Commission of Inquiry into Certain Events at the Prison for Women" was released in April 1996. The Honourable Louise Arbour, who at the time was a judge in the Ontario Court of Appeal and now sits on the United Nations Human Rights Violation Tribunal, was tasked with investigating incidents that involved violent confrontations between six female offenders and various correctional staff at the Prison for Women. The report also addressed the offenders' subsequent lengthy segregation, CSC's deployment of a male emergency response team, their role in strip-searching the female offenders, and CSC's response (Arbour 1996). Arbour ruled that many of the women's concerns were valid.

The CSC has advanced considerably since 1990, though critics argue that there is still room for improvement (Glube et al. 2006). CSC is considered a world leader in the provision and development of gender-informed programs for women. Not only does CSC offer programs that target risk factors directly related to criminal behaviour (e.g., the Women Offender Substance Abuse Program (WOSAP) and the Women's Violence Prevention Program (WVPP)), it also offers a number of programs that may be considered central to the criminal conduct of women (e.g., trauma programs and mother–child programs).

Canadian provincial governments have begun to recognize that correctional service delivery must be responsive to girls. As such, several informal working groups and girl-focused conferences have emerged across the country. Similarly, various non-governmental agencies are developing formal gender-informed policies (e.g., Elizabeth Fry Society of Peel-Halton 2005).

Global Developments

Significant strides have also occurred internationally. In December 2010, all 173 United Nations countries unanimously voted in favour of 70 rules to guide policy makers, legislators, sentencing authorities, and prison staff in reducing female incarceration and meeting the specific needs of imprisoned women (Penal Reform International 2013). These rules are known as the UN Bangkok Rules because HRH Princess Bajrakitiyabha of Thailand was instrumental in their development. In essence, the rules recognize that women have unique needs and vulnerabilities that require attention. The rules specify that incarcerated women require access to gender-specific healthcare (such as breast cancer screening) and should be treated humanely and with dignity. Thus, for example, incarcerated women are not to be restrained during labour and childbirth, placed in solitary confinement whilst breast feeding, or subject to strip searches by male staff. Importantly, the UN Bangkok Rules emphasize the need to maintain family connections between incarcerated women and their children in a manner that is mutually respectful and safe to both child and mother (Penal Reform International 2013).

Specific Treatment Targets

Research has identified various correctional treatment targets for girls and women. Some are also considered risk factors and were described in the earlier section "Factors Associated with Female Offending." However, there are a number of additional treatment targets that are not traditionally considered risk factors but could be conceptualized as non-criminogenic responsivity factors—factors that may not be directly related to criminal recidivism but if left unaddressed may impede correctional treatment and make it less effective in aiding offender reintegration into the community.

Applied correctional feminists have emphasized the following areas as especially salient to girls and/or women: childcare and prenatal services, parenting programs, female-only group programs, trauma programming, substance abuse treatment, education and employment training, gender-responsive medical (e.g., gynaecological) and mental-health care services (e.g., programming for borderline personality and depression), and service delivery that permits meaningful communication with staff characterized by empowerment and empathy (Ashley, Marsden, and Brady 2003; Bloom, Owen, and Covington 2003; Cusworth Walker, Muno, and Sullivan-Colglazier, 2015; Kennedy 2004; Koons et al. 1997; Morash, Bynam, and Koons 1998; Owen 1998; Richie 2001; Wellisch, Anglin, and Prendergast 1993). Additional proposed targets are more relevant during incarceration, such as protection against sexual harassment and abuse from staff, while others are more relevant in the community, such as protection from abusive partners, provision of safe and affordable housing, access to reliable transportation, and access to staff after hours (Ashley et al. 2003; Bloom, Owen, and Covington 2003).

Researchers also advocate that successful programming for girls and women must become more holistic in at least two important ways. First, it must target multiple needs simultaneously (e.g., substance abuse and mental health). Second, treatment must occur in an environment that is empowering and as such affords girls and women a voice in a safe setting characterized by mutual respect and understanding. This translates into gender-responsive training for staff that targets stereotypical beliefs about girls and women—that they are whiny, emotionally draining to work with, manipulative, needy—and provides knowledge and skills for dealing with a traumatized population (Bloom, Owen, and Rosenbaum 2003; Gaarder, Rodriguez, and Zatz 2004).

To date, researchers have not had ample opportunity to thoroughly investigate the extent to which targeting these factors can reduce recidivism in girls or women. The evidence we do have is encouraging, however. Ashley et al. (2003) narratively reviewed 38 substance abuse treatment studies that examined one or more of the above-noted factors. The authors concluded that substance abuse programming for women is most effective when it concurrently provides prenatal care, mental health care, women-specific comprehensive programming (e.g., children are integrated into the treatment effort and live with their mothers in the therapeutic community), and women-specific supplemental services (e.g., targeting breast health, breast self-examination, sexual and reproductive anatomy, sexually transmitted infections, HIV and AIDS prevention, assertiveness, and communication skills).

Gender Responsive Programming Example: *Moving On*

Moving On is a correctional treatment program built from the ground up specifically for women offenders. The program incorporates core elements from both the gender-neutral (cognitive behaviourism) and gender-responsive literatures (e.g., empowerment, relational focus). The primary goal of the program is to teach women how to draw on existing strengths and to access both personal and community resources (Van Dieten and MacKenna 2001). The program meets this objective by:

- Treating women with respect and dignity
- Providing a supportive, empathic, accepting, collaborative, and challenging environment
- Helping women build healthy and supportive networks
- Teaching decision-making, problem-solving, assertiveness, and emotional regulation skills
- Facilitating reintegration

Moving On is divided into the following nine treatment modules that are covered over 26 sessions.

- Setting the Context for Change
- Women in Society
- Taking Care of Yourself
- Family Messages
- Relationships
- Coping with Emotions and Harmful Self-Talk
- Problem-Solving
- Becoming Assertive
- Moving On

Importantly, the program is reducing reconviction rates. Gehring et al. (2009) evaluated the program in a sample of 111 Iowa probationers who completed the program with 111 Iowa probationers who did not complete any programming. The groups were matched on age, race, and risk level. As Figure 13.1 illustrates, the program significantly reduced reconvictions rates during the course of the follow-up period.

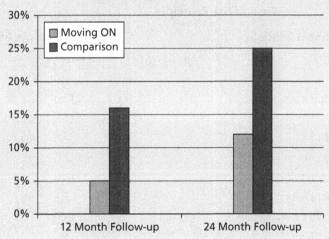

Figure 13.1 Conviction Rates for *Moving On* Completers and Comparison Group

Source: Gehring et al. (2009).

Although the development of programs built specifically for girls and women are in their infancy, there are a number of notable examples developed by Canadian researchers for both girls—Earlscourt Girls Connection program (EGC; Pepler, Walsh, and Levene 2004), *Girls Moving On* (Orbis Partners 2007a)—and women—*Moving On* (Van Dieten and MacKenna 2001), and *Women Offender Substance Abuse Program* (WOSAP; CSC 2007). These programs adopt an integrated approach, blending elements from gender-neutral correctional treatment literature (e.g., grounded in social learning theory and cognitive behaviourism [see Chapter 3] and gender-responsive literature [e.g., afford voice and enhance empowerment]). Notably, *Moving On* has been evaluated and has shown some promising results (see the Hot Topics box) (Gehring, Van Voorhis, and Bell 2009).

Although rigorous evaluations are lacking for programs designed specifically for girls or women, Dowden and Andrews (1999) conducted a meta-analytic review of gender-neutral correctional treatment programs that have targeted female offenders. Specifically, they explored whether treatment programs targeting female offenders (adhering to the principles of risk, need, and responsivity) yielded greater reductions in criminal recidivism than those that did not. The authors identified 26 unique treatment outcome studies comprised entirely (16 studies) or predominantly (10 studies) of female offenders. The main results of their meta-analysis are presented in Table 13.4.

The study demonstrated that programs adhering to the general responsivity principle generated a 25 percent (solely female) to 27 percent (predominantly female) reduction in criminal recidivism. Similarly, programs adhering to risk and/or need principles reduced recidivism by 19 to 26 percent. Studies with male offenders revealed comparable data

Table 13.4 Mean Effect Size Corresponding to Each Correctional Treatment Principle

Treatment Principle	Principle Adhered To	
	Yes (k)*	No (k)
Risk		
Predominantly female	.19 (36)	−.04 (9)
Solely female	.24 (18)	−.04 (6)
Need		
Predominantly female	.26 (21)	.04 (24)
Solely female	.23 (13)	.09 (11)
Responsivity		
Predominantly female	.27 (15)	.08 (30)
Solely female	.25 (8)	.12 (16)

*k refers to the number of studies that contributed to the mean effect size.

Source: Dowden and Andrews (1999).

(Andrews, Zinger et al. 1990). Dowden and Andrews' (1999) results are encouraging, but should be interpreted cautiously. As the authors note, the meta-analysis was based on a considerably small number of studies relative to comparable research with male offenders (i.e., 500+). Second, most of the studies were comprised of youthful female offenders. The extent to which the results generalize to adult female offender samples is largely unknown. As well, the majority of studies were published prior to 1990, so the meta-analysis did not permit a "fair test" of contemporary approaches.

Fortunately however, Gobéil, Blanchette and Stewart (forthcoming) conducted a recent meta-analysis examining the effectiveness of female offender programming. The results of 37 studies involving 22 000 women offenders revealed that the odds of community success were 22 to 35 percent higher for women who participated in correctional interventions versus those who did not. Interestingly, gender-informed and gender-neutral interventions produced similar effects. However, when the analyses were restricted to higher methodological rigor, gender-informed interventions were significantly more likely to be associated with reductions in recidivism. The You Be the Therapist box provides an opportunity to apply the material we have discussed so far.

Box 13.2

You Be the Therapist

Charlotte is a 21-year-old woman who has just been admitted to federal custody for six years. She was convicted of manslaughter, possession of drugs, vehicle theft, and armed robbery. During a cocaine high, she robbed a convenience store with a toy gun to obtain money for more drugs. She fled the store, drove away in a stolen car, and hit a pedestrian who later died of his injuries. Charlotte remembers no details of the incident.

Charlotte was repeatedly sexually abused by her stepfather between the ages of 10 and 12. Her mother was severely addicted to drugs and suffered from depression. Charlotte spent her childhood being bounced around between different foster care homes and residential facilities and could never adjust to life in these places. She was always full of rage and trusted no one. The only way she could cope with her emotions was either to cut her forearms until she bled, or run away to the streets. She spent the better part of her adolescence and early adulthood on the streets. Prostitution was her only means of making money as she had dropped out of high school long ago. Gradually she became addicted to cocaine as a means of coping with her depression. Her pimp could sometimes be very nice and bought her nice clothes, but she also lived in fear of his beatings. Charlotte feels hopeless about the future and has been put on 24-hour suicide watch.

Questions

Charlotte has only been in prison for 48 hours. What kind of intervention does she need? What are her treatment priorities? What is the best way to meet Charlotte's needs while in prison? What are some of the challenges in treating Charlotte?

Criticisms of the Gender-Neutral Correctional Treatment Model

A number of feminist scholars have been highly critical of the responsivity model in its application to females. The first criticism asserts that it is problematic because it targets individual change while simultaneously ignoring an individual's ecology, both immediate (e.g. partner, family, friends) and distal (e.g., society, cultural, political, economic) (Covington and Bloom 2003; Hannah-Moffat 2004; Kendall 2004; Pollack 2005; Shaw and Hannah-Moffat 2004). The second criticism argues that the RNR model was empirically informed by quantitative meta-analytic results. Kendall (2002; 2004) contends that using meta-analytic results to inform female-specific treatment strategies is unreliable because qualitative and small-scale studies are excluded. A third criticism against cognitive behaviourism stems largely from Kendall's (2002; 2004) distrust of science, particularly psychology. Kendall argues that science and empiricism reflect the values of the dominant class in society; namely, white middle-class men from the Western world. It would appear that there is much to be done in the field of female treatment and that perhaps the best path is an integrated one (Blanchette and Brown 2006).

FUTURE DIRECTIONS

THE STUDY OF FEMALE OFFENDING AND GENDER-RESPONSIVE CORRECTIONS IS EVOLVING steadily. However, much work remains. In particular, researchers and practitioners need to determine how best to meet the co-occurring, complex needs of female offenders that span both mental health and correctional jurisdictions. Similarly, more longitudinal research is needed to figure out whether or not girls and women have different strengths than their male counterparts. Longitudinal research is also needed to assess if and how risk factors interact differently depending upon gender. So, while severe family conflict might not be sufficient to catapult a youthful male toward a life of crime, perhaps it is sufficient for youthful females. Lastly, as the implementation of gender-responsive programs continues to grow, so does the need for corresponding rigorous evaluations to ensure that we are indeed improving the lives and safety of all Canadians.

SUMMARY

1. Girls and women commit substantially less crime and particularly less violent and less serious crime compared to boys and men. When girls and women commit crime, their motivations and situational contexts are sometimes different from that of their male counterparts (e.g., more relational in nature, directed against intimate partners), but sometimes similar (e.g., driven by a need to "save face" or restore personal reputation/integrity).

2. Gender-neutral and female-centred theories have been proposed to explain female criminal behaviour. Both perspectives have merit.

3. Girls and women share a number of risk factors with their male counterparts, such as criminal history and employment and education needs. However, there are a number of factors that appear to be more salient for females (e.g., family conflict).

4. Gender-neutral risk tools appear to predict criminal recidivism equally well for male and female offenders. However, gender-responsive tools are starting to surpass gender-neutral tools.

5. Girls and women have a number of programming needs that don't typically arise in the context of treating male offenders, such as protection from abusive partners or parenting needs. The number of gender-responsive programs is growing, along with the number of evaluations of these programs. Thus far, the evidence is encouraging.

6. Although girls and women share a number of similarities, there are some important developmental differences that have yet to be fully explored.

Discussion Questions

1. Do we need female-specific theories of crime or are traditional theories enough?

2. What are the advantages and disadvantages associated with using gender-neutral risk-assessment tools such as the LS/CMI versus gender-responsive risk-assessment tools such as the SPIn-W?

3. Throughout the chapter, we explored what the research has to say about whether girls and women have unique risk factors and treatment needs. Much of the discussion suggests that girls and women have many of same risk and need factors as their male counterparts. In contrast, the world (United Nations) as well as modern correctional agencies such as the CSC begin with the assumption that women have unique needs, as exemplified by statements such as "While CSC has come far in addressing the unique needs of women offenders..." (CSC 2006: 3). So if the real world has already decided that women have unique needs, should we continue our research?

4. Should female offenders be considered offenders or victims?

Chapter 14
Aboriginal Offenders

At the age of two, Victor Dellaire was removed from his parents' home by Child Welfare Services and spent the next 12 years in and out of foster homes where he experienced serious physical abuse. At 14, Victor ran away from his foster home and lived on the city streets for two years. While he attended school regularly as a child, he rarely showed up for classes once he was older and was frequently suspended for truancy and fighting. School took a back seat in Victor's life and he eventually dropped out. Victor's life gradually became centred on crime and alcohol abuse. He was often involved in the criminal justice system and ultimately found himself sentenced to an Aboriginal healing lodge. While in the lodge, Victor took part in a number of treatment programs, some to tackle his substance abuse issues and others to help him control his anger. He also took part in a variety of programs that taught him about his Aboriginal culture, which he had little knowledge of. An Elder at the lodge befriended Victor and introduced him to drumming. They often spoke about his upbringing, his experiences in foster care, and his ultimate path into crime. They spent time in sweat lodges, smoked tobacco together, and talked about what Victor needed to do to return to the right path. Over time, Victor learned to embrace his culture and devoted himself to giving back to his people. Today, Victor works at the lodge where he spent several years. He not only constructs the drums that are used during drumming classes, he teaches classes and talks to the inmates about his life and how he turned it around.

Learning Objectives

1   Describe why Aboriginal people might be overrepresented in the criminal justice system.

2   Describe the attempts that have been made to reduce Aboriginal overrepresentation.

3   Discuss the similarities and differences between Aboriginal and non-Aboriginal offenders with respect to their risk and need factors.

4   Explain the legal requirements to provide Aboriginal-specific correctional programs.

5   Describe what an Aboriginal healing lodge is and explain why such lodges are used.

INTRODUCTION

AS YOU WILL SEE THROUGHOUT THIS CHAPTER, VICTOR IS ONE OF MANY ABORIGINAL offenders in Canada who has come into contact with the law. In fact, for a variety of reasons we will explore, Aboriginals are more likely than non-Aboriginals to serve time in a Canadian correctional facility. When Aboriginal offenders do serve time, they are often exposed to the types of Aboriginal treatment programs described in the opening vignette. Like traditional correctional programs, Aboriginal treatment programs also aim to reform offenders so that they do not commit further crimes, but they also attempt to do this by reconnecting offenders with their Aboriginal culture. Not only is the provision of such programs to (appropriate) Aboriginal offenders a requirement in Canada, it reflects the generally held belief that loss of culture is at the heart of the Aboriginal offending problem.

In this chapter, we will examine Aboriginal offenders and offending. We will begin by exploring the issue of Aboriginal overrepresentation in the Canadian criminal justice system. We will describe why Aboriginal people may be more likely than non-Aboriginals to come into contact with the law and we will examine various attempts that have been made to reduce overrepresentation. We will then discuss the similarities and differences between Aboriginal and non-Aboriginal offenders with respect to childhood and adult risk factors and examine the applicability of traditional risk assessment instruments to Aboriginal offenders. Lastly, we will look at correctional treatment for Aboriginal offenders, including the need for Aboriginal-specific programs, what some of these programs look like, and whether these programs are having their intended effects.

CONTEXT

YOU MAY BE WONDERING WHY WE INCLUDE A CHAPTER IN THIS TEXTBOOK DEDICATED solely to Aboriginal offenders. There are many answers to this question. However, perhaps the most obvious has already been alluded to: within Canada, Aboriginal offenders are by far the most overrepresented group in our criminal justice system. This has been true for a long time, as it has been in other countries with indigenous populations (e.g., Jeffries and Stenning 2014; Welsh and Ogloff 2008). Unfortunately, despite attempts to reduce overrepresentation in Canada, the matter does not appear to be drastically improving (Jeffries and Stenning 2014; Roberts and Melchers 2003; Welsh and Ogloff 2008). In fact, many people believe that **Aboriginal overrepresentation** is one of the most important problems facing our criminal justice system (e.g., Corrado, Kuehn, and Margaritescu 2014; Owusu-Bempah and Wortley 2014).

One just has to look at the numbers to appreciate the magnitude of the problem. For example, according to recent statistics, Aboriginal people make up only about 3 percent of the general population in Canada. However, Aboriginal offenders make up approximately 18 percent of the federal inmate population (Correctional Service Canada 2013a) and 18 percent of the provincial/territorial inmate population (Perreault 2009). In addition, Aboriginals represent approximately 12 percent of offenders who are serving sentences in the community (Trevethan, Moore, and Rastin 2002). While the problem

Table 14.1 Percentage of Aboriginal Offenders in Each Canadian Province

Province	Total # of Offenders	% of Offenders That Are of Aboriginal Descent	Total # of Offenders That Are of Aboriginal Descent
Newfoundland	1199	6%	72
Prince Edward Island	803	NIL	NIL
Nova Scotia	1964	5%	98
New Brunswick	2273	5%	114
Quebec	21 735	2%	435
Ontario	32 815	10%	328
Manitoba	1393	59%	822
Saskatchewan	3850	76%	2926
Alberta	15 491	38%	5887
British Columbia	9628	20%	1926
Yukon	300	NIL	NIL
Northwest Territories	1594	49%	781
Total Incarcerated Population	**93 045**		**13 389**

Source: Correctional Service Canada (2013a).

of Aboriginal overrepresentation is evident across the country, the problem is much more obvious in the western half of Canada, particularly in the Prairie region (see Table 14.1; CSC 2013a; Johnson 2005; Trevethan, Moore, and Rastin 2002).

DEFINITIONS

BEFORE PROCEEDING, IT IS IMPORTANT TO UNDERSTAND WHAT WE MEAN IN THIS chapter when we use the term **Aboriginal** offender. According to Indian and Northern Affairs Canada (INAC 2004), three groups of Aboriginal people are formally recognized in Canada—Indian, Metis, and Inuit. As INAC (2004) notes, "These are three separate peoples with unique heritages, languages, cultural practices and spiritual beliefs." The term Indian is generally used for legal reasons (i.e., because such terminology is used in existing legislation, such as the *Indian Act*; INAC 2004). More recently, people in Canada have started to use the term First Nation instead of Indian to refer to Aboriginal Canadians who are not Metis or Inuit. In contrast to First Nation people, Metis are people who have mixed European and First Nation ancestry (INAC 2004). Finally, Inuit includes individual of Aboriginal ancestry who reside in Northern Canada, including Nunavut, Northwest Territories, Northern Quebec, and North Labrador (INAC 2004). In some cases, studies will separate Aboriginal people into these three groups; however, this is typically not the case. Thus, our use of the term Aboriginal throughout this chapter will refer to individuals belonging to any of the three groups described above.

WHY DO WE CARE?

NOT ONLY ARE ABORIGINAL CRIME RATES A CONCERN (IF THEY ARE IN FACT HIGHER than non-Aboriginal crime rates), but given the costs associated with incarceration and community sentences, Aboriginal overrepresentation is cause for concern from a purely financial perspective. However, perhaps more important than the costs associated with Aboriginal overrepresentation is the fact that Aboriginal people are disproportionately represented in the criminal justice system. This suggests that problems exist with the system and with society as a whole. If we belong to a just society that values fairness and equality, we should care that a particular group of individuals appears to be being discriminated against (either overtly or covertly, in terms of systemic biases). Potential problems in the criminal justice system (and in society more generally) need to be examined and corrected.

Attempts to do this have been made over several decades Not only is effort being put into understanding why we have an Aboriginal overrepresentation problem, but attempts are also being made to correct this. This includes the creation (and evaluation) of culturally sensitive assessment tools and treatment programs. Some of these tools and programs will be discussed in this chapter.

METHODOLOGY

AS IS THE CASE WHEN STUDYING OTHER OFFENDER POPULATIONS, METHODOLOGIES used by researchers to study Aboriginal offenders are varied. As you will see throughout this chapter, both quantitative and qualitative approaches to research are adopted (although, for reasons discussed below, qualitative approaches are frequently used). For example, quantitative approaches to research are popular when studying whether existing risk-assessment tools can be applied to Aboriginal offenders to accurately predict their risk of reoffending (e.g., Wormith and Hogg 2012), and meta-analyses of risk assessment studies are increasingly being published (e.g., Gutierrez, Wilson, Rugge, and Bonta 2013). In contrast, qualitative approaches to research are commonly used when studying the impact of culturally-specific treatment programs on Aboriginal offenders (e.g., Yuen and Pedlar 2009).

Despite the commonalities that exist between Aboriginal and non-Aboriginal research, most researchers who study Aboriginal issues argue that extra care is required when conducting research with Aboriginals. This is to ensure that researchers are sensitive to how the world views of Aboriginal people differ from the typical views held by non-Aboriginal researchers, and that we adequately capture such differences in the studies we produce (Stelmach 2009). One can imagine how a quantitative researcher might impose their world view on Aboriginal participants (no matter how well-intentioned they are) by constructing a set of inflexible, closed-ended questions to explore a topic, which do not allow the participant's "voice" to be heard. Indeed, it is for this reason that criminal justice researchers often use open interviews or focus groups to study Aboriginal offenders.

The complexity associated with Aboriginal research has led to the development of Aboriginal research protocols (e.g., Kenny 2004; Menzies 2001). Compared to quantitative methodologies commonly used in psychology; which often emphasize precision, control, and generalizability; protocols for Aboriginal research emphasize different aspects of the research process, such as developing trust with participants, understanding the impact of the research, and reporting back results (Kenny 2004). Unlike traditional research in psychology, proposed protocols for Aboriginal research also advocate a more holistic approach to research that captures critical aspects of Aboriginal identity. For example, Kenny argues that a framework for holistic Aboriginal research would include "the spiritual, physical, emotional and mental aspects of the person and the community in research protocols, methodologies and analyses" (2004: 8).

THEORIES OF ABORIGINAL OVERREPRESENTATION

GIVEN THE DATA IN TABLE 14.1, AN OBVIOUS QUESTION TO ASK IS WHY ABORIGINAL people are overrepresented in the Canadian criminal justice system. Unfortunately, there is no easy answer to this question.

Potential Explanations of Aboriginal Overrepresentation

Historically, four potential explanations have been proposed for Aboriginal overrepresentation (LaPrairie 1996):

1. A higher Aboriginal crime rate.
2. The commission by Aboriginal people of offences that are more likely to result in criminal justice processing.
3. Differential criminal justice processing as a result of racial discrimination.
4. Criminal justice policies and practices that have a differential impact on Aboriginal offenders due to their socio-economic conditions.

Higher Aboriginal Offending Rates There appears to be general agreement that the Aboriginal crime rate in Canada is significantly higher than the non-Aboriginal crime rate, especially when focusing on Aboriginal people living on reserves (Brzozowski, Taylor-Butts, and Johnson 2006; Ruddell, Lithopoulos, and Jones 2014). One estimate in Manitoba, for instance, put the 1989–90 provincial crime rate (excluding reserves) at 1003 offences per 10 000 people, whereas the estimated crime rate on reserves was 1505 offences per 10 000 people (Aboriginal Justice Inquiry 1999). Another more recent estimate put the 1996–97 crime rates in Saskatchewan at 1408 and 1407 offences per 10 000 people in urban and rural areas, respectively (Quann and Trevethan 2000). The corresponding crime rate on reserves was 3054 offences per 10 000 people. If these numbers are accurate, it appears that one of the reasons for Aboriginal overrepresentation is that the crime rate associated with Aboriginal people is simply higher. Note, however, that this does not necessarily mean that Aboriginal people are more inclined to commit crime. As discussed in more detail below, a range of other factors could potentially explain the higher crime rate observed for Aboriginal people.

A Tendency to Commit More Violent Crime There also seems to be agreement among researchers that the types of crime committed (or at least detected and recorded) by Aboriginal and non-Aboriginal offenders differ, and that the types of recorded crime committed by Aboriginal offenders are more likely to result in arrests and incarceration (Brzozowski et al. 2006; LaPrairie 1996; Moyer 1992). For example, compared to non-Aboriginal crime, significantly more Aboriginal crime is recorded as violent in nature. In Quann and Trevethan's (2000) study of recorded crime in Saskatchewan, for instance, on-reserve violent crime was five times higher than that in urban and rural areas. More recently, a survey conducted by Statistics Canada indicated that rates of violent crime committed on reserves were eight times higher for assaults, seven times higher for sexual assaults, and six times higher for homicides than rates in the rest of Canada (Statistics Canada 2006). Given these findings, it is perhaps unsurprising that Aboriginal overrepresentation exists.

Discrimination in the Criminal Justice System As noted above, disagreement emerges when attempts are made to understand the higher rate of recorded crime for Aboriginal people. Does the data presented in the previous paragraphs indicate that Aboriginal people actually commit more crime? Or, does it just appear as if they do because of criminal justice practices, some of which might discriminate against Aboriginal people?

There are clearly people who believe discrimination plays only a minor role in the Aboriginal overrepresentation problem. For example, according to Tonry (1994), the primary cause of overrepresentation is differences in offending patterns between Aboriginal and non-Aboriginal people, not racial discrimination. There is some empirical evidence to support this view. For instance, in contrast to what would be expected if discrimination was occurring in the criminal justice system, a number of studies have found that, on average, Aboriginal offenders receive significantly shorter custodial sentences than non-Aboriginal offenders (LaPrairie 1990, 1996; Stenning and Roberts 2001; York 1995), although this may not be true at the provincial/territorial level (Trevethan, Tremblay, and Carter 2000).

This seems to be the minority view, however. Provincial and federal government inquiries (and numerous court rulings) have consistently concluded that the overrepresentation of Aboriginal people in the Canadian criminal justice system is a result, to a significant degree, of discrimination (although not always overt discrimination) in the criminal justice system (e.g., Jeffries and Bond 2012; Owusu-Bempah and Wortley 2014; Rudin 2006). Aboriginal overrepresentation itself is typically used as evidence of this discrimination, but other potential sources have also been highlighted.

It has been argued, for example, that Aboriginal communities are subject to **overpolicing**, and that police officers use discretion differently depending on whether they are dealing with Aboriginal or non-Aboriginal people (Comack 2012; Corrado, Kuehn, and Margaritescu 2014; Cunneen, Allison, and Schwartz 2014). Signs of discrimination against Aboriginal offenders have also been recognized in other phases of the criminal justice system. For instance, one inquiry found that, compared to non-Aboriginal inmates, Aboriginal inmates reported spending significantly less time with lawyers preparing their case and were more likely to appear in court without a lawyer (Aboriginal Justice Inquiry 1999). The same inquiry found that Aboriginal offenders are often detained for longer periods of time before their trial begins. Razack (2011) conducted a study examining inquests into the deaths of Aboriginal people in custody. She argued that Aboriginal people are often neglected once incarcerated, and tend to experience a lack of care by the arresting authorities, compared to non-Aboriginal offenders. In British Columbia, for example, statistics show that Aboriginal offenders are twice as likely to die in custody compared to other groups, and Razack argues that many of these deaths appear to have been preventable. Other potential signs of discrimination toward Aboriginal offenders will be discussed throughout the chapter (e.g., the over-classification of female Aboriginal offenders with respect to security level placements; Webster and Doob 2004a).

The Socio-Economic Disadvantage of Aboriginal People There seems to be little doubt that, as a group, Aboriginal Canadians are more disadvantaged socio-economically than non-Aboriginal Canadians (Weinrath 2007). Data clearly indicate that the unemployment rate is significantly higher for Aboriginal people and that Aboriginal people earn significantly smaller incomes on average (Mendelson 2006; Perusse 2008). Aboriginal people are also less educated than non-Aboriginal people, with a much smaller number of Aboriginals finishing high school and very few completing a post-secondary degree (Hull 2005; Mendelson 2006). There also seems to be agreement that these socio-economic disadvantages make Aboriginal people more vulnerable to certain criminal justice practices (Fitzgerald and Carrington 2008). Consider the issue of fine defaults. The *Criminal Code* states that a term of imprisonment may be imposed if an individual is unable to pay their fine and if they refuse to work it off in a fine option program. Given that many Aboriginal people are disadvantaged socio-economically and are unable to pay their fine, this rule will likely impact Aboriginal individuals disproportionately (and may explain, to some extent, their overrepresentation in the prison system; Mann 2013).

Root Causes of Aboriginal Overrepresentation

While these issues may help explain Aboriginal overrepresentation, it is important to understand that they are simply symptoms of larger, more serious social problems. If Aboriginal overrepresentation is to be adequately dealt with, we must first understand the root causes of these problems (LaPrairie 1996). Unfortunately, we still don't fully understand why these problems exist, although we have some good ideas (Rudin 2006). For example, culture clash seems to play an important role. As Rudin argues, there is no question "… that Aboriginal concepts of justice and Western concepts of justice are very different" (p. 22). Consider Table 14.2, which lists some of the major conflicts between

Table 14.2 Conflicts between Aboriginal and Non-Aboriginal
Concepts of Justice

	Western Justice	Aboriginal Justice
Justice system	Adversarial	Non-confrontational
Guilt	European concept of guilty/not guilty	No concept of guilty/not guilty
Pleading guilty	The accused has the right against self-incrimination (it is not seen as dishonest to plead not guilty when one has actually committed the offence).	It is dishonest to plead not guilty if one has committed the crime.
Testifying	As part of the process, witnesses testify in front of the accused.	Reluctance to testify (it is confrontational to testify against the accused while in his/her presence).
Truth	Expectation to tell the "whole truth."	It is impossible to know the "whole truth" in any situation.
Witnesses	Only certain people are called to testify in relation to specific subjects.	Everyone is free to give their say. Witnesses do not want to appear adversarial and often make every attempt to give answers that please counsel, thus changing their testimony.
Eye contact	Maintaining eye contact conveys that one is being truthful.	Maintaining eye contact with a person of authority can be a sign of disrespect.
Verdict	Accused is expected to show, upon a verdict of guilty, remorse and a desire for rehabilitation.	Accused must accept what comes to him/her without a show of emotion.
Incarceration/probation	Means of punishing/rehabilitating offender.	Completely absolves Aboriginal offender of responsibility of restitution to victim.
Function of justice	To ensure conformity, punish deviant behaviour, and protect society.	To heal the offender and restore peace and harmony to the community.

Source: Mount Pleasant-Jette (1993), cited in Canadian Criminal Justice Association (2000).

Aboriginal and non-Aboriginal values in a court setting. It is not difficult to imagine scenarios in which Aboriginal offenders would be at a distinct disadvantage compared to non-Aboriginal offenders (Ross 1992). For instance, the Aboriginal view that maintaining eye contact with a person of authority can be a sign of disrespect could make Aboriginals seem more guilty (or at least more deceptive) in the eyes of Western jurors and judges.

However, while there is no doubt some merit to this line of thinking, the concept of culture clash fails to explain certain realities of the criminal justice situation in Canada. For example, as Rudin (2006) points out, in contrast to what would be expected by a culture clash explanation, many Aboriginals incarcerated in Canadian prisons hold a distinctly Western view of justice. Surveys of these individuals have found that they often possess little knowledge of Aboriginal traditions and have little contact with Aboriginal communities, likely because many were uprooted as children (Rudin 2006).

The impact of colonialism has also been proposed as a root cause of overrepresentation. As Rudin (2006) explains,

> ... colonial governments prior to 1867 and Canadian governments since that time pursued a generally single-minded policy aimed at ensuring the disappearance of Aboriginal people in Canada. ... Included in the process was the relocation of Aboriginal people to often marginal land bases, criminalization of spiritual practices, severe restrictions on fundamental rights and liberties of Aboriginal people with respect to freedom of speech and assembly, mobility, and voting. *Indian Act* provisions regarding enfranchisement forced Aboriginal people who had ambitions to move outside of the reserve community

Library and Archives of Canada

As part of colonial efforts to assimilate Aboriginal people into the non-Aboriginal culture, many Aboriginal children were sent away to residential schools.

and to give up their status, and discriminated against Aboriginal women and their children on the basis of the status of the man the woman married. (pp. 25–26)

The favoured explanation for how colonialism has led to Aboriginal overrepresentation in the criminal justice system relates directly to the disadvantages experienced by Aboriginal people that resulted from these efforts to eradicate them (Royal Commission on Aboriginal People 1996). Consider the impact of residential schooling. As part of colonial efforts, countless Aboriginal children went through the residential school system, where an attempt was made to remove their Aboriginal identity and assimilate them into the non-Aboriginal culture. Many of these children suffered serious mistreatment and these experiences have had a long-lasting, negative impact on their lives. While it is difficult to quantify this impact, it is also difficult to imagine that this experience does not play some role in explaining Aboriginal overrepresentation (Bracken, Deane, and Morrissette 2009; Waldram 2014). The criminal justice system has begun to take into account the role of residential schooling on Aboriginal offending. For example, in the 2012 case of *Ipeelee*, the Supreme Court noted that "…judges should take notice of the broader legacy of residential schools as a background factor in sentencing" (Roach 2014: 566).

Attempts to Reduce Aboriginal Overrepresentation

Gradually, researchers, practitioners, and policymakers have begun to recognize and understand the unique circumstances surrounding Aboriginal people, resulting in numerous initiatives to reduce the number of Aboriginals who come into contact with the law. Many changes to policing have been introduced (Clairmont 2006), such as the introduction of self-administered First Nations police services. Policies that ensure Aboriginal offenders are able to receive treatment that is culturally appropriate have also been developed (*Corrections and Conditional Release Act* 1992).

Changes have also been made to Canadian sentencing practices to help address Aboriginal overrepresentation. For example, in 1996, Parliament introduced Bill C-41, which discusses the principles and purposes of sentencing and introduced new sentencing options, such as the conditional

The Canadian Press/Troy Fleece

First Nations police services are now common in Canada.

(community) sentence. In section 718.2(*e*) of Bill C-41, which deals with the use of incarceration, the government included the qualification that "all available sanctions other than imprisonment that are reasonable in the circumstances should be considered for all offenders, *with particular attention to the circumstances of aboriginal offenders*." The Supreme Court of Canada interpreted this section in R. *v. Gladue* (1999) as an attempt to "ameliorate the serious problem of overrepresentation of aboriginal people in prison" (paragraph 93).

One significant result of this ruling was the development of courts in Canada that focus on processing Aboriginal offenders. Some of these courts are known as **Gladue Courts**. In a Gladue court, special cultural considerations and adverse background conditions are taken into account when assessing the case of an accused, which may work to mitigate or reduce the culpability of the offender. Examples of Gladue factors include, but are not limited to: substance abuse; poverty; racism; family breakdown; exposure to abuse; lack of employment; loss of identity, culture, and ancestral knowledge; family involvement in crime; and attendance at a residential school (Law Courts Education Society of B.C. 2009). Consideration of these factors will sometimes result in sentences that are more in line with traditional Aboriginal justice (e.g., restorative justice; Law Courts Education Society of B.C. 2009). However, a consideration of Gladue factors does not necessarily mean that Aboriginal offenders will always get off more lightly than non-Aboriginal offenders (e.g., if a very serious crime has been committed).

Unfortunately, there are reasons to be pessimistic about the impact of the Gladue decision. While the 1996 reforms introduced by Parliament led to a reduction in the use of prison sentences in general, Aboriginal overrepresentation continues to persist (Roberts and Melchers 2003). One problem is that while Gladue emphasized the need for judges to pay attention to the life circumstances of Aboriginal offenders, the decision did not provide a process for how to "gather this information, synthesize it, and provide it to the sentencing judge" (Rudin 2006: 48). Some scholars also argue that recent legislation (e.g., Bill C-10, or *The Safe Streets and Communities Act*) may work in opposition to Gladue. This bill gets "tough on crime" by increasing sentence length, making it more difficult for judges to have discretion when sentencing (Rudin 2013).

Let's see how you would do in identifying Gladue factors. Read about the case of Jeremy in the You Be the Assessor box and try to identify relevant factors that you would take into account when deciding how to proceed with this case.

Box 14.1

You Be the Assessor

Identifying Gladue Factors in Aboriginal Offenders

Jeremy is a 48-year-old Metis man who has been in and out of prison throughout his adult life. His criminal record is long and reveals a history of drug- and alcohol-related offences, assaults, and domestic violence. He is appearing in court today for his most recent offence, an armed robbery.

Box 14.1 (Continued)

He and two friends rushed into a bank carrying guns. While Jeremy stood guard at the door, his co-offenders threatened the bank tellers and ordered them to hand over the money in their tills.

Jeremy's life story—his path into crime—is a tragic one. He was born on a reserve just outside of Edmonton, Alberta. At the age of 5 he was removed from his parents' home and put into the foster care system. His father was a hunter and his mother, who had attended residential school, worked at a local store. Both of his parents abused alcohol and he was frequently left alone or was taken care of by his older siblings. His father was also regularly sent to prison, and Jeremy often witnessed domestic abuse in his home.

In foster care, Jeremy was frequently moved from home to home. In one of his early foster homes he was abused, both physically and sexually. As he grew older, requests to have him placed in other foster homes resulted from his uncontrollable aggression, which was directed either at other foster kids or his foster parents. He frequently ran away from foster homes, and the police were regularly called to try and locate him.

Jeremy always hated school. Nearly all the kids in his schools were non-Aboriginal and he never felt like he fit in. He frequently skipped school and would instead hang out on "the strip." He spent his afternoons drinking with friends or playing pool at the local pool hall. As he got older,

he found employment, but jobs never lasted long. He'd either stop showing up or he would be fired.

Jeremy's involvement in crime started early in his life. He stole things from the local store and vandalized his neighbourhood. He can't remember when he first started drinking, but that too began early in life. As a young man he frequently got into fights with people, usually when he was drunk, and his relationships with women were volatile, marked by emotional and physical abuse. He had little ability to control his anger and frequently acted impulsively. Care providers throughout his life frequently wondered whether this was the result of fetal alcohol syndrome. The most recent armed robbery was an example of this. It was a spur of the moment, unplanned decision—he and his co-offenders had no vehicle or escape plan and the police arrested them a few blocks from the bank with the stolen money in a backpack Jeremy was carrying.

Questions

As the judge in this case, you must decide what to do with Jeremy. What sorts of factors would you take into account when deciding on an appropriate sentence? What are some "traditional" factors that you would consider (e.g., crime severity)? What sorts of Gladue factors would you consider, and how would they influence your decisions?

FACTORS ASSOCIATED WITH OFFENDING AMONG ABORIGINALS

A SIGNIFICANT ASPECT OF REDUCING ABORIGINAL OVERREPRESENTATION IS TO develop an understanding of the risk factors most relevant to Aboriginal offenders and to determine how these risk factors influence their offending behaviour. Based on existing research, it is clear that Aboriginal offenders generally represent a high-risk group with respect to both their childhood and adult backgrounds, which leads to relatively high rates of offending and reoffending compared to their non-Aboriginal counterparts.

Childhood Risk Factors

When surveyed, a large proportion of Aboriginal offenders report serious childhood trauma that could potentially contribute to their later law-breaking behaviour. Disturbingly high levels of poverty are reported by Aboriginal offenders when recounting their childhood, for instance, as are high levels of parental absence, behavioural and learning problems, and abuse of all kinds (Johnston 1997, 2000). While similar traumas are also experienced by non-Aboriginal offenders, they appear to be experienced to a lesser degree (Corrado, Kuehn, and Margaritescu 2014; Rojas and Gretton 2007). For example, Trevethan and Moore (2013) found that significantly more Aboriginal than non-Aboriginal offenders were involved in the child welfare system when they were young (e.g., approximately 63 percent of Aboriginal offenders had been adopted or placed in foster/group homes at some point in their childhood, compared to 36 percent of non-Aboriginal offenders; see Figure 14.1). Relatedly, a significantly larger proportion of Aboriginal offenders reported that they had an unstable childhood, relative to non-Aboriginal offenders (36 percent vs. 26 percent). As outlined in Figure 14.2, nearly half of all Aboriginal offenders reported having had experienced an unstable adolescence, whereas only 32 percent of non-Aboriginal offenders reported similar circumstances.

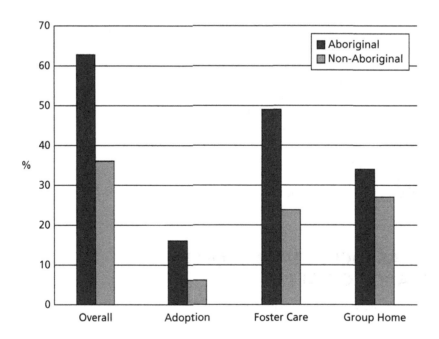

Figure 14.1 Percentage of Aboriginal and Non-Aboriginal Inmates who were Involved in the Child Welfare System

Source: Trevethan, Moore, Auger, et al. (2002), Figure 1.

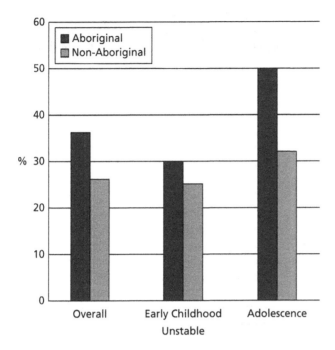

Figure 14.2 Percentage of Aboriginal and Non-Aboriginal Inmates Who Experienced Instability in their Childhood

Source: Trevethan, Moore, Auger, et al. (2002), Figure 2.

A larger proportion of Aboriginal offenders are also known to suffer from disorders such as fetal alcohol syndrome (FAS) or fetal alcohol spectrum disorder (FASD), which is associated with a range of problems, including juvenile delinquency and adult criminal behaviour (Boland, Duwyn, and Serin 2002; Scrim 2015). While the relationship between FAS/FASD and Aboriginal offending has been examined for some time, this issue continues to be the focus of much attention. The Hot Topics box further examines this issue.

Hot Topics

The Role of Fetal Alcohol Syndrome in Aboriginal Offending

The consumption of alcohol by a woman when she is pregnant can cause serious problems for the unborn child, leading to long-lasting consequences after birth. One such problem that has

implications for the criminal justice system is **fetal alcohol spectrum disorder (FASD)**, which can include **fetal alcohol syndrome (FAS)** (Ospina and Dennett 2013; Popova et al. 2011; Rojas and

Gretton 2007). FAS is diagnosed when there is a history of maternal alcohol consumption during pregnancy in addition to three criteria: prenatal and/or postnatal growth delay, characteristic cranio-facial anomalies, and central nervous system impairments (Boland et al. 2002).

The available research is clear that individuals diagnosed with FASD likely suffer from a range of problems. For example, Rangmar et al. (2015) found that adults suffering from FASD were more likely than a matched group of non-FASD adults (matched by age, gender, and birth place) to have received special education (25 percent vs. 2 percent), be unemployed (51 percent vs. 15 percent), and receive a disability pension (31 percent vs. 3 percent). The FASD group also had higher hospital admission rates for alcohol abuse (9 percent vs. 2 percent) and psychiatric disorders (33 percent vs. 5 percent).

Other studies have indicated that those with FASD are at a higher risk for coming into contact with the law as they often exhibit poor impulse control, poor social judgement, low tolerance, anger, and aggression (Townsend, Hammill, and White 2015). Indeed, studies have indicated that Aboriginal individuals with histories of FASD are overrepresented in the correctional system (Rojas and Gretton 2007). Popova and colleagues

(2011) conducted a systematic search of the literature and found that youths with FASD were an estimated nineteen times more likely to be incarcerated than youths without the diagnosis, in a given year. Similarly, Ospina and Dennett (2013) reported that over one quarter (26.9 percent) of Aboriginal youth within the correctional system had a diagnosis of FASD.

Although it is difficult to obtain a precise rate of the prevalence of FASD in Aboriginal people, estimates as high as 16 percent in Aboriginal communities have been reported in Canada (First Nations and Inuit Health Committee 2010). A recent meta-analysis found the rate of FASD on Aboriginal reserves to range from 1.5 percent to 10 percent, which is much higher than the rate of 0.02 percent to 0.5 percent found for non-Aboriginal individuals (Ospina and Dennett 2013). Given the potential link between FASD and crime, these figures represent a very serious problem for the Canadian criminal justice system and for the Aboriginal people of Canada. Increasingly, we will likely see FASD being raised as an issue in court in cases involving Aboriginal offenders. Indeed, there are very recent examples where arguments have been put forward by lawyers of Aboriginal offenders to have FASD be considered as a Gladue factor (Pacholik 2015).

Adult Risk Factors

In adulthood, Aboriginal offenders also exhibit a range of risk factors. However, many of these risk factors appear to be the same as those exhibited by non-Aboriginal offenders (Gutierrez et al. 2013). Bonta, LaPrairie, and Wallace-Capretta (1997) set out to determine whether a risk-assessment tool developed on non-Aboriginal offenders—the Manitoba Risk-Needs Scale—could be used successfully with Aboriginal offender populations. They collected data from 390 Aboriginal and 513 non-Aboriginal offenders and found that scores were significantly related to recidivism for both samples. In addition, they found that almost all of the scale items that predicted risk in the non-Aboriginal sample also predicted risk in the Aboriginal sample. Included among these factors were a history of substance abuse, prior criminal convictions, antisocial attitudes, and antisocial peers.

These findings suggest that predictors of recidivism may, at least to some extent, be independent of culture, as some researchers have argued (e.g., Andrews and Bonta 2010). This is not to say that Aboriginal-specific factors are totally unimportant, however. Recent research suggests there are a number of factors specific to Aboriginal offenders that may assist in predicting the likelihood of reoffending. For example, in a study by Sioui and Thibault (2002), participation in cultural and spiritual activities while incarcerated, and involvement in Aboriginal-specific education and employment programs, were related to decreases in recidivism for Aboriginal offenders.

ASSESSMENT APPROACHES AND EFFECTIVENESS

As indicated in other chapters, there are a number of risk-assessment instruments currently in use. Here we will focus on ones that are regularly used to assess Canadian offenders, including Aboriginal offenders on occasion: the Level of Service Inventory–Revised (LSI-R; or related tools), the Statistical Information on Recidivism Scale (SIR), and the Custody Rating Scale (CRS). Note that unlike the LSI–R and the SIR, the CRS is used for a very specific purpose (determining security classification), which is reflected in the type of risk it predicts (e.g., escape risk).

Level of Service Inventory–Revised (LSI–R)

The LSI–R is a 54-item risk-need assessment instrument designed for use with adult offenders (Andrews and Bonta 1995). The instrument taps into 10 dimensions related to risk and need factors and allows an offender's risk level to be categorized into five degrees, ranging from low to high. The LSI–R provides for professional discretion override, which allows administrators to consider special circumstances that may influence level of service decisions (Rugge 2006). Research has provided reasonably strong empirical support for the use of the LSI–R with non-Aboriginal offenders (e.g., Gendreau, Goggin, and Smith 2002; Wilson and Gutierrez 2014). Although more limited, some research has examined the applicability of the LSI–R to Aboriginal offenders.

Holsinger, Lowenkamp, and Latessa (2006) compared the predictive ability of the LSI–R with an Aboriginal and non-Aboriginal sample. The results suggested that the total risk score of the LSI–R retained predictive validity, even when ethnicity and sex were controlled for. Notably, however, predictive validity was better for Caucasian male and female offenders, relative to Aboriginal offenders. A similar result was obtained more recently when Wormith, Hogg, and Guzzo (2015) examined the predictive validity of the Level of Service/Case Management Inventory (LS/CMI), a recent version of the LSI–R. They tested the LS/CMI on a sample of Aboriginal ($n = 1692$) and non-Aboriginal offenders ($n = 24\ 758$). Consistent with Holsinger et al.'s (2006) findings, the results suggested that the predictive validity of the LS/CMI for predicting general reoffending in Aboriginal offenders was high, however, the tool predicted slightly better for non-Aboriginal offenders.

A recent meta-analysis produced results that are consistent with these studies (Wilson and Gutierrez 2014). The analysis examined 12 studies that explored the ability of the LSI to predict recidivism among Aboriginal and non-Aboriginal offenders. The results suggested that while the LSI did significantly predict recidivism for general offenses in Aboriginal offenders, the predictive accuracy for five of the eight subscales (Criminal History, Education/Employment, Companions, Alcohol/Drugs, and Procriminal Attitudes) was weaker compared to the strength of these scales for non-Aboriginal offenders. In other words, while the LSI can predict recidivism with Aboriginal offenders, it may do so with less accuracy. That being said, the LSI was found to be more useful for certain Aboriginal offenders (those with higher scores on the LSI). This suggests that Aboriginal offenders must be thought of as a heterogeneous group and that for some Aboriginal offenders, the LSI might have satisfactory predictive power.

Statistical Information on Recidivism (SIR) Scale

The SIR scale (Nuffield 1982) was developed to assist in parole decision making for federally sentenced offenders (Rugge 2006). The scale consists of 15 items, the majority of which are static (i.e., unchanging). Research has shown that the SIR scale demonstrates good psychometric properties with non-Aboriginal offenders, including reasonably high levels of predictive validity for general and violent recidivism (Bonta, Harman, Hann, and Cormier 1996; Hann and Harman 1989; Nafekh and Motiuk 2002; Nuffield 1982).

Although the SIR scale is typically not applied to Aboriginal offenders entering Correctional Service Canada institutions (Gutierrez et al. 2013), some research has reported reasonable evidence that it can be usefully applied to this population. Hann and Harman (1989, cited in Rugge 2006) tested the scale's applicability to female and Aboriginal offenders and found that there was a general correspondence between risk category and recidivism, although the relationship was not as strong as that found for non-Aboriginal offenders. As a follow-up, Hann and Harman (1993, cited in Rugge 2006) conducted another study examining the applicability of the SIR scale to male Aboriginal offenders. According to Rugge (2006), the "results indicated that the SIR scale had predictive value for the general release risk of Aboriginal offenders and that the predictive accuracy was comparable to the predictive accuracy of the scale for non-Aboriginal offenders" (pp. 17–18). Despite these results, the studies were not without limitation (e.g., small sample sizes). As a result, the authors were cautious in recommending the widespread application of the scale to the Aboriginal offender population.

In 2002, Nafekh and Motiuk tested several versions of the SIR scale on male Aboriginal offenders. Specifically, because the scale is not regularly administered to Aboriginals, an SIR–Proxy scale was developed and used, whereby scoring was done using information from intake assessments of Aboriginal offenders that approximated items on the SIR scale (using a non-Aboriginal sample, the SIR scale and the SIR–Proxy were found to produce similar results). A version of the SIR–Proxy that was calibrated on the offenders examined in the study was also used (referred to as the Recalibrated SIR). Using receiver operating characteristic (ROC) analysis—where accuracy scores, or AUCs, can range from

Table 14.3 Predictive Validity of the SIR Scale for Aboriginal and Non-Aboriginal Offenders

Criterion	Aboriginal	Non-Aboriginal
Any reconviction		
Correlation	−.42	−.46
AUC	.74	.77
Non-violent reconviction		
Correlation	−.27	−.38
AUC	.66	.73
Violent reconviction		
Correlation	−.21	−.19
AUC	.65	.65

Source: Rugge (2006).

.50 (chance accuracy) to 1.0 (perfect accuracy—tests of the SIR–Proxy on 6881 male non-Aboriginal offenders resulted in an AUC of .75 for general recidivism and .73 for violent recidivism (no AUC could be calculated for sexual recidivism). The corresponding values on the SIR–Proxy for 1211 male Aboriginal offenders were .68 for general recidivism, .65 for violent recidivism, and .60 for sexual recidivism. With respect to the Recalibrated SIR, an AUC of .75 was found for non-Aboriginal offenders when predicting general recidivism. The corresponding accuracy value for the Aboriginal offenders was .72.

Most recently, Bonta and Rugge (2004, cited in Rugge 2006) examined the predictive accuracy of the SIR scale using data from 940 male Aboriginal offenders. Bonta and Rugge's results "indicated that the SIR scale scores predicted any reconvictions and violent reconvictions equally well for both Aboriginal and non-Aboriginal male offenders" (Rugge 2006). However, "while the SIR scale predicted 'non-violent reconvictions' for both Aboriginal and non-Aboriginal males, results indicated that the prediction was better for non-Aboriginal males" (Rugge 2006: 18). See Table 14.3 for a summary of these results.

Custody Rating Scale (CRS)

The Custody Rating Scale (CRS) was adopted by Correctional Service Canada in the early 1990s for the purpose of making institutional security classification decisions (i.e., minimum, medium, or maximum; Blanchette, Verbrugge, and Wichmann 2002). The 12-item CRS consists of two subscales: the Institutional Adjustment (IA) subscale (including items such as history of institutional incidents and escape history) and the Security Risk (SR) subscale (including items such as number of prior convictions and severity of current offence) (Rugge 2006). The subscales consist of five items and seven items, respectively, with higher scores resulting in higher levels of classification. Since its implementation, there has been much debate as to whether the CRS is applicable for Aboriginal offenders, particularly females (Blanchette et al. 2002; Blanchette and Motiuk 2004; Canadian Human Rights Commission 2003; Webster and Doob 2004a, 2004b).

In the most comprehensive study of the CRS to date, Blanchette et al. (2002) examined the validity of using the CRS with female Aboriginal and non-Aboriginal offenders. Based on a sample of 68 Aboriginals and 266 non-Aboriginals, they found that the CRS designation distribution differed across Aboriginal and non-Aboriginal offenders, with Aboriginals being underrepresented in minimum security designations (20.6 percent) and overrepresented in both medium (70.6 percent) and maximum (8.8 percent) security designations (see data in the top two rows of Table 14.4). This pattern of results was also observed when actual placement decisions were examined (see data in the bottom two rows of Table 14.4).

As an additional sign of predictive accuracy, the percentage of female offenders in Blanchette et al.'s (2002) study who were involved in institutional incidents generally increased in the expected order for both Aboriginal and non-Aboriginal offenders at each CRS designation (see data in square brackets in Table 14.4), although there were more reported incidents for Aboriginal offenders classified as a minimum security risk (28.6 percent) than a medium security risk (26.8 percent). While this general trend is encouraging, it appears from this data that the CRS over-classifies Aboriginal offenders. In other words, a substantial portion of female Aboriginal offenders are designated to higher security levels than they need to be based on their rates of institutional misconduct. For example, the data in Table 14.4 indicates that Aboriginal offenders are more likely to be assigned (and placed) in medium security even though they are less likely to be involved in institutional incidents at this security level.

Table 14.4 Percentage of Aboriginal and Non-Aboriginal Offenders Designated and Placed in Minimum, Medium, and Maximum Security

	Sub-group	Security Level			
		Minimum (%)	Medium (%)	Maximum (%)	Total
CRS Designation	Aboriginal	20.6 [28.6]	70.6 [26.8]	8.8 [100]	(n = 68) [n = 61]
	Non-Aboriginal	55.3 [40]	42.8 [52.4]	1.9 [80]	(n = 266) [n = 230]
Actual Placement	Aboriginal	29.4 [16.7]	60.3 [30.6]	10.3 [100]	(n = 68) [n = 61]
	Non-Aboriginal	55.3 [38.5]	42.1 [53.5]	2.6 [85.7]	(n = 266) [n = 230]

Note: Percentage of institutional incidents within each security level is provided in square brackets.

Source: Blanchette et al. (2002).

In addition to these analyses, Blanchette et al. (2002) examined how Aboriginal and non-Aboriginal offenders scored on the two subscales of the CRS. When the 12 items making up the two scales were examined, Aboriginals scored significantly higher on six of them (non-significant differences were found for the other six, although Aboriginal offenders scored higher on five of these items as well). Blanchette et al. then calculated correlations between the subscale scores and various outcome measures for 61 of the Aboriginal offenders and 230 of the non-Aboriginal offenders. The IA subscale was moderately correlated with violent and non-violent incidents for both Aboriginal (.39 and .47, respectively) and non-Aboriginal offenders (.19 and .21, respectively). On the other hand, the SR subscale was correlated with violent and non-violent incidents for non-Aboriginal offenders (.18 and .19, respectively), but not for Aboriginal offenders (.01 and .05, respectively).

These sorts of findings have led to two approaches to try and rectify this problem. One approach has been to examine whether the problem of over-classification can be resolved if the CRS is used differently. For example, Barnum and Gobéil (2012) examined the validity of using the CRS in combination with professional judgement (from relevant staff) and psychological assessment. Using this approach, they found that both Aboriginal and non-Aboriginal offenders with higher security classifications had higher risk ratings, greater needs, lower reintegration potential, and lower motivation, relative to those with a lower security classification. Additionally, offenders with higher security classifications were more likely to be involved in serious institutional misconducts and were more likely to return to custody with a new offence; lower security classifications were associated with the granting of parole. These findings suggest that consideration of the CRS results in combination with professional judgement and psychological assessment is potentially a valid method for initial security classification of both Aboriginal and non-Aboriginal female offenders.

The other approach that has been taken involves the development of new instruments. Notably, a new instrument—the Security Reclassification Scale for Women (SRSW)— has been designed to classify female offenders' security levels after their initial security classification (Blanchette and Taylor 2007). This new instrument includes nine items (i.e., serious disciplinary convictions, segregation during the review period, regular prosocial family contact, etc.). Based on data from 103 non-Aboriginal offenders and 45 Aboriginal offenders, Blanchette and Taylor examined the predictive validity of the SRSW by studying various institutional outcome measures (e.g., any misconduct within a three-month follow-up period). Based on the entire group, AUCs for the new scale were fairly impressive: .74 for major institutional misconduct, .75 for minor institutional misconduct, and .75 for any institutional misconduct. When the offenders were separated into Aboriginal and non-Aboriginal samples the instrument was actually more accurate for Aboriginal offenders. The AUCs for minor misconducts were .72 and .75 for non-Aboriginal and Aboriginal offenders, respectively. For major misconducts, the difference was even more marked, with AUCs of .68 and .74 for non-Aboriginal and Aboriginal offenders, respectively.

Aboriginal-Specific Risk-Assessment Instruments

Although debate exists around the applicability of traditional risk-assessment tools to Aboriginal offenders (see the Media Spotlight box for one perspective), in light of the research described above, there appears to be at least some support for using such instruments with Aboriginal offenders. For example, it appears that the LSI tools can potentially be used to predict recidivism for Aboriginal offenders in Canada, although additional research is needed to confirm the validity of the LSI for female Aboriginal offenders. In addition, some studies have found that the SIR scale (or variations of this scale) has similar levels of predictive validity for Aboriginal and non-Aboriginal offenders, at least for predicting certain outcomes. While the CRS has been found to be problematic, especially when applied to female Aboriginal offenders, new risk-assessment tools (or combined approaches) for classifying female Aboriginal offenders appear to be more promising.

Media Spotlight

Judge Rules that Traditional Risk Assessment Tools are Unreliable for Aboriginal Offenders

A recent ruling by a Canadian judge (*Ewert v. Canada* 2015) has attracted the attention of the national news media (Quan 2015) and calls into question the applicability of traditional risk-assessment tools to Aboriginal offenders. The case highlights the level of disagreement that exists around this issue, even among researchers who study risk assessment.

The case involved a lawsuit brought forward by Jeffrey Ewert, a Metis man serving two life sentences in prison for second-degree murder and attempted murder. Ewert has spent 30 years in various federal correctional facilities and has been classified as either a medium or maximum security risk within those institutions. Although eligible for day parole since August 1996, and full parole since August 1999, he waived his right to each parole hearing and has never had one. Ewert claims that one of the reasons why he waived his rights was that "he was unlikely to be granted parole because he was assessed as too great a risk of reoffending" (paragraph 7).

Ewert's case revolves around the argument that the risk-assessment tools that have been applied to him, and used to make institutional decisions concerning him, were flawed because the tools cannot be applied reliably to Aboriginal offenders. The tools in question include those that we've been discussing throughout this book; tools such as the Psychopathy Checklist-Revised (PCL-R), the Violence Risk Appraisal Guide (VRAG), the Sex Offender Risk Appraisal Guide (SORAG), and the Static-99.

The case saw two leading Canadian risk-assessment researchers take the stand—Dr. Stephen Hart from Simon Fraser University on behalf of the Plaintiff (Ewert) and Dr. Marnie Rice from the Waypoint Centre for Mental Health Care for the defendant. While Hart argued that the risk-assessment tools in question are problematic when applied to Aboriginal offenders because they don't take into account "pronounced cultural differences between Aboriginals and non-Aboriginal groups" (paragraph 31), Rice argued that the test scores are reliable predictors of reoffending.

Despite the defendant's expert pointing out research like Olver et al.'s (2013) study of the PCL-R (discussed in the text), the presiding judge ultimately ruled in favour of the plaintiff. Judge Phelan ruled that the risk-assessment tools in question failed to consider the "special needs" of Aboriginals, lacked scientific rigour, and were susceptible to "cultural bias" (Quan 2015). The judge further noted that the use of the assessment tools in question violated the plaintiff's Section 7

Charter rights to life, liberty and security, and breached sections of the *Corrections and Conditional Release Act* (1992) because the tools were not responsive to the needs of Aboriginal people.

In his conclusion, Judge Phelan indicated that he intends to issue an order prohibiting Correctional Service Canada from using the assessment tools on Ewert, and any other Aboriginal inmates, until it conducts research that confirms the reliability of the tools with Aboriginal offenders.

Source: *Ewert v. Canada* (2015); Quan (2015).

One potential path for individuals who are interested in assessing the risk of Aboriginal offenders is to continue with the type of research described above. In this way, additional support for the use of traditional risk-assessment tools with Aboriginal offenders may gradually accumulate. For example, Olver, Neumann, Wong, and Hare (2013) recently examined the predictive ability of the Psychopathy Checklist–Revised (PCL–R) for Canadian male Aboriginal and non-Aboriginal offenders. The results suggested that the PCL–R total score could predict violent, nonviolent, and general criminal recidivism (AUC = .63–.70, Cohen's d = .28–.42) for both Aboriginal and non-Aboriginal offenders.

Another possible path also exists: to develop Aboriginal-specific risk assessment tools. Currently, very few Aboriginal-specific risk assessment instruments actually exist, and those that do exist are somewhat different from the instruments we have discussed in the sense that they are not formal scientific instruments for predicting risk and do not necessarily treat recidivism as the primary outcome of interest (Boer, Couture, Geddes, and Ritchie 2003).

One such instrument, the Yókw'tól, is a risk-management guide for incarcerated Aboriginal male and female violent offenders (Boer et al. 2003). Yókw'tól is a native word meaning "the understanding of one is complete." Unlike the majority of traditional risk-assessment instruments, where item selection is based on rigorous statistical testing, the content of the Yókw'tól is based primarily on input from Aboriginal Elders, Aboriginal staff, and Aboriginal offenders (this is not to say that there isn't empirical evidence to support many of the items included in the guide). It was designed to "provide guidance for the effective management of the offender both in the institution and the community" (Boer et al. 2003: 7). The Yókw'tól consists of 20 items that summarize the issues that must be addressed by Aboriginal offenders in order to return home in a safe manner. As can be seen in Table 14.5, both static and dynamic items are included, some of which are unique to Aboriginal offenders.

Table 14.5 Static and Dynamic Items Included in the Yókw'tól

1. Traditional teachings, ceremonies, and customs	11. Self-harm risk
2. Relationship of offender to heritage	12. Gains, insights, and behavioural changes
3. Child abuse history	13. Support for the victim(s)
4. Historical/generational issues	14. Support for the offender
5. Foster care history	15. Relevance of Sections 81/84 to offender
6. Family and marital relationships	16. Lifestyle stability
7. Alcohol and drug use	17. Self-support skills
8. Impulsive behaviour and violence	18. Supervision attitudes and compliance
9. Attitudes regarding offending	19. Risk-management plan
10. Psychological or psychiatric issues	20. Unique resiliency factors

Source: Adapted from Boer et al. (2003).

Like other risk-assessment instruments, these factors can be coded for on a periodic basis. With this tool, this is done by conducting an interview with the offender and an Elder and by consulting the offender's institutional file (Boer et al. 2003). The resulting scores can be used to guide treatment and supervision strategies that are jointly agreed to by the offender, the assessor, and the Elder to ensure that the offender will realize their full potential. While the Yókw'tól could theoretically be validated in the same manner as the other instruments we discussed, such scientific validation efforts have not taken place yet, nor has there been a rush to conduct them by the authors of the guide. The authors of the Yókw'tól do not see it as a scientific "instrument," but as a guideline to help Aboriginal offenders take responsibility for what they have done and make positive changes in their lives (Boer et al. 2003). Neither do the authors necessarily see the prediction of recidivism as the only outcome of interest when working with Aboriginal offenders. For example, they suggest a range of other variables that may be important to consider, including ". . . the willingness of Aboriginal people to be assessed; the willingness of such offenders to be honest with the interviewer; and the opinion of the individual offender that he has been interviewed with questions that seem relevant to him" (Boer et al. 2003: 5).

Risk of Reoffending among Aboriginal and Non-Aboriginal Offenders

The general finding of studies examining recidivism is that Aboriginal offenders tend to have higher recidivism rates than non-Aboriginal offenders (Rastin and Johnson 2002; Sioui and Thibault 2001; Wormith and Hogg 2012; Wormith, Hogg, and Guzzo 2015).

Sioui and Thibault (2002) examined the recidivism rates (i.e., technical violations and new offences) of 30 041 male offenders who were released on day parole, full parole, or statutory release from federal penitentiaries in Canada. Eighty-four percent were non-Aboriginal and the remaining 16 percent were Aboriginal. The researchers found that a larger proportion of Aboriginal offenders were readmitted to a federal institution within six months (18 percent vs. 11 percent for Aboriginal and non-Aboriginal offenders, respectively). This was true regardless of whether day parole (14 percent vs. 7 percent), full parole (21 percent vs. 9 percent), or statutory release (25 percent vs. 21 percent) was examined.

A more recent study conducted by Wormith and Hogg (2012) compared the recidivism rates of Aboriginal and non-Aboriginal offenders. Not only did they find that Aboriginal offenders have a higher rate of both general and violent reoffending, Aboriginal offenders also reoffended at a faster rate. Interestingly, their results showed that offenders placed on a custodial sentence were more likely to recidivate (74.6 percent) compared to those placed on probation (47.0 percent) and to those placed on a conditional sentence (48.5 percent). In addition, male offenders (60.7 percent) were significantly more likely to recidivate relative to females (45.9 percent).

TREATMENT ISSUES AND APPROACHES

GIVEN THAT ABORIGINAL OFFENDERS APPEAR TO BE MORE LIKELY TO REOFFEND than non-Aboriginal offenders, there is great value in examining ways to reduce their likelihood of recidivism. For the most part, research examining this issue has focused on whether culturally appropriate treatment programs (versus traditional correctional interventions) will help deal with the problem. As early as 1985, Correctional Service Canada began to introduce policies stressing the importance of Aboriginal culture, commenced an examination of the process Aboriginal offenders go through once they enter the criminal justice system, and started to work toward developing correctional programs that would meet the needs of these offenders. Since 1992, the provision of Aboriginal-specific programs has been a requirement under the *Corrections and Conditional Release Act*. Correctional Service Canada's own policy also recognizes the need for Aboriginal programs, stating that ". . . differences in cultural approaches to learning require different techniques and stipulates the requirement for regions to provide Aboriginal offenders with culturally-specific programs, activities, and Elder services" (Trevethan, Moore, and Allegri 2005: 3). One of the people responsible for carrying out many of the evaluations of these culturally specific programs is Shelley Trevethan (see the Canadian Researcher Profile box).

The Treatment Needs of Aboriginal Offenders

A focus on Aboriginal treatment makes sense considering the treatment needs of this population. Although Aboriginal and non-Aboriginal offenders often exhibit similar types of treatment needs while incarcerated, the level of need does not appear to be the same (LaPrairie 1996). Studies have consistently shown that larger proportions of

Box 14.3

Canadian Researcher Profile Shelley Trevethan

As you can see from the numerous references to her work throughout this chapter, one of the key figures in Aboriginal criminal justice research is Shelley Trevethan. Indeed, there is probably no other person in Canada who has conducted more research on the topic of Aboriginal offenders and their treatment.

Interestingly, Aboriginal issues weren't always the focus of Trevethan's research, although her passion has always been in the area of criminology. After completing a Bachelor's degree at Carleton University in criminology, Trevethan carried out her Master's research at UBC, where she studied psychopathy. Her M.A. thesis was titled

Courtesy of Dr. Shelley Trevethan

Shelley Trevethan

"Moral development in psychopathic, delinquent, and normal youths: An examination of moral reasoning in hypothetical and real-life dilemmas."

Soon after completing her M.A. thesis, Trevethan began her career as a psychologist, working in a variety of research positions within Statistics Canada, the Department of Justice, and the Public Service Commission. These positions gave her the opportunity to conduct research on a wide variety of topics, including Aboriginal issues, young offenders, access to justice, divorce, and other topics. Being able to work in different government departments gave her the unique opportunity to learn about all aspects of the criminal justice system.

One main topic that captured Trevethan's interest early on was the over-representation of Aboriginal people within the criminal justice system, both as offenders and as victims. The 1990s was an exciting time in Canada for those studying Aboriginal issues. There was a growing understanding of the devastating effects that colonization and residential schools had on Aboriginal people, and the over-representation of Aboriginal people in the criminal justice system was beginning to be addressed through the introduction of Aboriginal courts and culturally specific programs for Aboriginal offenders.

It was around this time that Trevethan moved into an exciting role as Director, Community/Aboriginal Research with the Correctional Service Canada. In this role, Trevethan led the agency's efforts to identify the needs of Aboriginal (and other ethnocultural) offenders through the conduct of research. Not only did she accomplish this, Trevethan's time at Correctional Service Canada also marked a period of very productive research for her.

During this time, Trevethan conducted some of her best-known studies. Together with her colleagues, she examined the childhood experiences

Box 14.3 (Continued)

of Aboriginal offenders, explored the treatment needs of these individuals, and evaluated a number of culturally specific rehabilitation programs, such as the *In Search of Your Warrior* program for violent male Aboriginal offenders and the *Tupiq* program for Inuit sex offenders. One of the most exciting aspects of this work was being able to examine the different needs of First Nations, Métis, and Inuit offenders—the first time such comprehensive work was undertaken at Correctional Service Canada. She also was responsible for establishing an Aboriginal Research Working Group that ensured input and collaboration from Aboriginal organizations on the research being conducted.

More recently, Trevethan has broadened her role and the impact that she can have on Aboriginal people in Canada, including offenders. Upon leaving Correctional Service Canada, she served for a short time as Senior Advisor in Health Canada's First Nation's and Inuit Health Branch, and then served as the Executive Director General at the Parole Board of Canada. In this role, she focused on ensuring Aboriginal offenders were involved in culturally appropriate hearing processes (such as Elder-assisted hearings) and

set up the Aboriginal Forum to gather input from Aboriginal organizations on the best approaches to address the over-representation of Aboriginal people in the correctional system.

Currently, Trevethan is the Executive Director of the Indian Residential Schools Adjudication Secretariat. Her mandate at the Secretariat is to resolve claims by Aboriginal people of abuse that occurred at residential schools. Through this work, Trevethan continues to serve the needs of Canada's Aboriginal people, as she has done over many years as a criminal justice researcher. She is currently examining the extent to which the Secretariat has achieved its objectives in resolving claims of abuse in residential schools and contributing to healing among survivors.

Trevethan has been fortunate in her career to have worked with numerous Aboriginal organizations and colleagues. It has become clear over her years of work in the area of Aboriginal issues that it is imperative to work in collaboration with Aboriginal organizations and communities when conducting research about Aboriginal issues. It helps to ensure a well-rounded perspective and to ensure that the research focuses on the most salient issues.

Aboriginal offenders are rated as being higher need than non-Aboriginal offenders. For example, Trevethan, Moore, and Rastin (2002) examined the treatment needs of Aboriginal and non-Aboriginal offenders (primarily male) serving time in federal custody. As illustrated in Figure 14.3, Aboriginal offenders were rated as higher need across a range of domains, with the exception of antisocial attitudes.

Very similar differences in need ratings between Aboriginal and non-Aboriginal offenders emerge for both female offenders (Dell and Boe 2000) and young offenders (Corrado and Cohen 2002).

Aboriginal and Non-Aboriginal Treatment Programs

Given their serious treatment needs, programming for Aboriginal offenders needs to be focused on. As mentioned earlier, there is a belief in Canada that part of the cause of Aboriginal offending is loss of culture. Thus, re-establishing a connection with Aboriginal

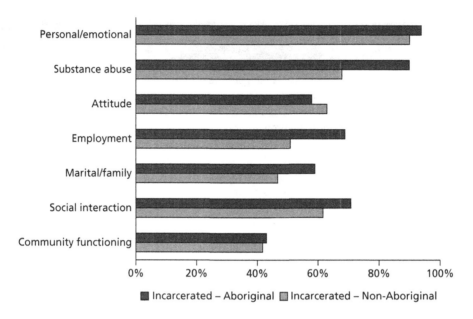

Figure 14.3 Need Ratings for Aboriginal and Non-Aboriginal Offenders in Federal Custody

Source: Trevethan, Moore, and Rastin (2002).

culture is viewed as part of the solution to the Aboriginal offending problem. A range of treatment programs tailored to Aboriginal offenders in provincial and federal custody, as well as in the community, has been developed. For example, in addition to traditional correctional interventions such as anger management and substance abuse programs (e.g., Ghelani 2010), Aboriginal offenders now have access to traditional spiritual practices, Aboriginal literacy classes, sweat lodge ceremonies, drumming classes, etc. (LaPrairie 1996). In fact, in a relatively recent survey of Aboriginal-specific programs in Canada, 23 healing programs were identified (13 federal and 10 provincial) (Epprecht 2000). Many of these programs are offered with Aboriginal healing lodges.

Aboriginal Healing Lodges

Section 81 of the *Corrections and Conditional Release Act* allows the Aboriginal community to take responsibility for overseeing Aboriginal offenders under certain conditions. This enables the provision of correctional services to Aboriginal offenders in a manner that respects their culture. These services are often provided in **Aboriginal healing lodges**. According to Correctional Service Canada (2009), healing lodges

> ... offer services and programs that reflect Aboriginal culture in a space that incorporates Aboriginal peoples' tradition and beliefs. In the healing lodge, the needs of

Some Aboriginal-specific treatment programs include teaching offenders about drumming and encouraging them to learn traditional songs.

> Aboriginal offenders serving federal sentences are addressed through Aboriginal teachings and ceremonies, contact with Elders and children, and interaction with nature. A holistic philosophy governs the approach, whereby individualized programming is delivered within a context of community interaction, with a focus on preparing for release. In the healing lodges, an emphasis is placed on spiritual leadership and on the value of the life experience of staff members, who act as role models. (p. 1)

There are a number of healing lodges across Canada. Some are managed directly by Correctional Service Canada, and others are managed by Aboriginal agencies or communities. While each is unique, they all focus on providing correctional services that are respectful of Aboriginal culture (Crutcher and Trevethan 2002). For example, while traditional correctional programs are offered to inmates, Aboriginal staff, including Elders, are often heavily involved in delivering the programs, especially those that instruct inmates in traditional values and spiritual practices (Trevethan, Crutcher, and Rastin 2002). Speaking about the programming offered in one of Canada's healing lodges, the Pê Sâkâstêw Healing Centre in Hobbema, Alberta, Rashid (2004) argues that it is believed ". . . by integrating the concepts of self-motivated healing, cultural identity, spirituality, and community re-connection, the Centre helps rebuild connections between troubled individuals and the communities they have become alienated from". Ultimately, it is hoped that by integrating traditional and cultural treatment options, the likelihood of Aboriginal reoffending will be reduced.

Does Paying Attention to Culture Matter?

While it is intuitively appealing to think that paying attention to culture matters in corrections, it is important that this issue be examined empirically. Do Aboriginal-specific treatment programs work? Do they work better than non-Aboriginal programs? What do we mean by "work"? It is possible for a program to "work" in the sense that it increases the connection that an Aboriginal offender feels to himself, his community, and/or his spirituality, but it may not actually lead to reductions in crime (i.e., the typical meaning of "work" in the Western correctional research tradition). See the Hot Topics box for a more detailed discussion of these issues as they relate to a particular program that is currently being offered.

On the positive side, there are a range of studies that report encouraging results. For example, when Aboriginal offenders are asked their views on the issue of culturally-based programming, it is clear that they appreciate their value (Waldram 2013). They report feeling more comfortable dealing with Aboriginal staff, for instance, and view them as

---

Hot Topics

Do Aboriginal-Specific Treatment Programs Work? An Evaluation of the *In Search of Your Warrior* Violence Prevention Program for Aboriginal Offenders

As indicated above, the delivery of culturally sensitive treatment to Aboriginal offenders in Canada is required. Given this, it is important to understand the impact that these programs actually have. If these programs can be shown to be effective, this may pave the road for the development of other new and innovative programs. If the programs are not having their intended impact, research can help identify why, and important improvements to the programs can be made.

One program that has been evaluated to some extent is the *In Search of Your Warrior* (ISOYW) program. This is a group-based, high-intensity violence prevention program designed by the Native Counselling Services of Alberta. It is intended to meet the needs of male Aboriginal offenders who have a history of violent behaviour (Laboucane-Benson 2002).

The foundation for the program is clearly based in the culture, teachings, and ceremonies of Aboriginal people. For example, the program immerses participants in a holistic healing approach that encompasses all aspects of the Medicine Wheel (i.e., physical, emotional, spiritual, and mental well-being) with an emphasis on controlling violent and aggressive behaviour (Trevethan, Moore, and Allegri 2005). With the assistance of an Aboriginal Elder, appropriate Aboriginal ceremonies and teachings are incorporated into the program and are used to engage the offender in the healing process. While it is often delivered in a typical classroom setting, the program is occasionally delivered in the wilderness, reflecting the strong connection with nature that is part of Aboriginal culture.

The structure of the program is similar to traditional correctional programs that target violent offenders, as are many of its treatment targets. Indeed, the program relies heavily on the theories, principles, and processes of traditional violence prevention programs (Trevethan et al. 2005). Over the course of many weeks (up to 75 sessions), participants engage in group therapy targeting eight components: 1) anger awareness; 2) violence awareness; 3) family of origin awareness; 4) self-awareness; 5) skill development; 6) group skill development; 7) cultural awareness; and 8) cognitive learning. The ultimate goal is to provide offenders with insight into their own behaviour and strategies for self-management so that violence can be reduced in their homes and communities upon release (Trevethan et al. 2005).

Several attempts have been made to evaluate this program. For example, Trevethan et al. (2005) reported positive changes for offenders who had completed the program—these offenders demonstrated lower need ratings for personal distress, family issues, substance abuse, community functioning, employment, social interactions, and pro-criminal attitudes. Naclia (2009) also reported positive results from his evaluation. For example, the program was perceived positively by participants he interviewed. In addition, the methods of intervention were thought to enable more trust in the counsellor–client relationship and most participants indicated that the cultural component of the programming assisted them with wellness, reintegration, and in dealing with interpersonal problems related to their incarceration. Positive behavioural and attitudinal changes in program participants were also observed by institutional staff. These changes related to greater control of anger, fewer confrontations in the institution, calmer temperament, and greater participation in programming.

Despite these findings, it is currently unclear whether the ISOYW program actually leads to reductions in crime. For example, in Trevethan et al.'s (2005) evaluation, they examined the recidivism rate of offenders taking part in the program along with a matched comparison group that did not take part in the program. No significant differences emerged between the two groups on readmission to federal custody at the end of a one-year follow-up (for technical violations or new offences, although a significantly smaller portion of ISOYW completers were readmitted for new violent offences). This suggests that while participants and staff may perceive value in the program, this value may not translate into significantly improved behaviour on the part of offenders upon completion of the program.

Source: Laboucane-Benson (2002); Naclia (2009); Trevethan, Moore, and Allegri (2005).

more trustworthy than non-Aboriginal staff (Johnston 1997). Aboriginal offenders also feel as though they get a lot out of Aboriginal treatment programs. For example, one study found that Aboriginal offenders felt that culturally-based programs enabled them to trust people more, stay out of trouble better, and deal more positively with their problems (Pfeifer and Hart-Mitchell 2001). Offenders in another study felt that Aboriginal programs helped them understand themselves better and were useful in alleviating anger and gaining control of their behaviour (Crutcher and Trevethan 2002). Female offenders in another study felt that the program they were involved in (*Native Sisterhood*) helped them overcome traumatic events from their past, and provided them a culturally relevant, supportive environment where they could speak about and overcome their mistakes (Yuen and Pedlar 2009).

These findings are obviously important, but they are subjective in nature. Studies have also been conducted that have used more objective measures to demonstrate the benefits associated with Aboriginal treatment programs. Some of these studies also reveal encouraging results. For example, Aboriginal offenders appear more likely to complete treatment when they are participating in culturally based programs (e.g., Ellerby and MacPherson 2002), which will potentially impact their likelihood of reoffending (Nunes and Cortoni 2006). Aboriginal offenders attending these programs also show improvement on treatment targets. In their study of a Native substance abuse pre-treatment program, for example, Weekes and Millson (1994) observed significant improvements on measures of knowledge and attitudes toward substance abuse, general problem-solving ability, and recognition of Native cultural factors.

These results all reflect positively on Aboriginal-specific programs and have led some researchers to conclude that, "Delivering institutional services and programs in a culturally sensitive manner and providing access to cultural practices may serve to heighten responsiveness to treatment among Aboriginal offenders" (Trevethan and Moore 2013: 245). However, it is unclear whether these findings translate into lower levels of recidivism and, more specifically, whether they result in less recidivism than non-Aboriginal programs. This issue has not been extensively explored, but there are a few studies that have addressed these questions and the results are not always positive.

For example, in an examination of the effectiveness of Aboriginal healing lodges to reduce reoffending, Trevethan, Crutcher, and Rastin (2002) found a higher rate of recidivism (19 percent) among healing-lodge residents compared to a sample of Aboriginal offenders serving time in minimum-security facilities (13 percent). Significant differences remained even when matching for risk to reoffend at intake. In addition, post-release, healing lodge residents were found to recidivate more quickly than Aboriginal offenders released from minimum security (275 days vs. 338 days). While these results are not promising, it should be noted that recidivism rates differed significantly across healing lodges in the study, ranging from 12 percent (Okimaw Ohci) to 30 percent (Wahpeton). In contrast, other studies provide a more positive picture when it comes to reoffending rates following participation in Aboriginal-specific treatment programs. Ellerby and MacPherson (2001), for example, found that traditional Aboriginal healing methods were more effective at reducing recidivism among Aboriginal sex offenders (8.1 percent) than non-Aboriginal approaches (25.5 percent). Likewise, Sioui and Thibault (2001) found that Aboriginal offenders who participated in programs with cultural activities demonstrated significantly lower levels of recidivism (3.6 percent) compared to those who did not participate (32.5 percent). Furthermore, Aboriginal offenders who participated in programs that included Elder involvement reoffended significantly less (12.9 percent) than offenders who did not (26.8 percent).

More recently, a study by Stewart, Hamilton, Wilton, Cousineau, and Varrette (2014) examined the effectiveness of the Tupiq program, which is designed for Inuit sex offenders and is facilitated by Inuit leaders. It combines cognitive-behavioural treatment methods and Inuit culture. The recidivism rate of 61 Inuit sex offenders who participated in the Tupiq program was compared with that of 114 Inuit sex offenders incarcerated during the same time period who had participated in an alternative sex-offender treatment program, or had not participated in any program. The findings showed that those who had participated in the Tupiq program had significantly lower rates of general and violent reoffending compared to those who had not received Tupiq programming.

It is not yet clear why some programs effectively reduce recidivism and others do not. In the future, an increased understanding of this issue may lead to the creation of more effective programs for Aboriginal offenders.

FUTURE DIRECTIONS

Despite the very serious problem of Aboriginal overrepresentation in this country, we know surprisingly little about the problem. More research is needed so that we can develop a better understanding of why Aboriginals come into contact with the criminal justice system in disproportionate numbers, and what can be done to help resolve this situation. As discussed throughout this chapter, several initiatives have already been put in place in an attempt to reduce Aboriginal overrepresentation (e.g., Gladue Courts). Future research will continue to monitor the impact of these initiatives. Researchers will also have to carefully track how other developments may unintentionally have a negative impact on attempts to reduce Aboriginal overrepresentation. For example, will the application of mandatory-minimum sentencing in The Safe Streets and Communities Act result in fewer alternative sentencing options (e.g., restorative justice) being considered for Aboriginal offenders? Additional research is also required to better understand how traditional risk-assessment tools can be applied to Aboriginal offenders, particularly female Aboriginal offenders. From this research, the need for more culturally sensitive risk assessment tools may become more apparent. Similarly, more research is needed to gain a greater understanding of the efficacy of Aboriginal treatment programs, including the impact that these programs have on recidivism.

SUMMARY

1. There are four common explanations for Aboriginal overrepresentation. These include: 1) a higher Aboriginal offending rate; 2) the commission by Aboriginal offenders of crimes that are more likely to result in prison sentences; 3) criminal justice policies and practices that have a differential impact on Aboriginal offenders due to their socio-economic conditions; and 4) differential processing through the criminal justice system as a result of discrimination.

2. A variety of attempts have been made to reduce Aboriginal overrepresentation in the criminal justice system, including various police reforms such as the introduction of

First Nations police services, the creation of Aboriginal courts, and legislation that requires that Aboriginal offenders have access to culturally appropriate treatment programs.

3. The risk and need factors exhibited by Aboriginal and non-Aboriginal offenders appear to be similar, but Aboriginal offenders often exhibit more serious problems in these areas. For example, childhood trauma and instability is experienced by both groups, but to a greater extent and in more serious forms for Aboriginal offenders.

4. In the mid-1980s, the Correctional Service Canada (CSC) began to seriously examine the problem of Aboriginal overrepresentation and introduced programs that would better meet the needs of these individuals. By 1992, the *Corrections and Conditional Release Act* stated explicitly that CSC must provide a range of Aboriginal-specific treatment programs. Currently, a range of such programs are available.

5. According to CSC, Aboriginal healing lodges offer services and programs to offenders that reflect Aboriginal culture in a space that incorporates Aboriginal traditions and beliefs. The delivery of such services is based on the belief that loss of culture is at the heart of Aboriginal offending and Aboriginal overrepresentation in the criminal justice system.

Discussion Questions

1. Imagine that the Supreme Court of Canada has just handed down their ruling in the case of *R. v. Gladue* (1999), which indicates that judges must consider alternatives to incarceration when sentencing offenders and must pay particular attention to the circumstances of Aboriginal offenders. What challenges might judges face when trying to implement this ruling? Are there things that could be done in Canada to overcome these challenges?

2. Should cultural, religious, and/or political orientations play a role in the treatment process for offenders? Why or why not?

3. Imagine you are a non-Aboriginal offender facing sentencing. Do you think you should be given the same sentencing options as an Aboriginal offender (e.g., the opportunity to serve your sentence in an Aboriginal healing lodge)? Why or why not?

4. CSC has just proposed a new treatment program for Aboriginal offenders serving time for violent offences. Imagine you are a forensic psychology student doing a summer practicum with CSC and are tasked with developing a study that would allow you to determine whether the new program is successful at reducing recidivism. What would this study look like?

Glossary

Aboriginal The original inhabitants of Canada, which includes three groups of people: Indian (First Nation), Metis, and Inuit.

Aboriginal healing lodge A facility in which offenders can be exposed to correctional services in an environment that incorporates Aboriginal traditions and beliefs.

Aboriginal overrepresentation Aboriginal people are incarcerated at levels higher than their proportion in the general population would predict.

adaptation Evolutionary concept that refers to traits or characteristics that eventually become commonplace in a given species because they somehow enhanced reproductive success in an ancestral environment.

adolescent-onset adolescent offenders Adolescent offenders who begin to show behavioural problems in their teen years.

aggression (specifically human aggression) Refers to the intent and action of inflicting harm on others either through physical means (e.g., punching, gun, knife, slap) or indirect means (e.g., damaging someone's reputation with disparaging gossip).

amino acids The basic proteins of life that are essentially the precursors to neurotransmitters. Amino acids are converted into neurotransmitters via enzymes.

ancestral environment An evolutionary term that refers to the hunter-and-gatherer era, from which most of our current-day adaptations are hypothesized to have evolved.

antisocial behaviour Generic term that encompasses a wide range of behaviours (e.g., hitting, slapping, punching, lying, cheating, stealing, running away, breaking and entering, homicide, and so forth).

antisocial personality disorder (ASPD) Official diagnosis defined in the Diagnostic and Statistical Manual of Mental Disorders (DSM-5), referring to a constellation of antisocial behaviours occurring during adulthood that have persisted for at least six months. Sometimes ASPD is used interchangeably with psychopathy, albeit incorrectly.

attachment Social bond proposed by Travis Hirschi in his social control theory, which refers to one's attachment to others (e.g., parents, friends, teachers).

attention deficit hyperactivity disorder (ADHD) Inattention and restlessness that is not developmentally appropriate.

aversive conditioning Procedure whereby an unpleasant stimulus (e.g., an electric shock) is presented while an individual is engaged in problematic behaviour (e.g., experiencing sexual arousal while observing child pornography) with the goal of creating an aversion to the activity.

behavioural genetics A sub-discipline of biology that studies how genes in humans and animals influence behaviour.

behavioural treatments For sex offenders, treatments that use conditioning to reduce deviant sexual interests or increase appropriate sexual interests.

behaviourism A school of thought in psychology that emphasizes the view that all behaviour can be described and studied scientifically without reference to internal psychological constructs such as the mind.

belief Social bond proposed by Travis Hirschi in his social control theory, which refers to one's conviction to the view that people should obey common rules (e.g., the law).

Big Four The four most strongly correlated risk factors, as identified through meta-analysis.

biosocial theory of crime Theory of crime proposed by Hans Eysenck that suggests that people commit crime as a result of the interaction between biologically determined characteristics (e.g., nervous system processing) and environmental stimuli (e.g., parental discipline).

blockage Some people may be blocked from meeting their sexual and emotional needs in prosocial ways (e.g., consenting sexual contact with adults).

causal mechanisms Processes that directly cause a behaviour (i.e., factor X causes factor Y). In order to confirm the existence of a causal mechanism, a research design is needed that allows for the independent variable to be manipulated by the experimenter. Ethically, however, we are unable to do this most of the time. For example, if we wanted to know beyond a doubt whether child abuse causes crime, we would have to randomly assign children to one of two conditions—an abuse and a non-abuse situation, and clearly this is not an option. There are reasonable proxy designs that get us closer to causality, such as treatment studies that use random assignment or comparison groups as well as longitudinal designs that examine whether naturally occurring changes in variable X are related to changes in variable Y.

Central Eight The eight most strongly identified risk factors, as identified through meta-analysis.

child-onset adolescent offenders Adolescent offenders who have behavioural problems starting very early in childhood.

classical conditioning A form of learning that takes place when an unconditioned stimulus (e.g., food) that produces an unconditioned response (e.g., salivation) is paired with a conditioned stimulus (e.g., a tone) such that, over time, a conditioned response (e.g., salivation) is reproduced using only the conditioned stimulus.

cognitive-behavioural therapy (CBT) Combines elements of cognitive and behavioural treatments to address psychological problems and abnormal behaviour.

cognitive social learning theory of crime A learning theory of crime that attends to both social and cognitive factors as well as behaviour.

commitment Social bond proposed by Travis Hirschi in his social control theory that refers to the time, energy, and effort one places in conventional behaviour (e.g., getting an education).

community notification Informing the public that a sex offender is being released to a particular city or neighbourhood.

community service Requirement by the courts to provide a form of service to the community (i.e., speaking to youth groups, cleaning up

public sites, etc.) in lieu of incarceration. Could be performed in conjunction with a probation or community supervision order.

conditioned response In classical conditioning, a response to a previously neutral stimulus turned conditioned stimulus (e.g., salivation is a conditioned response when it occurs after the presentation of a tone, which has become a conditioned stimulus by repeatedly pairing it with food, an unconditioned stimulus).

conditioned stimulus In classical conditioning, a previously neutral stimulus that comes to evoke a conditioned response after it is paired with an unconditioned stimulus (e.g., a tone becomes a conditioned stimulus that elicits a salivation response when repeatedly paired with food, an unconditioned stimulus).

Conduct Disorder (CD) Official diagnosis defined in the Diagnostic and Statistical Manual of Mental Disorders (DSM-5). It refers to a constellation of antisocial behaviours (e.g., stealing, getting into fights, using a weapon during a fight) occurring during childhood that have persisted for at least six months.

Conflict Tactics Scale (CTS) Scale designed to assess how a person and his or her partner resolve conflict; measures constructive problem solving, verbal aggression, and physical aggression.

conscience One component of the Freudian superego, which allows an individual to distinguish between right and wrong and inhibit id pursuits that are out of line with one's morals.

core correctional practice A combination of practices that correctional staff can use to more effectively interact with offenders and manage behaviour.

corporate crime Offences committed by organizations to advance their own interests.

correctional program A structured set of methods and activities delivered by skilled staff to provide opportunities for offenders to gain new attitudes and skills in order to reduce the likelihood of reoffending. Also referred to as appropriate service delivery, treatment program, or rehabilitation program.

correctional program officer Highly trained paraprofessional who delivers correctional programs to groups of offenders.

correctional psychology Application of psychology to the understanding of the assessment and management of individuals who engage in criminal behaviour.

correctional treatment plan Written plan that identifies an offender's criminogenic needs and treatment requirements. Typically includes the ranking of needs from most to least serious and an indication of the intensity of programming required based on risk assessment.

Corrections and Conditional Release Act Act brought into force on November 1, 1992, that governs corrections and the conditional release and detention of offenders. Its purpose is to contribute to the maintenance of a just, peaceful, and safe society by: (a) carrying out sentences imposed by courts through the safe and humane custody and supervision of offenders; and (b) assisting the rehabilitation of offenders and their reintegration into the community as law-abiding citizens through the provision of programs in penitentiaries and in the community.

crime desistance The cessation of criminal behaviour, most often described as a process of change rather than an instantaneous event.

criminal behaviour Intentional behaviour that, when detected, is sanctioned by the courts as a breach of society's established rules.

criminogenic needs/factors Changeable risk factors that, when reduced, result in reduced criminal behaviour. Sometimes referred to as dynamic risk factors.

cross-sectional research Type of research design whereby different groups of people who differ on a variable of interest (e.g., involvement in delinquent activity) are observed at a particular point in time to determine how they differ on some other variable (e.g., parental supervision) or set of variables.

custody classification Method of initially assessing inmate risks that balances security requirements with program needs. Placement considers both custody level and area within a prison.

Custody Rating Scale Statistical scale used by Correctional Service Canada to determine security placement.

delusion Erroneous beliefs that usually involve a misinterpretation of perceptions or experiences.

deterrence Expectation that increased costs (i.e., longer sentences) by the courts will suppress the frequency and/or severity of crime. The

impact of these costs on the particular individual involved with the courts is referred to as specific deterrence. The impact on the population as a whole is referred to as general deterrence.

deviant identification The process of identifying with a deviant role model (e.g., a criminal father).

Diagnostic and Statistical Manual of Mental Disorders (DSM) Manual published by the American Psychiatric Association that lists mental and personality disorders.

differential association theory Theory of crime proposed by Edwin Sutherland that suggests that people commit crime when they are exposed (e.g., in intimate group settings) to an excess of definitions (i.e., attitudes) that are favourable to law-breaking versus definitions that are unfavourable to law-breaking.

differential association-reinforcement theory Theory of crime proposed by Robert Burgess and Ron Akers that combines operant conditioning principles with differential association principles and suggests that people commit crime when criminal behaviour is more reinforced (e.g., in intimate group settings) than non-criminal behaviour.

disinhibition In Finkelhor's model, he noted that inhibitions against child sexual abuse are either circumvented or absent to allow an offender to act on his or her sexual interest in children.

diversion A decision not to prosecute a young offender but rather have him or her undergo an educational or community service program.

Domestic Violence Risk Appraisal Guide (DVRAG) Empirical actuarial risk-assessment instrument designed to estimate risk of spousal assault recidivism in adult male batterers.

Dopamine A brain neurotransmitter that helps control the brain's reward, motivation, and pleasure centres.

Drug treatment courts An alternative court system for substance abusers who commit non-violent crimes motivated by their addiction. The outcome is generally court-ordered community-based treatment rather than prison time.

Duluth model Treatment program for male batterers that believes abusers are overwhelmingly men who use violence to exercise control over women.

dynamic risk factors Risk factors that can change, unlike static factors, with such change related to reduced criminal behaviour.

dysphoric/borderline batterer Male batterer who is depressed and has borderline personality traits, primarily exhibits violence toward his intimate partner, and has problems with jealously and abandonment.

ecological model Model of family violence that examines the relationship between multiple levels of influence, including individual, relationship, community, and societal levels, in understanding family violence.

economic crime Criminal offences in which the primary motivation is economic gain.

effect size Outcome measure indicating the degree of the relationship between two variables *or* the impact of an intervention.

ego The conscious part of the Freudian personality, which acts as the mediator between the instinctual demands of the id and the social restrictions of the superego.

ego-ideal One component of the Freudian superego that represents the socially accepted standards that we all aspire to.

emotional congruence Perceived fit between an adult's emotional needs and a child's characteristics. Also referred to as emotional identification with children.

empirical actuarial approach Follows explicit rules about what factors to consider and how to combine those factors to arrive at a final estimate of risk. More specifically, a selection and combination of items are derived from their observed statistical relationship with recidivism. Provides tables linking scores to expected recidivism rates.

epidemiological Refers to research designs that utilize large representative samples of the general population (or, in some cases, the entire population) in order to study the incidence, prevalence, and/or nature of a disease or a particular behaviour (e.g., crime).

eugenics The belief that the evolution of the human species can be artificially improved by preventing individuals considered genetically "defective" from reproducing by methods such as forced sterilization.

evidence-based practice Body of research and replicable clinical knowledge that describes contemporary correctional assessment, programming, and supervision strategies that lead to improved correctional outcomes such as the rehabilitation of offenders and increased public safety.

ex-offender assistance Providing assistance in terms of accommodation, employment, and addictions counselling. Often provided by non-governmental agencies such as the Elizabeth Fry Society, the John Howard Society, and the St. Leonard's Society.

externalizing problems Behavioural difficulties such as delinquency, fighting, bullying, lying, and destructive behaviour.

extinction In classical conditioning, when the conditioned response no longer gets elicited by the conditioned stimulus as a result of the conditioned stimulus not being paired with an unconditioned stimulus (e.g., salivation—a conditioned response—no longer gets elicited by the presentation of a tone—a conditioned stimulus—because the tone has been repeatedly presented in the absence of the unconditioned stimulus, such as food).

extrajudicial measures Community options and less serious alternatives than youth court.

family-only batterer A male batterer who is typically not violent outside the home, has few psychopathological symptoms, and does not possess negative attitudes supportive of violence.

family-supportive interventions Interventions that connect at-risk families to various support services (e.g., child care, counselling, medical assistance) that may be available in their community.

federally sentenced women In Canada, offenders sentenced to periods of imprisonment of two years or more fall under federal jurisdiction. Those sentenced to less than two years are the responsibility of the provinces. Women sentenced to two years or more are collectively known as federally sentenced women.

female-salient predictor Risk factor that predicts recidivism in females and males but the strength of the association is significantly stronger for females.

feminism "A set of theories about women's oppression and a set of strategies for change" (Daly and Chesney-Lind 1988, 502). The common theme that binds feminist theories of female crime is the assumption that the oppression of women plays a central role in the explanation and prediction of female criminal conduct.

fetal alcohol syndrome (FAS) Disorder caused when a woman drinks alcohol during pregnancy. Diagnosed when the alcohol consumption results in prenatal and/or post-natal growth delay, characteristic cranio-facial anomalies, and central nervous system impairments. Prevalence rates of this disorder are known to be significantly higher in Aboriginal populations.

fetal alcohol spectrum disorder (FASD) Umbrella term used to describe a range of disabilities that may affect people whose mothers drank alcohol during pregnancy.

first-degree murder Murder is first-degree when it is planned and deliberate or under any of the following conditions: (a) the victim is a peace officer (e.g., police officer) or prison employee (e.g., correctional officer, institutional parole officer); or (b) the victim's death is caused while committing or attempting to commit the hijacking of an aircraft, sexual assault, kidnapping, hostage taking, criminal harassment, terrorist activity, use of explosives in association with a criminal organization, or intimidation.

forensic psychology Application of psychology to the legal system, intended to guide legal decision making.

fraud triangle A conceptualization of fraud that has three facets: 1) opportunity to commit fraud, 2) pressure to commit fraud, and 3) rationalization of the fraud.

gender informed Refers to research, risk tools, or treatment methods that were originally developed based on female-centred principles. The end result may or may not include hypothesized gender-specific factors (e.g., poverty) as well as gender neutral factors (e.g., criminal attitudes). Researchers and program developers initiated the process using contemporary female-focused theory and research. It doesn't matter if the final risk instrument, program, or policy resembles gender-neutral methods.

gender neutral Refers to research, risk assessment tools, or treatment methods originally grounded in theories or research that either implicitly or explicitly excluded the female perspective. The assumption of gender-neutral approaches is that there are no differences between males and females.

gender responsive Describes correctional assessment and programming strategies that have been designed to address hypothesized female-specific risk factors, treatment targets, or responsivity factors.

gender specificity Term used to describe a situation in which a risk factor or treatment approach is unique to one gender but not the other. For example, a risk factor that predicts crime only for females but not at all for males would be taken as evidence of gender specificity, in this case in favour of females. Risk factors may also possess gender specificity for males as well.

general deterrence The impact of a court-imposed cost (e.g., a sentence) on the population as a whole.

general responsivity Refers to the principle of delivering treatment programs in a manner that is consistent with offenders' learning styles (i.e., skills-based, cognitive-behavioural).

general theory of crime Theory of crime proposed by Michael Gottfredson and Travis Hirschi that suggests that people do not commit crime because they possess high levels of self-control.

generally violent/antisocial A male batterer who is violent inside and outside the home; engages in other criminal acts; has drug, alcohol, and impulsive problems; and possesses violence-supportive attitudes.

genotype An individual's complete genetic makeup regardless of whether a particular gene has a visible influence on an individual's functioning or behaviour; what's on the "inside" versus the "outside."

Gladue Court An Aboriginal persons court, which performs the same duties as a regular court but in a way that is in line with Aboriginal beliefs and traditions.

Good Lives Model In addition to focusing on the usual risk management issues, this model emphasizes helping offenders identify and achieve healthy goals that promote psychological well-being. This is expected to increase the motivation of offenders to participate and engage in treatment, as well as reduce their likelihood of reoffending because they learn how to achieve fundamental human needs through prosocial means rather than through offending.

HCR-20 A structured professional judgement instrument designed to assess risk for violence.

human trafficking The recruitment, transport, or harbouring of persons by means of threat, use of force, or other forms of coercion, abduction, fraud, or deception for the purpose of exploitation.

id The unconscious, instinctual part of the Freudian personality that seeks the immediate gratification of basic drives (e.g., aggression).

identity fraud The use of personal information without the person's knowledge or consent to commit various crimes under their name, such as fraud, theft, or forgery.

identity theft The collection, possession, and trafficking of personal information, which typically takes place independent of or in preparation for the commission of identity fraud.

incapacitation The incarceration of criminals to reduce the risk to the community.

incidence The number of *new* cases identified or reported at a given point in time, usually one year.

intimate partner violence Violence occurring between intimate partners who are living together or separated.

instigator In social learning theory, events in the environment or within the individual that trigger violence.

instrumental violence Premeditated violence ultimately aimed at achieving some secondary goal beyond harming the victim (e.g., money).

interactive Effects that are known to be multiplicative, exponential, or synergistic rather than merely additive. Thus while psychopathy and sexual deviance may elevate the risk of sexual recidivism by two points, in combination, the risk of sexual recidivism may increase by six points. Or, alternately, the noise level generated by two young toddlers is interactive in that "one boy" plus "one boy" doesn't equal two boys playing but seems more like six toddlers!

internalizing problems Emotional difficulties such as anxiety, depression, and obsessions.

involvement Social bond proposed by Travis Hirschi in his social control theory that refers to the time and energy one spends taking part in activities that are in line with the conventional interests of society (e.g., school).

longitudinal research Type of research design whereby a particular group of individuals are observed repeatedly over time.

learning theories Theories of crime that emphasize learning, such as the way in which information is encoded, processed, and retained in the process of becoming a criminal.

mass murder Killing three or more victims in a single location with no "cooling-off period" between murders.

mechanical approach Following explicit rules about what factors to consider and how to combine those factors to arrive at a final estimate of risk; the selection and combination of items are derived from theory or reviews of the empirical literature and no tables are provided.

mediators Variables that explain the relationship between variable X and Y. It might be concluded that variable X exerts its influence on variable Y through a third intervening variable—the mediator.

mens rea Legal term for criminal intent.

meta-analysis Quantitative method of combining the results of independent studies (usually drawn from published literature) and synthesizing summaries and conclusions that may be used to detect and evaluate trends.

Methadone maintenance program A drug treatment program for individuals with opiate-related addictions (e.g., heroin, oxycontin) that allows participants to take methadone, a synthetic drug substitute for opiates that eases withdrawal symptoms while also blocking the pleasurable effects of the opiate

moderators Variables that cause the relationship between variable A and B to vary as a function of a third variable—the moderator.

money laundering The process whereby money received through illegal activity is disguised to mask where it came from.

motivational interviewing A therapeutic technique that focuses on the provision of non-judgmental feedback regarding an person's risks and experience of problems. Avoids labels and confrontation and helps the offender generate goals for behaviour change.

natural selection Primary mechanism through which evolution created all species. Natural selection works by allowing the "trait" that bestowed a reproductive fitness advantage to be "selected" for in the sense that those with the trait lived long enough to procreate and pass it on to the next generation.

negative punishment In operant conditioning, a decrease in the likelihood of a behaviour being exhibited in the future due to the removal of a pleasant stimulus following the behaviour.

negative reinforcement In operant conditioning, an increase in the likelihood of a behaviour being exhibited in the future due to the removal of an aversive stimulus following the behaviour.

neurotic criminal An individual who commits crime as a result of a harsh superego, which is assumed to lead to pathological levels of unconscious guilt that can be resolved by receiving punishment (e.g., a legal sanction for a crime).

neurotransmitters The chemical messengers of the brain.

not criminally responsible on account of a mental disorder (NCRMD) Person who, due to a mental disorder at the time of an offence, is incapable of appreciating the nature and quality of the act or knowing that it was wrong.

observational learning Learning that occurs as a function of observing and often imitating behaviour exhibited by other people.

occupational crime Offences committed against businesses and government by those with a "higher" social status.

offender classification Sometimes referred to as custody classification, this process involves the assessment of offender risk and need levels in order to determine the appropriate security placement of incarcerated prisoners.

offender rehabilitation The delivery of correctional programming that targets criminogenic needs for the purpose of reducing rates of reoffending by program completers.

operant conditioning A form of learning that takes place by experiencing environmental consequences caused by behaviour, especially reinforcement and punishment.

oppositional defiant disorder (ODD) Pattern of negativistic, hostile, and defiant behaviour.

over-policing The practice of police targeting people of particular ethnic or racial backgrounds or who live in particular neighbourhoods.

paraphilias Sexual disorders characterized by recurrent, intense, sexually arousing fantasies, sexual urges, or behaviours generally involving 1) non-human objects, 2) the suffering or humiliation of oneself or one's partner, or 3) children or other non-consenting persons that occur over a period of at least six months.

parent-focused interventions Interventions directed at assisting parents to recognize warning signs for later juvenile violence and/or training parents to effectively manage any behavioural problems that arise.

parole officer With a background in social sciences, officers who supervise offenders, either in the community or federal prison, providing counselling and writing reports for various decision-makers (i.e., wardens, National Parole Board) regarding release suitability.

patriarchal theory Theory that suggests violence of men against their female partners is rooted in a broad set of cultural beliefs and values that support the male dominance of women.

pedophilia Sexual preference for children who have not yet begun puberty.

penile plethysmography (PPG) Measurement of penile tumescence (erection) during the presentation of various stimuli, such as descriptions of sexual activity. Deviant sexual interest is usually inferred from the amount of arousal in response to deviant stimuli relative to non-deviant stimuli.

pharmacological treatments In the case of sex offenders, treatment with drugs, usually with the goal of reducing sex drive (e.g., desire, arousal).

phenotypic An individual's observed properties or how one's genotype is actually expressed. For example, a genotype may have a recessive gene for blue eyes but a phenotype may be for brown eyes.

Personal, interpersonal, and community-reinforcement (PIC–R) theory An integrative and situational model of criminal behaviour that recognizes the influence of both historical and immediate factors in an individual arriving at the decision to engage in a criminal act and to view such behaviour as appropriate.

pleasure principle The driving force of the id, which leads people to seek immediate pleasure while trying to avoid pain.

polymorphism Biological term that refers to a situation where alternative versions of a discrete trait exist naturally in a given species. For example, a polymorphism exists for eye colour (e.g., blue eyes, brown eyes, green eyes) and blood type—A, B, AB, O). The contrasting forms are called morphs.

positive punishment In operant conditioning, a decrease in the likelihood of a behaviour being exhibited in the future due to the addition of an aversive stimulus following the behaviour.

positive reinforcement In operant conditioning, an increase in the likelihood of a behaviour being exhibited in the future due to the addition of a pleasant stimulus following the behaviour.

prevalence The *total* number of people who have experienced abuse or neglect in a specified time period.

price fixing Occurs when companies group together to sell the same product for the same price; there is no price variability for the consumer.

primary intervention strategies Strategies implemented prior to any violence occurring with the goal of decreasing its likelihood later.

proactive aggression Aggression directed at achieving a goal or receiving positive reinforcers.

professional override Provision within a decision-making process to permit trained staff, with well-articulated reasons, to arrive at a decision different than that recommended by the results of a standardized risk measure.

prostitution The provision of sexual services in exchange for money.

protective factor Variable or factor that, if present, decreases the likelihood of a negative outcome (such as antisocial behaviour and juvenile offending) or increases the likelihood of a positive outcome.

psychodynamic A school of thought in psychology developed by Sigmund Freud that emphasizes the role of conscious and unconscious psychological forces (forming a dynamic personality system) in understanding human behaviour.

psychodynamic theories Theories of crime that emphasize how psychodynamic processes, such as conscious and unconscious psychological forces, influence the development of criminal behaviour.

psychopath A personality disorder defined by a cluster of interpersonal, affective, behavioural, and antisocial traits.

psychopathy Typified by a constellation of affective, interpersonal, and behavioural characteristics such as superficial charm, grandiosity, manipulation and lying, absence of remorse, inability to feel empathy, impulsivity, risk-taking, irresponsibility, and living a parasitic lifestyle.

rape myths Beliefs that justify, excuse, or otherwise support rape.

rational choice model In criminology, the rational choice model assumes that crime is purposive behaviour designed to meet the offender's commonplace needs for such things as money, status, sex, and excitement. Meeting these needs through crime is considered a rational choice.

reactive violence An emotionally violent response to a perceived threat or frustration.

reality principle The driving force of the ego, which leads people to defer gratification until it is physically and socially safe to pursue it.

re-entry Involves the use of programs and community aftercare targeted at promoting the effective reintegration of offenders into communities upon release from prison.

regulator In social learning theory, the consequences of violence that result in an increase or decrease in the probability of future violence.

rehabilitative program See correctional program.

relapse prevention (RP) For sex offenders, RP focuses on addressing putative dynamic risk factors, identifying situational risk factors (e.g., high-risk situation), and developing ways to avoid or otherwise cope with these situational risk factors with the ultimate goal of avoiding recidivism.

reproductive fitness variance The range of possible offspring an organism can produce.

resilient A child who has multiple risk factors but can overcome them and prevail.

restitution Financial reimbursement for property damaged or lost by being a victim of crime.

restorative justice Emphasizes repairing the harm caused by crime. When victims, offenders, and community members meet voluntarily to decide how to achieve this, transformation can result.

retribution Considered a morally acceptable response to crime intended to satisfy an aggrieved party, including society, through the application of punishment or other sanctions, if proportionate.

risk assessment The determination of risk or probability of reoffending through the systematic review of static and dynamic factors.

risk factors Measurable constructs (e.g., criminal history, employment stability) that predict future criminal reoffending. In order to be deemed a risk factor, the construct must be measured before criminal reoffending is assessed. Thus, evidence for risk factors comes from predictive or longitudinal studies.

risk management The application of risk-assessment information to differentially allocate resources such as programming and supervision in order to manage changes in risk over time.

risk, needs, responsivity (RNR) An approach to intervention that asserts intervention should only target those at risk, should only target criminogenic needs, and should be applied in a manner consistent with cognitive-behavioural principles.

sanctions Terms used to describe punishment imposed by the courts.

secondary intervention strategies Strategies that attempt to reduce the frequency of violence.

selection pressures Recurring conditions in the ancestral environment that favoured certain traits (in a reproductive fitness sense) and thus promoted their eventual conversion into adaptations.

Self-Appraisal Questionnaire (SAQ) A self-report empirical risk-assessment instrument developed to estimate risk of violent and non-violent recidivism.

serial murder Killing three or more people, usually in different locations, with a cooling-off period between murders.

sex offender registries In many jurisdictions, sex offenders are required to register with the police upon release and to maintain current information about their address.

sexual deviancy A general term referring to a variety of deviant sexual interests and behaviours, such as sexual interest in children, sexual preoccupation, and sex as coping.

sex tourism Going to other countries to seek (often child) prostitution.

social control theory Theory of crime proposed by Travis Hirschi that suggests that people don't commit crimes because of social controls or the bonds people have to society.

social learning theory A theory of human behaviour that posits people develop skills, behaviours, and attitudes by how they are directly reinforced or punished for these skills, behaviours, and attitudes and by observing how others are similarly punished or reinforced.

sociopathy A dated term previously used to describe psychopathy. Often used interchangeably though incorrectly with psychopathy and antisocial personality disorder.

sociopath Label used to describe individuals who commit antisocial acts because of family or environmental factors.

specific deterrence The impact of court-imposed costs (e.g. a sentence) on the particular individual (offender) involved with the court.

specific responsivity Principle of delivering treatment programs in a manner that considers the unique aspects of the offenders, including gender, motivation, and strengths.

Spousal Assault Risk Assessment Guide (SARA) A structured professional judgment instrument consisting of both historical and dynamic risk factors designed to estimate risk for spousal assault recidivism.

spree murder Killing three or more victims at two or more locations with no cooling-off period between murders.

Static-99 An empirical actuarial risk-assessment instrument designed to estimate risk of sexual recidivism among adult sex offenders.

static risk factors Risk factors with a demonstrated correlation with criminal behaviour, but which cannot change over time or with intervention.

stigma Combination of stereotypes (i.e., cognitive labels used to describe a person), prejudices (i.e., negative emotions toward individuals), and discrimination (i.e., curtailing the rights and opportunities of individuals) toward a specific group.

structured professional judgment Incorporates features of both unstructured clinical judgment and the actuarial approach; there are explicit guidelines for which factors to consider (although additional factors may also be considered) but their combination is left up to the discretion of the assessor.

superego The part of the Freudian personality that acts as the moral regulator, making sure that we act in accordance with internalized group standards. Includes two sub-systems called the *conscience* and the *ego-ideal*.

tertiary intervention strategies Strategies that attempt to prevent violence from reoccurring.

theory of maternal deprivation A theory of crime proposed by John Bowlby that suggests that if children are not exposed to consistent and constant maternal care in their early years they will experience difficulties in developing the ability to establish meaningful prosocial relationships and, as a result, will be more likely to exhibit antisocial patterns of behaviour.

threat/control-override (TCO) symptoms Psychotic symptoms in which an individual feels that their self-control is overridden by outside forces or feels they will be harmed by others.

unconditioned response In classical conditioning, an unlearned response that occurs automatically following the presentation of an unconditioned stimulus (e.g., salivation is an unconditioned response to the presentation of food).

unconditioned stimulus In classical conditioning, a stimulus that unconditionally (i.e., automatically) triggers a response (e.g., food is an unconditioned stimulus that triggers salivation).

unfit to stand trial (UFST) Person who, due to a mental disorder, is unable to understand trial proceedings, interpret the consequences of a crime, or communicate with their counsel.

Uniform Crime Reporting (UCR) Survey Measures the incidence of crimes reported to police in a given year and some of the characteristics of those crimes. Includes offences against victims of all ages and incorporates the territories and the provinces.

unstructured clinical judgment Assessors arrive at an estimate of risk based on their own idiosyncratic decisions about what factors to consider and how to combine those factors.

vicarious conditioning A form of learning that takes place by observing the environmental consequences of other people's behaviour, especially reinforcement and punishment.

victim assistance Provision of information and support regarding the criminal justice process, which can occur from the time of an incident to the perpetrator's release into the community.

victim–offender mediation Face-to-face meeting in the presence of a trained mediator between the victim of a crime and the person who committed it. The offender and victim talk to each other about what happened, the effects of the crime on their lives, and their feelings about it.

Violence Risk Appraisal Guide—Revised (VRAG-R) Empirical actuarial risk-assessment instrument designed to estimate risk for violent recidivism.

Violence Risk Scale–Sexual Offender version (VRS-SO) Actuarial instrument consisting of both static and putatively dynamic factors designed to estimate risk of sexual recidivism.

References

Abel, E.L. 1980. *Marihuana: The first twelve thousand years*. New York: Springer.

Abel, G.G., Becker, J.V., and Cunningham-Rathner, J. 1984. "Complications, consent, and cognitions in sex between children and adults." *International Journal of Law and Psychiatry*. 7:89–103. DOI:10.1016/0160-2527(84)2990008-6.

Abel, G.G., Jordan, A., Rouleau, J.L., Emerick, R., Barboza-Whitehead, S., and Osborn, C. 2004. "Use of visual reaction time to assess male adolescents who molest children." *Sexual Abuse: A Journal of Research and Treatment*. 16(3):255–265. DOI: 10.1023/B:SEBU.0000029136.01177.51.

Aboriginal Justice Inquiry of Manitoba. 1999. *Report of the Aboriginal Justice Inquiry of Manitoba*. Retrieved January 12, 2009 (www.ajic.mb.ca/volume.html).

Abrahamsen, D. 1973. *The murdering mind*. New York, NY: Harper and Row, Publishers, pp. 9–10. Copyright © 1973 by David Abrahamsen, M.D.

Abrahamsen, D. 1985. *Confessions of Son of Sam*. New York, NY: Columbia University Press.

Adachi, P.J.C., and Willoughby, T. 2011. "The effect of video game competition and violence on aggressive behavior: Which characteristic has the greatest influence?" *Psychology of Violence*. 1(4):259–274. DOI: dx.doi.org/10.1037/a0024908.

Adler, F. 1975. *Sisters in crime*. New York, NY: McGraw-Hill.

Agnew, R. 1991. "A longitudinal test of social control theory and delinquency." *Journal of Research in Crime and Delinquency*. 28:126–156.

Agnew, R. 2006. *Pressured into crime: An overview of General Strain Theory*. Los Angeles, CA: Roxbury Publishing.

Akers, R.L. 1991. "Self-control as a general theory of crime." *Journal of Quantitative Criminology*. 7:201–211.

Akers, R.L. 1998. *Social learning and social structure: A general theory of crime and deviance*. Boston, MA: Northeastern University Press.

Akers, R.L. 2009. *Social learning and social structure: A general theory of crime and deviance*. New Brunswick, NJ: Transaction Publishers.

Akers, R.L., and Jensen, G.F. 2006. "The empirical status of social learning theory: The past, present, and future." In F.T. Cullen, J.P. Wright, and K.R. Blevins, eds. *Taking stock: The status of criminological theory*. pp. 37–76. New Brunswick., NJ: Transaction Publishers.

Akers, C., and Kaukinen, C. 2009. "The police reporting behavior of intimate partner violence victims." *Journal of Family Violence*. 24:159–171.

Akers, R.L., Krohn, M.D., Lanza-Kaduce, L., and Radosevich, M. 1979. "Social learning and deviant behavior: A specific test of a general theory." *American Sociological Review*. 44:636–655.

Akers, R.L., and Sellers, C.S. 2004. *Criminological theories: Introduction, evaluation, and application*. 4th ed. Los Angeles, CA: Roxbury Publishing Company.

Alberta Justice and Solicitor General (2015); British Columbia Ministry of Justice (2013); Manitoba Justice (2015); New Brunswick Public Safety (2015); Newfoundland Labrador Department of Justice and Public Safety (2015); Northwest Territories Department of Justice (2015); Nova Scotia Department of Justice Correctional Services (2013); Nunavut Department of Justice (2013); Ontario Ministry of Community Safety and Correctional Services (2015); Prince Edward Island Department of Justice and Public Safety (2015); Saskatchewan Ministry of Justice (2012); Sécurité Publique Québec (2015); Yukon Department of Justice (2014).

Alcoholics Anonymous. 2015. "Historical data: The birth of A.A. and its growth in the U.S./Canada." *Alcoholics Anonymous*. Retrieved October 28, 2015 (www.aa.org/pages/en_US/historical-data-the-birth-of-aa-and-its-growth-in-the-uscanada).

Amato, P.R., and Keith, B. 1991. "Parental divorce and the well being of children: A meta-analysis." *Psychological Bulletin*. 110:26–46.

American Psychiatric Association. 2013. *Diagnostic and Statistical Manual of Mental Disorders*, 5th ed. (DSM-5). Washington, DC: Author.

Amstutz, L.S., and Zehr, H. 1998. *Victim offender conferencing in Pennsylvania's juvenile justice system*. Harrisonburg, PA: Eastern Mennonite University, Conflict Transformation Program (www.emu.edu/cjp/pub/rjmanual.pdf).

Andershed, H. 2010. "Stability and change of psychopathic traits: What do we know?" In R.T. Salekin, and D.R. Lynam, eds. *Handbook of child and adolescent psychopathy*. pp. 233–250. New York, NY: Guilford Press.

Andershed, H., Kerr, M., Stattin, H., and Levander, S. 2002. "Psychopathic traits in non-referred youths: A new assessment tool." In E. Blaauw and L. Sheridan, eds. *Psychopaths—Current international perspectives*. pp. 131–158. Elsevier, The Hague.

Anderson, C.A., and Bushman, B.J. 2002. "Human aggression." *Annual Review of Psychology*. 53:27–51.

Anderson, C.A., and Dill, F.E. 2000. "Video games and aggressive thoughts, feelings, and behavior in the laboratory and in life." *Journal of Personality and Social Psychology*. 78:772–290.

Anderson, C.A., Shibuya, A., Ihori, N., Swing, E.L., Bushman, B.J., Nakamoto, A., Rothstein, H.R., & Salem, M. 2010. Violent video game effects on aggression, empathy, and prosocial behaviour in eastern and western countries: A meta-analytic review. *Psychological Bulletin*. 136:151–173.

Anderson, G.S. 2007. *Biological influences on criminal behavior*. Boca Raton, FL: Simon Fraser University Publications, CRC Press, Taylor and Francis Group.

Andrews, D.A. 1980. "Some experimental investigations of the principles of differential association through deliberate manipulations of the structure of service systems." *American Sociological Review*. 45:448–462.

Andrews, D.A. 1994. *An Overview of Treatment Effectiveness: Research and Clinical Principles*. Ottawa, ON: Carleton University Department of Psychology.

Andrews, D.A., and Bonta, J. 1995. *The Level of Service Inventory-Revised*. Toronto, ON: Multi-Health Systems.

Andrews, D.A., and Bonta, J. 2006. *The psychology of criminal conduct*. 4th ed. Cincinnati, Ohio: Anderson Publishing.

Andrews, D.A., and Bonta, J. 2010. *The psychology of criminal conduct*. 5th ed. New Providence, NJ: Matthew Bender and Company, Inc.

Andrews, D.A., Bonta, J., and Hoge, R.D. 1990. "Classification for effective rehabilitation: Rediscovering psychology." *Criminal Justice and Behavior*. 17:19–52.

Andrews, D.A., Bonta, J., and Wormith, S.J. 2004. *Level of Service/Case Management Inventory: An offender assessment system*. Toronto, ON: Multi-Health Systems.

Andrews, D.A., Bonta, J., Wormith, S.J., Guzzo, L., and Brews, A. 2008. *The relative and incremental predictive validity of gender-neutral and gender-informed risk/need*. Unpublished Manuscript. Carleton University.

Andrews, D.A., Guzzo, L., Raynor, P., Rowe, R.C., Rettinger, L.J., Brews, A., and Wormith, S. 2012. "Are the major risk/need factors predictive of both female and male offending? A test with the eight domains of the Level of Service/Case Management Inventory." *International Journal of Offender Therapy and Comparative Criminology*. 56:113–133. DOI: 10.1177/0306624X10395716.

Andrews, D.A., Zinger, I., Hoge, R.D., Bonta, J., Gendreau, P., and Cullen, F.T. 1990. "Does correctional treatment work? A clinically relevant and psychologically informed meta-analysis." *Criminology*. 28:369–404.

Aos, S., Miller, M., and Drake, E. 2006. *Evidence-based public policy options to reduce future prison construction, criminal justice costs and crime rates*. Olympia: Washington State Institute for Public Policy.

Arboleda-Florez, J. 1994. *An epidemiological study of mental illness in a remanded population and the relationship between mental condition and criminality*. Ph.D. diss. University of Calgary, Calgary, Alberta.

Arbour, L. 1996. "Commission of inquiry into certain events at the Prison for Women in Kingston." Catalogue No. JS42-73/1996E. Public Works and Government Services Canada. Retrieved March 1, 2009 (www.justicebehindthewalls.net/resources/arbour_report/arbour_rpt.htm).

Archer, J. 1991. "The influence of testosterone on human aggression." *British Journal of Psychology*. 82:1–28.

Archer, J. 1999. "Assessment of the reliability of the conflict tactics scales: A meta-analytic review." *Journal of Interpersonal Violence*. 14:1263–1289.

Archer, J. 2002. "Sex differences in physically aggressive acts between heterosexual partners: A meta-analytic review." *Aggression and Violence Behavior*. 7:313–351.

Archer, J. 2006. "Testosterone and human aggression: An evaluation of the challenge hypothesis." *Neuroscience and Biobehavioral Reviews*, 30, 319-345.

Arieti, S. 1963. "Psychopathic personality: Some views on its psychopathology and psychodynamics." *Comprehensive Psychiatry*. 4:301–312.

Armstrong, Todd A., and Brian B. Boutwell. 2012. "Low resting heart rate and rational choice: Integrating biological correlates of crime in criminological theories." *Journal of Criminal Justice*. 40:31–9.

Arnold, R. 1990. "Processes of victimization and criminalization of black women." *Social Justice*. 17:153–166.

Arredondo, D.E., and Butler, S.F. 1994. "Affective comorbidity in psychiatrically hospitalized adolescents with conduct disorder or oppositional defiant disorder: Should conduct disorder be treated with mood stabilizers?" *Journal of Child and Adolescent Psychopharmacology*. 4(3):151–158.

Ascend Counseling. 2015. "Ascend counseling programs." Retrieved May 14, 2015 (www.michigantreatment.com/programs.html).

Ashley, O.S., Marsden, M.E., and Brady, T.M. 2003. "Effectiveness of substance abuse treatment programming for women: A review." *American Journal of Drug and Alcohol Abuse*. 29:19–53.

Associated Press. 2005. "Canadian gets 10 years for sex crimes." *The Seattle Times*. Retrieved December 21, 2009 (www.thefreelibrary.com/Canadian+gets+10+years+for+sex+crimes.(Local+News)-a0132980734).

Astwood Strategy Corporation. 2002. *Canadian Police Survey on Youth Gangs*. Ottawa, ON: Public Safety Canada.

Augimeri, L., Farrington, D., Koegl, C., and Day, D. 2007. "The SNAP under 12 outreach project: Effects of a community based program for children with conduct problems." *Journal of Child and Family Studies*. 16:799–807.

Aurélius c. R. 2007 QCCA 1859 (CanLII). Retrieved November 4, 2015 (http://canlii.ca/t/1vd5w).

Austin, J. 1983. "Assessing the new generation of prison classification models." *Crime and Delinquency*. 29:561–576.

Babchishin, K.M., Nunes, K.L., and Kessous, N. 2014. "A multimodal examination of sexual interest in children: A comparison of sex offenders and non-sex offenders." *Sexual Abuse: A Journal of Research and Treatment*. 26(4):343–374. DOI: 10.1177/1079063213492343.

Babcock, J.C., Green, C.E., and Robie, C. 2004. "Does batterers' treatment work? A meta-analytic review of domestic violence treatment." *Clinical Psychology Review*. 23:1023–1053.

Babiak, P., and Hare, R.D. forthcoming. *The B-Scan 360 manual*. Manuscript in preparation.

Babiak, P., Neumann, C.S., and Hare, R.D. 2010. "Corporate psychopathy: Talking the walk." *Behavioral Sciences and the Law*. 28:174–193.

Baca-Garcia, E., Perez-Rodriguez, M.M., Basurte-Villamor, I., Fernandez del Moral, A,L., Gmenez-Arriero, M.A., Gonzalez de Rivera, J.L., Saiz-Ruiz, J., and Oquendo, M.A. 2007. "Diagnostic stability of psychiatric disorders in clinical practice." *British Journal of Psychiatry*. 190:210–216.

Baker, T., and Piquero, A.R. 2010. "Assessing the perceived benefits—Criminal offending relationship." *Journal of Criminal Justice*. 38:981–987. DOI:10.1016/j.jcrimjus.2010.06.015.

Bandura, A. 1965. "Influence of models' reinforcement contingencies on the acquisition of imitative responses." *Journal of Personality and Social Psychology*. 2:589–595.

Bandura, A. 1973. *Aggression: A social learning analysis*. Englewood Cliffs, NJ: Prentice Hall.

Bandura, A. 1977. *Social learning theory*. Orrville, OH: Prentice Hall.

Banse, R., Schmidt, A.F., and Clarbour, J. 2010. "Indirect measures of sexual interest in child sex offenders: A multimethod approach." *Criminal Justice and Behavior*. 37:319–335. DOI: 10.1177/0093854809357598.

Barbaree, H.E. 2005. "Psychopathy, treatment behavior, and recidivism: An extended follow-up to Seto and Barbaree." *Journal of Interpersonal Violence*. 20:1115–1131.

Barkley, R.A. 1997. "Attention-deficit/hyperactivity disorder." In E.J. Mash, and L.G. Terdal, eds. *Assessment of childhood disorders*. pp. 71–129. New York: Guilford Press.

Barnes, D.M. 1986. "Promising results halt trial of anti-AIDS drug." *Science*. 234:15–16. DOI: 10.1126/science.3529393.

Barnett, A., Blumstein, A., and Farrington, D.P. 1987. "Probabilistic models of youthful criminal careers." *Criminology*. 25:83–107.

Barnett, G.D., Wakeling, H., Mandeville-Norden, R., and Rakestrow, J. 2013. "Does change in psychometric test scores tell us anything about risk of reconviction in sexual offenders?" *Psychology, Crime and Law*. 19:85–110. DOI: /10.1080/1068316X.2011.607820.

Barnett, L., and Béchard, J. 2011. "Justice and human rights: Trafficking in persons and human smuggling." In *Current and Emerging Issues: 41ˢᵗ Parliament*. Ottawa: Library of Parliament. Retrieved November 24, 2015 (www.parl.gc.ca/content/lop/researchpublications/cei-10-e.htm).

Barnum, G., and Gobéil, R. 2012. *Research at a glance: Revalidation of the custody rating scale for Aboriginal and non-Aboriginal women offenders*. Research Report No. R-273. Ottawa, ON: Correctional Service Canada. Retrieved December 8, 2015 (www.csc-scc.gc.ca/005/008/092/005008-0273-eng.pdf).

Baron, S. 2013. "Legal and justice issues." In S. Gaetz, B. O'Grady, K. Buccieri, J. Karabanow, and A. Marsolais, eds. *Youth homelessness in Canada: Implications for policy and practice*. pp. 353–368. Retrieved November 5, 2015 (www.homelesshub.ca/sites/default/files/YouthHomelessnessweb.pdf).

Barron, C., and Lacombe, D. 2005. "Moral panic and the nasty girl." *The Canadian Review of Sociology and Anthropology*. 42:51–69.

Bartholow, B.D., Bushman, B.J., and Sestir, M.A. 2006. "Chronic violent video game exposure and desensitization to violence: Behavioral and event-related brain potential data." *Journal of Experimental Social Psychology*. 42:532–539.

Bartol, C.R., and Bartol, A.M. 2008. *Criminal behaviour: A psychosocial approach*. 8th ed. Pacific Grove, CA: Brooks/Cole.

Baughman, H.M., Dearing, S., Giammarco, E.A., and Vernon, P.A. 2012. "Relationships between bullying behaviours and the dark triad: A study with adults." *Personality and Individual Differnces*. 52:571–575.

Beaudette, J.N., Power, J., and Stewart, L.A. 2015. *National prevalence of mental disorders among incoming federally-sentenced men offenders*. Research Report No. R-357. Ottawa, ON: Correctional Service Canada.

Beaupré, P. 2015. *Family violence in Canada: A statistical profile, 2013*. Statistics Canada Catalogue no. 85-002-x. Ministry of Industry.

Beaver, K.M., Nedelec, J.L., Schwartz, J.A., and Connolly, E.J. 2014. "Evolutionary behavioural genetics of violent crime." In T.K. Shackelford, & R.D. Hansen, eds. *The evolution of violence*. pp. 117–135. New York: NY: Springer.

Beggs, S. M., and Grace, R. C. 2011. "Treatment gain for sexual offenders against children predicts reduced recidivism: A comparative validity study." *Journal of Consulting and Clinical Psychology*. 79:182–192. DOI: 10.1037/a0022900.

Beitchman, J.H., Zucker, K.J., Hood, J.E., DaCosta, G.A., Akman, D., and Cassavia, E. 1992. "A review of the long-term effects of child sexual abuse." *Child Abuse and Neglect*. 16:101–118.

Belknap, J. 2001. *The invisible woman: Gender, crime, and justice*. 2nd ed. California: Wadsworth Publishing Company.

Belknap, J. 2007. *The invisible woman: Gender, crime and justice*. 3rd ed. Belmont, CA: Thomson Wadsworth.

Benda, B.B. 2005. "Gender differences in life course theory of recidivism: A survival analysis." *International Journal of Offender Therapy and Comparative Criminology*. 493:325–342.

Benedetti, W. 2007. "Were video games to blame for massacre? Pundits rushed to judge industry, gamers in the wake of shooting." *NBC News*. Retrieved October 21, 2015 (www.nbcnews.com/id/18220228/ns/technology_and_science-games/t/were-video-games-blame-massacre/#.VaMEjRvbKM8).

Benson, M.L., and Moore, E. 1992. "Are white-collar and common offenders the same? An empirical and theoretical critique of a recently proposed general theory of crime." *Journal of Research in Crime and Delinquency*. 29:251–272.

Bergstrom, H., Forth, A., and Farrington, D. Forthcoming. 2016, "The psychopath: Continuity or change? The stability of psychopathic traits and predictors of stability." In D. Kapardis and D. Farrington, eds. *The psychology of crime, policing, and courts*. London, UK: Routledge.

Berkowitz, L. 1994. "On the escalation of aggression." In M. Potegal and J. Knutson, eds. *The dynamics of aggression: Biological and social processes in dyads and groups*. pp. 33–41. Hillsdale, NJ: Erlbaum.

Beryl, R., Chou, S., and Völlm, B. 2014. "A systematic review of psychopathy in women within secure settings." *Personality and Individual Differences*. 71:185–195.

Birbaumer, N., Veit, R., Lotze, M., Herrmann, C., Erb, M., Grodd, W., and Flor, H. 2005. "Deficient fear conditioning in psychopathy: A functional magnetic resonance imaging study." *Archives of General Psychiatry*. 62:799–805.

Bjerregaard, B., and Lizotte, A. 1995. "Gun ownership and gang membership." *The Journal of Criminal Law and Criminology*. 86:37–58. DOI: 10.2307/1143999.

Bjork, J.M., Dougherty, D.M., Moeller, F.G., and Swann, A.C. 2000. "Differential behavioural effects of plasma tryptophan depletion and loading in aggressive and non-aggressive men." *Neuropsychopharmacology*. 22:375–369.

Blackburn, R. 1995. *The psychology of criminal conduct: Theory, research and practice*. Chichester, UK: Wiley.

Blair, R.J.R. 1995. "A cognitive developmental approach to morality: investigating the psychopath." *Cognition*. 57:1–29.

Blair, R.J.R. 2006. "Subcortical brain systems in psychopathy: The amygdala and associated structures." In C.J. Patrick, ed. *Handbook of the psychopathy*. pp. 296–312. New York, NY: Guilford Press.

Blair, R.J.R. 2007. "The amygdala and ventromedial prefrontal cortex in morality and psychopathy." *Trends in Cognitive Sciences*. 11:387–392.

Blair, R.J.R., Colledge, E., Murray, L., and Mitchell, D.G.V. 2001. "A selective impairment in the processing of sad and fearful expressions in children with psychopathic tendencies." *Journal of Abnormal Child Psychology*. 294:491–498.

Blair, R.J.R., Jones, L., Clark, F., and Smith, M. 1997. "The psychopathic individual: A lack of responsiveness to distress cues." *Psychophysiology*. 34:192–198.

Blais, J., and Forth, A.E. 2014. "Potential labeling effects: Influence of psychopathy diagnosis, defendant age, and defendant gender on mock jurors' decisions." *Psychology, Crime and Law*. 20:116–134.

Blais, J., Solodukhin, E., and Forth, A. E. 2014. "A meta-analysis exploring the relationship between psychopathy and instrumental versus reactive violence." *Criminal Justice and Behavior*. 41:797–821.

Blanchette, K.D., and Brown, S.L. 2006. *The assessment and treatment of women offenders: An integrative perspective*. Wiley Series in Forensic Clinical Psychology. Chichester: John Wiley and Sons.

Blanchette, K.D., and Motiuk, L.L. 2004. "Taking down the straw man: A reply to Webster and Doob." *Canadian Journal of Criminology and Criminal Justice*. 46:621–630.

Blanchette, K.D., and Taylor, K.N. 2007. "Development and field test of a gender-informed security reclassification scale for female offenders." *Criminal Justice and Behaviour*. 34:362–379.

Blanchette, K.D., Verbrugge, P., and Wichmann, C. 2002. *The Custody Rating Scale, initial security placement, and women offenders*. Research Report No. R-127. Ottawa, ON: Correctional Service Canada.

Bland, R.C., Orn, H., and Newman, S.C. 1988. "Lifetime prevalence of psychiatric disorders in Edmonton." *Acta Psychiatrica Scandinavica*. 77(Suppl. 338):24–32.

Blickle, G., Schlegel, A., Fassbender, P., and Klein, U. 2006. "Some personality correlates of business white-collar crime." *Applied Psychology*. 55:220–233.

Bloom, B., Owen, B., and Covington, S.S. 2003. *Gender-responsive strategies for women offenders: Research, practice, and guiding principles for women offenders*. NIC Accession Number 018017. Retrieved August 15, 2005 (www.nicic.org).

Bloom, B., Owen, B., Rosenbaum, J., and Deschenes, E.P. 2003. "Focusing on girls and young women: A gendered perspective on female delinquency." *Women and Criminal Justice*. 14:117–136.

Blonigen, D.M., Hicks, B.M., Krueger, R.F., Patrick, C.J., and Iacono, W.G. 2005. "Psychopathic personality traits: Heritability and genetic overlap with internalizing and externalizing psychopathology." *Psychological Medicine*. 35:637–648.

Blonigen, D.M., Hicks, B.M., Krueger, R.F., Patrick, C.J., and Iacono, W.G. 2006. "Continuity and change in psychopathic traits as measured via normal-range personality: A longitudinal-biometric study." *Journal of Abnormal Psychology*. 1:85–95.

Blum, J., Ireland, M., and Blum, R. 2003. "Gender differences in juvenile violence: A report from Add Health." *Journal of Adolescent Health*. 32:234–240.

Blumstein, A., and Cohen, J. 1987. "Characterizing criminal careers." *Science*. 237:985–991.

Boccaccini, M.T., Murrie, D.C., Clark, J.W., and Cornell, D.G. 2008. "Describing, diagnosing, and naming psychopathy: How do youth psychopathy labels influence jurors?" *Behavioral Sciences and the Law*. 26:487–510.

Boe, R., Nafekh, M., Vuong, B., Sinclair, R., and Cousineau, C. 2003. *The changing profile of the federal inmate population: 1997 and 2002*. Research Report No. R-132. Ottawa, ON: Correctional Service Canada.

Boer, D., Couture, J., Geddes, C., and Ritchie, A. 2003. *Yókw'tól: Risk management guide for Aboriginal offenders*. Ottawa, ON: Correctional Service Canada.

Boer, D.P., Hart, S.D., Kropp, P.R., and Webster, C.D. 1997. *Manual for the Sexual Violence Risk—20: Professional guidelines for assessing risk of sexual violence*. Burnaby, BC: Mental Health, Law, and Policy Institute, Simon Fraser University.

Boland, F.J., Duwyn, M., and Serin, R. 2002. "Fetal alcohol syndrome: Understanding its impact." *Forum on Corrections*. 12:16–18.

Bonta, J. 1996. "Risk-needs assessment and treatment." In A. T. Harland, ed. *Choosing correctional options that work: Defining the demand and evaluating the supply*. pp. 18–32. Thousand Oaks, CA: Sage.

Bonta, J. 2007. Unpublished training presentation, National Parole Board of Canada.

Bonta, J., Blais, J., and Wilson, H.A. 2014. "A theoretically informed meta-analysis of the risk for general and violent recidivism for mentally disordered offenders." *Aggression and Violent Behavior*. 19, 278–287. DOI:10.1016/j.avb.2014.04.014.

Bonta, J., Bourgon, G., Rugge, T., Scott, T. L., Yessine, A. K., Gutierrez, L., and Li, J. 2011. "An experimental demonstration of training probation officers in evidence-based community supervision." *Criminal Justice and Behavior*. 38:1127–1148. DOI:10.1177/0093854811420678.

Bonta, J., Harman, W.G., Hann, R.G., and Cormier, R.B. 1996. "The prediction of recidivism among federally sentenced offenders: A re-validation of the SIR scale." *Canadian Journal of Criminology*. 38:61–79.

Bonta, J., LaPrairie, C., and Wallace-Capretta, S. 1997. "Risk prediction and re-offending: Aboriginal and non-aboriginal offenders." *Canadian Journal of Criminology*. 39:127–144.

Bonta, J., Law, M., and Hanson, R.K. 1998. "The prediction of criminal and violent recidivism among mentally disordered offenders: A meta-analysis." *Psychological Bulletin*. 123:123–142. DOI:10.1037/0033-2909.123.2.123.

Bonta, J., and Rugge, T. 2004. *The prediction of recidivism with Aboriginal offenders*. Unpublished manuscript.

Bonta, J., Rugge, T., Scott, T. L., Bourgon, G, and Yessine, A. K. 2008. "Exploring the black box of community supervision." *Journal of Offender Rehabilitation*. 47(3):248–270. DOI:10.1080/10509670802134085.

Bonta, J., Wallace-Capretta, S., and Rooney, J. 1998. *Restorative justice: An evaluation of the Restorative Resolutions Project*. Ottawa, ON: Solicitor General Canada.

Book, A.S., Starzyk, K.B., and Quinsey, V.L. 2001. "The relationship between testosterone and aggression: A meta-analysis." *Aggression and Violent Behavior*. 6:579–599.

Book, A.S., Visser, B. A., and Volk, A.A. 2015. "Unpacking 'evil': Claiming the core of the Dark Triad." *Personality and Individual Differences*. 73:29–38.

Borum, R., Bartel, P.A., and Forth, A.E. 2002. *Manual for the structured assessment of violent risk in youth (SAVRY), Consultation edition, Version 1*. Florida: University of South Florida.

Bourgon, G., and Armstrong, B. 2005. "Transferring the principles of effective treatment into a 'real world' prison setting." *Criminal Justice and Behavior*. 32:3–25.

Bourgon, G., Gutierrez, L., and Ashton, J. 2011. "The evolution of community supervision practice: The transformation from case manager to change agent." *Irish Probation Journal*. 8:28–48.

Bowen, E. 2011. "An overview of partner violence risk assessment and the potential role of female victim risk appraisals." *Aggression and Violent Behavior*. 16(3):214–226.

Bowker, L.H., Arbitell, M., and McFerron, J.R. 1988. "On the relationship between wife beating and child abuse." In K. Yllo and M. Bogard, eds., *Feminist perspectives on wife abuse*. pp. 158–174. Newbury Park, CA: Sage.

Bowlby, J. 1944. "Forty-four juvenile thieves: Their characteristics and home life." *International Journal of Psychoanalysis*. 25:19–53.

Bowlby, J. 1989. *The making and breaking of affectional bonds*. London, UK: Routledge.

Bowlby, J., Ainsworth, M., Boston, M., and Rosenbluth, D. 1956. "The effects of mother-child separation: A follow-up study." *British Journal of Medical Psychology*. 292:11–247.

Boyce, J. 2015. "Police-reported crime statistics in Canada, 2014." *Juristat*. 35. Catalogue No. 85-002-X. Statistics Canada, Canadian Centre for Justice Statistics. Retrieved July 23, 2015 (www.statcan.gc.ca/pub/85-002-x/2015001/article/14211-eng.pdf).

Boyce, J., Cotter, A., and Perreault, S. 2014. Police-reported crime statistics in Canada, 2013. *Juristat*. Statistics Canada, Canadian Centre for Justice Statistics. Retrieved May 20, 2015 (www.statcan.gc.ca/pub/85-002-x/2014001/article/14040-eng.htm).

Bracken, D., Deane, L., and Morrissette, L. 2009. "Desistance and social marginalization: The case of Canadian Aboriginal offenders." *Theoretical Criminology*. 13(1):61–78.

Brame, B., Nagin, D.S., and Tremblay, R.E. 2001. "Developmental trajectories of physical aggression from school entry to late adolescence." *Journal of Child Psychology and Psychiatry*. 42:503–512.

Brennan, S. 2011. *Family violence in Canada: A statistical profile, 2009*. Statistics Canada Catalogue no. 85-224-X. Ottawa: Ministry of Industry.

Brennan, S. 2012. "Youth court statistics in Canada, 2010/2011." *Juristat*. Catalogue no. 85-002-X. Ottawa ON: Statistics Canada. Retrieved October 26, 2015 (www.statcan.gc.ca/pub/85-002-x/2012001/article/11645-eng.htm).

Brennan, S., and Taylor-Butts, A. 2008. "Sexual assault in Canada: 2004 and 2007." Catalogue no. 85F0033M, no. 19. Statistics Canada: Canadian Centre for Justice Statistics.

Brennan, T. 1998. "Institutional classification of females: Problems and some proposals for reform." In R.T. Zaplin, ed. *Female offenders: Critical perspectives and effective interventions*. pp. 179–204. Gaithersburg, MD: Aspen Publishers.

Brewer, D.D., Hawkins, J.D., Catalano, R.F., and Neckerman, H.J. 1995. "Preventing serious, violent, and chronic juvenile offending: A review of evaluations of selected strategies in childhood, adolescence, and the community." In J.C. Howell, B. Krisberg, J.D. Hawkins, and J.J. Wilson, eds. *A Source Book: Serious, Violent, and Chronic Juvenile Offenders*. pp. 61–141. Thousand Oaks, CA: Sage.

Brink, J.H., Doherty, D., and Boer, A. 2001. "Mental disorder in federal offenders: A Canadian prevalence study." *International Journal of Law and Psychiatry*. 24:339–356.

Brink, J.H., Livingston, J., Desmarais, S., Greaves, C., Maxwell, V., Michalak, E., Parent, R., Verdun-Jones, S., and Weaver, C. 2011. *A Study of how people with mental illness perceive and interact with the police*. Calgary: Mental Health Commission of Canada. Retrieved September 27, 2015 (www.mentalhealthcommission.ca).

British Columbia Ministry of Justice. 2013. "Corrections." Retrieved October 21, 2015 (www.pssg.gov.bc.ca/corrections/index.htm).

Brook, M., Brieman, C.L., and Kosson, D. S. 2013. "Emotion processing in Psychopathy Checklist-assessed psychopathy: A review of the literature." *Clinical Psychology Review*. 33:979–995.

Brooks-Crozier, J. 2011. "The nature and nurture of violence: Early intervention services for the families of MAOA-low children as a means to reduce violent crime and the costs of violent crime." *Connecticut Law Review*. 44(2), 531–573.

Brown, G.R. 2004. "Gender as a factor in the response of the law-enforcement systems to violence against partners." *Sexuality and Culture*. 9:3–138.

Brown, J. 2004. "Challenges facing Canadian federal offenders newly released to the community: A concept map." *Offender Rehabilitation*. 39(1):19–35. DOI:0.1300/J076v39n01_02.

Brown, S., and Leedom, L.J. 2008. *Women who love psychopaths: Inside the relationships of inevitable harm*. Fairfield, CT: Health and Well-Being Publications.

Brown, S.L., and Forth, A.E. 1997. "Psychopathy and sexual assault: Static risk factors, emotional precursors, and rapist subtypes." *Journal of Consulting and Clinical Psychology*. 65:848–857.

Brown, S.L., and Motiuk, L.L. 2005. *The Dynamic Factor Identification and Analysis (DFIA) component of the Offender Intake Assessment (OIA) process: A meta-analytic, psychometric and consultative review*. Research Report No. R-164. Ottawa, ON: Research Branch, Correctional Service Canada.

Brown, S.L., and Motiuk, L.L. 2008. "Using dynamic risk factors to predict criminal recidivism in a sample of male and female offenders." In K.D. Blanchette, chair. *Classification for the prediction of recidivism in girls and women*. Symposium conducted at the 2008 69th Annual Conference of the Canadian Psychological Association (CPA), Halifax, NS.

Brown, S.L., St. Amand, M., and Zamble, E. 2009. "The dynamic prediction of criminal recidivism: A three-wave prospective study." *Journal of Law and Human Behavior*. 33:25–45. DOI:10.1007/s10979-008-9139-7.

Browne, A., and Finkelhor, D. 1986. "Impact of child sexual abuse: A review of the research." *Psychological Bulletin*. 99:66–77.

Brownmiller, S. 1975. *Against our will: Men, women and rape*. New York: Simon & Schuster.

Brzozowski, J., Taylor-Butts, A., and Johnson, S. 2006. "Victimization and offending among the Aboriginal population in Canada." *Juristat*. 26.

Buker, H. 2011. "Formation of self-control: Gottfredson and Hirschi's general theory of crime and beyond." *Aggression and Violent Behavior*, 16:265–276.

Bumby, K.M. 1996. "Assessing the cognitive distortions of child molesters and rapists: Developments and validation of the MOLEST and RAPE scales." *Sexual Abuse: A Journal of Research and Treatment*. 8:37–54.

Bunge, V.P, Johnson, H., and Baldé, T.A. 2005. *Exploring crime patterns in Canada*. Catalogue no. 85-561-MIE — No. 005. Statistics Canada. Retrieved September 23, 2015 (www.statcan.gc.ca/pub/85-561-m/85-561-m2005005-eng.pdf).

Bureind, J.W., and Bartusch, D.J. 2005. *Juvenile delinquency: An integrated approach*. Thousand Oaks, CA: Jones and Bartlett Publishers.

Burke, P., and Tonry, M. 2006. *Successful transition and reentry for safer communities: A call to action for parole*. Silver Spring, MD: Center for Effective Public Policy.

Burnett, R., and McNeill, F. 2005. "The place of the officer-offender relationship in assisting offenders to desist from crime." *Probation Journal*. 52:221–242. DOI:10.1177/0264550505055112.

Burt, S.A., Donnellan, M.B., Iacono, W.G., and McGue, M. 2011. "Age-of-onset or behavioral sub-types? A prospective comparison of two approaches to characterizing the heterogeneity within antisocial behavior." *Journal of Abnormal Child Psychology*. 39(5):633–644. DOI: dx.doi.org/10.1007/s10802-011-9491-9.

Bushman, B.J., and Anderson, C.A. 2001. "Media violence and the American public: Scientific facts versus media misinformation." *American Psychologist*. 56:477–489.

Buss, D.M. 2005. "Foundations of evolutionary psychology." In D.M. Buss, ed. *The handbook of evolutionary psychology*. pp. 5–145. Hoboken, New Jersey: John Wiley and Sons, Inc.

Butler, S., Baruch, G., Hickey, N., and Fonagy, P. 2011. "A randomized controlled trial of multisystemic therapy and a statutory therapeutic intervention for young offenders." *Journal of the American Academy of Child and Adolescent Psychiatry*. 50:1220–1235.

Cadoret, R.J., and Cain, C. 1980. "Sex differences in predictors of antisocial behavior in adoptees." *Archives of General Psychiatry*. 37:1171–1175.

Caldwell, M.F., McCormick, D., Wolfe, J., and Umstead, D. 2012. "Treatment-related changes in psychopathy features and behavior in adolescent offenders." *Criminal Justice and Behavior*. 39:144–155.

Caldwell, M., Skeem, J., Salekin, R., VanRybroek, G. 2006. "Treatment response of adolescent offenders with psychopathy features: A 2-year follow-up." *Criminal Justice and Behavior*. 33:571–596.

Callahan, E.J., and Leitenberg, H. 1973. "Aversion therapy for sexual deviation: Contingent shock and covert sensitization." *Journal of Abnormal Psychology*. 81:60–73.

Campbell, A. 1984. *The girls in the gang: A report from New York City*. Oxford, UK: Blackwell.

Campbell, A. 1995. "A few good men: Evolutionary psychology and female adolescent aggression." *Ethnology and Sociobiology*. 16:99–123.

Campbell, A. 1999. "Staying alive: Evolution, culture, and women's intrasexual aggression." *Behavioural and Brain Sciences*. 22:203–252.

Campbell, A. 2002. *A mind of her own: The evolutionary psychology of women*. Oxford: Oxford University Press.

Campbell, A., and Cross, C. 2012. "Women and aggression." In T.K., Shackelford and V.A. Weekes-Shackelford, eds. *The Oxford handbook of evolutionary perspectives on violence, homicide, and war*. pp. 197–217). Oxford: Oxford University Press.

Campbell, A., Muncer, S., and Bibel, D. 2001. "Women and crime: An evolutionary approach." *Aggression and Violent Behavior*. 6:481–497.

Campbell, M.A., French, S., and Gendreau, P. 2009. "The prediction of violence in adult offenders: A meta-analytic comparison of instruments and methods of assessment." *Criminal Justice and Behavior*. 36:567–590.

Campbell, N.A., Reece, J.B., and Mitchell, L.G. 1999. *Biology*. 5th ed. Menlo Park, CA: Addison Wesley Longman.

Campbell, N.M. 2008. *Comprehensive framework for paroling authorities in an era of evidence-based practice*. Washington, DC: National Institute of Corrections.

Canadian Anti-Fraud Centre. 2015. "Fraud types." Retrieved November 3, 2015 (www.antifraudcentre-centreantifraude.ca/fraud-escroquerie/index-eng.htm).

Canadian Centre on Substance Abuse. 2013. "Canadian low-risk drinking guidelines." Retrieved October 29, 2015 (www.ccsa.ca/Resource%20Library/2012-Canada-Low-Risk-Alcohol-Drinking-Guidelines-Brochure-en.pdf).

Canadian Charter of Rights and Freedoms. Part I of the Constitution Act, 1982, being Schedule B to the *Canada Act 1982* (UK), 1982, c 11.

Canadian Criminal Justice Association. 2000. "Part IV: Aboriginal people and the criminal justice system." In *Aboriginal people and the criminal justice system*. Retrieved December 7, 2015 (www.ccja-acjp.ca/en/abori4.html).

Canadian Human Rights Commission. 2003. "Protecting their rights: A systemic review of human rights in correctional services for federally sentenced women." Retrieved January 14, 2009 (www.chrc-ccdp.ca/legislation_policies/consultation_report-en.asp).

Canadian Institute for Health Information. 2006. "Health Care Spending to Reach $130 Billion This Year." Retrieved 21 March 2009 (http://secure.cihi.ca/cihiweb/dispPage.jsp?cw_page=media_08dec2004_e).

Canadian Press. 2007. "Some key dates in the Pickton case." *CTV News*. December 9, 2007. Retrieved August 13, 2009 (www.ctv.ca/servlet/ArticleNews/story/CTVNews/20071209/pickton_keydates_071209/20071209).

Canadian Press. 2014. "Marijuana: Key dates in the evolution of Canadian attitudes, laws." *CTV News*. Retrieved October 29, 2015 (www.ctvnews.ca/politics/marijuana-key-dates-in-the-evolution-of-canadian-attitudes-laws-1.1753702).

Canadian Psychological Association. 2000. *Canadian code of ethics for psychologists*. 3rd ed. Retrieved October 23, 2015 (www.cpa.ca/docs/File/Ethics/cpa_code_2000_eng_jp_jan2014.pdf).

Canadian Security Intelligence Service. 2012. *Public report 2010–2011*. Cat. No. PS71-2011. Ottawa: Public Works and Government Services Canada. Retrieved November 22, 2014 (www.csis-scrs.gc.ca/pblctns/nnlrprt/2010/index-en.php).

Canales, D.D., Olver, M.E., and Wong, S.C.P. 2009. "Construct validity of the Violence Risk Scale-Sexual Offender version for measuring sexual deviance." *Sexual Abuse: A Journal of Research and Treatment*. 21:474–492. DOI: 10.1177/1079063209344990.

Caplan, J.M. 2007. "What factors affect parole: A review of empirical research." *Federal Probation*. 71(1):16–19.

Cappadocia, M.C., Craig, W.M., and Pepler, D. 2013. "Cyberbullying: Prevalence, stability, and risk factors during adolescence." *Canadian Journal of School Psychology*. 28(2): 171–192. Retrieved April 30, 2015 (http://search.proquest.com/docview/1429633731?accountid=9894).

Carlen, P. 1988. *Women, crime and poverty*. Milton Keynes: Open University Press.

Carmichael, S., and A.R. Piquero. 2004. "Sanctions, perceived anger, and criminal offending." *Journal of Quantitative Criminology. Special Issue: Offender Decision Making*. 20:371–393. DOI:10.1007/s10940-004-5869-y.

Carney, M., Buttell, F., and Dutton, D. 2007. "Women who perpetrate intimate partner violence: A review of the literature with recommendations for treatment." *Aggression and Violent Behavior*. 12:108–115.

Carson, R.C., and Butcher, J.N. 1992. *Abnormal psychology and modern life.* 9th ed. New York, NY: HarperCollins.

Caspi, A., McClay, J., Moffitt, T.E., Mill, J., Martin, J., Craig, I.W., Taylor, A., and Poulton, R. 2002. "Role of genotype in the cycle of violence in maltreated children." *Science.* 297:851–854.

Cassel, E., and Bernstein, D.A. 2001. *Criminal behavior.* Boston, MA: Allyn and Bacon.

Cattaneo, L.B., Stuewig, J., Goodman, L. A., Kaltman, S., and Dutton, M.A. 2007. "Longitudinal helpseeking patterns among victims of intimate partner violence: The relationship between legal and extralegal services." *American Journal of Orthopsychiatry.* 77:467–477.

CBC News. 2008. "Medicine Hat man plotted with girlfriend to kill family: Crown." Retrieved August 31, 2009 (www.cbc.ca/canada/edmonton/story/2008/11/17/steinke-medhat.html).

CBC News. 2009. "Teen guilty of 1st-degree murder in death of Stefanie Rengel, 14." Retrieved August 31, 2009 (www.cbc.ca/canada/toronto/story/2009/03/20/murder-rengel-trial.html).

CBC News. 2010. "Col. Russell Williams timeline." Retrieved November 30, 2015 (www.cbc.ca/news/canada/col-russell-williams-timeline-1.913312).

CBC News. 2012. "Convicted 'sex tourist' released from prison." Retrieved November 22, 2014 (www.cbc.ca/news/canada/british-columbia/convicted-sex-tourist-released-from-prison-1.1183833).

CBC News. 2014. "Death of Lee Bonneau, 6, allegedly at hands of boy, 10, was avoidable, report says." Retrieved April 20, 2015 (www.cbc.ca/news/canada/saskatchewan/death-of-lee-bonneau-6-allegedly-at-hands-of-boy-10-was-avoidable-report-says-1.2643066).

CBC News. 2014b. "Kailey Oliver-Machado, Ottawa teen prostitution ringleader, gets 6½-year adult sentence." November 4. Retrieved December 2, 2015 (www.cbc.ca/news/canada/ottawa/kailey-oliver-machado-ottawa-teen-prostitution-ringleader-gets-6-year-adult-sentence-1.2822106).

CBC News. 2015. "Lee Bonneau inquest: 'Heartbreaking' case, coroner says." Retrieved April 20, 2015 (www.cbc.ca/news/canada/saskatchewan/lee-bonneau-inquest-heartbreaking-case-coroner-says-1.3037687).

Centre for Addiction and Mental Health. 2008. "Partying and getting drunk." Retrieved October 29, 2015 (www.camh.ca/en/hospital/health_information/a_z_mental_health_and_addiction_information/alcohol/Pages/binge_drinking.aspx).

Chadwick, N., DeWolf, A.H., and Serin, R.C. 2015. "Effectively training community supervision officers: A meta-analytic review of the impact on offender outcome." *Criminal Justice and Behavior.* 42(10):977–989. DOI: 10.1177/0-093854815595661.

Chan, K.L., Straus, M.A., Brownridge, D.A., Tiwari, A., and Leung, W.C. 2008. "Prevalence of dating partner violence and suicidal ideation among male and female university students worldwide." *Journal of Midwifery and Women's Health.* 53:529–537.

Chesney-Lind, M. 1986. "Women and crime: The female offender. Signs." *Journal of Women in Culture and Society.* 121:78–96.

Chesney-Lind, M., and Irwin, K. 2008. *Beyond bad girls: Gender, violence and hype.* New York, NY: Taylor and Francis Group.

Chesney-Lind, M., and Paramore, V.V. 2001. "Are girls getting more violent?" *Journal of Contemporary Criminal Justice.* 17:142–166.

Chesney-Lind, M., and Rodriguez, N. 1983. "Women under lock and key." *Prison Journal.* 63:47–65.

Cheverie, M., MacSwain, M., Farrell MacDonald, S., and Johnson, S. 2014. *Institutional adjustment of methadone maintenance treatment program (MMTP) participants.* Research Report No. R-323. Ottawa, ON: Correctional Service Canada.

Chiffriller, S.H., Hennessy, J.J., and Zappone, M. 2006. "Understanding a new typology of batterers: Implications for treatment." *Victims and Offenders.* 1:79–97.

Chilliwack Progress. 2015. "Police seize millions in drugs during Chilliwack bust." Author. March 18. Retrieved November 4, 2015 (www.theprogress.com/news/296768531.html).

Choy, O., Raine, A., Portnoy, J., Rudo-Hutt, A., Gao, Y., and Soyfer, L. 2015. "The mediating role of heart rate on the social adversity-antisocial behavior relationship: A Social Neurocriminology Perspective." *Journal of Research in Crime and Delinquency.* 52:303–341.

Clairmont, D. 2006. "Aboriginal policing in Canada: An overview of developments in First Nations." Retrieved January 12, 2009 (www.attorneygeneral.jus.gov.on.ca/inquiries/ipperwash/policy_part/research/pdf/Clairmont_Aboriginal_Policing.pdf).

Cleary Bradley, R.P., and Gottman, J.M. 2012. "Reducing situational violence in low-income couples by fostering healthy relationships." *Journal of Marital and Family Therapy.* 38:187–198.

Cleckley, H. 1941. *The mask of sanity: An attempt to clarify some issues about the so called psychopathic personality.* St. Louis: Mosby.

Cleckley, H. 1976. *The mask of sanity: An attempt to clarify some issues about the so called psychopathic personality.* 5th ed. St. Louis: Mosby.

Clinard, M.B., and Quinney, R. 1967. *Criminal behavior systems: A typology.* New York, NY: Holt, Rinehart, and Winston.

Cohen, A.J., Adler, N., Kaplan, S.J., Pelcovitz, D., and Mandel, F.G. 2002. "Interactional effects of marital status and physical abuse on adolescent psychopathology." *Child Abuse and Neglect.* 26:277–288.

Cohen, J. 1988. *Statistical power analysis for the behavioural sciences.* Hillsdale, NJ: Lawrence Erlbaum Associates.

Cohen, L., and Felson, M. 1979. "Social change and crime rate trends: A routine activity approach." *American Sociological Review.* 44:588–608.

Coid, J., and Yang, M. 2011. "The impact of psychopathy on violence among the household population of Great Britain." *Social Psychiatry and Psychiatric Epidemiology.* 46(6):473–80. DOI:10.1007/s00127-010-0212-4.

Coid, J., Yang, M., Ullrich, S., Zhang, T., Sizmur, S., Roberts, C., and Rogers, R.D. 2009. "Gender differences in structured risk assessment: Comparing the accuracy of five instruments." *Journal of Consulting and Clinical Psychology.* 77:237–348.

Coid, J., Yang, M., Ullrich, S., Roberts, A., and Hare, R.D. 2009. "Prevalence and correlates of psychopathic traits in the household population of Great Britain." *International Journal of Law and Psychiatry.* 32:65–73.

Coker, A.L., Smith, P.H., Thompson, M.P., McKeown, R.E., Bethea, L., and Davis, K.E. 2002. "Social support protects against the negative effects of partner violence on mental health." *Journal of Women's Health and Gender-based Medicine.* 11:465–476.

Coie, J.D., Belding, M., and Underwood, M. 1988. "Aggression and peer rejection in childhood." In B.B. Lahey and A.E. Kazdin, eds. *Advances in clinical child psychology.* Vol. II. pp. 125–158. New York, NY: Plenum.

Collins, J.M., and Schmidt, F.L. 1993. "Personality, integrity, and white-collar crime. A construct validity study." *Personnel Psychology.* 46:295–311.

College of Physicians and Surgeons Ontario. 2011. *Methadone maintenance treatment: Program standards and clinical guidelines.* 4th ed. Toronto, ON: Author. Retrieved October 29, 2015 (www.cpso.on.ca/uploadedFiles/members/MMT-Guidelines.pdf).

Comack E. 2012. *Racialized policing: Aboriginal people's encounters with the police.* Halifax, NS: Fernwood Publishing.

Community Care of North Carolina. 2013. "CCNC motivational interviewing (MI) resource guide: Everybody's motivated about something." Retrieved October 29, 2015 (www.communitycarenc.org/media/files/mi-guide.pdf).

Conference Board of Canada. 2012. "Mental health issues in the labour force: Reducing the economic impact on Canada." Retrieved December 9, 2015 (www.conferenceboard.ca/e-library/abstract.aspx?did=4957).

Conner, S. 1995. "Do your genes make you a criminal?" *The Independent.* Retrieved October 26, 2015 (www.independent.co.uk/news/uk/do-your-genes-make-you-a-criminal-1572714.html).

Controlled Drugs and Substances Act. 2015. SC 1996, c. 19. Retrieved October 29, 2015 (http://laws-lois.justice.gc.ca/eng/acts/c-38.8/).

Cook, A. 2014. *Risk assessment and management of group-based violence.* PhD diss. Simon Fraser University.

Coolidge, F.L., Marle, P.D., Van Horn, S.A., and Segal, D.L. 2011. "Clinical syndromes, personality disorders, and neurocognitive differences in male and female inmates." *Behavioral Sciences and the Law.* 29:741–751. DOI: 10.1002/bsl.997.

Cornell University Law School. 2015. "White-collar crime." *WEX Legal Dictionary.* Legal Information Institute (LII). Retrieved November 3, 2015 (www.law.cornell.edu/wex/white-collar_crime).

Cornish, D.B., and Clarke, R.V., eds. 1986. *The reasoning criminal: Rational choice perspectives on offending.* New York: Springer-Verlag.

Corrado, R.R., and Cohen, I.M. 2002. "Needs profile of serious and/or violent Aboriginal youth in prison." *Forum on Corrections Research.* 14:20–24.

Corrado, R.R., Kuehn, S., and Margaritescu, I. 2014. "Policy issues regarding the overrepresentation of incarcerated Aboriginal young offenders in a Canadian context." *Youth Justice.* 14(1):40–62.

Correctional Service Canada. 2006. "Ten-year status report on women's corrections 1996–2006." Correctional Service Canada: Author. Retrieved March 21, 2009 (www.csc-scc.gc.ca/text/prgrm/fsw/wos24/tenyearstatusreport_e.pdf).

Correctional Service Canada. 2007. "Women Offender Substance Abuse Program (WOSAP)." Retrieved July 6, 2009 (www.csc-scc.gc.ca/text/prgrm/fsw/fsw-eng.shtml).

Correctional Service Canada. 2009. *Healing lodges for Aboriginal federal offenders.* Ottawa, ON: Correctional Service Canada.

Correctional Service Canada. 2013a. "Aboriginal offender statistics." Retrieved December 2, 2015 (www.csc-scc.gc.ca/aboriginal/002003-1010-eng.shtml).

Correctional Service Canada. 2013b. "Federal Offender Population—2013: Warrant of Committal Admissions—Aboriginal Offenders." Retrieved October 29, 2015 (www.csc-scc.gc.ca/research/005008-3001-eng.shtml).

Correctional Service Canada. 2014a. "General crime prevention programs." Retrieved May 13, 2015 (www.csc-scc.gc.ca/correctional-process/002001-2005-eng.shtml).

Correctional Service Canada. 2014b. "National Substance Abuse Programs." Retrieved October 29, 2015 (www.csc-scc.gc.ca/correctional-process/002001-2009-eng.shtml).

Correctional Service Canada. 2015. *2015–16 Report on Plans and Priorities.* Retrieved October 21, 2015 (www.csc-scc.gc.ca/publications/005007-2603-eng.shtml).

Correctional Service Canada. 2015a. "Integrated correctional program model." Retrieved October 23, 2015 (www.csc-scc.gc.ca/correctional-process/002001-2011-eng.shtml).

Corrections and Conditional Release Act. 1992. S.C., c. 20. Retrieved December 7. 2015 (http://laws-lois.justice.gc.ca/eng/acts/C-44.6/).

Cortoni, F., Nunes, K., and Latendresse, M. 2006. *An examination of the effectiveness of the Violence Prevention Program.* Research Report No. R-178. Ottawa, ON: Correctional Service Canada.

Coté, G., and Hodgins, S. 1990. "Co-occurring mental disorders among criminal offenders." *Bulletin of American Academy of Psychiatry Law.* 18:271–281.

Cotter, A., and Beaupré, P. 2014. "Police-reported sexual offences against children and youth in Canada 2012." *Juristat.* 34. Catalogue No. 85-002-X. Statistics Canada, Canadian Centre for Justice Statistics. Retrieved May 17, 2015 (www.statcan.gc.ca/pub/85-002-x/2014001/article/14008-eng.htm).

Cotter, A., Greenland, J., and Karam, M. 2015. "Drug-related offences in Canada, 2013." *Juristat.* 35(1). Retrieved October 29, 2015 (www.statcan.gc.ca/pub/85-002-x/2015001/article/14201-eng.htm).

Cotton, D., and Coleman, T. 2008. *A study of police academy training and education for new police officers working with people with mental illness.* Report prepared on behalf of The Police/Mental Health Subcommittee of the Canadian Association of Chiefs of Police and The Mental Health and the Law Advisory Committee of the Mental Health Commission of Canada. Retrieved November 27, 2015 (www.mentalhealthcommission.ca/English/document/438/study-police-academy-training-and-education-new-police-officers-related-working-people-).

Cotton, D., and Coleman, T.G. 2010. "Canadian police agencies and their interactions with persons with a mental illness: A systems approach." *Police Practice and Research: An International Journal.* 11(4):301–314. DOI:10.1080/15614261003701665.

Costa, D.M., and Babcock, J.C. 2008. "Articulated thoughts of intimate partner abusive men during anger arousal: Correlates with personality disorder features." *Journal of Family Violence.* 23:395–402.

Covington, S.S. 2003. "A woman's journey home: Challenges for female offenders." In J. Travis and M. Waul, eds. *Prisoners once removed: The impact of incarceration and reentry on children, families, and communities.* pp. 67–103. Washington, DC: The Urban Institute.

Covington, S.S., and Bloom, B.E. 2003. "Gendered justice: Women in the criminal justice system." In B.E. Bloom, ed. *Gendered justice: Addressing female offenders*. pp. 3–23. Durham, NC: Carolina Academic Press.

Coy, E., Speltz, M.L., DeKlyen, M., and Jones, K. 2001. "Social-cognitive processes in preschool boys with and without oppositional defiant disorder." *Journal of Abnormal Child Psychology*. 29:107–119.

Cressey, D.R. 1973. *Other people's money: A study in the social psychology of embezzlement*. Montclair: Patterson Smith.

Crick, N.R., and Dodge, K.A. 1994. "A review and reformulation of social information-processing mechanisms in children's social adjustment." *Psychological Bulletin*. 115:74–101.

Criminal Code. 2015. RSC 1985, c. C-46. Retrieved October 30, 2015 (http://laws-lois.justice.gc.ca/eng/acts/C-46/).

Criminal Intelligence Service Canada. 2008. *Report on organized crime*. Cat. No. PS61-1/2008. Public Safety Canada.

Criminal Intelligence Service Canada. 2014. "Organized crime in Canada—Backgrounder." Government of Canada. Retrieved November 22, 2015 (www.cisc.gc.ca/media/2014/2014-08-22-eng.htm).

Crutcher, N., and Trevethan, S. 2002. "An examination of healing lodges for federal offenders in Canada." *Forum on Corrections Research*. 14:52–54.

CTVnews.ca. 2014. "Ottawa teen pimp ringleader sentenced as adult for 'despicable' crimes." November 4, 2014. Retrieved November 4, 2015 (www.ctvnews.ca/canada/ottawa-teen-pimp-ringleader-sentenced-as-adult-for-despicable-crimes-1.2085930).

Cullen, A.E., Clarke, A.Y., Kuipers, E., Hodgins, S., Dean, K., and Fahy, T. 2012. "A multisite randomized trial of a cognitive skills program for male mentally disordered offenders: Violence and behavior outcomes." *Consulting and Clinical Psychology*. 80(6):1114–20. DOI: 10.1037/a0030291.

Cullen, F.T. 2012. "Taking rehabilitation seriously: Creativity, science, and the challenge of offender change." *Punishment and Society*. 14:94–114. DOI: 10.1177/1462474510385973.

Cullen, F.T., Wright, J.P., Gendreau, P., and Andrews, D.A. 2003. "What correctional treatment can tell us about criminological theory: Implications for social learning theory." In R.L. Akers and G.F. Jensen, eds. *Social learning theory and the explanation of crime: A guide for the new century*. pp. 339–362. New Brunswick, NJ: Transaction Publishers.

Cummings, E.M., Davies, P.T., and Campbell, S.B. 2000. *Developmental psychopathology and family process: Theory, research, and clinical implications*. New York, NY: Guilford Press.

Cunneen, C., Allison, F., and Schwartz, M. 2014. "Access to justice for Aboriginal people in the Northern Territory." *Australian Journal of Social Issues*. 49(2):219–240.

Cusworth Walker, S., Muno, A., and Sullivan-Colglazier, C. 2015. "Principles in practice: A Multistate study of gender-responsive reforms in the juvenile justice system." *Crime and Delinquency*. 61:742–766. DOI: 10.1177/0011128712449712.

Cybercrime. http://www.international.gc.ca/crime/cyber_crime-criminalite.aspx?lang=eng with permission of the Department of Global Affairs Canada, Ottawa, 2016

Dadds, M.R., Allen, J.L., McGregor, K., Woolgar, M., Viding, E., and Scott, S. 2014. "Callous-unemotional traits in children and mechanisms of impaired eye contact during expressions of love: A treatment target?" *Journal of Child Psychology and Psychiatry*. 55:771–780.

Dadds, M.R., Cauchi, A.J., Wimalaweera, S., Hawes, D.J., and Brennan, J. 2012. "Outcomes, moderators, and mediators of empathic-emotion recognition training for complex conduct problems in childhood." *Psychiatry Research*. 199(3):201–207.

Dahlberg, L.L., and Krug, E.G. 2002. "Violence—A global health problem." In E. Krug et al., eds. *World report on violence and health*. pp. 1–56. Geneva, Switzerland: World Health Organization.

Daigle, L.E., Cullen, F.T., and Wright, J.P. 2007. "Gender differences in the predictors of juvenile delinquency: Assessing the generality-specificity debate." *Youth Violence and Juvenile Justice*. 5:254–286.

Daly, K. 1992. "Women's pathways to Felony court: Feminist theories of lawbreaking and problems of representation." *Review of Law and Women's Studies*. 2:11–52.

Daly, K. 1994. *Gender, crime and punishment*. New Haven, CT: Yale University Press.

Daly, K., and Chesney-Lind, M. 1988. "Feminism and Criminology." *Justice Quarterly*. 5(4):497–538.

Daly, M., and Wilson, M. 1988. *Homicide*. New York, NY: Aldine De Gruyter.

Dauvergne, M. 2013. "Youth court statistics in Canada, 2011/2012." Juristat. Canadian Centre for Justice Statistics, Statistics Canada. Catalogue no. 85-002-X. Retrieved April 20, 2015 (www.statcan.gc.ca/pub/85-002-x/2013001/article/11803-eng.htm).

Davidson, W.S., and Redner, R. 1988. "The prevention of juvenile delinquency: Diversion from the juvenile justice system." In R.H. Price, E.L. Cowen, R.P. Lorion, and J. Ramos-McKay, eds. *Fourteen ounces of prevention: A casebook for practitioners*. pp. 123–137. Washington, DC: American Psychological Association.

Dawkins, R. 1989. *The selfish gene*. 2nd ed. Oxford: Oxford University Press.

de Vogel, V., de Ruiter, C., Bouman, Y., and de Vries Robbé, M. 2009. *SAPROF: Guidelines for the assessment of protective factors for violence risk*. Utrecht, The Netherlands: Forum Educatief.

de Vries Robbé, M., de Vogel, V., and de Spa, E. 2011. "Protective factors for violence risk in forensic psychiatric patients: A retrospective validation of the SAPROF." *International Journal of Forensic Mental Health*. 10:178–186. DOI: 10.1080/14999013.2011.600232.

de Vries Robbé, M., de Vogel, V., and Douglas, K.S. 2013. "Risk factors and protective factors: A two-sided dynamic approach to violence risk assessment." *Journal of Forensic Psychiatry and Psychology*. 24:440–457. DOI:10.1080/14789949.2013.818162.

Decker, S., Melde, C., and Pyrooz, D. 2013. "What do we know about gangs and gang members and where do we go from here?" *Justice Quarterly*. 30:369–402. DOI:10.1080/07418825.2012.732101.

DeFries, J.D., and Fulker, D.W. 1985. "Multiple regression analysis of twin data." *Behaviour Genetics*. 15:467–473.

DeGue, S., and DiLillo, D. 2009. "Is animal cruelty a 'red flag' for family violence?: Investigating co-occurring violence toward children, partners, and pets." *Journal of Interpersonal Violence*. 24(6):1036–1056.

Dell, C.A., and Boe, R. 2000. *An examination of Aboriginal and Caucasian women offender risk and needs factors*. Research Report No. R-94. Ottawa, ON: Correctional Service Canada.

Dekovic, M. 1999. "Risk and protective factors in the development of problem behavior during adolescence." *Journal of Youth and Adolescence*. 28:667–685.

DeMatteo, D., Filone, S., and Davis, J. 2015. "Substance use and crime." In B.L. Cutler and P.A. Zapf, eds. *APA Handbook of Forensic Psychology. Volume 1: Individual and Situational Influences in Criminal and Civil Contexts*. pp. 325–349. Washington, DC: American Psychological Association.

DeMatteo, D., and Marczyk, G. 2005. "Risk factors, protective factors, and the prevention of antisocial behavior among juveniles." In K. Heilbrun, N. Goldstein, and R. Redding, eds. *Juvenile delinquency: Prevention, assessment, and intervention*. pp. 19–44. New York, NY: Oxford University Press.

Denham, S., and Almeida, M. 1987. "Children's social problem solving skills, behavioral adjustment, and interventions: A meta-analysis evaluating theory and practice." *Journal of Applied Developmental Psychology*. 8:391–409.

Department of Health and Human Services. 2001. *Youth violence: A report of the surgeon general*. Rockville, MD: Author.

Department of Justice. 2015. *Drug treatment court funding program*. Retrieved October 29, 2015 (www.justice.gc.ca/eng/fund-fina/gov-gouv/dtc-ttt.html).

Derogatis, L.R. 1993. *BSI: Administration, scoring and procedures manual*. 3rd ed. Minneapolis: National Computer Systems.

Desmarais, S.L., Nicholls, T.L., Wilson, C.M., and Brink, J. 2012. "Using dynamic and protective factors to predict inpatient aggression: Reliability and validity of START assessments." *Psychological Assessment*. 24(3):685–700. DOI: 10.1037/a0026668.

Desmarais, S.L., and Singh, J.P. 2013. *Instruments for assessing recidivism risk: A review of validation studies conducted in the U.S.* New York: Council of State Governments Justice Center.

DeWall, C.N., Baumeister, R.F., Stillman, T.F., Gailliot, M.T. 2007. "Violence restrained: Effects of self-regulation and its depletion on aggression." *Journal of Experimental Social Psychology*. 43:62–72.

Dixon, L., and Browne, K. 2003. "The heterogeneity of spouse abuse: A review." *Aggression and Violent Behavior*. 8:107–130.

Dobash, R., and Dobash, R.E. 1979. *Violence against wives: The case against the patriarchy*. New York, NY: Free Press.

Dobash, R.P., Dobash, R.E., Wilson, M., and Daly, M. 1992. "The myth of sexual symmetry in marital violence." *Social Problems*. 39:71–91.

Dodge, K.A. 1991. "The structure and function of reactive and proactive aggression." In D. Pepler and K. Rubin, eds. *The development and treatment of childhood aggression*. pp. 201–218. Hillsdale, NJ: Earlbaum.

Dodge, K.A. 2000. "Conduct disorder." In A.J. Sameroff, M. Lewis, and S.M. Miller, eds. *Handbook of developmental psychopathology*. 2nd ed. pp. 447–463. New York, NY: Kluwer Academic/Plenum Publishers.

Dodge, K.A., and Godwin, J. 2013. "Social-information-processing patterns mediate the impact of preventive intervention on adolescent antisocial behavior." *Psychological Science*. 24(4):456-465. DOI: dx.doi.org/10.1177/0956797612457394.

Dodge, K.A., Lochman, J.E., Harnish, J.D., Bates, J.E., and Pettit, G.S. 1997. "Reactive and proactive aggression

in school children and psychiatrically impaired chronically assaultive youth." *Journal of Abnormal Psychology*. 106:37–51.

Doherty, S., Ternes, M., and Matheson, F.I. 2014. "An examination of the effectiveness of the National Substance Abuse Program High Intensity (NSAP-H) on institutional adjustment and post-release outcomes. Research Report No. R-290. Ottawa, ON: Correctional Service Canada.

Donovan, D.M. 2013. "Evidence-based assessment: Strategies and measures in addictive behaviors." In B.S. McCrady and E.E. Epstein, eds. *Addictions: A comprehensive guidebook*. pp. 311–351. New York: Oxford University Press.

Doob, A., and C. Cesaroni. 2004. *Responding to youth crime in Canada*. Toronto: University of Toronto Press.

Doob, A., and Sprott, J.B. 1998. "Is the quality of youth violence becoming more serious?" *Canadian Journal of Criminology and Criminal Justice*. 40:185–194.

Dorminey, J., Flemming, A.S., Kranacher, M., and Riley, R.A. 2012. "The evolution of fraud theory." *Issues in Accounting Education*. 27:555–579. DOI: 10.2308/iace-50131.

Douglas, K.S., Cox, D.N., and Webster, C.D. 1999. "Violence risk assessment." *Legal and Criminological Psychology*. 4:149–184.

Douglas, K.S., Guy, L.S., and Hart, S.D. 2009. "Psychosis as a risk factor for violence to others: A meta-analysis." *Psychological Bulletin*. 135:679.

Douglas, K.S., Hart, S.D., Webster, C.D., and Belfrage, H. 2013. *HCR-20V3: Assessing risk for violence—User guide*. Burnaby BC, Canada: Mental Health, Law, and Policy Institute, Simon Fraser University.

Douglas, K.S., Hart, S.D., Webster, C.D., Belfrage, H., Guy, L.S., and Wilson, C.M. 2014. "Historical-Clinical-Risk Management-20, Version 3 (HCR-20V3): Development and overview." *International Journal of Forensic Mental Health*. 13(2): 93–108. DOI: 10.1080/14999013.2014.906519.

Douglas, K.S., and Skeem, J.L. 2005. "Violence risk assessment: Getting specific about being dynamic." *Psychology, Public Policy, and Law*. 11:347–383.

Douglas, K.S., Yeomans, M., and Boer, D.P. 2005. "Comparative validity analysis of multiple measures of violence risk in a sample of criminal offenders." *Criminal Justice and Behavior*. 32:479–510.

Dowden, C. 2005. *What works for women offenders? A meta-analytic exploration of gender-responsive treatment targets and their role in the delivery of effective correctional intervention*. Paper presented at What Works with Women Offenders: A Cross-National Dialogue about Effective Responses to Female Offenders. June 2015, Prato, Italy.

Dowden, C., and Andrews, D.A. 1999. "What works for female offenders: A meta-analytic review." *Crime and Delinquency*. 45:438–452.

Dowden, C., and Andrews, D.A. 2000. "Effective correctional treatment and violent reoffending." *Canadian Journal of Criminology*. 42:449–467.

Dowden, C., and Andrews, D.A. 2004. "The Importance of staff practice in delivering effective correctional treatment: A meta-analytic review of core correctional practice." *International Journal of Offender Therapy and Comparative Criminology*. 482:203–214.

Dowden, C., and Brown, S.L. 2002. "The role of substance abuse factors in predicting recidivism: A meta-analysis." *International Journal of Crime, Psychology, and Law*. 8:243–264.

Drake, E.K., Aos, S., and Miller. 2009. "Evidence-based public policy options to reduce crime and criminal justice costs: Implications in Washington State." *Victims and Offenders.* 4(2):170–196. DOI: 10.1080/15564880802612615.

Drews, K. 2013. "Conservatives slam Trudeau over marijuana legalization stance, saying drugs have 'harmful effect.'" *National Post.* July 26. Retrieved October 29, 2015 (http://news.nationalpost.com/news/canada/canadian-politics/conservatives-slam-trudeau-over-marijuana-legalization-stance-saying-drugs-have-harmful-effect).

Dunford, F.W. 2000. "The San Diego Navy Experiment: An assessment of interventions for men who assault their wives." *Journal of Consulting and Clinical Psychology.* 68:468–476.

Duntley, J.D., and Buss, D.M. 2008. "The origins of homicide." In J.D. Duntley and T.K. Shackelford, eds. *Evolutionary forensic psychology: Darwinian foundations of crime and law.* pp. 41–64. Oxford, NY: Oxford University Press.

Durrant, R., and Thakker, J. 2003. *Substance use and abuse: Cultural and historical perspectives.* Thousand Oaks, CA: Sage.

Durrant, R., and Ward, T. 2015. *Evolutionary criminology: Towards a comprehensive explanation of crime.* Amsterdam: Elsevier Inc.

Dutton, D.G. 1995. *The domestic assault of women: Psychological and criminal justice perspectives.* Vancouver, BC: UBC Press.

Dutton, D.G., and Browning, J.J. 1988. "Concern for power, fear of intimacy, and aversive stimuli for wife assault." In G.J. Hotaling, D. Finkelhor, J.T. Kirkpatrick, and M.A. Strausm, eds. *Family abuse and its consequences: New directions in research.* pp. 163–175. Newbury Park, CA: Sage.

Dutton, D.G., and Corvo, K. 2006. "Transforming a flawed policy: A call to revive psychology and science in domestic violence research and practice." *Aggression and Violent Behavior.* 11:457–483.

Dutton, D.G., and Corvo, K. 2007. "The Duluth Model: A data-impervious paradigm and a failed strategy." *Aggression and Violent Behavior.* 16:658–667.

Earlscourt Child and Family Centre. 2001a. *SNAP children's group manual.* Toronto, ON: Earlscourt Child and Family Centre.

Earlscourt Child and Family Centre. 2001b. *SNAP parent group manual.* Toronto, ON: Earlscourt Child and Family Centre.

Easteal, P. 1991. "Premenstrual syndrome (PMS) in the courtroom." *Women and the Law.* 165–172.

Easton, S., Furness, H., and Brantingham, P. 2014. "The cost of crime in Canada: 2014 report." Fraser Institute. Retrieved October 30, 2015 (www.fraserinstitute.org/research/cost-crime-canada-2014-report).

Ebata, A.T., Peterson, A.C., and Conger, J.J. 1990. "The development of psychopathology in adolescence." In J. Rolf, A.S. Masten, D. Cicchetti, K. Nuechterlein, and S. Weintraub, eds. *Risk and protective factors in the development of psychopathology.* pp. 308–333. Cambridge, MA: Cambridge University Press.

Edens, J.F., Campbell, J.S., and Weir, J.M. 2007. "Youth psychopathy and criminal recidivism: A meta-analysis of the Psychopathy Checklist measures." *Law and Human Behavior.* 31:53–75.

Edens, J.F., Guy, L.S., and Fernandez, K. 2003. "Psychopathic traits predict attitudes toward a juvenile capital murderer." *Behavioral Sciences and the Law.* 21:807–828.

Edens, J.F., Skeem, J.L., Cruise, K.R., and Cauffman, E. 2001. "Assessment of 'juvenile psychopathy' and its association with violence: A critical review." *Behavioral Sciences and the Law: Special Issue: Youth Violence.* 19:53–80.

Elia, J., Ambrosini, P., and Berrettini, W. 2008. "ADHD characteristics: Concurrent co-morbidity patterns in children and adolescents." *Child Adolescent Psychiatry Mental Health.* 2(1):15.

Elizabeth Fry Society of Peel-Halton. 2005. *Structured Decision Making Model for Girls in the Youth Justice System.*

Ellerby, L.A., and MacPherson, M. 2002. *Exploring the profile of Aboriginal sex offenders: Contrasting Aboriginal and non-Aboriginal sexual offenders to determine unique client characteristics and potential implications for sex offender assessment and treatment strategies.* Research Report No. R-122. Ottawa, ON: Correctional Service Canada. Retrieved December 8, 2015 (www.csc-scc.gc.ca/research/r122-eng.shtml).

Elliott, D.S., Huizinga, D., and Ageton, S.S. 1985. *Explaining delinquency and drug use.* Thousand Oaks, CA: Sage.

Elliott, I., and Beech, A. 2009. "Understanding online child pornography use: Applying sexual offense theory to internet offenders." *Aggression and Violent Behavior.* 14:180–193.

Ellis, D. 1989. "Male abuse of a married or cohabiting female partner: The application of sociological theory to research findings." *Violence and Victims.* 4:235–255.

Employment and Social Development Canada. 2015. "Security—Victims of property crime." Retrieved November 3, 2015 (http://well-being.esdc.gc.ca/misme-iowb/.3ndic.1t.4r@-eng.jsp?iid=60).

Environics Institute. 2010. "Focus Canada 2010: Public opinion research on the record: Serving the public interest." Kingston ON: Queen's University. Retrieved October 30, 2015 (www.queensu.ca/cora/_files/fc2010report.pdf).

Epprecht, N. 2000. "Programs for Aboriginal offenders: A national survey." *Forum on Corrections Research.* 12:45-47.

Erickson, P.G., and Butters, J.E. 2006. "Youth, weapons, and violence in Toronto and Montreal." Report prepared for Public Safety Canada, Ottawa.

Ewert v. Canada. 2015. FC 1093 (CanLII). Retrieved December 8, 2015 (http://canlii.ca/t/gl9d9).

Eysenck, H.J. 1977. *Crime and personality.* 2nd ed. London, UK: Routledge.

Fagan, J. 1989. "The social organization of drug use and drug dealing among urban gangs." *Criminology.* 27:633–670. DOI: 10.1111/j.1745-9125.1989.tb01049.x.

Fagot, B.I., and Kavanagh, K. 1990. "The prediction of anti-social behaviour from avoidant attachment classifications." *Child Development.* 61:864–873.

Fals-Stewart, W., Birchler, G.R., and Kelley, M.L. 2003. "The timeline follow back spousal violence interview to assess physical aggression between intimate partners: Reliability and validity." *Journal of Family Violence.* 18:131–142.

Farr, K.A. 2000. "Classification of female inmates: Moving forward." *Crime and Delinquency.* 461:3–17.

Farrall, S. 2004. "Social capital and offender reintegration: Making probation desistance focussed." In S. Maruna and R. Immarigeon, eds. *After Crime and Punishment: Pathways to Offender Reintegration.* pp. 57–84. Cullompton: Willan Publishing.

Farrar-Owens, M. 2012. *Use of offender risk assessment in Virginia.* Paper presented at the National Association of Sentencing Commissions annual conference, Chicago, Illinois.

Farrell, A., and Bruce, S. 1997. "Impact of exposure to community violence on violent behavior and emotional distress among urban adolescents." *Journal of Clinical Child Psychology.* 26:2–14.

Farrington, D.P. 1989. "Early predictors of adolescent aggression and adult violence." *Violence and Victims.* 4:79–100.

Farrington, D.P. 1995. "The development of offending and antisocial behavior from childhood: Key findings from the Cambridge Study in Delinquent Development." *Journal of Child Psychology and Psychiatry.* 36:929–964.

Farrington, D.P. 2003. "Key results for the first forty years of the Cambridge Study in Delinquent Development." In T.P. Thornberry and M.D. Krohn, eds. *Taking stock of delinquency: An overview of findings from contemporary longitudinal studies.* New York, NY: Kluver Academic/Plenum Publishers.

Farrington, D.P. 2006. "Family background and psychopathy." In C. Patrick, ed. *Handbook of psychopathy.* pp. 229–250. New York, NY: Guilford Press.

Farrington, D.P., and Painter, K.A. 2004. "Gender differences in offending: Implications for risk-focused prevention." Retrieved August 22, 2005 (www.homeoffice.gov.uk/rds/pdfs2/rdsolr0904.pdf).

Farrington, D.P., and West, D.J. 1993. "Criminal, penal and life histories of chronic offenders: Risk and protective factors and early identification." *Criminal Behaviour and Mental Health.* 3:492–523.

Fazel, S., and Danesh, J. 2002. "Serious mental disorder in 23,000 prisoners: A systematic review of 62 surveys." *Lancet.* 359:545–550.

Feder, L., and Wilson, D.B. 2005. "A meta-analytic review of court-mandated batterer intervention programs: Can courts affect abusers' behavior?" *Journal of Experimental Criminology.* 1(2):239–262.

Federal Bureau of Prisons. 2012. "Substance abuse treatment." National Institute of Corrections. Retrieved November 2, 2015 (www.bop.gov/inmates/custody_and_care/substance_abuse_treatment.jsp).

Feinman, C. 1986. *Women in the criminal justice system.* 2nd ed. New York, NY: Praeger Publishers.

Feldman, M.P. 1977. *Criminal behavior: A psychological analysis.* Hoboken, NJ: John Wiley and Sons, Inc.

Felson, R.B., and Cares, A.C. 2005. "Gender and the seriousness of assaults on intimate partners and other victims." *Journal of Marriage and Family.* 675:182–195.

Ferguson, C.J., San Miguel, C., Garza, A., and Jerabeck, J.M. 2012. "A longitudinal test of video game violence influences on dating and aggression: A 3-year longitudinal study of adolescents." *Journal of Psychiatric Research.* 46(2):141–146. DOI: dx.doi.org/10.1016/j.jpsychires.2011.10.014.

Ferguson, D.M., and Horwood, L.J. 1998. "Early conduct problems and later life opportunities." *Journal of Child Psychology and Psychiatry.* 39:1097–1108.

Fergusson, D.M., and Lynskey, M.T. 1997. "Early reading difficulties and later conduct problems." *Journal of Child Psychology and Psychiatry.* 38:899–907.

Fergusson, D.M., and Woodward, L.J. 2000. "Educational, psychological, and sexual outcomes of girls with conduct problems in early adolescence." *Journal of Child Psychology and Psychiatry.* 41:779–792.

Feshbach, S. 1964. "The function of aggression and the regulation of aggressive drive." *Psychological Review.* 71:257–272.

Few, L.R., Lynam, D.R., Maples, J.L., MacKillop, J., and Miller, J.D. 2015. "Comparing the utility of DSM-5 section II and III antisocial personality disorder diagnostic approaches for capturing psychopathic traits." *Personality Disorders: Theory, Research, and Treatment.* 6(1):64–74.

Finckenauer, J. 1982. *Scared Straight and the Panacea Phenomenon.* Englewood Cliffs, NJ: Prentice Hall.

Finkelhor, D. 1984. *Child sexual abuse: New theory and research.* New York, NY: Free Press.

Finkelhor, D., and Jones, M. 2008. "Good news: Child victimization has been declining. Why?" In D. Finkelhor, ed. *Childhood victimization: Violence, crime and abuse in the lives of young people.* pp. 142–147. New York: Oxford University Press.

First Nations and Inuit Health Committee. 2010. Addendum to "Position statement: Fetal alcohol syndrome." *Paediatric Child Health.* 7(3):161–174. Retrieved December 7, 2015 (www.cps.ca/documents/position/fetal-alcohol-syndrome#addendum).

Fischer, B. 2000. "Prescriptions, power and politics: The turbulent history of methadone maintenance in Canada." *Public Health Policy.* 21(2):187–210.

Fitzgerald, R.T., and Carrington, P.J. 2008. "The neighbourhood context of urban Aboriginal crime." *Canadian Journal of Criminology and Criminal Justice.* 50(5):523–557.

Flannery, D.J., and Williams, L. 1999. "Effective youth violence prevention." In T. Gullotta and S.J. McElhaney, eds. *Violence in homes and communities: Prevention, intervention, and treatment.* Thousand Oaks, CA: Sage.

Flight, J.I., and Forth, A.E. 2007. "Instrumentally violent youths: The roles of psychopathic traits, empathy, and attachment." *Criminal Justice and Behavior.* 34:739–751.

Foglia, W.D. 1997. "Perceptual difference and the mediating effect of internalized norms among inner-city teenagers." *Journal of Research in Crime and Delinquency.* 34:414–442.

Foley, D.L., Eaves, L.J., Wormley, B., Silberg, J.L., Maes, H.H., Kuhn, J., and Riley, B. 2004. "Childhood adversity, monoamine oxidase A genotype, and risk for conduct disorder." *Archives of General Psychiatry.* 61:738–744.

Follingstad, D.R., Helff, C.M., Binford, R.V., Runge, M.M., and White, J. D. 2004. "Lay persons' versus psychologists' judgments of psychologically aggressive actions by a husband and wife." *Journal of Interpersonal Violence.* 19:916–942.

Fontaine, N.M.G., Rijsdijk, F.V., McCrory, E.M.J.P., and Viding, E. 2010. "Etiology of different developmental trajectories of callous-unemotional traits." *Journal of the American Academy of Child and Adolescent Psychiatry.* 49:656–664.

Fontaine, R.G., Burks, V.S., and Dodge, K.A. 2002. "Response decision processes and externalizing behavior problems in adolescents." *Development and Psychopathology.* 14:107–122.

Foreign Affairs, Trade and Development Canada. 2015. "Cybercrime." Government of Canada. Retrieved November 3, 2015 (www.international.gc.ca/crime/cyber_crime-criminalite.aspx?lang=eng).

Forsman, M., Lichtenstein, P., Andershed, H., and Larsson, H. 2008. "Genetic effects explain the *stability* of psychopathic personality from mid- to late-adolescence." *Journal of Abnormal Psychology.* 117:606–617.

Forth, A.E., Kosson, D.S., and Hare, R.D. 2003. *The Psychopathy Checklist: Youth Version.* Toronto, ON: Multi-Health Systems.

Fowles, D.C. 1988. "Psychophysiology and psychopathology: A motivational approach." *Psychophysiology.* 25:373–391.

Fox, J.A., and Levin, J. 1998. "Multiple homicide: Patterns of serial and mass murder." *Crime and Justice.* 23:407–455.

Fox, L., and Sugar, F. 1990. *Survey of federally sentenced Aboriginal women in the community.* Ottawa: Correctional Service Canada.

Francis, P., Black, S., Johnson, S., and Payette, T. (n.d.). "Evaluation of methadone maintenance treatment services: First voice." Halifax NS: Capital Health Addiction Prevention and Treatment Services. Retrieved October 29, 2015 (www.cdha.nshealth.ca/system/files/sites/documents/evaluation-methadone-maintenance-treatment-services.pdf).

Frazzetto, G., Lorenzo, G.D., Carola, V., Proietti, L., Sokolwska, E., Siracusano, A., Gross, C., and Troisi, A. 2007. "Early trauma and increased risk for physical aggression during adulthood: The moderating role of MAOA genotype." *PLoS ONE,* 5, e486. Available at (www.pubmedcentral.nih.gov/picrender.fcgi?artid=1872046andblobtype=pdf).

Freeman, R.B. 1996. "Why do so many young American men commit crimes and what might we do about it?" *Journal of Economic Perspectives.* 10:25–42.

Freeman, N.J. 2012. "Notification laws: Rearrest of convicted sex offenders." *Crime and Delinquency.* 58(4):539–564. DOI: 10.1177/0011128708330852.

French, S., and Gendreau, P. 2003. *"Safe and humane corrections through effective treatment." Correctional Service Canada.* Research Report No. R-139.

Freud, S. 1901. *The psychopathology of everyday life.* New York, NY: Macmillan.

Freud, S. 1916. "Some character types met with in psychoanalytic work." *Standard Edition.* 14:309–336.

Freud, S. 1923. *The ego and the id.* London, UK: Hogarth Press.

Freud, S. 1953. *A general introduction to psychoanalysis.* New York, NY: Permabooks.

Freund, K., and Kuban, M. 1994. "The basis of the abused abuser theory of pedophilia: A further elaboration on an earlier study." *Archives of Sexual Behavior.* 23:553–563. DOI: 10.1007/BF01541497.

Freund, K., Watson, R., and Dickey, R. 1990. "Does sexual abuse in childhood cause pedophilia: An exploratory study." *Archives of Sexual Behavior.* 19:557–568. DOI: 10.1007/BF01542465.

Frick, P.J. 1994. "Family dysfunction and the disruptive disorders: A review of recent empirical findings." In T.H. Ollendick and R.J. Prinz, eds. *Advances in clinical child psychology.* Vol. 16. New York, NY: Plenum.

Frick, P.J., and Hare, R.D. 2001. *The Antisocial Process Screening Device.* Toronto, ON: Mental Health Systems.

Frick, P.J., Kimonis, E.R., Dandreaux, D.M., and Farrell, J.M. 2003. "The 4 year stability of psychopathic traits in non-referred youth." *Behavioral Sciences and the Law.* 21:1–24.

Frick, P.J., Lahey, B.B., Loeber, R., Stouthamer, M., Christ, M.A.G., and Hanson, K. 1992. "Familial risk factors to oppositional defiant disorder and conduct disorder: Parental psychopathology and maternal parenting." *Journal of Consulting and Clinical Psychology.* 60:49–55.

Frick, P.J., and Marsee, M.A. 2006. "Psychopathic traits and developmental pathways to antisocial behavior in youth." In C. J. Patrick, ed. *Handbook of psychopathy.* pp. 355–374. New York, NY: Guilford Press.

Friend, D.J., Cleary Bradley, R.P., Thatcher, R., and Gottman, J.M. 2011. "Typologies of intimate partner violence: Evaluation of a screening instrument for differentiation." *Journal of Family Violence.* 26:551–563.

Fulero, S. 1995. "Review of the Hare Psychopathy Checklist-Revised." In J.C. Conoley, and J.C. Impara, eds. *Twelfth Mental Measurements Yearbook.* pp. 453–454. Lincoln, NE: Buros Institute Mental Measures.

Furnham, A., Richards, S C., and Paulhus, D.L. 2013. "The dark triad of personality: A 10 year review." *Social and Personality Psychology Compass.* 7:199–216.

Gaarder, E., and Belknap, J. 2004. "Little women: Girls in adult prison." *Women and Criminal Justice.* 152:5–80.

Gaarder, E., Rodriguez, N., and Zatz, M. 2004. "Criers, liars, and manipulators: Probation officers' views of girls." *Justice Quarterly.* 21:547–578.

Gabarino, J. 2007. *See Jane hit: Why girls are growing more violent and what we can do about it.* New York: Penguin Books.

Gabora, N., Stewart, L., Lilley, K., and Allegri, N. 2007. *A profile of female perpetrators of intimate partner violence: Implications for treatment.* R-175. Ottawa, ON: Correctional Services of Canada.

Gannon, M., and Mihorean, K. 2005. "Criminal victimization in Canada, 2004." *Juristat.* 257:1–27. Catalogue no. 85-002-XPE. Ottawa, ON: Statistics Canada.

Gannon, T.A., Ward, T., and Collie, R. 2007. "Cognitive distortions in child molesters: Theoretical and research developments over the past two decades." *Aggression and Violent Behavior.* 12:402–416. DOI:10.1016/j.avb.2006.09.005.

Garmezy, N. 1985. "Stress-resistant children: The search for protective factors." In J.E. Stevenson, ed. *Recent research in developmental psychopathology.* pp. 213–233. New York, NY: Pergamon.

Garmezy, N. 1991. "Resilience in children's adaptation to negative life events and stressed environments." *Pediatric Annuals.* 20:460–466.

Gaylord, M.S., and Galliher, J.F. 1988. *The criminology of Edward Sutherland.* New Brunswick, NJ: Transaction Publishers.

Gehring, K.S., Van Voorhis, P., and Bell, V.R. 2009. '*What Works' for female probationers? An evaluation of the Moving On program.* Retrieved December 3, 2015 (www.uc.edu/content/dam/uc/womenoffenders/docs/MOVING%20ON.pdf).

Gendreau, P., and Andrews, D.A. 1991. "Tertiary prevention: What the meta-analyses of the offender treatment literature tell us about 'what works.'" *Canadian Journal of Criminology.* 32:173–184.

Gendreau, P. 1996. "The principles of effective intervention with offenders." In A. T. Harland, ed. *Choosing correctional options that work: Defining the demand and evaluating the supply.* pp. 117–130. Thousand Oaks, CA: Sage Publications.

Gendreau, P., French, S., and Gionet, A. 2004. "What works (what doesn't work): The principles of effective correctional treatment." *Journal of Community Corrections.* XIII(Spring):4–30.

Gendreau, P. French, S., Taylor, A. 2002. *What works what doesn't work.* Invited submission to the International

Community Corrections Association Monograph Series Project.

Gendreau, P., Goggin, C., and Cullen, F. 1999. "The effects of prison sentences on recidivism." Ottawa, ON: Solicitor General Canada.

Gendreau, P., Goggin, C., Cullen, F.T., and Paparozzi, M. 2001. "The effects of community sanctions and incarceration on recidivism." In L.L. Motiuk and R.C. Serin, eds. Compendium 2000 on effective correctional programming. Ottawa, ON: Correctional Service Canada.

Gendreau, P., Goggin, C., and Smith, P. 2002. "Is the PCL-R really the 'unparalleled' measure of offender risk?" Criminal Justice and Behaviour. 29:397–426.

Gendreau, P., Little, T., and Goggin, C. 1996. "A meta-analysis of predictors of adult offender recidivism: What works!" Criminology. 34:575–607.

Gendreau, P., and Ross, R.R. 1979. "Effective correctional treatment: Bibliotherapy for cynics." Crime and Delinquency. 25:463–489.

Ghelani, A. 2010. "Evaluating Canada's drug prevention strategy and creating a meaningful dialogue with urban Aboriginal youth." Social Work with Groups. 34(1):4–20.

Gilfus, M. 1992. "From victims to survivors to offenders: Women's routes of entry into street crime." Women and Criminal Justice. 4:63–89.

Glaser, D. 1956. "Criminality theories and behavioral images." American Journal of Sociology. 61:441.

Glenn, A. L., Raine, A., and Laufer, W.S. 2011. "Is it wrong to criminalize and punish psychopaths?" Emotion Review. 3:302–304.

Globe and Mail. 2013. "By the numbers: Canada's medical marijuana use." Retrieved November 6 (www.theglobeandmail.com/news/national/by-the-numbers-canadas-medical-marijuana-use/article14694389/).

Gleuck, S., and Glueck, E. 1950. Unravelling juvenile delinquency. Cambridge, MA: Harvard University Press.

Glueck, S., and Glueck, E. 1968. Delinquents and non-delinquents in perspective. Cambridge, MA: Harvard University Press.

Glube, C., Michèle, A., Henriksen, S., and Stobbe, B. 2006. Moving Forward with Women's Corrections: Expert Committee Review of the Correctional Service Canada's Ten-Year Status Report on Women's Corrections 1996–2006. Correctional Service Canada. Retrieved December 3, 2015 (www.csc-scc.gc.ca/publications/fsw/wos29/wos29-eng.shtml).

Gobéil, R., and Blanchette, K. 2007. "Re-validation of a gender-informed security classification scale for women inmates." Journal of Contemporary Criminal Justice. 23:296–309.

Gobéil, R. 2011. Research at a glance: Use of the Custody Rating Scale with male offenders. Research Report No. R-257. Ottawa, ON: Correctional Service Canada. Retrieved December 8, 2015 (www.csc-scc.gc.ca/005/008/092/005008-0257-eng.pdf).

Gobéil, R., Blanchette, K., and Stewart, L. Forthcoming. "A meta-analytic review of correctional interventions for women offenders: Gender-neutral versus gender-informed interventions." Criminal Justice and Behavior.

Goldstein, P.J. 1985. "The drugs/violence nexus: A tripartite conceptual framework." Journal of Drug Issues. 15:493–506.

Gollom, M. 2015. "Mike Duffy trial: Crown dogs suspended senator over Peterborough trip." CBC News. May 5. Retrieved November 2, 2015 (www.cbc.ca/news/politics/mike-duffy-trial-crown-dogs-suspended-senator-over-peterborough-trip-1.3061069).

Gondolf, E.F. 1985. Men who batter: An integrated approach for stopping wife abuse. Holmes Beach, CA: Learning Publications.

Gondolf, E.F. 1988. "Who are those guys? Toward a behavioral typology of batterers." Violence and Victims. 3:187–203.

Goode, E., ed. 2008. Out of control: Assessing the general theory of crime. Palo Alto, CA: Stanford University Press.

Gottfredson, M.R., and Hirschi, T. 1990. A general theory of crime. Stanford, CA: Stanford University Press.

Gottman, J.M., Jacobson, N.S., Rushe, R.H., Shortt, J., Babcock, J., La Tailade, J.J,. et al. 1995. "The relationship between heart rate reactivity, emotionally aggressive behavior, and general violence in batterers." Journal of Family Psychology. 9:227–248.

Government of Canada. 2009. "National Victims of Crime Awareness Week." Retrieved January 25, 2009 (www.victimsweek.gc.ca/archives_2006/fact-sheets/p2.html).

Government of Canada. 2013. Marijuana for Medical Purposes Regulations. SOR/2013-119. Retrieved October 29, 2015 (http://laws-lois.justice.gc.ca/eng/regulations/SOR-2013-119/index.html).

Government of Canada. 2015a. "Summary of results for 2013." Canadian tobacco, alcohol and drug survey. Retrieved October 29, 2015 (http://healthycanadians.gc.ca/science-research-sciences-recherches/data-donnees/ctads-ectad/summary-sommaire-2013-eng.php).

Government of Canada. 2015b. "National anti-drug strategy." Retrieved October 29, 2015 (www.healthycanadians.gc.ca/anti-drug-antidrogue/index-eng.php).

Government of Canada. 2015c. "Rates of pay for public service employees." Retrieved October 22, 2015 (www.tbs-sct.gc.ca/pubs_pol/hrpubs/coll_agre/rates-taux-eng.asp).

Grasmick, H.G., Tittle, C.R., Bursik, R.J., and Arneklev, B.J. 1993. "Testing the core empirical implications of Gotteredson and Hirschi's general theory of crime." Journal of Research in Crime and Delinquency. 30:5–29.

Gray, J.A., and McNaughton, N. 2000. The neuropsychology of anxiety: An enquiry into the functions of the septohippocampal system. 2nd ed. Oxford: Oxford University Press.

Green, D.L., and Pomeroy, E. C. 2007. "Crime victimization: Assessing differences between violent and nonviolent experiences." Victims and Offenders. 2:63–76.

Green, G.S. 1997. Occupational crime. 2nd ed. Chicago: Nelson-Hall.

Green, L., and Campbell, M.A. 2006. "Gender influences and methodological considerations in adolescent risk-need assessment: A meta-analysis." Paper presented at the 67th annual meeting of the Canadian Psychological Association, Calgary, AB.

Greenfeld, L.A., and Snell, T.L. 1999. Women offenders. Special Report NCJ 175688. Bureau of Justice Statistics, U.S. Department of Justice. Retrieved Sept. 15, 2005 (www.ojp.usdoj.gov/bjs/abstract/wo.htm).

Grenier, E. 2013. "Majority of Canadians want to loosen marijuana laws: polls." Globe and Mail. Retrieved October 29, 2015 (www.theglobeandmail.com/news/politics/majority-of-canadians-want-to-loosen-marijuana-laws-polls/article14010389/).

Grekul, J., and LaBoucane-Benson, P. 2006. An investigation into the formation and recruitment process of Aboriginal gangs in Western Canada. Cat. No. JS42-110/2002. Ottawa: Public Safety Canada.

Gress, C.L.Z. 2005. "Viewing time measures and sexual interest: Another piece of the puzzle." *Journal of Sexual Aggression.* 11:117–125. DOI: 10.1080/13552600500063666.

Gricar, B. 1983. "A preliminary theory of compliance with OSHA regulation." *Research in Corporate Social Performance and Policy.* 5:121–141.

Gutierrez, L., and Bourgon, G. 2009. *Drug treatment courts: A quantitative review of study and treatment quality.* User Report 2009-04. Ottawa: Public Safety Canada. Retrieved October 29, 2015 (www.publicsafety.gc.ca/cnt/rsrcs/pblctns/2009-04-dtc/index-eng.aspx).

Gutierrez, L., Wilson, H.A., Rugge, T., and Bonta, J. 2013. "The prediction of recidivism with Aboriginal offenders: A theoretically informed meta-analysis." *Canadian Journal of Criminology and Criminal Justice.* 55(1):55–99.

Gutowski, C., and Mills, S. 2014. "Serial Killer Brian Dugan Gives 1st Prison Interview: 'I Could Not Stop.'" *Chicago Tribune.* December 13. Retrieved October 14, 2015 (www.chicagotribune.com/news/ct-brian-dugan-serial-killer-interview-met-20141212-story.htm/).

Guy, L.S., Edens, J.F., Anthony, C., and Douglas, K.S. 2005. "Does psychopathy predict institutional misconduct among adults? A meta-analytic investigation." *Journal of Consulting and Clinical Psychology.* 73:1056–1064.

Hall, G.C.N., and Hirschman, R. 1991. "Towards a theory of sexual aggression: A quadripartite model." *Journal of Consulting and Clinical Psychology.* 59:662–669.

Hall, G.C.N., and Hirschman, R. 1992. "Sexual aggression against children: A conceptual perspective of etiology." *Criminal Justice and Behavior.* 19:8–23.

Hamberger, J.E., and Hastings, L.K. 1994. "Psychosocial modifiers of psychopathology for domestically violent and nonviolent men." *Psychological Reports.* 74:112–114.

Hanby, L. 2013. *A longitudinal study of dynamic risk, protective factors, and criminal recidivism: Change over time and the impact of assessment timing.* Ph.D. diss. Carleton University.

Hangen, E. 1994. *D.S.S. interagency domestic violence team pilot project: Program data evaluation.* Boston: Massachusetts Department of Social Services.

Hann, R.G., and Harman, W.G. 1989. *Release risk prediction: Testing the Nuffield scoring system for Native and female inmates.* User Report No. 1989-4. Ottawa, ON: Solicitor General Canada.

Hann, R.G., and Harman, W.G. 1993. *Predicting release risk for Aboriginal penitentiary inmates.* User Report No. 1993-12. Ottawa, ON: Solicitor General Canada.

Hannah-Moffat, K. 2004. "Gendering risk at what cost: Negotiations of gender and risk in Canadian women's prisons." *Feminism and Psychology.* 142:243–249.

Hannah-Moffat, K., and Maurutto, P. 2003. *Youth Risk/Need Assessment: An overview of issues and practices.* Department of Justice Canada, Youth Justice Research. RR03YJ-4e. Retrieved March 21, 2009 (www.justice.gc.ca/eng/rp-pr/cj-jp/yj-jj/rr03_yj4-rr03_jj4/rr03_yj4.pdf).

Hanson, R.K. 1997. *The development of a brief actuarial risk scale for sexual offense recidivism.* Ottawa, ON: Ministry of Public Safety.

Hanson, R.K. 2009. "The psychological assessment of risk for crime and violence." *Canadian Psychology.* 50(3): 172–182. DOI:10.1037/a0015726.

Hanson, R.K. 2008. "What statistics should we use to report predictive accuracy?" *Crime Scene.* 151:15–17.

Hanson, R.K., Bourgon, G., Helmus, L., and Hodgson, S. 2009. *A meta-analysis of the effectiveness of treatment for sexual offenders: Risk, need, and responsivity.* Corrections Research User Report No. 2009-01. Ottawa, ON: Public Safety Canada.

Hanson, R.K., Bourgon, G., Helmus, L., and Hodgson, S. 2009a. "The principles of effective correctional treatment also apply to sexual offenders: A meta-analysis." *Criminal Justice and Behavior.* 36(9):865–891.

Hanson, R.K., Broom, I., and Stephenson, M. 2004. "Evaluating community sex offender treatment programs: A 12-year follow-up of 724 offenders." *Canadian Journal of Behavioural Science.* 36:87–96.

Hanson, R.K., and Bussière, M.T. 1998. "Predicting relapse: A meta-analysis of sexual offender recidivism studies." *Journal of Consulting and Clinical Psychology.* 66:348–362.

Hanson, R.K., Gordon, A., Harris, A.J.R., Marques, J.K., Murphy, W., Quinsey, V.L., and Seto, M.C. 2002. "First report of the collaborative outcome data project on the effectiveness of treatment for sex offenders." *Sexual Abuse: A Journal of Research and Treatment.* 14:169–194.

Hanson, R.K., Harris, A.J.R., Scott, T.L., and Helmus, L. 2007. *Assessing the risk of sexual offenders on community supervision: The Dynamic Supervision Project.* Report No. 2007-06. Ottawa, ON: Public Safety Canada.

Hanson, R.K., Helmus, L., and Bourgon, G. 2007. *The validity of risk assessments for intimate partner violence: A meta-analysis.* Public Safety Canada 2007-07.

Hanson, R.K., and Morton-Bourgon, K.E. 2004. *Predictors of sexual recidivism: An updated meta-analysis.* Ottawa, ON: Public Safety Canada.

Hanson, R.K., and Morton-Bourgon, K.E. 2009. "The accuracy of recidivism risk assessments for sexual offenders: A meta-analysis of 118 prediction studies." *Psychological Assessment.* 21:1–21.

Hanson, R.K., and Thornton, D. 1999. *Static-99: Improving actuarial risk assessments for sex offenders.* User Report 99-02. Ottawa: Department of the Solicitor General of Canada.

Hanson, R.K., and Thorton, D. 2000. "Improving risk assessments for sex offenders: A comparison of three actuarial scales." *Law and Human Behavior.* 24:119–136.

Hardyman, P.L. 2001. *Validation and refinement of objective prison classification systems for women: The experience of four states and common themes.* Washington, DC: The Institute on Crime, Justice and Corrections, National Institute of Corrections.

Hardyman, P., and Van Voorhis, P. 2004. *Developing gender specific classification systems for women offenders.* Washington, DC: National Institute of Corrections.

Hare, R.D. 1978. "Electrodermal and cardiovascular correlates of psychopathy." In R.D. Hare and D. Schalling, eds. *Psychopathic behavior: Approaches to research.* pp. 107–144. New York, NY: Wiley.

Hare, R.D. 1980. "A research scale for the assessment of psychopathy in criminal populations." *Personality and Individual Differences.* 1:111–119.

Hare, R.D. 2003. *Hare Psychopathy Checklist-Revised (PCL-R).* 2nd ed. Toronto, ON: Multi-Health Systems.

Hare, R.D., Clark, D., Grann, M., and Thornton, D. 2000. "Psychopathy and the predictive validity of the PCL-R: An international perspective." *Behavioral Sciences & the Law.* 18:623–645.

Hare, R.D., and Neumann C.S. 2008. "Psychopathy as clinical and empirical construct." *Annual Review of Clinical Psychology.* 4:217–246. DOI: 10.1146/annurev.clinpsy.3.022806.091452.

Harlow, C.W. 1999. *Prior abuse reported by inmates and probationers. Bureau of Justice Statistics: Selected Findings.* Report No. NCJ 172879. U.S. Department of Justice: Office of Justice Programs.

Harper, R, and Murphy, R. 2000. "An analysis of drug trafficking." *British Journal of Criminology.* 40:746–749.

Harpur, T.J., and Hare, R.D. 1994. "Assessment of psychopathy as a function of age." *Journal of Abnormal Psychology.* 103:604–609.

Harris, A.J., Levenson, J.S., and Ackerman, A.R. 2014. "Registered sex offenders in the United States: Behind the numbers." *Crime and Delinquency.* 60(1):3–33. DOI: 10.1177/0011128712443179.

Harris, B. 1979. "Whatever happened to Little Albert?" *American Psychologist.* 34:151–160.

Harris, G. T., and Rice, M.E. 2003. "Actuarial assessment of risk among sex offenders." *Annals of the New York Academy of Sciences.* 989:198–210. DOI: 10.1111/j.1749-6632.2003.tb07306.x.

Harris, G.T., and Rice, M.E. 2015. "Progress in violence risk assessment and communication: Hypothesis versus evidence." *Behavioral Sciences and the Law.* 33:128–145.

Harris, G.T., Rice, M.E., and Lalumière, M. 2001. "Criminal violence: The roles of psychopathy, neurodevelopmental insults, and antisocial parenting." *Criminal Justice and Behavior.* 28:402–426.

Harris, G.T., Rice, M.E., and Quinsey, V.L. 1993. "Violent recidivism of mentally disordered offenders: The development of a statistical prediction instrument." *Criminal Justice and Behavior.* 20:315–335.

Harris, G.T., Rice, M.E., Quinsey, V.L., and Chaplin, T.C. 1996. "Viewing time as a measure of sexual interest among child molesters and normal heterosexual men." *Behavior Research and Therapy.* 34:389–394.

Harris, G.T., Rice, M.E., Quinsey, V.L., and Cormier, C.A. 2015. *Violent offenders: Appraising and managing risk.* 3rd ed. Washington, DC: American Psychological Association. DOI:10.1037/14572-000.

Harris, G.T., Rice, M.E., Quinsey, V.L., Lalumière, M.L., Boer, D., and Lang, C. 2003. "A multi-site comparison of actuarial risk instruments for sex offenders." *Psychological Assessment.* 15:413–425.

Hart, S.D., Cox, D., and Hare, R.D. 1995. *Manual for the Psychopathy Checklist: Screening Version PCL: SV.* Toronto, ON: Multi-Health Systems.

Hart S.D., Roesch R., Corrado, R.R., and Cox, D.N. 1993. "The Referral Decision Scale: A validation study." *Law and Human Behavior.* 17(6):611–623.

Hart, S.D., Watt, K.A., and Vincent, G.M. 2002. "Commentary on Seagrave and Grisso: Impressions of the state of the art." *Law and Human Behavior.* 26:241–245.

Hartvig, P., and Kjelsberg, E. 2008. "Penrose's Law revisited: The relationship between mental institution beds, prison population and crime rate." *Nordic Journal of Psychiatry.* 63(1):51–6. DOI:10.1080/08039480802298697.

Hastings, R., Dunbar, L., and Bania, M. 2011. *Leaving criminal youth gangs: Exit strategies and programs.* Ottawa, ON: Crime Prevention Ottawa.

Hawes, S.W., Boccaccini, M.T., and Murrie, D.C. 2013. "Psychopathy and the combination of psychopathy and sexual deviance as predictors of sexual recidivism: Meta-analytic findings using the Psychopathy Checklist—Revised." *Psychological Assessment.* 25(1):233–243.

Hawes, D.J., Price, M.J., and Dadds, M.R. 2014. "Callous-unemotional traits and the treatment of conduct problems in childhood and adolescence: A comprehensive review." *Clinical Child and Family Psychology Review.* 17:248–267.

Hawkins, J.D., Herrenkohl, T.L., Farrington, D.P., Brewer, D., Catalano, R.F., and Harachi, T.W. 1998. "A review of predictors of youth violence." In R. Loeber and D.P. Farrington, eds. *Serious and Violent Juvenile Offenders: Risk Factors and Successful Interventions.* pp. 106–146. Thousand Oaks, CA: Sage Publications.

Hawkins, J.D., Herrenkohl, T.I., Farrington, D.P., Brewer, D., Catalano, R.F., Harachi, T.W., et al. 2000. *Predictors of youth violence.* Juvenile Justice Bulletin. Washington, DC: U.S. Department of Justice, Office of Justice Programs, Office of Juvenile Justice and Delinquency Prevention.

Health and Welfare Canada. 1990. *Mental health services in Canada.* Ottawa: Minister of Supply and Services Canada.

Health Canada. 2003. *The consequences of child maltreatment: A reference guide for health practitioners.* Report prepared by Jeff Latimer. Ottawa, ON: Health Canada.

Health Canada. 2014. "Canadian alcohol and drug use monitoring survey." Retrieved October 29, 2015 (www.hc-sc.gc.ca/hc-ps/drugs-drogues/stat/_2012/summary-sommaire-eng.php).

Health Canada. 2015a. "Authorized licensed producers under the *Marihuana for Medical Purposes Regulations.*" Retrieved October 29, 2015 (http://hc-sc.gc.ca/dhp-mps/marihuana/info/list-eng.php).

Health Canada. 2015b. "Medical Use of Marijuana." Retrieved October 29, 2015 (http://hc-sc.gc.ca/dhp-mps/marihuana/index-eng.php).

Heinze, P., Allen, R., Magai, C., and Ritzler, B. 2010. "'Let's get down to business': A validation study of the Psychopathic Personality Inventory among a sample of MBA students." *Journal of Personality Disorders.* 24:487–498.

Helmus, L., and Bourgon, G. 2011. "Taking stock of 15 years of research on the Spousal Assault Risk Assessment Guide (SARA): A critical review." *International Journal of Forensic Mental Health.* 10:64–75.

Helmus, L M., and Forrester, T. 2014. "Validation of the Static Factors Assessment (SFA) risk scale for federally sentenced offenders in Canada." Working paper.

Helmus, L., Hanson, R.K., Babchishin, K.M., and Mann, R.E. 2013. "Attitudes supportive of sexual offending predict recidivism: A meta-analysis." *Trauma, Violence, and Abuse.* 14(1):34–53. DOI: 10.1177/1524838012462244.

Hemmati, T. 2006. *The nature of Canadian urban gangs and their use of firearms: A review of the literature and police survey.* Report No. rr07-1e. Department of Justice Canada. Retrieved November 4, 2015 (www.justice.gc.ca/eng/rp-pr/csj-sjc/crime/rr07_1/toc-tdm.html).

Henggeler, S.W., and Borduin, C.M. 1990. *Family therapy and beyond: A multisystemic approach to treating the behavior problems of children and adolescents.* Pacific Grove, CA: Brooks/Cole.

Henggeler, S.W., Melton, G.B., and Smith, L.A. 1992. "Family preservation using multisystemic therapy: An effective alternative to incarcerating serious juvenile offenders." *Journal of Consulting and Clinical Psychology.* 60:953–961.

Henggeler, S.W., Schoenwald, S.K., Borduin, C.M., Rowland, M.D., and Cunningham, P.B. 1998. *Multisystemic treatment of antisocial behavior in children and adolescents.* New York, NY: Guilford Press.

Henggeler, S.W., Schoenwald, S.K., and Pickrel, S.A.G. 1995. "Multisystemic therapy: Bridging the gap between university and community bad treatment." *Journal of Consulting and Clinical Psychology.* 63:709–717.

Henry, B., Avshalom, C., Moffitt, T.E., and Silva, P.A. 1996. "Temperamental and familial predictors of violent and non-violent criminal convictions." *Developmental Psychology.* 32:614–623.

Henry, B., Caspi, A., Moffitt, T.E., and Silva, P.A. 1996. "Temperamental and familial predictors of violent and nonviolent criminal convictions: Age 3 to age 18." *Developmental Psychology.* 32:614–623.

Henry, B., and Moffitt, T.E. 1997. "Neuropsychological and neuroimaging studies of juvenile delinquency and adult criminal behaviour." In D.M. Stoff, J. Breiling, and J.D. Maser, eds. *Handbook of Antisocial Behavior.* pp. 280–287. New York, NY: Wiley.

Herrenkohl, T., Maguin, E., Hill, K., Hawkins, J., Abbott, R., and Catalano, R. 2000. "Developmental risk factors for youth violence." *Journal of Adolescent Health.* 26:176–186.

Hersh, K., and Borum, R. 1998. "Command hallucinations, compliance, and risk assessment." *Journal of the American Academy of Law.* 26:353–359.

Hervé, H. 2007. "Psychopathic subtypes: Historical and contemporary perspectives." In H. Hervé and J.C. Yuille, eds. *The psychopath: Theory, research, and practice.* pp. 431-460. Mahwah, NJ: Lawrence Erlbaum.

Hessing, D., Junger, M., Pickering, L., and Vazsonyi, A. 2001. "An empirical test of a general theory of crime: A four-nation comparative study of self-control and the prediction of deviance." *Journal of Research in Crime and Delinquency.* 38:91–131.

Hill, C., Kelley, P., Agle, B., Hitt, M., and Hoskisson, R. 1992. "An empirical examination of the causes of corporate wrongdoing in the United States." *Human Relations.* 45:1055–1076.

Hill, K.G., Howell, J., Hawkins, J., and Battin-Pearson, S. 1999. "Childhood risk factors for adolescent gang membership: Results from the Seattle Social Development Project." *Journal of Research in Crime and Delinquency.* 36:300–322.

Hilton, N.Z. 1993. "Childhood sexual victimization and lack of empathy in child molesters: Explanation or excuse?" *International Journal of Offender Therapy and Comparative Criminology.* 37:287–296.

Hilton, N.Z., Harris, G.T., Rice, M.E., Houghton, R.E., and Eke, A.W. 2008. "An in-depth risk assessment for wife assault recidivism: The Domestic Violence Risk Appraisal Guide." *Law and Human Behavior.* 32:150–163.

Hilton, N.Z., Harris, G.T., Rice, M.E., Lang, C., Cormier, C.A., and Lines, K.J. 2004. "A brief actuarial assessment for the prediction of wife assault recidivism: The Ontario Domestic Assault Risk Assessment." *Psychological Assessment.* 16:267–275.

Hinckers, A.S., Laucht, M., Schmidt, M.H., Mann, K.F., Schumann, G., Schuckit, M.A., and Heinz, A. 2006. "Low level of response to alcohol as associated with serotonin transporter genotype and high alcohol intake in adolescents." *Biological Psychiatry.* 60:282–287. DOI:10.1016/j.biopsych.2005.12.009.

Hinduja, S. 2006. "A critical examination of the digital music phenomenon." *Critical Criminology.* 14:387–409.

Hinshaw, S.P. 1992. "Externalizing behavior problems and academic underachievement in childhood and adolescence. Causal relationships and underlying mechanisms." *Psychological Bulletin.* 111:127–155.

Hinshaw, S.P., Lahey, B.B., and Hart, E.K. 1993. "Issues of taxonomy and comorbidity in the development of conduct disorder." *Development and Psychopathology.* 5:31–49.

Hipwell, A.E., and Loeber, R. 2006. "Do we know which interventions are effective for disruptive and delinquent girls?" *Clinical Child and Family Psychology Review.* 9:221–255.

Hirschi, T. 1969. *Causes of delinquency.* New Brunswick, NJ: Transaction Publishers.

Hirschi. T. 2002. *Causes of delinquency.* New Brunswick, NJ: Transaction Publishers.

Hirschi, T., and Selvin, H.C. 1967. *Delinquency research: An appraisal of analytic methods.* New York, NY: The Free Press.

History of Madness. 2015. "L'Institut universitaire en santé mentale de Québec: Deinstitutionalization." Retrieved September 23, 2015 (http://historyofmadness.ca/index.php?option=com_contentandview=articleandid=62andItemid=43andlang=enandlimitstart=7).

Hobson, J., Shine, J., and Roberts, R. 2000. "How do psychopaths behave in a prison therapeutic community?" *Psychology, Crime, and Law.* 6:139–154.

Hodgins, S., and Côté, G. 1990. "The prevalence of mental disorders among penitentiary inmates." *Canada's Mental Health.* 38:1–5.

Hodgins, S., Hiscoke, U., and Freese, R. 2003. "The antecedents of aggressive behavior among men with schizophrenia: A prospective investigation of patients in community treatment." *Behavioral Sciences and the Law.* 21:523–546.

Hodgins, S., Mednick, S.A., Brennan, P., Schulsinger, F., and Engberg, M. 1996. "Mental disorder and crime: Evidence from a Danish birth cohort." *Archives of General Psychiatry.* 53:489–96.

Hoffman, P.B., and Beck, J.L. 1984. "Burnout: Age at release from prison and recidivism." *Journal of Criminal Justice.* 12:617–623.

Hoge, R.D., and Andrews, D.A. 1996. *Assessing the youthful offender: Issues and techniques.* New York, NY: Plenum.

Hoge, R.D., and Andrews, D.A. 2002. *The Youth Level of Service/Case Management Inventory.* Toronto, ON: Multi-Health Systems.

Hoge, R.D., and Andrews, D.A. 2011. *Youth Level of Service/Case Management Inventory (2nd ed.): YLS/CMI 2.0 interview guide.* Toronto: Multi-Health Systems.

Hoge, R.D., Andrews, D.A., and Leschied, A.W. 1996. "An investigation of risk and protective factors in a sample of youthful offenders." *Journal of Child Psychology and Psychiatry.* 37:419–424.

Hogg, S. 2011. *The Level of Service Inventory (Ontario Revision) scale validation for gender and ethnicity: Addressing reliability and predictive validity.* M.A. thesis, University of Saskatchewan.

Hollin, C.R. 1989. *Psychology and crime: An introduction to criminological psychology.* London, UK: Routledge.

Holsinger, A.M., Lowenkamp, C.T., and Latessa, E.J. 2006. "Exploring the validity of the Level of Service Inventory–Revised with Native American offenders." *Journal of Criminal Justice.* 34:331–337.

Holsinger, K., Belknap, J., and Sutherland, J. 1999. *Assessing the gender specific program and service needs for adolescent females in the juvenile justice system.* Columbus, OH: Office of Criminal Justice Services.

Holtfreter, K. 2005. "Is occupational fraud 'typical' white-collar crime? A comparison of individuals and organizational characteristics." *Journal of Criminal Justice.* 33:353–365.

Holtfreter, K., and Cupp, R. 2007. "Gender and risk assessment." *Journal of Contemporary Criminal Justice.* 23:363–382.

Holtfreter, K., and Morash, M. 2003. "The needs of women offenders: Implications for correctional programming." *Women and Criminal Justice.* 14:137–160.

Holtfreter, K., Reisig, M.D., and Morash, M. 2004. "Poverty, state capital, and recidivism among women offenders." *Criminology and Public Policy.* 32:185–208.

Holtfreter, K., Reisig, M., Piquero, N., and Piquero, A. 2010. "Low self-control and fraud: Offending, victimization, and their overlap." *Criminal Justice and Behavior.* 37: 188–203. DOI:10.1177/0093854809354977.

Holtfreter, K., Van Slyke, S., Bratton, J., and Gertz, M. 2008. "Public persceptions of white-collar crime and punishment." *Journal of Criminal Justice.* 36:50–60.

Holtzworth-Munroe, A., Meehan, J.C., Herron, K., Rehman, U., and Stuart, G.L. 2003. "Do subtypes of martially violent men continue to differ over time." *Journal of Consulting and Clinical Psychology.* 714:728–740.

Holtzworth-Munroe, A., and Stuart, G.L. 1994. "Typologies of male batterers: Three subtypes and the differences among them." *Psychological Bulletin.* 116:476–497.

Hood, R. 2002. *The Death Penalty: A Worldwide Perspective.* 3rd ed. Oxford: Oxford University Press.

Hotton Mahony, T. 2011. "Women and the criminal justice system." In Statistics Canada, *Women in Canada: A gender-based statistical.* Catalogue No. 89-503-X. Retrieved December 2, 2015 (www.statcan.gc.ca/pub/89-503-x/2010001/article/11416-eng.pdf).

Howe, J., Falkenbach, D., and Massey, C. 2014. "The Relationship among Psychopathy, Emotional Intelligence, and Professional Success in Finance." *International Journal of Forensic Mental Health.* 13(4):337–347.

Howell, J. 2005. "Moving risk factors into developmental theories of gang Membership." *Youth Violence and Juvenile Justice.* 3:334–354.

Howsen, R.M., and Jarrell, S.B. 1987. "Some determinants of property crime: Economic factors influence criminal behavior but cannot completely explain the syndrome." *American Journal of Economics and Sociology.* 46:445–457.

Hubbard, D.J., and Pratt, T.C. 2002. "A meta-analysis of the predictors of delinquency among girls." *Journal of Offender Rehabilitation.* 34:1–13.

Hudson, S.M., Wales, D.S., Bakker, L., and Ward, T. 2002. "Dynamic risk factors: The Kia Marama evaluation." *Sexual Abuse: A Journal of Research and Treatment.* 14:103–119. DOI: 10.1177/107906320201400203.

Huesmann, L.R., Eron, L.D., Lefkowitz, M.M., and Walder, L.O. 1984. "Stability of aggression over time and generations." *Developmental Psychology.* 20:1120–1134.

Hughes, H.M. 1988. "Psychological and behavioral correlates of family violence in child witnesses and victims." *American Journal of Orthopsychiatry.* 58:77–90.

Hughes, V. 2010. "Science in court: Head case." *Nature.* 464:340–342. Retrieved October 14, 2015 (www.nature.com/news/2010/100317/full/464340a.html#close).

Hull, J. 2005. *Post-secondary education and labour market outcomes Canada, 2001.* Ottawa, ON: Minister of Indian Affairs and Northern Development.

Hunnicutt, G., and Broidy, L.M. 2004. "Liberation and economic marginalization: A reformulation and test of formerly? Competing models." *Journal of Research in Crime and Delinquency.* 412:130–155.

Huss, M.T. 2009. *Forensic psychology: Research, clinical practice and applications.* Chichester: Wiley-Blackwell.

Hussong, A.M., Curran, P.J., Moffitt, T.E., Caspi, A., and Carrig, M.M. 2004. "Substance abuse hinders desistance in young adults' antisocial behavior." *Development and Psychopathology.* 16:1029–1046.

Huizinga, D., Esbensen, F., and Weiher, A.W. 1991. "Are there multiple paths to delinquency?" *Journal of Criminal Law and Criminology.* 82:83–118.

Huizinga, D., Weiher, A.W., Espitiru, R., and Esbensen, F. 2003. "Delinquency and crime: Some highlights from the Denver youth study." In T. P. Thornberry and M. D. Krohn, eds. *Taking stock of delinquency: An overview of findings from contemporary longitudinal studies.* pp. 47–91. New York: Kluwer Academic/Plenum Publishers. DOI: 10.1007/0-306-47945-1_3.

Inciardi, J., Lockwood, D., and Pottieger, A.E. 1993. *Women and crack-cocaine.* New York, NY: Macmillan.

Indian and Northern Affairs Canada. 2004. Words first: An evolving terminology relating to Aboriginal peoples in Canada. Retrieved December 3, 2015 (http://publications.gc.ca/collections/Collection/R2-236-2002E.pdf).

Iowa Department of Human Rights. 2011. *Final report: Outcomes of mandatory minimum sentences for drug traffickers.* NCJRS Publication No. NCJ 238733. Iowa: Public Safety Advisory Board. May 14, 2015 (https://humanrights.iowa.gov/sites/default/files/media/PSAB_MandatoryMinimumReport2011.pdf).

Irish, L., Kobayashi, I., and Delahanty, D. L. 2010. "Long-term physical health consequences of childhood sexual abuse: A meta-analytic review." *Journal of Pediatric Psychology.* 35(5):450–461. DOI: dx.doi.org/10.1093/jpepsy/jsp118.

Jaccarino, M. 2013. "'Training simulation:' Mass killers often share obsession with violent video games." *Fox News.* Retrieved October 21, 2015 (www.foxnews.com/tech/2013/09/12/training-simulation-mass-killers-often-share-obsession-with-violent-video-games/).

Jaffee, S.R., Caspi, A., Moffitt, T.E., Dodge, K.A., Rutter, M., Taylor, A., et al. 2005. "Nature X Nurture: Genetic vulnerabilities interact with physical maltreatment to promote conduct problems." *Development and Psychopathology.* 17:67–84.

James, L., Brody, D., and Hamilton, Z. 2013. "Risk factors for domestic violence during pregnancy: A meta-analytic review." *Violence and Victims.* 28(3):359–80.

James, J., and Meyerding, J. 1977. "Early sexual experiences and prostitution." *American Journal of Psychiatry.* 134:1381–1385.

Jeffery, C.R. 1965. "Criminal behavior and learning theory." *Journal of Criminal Law, Criminology, and Police Science.* 56:294–300.

Jeffries, S., and Bond, C.E. 2012. "The impact of Indigenous status on adult sentencing: A review of the statistical research literature from the United States, Canada, and Australia." *Journal of Ethnicity in Criminal Justice.* 10(3):223–243.

Jeffries, S., and Stenning, P. 2014. "Sentencing Aboriginal offenders: Law, policy, and practice in three countries." *Canadian Journal of Criminology and Criminal Justice.* 56(4):447–494.

Jespersen, A.F., Lalumière, M.L., and Seto, M.C. 2009. "Sexual abuse history among adult sex offenders and non-sex offenders: A meta-analysis." *Child Abuse and Neglect.* 33:179–192.

Jessor, R., Van Den Bos, J., Vanderryn, J., Costa, F.M., and Turbin, M.A. 1995. "Protective factors in adolescent problem behavior: Moderator effects and developmental change." *Developmental Psychology.* 31:923–933.

John Howard Society of Southeastern New Brunswick. 2013. "Our programs." Retrieved May 13, 2015 (http://mesacc. libguides.com/c.php?g=255783andp=1707689).

Johansson, P., and Kempf-Leonard, K. 2009. "A gender-specific pathway to serious, violent, and chronic offending? Exploring Howell's risk factors for serious delinquency." *Crime and Delinquency.* 55:216–240.

Johnson, H. 2004. *Drugs and crime: A study of incarcerated female offenders.* Research and Public Policy Series, No.63. Australian Institute of Criminology.

Johnson, H. 2006. "Concurrent drug and alcohol dependency and mental health among incarcerated women." *Australian and New Zealand Journal of Criminology.* 1–22. Retrieved April 11, 2009 (http://findarticles. com/p/articles/mi_hb3370/is_2_39/ai_n29294216/ pg_2/?tag=content;col1).

Johnson, R.E. 1979. *Juvenile delinquency and its origins.* Cambridge, UK: Cambridge University Press.

Johnson, S. 2005. "Returning to correctional services after release: A profile of Aboriginal and non-Aboriginal adults involved in Saskatchewan corrections from 1999/00 to 2003/04." *Juristat.* 25.

Johnston, J.C. 1997. *Aboriginal offender survey: Case files and interview sample.* Research Report No. R-61. Ottawa, ON: Correctional Service Canada.

Johnston, J.C. 2000. "Aboriginal federal offender surveys: A synopsis." *Forum on Corrections Research.* 12:25–27.

Jolliffe, D., and Farrington, D.P. 2007. *A systematic review of the national and international evidence on the effectiveness of interventions with violent offenders.* Ministry of Justice Research Series 16/07.

Jonason, P.K., Li, N.P., and Buss, D.M. 2010. "The costs and benefits of the Dark Triad: Implications for mate poaching and mate retention tactics." *Personality and Individual Differences,* 48:373–378.

Jonason, P.K., Lyons, M., and Blanchard, A. 2015. "Birds of a 'bad' feather flock together: The Dark Triad and mate choice." *Personality and Individual Differences.* 78:34-38.

Jones, D.N., and Paulhus, D.L. 2010. "Differential provocations trigger aggression in psychopaths and narcissists." *Social Psychological and Personality Science.* 1:33–45.

Jones, N.J., Brown, S.L., Robinson, D., and Frey, D. 2015. "Incorporating strengths into quantitative assessments of criminal risk for adult offenders: The Service Planning Instrument." *Criminal Justice and Behavior.* 42:321–338. DOI: 10.1177/009385-4814547041.

Jones, S., and Cauffman, E. 2008. "Juvenile psychopathy and judicial decision making: An empirical analysis of an ethical dilemma." *Behavioral Science and the Law.* 26:151–165.

Junginger, J. 1995. "Command hallucinations and the prediction of dangerousness." *Psychiatric Services.* 46:911–914.

Junginger, J., Claypoole, K., Laygo, R., Crisanti, A. 2006. "Effects of serious mental illness and substance abuse on criminal offences." *Psychiatric Services.* 57:879–882.

Kalmuss, D.S. 1984. "The intergenerational transmission of marital aggression." *Journal of Marriage and the Family.* 46:11–19.

Kandel, D.B., and Adler, I. 1982. "Socialization into marijuana use among French adolescents: A cross-cultural comparison with the United States." *Journal of Health and Social Behavior.* 23:295–309.

Kandel, E., and Freed, D. 1982. "Frontal-lobe dysfunction and antisocial behavior." *Journal of Clinical Psychology.* 45:404–413.

Kandel, E., Mednick, S.A., Kikegaard-Sorensen, L., Hutchings, B., Knop, J., Rosenberg, R., et al. 1988. "IQ as a protective factor for subjects at high risk for antisocial behavior." *Journal of Consulting and Clinical Psychology.* 56:224–226.

Kantor, G.K., Jasinski, J.L., and Aldaraondo, E. 1994. "Sociocultural status and incidence of marital violence in Hispanic families." *Violence and Victims.* 9:207–222.

Kaplan, H.S., and Gangestad, S.W. 2005. "Life history theory and evolutionary psychology." In D.M. Buss, ed. *The handbook of evolutionary psychology.* pp. 68–118. Hoboken, NJ: John Wiley and Sons, Inc.

Kapur, S., Phillips, K.S., Insel, A.G., and Mol, T.R. 2012. "Why has it taken so long for biological psychiatry to develop clinical tests and what to do about it?" *Mol Psychiatry.* 17(12):1174–1179. DOI:10.1038/mp.2012.105.

Karandikar, S., and Próspero, M. 2010. "From client to pimp: Male violence against female sex workers." *Journal of Interpersonal Violence.* 25(2):257–273. DOI: dx.doi. org/10.1177/0886260509334393.

Karpman, B. 1948. "The myth of the psychopathic personality." *American Journal of Psychiatry.* 104 3(9):523–534.

Kazdin, A.E. 1996. *Conduct disorders in childhood and adolescence.* 2nd ed. Thousand Oaks, CA: Sage.

Kazdin, A.E., Kraemer, H.C., Kessler, R.C., Kupfer, D.J., and Offord, D.R. 1997. "Contributions of risk factor research to developmental psychopathology." *Clinical Psychology Review.* 17:375–406.

Kelly, K., and Caputo, T. 2005. "The linkages between street gangs and organized crime: The Canadian experience." *Journal of Gang Research.* 13:17–31.

Kelly, J.B., and Johnson, M.P. 2008. "Differentiation among types of intimate partner violence: Research update and implications for intervention." *Family Court Review.* 46:476–499.

Kendall, K. 2002. "Time to think again about cognitive behavioural programmes." In P. Carlen, ed. *Women and punishment: The struggle for justice.* pp. 182–198. Cullompton, Devon, UK: Willan Publishing.

Kendall, K. 2004. "Dangerous thinking: A critical history of correctional cognitive behaviouralism." In G. Mair, ed. *What matters in probation.* pp. 53–89. Cullompton, Devon, UK: Willan Publishing.

Kendell, R., and Jablensky, A. 2003. "Distinguishing between the validity and utility of psychiatric diagnoses." *American Journal of Psychiatry.* 160:2–12.

Kendler, K.S. 2001. "Twin studies of psychiatric illness." *Archives of General Psychiatry.* 58:1005–1014. DOI: 10.1001/archpsyc.58.11.1005.

Kendler, K.S., Karkowski, L.M., Neale, M.C., and Prescot, C.A. 2000. "Illicit psychoactive substance use, heavy use, abuse, and dependence in a U.S. population-based sample of male twins." *Archives of General Psychiatry.* 57:261–269. DOI:10.1001/archpsyc.57.3.261.

Kendler, K.S., Neale, M.C., Heath, A.C., Kessler, R.C., and Eaves, L.J. 1994. "A twin-family study of alcoholism in women." *American Journal of Psychiatry.* 151:707–715.

Kennealy, P.J., Skeem, J.L., Eno Louden, J., and Manchak, S.M. 2012. "Firm, fair, and caring officer–offender relationships protect against supervision failure." *Law and Human Behavior.* 36:496–505. DOI:10.1037/h0093935.

Kennedy, S.M. 2004. "A practitioner's guide to responsivity: Maximizing treatment effectiveness." *Journal of Community Corrections, XIII.* 7–9:22–30.

Kenny, C. 2004. *A holistic framework for Aboriginal policy research.* Ottawa, ON: Status of Women in Canada.

Kiehl, K.A. 2006. "A cognitive neuroscience perspective on psychopathy: Evidence for paralimbic system dysfunction." *Psychiatry Research.* 142:107–128.

Kiehl, K.A., Smith, A.M., Hare, R.D., Forster, B.B., Brink, J., and Liddle, P.F. 2001. "Limbic abnormalities in affective processing by criminal psychopaths as revealed by functional magnetic resonance imaging." *Biological Psychiatry.* 50:677–684.

Kim, T.E., and Goto, S.G. 2000. "Peer delinquency and parental social support as predictors of Asian American adolescent delinquency." *Deviant Behavior.* 21:331–348.

Kimonis, E.R., Bagner, D. M., Linares, D., Blake, C.A., and Rodriguez, G. 2014. "Parent training outcomes among young children with callous–unemotional conduct problems with or at risk for developmental delay." *Journal of Child and Family Studies.* 23:437–448.

Kimonis, E.R., Frick, P.J., Fazekas, H., and Loney, B.R. 2006. "Psychopathic traits, aggression, and the processing of emotional stimuli in non-referred children." *Behavioral Sciences and the Law.* 24:21–37.

Kirby, J.L. 2006. "Out of the shadows at last: Transforming Mental Health, Mental Illness and Addiction Services in Canada." Retrieved September 23, 2015 (www.parl.gc.ca/Content/SEN/Committee/391/soci/rep/rep02may06-e.htm).

Kirkman, C.A. 2005. "From soap opera to science: Towards gaining access to the psychopaths who live amongst us." *Psychology and Psychotherapy: Theory, Research and Practice.* 78:379–396.

Klemke, L.W. 1982. "Reassessment of Cameron's apprehension-termination of shoplifting finding." *California Sociologist.* 5:88–95.

Klemp-North, M. 2007. "Theoretical foundations of gang membership." *Journal of Gang Research.* 14:11–26.

Knabb, J.J., Welsh, R.K., and Graham-Howard, M.L. 2011. "Treatment alternatives for mentally disordered offenders: A literature review." *Psychology.* 2:122–131.

Kong, R., and AuCoin, K. 2008. "Female offenders in Canada." *Juristat.* Catalogue no. 85-002-XIE. Ottawa, ON: Statistics Canada.

Koons, B.A., Burrow, J.D., Morash, M., and Bynum, T. 1997. "Expert and offender perceptions of program elements linked to successful outcomes for incarcerated women." *Crime and Delinquency.* 434:515–532.

Kochanska, G. 1993. "Toward a synthesis of parental socialization and child temperament in early development of conscience." *Child Development.* 64:325–347.

Kochanska, G. 1994. "Beyond cognition: Expanding the search for the early roots of internalization and conscience." *Developmental Psychology.* 30:20–22.

Kochanska, G., Murray, K.T., and Coy, K.C. 1997. "Inhibitory control as a contributor to conscience in childhood: From toddler to early school age." *Child Development.* 68:263–277.

Koegl, C.J., and Day, D.M. 2015. *The monetary cost of criminal offending in Ontario.* Ottawa, ON: Public Safety Canada.

Koegl, C.J., Farrington, D.P., Augimeri, L.K., and Day, D.M. 2008. "Evaluation of a targeted cognitive-behavioral program for children with conduct problems--the SNAP® under 12 outreach project: Service intensity, age and gender effects on short- and long-term outcomes." *Clinical Child Psychology and Psychiatry.* 13(3):419–434. DOI: dx.doi.org/10.1177/1359104508090606.

Kondro, W. 2015. "Health system's deficiencies clear to Canadians." *iPolitics.* Retrieved October 30, 2015 (http://ipolitics.ca/2015/06/14/health-systems-deficiencies-clear-to-canadians/).

Kouyoumdjian, F.G., Calzavara, L.M., Kiefer, L., Main, C., and Bondy, S.J. 2014. "Drug use prior to incarceration and associated socio-behavioural factors among males in a provincial correctional facility in Ontario, Canada." *Canadian Journal of Public Health,* 105(3):198–202.

Kraemer, H.C., Kazdin, A.E., Offord, D.R., Kessler, R.C., Jensen, P.S., and Kupler, D.J. 1997. "Coming to terms with the terms of risk." *Archives of General Psychiatry.* 54:337–343. DOI: 10.1001/archpsyc.1997.01830160065009.

Kramer-Kuhn, A. 2013. "Family processes as moderators of the impact of peer, social, and neighborhood influences on adolescent aggression." Ph.D. diss. Virginia Commonwealth University. Available from PsycINFO (1634754665; 2014-99221-041).

Kropp, P.R., Hart, S.D., Webster, C.D., and Eaves, D. 1999. *Manual for the Spousal Assault Risk Assessment Guide.* 3rd ed. Toronto, ON: Multi-Health Systems.

Kruttschnitt, C. 1996. "Contributions of quantitative methods to the study of gender and crime, or bootstrapping our way into the theoretical thicket." *Journal of Quantitative Criminology.* 12:135–161.

Kruttschnitt, C. 2001. "Gender and violence." In C.M. Renzetti and L. Goodstein, eds. *Women, crime, and criminal justice: Original Feminist Readings.* pp. 77–92. Los Angeles: Roxbury Publishing Company.

Kshetri, N. 2010. *The global cyber-crime industry: Economic, institutional, and strategic perspectives.* Heidelberg: Springer-Verlag.

Kumpfer, K.L., and Alvarado, R. 2003. "Family-strengthening approaches for the prevention of youth problem behaviors." *American Psychologist.* 58:457–465.

Kunic, D., and Grant, B. 2007. *The computerized assessment of substance abuse (CASA): Results from the demonstration project 2006.* Research Report No. R-173. Correctional Service Canada. Retrieved October 29, 2015 (www.csc-scc.gc.ca/research/092/r173_e.pdf).

Kuziemko, I., and Levitt, S. 2004. "An empirical analysis of imprisoning drug offenders." *Journal of Public Economics.* 88:2043–2066.

Kwong, M. 2015. "Canada's gang hotspots—are you in one?" *CBC News Canada.* Retrieved May 14, 2015 (www.cbc.ca/news/canada/canada-s-gang-hotspots-are-you-in-one-1.2912442).

LaBoucane-Benson, P. 2002. "In Search of Your Warrior program." *Forum on Corrections Research.* 14:40–41.

LaGrange, R.L., and White, H.R. 1985. "Age differences in delinquency: A test of theory." *Criminology.* 23:19–45.

Lahey, B.B., Waldman, I.D., and McBurnett, K. 1989. "The development of antisocial behaviour: An integrative causal model." *Journal of Child Psychology and Psychiatry.* 40:669–682.

Laird, R.D., Jordan, K.Y., Dodge, K.A., Petit, G.S., and Bates, J.E. 2001. "Peer rejection in childhood, involvement with antisocial peers in early adolescence and the development of externalizing behavior problems." *Development and Psychopathology.* 13:337–354.

Lalumière, M.L., Harris, G.T., Quinsey, V.L., and Rice, M.E. 2005. *The causes of rape: Understanding individual differences in male propensity for sexual aggression.* Washington, DC: American Psychological Association.

Lalumière, M.L., and Quinsey, V.L. 1994. "The discriminability of rapists from non-sex offenders using phallometric measures: A meta-analysis." *Criminal Justice and Behavior.* 21:150–175.

Lalumière, M.L., Quinsey, V.L., Harris, G.T., Rice, M.E., and Trautrimas, C. 2003. "Are rapists differentially aroused by coercive sex in phallometric assessments?" In R. Prentky, E. Janus, and M.C. Seto, eds. *Sexually coercive behavior: Understanding and management.* pp. 211–224. New York, NY: Annals of the New York Academy of Sciences.

Lambert, M.J. 1992. "Psychotherapy outcome research: Implications for integrative and eclectical therapists." In J.C. Norcross and M.R. Goldfried, eds. *Handbook of psychotherapy integration.* pp. 94–129. New York, NY: Basic Books, Inc.

Lange, P.J. 1994. "The varieties of emotional experiences: A mediation on James-Lange theory." *Psychological Review.* 101:211–221.

Langton, C.M., Barbaree, H.E., Harkins, L., and Peacock, E.J. 2006. "Sex offenders response to treatment and its association with recidivism as a function of psychopathy." *Sexual Abuse: A Journal of Research and Treatment.* 181:99–120.

Lansford, J.E., Miller-Johnson, S., Berlin, L. J., Dodge, K.A., Bates, J.E., and Pettit, G.A. 2007. "Early physical abuse and later violent delinquency: A prospective longitudinal study." *Child Maltreatment.* 12:233–245.

LaPrairie, C. 1990. "The role of sentencing in the over-representation of Aboriginal people in correctional institutions." *Canadian Journal of Criminology.* 32:429–440.

LaPrairie, C. 1996. *Examining Aboriginal corrections.* Ottawa, ON: Solicitor General Canada.

Larsson, H., Andershed, H., and Lichtenstein, P. 2006. "A genetic factor explains most of the variation in the psychopathic personality." *Journal of Abnormal Psychology.* 115:221–230.

Lasher, M.P., and McGrath, R.J. 2012. "The impact of community notification on sex offender reintegration: A quantitative review of the research literature." *International Journal of Offender Therapy and Comparative Criminology.* 56(1):6–28. DOI: 10.1177/0306624X10387524.

Latimer, J., and Desjardins, N. 2007. *The 2007 National Justice Survey: Tackling crime and public confidence.* Research Report No. 07-4e. Ottawa, ON: Department of Justice. Retrieved October 30, 2015 (http://www.justice.gc.ca/eng/rp-pr/csj-sjc/jsp-sjp/rr07_4/rr07_4.pdf).

Latimer, J., Dowden, C., and Muise, D. 2005. "The effectiveness of restorative justice practices: A meta-analysis." *The Prison Journal.* 85:127–44.

Latimer, J., Kleinknecht, S., Hung, K., and Gabor, T. 2003. *Self-reported delinquency in Canada: An analysis of the National Longitudinal Survey of Children and Youth.* Ottawa, ON: Department of Justice.

Law Courts Education Society of B.C. 2009. *Gladue and Aboriginal sentencing.* Retrieved January 14, 2009 (http://216.197.122.213/gladue_sentencing).

Laws, D.R., Hanson, R.K., Osborn, C.A., and Greenbaum, P.E. 2000. "Assessment of sexual arousal and a self-report measure of sexual preference." *Journal of Interpersonal Violence.* 15:1297–1312.

Laws, D.R., and Marshall, W.L. 1990. "A conditioning theory of the etiology and maintenance of deviant sexual preference and behaviour." In H.E. Barbaree, W.L. Marshall, and D.R. Laws, eds. *Handbook of sexual assault: Theories and treatment of the offender.* pp. 209–229. New York, NY: Plenum.

Laws, D.R., Meyer, J., and Holmen, M.L. 1978. "Reduction of sadistic arousal by olfactory aversion: A case study." *Behaviour Research and Therapy.* 16:281–285.

Leadbeater, B.J., Kuperminc, G.P., Blatt, S.J., and Hertzog, C. 1999. "A multivariate model of gender differences in adolescents' internalizing and externalizing problems." *Developmental Psychology.* 35:1268–1282.

LeBel, T.P., Burnett, R., Maruna, S., and Bushway, S. 2008. "The 'Chicken and Egg' of Subjective and Social Factors in Desistance From Crime." *European Journal of Criminology.* 5(2):131–159. DOI:10.1177/1477370807087640.

Lee, J.K.P., Jackson, H., Pattison, P., and Ward, T. 2002. "Developmental risk factors for sexual offending." *Child Abuse and Neglect.* 26:73–92. DOI: 10.1016/S0145-2134(01)00304-0.

Lee, K., and Ashton, M. C. 2004. "Psychometric properties of the HEXACO personality inventory." *Multivariate Behavioral Research,* 39:329–358.

Lee, T., Chong, S.A., Chan, Y.H., and Sathyadevan, G. 2004. "Command hallucinations among Asian patients with schizophrenia." *Canadian Journal of Psychiatry.* 49:838–842.

Leeder, E., ed. 2004. *Inside and out: Women, prison, and therapy.* Binghamton, NY: Haworth Press, Inc.

Leistico, A.R., Salekin, R.T., DeCoster, J., and Rogers, R. 2008. "A large-scale meta-analysis relating the Hare measures of psychopathy to antisocial conduct." *Law and Human Behavior.* 32:28–45.

Leonard, E. 1982. *Women, crime and society.* New York, NY: Longman.

Leschied, A.W., and Cunningham, A. 2002. *Seeking effective interventions for serious young offenders: Interim results of a four-year randomized study of multisystemic therapy in Ontario, Canada.* London, ON: Centre for Children and Families in the Justice System.

Letourneau, E.J. 2002. "A comparison of objective measures of sexual arousal and interest: Visual reaction time and penile plethysmography." *Sexual Abuse: A Journal of Research and Treatment.* 14(3):207–223. DOI: 10.1177/107906320201400302.

Leve, L.D., and Chamberlain, P. 2005. "Girls in the juvenile justice system: Risk factors and clinical implications." In D. Pepler, K. Madsen, C. Webster, and K. Levine, eds. *Development and treatment of girlhood aggression.* pp. 191–215. Mahwah, NJ: Lawrence Erlbaum.

Levenson, J.S., Brannon, Y.N., Fortney, T., and Baker, J. 2007. "Public perceptions about sex offenders and community protection policies." *Analyses of Social Issues and Public Policy.* 7:137–161.

Levenson, J.S., D'Amora, D.A., Hern, A.L. 2007. "Megan's Law and its impact on community re-entry for sex offenders." *Behavioral Sciences and the Law.* 25:587–602.

Lewis, M. 2015. *The biology of desire: Why addiction is not a disease.* Doubleday Canada.

Li, G. 2008. "Homicide in Canada, 2007." *Juristat.* 289:1–26. Ottawa, ON: Statistics Canada Catalogue no. 85-002-X.

Liebling, A. 2006. "Why fairness matters in criminal justice." In N. Padfield, ed. *Who to Release? Parole, fairness and criminal justice.* pp. 63–71. Portland, Oregon: Willan Publishing.

Lilienfeld, S.O. 1992. "The association between antisocial personality and somatization disorders: A review and integration of theoretical models." *Clinical Psychology Review.* 12:641–662.

Lilienfeld, S.O., and Fowler, K.A. 2006. "The self-report assessment of psychopathy: Problems, pitfalls, and promises." In C.J. Patrick, ed. *Handbook of the psychopathy.* pp. 107–132. New York, NY: Guilford Press.

Lilienfeld, S.O., and Widows, M. 2005. *Professional Manual for the Psychopathic Personality Inventory-Revised (PPI-R).* Lutz, Florida: Psychological Assessment Resources.

Lilly, J.R., Cullen, F.T., and Ball, R.A. 2006. *Criminological theory: Context and consequences.* 4th ed. Thousand Oaks, CA: Sage.

Link, B., Monahan, J., Stueve, A., and Cullen, F. 1999. "Real in their consequences: A sociological approach to understanding the association between psychotic symptoms and violence." *American Sociological Review.* 64:316–332.

Link, B., and Stueve, A. 1994. "Psychotic symptoms and the violent/illegal behavior of mental patients compared to community controls." In J. Monahan and H. Steadman, eds. *Violence and mental disorder.* Chicago, IL: University of Chicago Press.

Link, B., Stueve, A., and Phelan, J. 1998. "Psychotic symptoms and violent behaviors: Probing the components of 'threat/control-override' symptoms." *Social Psychiatry and Psychiatric Epidemiology.* 33:S55–S60.

Linnoila, M., Virkkunen, M., Scheinin, M., Nuutila, A., Rimon, R., and Goodwin, F.K. 1983. "Low cerebrospinal fluid 5-hydroxyindolacetic acid concentration differentiates impulsive from non-impulsive violent behavior." *Life sciences.* 33:2609–2614.

Lipsey, M.W., and Derzon, J.H. 1998. "Predictors of violent or serious delinquency in adolescence and early adulthood: A synthesis of longitudinal research." In R. Loeber and D.P. Farrington, eds. *Serious and Violent Juvenile Offenders: Risk Factors and Successful Interventions.* pp. 86–105. Thousand Oaks, CA: Sage.

Liska, A.E., and Reed, M.D. 1985. "Ties to conventional institutions and delinquency: Estimating reciprocal effects." *American Sociological Review.* 50:547–560.

Lloyd, C. 1995. "To scare straight or educate? The British experience of day visits to prison for young people." Home Office Research Study no. 149. London: Home Office.

Lloyd, C.D., Hanby, L.J., and Serin, R.C. 2014. "Rehabilitation group co-participants' risk levels are associated with offenders' treatment performance, treatment change, and recidivism." *Journal of Consulting and Clinical Psychology.* 82:298–311. dx.doi.org/10.1037/a0035360.

Lloyd, C.D., Hanson, R.K., and Serin, R.C. 2015. *"Dynamic" stipulates that reassessment matters: Examining the hypothesis that repeated measurement enhances the prediction of recidivism.* Paper presented at the American Psychology-Law Society Annual Convention, San Diego, CA.

Lochman, J.E., Whidby, J.M., and Fitzgerald, D.P. 2000. "Cognitive-behavioural assessment and treatment with aggressive children." In P. Kendall, ed. *Child and Adolescent Therapy: Cognitive Behavioural Procedures.* 2nd ed. pp. 31–87. New York, NY: Guilford Press.

Loeber, R., and Farrington, D.P. 1998a. "Never too early, never too late: Risk factors and successful interventions for serious and violent juvenile offenders." *Studies on Crime and Crime Prevention.* 7:7–30.

Loeber, R., and Farrington, D.P. 2000. "Young children who commit crime: Epidemiology, developmental origins, risk factors, early interventions, and policy implications." *Development and Psychopathology.* 12:737–762.

Loeber, R., Green, S.M., Lahey, B.B., Christ, M.A.G., and Frick, P.J. 1992. "Developmental sequences in the age of onset of disruptive child behaviors." *Journal of Child and Family Studies.* 1:21–41.

Loeber, R., and Stouthamer-Loeber, M. 1986. "Family factors as correlates and predictors of juvenile conduct problems and delinquency." In M. Tonry and N. Morris, eds. *Crime and justice: An annual review of research.* Volume 7. pp. 29–159. Chicago, IL: Chicago University Press.

Lombroso, C. 2006. *Criminal Man.* M. Gibson, N. Hahn Rafter, & M. Seymour, Trans. Durham, NC: Duke University Press. Original work published 1895.

Lombroso, C., and Ferrero, G. 1895. *The female offender.* London: T. Fisher Unwin.

Lombroso, C., and Ferrero, G. 2004. *Criminal Woman, the Prostitute, and the Normal Woman.* N.H. Rafter and M. Gibson, Trans. Durham and London: Duke University Press. Original work published 1893.

Loney, B.R., Frick, P.J., Clements, C.B., Ellis, M.L., and Kerlin, K. 2003. "Callous/unemotional traits, impulsivity, and emotional processing in antisocial adolescents." *Journal of Clinical Child and Adolescent Psychology.* 32:66–80.

Longshore, D., Turner, S. 1998. "Self-control and criminal opportunity: Cross-sectional test of the General Theory of Crime." *Criminal Justice and Behavior.* 25:81–98. DOI: 10.1177/0093854898025001005.

Loos, M.E., and Alexander, P.C. 1997. "Differential effects associated with self-reported histories of abuse and neglect in a college sample." *Journal of Interpersonal Violence.* 12:340–360.

Lopez, J.M.O., Redondo, L.M., and Martin, A.L. 1989. "Influence of family and peer group on the use of drugs by adolescents." *The International Journal of the Addictions.* 24:1065–1082.

Lorber, M.F. 2004. "Psychophysiology of aggression, psychopathy, and conduct problems: A meta-analysis." *Psychological Bulletin.* 130:531–552.

Lösel, F. 1995. "The efficacy of correctional treatment: A review and synthesis of meta-evaluations." In J. McGuire, ed. *What Works: Reducing Re-offending. Guidelines from research and practice.* Chichester: Wiley.

Lösel, F., and Farrington, D.P. 2012. "Direct protective and buffering protective factors in the development of youth violence." *American Journal of Preventative Medicine.* 43(2):8–23. DOI: 10.1016/j.amepre.2012.04.029.

Lösel, F., and Schmucker, M. 2005. "The effectiveness of treatment for sexual offenders: A comprehensive meta-analysis." *Journal of Experimental Criminology.* 1:117–146.

Low, B.S. 2000. *Why sex matters.* Princeton, NJ: Princeton University Press.

Lowenkamp, C.T., Holsinger, A.M., and Latessa, E.J. 2001. "Risk/need assessment, offender classification, and the role of childhood abuse." *Criminal Justice and Behavior.* 285:543–563.

Lowenkamp, C.T., Holsinger, A., Robinson, C.R., and Alexander, M. 2012. "Diminishing or durable treatment effects of STARR? A research note on 24-month re-arrest rates." *Journal of Crime and Justice.* 37:275–283. DOI: 10.1080/0735648X.2012.753849.

Lowenkamp, C.T., Latessa, E.J., and Smith, P. 2006. "Does correctional program quality really matter? The importance of adhering to the principles of effective intervention." *Criminology and Public Policy.* 5:201–220.

Loza, W. 2005. *The Self-Appraisal Questionnare SAQ: A tool for assessing violent and non-violent recidivism.* Toronto, ON: Multi-Health Systems.

Loza, W., Dhaliwal, G., Kroner, D.G., and Loza-Fanous, A. 2000. "Reliability, construct, and concurrent validities of the Self-Appraisal Questionnaire: A tool for assessing violent and nonviolent recidivism." *Criminal Justice and Behavior.* 27:356–374.

Luciani, F. 2001. "Initiating safe reintegration: A decade of Custodial Rating Scale results." *Forum on Corrections Research.* 13:8–10.

Lucy Faithful Foundation, The. n.d. "Inform plus: The information forum for individuals with internet problems." Retrieved May 14, 2015 (www.lucyfaithfull.org.uk/inform_plus.htm).

Luke, K.P. 2008. "Are girls really becoming more violent?" *Journal of Women and Social Work.* 23:38–50.

Lundahl, B.W., Kunz, C., Brownell, C., Tollefson, D., and Burke, B.L. 2010. "A meta-analysis of motivational interviewing: Twenty-five years of empirical studies." *Research on Social Work Practice.* 20(2):137–160.

Lykken, D.T. 1995. *The antisocial personalities.* Mahwah, NJ: Erlbaum.

Lynam, D.R. 1997. "Pursuing the psychopath: Capturing the fledgling psychopath in a nomological net." *Journal of Abnormal Psychology.* 106:425–438.

Lynam, D.R., Charnigo, R., Moffitt, T.E., Raine, A., Loeber, R., and Stouthamer-Loeber, M. 2009. "The stability of psychopathy across adolescence." *Development and Psychopathology.* 21:1133–1153.

Lynam, D.R., Loeber, R., and Stouthamer-Loeber, M. 2008. "The stability of psychopathy from adolescence into adulthood: The search for moderators." *Criminal Justice and Behavior.* 35:228–243.

Lyons, M.J. 1996. "A twin study of self-reported criminal behavior." *Ciba Foundation Symposium.* 194:61–70.

MacDonald, S.F. 2014. "Lifetime substance use patterns of women offenders." *Research in Brief.* 14(24). Correctional Service Canada. Retrieved October 29, 2015 (www.csc-scc.gc.ca/005/008/092/005008-rs14-24-eng.pdf).

MacDonald, S.F., Mullins, P., and Ternes, M. 2011. "Offender satisfaction with the Computerized Assessment of Substance Abuse (CASA)." *Research Snippets.* No. 11-3. Correctional Service Canada. Retrieved October 29, 2015 (www.csc-scc.gc.ca/005/008/092/rs11-03-eng.pdf).

MacSwain, M., Cheverie, M., Farrell MacDonald, S., and Johnson, S. 2014. "Characteristics of women participants in the Methadone Maintenance Treatment Program (MMTP)." *Research at a Glance.* R-307. Correctional Service Canada. Retrieved October 29, 2015 (www.csc-scc.gc.ca/005/008/092/005008-0307-eng.pdf).

MacSwain, M., Farrell MacDonald, F., and Cheverie, M. 2014. *Post-release outcomes of Methadone Maintenance Treatment Program (MMTP) participants: A comparative study.* Research Report No. R-322.Ottawa, ON: Correctional Service Canada.

Magaletta, P., and Boothby, J. 2003. "Correctional mental health professionals." In T.J. Fagan and R.K. Ax, eds. *Correctional Mental health handbook.* Sage.

Maidment, M.R. 2006. "'We're not all that criminal': Getting beyond the pathologizing and individualizing of women's crime." In E. Leeder, ed. *Inside and out: Women, prison, and therapy.* pp. 35–56. Binghamton, New York, NY: Haworth Press, Inc.

Makarios, M., Sperber, K.G., and Latessa, E.J. 2014. "Treatment dosage and the risk principle: A refinement and extension." *Journal of Offender Rehabilitation.* 53(5):334–350. DOI: 10.1080/10509674.2014.922157.

Malamuth, N.M. 2003. "Criminal and noncriminal sexual aggressors: Integrating psychopathy in a hierarchical-mediational confluence model." In R.A. Prentky, E.S. Janus, and M.C. Seto, eds. *Annals of the New York Academy of Sciences.* Vol. 989. "Sexually coercive behavior: Understanding and management." pp. 35–58. New York, NY: New York Academy of Sciences.

Maletzky, B. 1991. *Treating the sexual offender.* Newbury Park, CA: Sage Publications.

Mamalian, C.A. 2011. *State of the science of pretrial risk assessment.* Bureau of Justice Assistance, U.S. Department of Justice. Retrieved November 1, 2015 (www.bja.gov/publications/pji_pretrialriskassessment.pdf).

Manders, W.A., Dekovi'c, M., Asscher, J.J., van der Laan, P.H., and Prins, P.J. 2013. "Psychopathy as predictor and moderator of multisystemic therapy outcomes among adolescents treated for antisocial behavior." *Journal of Abnormal Child Psychology.* 41:1–12.

Manitoba Justice. 2015. "Manitoba corrections." Retrieved October 21, 2015 (www.gov.mb.ca/justice/manitoba_corrections/index.html).

Mann, M. 2013. "Incarceration and the Aboriginal offender: Potential impacts of the tackling violent crime act and the corrections review panel recommendations." In J.P. White and J. Bruhn, eds. *Aboriginal Policy Research: Exploring the Urban Landscape.* pp. 233–253. Toronto, ON: Thompson Educational Publishing, Inc.

Mann, R., Webster, S., Wakeling, H., and Marshall, W. 2007. "The measurement and influence of child sexual abuse supportive beliefs." *Psychology, Crime and Law.* 13:443–458.

Marriage, K., Fine, S., Moretti, M.M, and Haley, G. 1986. "Relationship between depression and conduct disorder in children and adolescents." *Journal of the American Academy of Child Psychiatry.* 25:687–691.

Marshall, W.L. 1971. "A combined treatment method for certain sexual deviations." *Behaviour Research and Therapy.* 9:292–294.

Marshall, W.L., and Barbaree, H.E. 1990. "An integrated theory of the etiology of sexual offending." In W.L. Marshall, D.R. Laws, and H.E. Barbaree, eds. *Handbook of sexual assault: Issues, theories, and treatment of the offender.* pp. 257–275. New York, NY: Plenum.

Marshall, W.L., and Lippens, K. 1977. "The clinical value of boredom: A procedure for reducing inappropriate sexual interests." *Journal of Nervous and Mental Diseases.* 165:283–287.

Marshall, W.L., and Marshall, L.E. 2007. "The utility of the random controlled trial for evaluating sexual offender treatment: The gold standard of an inappropriate strategy?" *Sexual Abuse: A Journal of Research and Treatment.* 19:175–191.

Marshall, W.L., and Marshall, L.E. 2008. "Good clinical practice and the evaluation of treatment: A response to Seto et al." *Sexual Abuse: A Journal of Research and Treatment.* 20:256–260.

Marshall, W.L., and McGuire, J. 2003. "Effect sizes in the treatment of sexual offenders." *International Journal of Offender Therapy and Comparative Criminology.* 47(6):653–663. DOI: 10.1177/0306624X03256663.

Marshall, W.L., Serran, G.A., Fernandez, Y.M., Mulloy, R., Mann, R.E., and Thornton, D. 2003. "Therapist characteristics in the treatment of sexual offenders: Tentative data on their relationship with indices of behaviour change." *Journal of Sexual Aggression.* 9:25–30.

Marshall, W.L., Ward, T., Mann, R.E., Moulden, H., Fernandez, Y.M., Serran, G., and Marshall, L.E. 2005. "Working positively with sexual offenders: Maximizing the effectiveness of treatment." *Journal of Interpersonal Violence.* 20:1096–1114.

Martin, S.E., Annan, S., and Forst, B. 1993. "The special deterrent effects of a jail sanction on first-time drunk drivers: A quasi experimental study." *Accident Analysis and Prevention.* 25:561–8.

Martinson, R. 1974. "What works? Questions and answers about prison reform." *The Public Interest.* 10:22–54.

Martinson, R. 1979. "New findings, new views: A note of caution regarding sentencing reform." *Hofstra Law Review.* 7:243–58.

Maruna, S. 2001. *Making good: How ex-convicts reform and rebuild their lives.* Washington, DC: American Psychological Association.

Maruna, S. 2010. *Understanding desistance from crime.* Report for the Ministry of Justice and National Offender Management Services. Retrieved November 2, 2015 (www.safeground.org.uk/wp-content/uploads/Desistance-Fact-Sheet.pdf).

Masten, A., and Coatsworth, J. 1998. "The development of competence in favorable and unfavorable environments: Lessons from research on successful children." *American Psychologist.* 53:205–220.

Mathieu, C., Neumann, C.S., Hare, R.D., and Babiak, P. 2014. "A dark side of leadership: Corporate psychopathy and its influence on employee well-being and job satisfaction." *Personality and Individual Differences.* 59:83–88.

McDermott, R., Tingley, D., Cowden, J., Frazzetto, G., and Johnson, D.D.P. 2009. "Monoamine oxidase A gene MAOA predicts behavioural aggression following provocation." *Proceeds of the National Academy of Sciences of the United States of America.* 106:2118–2123.

Matsueda, R.L. 1982. Testing control theory and differential association: A causal modelling approach. *American Sociological Review.* 47:489–504.

Matsueda, R.L., Kreager D.A., and Huizinga, D. 2006. "Deterring delinquents: A rational choice model of theft and violence." *American Sociological Review.* 71:95–122. DOI:10.1177/000312240607100105.

Matthiessen, P. 1962. *Under the mountain wall: A chronicle of two seasons in the stone age.* New York, NY: Viking.

McCord, J., Widom, C.S., and Crowell, N.A., eds. 2001. *Juvenile Crime, Juvenile Justice. Panel on Juvenile Crime: Prevention, Treatment, and Control.* Washington, DC: National Academy Press.

McCormick, S., Peterson-Badali, M., and Skilling, T.A. 2015. "Mental health and justice system involvement: A conceptual analysis of the literature." *Psychology, Public Policy, and Law.* 21(2):213–225. DOI: dx.doi.org/10.1037/law0000033.

McDonald, R., Dodson, M.C., Rosenfield, D., and Jouriles, E.N. 2011. "Effects of a parenting intervention on features of psychopathy in children." *Journal of Abnormal Child Psychology.* 39:1013–1023.

McGrath, R.J., Cumming, G.F., Burchard, B.L., Zeoli, S., and Ellerby, L. 2010. *Current practices and emerging trends in sexual abuser management.* Brandon, VT: Safer Society Press.

McGrath, R., Hoke, S., and Lasher, M. 2013. *VASOR-2: Vermont Assessment of Sex Offender Risk-2 Manual.* Middlebury, VT: Author.

McGuire, J. 1995. *What Works: Reducing Re-offending. Guidelines from Research and Practice.* Chichester: Wiley.

McGuire, J. 2001. "Defining correctional programs." In L.L. Motiuk and R.C. Serin, eds. *Compendium 2000 on effective correctional programming.* Ottawa, ON: Correctional Service Canada.

McGuire, J. 2002. "Criminal sanctions versus psychologically-based interventions with offenders: A comparative empirical analysis." *Psychology, Crime, and Law.* 8:183–208.

McGuire, J. 2004. *Understanding psychology and crime: Perspectives on theory and action.* New York, NY: McGraw Hill.

McGuire, R.J., Carlisle, J.M., and Young, B.G. 1965. "Sexual deviation as conditioned behaviour: A hypothesis." *Behaviour Research and Therapy.* 2:185–190.

McKie, David. 2013. "Date rape drug busts put China at top of border agency's list." CBC News. March 28. Retrieved November 4, 2015 (www.cbc.ca/news/politics/date-rape-drug-busts-put-china-at-top-of-border-agency-s-list-1.1400074).

McMahon, R.J. 1994. "Diagnosis, assessment, and treatment of externalizing problems in children: The role of longitudinal data." *Journal of Consulting and Clinical Psychology.* 62:901–917.

McMurran, M. 2009. "Motivational interviewing with offenders: A systematic review." *Legal and Criminological Psychology.* 14(1):83–100.

McMurran, M. 2012. "Youth, alcohol, and aggression." In F. Losel, A. Bottoms, and D.P. Farrington, eds. *Young Adult Offenders: Lost in Transition?* London: Taylor and Francis.

McMurran, M. 2013. "Treatment for offenders in prison and the community." In M. McMurran ed. *Alcohol-related violence: Prevention and treatment.* pp. 205–225. Malden: MA: Wiley Series in Forensic Clinical Psychology.

McNeil, D.E., and Binder, R.L. 2007. "Effectiveness of a mental health court in reducing criminal recidivism and violence." *American Journal of Psychiatry.* 164:1395–1403.

McNeill, F. 2004. "Desistance, rehabilitation and correctionalism: Developments and prospects in Scotland." *Howard Journal of Criminal Justice.* 43:420–436.

McNeill, F., and Weaver, B. 2010. "Changing lives? Desistance research and offender management." Report No. 3/2010. Scotland: Scottish Centre for Crime and Justice Research.

McPhail, I.V., Hermann, C.A., and Nunes, K.L. 2013. "Emotional congruence with children and sexual offending against children: A meta-analytic review." *Journal of Consulting and Clinical Psychology*. 81:737–749. DOI: 10.1037/a0033248.

Mears, D.P., Ploeger, M., and Warr, M. 1998. "Explaining the gender gap in delinquency: Peer influence and moral evaluations of behaviour." *Journal of Research in Crime and Delinquency*. 35:251–266.

Mednick, S.A., Gabrielli, W.F.J., and Hutchings, B. 1984. "Genetic influences in criminal convictions: Evidence from an adoption cohort." *Science*. 224:891–894.

Mednick, S., and Kandel, E. 1988. "Congenital determinants of violence." *Bulletin of the American Academy of Psychiatry and the Law*. 16:101–109.

Meissner, D. 2014. "Sexting B.C. teen found guilty of child pornography." *CTV News Vancouver*. Retrieved April 20, 2015 (http://bc.ctvnews.ca/sexting-b-c-teen-found-guilty-of-child-pornography-1.1633678).

Melde, C., Taylor, T., and Esbensen, F. 2009. "'I got your back': An examination of the protective function of gang membership in adolescence." *Criminology*. 47:565–594.

Mellor, B., MacRae, L., Pauls, M., and Hornick, J.P. 2005. *Youth gangs in Canada: A preliminary review of programs and services*. Ottawa: Public Safety and Emergency Preparedness Canada.

Meloy, J.R., and Gacono, C.B. 1997. "A neurotic criminal: 'I've learned my lesson . . .' ." In J.R. Meloy, M.W. Acklin, C.B. Gacono, J.F. Murray, and C.A. Peterson, eds. *Contemporary Rorschach interpretation*. pp. 289–300. Mahwah, NJ: Lawrence Erlbaum Associates.

Melton, G.B., Petrila, J., Poythress, N.G., and Slobogin, C. 1997. *Psychological evaluations for the courts: A handbook for mental health professionals and lawyers*. 2nd ed. New York, NY: Guilford Press.

Mendelson, M. 2006. *Aboriginal peoples and postsecondary education in Canada*. Ottawa, ON: The Caledon Institute of Social Policy.

Mental Health Commission of Canada. 2013. *Opening minds: Interim report*. Retrieved September 25, 2015 (www.mentalhealthcommission.ca/English/initiatives-and-projects/opening-minds/opening-minds-interim-report).

Mental Health Commission of Canada. 2014. *Balancing individual safety, community safety and quality of life*. Retrieved September 27, 2015 (www.mentalhealthcommission.ca).

Menzies, C.R. 2001. "Reflections on research with, for, and among Indigenous peoples." *Canadian Journal of Native Education*. 25(1):19–36.

Merton, R. 1938. "Social structure and anomie." *American Sociological Review*. 3:672–682.

Merton, R.K. 1957. *Social Theory and Social Structure*. New York, NY: Free Press.

Miller, E. 1986. *Street woman*. Philadelphia: Temple University Press.

Miller, M., and Neaigus, A. 2002. "An economy of risk: Resource acquisition strategies of inner city women who use drugs." *International Journal of Drug Policy*. 13:409–418.

Miller, S.L., and Burack, C. 1993. "A critique of Gottfredson and Hirschi's general theory of crime: Selective inattention to gender and power positions." *Women and Criminal Justice*. 4:115–134.

Millon, T., Simonsen, E., and Birket-Smith, M. 2002. "Historical conceptions of psychopathy in the United States and Europe." In T. Millon, E. Simonsen, M. Birket-Smith, and R.D. Davis, eds. *Psychopathy: Antisocial, criminal, and violent behaviour*. pp. 3–31. New York, NY: Guilford Press.

Millon, T., Simonsen, E., Birket-Smith, M., and Davis, R.D. 1998. *Psychopathy: Antisocial, criminal, and violent behaviour*. New York, NY: Guilford Press.

Mills, J.F., Kroner, D.G., and Morgan R.D. 2011. *The clinician's guide to violence risk assessment*. New York: Guilford.

Mishra, S., and Lalumière, M.L. 2008. "Risk-taking, antisocial behavior, and life histories." In J.D. Duntley and T.K. Shackelford, eds. *Evolutionary forensic psychology: Darwinian foundations of crime and law*. pp. 139–159. Oxford, NY: Oxford University Press.

Mitchell, K.J., and Finkelhor, D. 2001. "Risk of crime victimization among youth exposed to domestic violence." *Journal of Interpersonal Violence*. 16:944–964.

Mitchell, O., Wilson, D.B., and Mackenzie, D.L. 2006. "The effectiveness of incarceration-based drug treatment on criminal behaviour." *Campbell Systematic Reviews*. 2006:11. Retrieved October 29, 2015 (www.ncjrs.gov/App/publications/abstract.aspx?ID=232369).

Mitchell, S., and Rosa, P. 1979. "Boyhood behavior problems as precursors of criminality: A fifteen-year follow-up study." *Journal of Child Psychology and Psychiatry*. 22:19–33.

Mobley v. The State. 1995. 265 Ga. 292, S94P1271.

Moffitt, T.E. 1983. "The learning theory model of punishment: Implications for delinquency deterrence." *Criminal Justice and Behavior*. 10:131–158.

Moffitt, T.E. 1993. "Adolescence-limited and life-course-persistent antisocial behavior: A developmental taxonomy." *Psychological Bulletin*. 100:674–701.

Moffitt, T.E. 2005. "The new look of behavioural genetics in developmental psychopathology: Gene-environment interplay in antisocial behaviours." *Psychological Bulletin*. 131:533–554.

Moffitt, T.E., and Caspi, A. 2001. "Childhood predictors differentiate life-course persistent and adolescence-limited antisocial pathways among males and females." *Development and Psychopathology*. 13:355–375.

Moffitt, T.E., Caspi, A., Harrington, H., and Milne, B.J. 2002. "Males on the life-course-persistent and adolescence limited antisocial pathways: Follow-up age 26 years." *Development and Psychopathology*. 14:179–207.

Moffitt, T.E., Caspi, A., Rutter, M., and Silva, P.A. 2001. *Sex difference in antisocial behaviour: Conduct disorder, delinquency, and violence in the Dunedin Longitudinal Study*. Cambridge: Cambridge University Press.

Moffitt, T.E., and Henry, B. 1989. "Neurological assessment of executive functions in self-reported delinquents." *Developmental and Psychopathology*. 1:105–118.

Mokros, A., Gebhard, M., Heinz, V., Marschall, R.W., Nitschke, J., Glasgow, D.V., Gress, C.L.Z., and Laws, D.R. 2012. "Computerized assessment of pedophilic sexual interest through self-report and viewing time: Reliability, validity, and classification accuracy of the Affinity program." *Sexual Abuse: A Journal of Research and Treatment*. 25(3): 230–258. DOI: 10.1177/1079063212454550.

Monahan, J., Steadman, H.J., Silver, E., Appelbaum, P.S., Robbins, P.C., Mulvey, E.P., et al. 2001. *Rethinking risk assessment: The MacArthur study of mental disorder and violence*. New York, NY: Oxford University Press.

Moore, T.M., Scarpa, A., and Raine, A. 2002. "A meta-analysis of serotonin metabolite 5-H1AA and antisocial behavior." *Aggressive Behaviour*. 28:299–316.

Morash, M., Bynam, T.S., and Koons, B.A. 1998. *Women offenders: Programming needs and promising approaches.* Research in Brief. Washington, DC: National Institute of Justice.

Moretti, M.M., Obsuth, I., Odgers, C.L., and Reebye, P. 2006. "Exposure to maternal vs. paternal partner violence, PTSD, and aggression in adolescent girls and boys." *Aggressive Behavior.* 32:385–395.

Moretti, M.M., Odgers, C.L., and Jackson, M.A. 2004. "Girls and aggression: A point of departure." In M.M. Moretti, C.L. Odgers, and M.A. Jackson, eds. *Girls and aggression: Contributing factors and intervention principles.* pp. 1–6. New York, NY: Kluwer Academic/Plenum Publishers.

Morgan, A.B., and Lilienfeld, S.O. 2000. "A meta-analytic review of the relation between antisocial behavior and neuropsychological measures of executive function." *Clinical Psychology Review.* 20:113–136.

Morgan, P. 1975. *Child care: Sense and fable.* London, UK: Temple Smith.

Morris, R.R. 1987. *Women, crime and criminal justice.* Oxford: Basil Blackwell.

Morse, S.J. 2008. "Psychopathy and criminal responsibility." *Neuroethics.* 1:205–212.

Mossman, D. 1994. "Assessing predictions of violence: Being accurate about accuracy." *Journal of Consulting and Clinical Psychology.* 62:783–792.

Motiuk, L.L. 1997. "Classification for correctional programming: The Offender Intake Assessment OIA process." *Forum on Corrections Research.* 9:18–22.

Motiuk, L.L., Cousineau, C., and Gileno, J. 2005. *The Safe Return of Offenders to the Community Statistical Overview.* Correctional Service Canada.

Motiuk, L.L., Luciani, F., Serin, R.C., and Vuong, B. 2001. "Federal Offender Population Movement: A Study of Minimum-security Placements." Research Report R-107. Correctional Service Canada.

Motiuk, L.L., and Porporino, F.J. 1991. *The prevalence, nature and severity of mental health problems among federal male inmates in Canadian penitentiaries.* R-24. Ottawa, ON: Correctional Service Canada.

Motiuk, L.L., and Serin, R.C. 2001. *Compendium 2000 on effective correctional programming.* Ottawa ON: Correctional Service Canada. Retrieved November 2, 2015 (www.csc-scc.gc.ca/research/compendium/2000/index-eng.shtml).

Mount Pleasant-Jette, C. 1993. "Creating a climate of confidence: Providing services within Aboriginal communites." In National Round Table on Economic Issues and Resources (Royal Commission on Aboriginal Issues: Ottawa, April 27–29, 1993). p. 11.

Moyer, S. 1992. "Race, gender, and homicide: Comparisons between Aboriginals and other Canadians." *Canadian Journal of Criminology.* 34:387–402.

Moyers, T.B., and Glynn, L.H. 2013. "Enhancing motivation for treatment and change." In B.S. McCrady and E.E. Epstein, eds. *Addictions: A comprehensive guidebook.* 2nd ed. pp. 377–390. New York: Oxford University Press.

Muncie, J. 2001. "The construction and deconstruction of crime." In J. Muncie and E. McLaughline, eds. *The problem of crime.* 2nd ed. London, Sage Publications in association with the Open University.

Muller, J.L., Sommer, M., Wagner, V., Lange, K., Taschler, H., and Roder, C.H. 2003. "Abnormalities in emotion processing within cortical and subcortical regions in criminal psychopaths: Evidence from a functional magnetic resonance imaging study using pictures with emotional content." *Biological Psychiatry.* 54(2):152–162.

Multi-Health Systems. 2005. *Controlling Anger and Learning to Manage It CALM Program: Corrections Version.* Winogron, Van Dieten, Gauzas, and Grisim.

Mulvey, E. 2005. "Risk assessment in juvenile justice policy and practice." In K. Heilbrun, N. Goldstein, and R. Redding. eds. *Juvenile Delinquency: Prevention, Assessment, and Intervention.* pp. 209–231. New York, NY: Oxford University Press.

Mulvey, E.P., Arthur, M.W., and Reppucci, N.D. 1993. "The prevention and treatment of juvenile delinquency: A review of the research." *Clinical Psychology Review.* 13:133–167.

Muñoz, L.C., and Frick, P.J. 2007. "The reliability, stability, and predictive utility of the self-report version of the Antisocial Process Screening Device." *Scandinavian Journal of Psychology.* 48:299–312.

Murnen, S.K., Wright, C., and Kaluzny, G. 2002. "If 'boys will be boys,' then girls will be victims? A meta-analytic review of the research that relates masculine ideology to sexual aggression." *Sex Roles.* 46:359–375.

Murphy, L., Fedoroff, J. P., and Martineau, M. 2009. "Canada's sex offender registries: Background, implementation, and social policy considerations." *The Canadian Journal of Human Sexuality.* 18(1–2):61–72.

Murrie, D.C., Boccaccini, M.T., McCoy, W., and Cornell, D. 2007. "Diagnostic labeling in juvenile court: How do psychopathy and conduct disorder findings influence judges." *Journal of Clinical Child and Adolescent Psychology.* 36:228–241.

Murrie, D.C., Cornell, D.G., and McCoy, W. 2005. "Psychopathy, conduct disorder, and stigma: Does diagnostic labeling influence juvenile probation officer recommendations." *Law and Human Behavior.* 29:323–342.

Naclia, K.B. 2009. *Culturally-specific programming: A qualitative analysis f the CSC program "In Search of Your Warrior."* M.A. Thesis, University of Regina. Retrieved December 8, 2015 (www.collectionscanada.gc.ca/obj/thesescanada/vol2/002/MR65670.PDF).

Naffine, N. 1987. *Female crime: The construction of women in criminology.* Sydney: Allen and Unwin.

Nafekh, M., and Motiuk, L. 2002. *The Statistical Information on Recidivism–Revised 1 SIR-R1 Scale: A psychometric examination.* Research Report No. R-126. Ottawa, ON: Correctional Service Canada.

Nafekh, M., Allegri, N., Fabisiak, A., Batten, D., Stys, Y., Li, H., Jensen, T., Loree, E., Henighan, M., Chappell, M., and Scarfone, C. 2009. *Evaluation report: Correctional Service Canada's correctional programs.* Ottawa, ON: Correctional Service Canada. Retrieved November 2, 2014 (www.cscscc.gc.ca/text/pa/cop-prog/cop-prog-eng.pdf).

Nathanson, C., Paulhus, D.L., and Williams, K.M. 2006. "Predictors of a behavioral measure of scholastic cheating: Personality and competence but not demographics." *Contemporary Educational Psychology.* 31:97–122.

National Crime Prevention Council. 1995. *Risk or threat to children.* Ottawa, ON: National Crime Prevention Council.

National Crime Prevention Council. 1997. *Preventing crime by investing in families and communities: Promoting positive outcomes in youth twelve- to eighteen-years-old.* Ottawa, ON: National Crime Prevention Council.

National Institute of Corrections. 2009. Implementing Evidence-Based Policy and Practice in Community Corrections. 2nd ed. Washington DC: Author. Retrieved November 2, 2015 (http://static.nicic.gov/Library/024107.pdf).

National Institute of Corrections. 2012. *Thinking for a Change (T4C) 3.1.* Retrieved October 23, 2015 (http://static.nicic.gov/Library/025057/default.html).

National Institute on Drug Abuse. 2014. "The science of drug abuse and addiction: The basics." In *The National Institute on Drug Abuse media guide*. pp. 1–8. Retrieved October 28, 2015 (www.drugabuse.gov/sites/default/files/mediaguide_web_1.pdf).

Needlemann, H., Riess, J., Tobin, M., Biesecker, G., and Greenhouse, J. 1996. "Bone lead levels and delinquent behavior." *Journal of the American Medical Association.* 275(5):363–369.

Neumann, C.S., Schmitt, D.S., Carter, R., Embley, I., and Hare, R.D. 2012. "Psychopathic traits in females and males across the globe." *Behavioral Sciences and the Law.* 30:557–574.

New Brunswick Public Safety. 2015. "Corrections." Retrieved October 21, 2015 (www2.gnb.ca/content/gnb/en/departments/public_safety/safety_protection/content/corrections.html).

Newfoundland Labrador Department of Justice and Public Safety. 2015. "Corrections." Retrieved October 21, 2015 (www.justice.gov.nl.ca/just/corrections/index.html).

Newman, J.P., Brinkley, C.A., Lorenz, A.R., Hiatt, K.D., and MacCoon, D.G. 2007. "Psychopathy as psychopathology: Beyond the clinical utility of the Psychopathy Checklist-Revised." In H. Hervé and J.C. Yuille, eds. *The psychopath: Theory, research, and practice*. pp. 173–206. Mahwah, NJ: Lawrence Erlbaum.

Newman, J.P., and Wallace, J.F. 1993. "Psychopathy and cognition." In P.C. Kendall and K.S. Dobson, eds. *Psychopathology and cognition*. pp. 293–349. New York, NY: Academic Press.

Newman, G. 1976. *Comparative deviance: Perception and law in six cultures*. New York, NY: Elsevier.

Newman, G. 1977. "Social institutions and the control of deviance: A cross-national opinion survey." *European Journal of Social Psychology.* 7:39–59.

Nicholls, T.L., Brink, J., Desmarais, S.L., Webster, C.D., and Martin, M.L. 2006. "The Short-Term Assessment of Risk and Treatability (START): A prospective validation study in a forensic psychiatric sample." *Assessment.* 13:313–327. DOI: 10.1177/1073191106290559.

Nicholls, T.L., Roesch, R., Olley, M.C., Ogloff, J.R.P., and Hemphill, J.F. 2005. *Jail Screening Assessment Tool (JSAT)*. Proactive Resolutions. Retrieved November 25, 2015 (http://proactive-resolutions.com/shop/jail-screening-assessment-tool-jsat/).

Niehoff, D. 1999. "Seeds of controversy." In *The biology of violence: How understanding the brain, behavior, and environment can break the vicious circle of aggression*. pp. 1–30. New York, NY: Free Press.

Northwest Territories Department of Justice. 2015. "Corrections and probation." Retrieved October 21, 2015 (www.justice.gov.nt.ca/en/browse/corrections-and-probation/).

Norton-Hawk, M. 2004. "A comparison of pimp- and non-pimp-controlled women." *Violence Against Women.* 10(2):189–194. DOI: dx.doi.org/10.1177/1077801203260949.

Nova Scotia Department of Justice Correctional Services. 2013. "Correctional services." Retrieved October 21, 2015 (http://novascotia.ca/just/Corrections/).

Nuffield, J. 1982. *Parole decision-making in Canada*. Ottawa, ON: Solicitor General Canada.

Nunavut Department of Justice. 2013. "Corrections." Retrieved October 21, 2015 (www.justice.gov.nu.ca/apps/authoring/dspPage.aspx?page=corrections).

Nunes, K.L., and Cortoni, F.A. 2006. *The heterogeneity of treatment non-completers*. Research Report No. R-176. Ottawa, ON: Correctional Service Canada.

Nunes, K.L., and Cortoni, F. 2008. "Dropout from sex offender treatment and dimensions of risk of sexual recidivism." *Criminal Justice and Behavior.* 35:24–33.

Nunes, K.L., Cortoni, F., and Serin, R.C. 2010. "Screening offenders for risk of dropout and expulsion from correctional programs." *Legal and Criminological Psychology.* 15:341–356.

Nunes, K.L., Firestone, P., Wexler, A.F., Jensen, T.L., and Bradford, J.M. 2007. "Incarceration and recidivism among sexual offenders." *Law and Human Behavior.* 31:305–318.

Nunes, K.L., Hermann, C.A., Malcom, J.R., and Lavoie, K. 2013. "Childhood sexual victimization, pedophilic interest, and sexual recidivism." *Child Abuse and Neglect.* 37:703–711. DOI: dx.doi.org/10.1016/j.chiabu.2013.01.008.

Nunes, K.L., Hermann, C.A., and Ratcliffe, K. 2013. "Implicit and explicit attitudes towards rape are associated with sexual aggression." *Journal of Interpersonal Violence.* 28:2657–2675. DOI: 10.1177/0886260513487995.

Nunes, K.L., Hermann, C.A., White, K., Pettersen, C., and Bumby, K. 2016. Attitude may be everything, but is everything an attitude? Cognitive distortions may not be evaluations of rape. *Sexual Abuse: A Journal of Research and Treatment*. Advance online publication.

Nunes, K. L., Pettersen, C., Hermann, C. A., Looman, J., & Spape, J. (2014). Does change on the MOLEST and RAPE scales predict sexual recidivism? *Sexual Abuse: A Journal of Research and Treatment*. Advance online publication. doi: 10.1177/1079063214540725

Nutt, D.J., Lingford-Huges, A., Erritzoe, D., and Stokes, P.R. 2015. "The dopamine theory of addiction: 40 years of highs and lows." *Neuroscience.* 16:1–8.

Nye, F.I. 1982. *Family relationships: Rewards and costs.* Beverly Hills, CA: Sage Publications.

Odgers, C. L., Moretti, M.M., Burnette, M.L., Chauhan, P., Waite, D., and Reppucci, N.D. 2007. "A latent variable modeling approach to identifying subtypes of serious and violent female juvenile offenders." *Aggressive Behaviour.* 33:1–14.

Odgers, C.L., Moretti, M.M., and Reppucci, N.D. 2005. "Examining the science and practice of violence risk assessment with female adolescents." *Law and Human Behavior.* 29:7–27.

Office of the Correctional Investigator. 2014. *A three year review of federal inmate suicides (2011–2014): Final report.* Cat. No.: PS104-11/2014E-PDF. Ottawa: Government of Canada. Retrieved November 20, 2015 (www.oci-bec.gc.ca/cnt/rpt/pdf/oth-aut/oth-aut20140910-eng.pdf).

Offord, D.R., Lipman, E.L., and Duku, E.K. 2001. "Epidemiology of problem behaviour up to age 12 years." In R. Loeber and D.P. Farrington, eds. *Child Delinquents.* pp. 95–234. Thousand Oaks, CA: Sage.

Ogloff, J.R., Talevski, D., Lemphers, A., Wood, M., and Simmons, M. 2015. "Co-occurring mental illness, substance use disorders, and antisocial personality disorder among clients of forensic mental health services." *Psychiatric Rehabilitation Journal.* 31(1):16–23. DOI: 10.1037/prj0000088.

Olver, M.E., Neumann, C.S., Wong, S.C., and Hare, R.D. 2013. "The structural and predictive properties of the Psychopathy Checklist–Revised in Canadian Aboriginal and non-Aboriginal offenders." *Psychological Assessment.* 25(1):167.

Olver, M.E., Nicholaichuk, T.P., Kingston, D.A., and Wong S.C.P. 2014. "A multisite examination of sexual violence risk and therapeutic change." *Journal of Consulting and Clinical Psychology.* 82:312–324.

Olver, M.E., Stockdale, K.C., and Wormith, J.S. 2009. "Risk assessment with young offenders: A meta-analysis of three assessment measures." *Criminal Justice and Behavior.* 36:329–353.

Olver, M.E., Stockdale, K.C., and Wormith, J.S. 2011. "A meta-analysis of predictors of offender treatment attrition and its relationship to recidivism." *Journal of Consulting and Clinical Psychology.* 79:6–21.

Olver, M.E., and Wong, S.C.P. 2006. "Psychopathy, sexual deviance, and recidivism among sex offenders." *Sexual Abuse: A Journal of Research and Treatment.* 18:65–82.

Olver, M.E., and Wong, S.C.P. 2009. "Therapeutic responses of psychopathic sexual offenders: Treatment attrition, therapeutic change, and long-term recidivism." *Journal of Consulting and Clinical Psychology.* 77:328–336.

Olver, M.E., and Wong, S. 2011. "Predictors of sex offender treatment dropout: psychopathy, sex offender risk, and responsivity implications." *Psychology, Crime and Law,* 17:57–471.

Olver, M.E., Wong, S.C.P., Nicholaichuk, T., and Gordon, A. 2007. "The validity and reliability of the Violence Risk Scale–Sexual Offender Version: Assessing sex offender risk and evaluating therapeutic change." *Psychological Assessment.* 19:318–329.

O'Malley, P., Coventry, G., and Walters, R. 1993. "Victoria's Day in Prison Program: An evaluation and critique." *Australian and New Zealand Journal of Criminology.* 26:171–83.

Ontario Ministry of Community Safety and Correctional Services. 2015. "Correctional services." Retrieved October 21, 2015 (www.mcscs.jus.gov.on.ca/english/corr_serv/adult_off/facilities/corr_centres/corr_centres.html).

Oram, S., Trevillion, K., Khalifeh, H., Feder, G., and Howard, L.M. 2014. "Systematic review and meta-analysis of psychiatric disorder and the perpetration of partner violence." *Epidemiology and Psychiatric Sciences.* 23(4):361–376.

Orbis Partners. 2003. *Service Planning Instrument (SPIn).* Ottawa, ON: Author.

Orbis Partners. 2007a. *Girls Moving On.* Ottawa, ON: Author.

Orbis Partners. 2007b. *Service Planning Inventory for Women SPIn-W.* Ottawa, ON: Author.

Orbis Partners. 2007c. *Youth Assessment and Screening Instrument: Girls (YASI-G).* Ottawa, Ontario, Canada: Author.

Ortiz, J., and Raine, A. 2004. "Heart rate level and antisocial behavior in children and adolescents: A meta-analysis." *Journal of the American Academy of Child and Adolescent Psychiatry.* 43:154–162.

Osher, F., Scott, J.E., Steadman, H.J., and Robbins, P.C. 2006. *Validating a brief jail mental health screen: Final technical report.* U.S. Department of Justice.

Ospina, M., and Dennett, L. 2013. *Systematic review on the prevalence of Fetal Alcohol Spectrum disorders.* Institute of Health Economics Alberta Canada. Retrieved December 7, 2015 (http://fasd.alberta.ca/documents/Systematic_Prevalence_Report_FASD.pdf).

Ostrom, B., Kleiman, M., Cheesman, F., Hansen, R., and Kauder, N. 2002. "Offender risk assessment in Virginia: A three-stage evaluation: Process of sentencing reform, empirical study of diversion and recidivism, benefit-cost analysis." National Center for State Courts. Retrieved May 14, (www.vcsc.virginia.gov/risk_off_rpt.pdf).

Overall, J.E., and Gorham, D.R. 1962. "The Brief Psychiatric Rating Scale." *Psychological Reports.* 24:97–99.

Owen, B. 1998. *In the mix: Struggle and survival in a women's prison.* Albany: State University of New York Press.

Owen, B. 2001. "Perspectives on women in prison." In C.M. Renzetti and L. Goodstein, eds. *Women, crime, and criminal justice: Original feminist readings.* pp. 243–254. Los Angeles: Roxbury.

Owusu-Bempah, A., and Wortley, S.C.O.T. 2014. "Race, crime, and criminal justice in Canada." In S. M. Bucerius and M. Tonry, eds. *The Oxford handbook of ethnicity, crime and immigration.* pp. 281–320. New York, NY: Oxford University Press.

Oxford, M.C., Cavell, T.A., and Hughes, J.N. 2003. "Callous/unemotional traits moderate the relation between ineffective parenting and child externalizing problems: A partial replication and extension." *Journal of Clinical Child and Adolescent Psychology.* 32:577–585.

Oxford Dictionary. n.d. "Drug." Retrieved October 28, 1015 (www.oxforddictionaries.com/definition/english/drug).

Pacholik, B. 2015. "Sask. top court declines to hear appeal of troubled offender." *Regina Leader-Post.* September 9. Retrieved December 7, 2015 (www.leaderpost.com/health/sask+court+declines+hear+appeal+troubled+offender/11354455/story.html).

Palmer, T. 1975. "Martinson re-visited." *Journal of Research in Crime and Delinquency.* 12:133–52.

Palumbi, S.R. 2002. *The evolution explosion: How humans cause rapid evolutionary change.* New York: Norton, W.W., and Company Inc.

Paolucci, E.O., Genuis, M.L., and Violato, C. 2001. "A meta-analysis of the published research on the effects of child sexual abuse." *The Journal of Psychology.* 135:17–36.

Paparozzi, M.A., and Caplan, J.M. 2009. "A profile of paroling authorities in America: The strange bedfellows of politics and professionalism." *The Prison Journal.* 89(4):401–425. DOI: http://dx.doi.org/10.1177/0032885509349559.

Pardini, D.A., Lochman, J.E., and Frick, P.J. 2003. "Callous/unemotional traits and social cognitive processes in adjudicated youth." *Journal of the American Academic of Child and Adolescent Psychiatry.* 42:364–371.

Parker, J.G., and Asher, S.R. 1987. "Peer relations and later personal adjustment: Are low accepted children at risk?" *Psychological Bulletin.* 102:357–389.

Parole Board Canada. 2014. Performance monitoring report 2013–2014. Retrieved October 26, 2015 (www.pbc-clcc.gc.ca/rprts/pmr/pmr_2013_2014/index-eng.shtml). Government of Canada.

Partridge, G.E. 1930. "Current Conceptions of Psychopathic Personality." *American Journal of Psychiatry.* 1(87):53–99.

Passingham, R.A. 1972. "Crime and personality: A review of Eysenck's theory." In V.D. Nebylitsyn and J.A. Gray, eds. *Biological basis of individual behavior.* New York, NY: Academic Press.

Patrick, C.H. 1952. *Alcohol, culture, and society.* Durham: NC: Duke University Press.

Patrick, C.J., Fowles, D.C., and Krueger, R.F. 2009. "Triarchic conceptualization of psychopathy: developmental origins of disinhibition, boldness, and meanness." *Development and Psychopathology.* 21(3):913–38. DOI: 10.1017/S0954579409000492.

Patterson, G.R. 1982. *Coercive family process.* Eugene, OR: Castalia.

Patterson, G.R., Reid, J.B., and Dishion, T.J. 1998. *Antisocial boys.* Eugene, OR: Castalia.

Paulhus, D.L., Hemphill, J.F., and Hare, R.D. (forthcoming). *Manual for the Self-Report Psychopathy Scale.* Toronto, ON: Multi-Health Systems.

Paulhus, D.L., and Williams, K.M. 2002. "The dark triad of personality: Narcissism, Machiavellianism, and psychopathy." *Journal of Research in Personality.* 36:556–563.

Peper, J.S., and Dahl, R.E. 2013. "The teenage brain: Surging hormones—Brain-behaviour interactions during puberty." *Current Directions in Psychological Science.* 22:134–139.

Penal Reform International. 2013. *The U.N. Bangkok Rules on Women Offenders and Prisoners: A short guide.* Retrieved December 3, 2015 (www.penalreform.org/resource/united-nations-bangkok-rules-women-offenders-prisoners-short/).

Pepler, D.J., Walsh, M.M., and Levene, K.S. 2004. "Intervention for aggressive girls: Tailoring and measuring the fit." In M.M. Moretti, C.L. Odgers, and M.A. Jackson, eds. *Girls and Aggression: Contributing factors and intervention principles.* pp. 131–145. New York, NY: Kluwer.

Pernanen, K., Cousineau, M.M., Brochu, S., Sun, F. 2002. *Proportions of crimes associated with alcohol and drugs in Canada.* Ottawa, ON: Canadian Centre on Substance Abuse.

Perreault, S. 2009. "The incarceration of Aboriginal people in adult correctional services." *Juristat.* Report No. 85-002-X. Retrieved December 3, 2015 (www.statcan.gc.ca/pub/85-002-x/2009003/article/10903-eng.htm).

Perreault, S., and Brennan, S. 2010. "Criminal victimization in Canada, 2009." *Juristat.* Summer 2010. Catalogue No. 85-002-X. Statistics Canada. Retrieved November 24, 2015 (www.statcan.gc.ca/pub/85-002-x/2010002/article/11340-eng.htm).

Perrone, D., Sullivan, C.J., Pratt, T.C., and Margaryan, S. 2004. "Parental efficacy, self-control, and delinquency: A test of general theory of crime on a nationally representative sample of youth." *International Journal of Offender Therapy and Comparative Criminology.* 48:298–312.

Perusse, D. 2008. *Aboriginal people living off-reserve and the labour market: Estimates from the Labour Force Survey, 2007.* Ottawa, ON: Statistics Canada.

Petersilia, J. 2001. "Prisoner reentry: Public safety and reintegration challenges." *The Prison Journal.* 81:360–375. DOI:10.1177/0032885501081003004.

Petrosino, A. 2000. "Answering the why question in evaluation: The causal-model approach." *Canadian Journal of Program Evaluation.* 15:1–24.

Petrosino, A., Turpin-Petrosino, C., and Buehler, J. 2003. "Scared straight and other juvenile awareness programs for preventing juvenile delinquency: A systematic review of the randomized experimental evidence."

Annals of the American Academy of Political and Social Science. 589:41–62.

Petrosino, A., Turpin-Petrosino, C., Hollis-Peel, M.E., and Lavenberg, J.G. 2013. "'Scared Straight' and other juvenile awareness programs for preventing juvenile delinquency." *Cochrane Database of Systematic Reviews 2013.* 4. Art. No.: CD002796. DOI: 10.1002/14651858.CD002796.pub2.

Petrunik, M., Murphy, L., and Fedoroff, J.P. 2009. "American and Canadian approaches to sex offenders: A study of the politics of dangerousness." *Federal Sentencing Reporter.* 21(2):111–123. DOI: 10.1525/fsr.2008.21.2III.

Pfeifer, J., and Hart-Mitchell, R. 2001. *Evaluating the effect of healing lodge residency on adult offenders.* Regina, SK: Canadian Institute for Peace, Justice and Security, University of Regina.

Pihl, R.O. 2009. "Substance abuse: Etiological considerations." In P.H. Blaney and T. Millon, eds. *Oxford textbook of psychopathology.* pp. 253–279. New York, NY: Oxford University Press.

Pinker, S. 2011. *The better angels of our nature: Why violence has declined.* New York, New York: Penguin.

Pithers, W.D. 1990. "Relapse prevention with sexual aggressors: A method for maintaining therapeutic gain and enhancing external supervision." In W.L. Marshall, D.R. Laws, and H.E. Barbaree, eds. *Handbook of sexual assault: Issues, theories and treatment of the offender.* pp. 343–361. New York, NY: Plenum.

Pithers, W.D., Marques, J.K., Gibat, C.C., and Marlatt, G.A. 1983. "Relapse prevention: A self-control model of treatment and maintenance of change for sexual aggressives." In J. Greer, and I.R. Stuart, eds. *The sexual aggressor: Current perspectives on treatment.* pp. 292–310. New York, NY: Van Nostrand Reinhold.

Piquero, A.R. 2008. "Taking stock of developmental trajectories of criminal activity over the life course." In A.M. Liberman, ed. *The long view of crime: A synthesis of longitudinal research.* New York, NY: Springer.

Piquero, A.R., Blumstein, A., Brame, R., Haapanen, R., Mulvey, E.P., and Nagin, D.S. 2001. "Assessing the impact of exposure time and incapacitation on longitudinal trajectories of criminal offending." *Journal of Adolescent Research.* 16:54–74.

Piquero, A.R., Jennings, W., and Farrington, D.P. 2010. "On the malleability of self-control: Theoretical and policy implications regarding a general theory of crime." *Justice Quarterly.* 27:803–834.

Plomin, R., DeFries, J.C., McClearn, G.E., and McGuffin, P. 2001. *Behavioral Genetics.* 4th ed. New York, NY: Worth.

Polaschek, D.L.L. 2012. "An appraisal of the risk–need–responsivity (RNR) model of offender rehabilitation and its application in correctional treatment." *Legal and Criminological Psychology.* 17:1–17. DOI: 10.1111/j.2044-8333.2011.02038.x.

Polaschek, D.L.L., Calvert, S.W., and Gannon, T.A. 2009. "Linking violent thinking: Implicit theory-based research with violent offenders." *Journal of Interpersonal Violence.* 24: 75–96.

Polaschek, D.L.L., and Collie, R.M. 2004. "Rehabilitating serious violent adult offenders: An empirical and theoretical stocktake." *Psychology, Crime and Law.* 10:321–334.

Polaschek, D.L.L., Collie, R.M., and Walkey, F.H. 2004. "Criminal attitudes to violence: Development and preliminary validation of a scale for male prisoners." *Aggressive Behavior.* 30:484–503. DOI: 10.1002/ab.20081.

Poldrack, R.A. 2009. "Neuroimaging: Separating the Promise from the Pipe Dreams, Dana Foundation." Retrieved July 8, 2009 (www.dana.org/news/cerebrum/detail.aspx?id=22220).

Pollack, O. 1950. *The criminality of women.* Philadelphia: University of Philadelphia Press.

Pollack, S. 2005. "Taming the shrew: Regulating prisoners through women-centered mental health programming." *Critical Criminology.* 13:71–87.

Popova, S., Lange, S., Bekmuradov, D., Mihic, A., and Rehm, J. 2011. "Fetal alcohol spectrum disorder prevalence estimates in correctional systems: A systematic literature review." *Canadian Journal of Public Health.* 102(5):336–340.

Porporino, F.J., and Motiuk, L.L. 1995. "The prison careers of mentally disordered offenders." *International Journal of Law Psychiatry.* 18(1):29–44.

Porter, S., Birt, A.R., and Boer, D.P. 2001. "Investigation of the criminal and conditional release histories of Canadian federal offenders as a function of psychopathy and age." *Law and Human Behavior.* 25:647–661.

Porter, S., Fairweather, D., Drugge, J., Hervé, H., Birt, A., and Boer, D. P. 2000. "Profiles of psychopathy in incarcerated sexual offenders." *Criminal Justice and Behavior.* 27:216–233.

Portnoy, J., Raine, A., Chen, F.R., Pardini, D. Loeber, R., and Jennings, R. 2014. "Heart rate and antisocial behaviour: The mediating role of impulsive sensation seeking." *Criminology.* 52:292–311.

Postmus, J.L., Severson, M., Berry, M., and Yoo, J.A. 2009. "Women's experiences of violence and seeking help." *Violence Against Women.* 15:852–868.

Pozzulo, J., Bennell, C., and Forth, A.E. 2008. *Forensic psychology.* Toronto, ON: Pearson.

Pozzulo, J., Bennell, C., and Forth, A. 2015. *Forensic Psychology.* 4th Ed. Toronto, ON: Pearson.

Pratt, T.C., and Cullen, F.T. 2000. "The empirical status of Gottfredson and Hirschi's general theory of crime: A meta-analysis." *Criminology.* 38:931–964.

Pratt, T.C., Sellers, C.S., Cullen, F.T., Winfree, L.T., and Madensen, T.D. 2005. *The empirical status of social learning theory: A meta-analysis.* Unpublished manuscript. Washington State University, Pullman, Washington.

Prell, L. 2013. *Iowa parole risk assessment: Construction and validation.* Iowa: Iowa Department of Corrections.

Prescott, C.A., Caldwell, C.B., Carey, G., Vogler, G.P., Trumbetta, S.L., and Gottesman, I.I. 2005. "The Washington University twin study of alcoholism." *American Journal of Medical Genetics Part B (Neuropsychiatric Genetics).* 134B:45–55. DOI:10.1002/ajmg.b.30124.

Pressman, D.E. 2009. *Risk assessment decisions for violent political extremism.* User Report 2009-02. Ottawa: Public Safety Canada.

PricewaterhouseCoopers. 2015. "Global Economic Crime 2014 Survey: Fraud, Corruption and Cybercrime." PwC Forensic Services. Retrieved November 22, 2015 (www.pwc.com/gx/en/services/advisory/consulting/forensics/economic-crime-survey.html).

Prince Edward Island Department of Justice and Public Safety. 2015. "Community and correctional services." Retrieved October 21, 2015 (www.gov.pe.ca/jps/cacs-info/dg.inc.php3).

Proudfoot, S. 2009. "Girl violence increasing in 'lethality,' experts say." *Ottawa Citizen.* March 21.

Public Health Agency of Canada. 2009. "Chapter 3—The Health of Canadian Children." In *The Chief Public Health Officer's report on the state of public health in Canada 2009: Growing up well.* Ottawa, ON: Author. Retrieved November 2, 2015 (www.phac-aspc.gc.ca/cphorsphc-respcacsp/2009/fr-rc/cphorsphc-respcacsp06-eng.php).

Public Safety Canada. 2005. "Fast facts: A day in the life of an inmate." Retrieved October 23, 2015 (www.publicsafety.gc.ca/lbrr/archives/cff-1-2005%20e-eng.pdf). Public Works and Government Services Canada. Catalogue no. PS3-2/ 1·200SE Q-662·39876·9.

Public Safety Canada. 2007. *Corrections and conditional release statistical overview 2007.* Public Works and Government Services Canada. Catalogue no. PS1-3/2007E. Retrieved March 20, 2009 (www.publicsafety.gc.ca/cnt/rsrcs/pblctns/2007-ccrs/index-eng.aspx).

Public Safety Canada. 2007a. *Youth gangs in Canada: What do we know?* Ottawa, ON: Public Safety Canada. Public Works and Government Services Canada. Catalogue no. PS4-37/2-2007E-PDF. Retrieved April 27, 2015 (www.publicsafety.gc.ca/cnt/rsrcs/pblctns/gngs-cnd/gngs-cnd-eng.pdf).

Public Safety Canada. 2007b. *Youth gang involvement: What are the risk factors?* Public Works and Government Services Canada. Catalogue no. PS4-37/1-2007E-PDF. Retrived April 27, 2015 (www.publicsafety.gc.ca/cnt/rsrcs/pblctns/yth-gng-nvlvmnt/index-eng.aspx).

Public Safety Canada. 2008. *Corrections and conditional release statistical overview 2008.* Public Works and Government Services Canada. Catalogue no. PS1-3/2008E-PDF. Retrieved October 14, 2015 (www.publicsafety.gc.ca/cnt/rsrcs/pblctns/2008-ccrs/index-eng.aspx).

Public Safety Canada. 2009. *Corrections and conditional release statistical overview 2009.* Public Works and Government Services Canada. Catalogue no. PS1-3/2009E. Retrieved November 27, 2015 (www.publicsafety.gc.ca/cnt/rsrcs/pblctns/2008-ccrs/index-eng.aspx).

Public Safety Canada. 2014. *Corrections and conditional release statistical overview 2013.* Retrieved October 14, 2015 (www.publicsafety.gc.ca/cnt/rsrcs/pblctns/2009-ccrs/index-eng.aspx). Public Works and Government Services Canada. Catalogue no. PS1-3/2013E-PDF.

Public Safety Canada. 2015a. *Corrections and Conditional Release Statistical Overview 2014.* Retrieved October 29, 2015 (https://assets.documentcloud.org/documents/2110762/ps-sp-1483284-v1-corrections-and-conditional.pdf).

Public Safety Canada. 2015b. "Offender accountability." Retrieved October 23, 2015 (www.publicsafety.gc.ca/cnt/nws/nws-rlss/2012/20120509-1-eng.aspx).

Quan, D. 2015. "Test to predict if inmates will reoffend unreliable for aboriginal offenders, judge rules." *National Post.* September 24. Retrieved December 12, 2015 (http://news.nationalpost.com/news/canada/tests-to-predict-if-inmates-will-reoffend-unreliable-for-aboriginal-offenders-judge-rules).

Quann, N., and Trevethan, S. 2000. *Police-reported Aboriginal crime in Saskatchewan.* Ottawa, ON: Statistics Canada.

Queen's University. 2006. "Canadian Public Opinion Trends: Federal Government Spending: The Justice System." *Canadian Opinion Research Archive.* Retrieved March 21, 2009 (www.queensu.ca/cora/_trends/Spend_Justice.htm).

Quinn, P.D., and Fromme, K. 2010. "Self-regulation as a protective factor against risky drinking and sexual behaviour." *Psychology of Addictive Behaviours.* 24:376–385. DOI: 10.1037/a0018547.

Quinsey, V.L., Bergersen, S.G., and Steinman, C.M. 1976. "Changes in physiological and verbal responses of child molesters during aversion therapy." *Canadian Journal of Behavioral Science.* 8:202–212.

Quinsey, V.L., Harris, G.T., Rice, M.E., and Cormier, C.A. 2006. *Violent offenders: Appraising and managing risk.* 2nd ed. Washington, DC: American Psychological Association.

Quinsey, V.L., Skilling, T.A., Lalumière, M.L., and Craig, W. 2004. *Juvenile delinquency: Understanding the origins of individual differences.* Washington, DC: American Psychological Association.

Quinsey, V.L., Skilling, T.A., Lalumière, M.L., and Craig, W. 2004a. "Sex differences in aggression and female delinquency." In *Juvenile delinquency: Understanding the origins of individual differences.* pp. 115–136. Washington, DC: American Psychological Association.

R. v. Gladue. 1999. 1 SCR 688.

R. v. H.E. 2015. ONCA 531. Retrieved November 24, 2015 (www.canlii.org/en/on/onca/doc/2015/2015onca531/2015onca531.html?resultIndex=1).

R. v. Lindsay. 2005. CanLII 24240 (ON SC).

R. v. Smith. 2015. SCC 34. Retrieved October 29, 2015 (https://scc-csc.lexum.com/scc-csc/scc-csc/en/item/15403/index.do).

Rabinovitch, J., and Strega, S. 2004. "The PEERS story: Effective services sidestep the controversies." *Violence against women.* 10:140–159.

Raine, A. 1993. "Genetics and crime." In *The psychopathology of crime: Criminal behaviour as a clinical disorder.* pp. 47–78. San Diego, CA: Academic Press.

Raine, A. 1997. "Crime, conditioning, and arousal." In H. Nyborg, ed. *The scientific study of human nature: Tribute to Hans J. Eysenck.* pp. 122–141. Oxford, UK: Elsevier.

Raine, A. 2008. "From genes to brain to antisocial behaviour." *Current Directions in Psychological Science.* 17:323–328.

Raine, A. 2013. *The anatomy of violence: the biological roots of crime.* London: Allen Lane.

Raine, A., and Venables, P.H. 1981. "Classical conditioning and socialization—A biosocial interaction?" *Personality and Individual Differences.* 2:273–283.

Ramírez, J.M., and Andreu, J.M. 2006. "Aggression, and some related psychological constructs (anger, hostility, and impulsivity): Some comments from a research project." *Neuroscience and Biobehavioral Reviews.* 30(3):276–291.

Rangmar, J., Hjern, A., Vinnerljung, B., Strömland, K., Aronson, M., and Fahlke, C. 2015. "Psychosocial outcomes of Fetal Alcohol Syndrome in adulthood." *Pediatrics.* 135(1): e52–e58.

Rappaport, J. 1987. "Terms of empowerment/exemplars of prevention: Toward a theory for community psychology." *American Journal of Community Psychology.* 15(2)1:21–148.

Rashid, A. 2004. *A visit to the Pê Sâkâstêw healing centre: Not your ordinary prison.* Retrieved January 14, 2009 (http://maritimes.indymedia.org/news/2004/01/7234.php).

Rastin, C., and Johnson, S. 2002. "Inuit sexual offenders: Victim, offence, and recidivism characteristics." *Forum on Corrections Research.* 14.

Razack, S.H. 2011. "Timely deaths: Medicalizing the deaths of Aboriginal people in police custody." *Law, Culture and the Humanities.* 9(2):352–374. DOI: 10.1177/1743872111407022.

Rees-Jones, A., Gudjonsson, G., and Young, S. 2012. "A multi-site controlled trial of a cognitive skills program for mentally disordered offenders." *BMC Psychiatry.* 12:44. DOI: 10.1186/1471-244-12-44.

Reeves, S.J., Polling, C., Stokes, P.R., Lappin, J.M., Shotbolt, P.P., Mehta, M.A., Howes, O.D., and Egerton, A. 2012. "Limbic striatal dopamine D2/3 receptor availability is associated with non-planning impulsivity in healthy adults after exclusion of potential dissimulators." *Psychiatry Research.* 202:60–64.

Rehm, J., Baliunas, D., Brochu, S., Fischer, B., Gnam, W., Patra, J., Popova, S., Sanocinska-Hart, A., Taylor, B., Adlaf, E., Recel, M., and Single, E. (2006). *The cost of substance abuse in Canada 2002.* Canadian Centre on Substance Abuse. Retrieved October 29, 2015 (www.ccsa.ca/Resource%20Library/ccsa-011332-2006.pdf).

Reiss, A.J. 1951. "Unraveling juvenile delinquency. II. An appraisal of the research methods." *American Journal of Sociology.* 57:115–120.

Reisig, M.D., Holtfreter, K., and Morash, M. 2006. "Assessing recidivism risk across female pathways to crime." *Justice Quarterly.* 23:384–405.

Resick, P.A. 1993. "The psychological impact of rape." *Journal of Interpersonal Violence.* 8:223–255.

Rettinger, L.J., and Andrews, D.A. 2010. "General risk and need, gender specificity, and the recidivism of female offenders." *Criminal Justice and Behaviour.* 37:29–46. DOI: 10.1177/0093854809349438.

Rhee, S.H., and Waldman, I.D. 2002. "Genetic and environmental influences on antisocial behavior: A meta-analysis of twin and adoption studies." *Psychological Bulletin.* 128:490–529.

Rice, M.E., and Harris, G.T. 1997. "Cross-validation and extension of the Violence Risk Appraisal Guide or child molesters and rapists." *Law and Human Behavior.* 21:231–241.

Rice, M.E., and Harris, G.T. 2003. "The size and sign of treatment effects in sex offender therapy." *Annals of the New York Academy of Sciences.* 989:428–440. DOI: 10.1111/j.1749-6632.2003.tb07323.x.

Rice, M.E., and Harris, G.T. 2005. "Comparing effect sizes in follow-up studies: ROC area, Cohen's *d*, and *r.*" *Law and Human Behavior.* 295:615–620.

Rice, M.E., Harris, G.T., and Cormier, C.A. 1992. "An evaluation of a maximum security therapeutic community for psychopaths and other mentally disordered offenders." *Law and Human Behavior.* 16:399–412.

Rice, M.E., Harris, G.T., and Lang, C. 2013. "Validation of a revision to the VRAG and SORAG: The Violence Risk Appraisal Guide—Revised (VRAG-R)." *Psychological Assessment.* 25:951–965. DOI: 10.1037/a0032878.

Richie, B. 2001. "Challenges incarcerated women face as they return to their communities: Findings from life history interviews." *Crime and Delinquency.* 47:368–389.

Richie, B.E. 1996. *Compelled to crime: The gender entrapment of black battered women.* New York, NY: Routledge.

Rideauwood Addiction and Family Services. 2015. "Ottawa drug treatment court." Retrieved May 14, 2015 (www.rideauwood.org/ottawa-drug-treatment-court-2/).

Riina, E.M., Martin, A., and Brooks-Gunn, J. 2014. "Parent-to-child physical aggression, neighborhood cohesion, and development of children's internalizing and externalizing." *Journal of Applied Developmental Psychology.* 35(6):468–477. DOI: dx.doi.org/10.1016/j.appdev.2014.04.005.

Riley, D. 1998. *Drugs and drug policy in Canada: A brief review and commentary*. Canadian Foundation for Drug Policy and International Harm Reduction Association. Retrieved November 22, 2015 (www.parl.gc.ca/Content/SEN/Committee/362/ille/rep/rep-nov98-e.htm).

Roach, K. 2014. "Blaming the victim: Canadian law, causation, and residential schools." *University of Toronto Law Journal*. 64(4):566–595.

Roberts, A.R. 2007. "Domestic violence continuum, forensic assessment, and crises intervention." *Families in Society: The Journal of Contemporary Social Services*. 88:30–43.

Roberts, A.R., and Roberts, B. 2005. *Ending intimate abuse: Practical guidance and survival strategies*. New York, NY: Oxford University Press.

Roberts, A., Yang, M., Zhang, T., and Coid, J. 2008. "Personality disorder, temperament and childhood adversity: Findings from a cohort of prisoners in England and Wales." *Journal of Forensic Psychiatry and Psychology*. 19:460–483.

Roberts, J.V., Crutcher, N., and Verbrugge, P. 2007. "Public attitudes to sentencing in Canada: Exploring recent findings." *Canadian Journal of Criminology and Criminal Justice*. 491:75–107.

Roberts, J.V., and Melchers, R. 2003. "The incarceration of Aboriginal offenders: An analysis of trends, 1978–2001." *Canadian Journal of Criminology and Criminal Justice*. 45:211–242.

Robins, L.N. 1986. "The consequences of conduct disorder in girls." In D. Olweus, J. Block, and M. Radke-Yarrow, eds. *Development of antisocial and prosocial behaviour*. pp. 385–408. New York, NY: Academic Press.

Robinson, C.R., Lowenkamp, C.T., Holsinger, A.M., VanBenschoten, S., Alexander, M., and Oleson, J.C. 2012. "A random study of Staff Trained at Reducing Re-arrest (STARR): Using core correctional practices in probation interactions." *Journal of Crime and Justice*. 35:167–188. DOI:10.1080/0735648X.2012.674823.

Robinson, D., and Porporino, F.J. 2001. "Programming in cognitive skills: The reasoning and rehabilitation program." In C.R. Hollin, ed. *Handbook of offender assessment and treatment*. London: Wiley.

Robinson, D., and Taylor, J. 1995. *Incidence of family violence perpetrated by federal offenders: A file review study*. FV-03. Correctional Service Canada.

Rockett, J., Murrie, D.C., and Boccaccini, M.T. 2007. "Diagnostic labeling in juvenile justice settings: Do psychopathy and conduct disorder findings influence clinicians." *Psychological Services*. 4:107–122.

Rogers, R., Gillis, R., Turner, R., and Frise-Smith, T. 1990. "The clinical presentation of command hallucinations in a forensic population." *American Journal of Psychiatry*. 147:1304–1307.

Rogers, R., Sewell, K.W., Ustad, K., Reinhardt, V., Edwards, W. 1995. "The Referral Decision Scale with mentally disordered inmates." *Law and Human Behavior*. 19(5):481–492.

Rojas, E., and Gretton, H. 2007. "Background, offence characteristics, and criminal outcomes of Aboriginal youth who sexually offend: A closer look at Aboriginal youth intervention needs." *Sexual Abuse: A Journal of Research and Treatment*. 19(3):257–283.

Rosenbaum, J.L., and Lasley, J.R. 1990. "School, community context, and delinquency: Rethinking the gender gap." *Justice Quarterly*. 7:493–513.

Ross, R. 1992. *Dancing with a ghost: Exploring Indian reality*. Markham, ON: Reed Books Canada.

Royal Canadian Mounted Police. 2015a. "Bullying and Cyberbullying." Retrieved November 3, 2015 (www.rcmp-grc.gc.ca/cycp-cpcj/bull-inti/index-eng.htm).

Royal Canadian Mounted Police. 2015b. "Cybercrime: An overview of incidents and issues in Canada." Retrieved November 3, 2015 (www.rcmp-grc.gc.ca/pubs/cc-report-rapport-cc-eng.htm).

Royal Canadian Mounted Police. 2015c. "Definitions and terms: National identity crime strategy." Retrieved November 3, 2015 (www.rcmp-grc.gc.ca/pubs/cc-dc/strat/def-ter-eng.htm).

Royal Canadian Mounted Police. 2015d. "Drugs and Alcohol." Retrieved October 29, 2015 (www.rcmp-grc.gc.ca/cycp-cpcj/dr-al/index-eng.htm).

Royal Commission on Aboriginal Peoples. 1996. *Bridging the cultural divide: A report on Aboriginal people and the criminal justice system in Canada*. Ottawa, ON: Ministry of Supply and Services.

Ruddell, R., Lithopoulos, S., and A. Jones, N. 2014. "Crime, costs, and well-being: Policing Canadian Aboriginal communities." *Policing: An International Journal of Police Strategies and Management*. 37(4):779–793.

Rudin, J. 2006. *Aboriginal peoples and the criminal justice system*. Retrieved December 7, 2015 (http://www.archives.gov.on.ca/en/e_records/ipperwash/policy_part/research/pdf/Rudin.pdf).

Rudin, J. 2013. "There must be some kind of way out of here: Aboriginal over-representation, Bill C-10, and the *Charter of Rights*." *Canadian Criminal Law Review*. 17(3):349–363.

Rudolph, K.D., and Asher, S.R. 2000. "Adaptation and maladaptation in the peer system: Developmental processes and outcomes." In A.J. Sameroff, M. Lewis, and S.M. Miller, eds. *Handbook of developmental psychopathology*. 2nd ed. pp. 157–175. New York, NY: Kluwer Academic/Plenum Publishers.

Rugge, T. 2006. "Risk assessment of male Aboriginal offenders: A 2006 perspective." User Report No. 2006-01. Ottawa, ON: Public Safety Canada.

Rugge, T., Bonta, J., and Wallace-Capretta, S. 2005. *Evaluation of the Collaborative Justice Project: A restorative justice program for serious crime*. Ottawa, ON: Public Safety and Emergency Preparedness Canada.

Rumsey, J.M., and Rapoport, J.L., eds. 1983. *Nutrition and the Brain*. New York, NY: Raven Press.

Rutter, M. 1981. *Maternal deprivation reassessed*. 2nd ed. Harmondsworth, UK: Penguin.

Rutter, M. 1990. "Psychosocial resilience and protective mechanisms." In J. Rolf, A.S. Masten, D. Cicchetti, K. Nuechterlein, and S. Weintraub, eds. *Risk and protective factors in the development of psychopathology*. pp. 181–214. Cambridge, MA: Cambridge University Press.

Rutter, M., ed. 1995. *Psychosocial disturbances in young people: Challenges for prevention*. Cambridge, MA: Press Syndicate of the University of Cambridge.

Salihovic, S., Özdemir, M., Kerr, M. 2014. "Trajectories of adolescent psychopathic traits." *Journal of Psychopathology and Behavioural Assessment*. 36:47–59.

Sampson, R.J., and Laub, J.H. 1995. *Crime in the making: Pathways and turning points through life*. Cambridge, MA: Harvard University Press.

Sampson, R.J., Raudenbush, S.W., and Earls, F. 1997. "Neighbourhoods and violent crime: A multilevel study of collective efficacy." *Science*. 277:918–924.

Sandler, J.C., Freeman, N.J., Socia, K.M. 2008. "Does a watched pot boil? A time-series analysis of New York

State's sex offender registration and notification law." *Psychology, Public Policy, and Law.* 14:284–302.

Saskatchewan Ministry of Justice. 2012. "Corrections and policing." Retrieved October 21, 2015 (www.justice. gov.sk.ca/CP).

Savoie, J. 2007. "Youth self-reported delinquency, Toronto, 2006." *Juristat.* 27:6. Canadian Centre for Justice Statistics. Catalogue no. 85-002-XPE. Ottawa, ON: Ministry of Industry.

Sawatsky, M.L., Dawson, S.J., and Lalumière, M.L. 2015. "Consensual victim-perpetrator intercourse following nonconsensual sex: The impact of prior relationship." *Journal of Sex Research.* 22:1–10.

Sawyer, S., Metz, M.E., Hinds, J.D., and Brucker, R.A. Jr. 2001. "Attitudes towards prostitution among males: A 'consumers' report." *Current Psychology.* 20(4):363–376. DOI: dx.doi.org/10.1007/s12144-001-1018-z.

Schechter, M.T., and Kendall, P. 2011. "Is there a need for heroin substitution treatment in Vancouver's downtown eastside? Yes there is, and in many other places too." *Canadian Journal of Public Health.* 102(2):87–90.

Schmidt, A.F., Gykiere, K., Vanhoeck, K., Mann, R.E., and Banse, R. 2014. "Direct and indirect measurement of sexual maturity preferences differentiate subtypes of sexual abusers." *Sexual Abuse: A Journal of Research and Treatment.* 26(2):107–128. DOI: 10.1177/1079063213480817.

Schmitt, D.P. 2005. "Sociosexuality from Argentina to Zimbabwe: A 48-nation study of sex, culture, and strategies of human mating." *Behavioural Brain Sciences.* 28:247–311.

Schoenthaler, S.J. 1983. "Diet and crime, an empirical examination of the value of nutrition in the control and treatment of incarcerated juvenile offenders." *International Journal of Biosocial Research.* 4:25–39.

Schoepfer, A., Carmichael, S., and Piquero, N.L. 2007. "Do perceptions of punishment vary between white-collar and street crimes." *Journal of Criminal Justice.* 35:151–163.

Schulz, S. 2006. *Beyond self-control: Analysis and critique of Gottfredson and Hirschi's general theory of crime.* Berlin, Germany: Duncker and Homblot.

Schwalbe, C.S. 2008. "A meta-analysis of juvenile justice risk assessment instruments." *Criminal Justice and Behaviour.* 35:1367–1381.

Schwartz, D., Dodge, K.A., Coie, J.D., Hubbard, J.A., Cillessen, A.H.N., Lemerise, E.A., and Batemean, H. 1998. "Social-cognitive and behavioral correlates of aggression and victimization in boys' play groups." *Journal of Abnormal Child Psychology.* 26:431–440.

Scrim, K. 2015. "Aboriginal victimization in Canada: A summary of the literature." *Victims of Crime Research Digest.* 3. Department of Justice. Retrieved December 7, 2015 (http://www.justice.gc.ca/eng/rp-pr/cj-jp/victim/rd3-rr3/p3.html).

Seagrave, D., and Grisso, T. 2002. "Adolescent development and the measurement of juvenile psychopathy." *Law and Human Behavior.* 26:219–239.

Sealy, P.S., and Whitehead, P.C. 2004. "Forty years of deinstitutionalization of psychiatric services in Canada: An empirical assessment." *Canadian Journal of Psychiatry.* 49:249–257.

Seara-Cardoso, A., and Viding, E. 2014. "Functional neuroscience of psychopathic personality in adults." *Journal of Personality.* DOI: 10.1111/jopy.12113.

Sécurité Publique Québec. 2015. "Services correctionnels." Retrieved October 21, 2015 (www.securitepublique. gouv.qc.ca/services-correctionnels.html).

Seguin, J., Pihl, R., Harden, P., Tremblay, R., and Boulerice, B. 1995. "Cognitive and neuropsychological characteristics of physically aggressive boys." *Journal of Abnormal Psychology.* 104:614–624.

Sellers, C.S., and Akers, R.L. 2005. "Social learning theory: Correcting misconceptions." In S. Henry, and M. Lanier, eds. *The essential criminology reader.* pp. 89–99. Boulder, CO: Westview Press.

Serin, R.C. 2005. *Evidence-based practice: Principles for enhancing correctional results in prisons.* Washington, DC: National Institute of Corrections. Retrieved November 2, 2015 (https://s3.amazonaws.com/static.nicic.gov/Library/023360.pdf).

Serin, R. 2007. *The Dynamic Risk Assessment Scale for Offender Re-Entry (DRAOR).* Unpublished scale. Carleton University, Ottawa, Ontario.

Serin, R.C., Chadwick, N., and Lloyd, C.D. Forthcoming. "Dynamic risk and protective factors." *Psychology, Crime and Law.*

Serin, R.C., Gobeil, R., and Sutton, J. 2009. *Practice manual for use with release decision making worksheet.* Unpublished manuscript. National Parole Board of Canada and Correctional Service Canada. Ottawa, ON: Carleton University.

Serin, R.C., Lloyd, C.D., and Hanby, L.J. 2010. "Enhancing offender re-entry: An integrated model for enhancing offender re-entry." *European Journal of Probation.* 2(2):53–75. DOI: 10.1177/206622031000200205.

Serin, R.C., and Lloyd, C.D. 2009 "Examining models of offender change: Bridging the process from antisocial to prosocial." *Psychology, Crime and Law.* 15:347–364.

Serin, R.C., Mailloux, D.L., Kennedy, S.M. 2007. "Development of a clinical rating scale for offender readiness: Implications for assessment and offender change." Issues in Forensic Psychology. 7:70–80.

Seto, M.C. 2001. "The value of phallometry in the assessment of male sex offenders." *Journal of Forensic Psychology Practice.* 1:65–75.

Seto, M.C. 2008. *Pedophilia and sexual offending against children: Theory, assessment, and intervention.* Washington, DC: American Psychological Association.

Seto, M.C. 2013. *Internet sex offenders.* Washington, DC: American Psychological Association.

Seto, M.C., Harris, G.T., Rice, M.E., and Barbaree, H.E. 2004. "The Screening Scale for Pedophilic Interests predicts recidivism among adult sex offenders with child victims." *Archives of Sexual Behavior.* 33:455–466. DOI: 10.1023/B:ASEB.0000037426.55935.9c.

Seto, M.C., and Lalumière, M.L. 2001. "A brief screening scale to identify pedophilic interests among child molesters." *Sexual Abuse: A Journal of Research and Treatment.* 13:15–25. DOI: 10.1023/A:1009510328588.

Seto, M.C., and Lalumière, M.L. 2010. "What is so special about male adolescent sexual offending? A review and test of explanations using meta-analysis." *Psychological Bulletin.* 136:526–575. DOI: 10.1037/a0019700.

Seto, M.C., Marques, J.K., Harris, G.T., Chaffin, M., Lalumière, M.L., Miner, M.H. et al. 2008. "Good science and progress in sex offender treatment are intertwined: A response to Marshall and Marshall 2007." *Sexual Abuse: A Journal of Research and Treatment.* 20:247–255.

Seto, M.C., Murphy, W.D., Page, J., and Ennis, L. 2003. "Detecting anomalous sexual interests in juvenile sex offenders." *Annals of the New York Academy of Sciences.* 989:118–130. DOI: 10.1111/j.1749-6632.2003.tb07298.x.

Shackelford, T.K., and Duntley, J.D. 2008. "Evolutionary forensic psychology." In J.D. Duntley and T.K. Shackelford, eds. *Evolutionary forensic psychology: Darwinian foundations of crime and law.* pp. 3–19. Oxford NY: Oxford University Press.

Shadish, W.R., Cook. T.D., and Campbell, D.T. 2002. *Experimental and quasi-experimental designs for generalized causal inference.* Belmont, CA: Wadsworth.

Shapland, J., Atkinson, A., Atkinson, H., Dignan, J., Edwards, L., Hibbert, J., Howes, M., Johnstone, J., Robinson, G., and Sorsby, A. 2008. "Does restorative justice affect reconviction? The fourth report from the evaluation of three schemes." Ministry of Justice Research Series 10/08: National Offender Management Service (www.justice.gov.uk/publications/docs/restorative-justice-report_06-08.pdf).

Shaw, M. 1991. *Survey of Federally Sentenced Women: Reports to the Task Force on Federally Sentenced Women on the Prison Survey.* User Report 1991–4. Ottawa, ON: Ministry of the Solicitor General.

Shaw, M., and Hannah-Moffat, K. 2004. "How cognitive skills forgot about gender and diversity." In G. Mair, ed. *What matters in probation.* pp. 90–121. Cullompton, Devon: Willan Publishing.

Short, T., Thomas, S., Mullen, P., and Ogloff, J.R.P. 2013. "Comparing violence in schizophrenia patients with and without comorbid substance-use disorders to community controls." *Acta Psychiatrica Scandinavica,* 128:1-8. DOI: 10.1111/ACPS.12066.

Shurman, L.A., and Rodriguez, C.M. 2006. "Cognitive-affective predictors of women's readiness to end domestic violence relationships." *Journal of Interpersonal Violence.* 21:1417–1439.

Silbert, M.H., and Pines, A.M. 1981. "Sexual abuse as an antecedent to prostitution." *Child abuse and Neglect.* 5:407–411.

Simkins, S., and Katz, S. 2002. "Criminalizing abused girls." *Violence Against Women.* 8:1474–1499.

Simon, R.J. 1975. *Women and crime.* Lexington, MA: Lexington Books.

Simon, T.R., Anderson, M., Thompson, M.P., Crosby, A.E., Shelley, G., and Sacks, J.J. 2001. "Attitudinal acceptance of intimate partner violence among U.S. adults." *Violence and Victims.* 16:115–126.

Simourd, L., and Andrews, D.A. 1994. "Correlates of delinquency: A look at gender differences." *Forum on Corrections Research.* 6(1):26–31.

Simpson, D.W., and Christensen, A. 2005. "Spousal agreement regarding relationship aggression on the Conflict Tactics Scale-2." *Psychological Assessment.* 17:423–432.

Simpson, J.A., Griskevicius, V., Kuo, S.I., Sung, S., and Collins, W.A. 2012. "Evolution, stress, and sensitive periods: The influence of unpredictability in early versus late childhood on sex and risky behaviour." *Developmental Psychology.* 3:674–686.

Simpson, K., and Blevins, J. 1999. "Did Harris preview massacre on 'Doom.'" *Denver Post.* Retrieved October 21, 2015 (http://extras.denverpost.com/news/shot0504f.htm).

Sinha, R., and Easton, C. 1999. "Substance Abuse and criminality." *The Journal of the American Academy of Psychiatry and the Law.* 27:513–526.

Sioui, R., and Thibault, J. 2001. *Pertinence of cultural adaptation of Reintegration Potential Reassessment RPR scale to Aboriginal context.* Research Report No. R-109. Ottawa, ON: Correctional Service Canada.

Sioui, R., and Thibault, J. 2002. "Examining reintegration potential for Aboriginal offenders." *Forum on Corrections Research.* 14:49–51.

Skeem, J., Eno Louden, J., Polasheck, and Camp, J. 2007. "Relationship quality in mandated treatment: Blending care with control." *Psychological Assessment.* 19:397–410.

Skeem, J., and Manchak, S. 2008. "Back to the future: From Klockars' model of effective supervision to evidence-based practice in probation." *International Journal of Offender Rehabilitation.* 47:220–247.

Skeem, J., Schugert, C., Odgers, C., Mulvey, E., Garnder, W., and Lidz, C. 2006. "Psychiatric symptoms and community violence among high-risk patients: A test of the relationship at the weekly level." *Journal of Consulting and Clinical Psychology.* 74:967–979.

Skeem, J., Winter, E., Kennealy, P., Eno Louden, J., and Tatar, J. 2014. "Offenders with mental illness have criminogenic needs, too: Toward recidivism reduction." *Law and Human Behavior.* 38:212–224.

Skinner, B.F. 1953. *Science and human behavior.* New York, NY: Macmillan.

Skinner, H.A. 1982. "The Drug Abuse Screening Test." *Addictive Behaviours.* 7(4):363–371.

Skinner, H.A., and Allan, B.A. 1982. "Alcohol dependence syndrome: Measurement and validation." *Journal of Abnormal Psychology.* 91:199–209.

Skolnick Weisberg, D., Keil, F.C., Goodstein, J., Rawson, E., and Gray, J.R. 2008. "The seductive allure of neuroscience explanations." *Journal of Cognitive Neuroscience.* 20:470–477.

Smart, C. 1976. *Women, crime and criminology: A feminist critique.* London: Routledge and Kegan Paul.

Smart, C. 1982. "The new female offender: Reality or myth?" In B.R. Price and N. Sokoloff, eds. *The criminal justice system and women.* pp. 105–116. New York, NY: Clark Boardman.

Smigel, E.O. 1956. "Public attitudes toward stealing as related to the size of the victim organization." *American Sociological Review.* 21:3–20.

Smigel, E.O., and Ross, H.L. 1970. *Crimes against bureaucracy.* New York, NY: Van Nostraand Reinhold.

Smith, M.L., and Glass, G.V. 1977. "Meta-analysis of psychotherapy outcome studies." *American Psychologist.* 32:752–760. DOI: 10.1037/0003-066X.32.9.752.

Smith, P., Cullen, F.T., and Latessa, E.J. 2009. "Can 14,737 women be wrong? A meta-analysis of the LSI-R and recidivism for female offenders." *Criminology and Public Policy.* 8(1):183–208. DOI: 10.1111/j.1745-9133.2009.00551.x.

Smith, P., Gendreau, P., and Swartz, K. 2009. "Validating the principles of effective intervention: A systematic review of the contributions of meta-analysis in the field of corrections." *Victims and Offenders.* 4:148–169.

Smith, P., Goggin, C., and Gendreau, P. 2002. *The effects of prison sentences and intermediate sanctions on recidivism: General effects and individual differences.* Ottawa, ON: Public Safety Canada.

Smith, S.T., Edens, J.F., Clark, J., and Rulseh, A. 2014. "'So, what is a psychopath?' venireperson perceptions, beliefs, and attitudes about psychopathic personality." *Law and Human Behavior.* 38:490–500.

Smith Slep, A.M., and O'Leary, S.G. 2005. "Parent and partner violence in families with young children: Rates, patterns, and connections." *Journal of Consulting and Clinical Psychology.* 73:435–444.

Snyder, H.N., and Sickmund, M. 2006. *Juvenile Offenders and Victims: 2006 National Report.* Washington, DC: U.S. Department of Justice, Office of Juvenile Justice and Delinquency Prevention.

Somech, L.Y., and Elizur, Y. 2012. "Promoting self-regulation and cooperation in pre-kindergarten children with conduct problems: A randomized controlled trial." *Journal of the American Academy of Child and Adolescent Psychiatry.* 51:412–422.

Spergel, I. 2007. *Reducing youth gang violence: The Little Village gang violence reduction project.* Lanham, MD: Rouman, Altamira Press.

Standing Committee on Justice and Human Rights. 2012. *The state of organized crime in Canada: Report of the Standing Committee on Justice and Human Rights.* Parliament of Canada. 41st Parliament, 1st Session. Retrieved November 22, 2015 (www.parl.gc.ca/HousePublications/Publication.aspx?DocId=5462995&File=39).

Stare, B.G., and Fernando, D.M. 2014. "Intimate partner violence typology and treatment: A brief literature review." *The Family Journal.* 22(3):298–303.

Statistics Canada. 1999. "General Social Survey—Victimization." Retrieved October 21, 2015 (www23.statcan.gc.ca/imdb/p2SV.pl?Function=getSurvey&SurvId=1715&InstaId=5267).

Statistics Canada. 2004. *General Social Survey.* Retrieved October 21, 2015 (www.statcan.gc.ca/pub/89f0115x/89f0115x2004001-eng.pdf).

Statistics Canada. 2005a. "International criminal victimization survey and European survey on crime and safety." Retrieved March 21, 2009 (www.statcan.gc.ca/pub/85-002-x/2008010/article/10745-eng.htm#a1).

Statistics Canada. 2006. "Aboriginal people as victims and offenders." *The Daily.* Retrieved January 14, 2009 (www.statcan.gc.ca/daily-quotidien/060606/dq060606b-eng.htm).

Statistics Canada. 2009. *Measuring Crime in Canada: Introducing the Crime Severity Index and Improvements to the Uniform Crime Reporting Survey.* Retrieved June 10, 2009 (www.statcan.gc.ca/pub/85-004-x/85-004-x2009001-eng.pdf).

Statistics Canada. 2011. *Family violence in Canada: A statistical profile.* Canadian Centre for Justice Statistics. Catalogue No. 85-224-X. Retrieved November 24, 2015 (www.statcan.gc.ca/pub/85-224-x/85-224-x2010000-eng.pdf).

Statistics Canada 2014a. "Homicide survey, victims and persons accused of homicide, by age group and sex, Canada annual (number)." CANSIM Table 253-0003. Retrieved December 2, 2015 (www5.statcan.gc.ca/cansim/a26?lang=eng&retrLang=eng&id=2530003).

Statistics Canada. 2014b. "Incident-based crime statistics, by detailed violations, annual." CANSIM Table 252-0051. Retrieved October 29, 2015 (www5.statcan.gc.ca/cansim/a26?lang=eng&id=2520051).

Statistics Canada. 2015a. "Adult correctional services, community admissions to provincial and territorial programs by sex." CANSIM Table 251-0025. Retrieved December 2, 2015 (www5.statcan.gc.ca/cansim/a26?lang=eng&retrLang=eng&id=2510025&pa).

Statistics Canada. 2015b. "Adult correctional services, custodial admissions to provincial and territorial programs by sex." CANSIM Table 251-0021. Retrieved December 2, 2015 (www5.statcan.gc.ca/cansim/a26?lang=eng&retrLang=eng&id=2510021&pa).

Statistics Canada. 2015c. "Adult correctional statistics in Canada 2013/2014." *Juristat.* Catalogue No. 85-002-x. Retrieved December 2, 2015 (www.statcan.gc.ca/pub/85-002-x/2015001/article/14163-eng.htm).

Statistics Canada. 2015d. "Police-reported crime statistics, 2014." Retrieved October 21, 2015 (www.statcan.gc.ca/daily-quotidien/150722/dq150722a-eng.htm).

Statistics Canada. 2015e. "Youth correctional statistics in Canada, 2013/2014." *Juristat.* Catalogue No. 85-002-x. Retrieved December 2, 2015 (www.statcan.gc.ca/pub/85-002-x/2015001/article/14164-eng.htm).

Steering Committee of the Physicians' Health Study Research Group. 1988. "Preliminary report: Findings from the aspirin component of the ongoing Physicians' Health Study." *New England Journal of Medicine.* 318(4):262–264. DOI: 10.1056/NEJM198801283180431.

Steffensmeier, D., and Allan, E. 1996. "Gender and crime: Toward a gendered theory of female offending." *Annual Sociological Review.* 22:459–487.

Steffensmeier, D., Schwartz, J., Zhong, H., and Ackerman, J. 2005. "An assessment of recent trends in girls' violence using diverse longitudinal sources: Is the gender gap closing?" *Criminology.* 43:355–406.

Steinberg, L. 2002. "The juvenile psychopath: Fads, fictions, and facts." *National Institute of Justice Perspectives on Crime and Justice: 2001 Lecture Series.* Vol. V.:35–64.

Stelmach, B. 2009. "Research or in-search? A non-Aboriginal researcher's retrospective of a study on Aboriginal parental involvement." *First Nations Perspectives.* 2:35–56.

Stenning, P., and Roberts, J.V. 2001. "Empty promises: Parliament, the Supreme Court, and the sentencing of Aboriginal offenders." *Saskatchewan Law Review.* 64:137–168.

Stewart, L.A., Hamilton, E., Wilton, G., Cousineau, C., and Varrette, S.K. 2015. "The effectiveness of the Tupiq program for Inuit sex offenders." *International Journal of Offender Therapy and Comparative Criminology.* 59(12):1338–1357. DOI: 10.1177/0306624X14536374.

Stewart, L., Gabora, N., Kropp, R., and Lee, Z. 2008. *Family violence programming: Treatment outcome for Canadian federally sentenced offenders.* Correctional Service Canada R-174.

Stockdale, K.C., Olver, M.E., and Wong, S.C.P. 2010. "The Psychopathy Checklist: Youth Version and adolescent and adult recidivism: Considerations with respect to gender, ethnicity, and age." *Psychological Assessment.* 22(4):768–781.

Storms, M.D. 1981. "A theory of erotic orientation development." *Psychological Review.* 88:340–353.

Straus, M.A. 1977. "A sociological perspective on the prevention and treatment of wife beating." In M. Roy, ed. *Battered women.* pp. 194–239. New York, NY: Van Nostrand Reinhold.

Straus, M.A. 1979. "Measuring intrafamily conflict and violence: The conflict tactics CT scales." *Journal of Marriage and the Family.* 41:75–88.

Straus, M.A. 2008. "Dominance and symmetry in partner violence by male and female university students in 32 nations." *Children and Youth Services Review.* 30:252–275.

Straus, M.A., Gelles, R.J., and Steinmetz, S. 1980. *Behind closed doors: Violence in the American family.* Garden City, NY: Anchor/Doubleday.

Straus, M.A., Hamby, S.L., Boney-McCoy, S., and Sugerman, D.B. 1996. "The revised conflict tactics scale CTS2:

Development and preliminary psychometric data." *Journal of Family Issues.* 17:283–316.

Strub, D.S., Douglas, D.S., and Nicholls, T.L. 2014. "The Validity of Version 3 of the HCR-20 violence risk assessment scheme amongst offenders and civil psychiatric patients." *International Journal of Forensic Mental Health.* 13:148–159. DOI: 10.1080/14999013.2014.911785.

Suh, E., and Abel, E.M. 1990. "The impact of spousal violence on the children of the abused." *Journal of Independent Social Work.* 4(4):27–34.

Strickland, C.M., Drislane, L.E., Lucy, M., Krueger, R.F., and Patrick, C.J. 2013. "Characterizing psychopathy using DSM-5 personality traits." *Assessment.* 20:327–338.

Sutherland, E.H. 1947. *Principles of criminology.* 4th ed. Philadelphia, PA: J.B. Lippincott Company.

Sutherland, E.H. 1949. *White-collar crime.* New York, NY: Dryden Press.

Sutherland, E.H. 1983. *White collar crime: The uncut version.* New Haven, CT: Yale University Press.

Sutherland, E.H., and Cressey, D.R. 1970. *Principles of criminology.* 6th ed. New York, NY: Lippincott.

Swanson, J., Estroff, S., Swartz, M., Borum, R., Lachicotte, W., Zimmer, C., and Wagner, R. 1997. "Violence and severe mental disorder in clinical and community populations: The effects of psychotic symptoms, comorbidity, and lack of treatment." *Psychiatry.* 60:1–22.

Swanson, J.W., Swartz, M.S., Van Dorn, R.A., Elbogen, E.B., Wagner, H.R., Rosenheck, R., Stroup, S., and Liberman, J. 2006. "A national study of violent behavior in persons with schizophrenia." *Archives of General Psychiatry.* 63:490–499.

Tarling, R. 1993. *Analysing crime: Data, models and interpretations.* London: Home Office.

Task Force on Federally Sentenced Women. 1990. "Creating choices: Report of the Task Force on Federally Sentenced Women." Retrieved March 20, 2009 (www.csc-scc.gc.ca/text/prgrm/fsw/choices/toce-eng.shtml).

Taxman, F.S. 2012. "Crime control in the twenty-first century: Science-based supervision (SBS)." *Journal of Crime and Justice.* 35(2):135–144. DOI: 10.1080/0735648X.2012.686583.

Taxman, F.S., Shepardson, E.S., Delano, J., Mitchell, S., Byrne, J.M., Gelb, A., and Gornik, M. 2004. *Tools of the trade.* Washington, DC: National Institute of Corrections.

Taylor, I., Walton, P., and Young, J. 1973. *The new criminology.* London, U.K.: Routledge and Kegan Paul.

Taylor, J., Iacono, W.G., and McGue, M. 2000. "Evidence for a genetic etiology of early-onset delinquency." *Journal of Abnormal Psychology.* 1094:634–643.

Taylor, J., Loney, B.R., Bobadilla, L., Iacono, W.G., and McGue, M. 2003. "Genetic and environmental influences on psychopathy trait dimensions in a community sample of male twins." *Journal of Abnormal Child Psychology.* 31:633–645.

Teasdale, D., Silver, E., and Monahan, J. 2006. "Gender, threat/control-override delusions and violence." *Law and Human Behavior.* 30:649–658.

Teplin, L.A. 1984. "Managing disorder: Police handling of the persons with mental illness." In L. Teplin, ed. *Mental health and criminal justice.* pp. 157–175. Beverly Hills, CA: Sage.

Teplin, L.A. 1990. "The prevalence of mental disorder among urban jail detainees: Comparison with the Epidemiologic Catchment Area Program." *American Journal of Public Health.* 80:663–669.

Teplin, L.A., Swartz, J.A. 1989. "Screening for severe mental disorder in jails." *Law and Human Behavior.* 13:1–18.

Ternes, M., and Johnson, S. 2011. "Linking type of substance use and type of crime in male offenders." *Research Snippet.* 11(6). Correctional Service Canada. Retrieved October 29, 2015 (www.csc-scc.gc.ca/005/008/092/rs11-06-eng.pdf).

Ternes, M., Johnson, S., and Weekes, J. 2011. "The validity of self-reported drug use with male offenders." Research Snippet No. RS-11-05. Correctional Service Canada. Retrieved November 2, 2015 (www.csc-scc.gc.ca/research/005008-rs11-05-eng.shtml).

Ternes, M., Doherty, S., and Matheson, F.I. 2014. *An examination of the effectiveness of the National Substance Abuse Program Moderate Intensity (NSAP-M) on institutional adjustment and post-release outcomes.* Research Report No. R-291. Ottawa, ON: Correctional Service Canada.

Thomas, W.I. 1923. *The unadjusted girl.* Boston, MA: Little, Brown and Company.

Thompson, E. 2013. "What's the cost of a life of crime?" *Law Times.* Retrieved October 26, 2015 (www.lawtimesnews.com/201305203229/headline-news/whats-the-cost-of-a-life-of-crime).

Thompson, J., McConnel, A., Paquin-Marseille, L. 2013. "The Security Reclassification Scale (SRSW) for shorter review periods among federal women offenders." Research Report R286. Ottawa, ON: Correctional Service Canada.

Thornberry, T.P. 1987. "Toward an interactional theory of delinquency." *Criminology.* 25, 863–891.

Thornberry, T.P. 1996. "Toward an interactional theory of delinquency." In P. Cordella and L. Siegel, eds. *Readings in contemporary criminological theory.* pp. 223–239. Boston, MA: Northeastern University Press.

Thornberry, T.P., Huizinga, D., and Loeber, R. 1995. "The prevention of serious delinquency and violence: Implications from the program of research on the causes and correlates of delinquency." In J.C. Howell, B. Krisberg, J.D. Hawkins, and J.J. Wilson, eds. *A Sourcebook: Serious, violent, and chronic juvenile offenders.* pp. 213–237. Thousand Oaks, CA: Sage.

Thornberry, T.P., and Krohn, M.S. 2001. "The developmental of delinquency: An interactional perspective." In S.O. Whit, ed. *Handbook of youth and justice.* pp. 289–305. New York: Plenum.

Thornberry, T.P., and Krohn, M.D., eds. 2003. *Taking stock of delinquency: An overview of findings from contemporary longitudinal studies.* New York, NY: Kluwer Academic.

Thornton, D., Mann, R., Webster, S., Blud, L., Travers, R., Friendship, C., and Erikson, M. 2003. "Distinguishing and combining risks for sexual and violent recidivism." In R.A. Prentky, E.S. Janus and M.C. Seto, eds. *Sexually coercive behavior: Understanding and management.* pp. 225–235. Annals of the New York Academy of Sciences, Volume 989. New York, NY: New York Academy of Sciences.

Tittle, C.R., Villimez, W.J., and Smith, D.A. 1978. "The myth of social class and criminality: An empirical assessment of the empirical evidence." *American Sociological Review.* 43:643–656.

Tong, L.S.J., and Farrington, D.P. 2006. "How effective is the 'Reasoning and Rehabilitation' programme in reducing reoffending? A meta-analysis of evaluations in four countries." *Psychology, Crime and Law.* 12:3–24.

Tonry, M. 1994. "Editorial: Racial disparities in courts and prisons." *Criminal Behaviour and Mental Health.* 4:158–162.

Tooby, J., and Cosmides, L. 2005. "Conceptual foundations of evolutionary psychology." In D.M. Buss, ed. *The handbook of evolutionary psychology.* pp. 5–67. Hoboken, NJ: John Wiley and Sons, Inc.

Toronto Drug Treatment Court. 2015. "Step by step through the TDTC treatment process." Retrieved May 14, 2015 (www.tdtc.ca/treatment/stepbystep).

Townsend, C., Hammill, K., and White, P. 2015. "Fetal alcohol disorder, disability and the criminal justice system." *Indigenous Law Bulletin.* 8(17):30–33.

Travis, J., Solomon, A.L., and Wahl, M. 2001. *From prison to home: The dimensions and consequences of prisoner reentry.* The Urban Institute (www.urban.org/url.cfm?ID=410098.html).

Treasury Board of Canada Secretariat. 2015. *National anti-drug strategy: Plans, spending and Results.* Retrieved October 29, 2015 (www.tbs-sct.gc.ca/hidb-bdih/initiative-eng.aspx?Hi=28).

Trevethan, S., Crutcher, N., and Rastin, C.J. 2002. *An examination of healing lodges for federal offenders in Canada.* Research Report No. R-130. Ottawa, ON: Correctional Service Canada.

Trevethan, S., and Moore, J. 2013. "Childhood experiences of Aboriginal offenders." In J.P. White, P. Maxim, and D.J.K. Beavon, eds. *Aboriginal policy research: Setting the stage for change.* pp. 245–255. Toronto, ON: Thompson Educational Publishing, Inc.

Trevethan, S., Moore, J., and Allegri, N. 2005. *The "In Search of Your Warrior" program for Aboriginal offenders: A preliminary evaluation.* Research Report No. R-172. Ottawa, ON: Correctional Service Canada.

Trevethan, S., Moore, J., Auger, S., MacDonald, M., and Sinclair, J. 2002. "Childhood experiences affect Aboriginal offenders." *Forum on Corrections Research.* 14(3):7–9. Retrieved December 7, 2015 (www.csc-scc.gc.ca/research/forum/e143/e143c-eng.shtml).

Trevethan, S., Moore, J., and Rastin, C.J. 2002. "A profile of Aboriginal offenders in federal facilities and serving time in the community." *Forum on Corrections Research.* 14:17–19.

Trevethan, S., Tremblay, S., and Carter, J. 2000. *The overrepresentation of Aboriginal people in the justice system.* Ottawa, ON: Statistics Canada.

Trevino, L.K., and Victor, B. 1992. "Peer reporting of unethical behavior: A social context perspective." *Academy of Management Journal.* 35:38–64.

Trifilieff, P., and Martinez, D. 2014 "Imaging addiction: D2 receptors and dopamine signaling in the striatum as biomarkers for impulsivity." *Neuropharmacology.* 76:498–509.

Trinh, J. 2015. "Ottawa's gang violence result of power struggles over drug trade, rivalries." *CBC News.* Retrieved October 21, 2015 (www.cbc.ca/news/canada/ottawa/ottawa-s-gang-violence-result-of-power-struggles-over-drug-trade-rivalries-1.2940201).

Turnbull, S.R., 2004. *Genghis Khan and the Mongol conquests, 1190–1400.* New York, NY: Routledge.

Turnipseed, D.L., and Cohen, S.R. 2015. "Academic entitlement and socially aversive personalities: Does the dark triad predict academic entitlement?" *Personality and Individual Differences.* 82:72–75.

Ullrich, S., and Coid, J. 2011. "Protective factors for violence among released prisoners—Effects over time and interactions with static risk." *Journal of Consulting and Clinical Psychology.* 79(3):381–390. DOI: 10.1037/a0023613.

United Nations Office on Drugs and Crime. 2015. "Human trafficking." Retrieved November 4, 2015 (www.unodc.org/unodc/en/human-trafficking/what-is-human-trafficking.html).

Vale, E.L.E., and Kennedy, P.J. 2004. "Adolescent drug trafficking trends in the United Kingdom—a 10-year retrospective analysis." *Journal of Adolescence.* 27:749–754.

Vasilaki, E.I., Hosier, S.G., and Cox, W.M. 2006. "The efficacy of motivational interviewing as a brief intervention for excessive drinking: A meta-analytic review." *Alcohol and Alcoholism.* 41(3):328–335.

Van Baardewijk, Y., Vermeiren, R., Stegge, H., and Doreleijers, T. 2011. "Self-reported psychopathic traits in children: Their stability and concurrent and prospective association with conduct problems and aggression." *Journal of Psychopathology and Behavioral Assessment.* 33:236–245.

van der Stouwe, T., Asscher, J.J., Stams, G.J.J.M., Dekovi´c, M., and van der Laan, P. 2014. "The effectiveness of multisystemic therapy (MST): A meta-analysis." *Clinical Psychology Review.* 34(6):468–481. DOI: dx.doi.org/10.1016/j.cpr.2014.06.006.

Van Dieten, M., and MacKenna, P. 2001. *Moving On facilitator's guide.* Toronto, ON: Orbis Partners, Inc.

Van Dorn, R., Volavka J., Johnson, N. 2012. "Mental disorder and violence: Is there a relationship beyond substance use?" *Social Psychiatry and Psychiatric Epidemiology.* 47:487–503.

Van Voorhis, P. 2012. "On behalf of women offenders: Women's place in the science of evidence-based practice." *Criminology and Public Policy.* 11:111–145. DOI: 10.1111/j.1745-9133.2012.00793.x.

Van Voorhis, P., Bauman, A., Brushett, R. 2013a. *Revalidation of the Women's Risk Needs Assessment: Institutional Results Final Report November 2013.* Retrieved December 3, 2015 (www.uc.edu/content/dam/uc/womenoffenders/docs/Probation%20Final%20Report%202013%20WEB.pdf).

Van Voorhis, P., Bauman, A., Brushett, R. 2013b. *Revalidation of the Women's Risk Needs Assessment: Probation Results Final Report January 2013.* Retrieved December 3, 2015 (www.uc.edu/content/dam/uc/womenoffenders/docs/Prison%20FINAL%20REPORT%202013%20WEB.pdf).

Van Voorhis, P., and Gehring, K.S. 2014. "Defendants needs and pretrial failure: Additional risk factors for female and male pretrial defendants." *Criminal Justice and Behavior.* 41(8):943–970. DOI: 10.1177/0093854814538022.

Van Voorhis, P., Salisbury, E., Wright, E., and Bauman, A. 2008. "Achieving accurate pictures of risk and identifying gender responsive needs: Two new assessments for women offenders." National Institute of Corrections. Retrieved September 02, 2008 (http://community.nicic.org/files/folders/tools_for_evidence_based_decision_making_in_local_justice_systems/entry7534.aspx).

Van Voorhis, P., Wright, E.M., Salisbury, E., and Bauman, A. 2010. "Women's risk factors and their contributions to existing risk/needs assessment." *Criminal Justice and Behavior.* 37:261–288. DOI: 10.1177/0093854809357442.

Vance, J.P. 2001. "Neurobiological mechanisms of psychosocial resiliency." In J.M. Richman and M.W. Fraser, eds.

The context of youth violence: Resilience, risk, and protection. pp. 43–81. Westport, CN: Praeger.

VanMastrigt, S.B., and Farrington, D.P. 2009. "Co-offending, age, gender and crime type: Implications for criminal justice policy." British Journal of Criminology. 49(4):552–573. DOI: 10.1093/bjc/azp021.

VanNostrand, M., and Keebler, G. 2009. "Pretrial risk assessment in the federal court." Federal Probation. 73:3.

Veysey, B.M., Steadman, H.J., Morrissey, J.P., Johnson, M., Beckstead, J.W. 1998. "Using the Referral Decision Scale to screen mentally ill jail detainees: Validity and implementation issues." Law and Human Behavior. 22(2):305–315.

Vidal, S., and Skeem, J.L. 2007. "Effect of psychopathy, abuse, and ethnicity on juvenile probation officers decision-making and supervision strategies." Law and Human Behavior. 31:479–498.

Viding, E., Blair, R.J.R., Moffitt, T.E., and Plomin, R. 2005. "Evidence for substantial genetic risk for psychopathy in 7-year-olds." Journal of Child Psychology and Psychiatry. 46:592–597.

Vieira, T., Skilling, T.A., and Peterson-Badali, M. 2009. "Matching services with youths' treatment needs: Predicting treatment success with young offenders." Criminal Justice and Behavior. 36:385–401.

Viljoen, J.L., Mordell, S., and Beneteau, J.L. 2012. "Prediction of adolescent sexual reoffending: A meta-analysis of the J-SOAP-II, ERASOR, J-SORRAT-II, and Static-99." Law and Human Behavior. 36:423–438.

Vitacco, M.J., Erickson, S.K., and Lishner, D.A. 2013. "Comment: Holding psychopaths morally and criminally culpable." Emotion Review. 5:423–425.

Volkow, N.D. 2014. Prescription Opioid and Heroin Abuse. Testimony to Congress. National Institute on Drug Abuse. Retrived October 30, 2015 (www.drugabuse.gov/about-nida/legislative-activities/testimony-to-congress/2015/prescription-opioid-heroin-abuse).

Volkow, N.D., Wang, G.J., Begleiter, H., Porjesz, B., Fowler, J.S., Telang, F., Wong, C., Ma, Y., Logan, J., Goldstein, R., Alexoff, D., Thanos, P.K. 2006. "High levels of dopamine D2 receptors in unaffected members of alcoholic families: Possible protective factors." Archives of General Psychiatry. 63:999–1008.

Wada, F., Longe, O., and Danquah, P. 2012. "Action speaks louder than words—Understanding cyber criminal behavior using criminological theories." Journal of Internet Banking and Commerce. 17:1–12.

Wadsworth, M.E.J. 1976. "Delinquency, pulse rates, and early emotional deprivation." British Journal of Criminology. 16:245–256.

Wakeling, H., Beech, A.R., and Freemantle, N. 2013. "Investigating treatment changes and its relationship to recidivism in a sample of 3773 sex offenders in the UK." Psychology, Crime, and Law. 19(3):233–252. DOI: 10.1080/1068316X.2011.626413.

Wakeman, S.E., Bowman, S.E., McKenzie, M., Jeronimo, A., and Rich, J.D. 2009. "Preventing death among the recently incarcerated: An argument for naloxone prescription before release." Journal of Addictive Disease. 28:124–129.

Waldram, J.B. 2013. "Transformative and restorative processes: Revisiting the question of efficacy of indigenous healing." Medical Anthropology. 32(3):191–207.

Waldram, J.B. 2014. "Healing history? Aboriginal healing, historical trauma, and personal responsibility." Transcultural Psychiatry. 51(3):370–386.

Wallace, J. 2008. "Even inmates eat better than seniors in nursing homes." Kingston Whig Standard. Thursday, August 10, 2006, p. 4.

Wallace, J.F., and Newman, J.P. 2004. "A theory-based treatment model for psychopathy." Cognitive and Behavioral Practice. 11:178–189.

Walsh, A., and Beaver, K.M., 2008. "The promise of evolutionary psychology for criminology: The examples of gender and age." In J.D. Duntley and T.K. Shackelford, eds. Evolutionary forensic psychology: Darwinian foundations of crime and law. pp. 20–40. Oxford, NY: Oxford University Press.

Walters, G.D. 2002. Criminal belief systems: An integrated-interactive theory of lifestyles. Westport, CT: Greenwood.

Walters, G.D. 2003a. "Predicting criminal justice outcomes with the Psychopathy Checklist and Lifestyle Criminality Screening form: A meta-analytic comparison." Behavioral Sciences and the Law. 21:89–102.

Walters, G.D. 2003b. "Predicting institutional adjustment and recidivism with the Psychopathy Checklist factor scores: A meta-analysis." Law and Human Behavior. 27:541–558.

Walters, S.T., Lark, M.D., Gingerich, R., and Meltzer, M.L. 2007. Motivating offenders to change: A guide for probation and parole. Washington, DC: National Institute of Corrections. Retrieved November 2, 2015 (http://static.nicic.gov/Library/022253.pdf).

Ward, T., and Gannon, T.A. 2006. "Rehabilitation, etiology, and self-regulation: The comprehensive good lives model of treatment for sexual offenders." Aggression and Violent Behavior. 11:77–94.

Ward, T., and Marshall, W.L. 2007. "Narrative identity and offender rehabilitation." International Journal of Offender Therapy and Comparative Criminology. 51:279–297.

Ward, T., Melser, J., and Yates, P.M. 2007. "Reconstructing the risk-need-responsivity model: A theoretical elaboration and evaluation." Aggression and Violent Behavior. 12:208–228.

Ward, T., and Siegert, R. J. 2002. "Toward a comprehensive theory of child sexual abuse: A theory knitting perspective." Psychology, Crime and Law. 8:319–351. DOI: 10.1080/10683160208401823.

Warren, J.I., Burnette, M., South, S.C., Chauhan, P., Bale, R., and Friend, R. 2002. "Personality disorders and violence among female prison inmates." Journal of the American Academy of Psychiatry and Law. 30:502–509.

Waschbusch, D.A. 2002. "A meta-analytic examination of comorbid hyperactive-impulsive-attention problems and conduct problems." Psychological Bulletin. 128:118–150.

Wasserman, G.A., Mcreynolds, L.S., Schwalbe, C.S. 2010. "Psychiatric disorder, comorbidity, and suicidal behavior in juvenile justice youth." Criminal Justice and Behavior. 12:1361–1376. DOI: 10.1177/0093854810382751.

Watson, J.B., and Rayner, R. 1920. "Conditioned emotional reactions." Journal of Experimental Psychology. 3:1–14.

Webb, R.C. 1999. Psychology of the consumer and its development: An introduction. New York, NY: Kluwer Academic.

Weber, S., Habel, U., Amunts, K., and Schneider, F. 2008. "Structural brain abnormalities in psychopaths—A review." Behavioral Sciences and the Law. 26:7–28.

Webster, C.D. 2003. Flowchart of assessments and decisions for mentally disordered offenders. Unpublished document.

Webster, C.D., Douglas, K.S., Eaves, D., and Hart, S.D. 1997. *HCR-20: Assessing risk for violence.* Version 2. Burnaby, BC: Mental Health, Law, and Policy Institute, Simon Fraser University.

Webster, C.D., Martin, M., Brink, J., Nicholls, T.L., and Desmarais, S.L. 2009. *Manual for the Short-Term Assessment of Risk and Treatability (START) (Version 1.1).* Port Coquitlam, BC: Forensic Psychiatric Services Commission and St. Joseph's Healthcare.

Webster, C.M., and Doob, A.N. 2004a. "Classification without validity or equity: An empirical examination of the Custody Rating Scale for federally sentenced women offenders in Canada." *Canadian Journal of Criminology and Criminal Justice.* 46:395–421.

Webster, C.M., and Doob, A.N. 2004b. "Taking down the straw man or building a house of straw? Validity, equity and the Custody Rating Scale." *Canadian Journal of Criminology and Criminal Justice.* 46:631–638.

Webster-Stratton, C. 1992. *The incredible years: A trouble shooting guide for parents of children ages 3-8 years.* Toronto, ON: Umbrella Press.

Webster-Stratton, C., and Hammond, M. 1997. "Treating children with early-onset conduct problems: A comparison of child and parenting training interventions." *Journal of Consulting and Clinical Psychology.* 65:93–109.

Weekes, J., and Millson, W. 1994. *The Native offender substance abuse pre-treatment program: Intermediate measures of program effectiveness.* Research Report No. R-35. Ottawa, ON: Correctional Service Canada.

Weinrath, M. 2007. "Sentencing disparity: Aboriginal Canadians, drunk driving, and age." *Western Criminology Review.* 8:16–28.

Weisburd, D., and Chayet, E. 1995. "Specific deterrence in a sample of offenders convicted of white-collar crimes." *Criminology.* 33:587–607.

Weisburd, D., Wheeler, S., Waring, E., and Bode, N. 1991. *Crimes of the middle-classes: White-collar offenders in the federal courts.* New Haven, CT: Yale University Press.

Wellisch, J., Anglin, M.D., and Prendergast, M.L. 1993. "Treatment strategies for drug-abusing women offenders." In J.A. Inciardi, ed. *Drug treatment and criminal justice.* pp. 5–25. Newbury Park, CA: Sage Publications.

Welsh, A., and Ogloff, J.R. 2008. "Progressive reforms or maintaining the status quo? An empirical evaluation of the judicial consideration of Aboriginal status in sentencing decisions." *Canadian Journal of Criminology and Criminal Justice.* 50(4):491–517.

Werner, E. 2000. "Protective factors and individual resilience." In J. Shonkoff and S. Meisels, eds. *Handbook of early childhood intervention.* 2nd ed. Cambridge: Cambridge University Press.

Whitaker, D.J., Le, B., Hanson, R.K., Baker, C.K., McMahon, P.M., Ryan, G., et al. 2008. "Risk factors for the perpetration of child sexual abuse: A review and meta-analysis." *Child Abuse and Neglect.* 32:529–548.

White, R.J., and Gondolf, E.W. 2000. "Implications of personality profiles for batterer treatment." *Journal of Interpersonal Violence.* 15:467–486.

Whitlock, F.A. 1982. "A note on moral insanity and psychopathic disorders." *The Psychiatrists,* 6(4):57–59.

Wichmann, C., Serin, R.C., Motiuk, L.L. 2000. *Predicting suicide attempts among male offenders in federal penitentiaries.* Research Report No. R-91. Ottawa, ON: Correctional Service Canada.

Widom, C.S. 1989. "The cycle of violence." *Science.* 244:160–166.

Widom, C.S. 1997. "Child abuse, neglect and witnessing violence." In D.M. Stoff, J. Breiling, and J.D. Maser, eds. *Handbook of Antisocial Behavior.* pp. 159–170. New York, NY: Wiley.

Wilcox, P., Madensen, T., and Tillyer, M. 2007. "Guardianship in context: Implications for burglary victimization and prevention." *Criminology.* 45:771–803.

Williams, K.M., Nathanson, C., and Paulhus, D.L. 2010. "Identifying and profiling scholastic cheaters: Their personality, cognitive ability, and motivation." *Journal of Experimental Psychology: Applied.* 16:293–307.

Williams, S.L., and Frieze, I.H. 2005. "Patterns of violent relationship, psychological distress, and marital satisfaction in national sample of men and women." *Sex Roles.* 52:771–785.

Wilson, H.A., and Gutierrez, L. 2014. "Does one size fit all? A meta-analysis examining the predictive ability of the Level of Service Inventory (LSI) with Aboriginal offenders." *Criminal Justice and Behavior February.* 41(2):196–219.

Wilson, J.Q., and Herrnstein, R.J. 1985. *Crime and human nature.* New York, NY: Simon and Schuster.

Winfield, L. 1994. *NCREL Monograh: Developing resilience in urban youth.* NCREL: Urban Education Monograph Series.

Wolf, D.T., and Hermanson, D.R. 2004. "The fraud diamond: Considering the four elements of fraud." *The CPA Journal.* December: 38–42.

Wolfgang, M.E. 1958. *Patterns in criminal homicide.* Philadelphia, PA: University of Pennsylvania Press.

Wohlbold, E., LeMay, K., and Harrison-Baird, C. 2014. *Local safety audit report: Towards the prevention of trafficking in persons and related exploitation in the Ottawa area.* Ottawa: PACT Ottawa. Retrieved November 22, 2015 (www.pact-ottawa.org/uploads/7/6/4/6/7646662/impact_report_final_03182015.pdf).

Wong, S.C.P., Gordon, A., Gu, D., Lewis, K., and Olver, M.E. 2012. "The effectiveness of violence reduction treatment for psychopathic offenders: Empirical evidence and a treatment model." *International Journal of Forensic Mental Health.* 11:336–349.

Wong, S., and Hare, R.D. 2005. *Guidelines for a psychopathy treatment program.* Toronto, ON: Multi-Health Systems.

Wong, S., Olver, M.E., Nicholaichuk, T.P., and Gordon, A. 2003. *The Violence Risk Scale—Sexual Offender version VRS–SO.* Saskatoon, SK: Regional Psychiatric Centre and University of Saskatchewan.

Wooldredge, J.D. 1988. "Differentiating the effects of juvenile court sentences on eliminating recidivism." *Journal of Research in Crime and Delinquency.* 25:264–300.

Wootton, J.M., Frick, P.J., Shelton, K.K., and Silverthorn, P. 1997. "Ineffective parenting and childhood conduct problems: The moderating role of callous-unemotional traits." *Journal of Consulting and Clinical Psychology.* 65:301–308.

World Health Organization. 2005. *WHO multi-site study on women's health and domestic violence against women.* Geneva: World Health Organization.

World Health Organization. 2013. *Global and regional estimates of violence against women: Prevalence and health effects of intimate partner violence and non-partner sexual violence.* Geneva: World Health Organization.

World Health Organization. 2015. "Substance abuse." Retrieved October 29, 2015 (www.who.int/topics/substance_abuse/en/).

Worling, J.R., and Curwen, T. 2001. "Estimate of Risk of Adolescent Sexual Offense Recidivism (ERASOR; Version 2.0)." In M.C. Calder, ed. *Juveniles and children who sexually abuse: Frameworks for assessment.* pp. 372–397. Lyme Regis, UK: Russell House.

Wormith, J.S., Ferguson, M., and Bonta, J. 2013. "Offender classification and case management and their application in Canadian corrections." In J. Winterdyk and M. Weinrath, eds. *Adult corrections in Canada: A comprehensive overview.* Whitby, ON: deSitter.

Wormith, J.S., and Hogg, S. 2012. *The predictive validity of Aboriginal offender recidivism with a general risk/needs assessment inventory.* University of Saskatchewan Department of Psychology. Retrieved December 3, 2015 (www.usask.ca/cfbsjs/research/pdf/research_reports/LSI-OR%20 Aboriginal%20Paper%20w%20Abstract.pdf).

Wormith, J.S., Hogg, S., and Guzzo, L. 2012. "The predictive validity of a general risk/needs assessment inventory on sexual offender recidivism and an exploration of the professional override." *Criminal Justice and Behavior.* 39(12):1511–1538. DOI:10.1177/0093854812455741.

Wormith, J.S., Hogg, S.M., and Guzzo, L. 2015. "The predictive validity of the LS/CMI with Aboriginal offenders in Canada." *Criminal Justice and Behavior.* 42(5): 481–508.

Wyrick, P., and Howell, H. 2004. "Strategic risk-based response to youth gangs." *National Criminal Justice Reference Service.* Retrieved October 21, 2015 (www.ncjrs.gov/html/ojjdp/203555/jj3.html).

Yukon Department of Justice. 2014. "Corrections." Retrieved October 21, 2015 (www.justice.gov.yk.ca/prog/cor/index.html).

Xantidis, L., and McCabe, M.P. 2000. "Personality characteristics of male clients of female commercial sex workers in Australia." *Archives of Sexual Behavior.* 29:165–176.

Yang, Y., and Raine, A. 2009. "Prefrontal structural and functional brain imaging findings in antisocial, violent, and psychopathic individuals: A meta-analysis." *Psychiatry Research: Neuroimagining.* 174:81–88.

Yesberg, J.A., Scanlan, J., Hanby, L.J., Serin, R.C., and Polaschek, D.L.L. 2015. "Predicting women's recidivism: Validating a dynamic community-based 'gender-neutral' tool." *Probation Journal.* 62(1):33–48. DOI: 10.1177/026 4550514562851026455051456 2851.

Yessine, A., and Kroner, D.G. 2004. *Altering antisocial attitudes among federal male offenders on release: A preliminary analysis of the counter-point community program.* Research Report No. R-152. Ottawa, ON: Correctional Service Canada (www.csc-scc.gc.ca/text/rsrch/reports/r152/r152_e.pdf).

Yllo, K., and Straus, M.A. 1990. "Patriarchy and violence against wives: The impact of structural and normative factors." In M. Straus and R. Gelles, eds. *Physical violence in American families.* pp. 383–399. New Brunswick, JH: Transaction.

York, P. 1995. *The Aboriginal offender: A comparison between Aboriginals and non-Aboriginal offenders.* Ottawa, ON: Solicitor General of Canada.

Young Offenders Act. RSC 1985, c Y-1. Retrieved October 26, 2015 (http://canlii.ca/t/kmfv).

Youth Criminal Justice Act. SC 2002, c 1, Retrieved October 26, 2015 (http://canlii.ca/t/52hl0).

Yuen, F., and Pedlar, A. 2009. "Leisure as a context for justice: Experiences of ceremony for Aboriginal women in prison." *Journal of Leisure Research.* 41(4):547–564.

Zador, D., and Sunjic, S. 2000. "Deaths in methadone maintenance treatment in New South Wales, Australia 1990–1995." *Addiction.* 95(1):77–84.

Zehr, H. 1990. *Changing lenses: A new focus for criminal justice.* Scottsdale, PA: Herald Press.

Zehr, H. 2002. "Journey to belonging." In Elmar G. M. Weitekamp and Hans-Jürgen Kerne, eds. *Restorative justice: Theoretical foundations.* pp. 21–31. Portland, OR: Willan Publishing.

Zerjal, T. et al. 2003. "The genetic legacy of the Mongols." *American Journal of Genetics.* 72:717–721.

Zevitz, R.G. 2006. "Sex offender community notification: Its role in recidivism and offender reintegration." *Criminal Justice Studies.* 19:193–208.

Zinger, I., and Forth, A.E. 1998. "Psychopathy and Canadian criminal proceedings: The potential for human rights abuses." *Canadian Journal of Criminology.* 40:237–276.

Name Index

Note: Key Terms and their page numbers appear in bold face.

Boccaccini, M.T., 338, 364
Bode, N., 166
Boe, R., 390, 392, 435
Boer, A., 292, 298, 299
Boer, D.P., 242, 341, 363, 364, 367, 431, 432
Boland, F.J., 423, 424
Bond, C.E., 415
Bondy, S.J., 205
Boney-McCoy, S., 260
Bonta, J., 15, 16, 25, 27, 29, 30, 35, 63, 70, 72, 73, 81, 82, 84, 88, 91, 92, 101, 102, 103, 111, 112, 115, 117, 118, 119, 120, 121, 122, 123, 127, 130, 191, 200, 211, 246, 250, 305, 306, 308, 315, 317, 365, 377, 388, 389, 390, 391, 392, 394, 396, 397, 407, 413, 424, 425, 426
Book, A.S., 40, 336
Boothby, J., 14
Borduin, C.M., 160
Borum, R., 155, 307
Boston, M., 70
Boulerice, B., 144
Bouman, Y., 309, 312, 313
Bourgon, G., 26, 121, 128, 130, 277, 277n, 377
Bowen, E., 274
Bowker, L.H., 273
Bowlby, J., 68, 70
Bowman, S.E., 210
Boyce, J., 6, 230, 353
Bracken, D., 419
Bradford, J.M., 372
Brady, T.M., 404
Brame, B., 140
Brame, R., 15, 113, 114
Brannon, Y.N., 366, 372
Brantingham, P., 6
Bratton, J., 170
Brennan, J., 347
Brennan, P., 299
Brennan, S., 139, 231, 259, 352, 353, 366
Brennan, T., 401
Brewer, D.D., 143, 144, 146, 148, 149
Brews, A., 390, 392, 394
Brieman, C.L., 326
Brink, J.H., 292, 293, 295, 296, 299, 306, 309, 312, 313, 329
Brinkley, C.A., 327
Brochu, S., 205, 211
Brody, D., 273
Broidy, L.M., 386, 388, 394
Brook, M., 326
Brooks-Crozier, J., 41
Brooks-Gunn, J., 149
Broom, I., 376
Brown, G.R., 265
Brown, J., 293
Brown, S.L., 35, 58, 104, 107, 211, 326, 341, 382, 388, 389, 390, 391, 392, 393, 394, 398, 408
Browne, A., 354
Browne, K., 280
Brownell, C., 219
Browning, J.J., 270
Brownridge, D.A., 261, 262
Bruce, S., 146
Brucker, R.A. Jr., 177
Brushett, R., 399, 399n
Brzozowski, J., 414, 415

Bu, D., 344
Buehler, J., 157
Buker, H., 76
Bumby, K.M., 365
Bunge, V.P., 291
Burack, C., 390
Burchard, B.L., 362, 365
Bureind, J.W., 73
Burke, B.L., 219
Burke, P., 106
Burks, V.S., 142
Burnett, R., 114, 115
Burnette, M.L., 303n, 304, 388
Burrow, J.D., 391, 404
Bursik, R.J., 75
Burt, S.A., 140
Bushman, B.J., 86, 87, 143, 232, 233
Bushway, S., 115
Buss, D.M., 48, 49, 57, 336
Bussière, M.T., 372
Butcher, J.N., 144, 147, 148
Butler, S.F., 153, 347
Buttell, F., 264, 265
Butters, J.E., 146
Bynam, T.S., 404
Bynum, T., 391, 404
Byrne, J.M., 112, 120

C

Cadoret, R.J., 141
Cain, C., 141
Caldwell, C.B., 208
Caldwell, M.F., 344
Callahan, E.J., 373
Calvert, S.W., 235
Calzavara, L.M., 205
Camp, J., 130
Campbell, A., 58, 234, 386, 390, 391, 392, 398
Campbell, D.T., 234
Campbell, J.S., 341, 342, 390
Campbell, M.A., 238, 246, 390, 391, 392, 398
Campbell, N.A., 39, 40, 42, 48, 49, 54
Campbell, N.M., 106
Campbell, S.B., 144
Canales, D.D., 363
Caplan, J.M., 106
Cappadocia, M.C., 174
Caputo, T., 184
Cares, A.C., 265
Carey, G., 208
Carlen, P., 386, 388
Carlisle, J.M., 78
Carmichael, S., 111, 170
Carney, M., 264, 265
Carola, V., 39
Carrig, M.M., 15
Carrington, P.J., 416
Carson, R.C., 144, 147, 148
Carter, J., 415
Carter, R., 325
Caspi, A., 15, 38, 39, 40, 140, 238, 365, 383, 395
Cassavia, E., 354
Cassel, E., 76, 85
Catalano, R.F., 143, 144, 146, 148, 149
Cattaneo, L.B., 269

Cauchi, A.J., 347
Cauffman, E., 337, 338, 339
Cavell, T.A., 328
Cesaroni, C., 111
Chadwick, N., 106, 107, 130, 309, 314
Chaffin, M., 376
Chamberlain, P., 395
Chan, K.L., 261, 262
Chan, Y.H., 307
Chaplin, T.C., 363
Chappell, M., 127n, 128
Charnigo, R., 339, 340
Chauhan, P., 303n, 304, 388
Chayet, E., 110
Cheesman, F., 190
Chen, F.R., 44
Chesney-Lind, M., 385, 386, 388
Cheverie, M., 209, 218, 219
Chiffriller, S.H., 282
Chong, S.A., 307
Chou, S., 325
Choy, O., 44
Christ, M.A.G., 141, 152
Christensen, A., 260
Cillessen, A.H.N., 142
Clairmont, D., 419
Clarbour, J., 362, 363
Clark, D., 343
Clark, F., 327, 328
Clark, J.W., 323, 323n, 338
Clark, M.D., 130
Clarke, A.Y., 315
Clarke, R.V., 188
Claypoole, K., 309
Cleary Bradley, R.P., 282, 283
Cleckley, H., 321, 326, 343
Clements, C.B., 328
Clinard, M.B., 166
Coatsworth, J., 154
Cohen, A.J., 144
Cohen, I.M., 435
Cohen, J., 14, 43, 250, 251
Cohen, L., 187
Cohen, S.R., 336
Coid, J., 107, 303n, 324, 390
Coie, J.D., 142, 146
Coker, A.L., 269
Coleman, T.G., 295
Colledge, E., 328
Collie, R.M., 236, 250, 365
Collins, J.M., 169
Collins, W.A., 52
Comack, E., 416
Conger, J.J., 146, 152
Conner, S., 41
Connolly, E.J., 38
Cook, A., 191, 192
Cook. T.D., 234
Coolidge, F.L., 324
Cormier, C.A., 101, 254, 274, 343
Cormier, R.B., 426
Cornell, D.G., 338
Cornish, D.B., 188
Corrado, R.R., 310, 411, 416, 422, 435
Cortoni, F.A., 251, 253, 376, 440
Corvo, K., 271, 278
Cosmides, L., 48, 49
Costa, D.M., 270
Costa, F.M., 148

Helff, C.M., 265
Helmus, L M., 26, 103, 191, 277, 277n, 365, 367, 377
Hemmati, T., 186n
Hemphill, J.F., 310, 311n, 333
Henggeler, S.W., 160
Henighan, M., 127n, 128
Hennessy, J.J., 282
Henriksen, S., 403
Henry, B., 45, 141, 146, 238
Hermann, C.A., 364, 366
Hermanson, D.R., 187
Hern, A.L., 371, 372
Herrenkohl, T., 143
Herrenkohl, T.I., 146, 148, 149
Herrenkohl, T.L., 143, 144
Herrmann, C., 45, 329
Herrnstein, R.J., 82
Herron, K., 280
Hersh, K., 307
Hertzog, C., 147
Hervé, H., 320, 363
Hessing, D., 75
Hiatt, K.D., 327
Hibbert, J., 117
Hickey, N., 347
Hicks, B.M., 328, 329
Hill, C., 170
Hill, K.G., 143, 145
Hilton, N.Z., 274, 364
Hinckers, A.S., 208, 213
Hinds, J.D., 177
Hinduja, S., 189
Hinshaw, S.P., 140, 144
Hipwell, A.E., 393, 398
Hirschi, T., 70, 72, 73, 74, 75, 88, 92, 381, 390
Hirschman, R., 356, 365
Hiscoke, U., 307
Hitt, M., 170
Hjern, A., 424
Hobson, J., 343
Hodgins, S., 292, 298, 299, 307, 308, 315
Hodgson, S., 26, 377
Hoffman, P.B., 114
Hoge, R.D., 120, 144, 147, 148, 156, 250, 377, 396, 407
Hogg, S., 102, 103, 413, 425, 432, 433
Hoke, S., 191
Hollin, C.R., 79
Hollis-Peel, M.E., 157
Holmen, M.L., 373
Holsinger, A.M., 130, 392, 425
Holsinger, K., 385
Holtfreter, K., 168, 169, 170, 189, 394, 397, 398
Holtzworth-Munroe, A., 280
Hood, J.E., 354
Hood, R., 110
Hornick, J.P., 184, 185, 186n
Horwood, L.J., 145, 149
Hosier, S.G., 220
Hoskisson, R., 170
Hotton Mahony, T., 382, 383
Houghton, R.E., 274
Howard, L.M., 261
Howe, J., 335, 335n
Howell, H., 89
Howell, J., 89, 145

Howes, M., 117
Howes, O.D., 207
Howsen, R.M., 189
Hubbard, D.J., 390, 392, 393, 398
Hubbard, J.A., 142
Hudson, S.M., 365
Huesmann, L.R., 142
Hughes, H.M., 273
Hughes, J.N., 328
Hughes, V., 332n
Huizinga, D., 110, 111, 142, 144, 148
Hull, J., 416
Hung, K., 146
Hunnicutt, G., 386, 388, 394
Huss, M.T., 14
Hussong, A.M., 15
Hutchings, B., 37, 147, 148

I

Iacono, W.G., 38, 140, 328, 329
Ihori, N., 86, 87
Inciardi, J., 392
Insel, A.G., 288
Ireland, M., 144
Irish, L., 354
Irwin, K., 385

J

Jablensky, A., 288
Jaccarino, M., 86
Jackson, H., 364
Jackson, M.A., 388
Jaffee, S.R., 38
James, J., 388
James, L., 273
Jarrell, S.B., 189
Jasinski, J.L., 272
Jeffery, C.R., 82
Jeffries, S., 411, 415
Jennings, R., 44
Jennings, W., 76
Jensen, G.F., 83
Jensen, P.S., 365
Jensen, T.L., 127n, 128, 372
Jerabeck, J.M., 143
Jeronimo, A., 210
Jespersen, A.F., 364
Jessor, R., 148
Johansson, P., 391
Johnson, D.D.P., 39
Johnson, H., 205, 291, 391, 392, 414
Johnson, M.P., 281, 310
Johnson, N., 261
Johnson, R.E., 84
Johnson, S., 205, 209, 212, 215, 218, 219, 412, 414, 415, 432
Johnston, J.C., 117, 422, 439
Jolliffe, D., 250, 251, 251n, 252n 253, 254
Jonason, P.K., 336
Jones, D.N., 336
Jones, K., 142
Jones, L., 327, 328, 353
Jones, N.J., 107, 414
Jones, S., 338
Jordan, A., 363
Jordan, K.Y., 145

Jouriles, E.N., 347
Junger, M., 75
Junginger, J., 307, 309

K

Kalmuss, D.S., 271
Kaltman, S., 269
Kaluzny, G., 365
Kandel, D.B., 88
Kandel, E., 46, 47, 143, 147, 148
Kantor, G.K., 272
Kaplan, H.S., 52
Kaplan, S.J., 144
Kapur, S., 288
Karam, M., 205
Karandikar, S., 177
Karkowski, L.M., 208
Karpman, B., 321
Katz, S., 388
Kauder, N., 190
Kaukinen, C., 263
Kavanagh, K., 144
Kazdin, A.E., 160, 365
Keebler, G., 103
Keil, F.C., 331
Keith, B., 144
Kelley, M.L., 260
Kelley, P., 170
Kelly, J.B., 281
Kelly, K., 184
Kempf-Leonard, K., 391
Kendall, K., 397, 408
Kendall, P., 219
Kendell, R., 288
Kendler, K.S., 208
Kennealy, P.J., 130, 316
Kennedy, P.J., 183
Kennedy, S.M., 404
Kenny, C., 414
Kerlin, K., 328
Kerr, M., 337, 340
Kessler, R.C., 143, 208, 365
Kessous, N., 363
Khalifeh, H., 261
Kiefer, L., 205
Kiehl, K.A., 329
Kikegaard-Sorensen, L., 147, 148
Kim, T.E., 88
Kimonis, E.R., 328, 340, 347
Kingston, D.A., 240, 369
Kirby, J.L., 286
Kirkman, C.A., 325
Kjelsberg, E., 287
Kleiman, M., 190
Klein, U., 169
Kleinknecht, S., 146
Klemke, L.W., 110–
Klemp-North, M., 190
Knabb, J.J., 315
Knop, J., 147, 148
Kobayashi, I., 354
Kochanska, G., 327, 327n
Koegl, C.J., 6, 159
Kondro, W., 3
Kong, R., 382, 384, 390
Koons, B.A., 391, 404
Kosson, D.S., 326, 337, 339
Kouyoumdjian, F.G., 205

Subject Index

Note: Page numbers followed by *f* or *t* represent figures or tables respectively.

E

Earlscourt Girls Connection program (EGC), 406
ecological model, of family violence, 272, 272f
economic crime, 165–196
    assessment approaches, 190–192
    categories of, 167–186
    corporate crimes, 168
    cybercrime, 173–176, 174t, 188
    defined, 166
    fraud, 171–173
    fraud triangle, 187–188, 187f
    historical context, 166
    individual crime, 168
    introduction, 165–166
    occupational crimes, 168
    organizational crime, 167
    organized crime. see organized crime
    professional crime, 168
    property crime, 171
    prostitution, 176–178
    research methods, 167
    risk factors, 189–190
    routine activity theory, 187
    state-authority crime, 168
    theft, 170–171
    theories of, 186–189
    treatment approaches, 192–196
economic marginalization, 394
education, white-collar offenders, 169
effect sizes, 25–26, 250, 251, 251t
    for spousal assault recidivism, 277t
    for violent recidivism, 252t
ego, 67
ego-ideal, 67
electrodermal activity (EDA), 43–44
Elizabeth Fry Society, 116
emotion, 327, 327f
emotional congruence, 357
    with children, 366
emotional funnel system, 271
empirical actuarial instruments, 241, 367
empirical actuarial tools, 101
Employment and Social Development Canada, 171
employment difficulties, 394
endocrine system, 40
epidemiological, 39
Estimate of Risk of Adolescent Sexual Offense Recidivism (ERASOR), 369–371
eugenics, 34
evidence-based practice, 96, 112. see also correctional practice
evolutionary theories of crime, 47–59
    antisocial behaviour, 52
    criticisms, 50–51
    determinism, 50
    evolution, and crime, 51
    female-perpetrated crime, 58–59
    homicide, 56–58
    life history theory, 52
    naturalistic fallacy, 50
    natural selection, 48–51
    psychopathy, 52, 54, 55–56
    rape, 357–358
    research methodology, 51–59
    violent crime, 233–234
ex-offender assistance, 116–117
externalizing problems, 152
external punishment, 271
external validity, 234
extrajudicial measures, 135
Eysenck, Hans, 77, 78–80

F

Fabrikant, Valery, 227
familial protective factors, 148
familial risk factors, 144
family-only batterer, 280
family-supportive interventions, 157
family violence. see intimate partner violence (IPV)
Family Violence Prevention Program, 278
Fast Track program, 158
federal corrections, 7–8, 9t
federally sentenced women, 399
The Female Offender (Lombroso and Ferrero), 380
female offenders, 379–408
    antisocial personality, 390
    applied correctional feminists, 404
    childhood maltreatment, 392–393
    community functioning, 394
    community/structural risk factors, 394
    criminal attitudes, 390–391
    criminal friends, relationships with, 393
    criminal history, 390
    defined, 381
    disempowerment, 391
    economic marginalization, 394
    employment difficulties, 394
    familial risk factors, 392–393
    federally sentenced women, 399
    feminist pathways research, 388
    gender-informed risk instrument, 398–400
    gender-neutral risk-assessment instruments, 396–398
    girls, and violent crime, 384–385
    Hare Psychopathy Checklist-Revised (PCL-R), 390
    high risk female offender, 390
    historical context, 380–381
    impulsivity, 390
    individual risk factors, 390–392
    intimate partners, negative relationships with, 393
    introduction, 380
    length of sentences, 23
    Level of Service/Case Management Inventory (LS/CMI), 396–397, 397t
    mental health issues, 391–392
    nature of female-perpetrated crime, 382–384
    negative parental factors, 393
    over-classification hypothesis, 401
    patriarchy, 394
    personality disorders in, prevalence rates of, 303t
    PIC-R theory, 388–389
    prevalence of female-perpetrated crime, 382–384
    Prison for Women (P4W), 401–403
    protective factors, 395
    qualitative approach, 386
    quantitative approach, 386
    relational risk factors, 393
    risk assessment, 395–400
    risk assessment instruments, 396–400
    risk factors, 389–395
    school performance, 394
    Security Reclassification Scale for Women (SRSW), 399–400, 400t
    self-efficacy, 391
    self-esteem, 391
    Service Planning Inventory for Women (SPIn-W), 399
    substance abuse, 392
    targets of correctional treatment, 404–407
    theories of, 386–389
    treatment, 400–408
    Women's Risk Need Assessment (WRNA), 398–399, 399t
    Youth Assessment Screening Inventory for Girls (YASI-G), 399
    Youth Level of Service/Case Management Inventory (YLS/CMI 2.0), 396–397, 397t
"Female Offenders in Canada" report, 384
female-perpetrated crime, 58–59
female-perpetrated crimes, 385–386
female-salient predictor, 392
feminism, 381, 404
feminist pathways research, 388
fetal alcohol spectrum disorder, 47, 423–424
fetal alcohol syndrome, in Aboriginal offenders, 423–424
Finkelhor's model, 357
first-degree murder, 226–227
First Nations police services, 419
forensic psychology, 14
fraternal twins, 36–37
fraud, 171–173, 189
    assessment, 190
    identity theft, 171–173
    interventions, 193
    mass marketing fraud, 183–184
    mortgage fraud, 184
    organized crime and, 183–184
    payment card fraud, 184
    types of, 173. see also specific types
fraud triangle, 187–188, 187f
fraudulent bankruptcy, 173
French, Kristen, 1
Freud, Sigmund, 63–64

G

Gage, Phineas, 44–45
Galton, Francis, 34
gangs, 188–189, 190
    assessment, 191, 192
    interventions, 196
    membership in Canada, 179
    street, and organized crime, 184–186, 185–186t
    youth, 89, 145–146